An Introduction to

Graph Theory

S Pirzada
Professor of Mathematics
University of Kashmir

Universities Press

UNIVERSITIES PRESS (INDIA) PRIVATE LIMITED

Registered Office
3-6-747/1/A & 3-6-754/1, Himayatnagar, Hyderabad 500 029 (A.P.), India
info@universitiespress.com; www.universitiespress.com

Distributed by
Orient Blackswan Private Limited

Registered Office
3-6-752 Himayatnagar, Hyderabad 500 029 (A.P.) India

Other Offices
Bangalore / Bhopal / Bhubaneshwar / Chennai
Ernakulam / Guwahati / Hyderabad / Jaipur / Kolkata
Lucknow / Mumbai / New Delhi / Noida / Patna

ISBN 978 81 7371 760 4

Typeset in Adobe Garamond Pro BT 11.5/13.5 *by*
OSDATA, Hyderabad

Printed at
Graphica Printers and Binders
Hyderabad 500 013

Published by
Universities Press (India) Private Limited
3-6-747/1/A & 3-6-754/1, Himayatnagar,
Hyderabad 500 029 (A.P.), India.

Table of Contents

Preface

Graph theory has always attracted the attention of mathematicians and has a glorious history dotted with milestones—Euler's solution to the seven bridges of Königsberg, as early as 1756 and more recently, the elusive proof of the four colour theorem in 2000. The subject continues to evolve rapidly under the growing interest evinced by mathematicians, scientists and engineers in the past few decades in its powerful combinatorial methods, which have been put to use in diverse and often unexpected applications in science, engineering and technology. In computer science, for instance, it is used to design efficient algorithms and solve some of the most complex (NP-complete) problems that are essentially graph-theoretic in nature. New proofs and significant results are being discovered in a variety of areas of pure mathematics. As a result, graph theory is becoming a vital component of the mathematics and computer sciences curriculum of colleges all over the world.

This book has grown from my experience of several years of teaching various topics in graph theory at both the graduate and undergraduate levels. My attempt has been to provide the latest and best available information on the subject in such a manner so as to make the learning experience as beneficial as possible for a beginner.

This book is primarily intended for use as a textbook at the graduate level (for students pursuing masters in mathematics and computer science), with the first eleven chapters forming a one-year course. In India, the model syllabus for graduate level mathematics proposed by the University Grants Commission includes graph theory as a recommended course. However, the first eight chapters may be used as a one-semester course at the undergraduate level for students of computer science and engineering. The final sections of many chapters introduce advanced topics and unsolved problems that are the object of current research in graph theory. Thus, the book can also be used by students pursuing research work in M. Phil and Ph. D. programmes.

There are many new topics in this book that have not appeared before in print: new proofs of various classical theorems, signed degree sequences, criteria for graphical sequences, eccentric sequences, matching and decomposition of planar graphs into trees, and scores in digraphs.

Many earlier books, monographs and articles have been used in the preparation of this book and I have included a comprehensive bibliography at the end of the book.

My sincere thanks go to Merajuddin (AMU, Aligarh), M. A. Sofi (University of Kashmir), Petrovic Vojislav (Novi Sad University), Ivanyi Antal (Eotvos Lorand University, Hungary), Zhou Guofei (Nanjing University, China) and M. R. Sridharan (IIT, Kanpur) for their valuable suggestions and encouragement. I thank all my friends and colleagues, especially T. A. Chishti (University of Kashmir) for supporting my work and my research students, especially T. A. Naikoo, for help in drawing the figures and carefully proofreading the manuscript. I am grateful to my family for their love and support during the time this book was being written. Finally, it is a pleasure to thank the management and staff of Orient BlackSwan and Universities Press (India) for their interest, cooperation and fine workmanship.

S. Pirzada

1. Introduction

Graph theory owes its evolution to the study of some physical problems involving sets of objects and binary relations among them. It is difficult to pinpoint its formulation to a single source; in fact, graph theory can be said to have been discovered many times, each discovery being independent of the other. The earliest known studies appear in the works of Euler, Kirchoff, Cayley and Hamilton. The twentieth century witnessed considerable activity in this area, with new discoveries and proofs being proposed as solutions to classical problems including the celebrated four colour problem.

1.1 Basic Concepts

Let V be a nonempty set. The cartesian product of V with itself, denoted by $V \times V$, is the set of all unordered pairs of elements of V. That is, $V \times V = \{(u, v) : u, v \in V\}$. We denote by $V_{(2)}$ the set of unordered pairs of distinct elements of V, by $V_{[2]}$ the set of unordered pairs of elements of V, not necessarily distinct, and by $V^{(2)}$ the set of ordered pairs of distinct elements of V.

Definition: A simple graph (or briefly, a graph) G is a finite nonempty set V together with a symmetric, irreflexive relation R on V. The elements of the set V are called the *vertices* of the graph and the relation R is called the *adjacency relation*. If u is related to v by R, then u is said to be *adjacent* to v and we write uRv. An example of a simple graph is given in Figure 1.1(a).

Since R is a symmetric relation, it defines a subset E of $V_{(2)}$. The elements of the set E are called the *edges* of the graph.

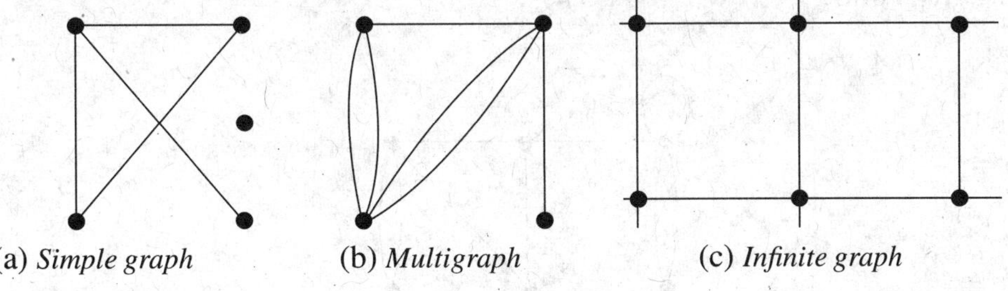

(a) *Simple graph* (b) *Multigraph* (c) *Infinite graph*

Fig. 1.1

From the above definition, we observe that a graph G is a pair (V, E), where V is a nonempty set whose elements are called the vertices of G and E is a subset of $V_{(2)}$ whose elements are called the edges of G.

We observe that there is an incidence relation I between the vertex set V and the edge set E of a graph. If the element $e \in E$, there is a pair of distinct vertices u and v such that $e = \{u, v\}$. The vertices u and v are called *end vertices* of e, and u and v are said to be *incident* with e (uIe and vIe). Also, e is said to be incident with u and v, and in that case we write $eI'u$ and $eI'v$, where I' is the relation converse to I.

A graph with a finite number of vertices and finite number of edges is called a *finite graph*, otherwise it is an *infinite graph* (Figure 1(c)).

We represent a graph G with vertex set V and edge set E by $(V(G), E(G))$ or $G(V, E)$. Since we are only going to deal with finite graphs, we write $V(G) = \{v_1, v_2, \ldots, v_n\}$, $E(G) = \{e_1, e_2, \ldots, e_m\}$.

We define $|V| = n$ to be the *order* of G and $|E| = m$ to be the *size* of G. Such a graph is called an (n, m) graph. If there is an edge e between the vertices u and v, we briefly write $e = uv$ and say edge e joins the vertices u and v. A vertex is said to be *isolated* if it is not adjacent to any other vertex.

Multigraph: A multigraph is a pair (V, E), where V is a nonempty set of vertices and E is a multiset of edges, being a multi-subset of $V_{[2]}$. The number of times an edge $e = uv$ occurs in E is called the *multiplicity* of e and edges with multiplicity greater than one are called *multiple edges*. An example of a multigraph is given in Figure 1(b).

General graph: A general graph is a pair (V, E), where V is a nonempty set of vertices and E is a multiset of edges, being a multi-subset of $V_{(3)}$. An edge of the form $e = uu$, $u \in V$ is called a *loop*. An edge which is not a loop is called a *proper edge* or *link*. The number of times edge e occurs is called its multiplicity, and proper edges with multiplicity greater than one are called multiple edges. Loops with multiplicity greater than one are called *multiple loops* (Fig. 1.2).

If $u, v \in V$ in a general graph or multigraph G, then the multiplicity of the edge uv is denoted by $q_G[u, v]$. If uv is not an edge, then $q_G[u, v] = 0$. Similarly, if u is a vertex of a general graph G, then the number of loops at u in G is denoted by $q_G[u]$.

The graph obtained by replacing all multiple edges by single edges in a multigraph G is called the *underlying graph* of G. Similarly, if G is a general graph, the graph H obtained by removing all its loops and replacing all multiple edges by single edges is called the underlying graph of G.

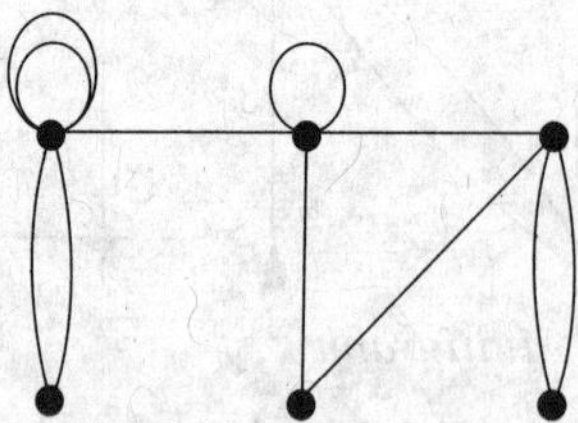

Fig. 1.2 *General graph*

1.2 Degrees

In a graph G, the degree of a vertex v is the number of edges of G which are incident to v and is denoted by $d(v)$ or $d(v|G)$. We have $d(v) = |\{e \in E: e = uv, \text{ for } u \in V\}|$. The *minimum degree* and the *maximum degree* of a graph G are denoted by $\delta(G)$ and $\Delta(G)$ respectively. In the graph of Figure 1.3(a), $d(v_1) = d(v_3) = d(v_6) = 3$, $d(v_2) = 1$, $d(v_4) = 0$ and $d(v_5) = 2$.

A graph is said to be *regular* if all its vertices are of same degree and *k-regular* if all its vertices are of degree k. A 3-regular graph is also called a *cubic graph*. A vertex with degree zero is an *isolated vertex*, a vertex with degree one is a *pendant vertex* and the unique edge incident to a pendant vertex is a *pendant edge*. A vertex of odd degree is an *odd vertex* and a vertex of even degree is an *even vertex*. In Figure 1.3(a), v_4 is an isolated vertex and v_2 is a pendant vertex. The graph shown in Figure 1.3(b) is 2-regular and that given in Figure 1.3(c) is 3-regular, i.e., cubic.

In a general graph G, a loop incident to a vertex v is counted as two edges incident to v. Therefore $d(v)$ is the number of non-loop edges incident to v plus twice the number of loops at v.

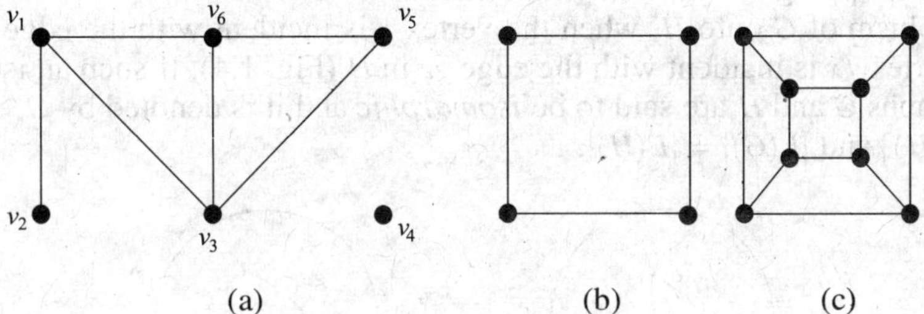

Fig. 1.3 *Graphs (b) and (c) are regular*

The following result is due to Euler [73].

Theorem 1.1 The sum of the degrees of a graph is even, being twice the number of edges.

Proof Let m be the number of edges in a graph $G(V, E)$. Since each edge contributes two to the degrees, one at the beginning vertex and one at the end vertex of the edge, the sum of the degrees is even and equal to twice the number of edges. Hence,

$$\sum_{v \in V} d(v) = 2m. \qquad \square$$

Theorem 1.2 In any graph there is an even number of vertices of odd degree.

Proof Let $G(V, E)$ be a graph and $d(v)$ be the degree of the vertex $v \in V$. Let $|E| = m$.

Then $\sum_{v \in V} d(v) = 2m$ and therefore,

$$\underbrace{\sum d(v_j)}_{\substack{\text{odd degree}\\ \text{vertices}\\ \text{I}}} + \underbrace{\sum d(v_k)}_{\substack{\text{even degree}\\ \text{vertices}\\ \text{II}}} = 2m. \tag{1.2.1}$$

Since the right hand side of (1.2.1) is even, and (II) in (1.2.1) is also even, therefore (I) in (1.2.1) is even. Hence,

$$\sum_{\substack{\text{odd degree}\\ \text{vertices}}} d(v_j) = \text{even number.}$$

This is only possible when the number of vertices with odd degree is even. ❑

1.3 Isomorphism

Let G and H be general graphs. Let f be a one–one mapping of $V(G)$ onto $V(H)$, and g be a one–one mapping of $E(G)$ onto $E(H)$. Let θ denote the ordered pair (f, g). Then θ is an isomorphism of G onto H, when the vertex x is incident with the edge e in G if and only if the vertex fx is incident with the edge ge in H (Fig. 1.4). If such an isomorphism θ exists, the graphs G and H are said to be *isomorphic* and it is denoted by $G \cong H$. We have, $|V(G)| = |V(H)|$ and $|E(G)| = |E(H)|$.

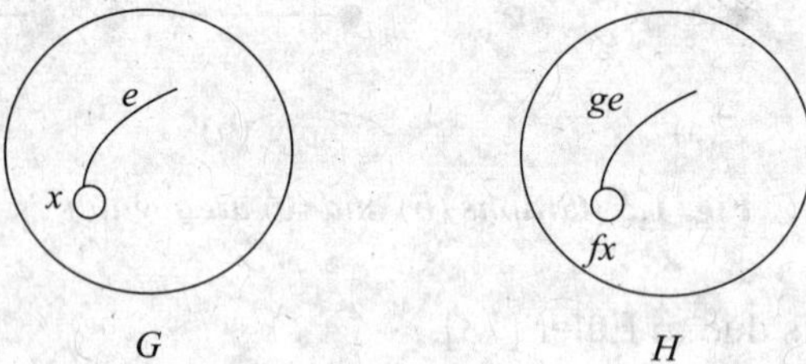

Fig. 1.4

We can think θ to be an operation transforming G into H and write $\theta G = H$. Also, we write $\theta v = fv$ and $\theta e = ge$ for each vertex v and each edge e of G. Clearly, G and H can be represented by the same diagram. The representative of an edge or vertex x of G can be reinterpreted as the representative of θx in H.

An isomorphism of a graph G onto itself is called an *automorphism* of G. Any graph G has the *identical* or *trivial automorphism* I such that $Ix = x$ for each edge or each vertex x of G.

Clearly, two graphs G and G' are *isomorphic* to each other if there is a one–one correspondence between their vertices, and between their edges such that the incidence relationship is preserved. For example, the graphs shown in Figure 1.5(a), Figure 1.5(b) and Figure 1.5(c) are isomorphic.

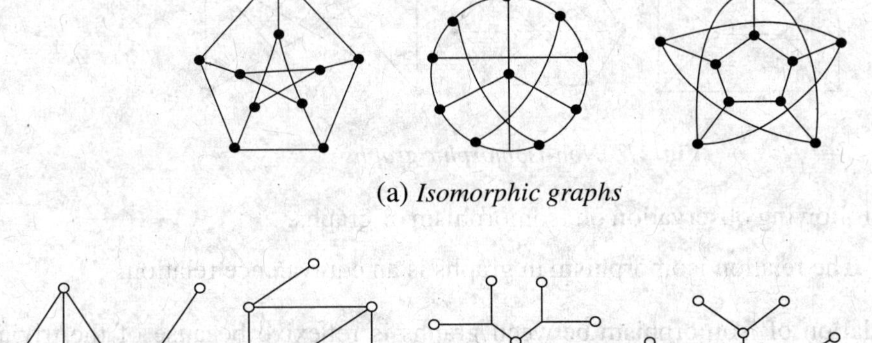

(a) *Isomorphic graphs*

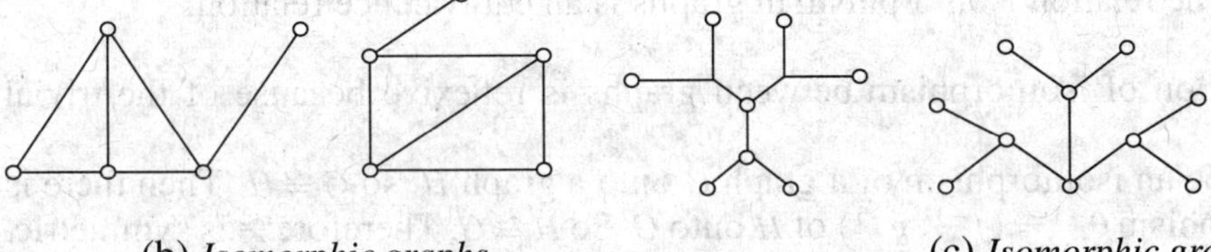

(b) *Isomorphic graphs* (c) *Isomorphic graphs*

Fig. 1.5

It follows from the definition of isomorphism that two isomorphic graphs have

i. the same number of vertices,

ii. the same number of edges, and

iii. an equal number of vertices with a given degree.

However, these conditions are not sufficient. To see this, consider the two graphs given in Figure 1.6.

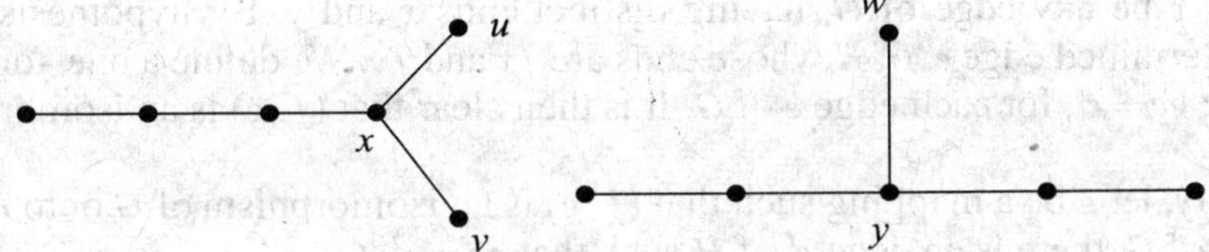

Fig. 1.6 *Non-isomorphic graphs*

These graphs satisfy all the three conditions, but they are not isomorphic because the vertex x in (a) corresponds to vertex y in (b) as there are no other vertices of degree three, and in (b) there is only one pendant vertex w adjacent to y, while in (a) there are two pendant vertices u and v adjacent to x.

The graphs in Figure. 1.7 also satisfy conditions (i), (ii) and (iii) but are not isomorphic.

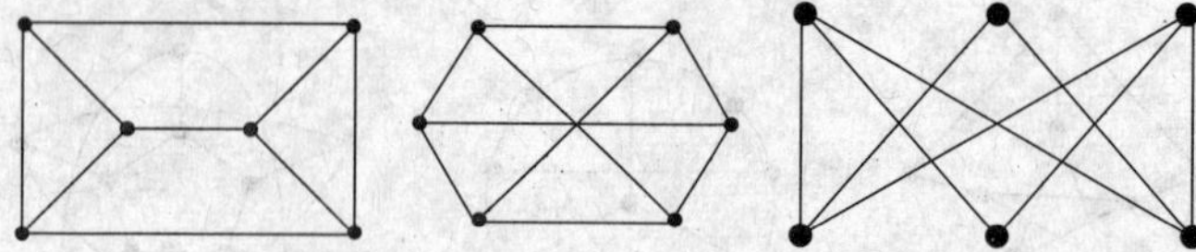

Fig. 1.7 *Non-isomorphic graphs*

We have the following observation on isomorphism of graphs.

Theorem 1.3 The relation isomorphism in graphs is an equivalence relation.

Proof The relation of isomorphism between graphs is reflexive because of the trivial automorphisms.

Let $\theta = (f, g)$ be an isomorphism of a graph G onto a graph H, so $G \cong H$. Then there is an inverse isomorphism $\theta^{-1} = (f^{-1}, g^{-1})$ of H onto G. So $H \cong G$. Therefore $\cong$ is symmetric.

Now, let $\theta = (f, g)$ be an isomorphism of G onto H, and $\phi\theta = (f_1 f, g_1 g)$ of G onto K. Here $f_1 f$ is a mapping obtained by applying first f and then f_1. Similarly, $\phi\theta$ is the isomorphism obtained applying first θ and then ϕ. Thus $\cong$ is transitive.

Hence the relation isomorphism is an equivalence relation. ❑

Remark The multiplication of the isomorphism defined above is associative.

Since the relation isomorphism is an equivalence relation, it partitions the class of all graphs into disjoint nonempty subclasses called *isomorphism classes*, such that two graphs belong to the same isomorphism class if and only if they are isomorphic.

Theorem 1.4 Let G and H be graphs and let f be a one–one mapping $V(G)$ onto $V(H)$ such that two distinct vertices x and y of G are adjacent if and only if the corresponding vertices fx and fy of H are adjacent in H. Then there is a uniquely determined one–one mapping g of $E(G)$ onto $E(H)$ such that (f, g) is an isomorphism of G onto H.

Proof Let e be any edge of G, having distinct ends x and y. By hypothesis, there is a uniquely determined edge e' of H whose ends are fx and fy. We define a one–one mapping g by the rule $ge = e'$, for each edge e of G. It is then clear that (f, g) is an isomorphism of G onto H.

Conversely, let g be a mapping such that (f, g) is an isomorphism of G onto H. Then for each edge e of G, there is an edge e' of H such that $ge = e'$. ❑

An isomorphism of a graph G onto a graph H is defined as a one–one mapping of $V(G)$ onto $V(H)$ that preserves adjacency. This specialisation can be regarded as an application of Theorem 1.4.

Definition: Two graphs $G(V, E)$ and $H(U, F)$ are label-isomorphic if and only if $V = U$, and for any pair u, v in V, $uv \in E$ if and only if $uv \in F$. The graphs of Figure 1.8 are isomorphic, but not label-isomorphic.

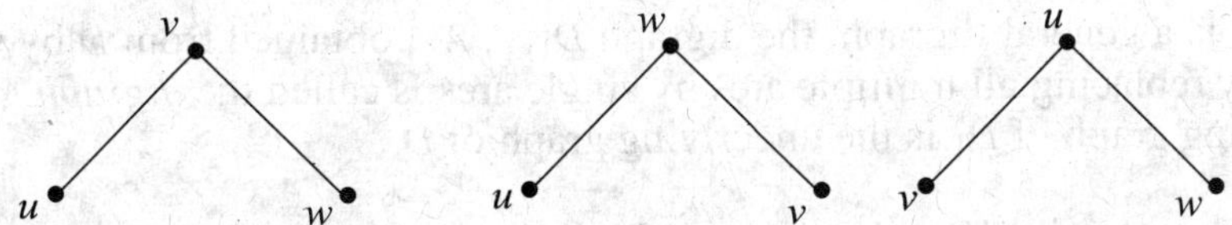

Fig. 1.8 *Isomorphic but not label-isomorphic graphs*

Definition: A graph invariant is a function f from the set of all graphs to any range of values (numerical, vectorial or any other) such that f takes the same value on isomorphic graphs. When the range of values is numerical (real, rational or integral) the invariant is called a *parameter*. The order and size of a graph are *graph parameters*.

1.4 Types of graphs

Simple directed graph or simple digraph: A simple digraph (or simply digraph) D is a pair (V, A), where V is a nonempty set of vertices and A is a subset of $V^{(2)}$ whose elements are called *arcs* of D.

Multidigraph: A multidigraph D is a pair (V, A), where V is a nonempty set of vertices, and A is a multiset of arcs of $V^{(2)}$. The number of times an arc occurs in D is called its multiplicity and arcs with multiplicity greater than one are called multiple arcs of D.

General digraph: A general digraph D is a pair (V, A), where V is a nonempty set of vertices, and A is a multiset of arcs, being a multisubset $V \times V$. An arc of the form uu is called a *loop* of D and arcs which are not loops are called *proper arcs* of D. The number of times an arc occurs is called its multiplicity. A loop with multiplicity greater than one is called a *multiple loop*.

An arc $(u, v) \in A$ of a digraph is denoted by uv, implying that it is directed from u to v, u being the *initial vertex* and v the *terminal vertex*. Clearly, a digraph represents an irreflexive binary relation on V.

Various types of digraphs are shown in Figure 1.9.

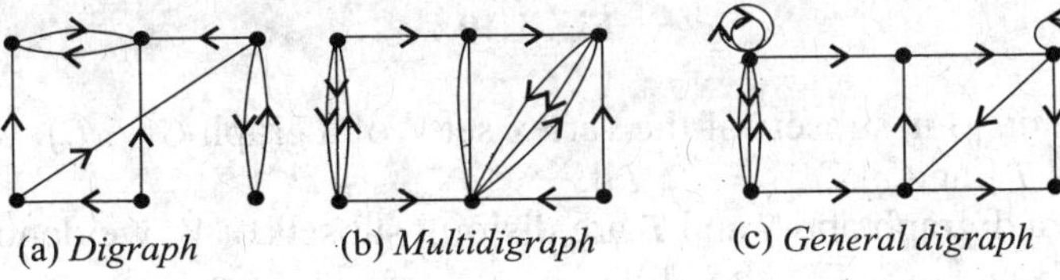

(a) *Digraph* (b) *Multidigraph* (c) *General digraph*

Fig. 1.9

If $D(V, A)$ is a digraph, the graph $G(V, E)$, where $uv \in E$ whenever uv or vu or both are in A, is called the underlying graph of D (also called the *covering graph* $C(D)$ of D).

If $D(V, A)$ is a general digraph, the digraph $D_1(V, A_1)$ obtained from D by removing all loops, and by replacing all multiple arcs by single arcs is called the *digraph underlying D*. The underlying graph of D_1 is the underlying graph of D.

Mixed graph: A mixed graph $G\{V, A \cup E\}$ consists of a nonempty set V of vertices, a set A of arcs $(A \subseteq V^{(2)})$, and a set E of edges $(E \subseteq V_{(2)})$, such that if $uv \in E$ then neither uv, nor vu is in A.

We call a general, multi and simple graph a *g*-graph, *m*-graph and *s*-graph respectively.

Subgraphs: A subgraph of a graph $G(V, E)$ is a graph $H(U, F)$ with $U \subseteq V$ and $F \subseteq E$. We denote it by $H < G$ (G is also called the *super graph* of H.) If $U = V$, then H is called the *spanning subgraph* of G, and is denoted by $H \leq G$. Here G is called the *spanning super graph* of H and is denoted by $G \geq H$.

If F consists of all edges of G joining pairs of vertices of U, then H is called the *vertex induced subgraph* of G and is denoted by $H = < U >$. If $F \subseteq E$, and U is the set of end vertices of the edges of F, then $H(U, F)$ is called an *edge induced subgraph* of G and is denoted by $H = < F >$. These definitions are illustrated in Figure 1.10.

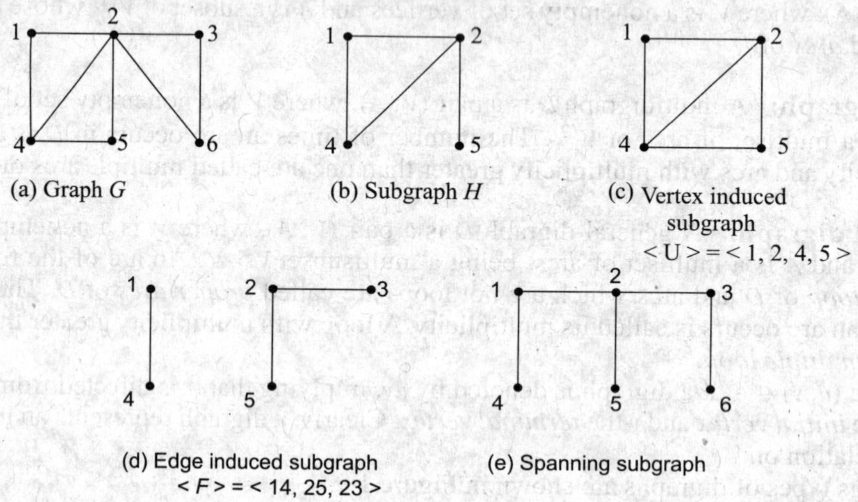

Fig. 1.10

If S and T are two disjoint subsets of the vertex set V of a graph $G(V, E)$, we define $[S, T] = \{uv \in E : u \in S, v \in T\}$ and $q[S, T] = |[S, T]|$.

If $D = (V, A)$ is a digraph and S and T are disjoint subsets of V, we denote $(S, T) = \{uv \in A : u \in S \text{ and } v \in T\}$ and $q(S, T) = |(S, T)|$.

Complete graph: A graph of order n with all possible edges $m = n(n-1)/2$ is called a complete graph of order n and is denoted by K_n. A graph of order n with no edges is called an *empty graph* and is denoted by $\overline{K_n}$. Each graph of order n is clearly a spanning subgraph of K_n. Some examples of complete graphs are shown in Figure 1.11.

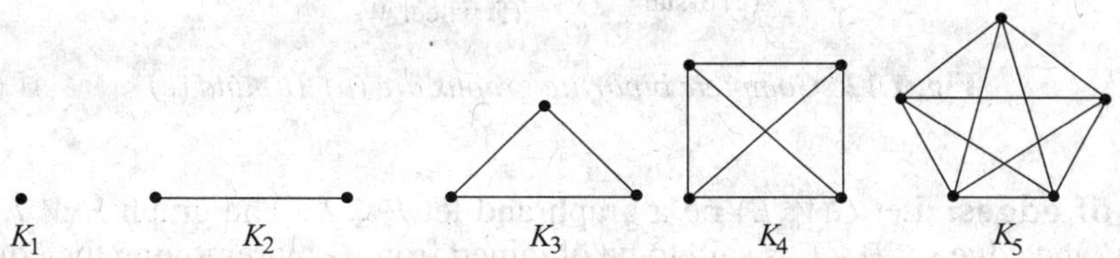

Fig. 1.11 *Complete graphs*

r-partite graph: A graph $G(V, E)$ is said to be r-partite (where r is a positive integer) if its vertex set can be partitioned into disjoint sets $V_1, V_2, \ldots, V_r$ with $V = V_1 \cup V_2 \cup \ldots \cup V_r$ such that uv is an edge of G if u is in some V_i and v in some V_j, $i \neq j$. That is, every induced subgraph $< V_i >$ is an empty graph. We denote an r-partite graph by $G(V_1, V_2, \ldots, V_r, E)$.

If an r-partite graph has all possible edges, that is, $uv \in E$, for every $u \in V_i$ and every $v \in V_j$, for all $i, j, i \neq j$, then it is called a *complete r-partite graph*. If $|V_i| = n_i$, we denote it by $K_{n_1, n_2, \ldots, n_r}$.

Bipartite graph: A graph $G(V, E)$ is said to be bipartite, or 2-partite, if its vertex set can be partitioned into two different sets V_1 and V_2 with $V = V_1 \cup V_2$, such that $uv \in E$ if $u \in V_1$ and $v \in V_2$. The bipartite graph is said to be *complete* if $uv \in E$, for every $u \in V_1$ and every $v \in V_2$. When $|V_1| = n_1$, $|V_2| = n_2$, we denote the complete bipartite graph by K_{n_1,n_2}. For example, $K_{2,2}$ and $K_{2,3}$ are shown in Figure 1.12(a) and (b).

The complete bipartite graph $K_{1,n}$ is called an *n-star* or *n-claw*. For example, 3-star can be seen in Figure 1.12(e).

Complement of a graph: The complement $\overline{G}(V, \overline{E})$ of a graph $G(V, E)$ is the graph having the same vertex set as G, and its edge set $\overline{E}$ is the complement of E in $V_{(2)}$, that is, uv is an edge of $\overline{G}$ if and only if uv is not an edge of G. In Figure 1.12(c) and (d) the complements of K_4 and $K_{2,3}$ respectively are shown.

A graph G is said to be *self-complementary* if $\overline{G} \cong G$. The complement K_n of the complete graph of order n is clearly the empty graph of order n.

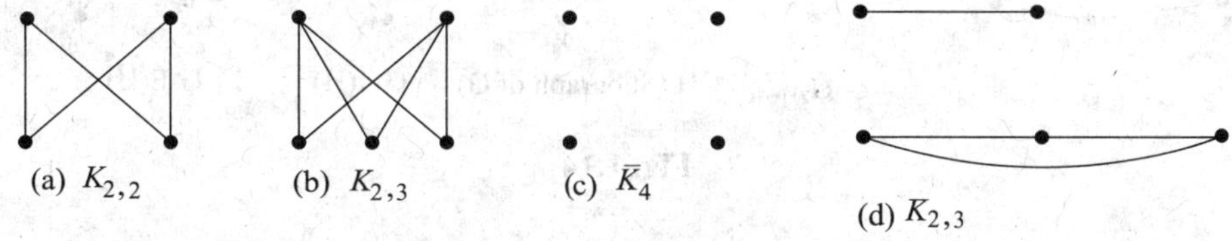

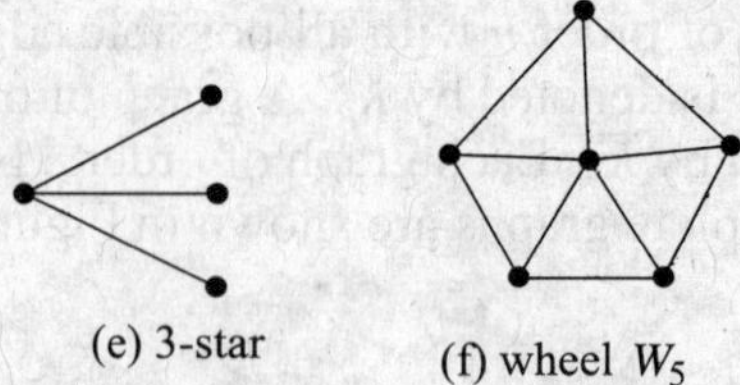

Fig. 1.12 *Complete bipartite graphs are (a), (b) and (e)*

Removal of edges: Let $G(V, E)$ be a graph and let $F \subseteq E$. The graph $H(V, E-F)$ with vertex set V and edge set $E-F$ is said to be obtained from G by removing the edges in F. It is denoted by $G-F$. If F consists of a single edge e of G, the graph obtained by removing e is denoted by $G-e$.

Now, $G-F$ may contain isolated vertices which are not isolated vertices of G. The graph obtained by removing these newly created isolated vertices from $G-F$ is denoted by $G\setminus F$. Similarly, the graph obtained by removing isolated vertices from $G-e$ is denoted by $G\setminus e$. Figure 1.13 illustrates this operation.

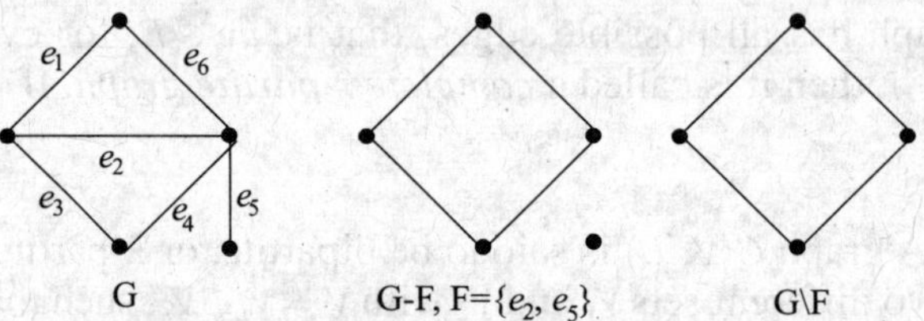

Fig. 1.13

Removal of vertices: Let $G(V, E)$ be a graph and let $v \in V$. Let E_v be the set of all edges of G incident with v. The graph $H(V-\{v\}, E-E_v)$ is said to be obtained from G by the removal of the vertex v and is denoted by $G-v$.

If U is a subset of V, the graph obtained by removing the vertices of G which are in U is denoted by $G-U$. If H is a subgraph of G, we denote $G-V(H)$ by $G-H$, and $G-E(H)$ by $\overline{H}(G)$. Here $\overline{H}(G)$ is called the *relative complement* of H in G (Fig. 1.14).

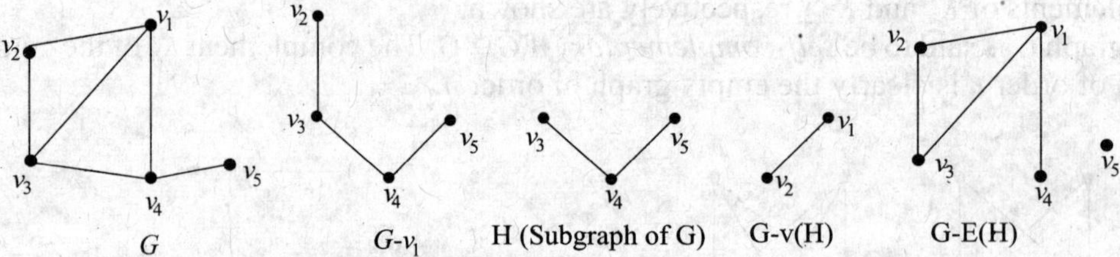

Fig. 1.14

Addition of edges: Let $G(V, E)$ be a graph and let f be an edge of $\overline{G}$. The graph $H(V, E \cup \{f\})$ is said to be obtained from G by the addition of the edge f and is denoted by $G+f$. If F is a subset of edges of $\overline{G}$, the graph obtained from G by adding the edges of F is denoted by $G+F$ (Fig. 1.15(a) and (b)).

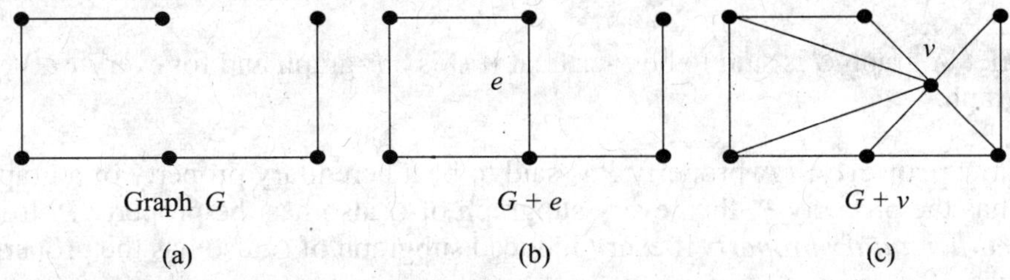

Fig. 1.15

Addition of vertices: Let $G(V, E)$ be a graph and let $v \notin V$. The graph H with vertex set $V \cup \{v\}$ and edge set $E \cup \{uv$, for all $u \in V\}$ obtained from G by adding a vertex v, is denoted by $G+v$. Thus $G+v$ is obtained from G by adding a new vertex and joining it to all vertices of G. For illustration, refer to Figure 1.15(c).

Join of graphs: Let $G(V, E)$ and $H(U, F)$ be two graphs with disjoint vertex sets ($V \cap U = \Phi$). The join of G and H denoted by GVH is the graph with vertex set $V \cup U$ and edge set E⊔ F ⊔[V, U]. So the join is obtained from G and H by joining every vertex of G to each vertex of H by an edge. Clearly, $G+v = GVK_1 = GV\overline{K_1}$. This operation is illustrated in Figure 1.16.

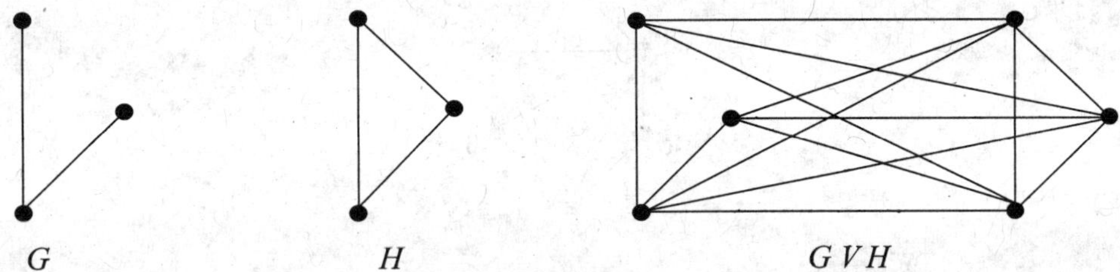

Fig. 1.16

1.5 Graph properties

Parametric property: A property P is called a parametric property of a graph if for a graph G having property P, every graph isomorphic to G also has property P. A graph with property P is denoted as P-graph. A subgraph H of a graph G is said to be *maximal* with respect to a property P (or P-maximal) if H is a P-graph, and there is no subgraph K of G having property P which properly contains H. So H is P-maximal if H is a P-graph, and for every $e \in E(G) - E(H)$, $H + e$ is not a P-graph, that is, the addition of any edge to H destroys the property P of H. A subgraph H of a graph G is said be *minimal* with respect to a property P (or P-minimal) if H is a P-graph and H has no proper subgraph K which is also a P-graph. So H is minimal if and only if H is a P-graph, and for every $e \in E(H)$, $H - e$ is not a P-graph, that is, if and only if the removal of any edge destroys the property P.

P-critical: A graph G is said to be P-critical if G is a P-graph and for every $v \in V$, $G - v$ is not a P-graph.

Hereditary property: A property P is said to be a hereditary property of a graph G if a graph G has the property P, then every subgraph of G also has the property P. It is called an *induced-hereditary property* if every induced subgraph of G also has the property.

Monotone property: A property P is said to be a monotone property of a graph G, if G has the property P, then for every $e \in E(\overline{G})$, $G + e$ also has the property P.

A vertex subset U of a graph G is said to be an *independent set* of G if the induced subgraph $< U >$ is an empty graph. An independent set of G with maximum number of vertices is called a *maximum independent set* (MIS) of G. The number of vertices in a *MIS* of G is called the *independence number* of G and is denoted by $\alpha_0(G)$.

A maximal complete subgraph of G is a *clique* of G. The order of a maximum clique of G is the *clique number* of G and is denoted by $w(G)$. Consider the graph given in Figure 1.17. Here $\{1, 4\}$ is independent set, $\{1, 3, 5\}$ is an *MIS*, $\alpha_0(G) = 3$, $\{1, 2, 6\}$ is a clique, $\{2, 3, 4, 6\}$ is a maximum clique and $w(G) = 4$.

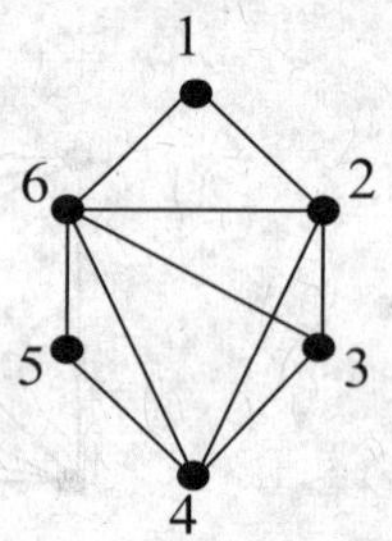

Fig. 1.17

The property of being a complete subgraph is an induced hereditary property. The property of being a planar graph is hereditary and the property of being a nonplanar graph is a monotone property.

1.6 Paths, Cycles and Components

The incidence relation I between the elements of V and the elements of E induced by the adjacency relation R further induces an adjacency relation among the edges, namely, two edges e and f are adjacent if and only if they have an end vertex in common. This relation is denoted by L. Two edges e and f of a graph $G(V, E)$ are adjacent if and only if $e = uv$ and $f = vw$, for some three vertices u, v, w. If e and f are adjacent, it is denoted by eLf.

Walks: An alternating sequence of vertices and edges, beginning and ending with vertices such that no edge is traversed or covered more than once is called a walk. A vertex may appear more than once in a walk. $v_1e_1v_2e_2v_3 \ldots v_ke_kv_{k+1}$ is called a $v_1 - v_{k+1}$ walk W, v_1 and v_{k+1} are called the *initial* and *terminal vertices* of the walk W, and k, the number of edges in W is called *length* of W. The walk is said to be *open* if v_1 and v_{k+1} are distinct, and *closed* if $v_1 = v_{k+1}$. If v_r and v_s are two vertices in W, $s > r$, then the walk $v_re_rv_{r+1}e_{r+1} \ldots e_{s-1}v_s$ is called a *subwalk* of W, or $v_r - v_s$ *section* of W, and is denoted by $Wv_r - v_s$. The walk $v_{k+1}e_kv_k \ldots e_1v_1$ is called the *reverse walk* of W and is denoted by W^{-1}.

Paths: A path is an open walk in which no vertex (and therefore no edge) is repeated. A closed walk in which no vertex (and edge) is repeated is called a *cycle*. A path of length n is called an *n-path* and is denoted by P_n. A cycle of length n is called an *n-cycle* and is denoted by C_n. A loop is 1-cycle and a pair of edges joining two vertices form a 2-cycle. An n-cycle is proper only if $n \geq 3$.

As the edges and vertices in a path or cycle are not repeated, these are denoted by the sequence of vertices only. For example $u_1u_2 \ldots u_k$, where $u_i \in V$ is a $k-1$ path.

Two distinct vertices u and v of a graph G are said to be *connected* or *joined* if there is a $u - v$ walk in G. By convention, a vertex is connected to itself. A graph is said to be connected if every two of its vertices are connected, otherwise it is *disconnected*. The relation of connectedness is an equivalence relation on the vertex set V of a graph. The graphs induced on the equivalence classes of this relation are called the *components* of the graph.

Component of a graph: A maximal connected subgraph of a graph G is called a component of G. A component which is K_1 is called a *trivial component*. The number of components of a graph G is denoted by $k(G)$. A component of G with an odd (even) number of vertices is called an *odd (even) component* of G. The number of odd components of G is denoted by $k_0(G)$. Consider the graph shown in Figure 1.18. Here $v_1e_1v_2e_2v_3e_3v_4e_4v_2e_5v_5e_6v_6$ is a walk, $v_1e_1v_2e_2v_3e_3v_4$ is a path and $v_2e_2v_3e_3v_4e_4v_2$ is a 3-cycle.

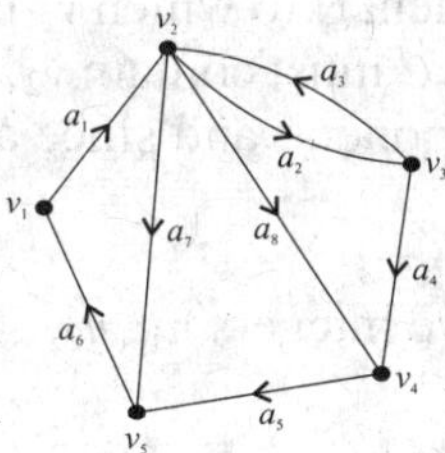

Fig. 1.18

Union of graphs: Let $G(V, E)$ and $H(U, F)$ be two graphs with $V \cap U = \Phi$. The union of G and H, denoted by $G \cup H$, is the graph with vertex set $V \cup U$ and edge set $E \cup F$. Clearly, when G and H are connected graphs, $G \cup H$ is a disconnected graph whose components are G and H (Fig. 1.19).

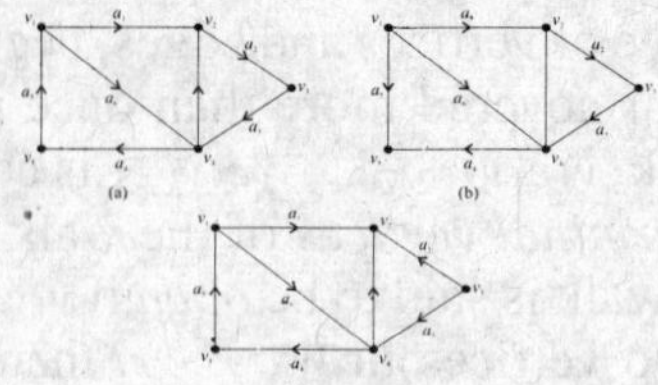

Fig. 1.19

A graph G which has k components, all isomorphic to H, is $H \cup H \cup \ldots \cup H$, or $G = kH$. We write $G = k_1G_1 \cup k_2G_2 \cup \ldots \cup k_rG_r$, if G has k_i components isomorphic to G_i, $1 \le i \le r$.

Theorem 1.5 A graph G is disconnected if and only if its vertex set V can be partitioned into two nonempty, disjoint subsets V_1 and V_2, such that there exists no edge in G whose one end vertex is in V_1 and the other in V_2.

Proof Let G be a graph whose vertex set can be partitioned into two nonempty disjoint subsets V_1 and V_2, so that no edge of G has one end in V_1 and the other in V_2. Let v_1 and v_2 be any two vertices of G such that $v_1 \in V_1$ and $v_2 \in V_2$. Then there is no path between vertices v_1 and v_2, since there is no edge joining them. This shows that G is disconnected.

Conversely, let G be a disconnected graph. Consider a vertex v in G. Let V_1 be the set of all vertices that are joined by paths to v. Since G is disconnected, V_1 does not contain all vertices of G. Let V_2 be the set of the remaining vertices. Clearly, no vertex in V_1 is joined to any vertex in V_2 by an edge, proving the converse. ❑

Theorem 1.6 If a graph has exactly two vertices of odd degree, they must be connected by a path.

Proof Let G be a graph with all its vertices of even degree, except for v_1 and v_2 which are of odd degree. Consider the component C to which v_1 belongs. Then C has an even number of vertices of odd degree. Therefore C must contain v_2, the only other vertex of odd degree. Thus v_1 and v_2 are in the same component, and since a component is connected, there is a path between v_1 and v_2. ❑

Lemma 1.1 For any set of positive integers $n_1, n_2, \ldots, n_k$

$$\sum_{i=1}^{k} n_i^2 \le \left(\sum_{i=1}^{k} n_i\right)^2 - (k-1)\left(2\sum_{i=1}^{k} n_i - k\right).$$

Proof We have, $\sum\limits_{i=1}^{k}(n_i - 1) = \sum\limits_{i=1}^{k} n_i - k$.

Squaring both sides, we get

$$\left[\sum_{i=1}^{k}(n_i-1)\right]^2 = \left[\sum_{i=1}^{k}n_i-k\right]^2,$$

$$\text{or } [(n_1-1)+(n_2-1)+\ldots+(n_k-1)]^2 = \left(\sum_{i=1}^{k}n_i\right)^2 - 2k\sum_{i=1}^{k}n_i+k^2,$$

$$\text{or } (n_1-1)^2+(n_2-1)^2+\ldots+(n_k-1)^2+\sum_{i=1}^{k}\sum_{\substack{j=1\\ i\neq j}}^{k}(n_i-1)(n_j-1) = \left(\sum_{i=1}^{k}n_i\right)^2 - 2k\sum_{i=1}^{k}n_i+k^2.$$

$$\text{Therefore, } \sum_{i=1}^{k}n_i^2 - 2\sum_{i=1}^{k}n_i+k+\sum_{i=1}^{k}\sum_{\substack{j=1\\ i\neq j}}^{k}(n_i-1)(n_j-1) = \left(\sum_{i=1}^{k}n_i\right)^2 - 2k\sum_{i=1}^{k}n_i+k^2,$$

$$\text{or } \sum_{i=1}^{k}n_i^2 \leq 2\sum_{i=1}^{k}n_i-k+\left(\sum_{i=1}^{k}n_i\right)^2 - 2k\sum_{i=1}^{k}n_i+k^2,$$

$$\text{or } \sum_{i=1}^{k}n_i^2 \leq \left(\sum_{i=1}^{k}n_i\right)^2 - (k-1)\left(2\sum_{i=1}^{k}n_i-k\right).$$ ❑

Theorem 1.7 A graph with n vertices and k components cannot have more than $\frac{1}{2}(n-k)(n-k+1)$ edges.

Proof The number of components is k and let the number of vertices in ith component be n_i, $1 \leq i \leq k$.

So, $n_1+n_2+\ldots+n_k = \sum_{i=1}^{k}n_i = n$.

Now, a component with n_i vertices will have the maximum possible number of edges when it is complete, and in that case it has $\frac{1}{2}n_i(n_i-1)$ edges.

Thus the maximum number of edges in $G = \frac{1}{2}\sum_{i=1}^{k}n_i(n_i-1)$

$$= \frac{1}{2}\sum_{i=1}^{k}n_i^2 - \frac{1}{2}\sum_{i=1}^{k}n_i \leq \frac{1}{2}\left\{\left(\sum_{i=1}^{k}n_i\right)^2 - (k-1)\left(2\sum_{i=1}^{k}n_i-k\right)\right\} - \frac{1}{2}\sum_{i=1}^{k}n_i$$

$$= \frac{1}{2}\{n^2-(k-1)(2n-k)\} - \frac{1}{2}n = \frac{1}{2}\left[n^2-2nk+k^2+n-k\right] = \frac{1}{2}(n-k)(n-k+1).$$ ❑

The following result is due to Turan [240].

Theorem 1.8 The maximum number of edges among all n vertex graphs with no triangles is $\left[\frac{n^2}{4}\right]$, where $\left[\frac{n^2}{4}\right]$ is the greatest integer not exceeding the number $\frac{n^2}{4}$.

Proof The result is proved by induction, taking the cases of n odd and n even separately.

Let n be even. The result is obvious for small values of n. Assume the result to be true for all even $n \leq 2p$. We then prove it for $n = 2p+2$. So assume G is a graph with $n = 2p+2$ vertices and no triangles. Since G is not totally disconnected, there are adjacent vertices u and v. The subgraph $G' = G - \{u, v\}$ has $2p$ vertices and no triangles, so that by the induction hypothesis, G' has at most $\left[\frac{4p^2}{4}\right] = p^2$ edges.

There can be no vertex w such that u and v are both adjacent to w, for then u, v and w form a triangle of G. Therefore, if u is adjacent to k vertices of G', v is adjacent to at most $2n - k$ vertices. Then G has at most

$$p^2 + k + (2p - k) + 1 = p^2 + 2p + 1 = (p+1)^2 = \frac{n^2}{4} = \left[\frac{n^2}{4}\right] \text{ edges.}$$

It can be shown that for all even p, there exists a $(p, \frac{p^2}{4})$ graph with no triangles. Such a graph is formed as follows. Take two sets V_1 and V_2 of $\frac{p}{2}$ vertices each, and join each vertex of V_1 with each vertex of V_2. ❑

Example When $n = 6$, the graph formed is shown in Figure 1.20.

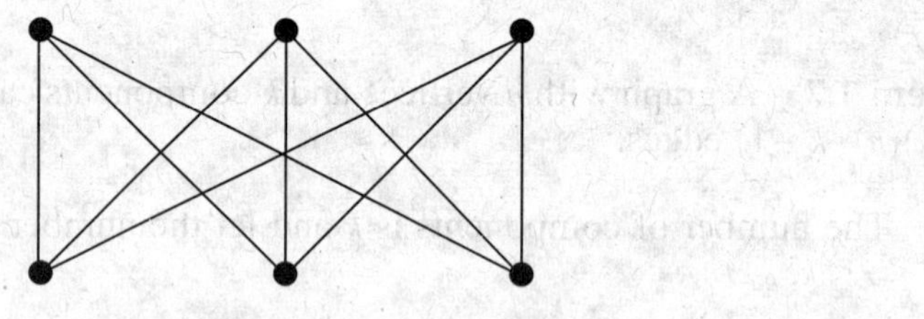

Fig. 1.20

The following result due to Konig [130] characterises bipartite graphs.

Theorem 1.9 A graph is bipartite if and only if it contains no odd cycles.

Proof Let G be a bipartite graph. Then its vertex set V can be partitioned into two sets V_1 and V_2, so that every edge of G joins a vertex of V_1 with a vertex of V_2. Thus every cycle $v_1 v_2 \ldots v_n v_1$ in G has its oddly subscripted vertices in V_1, say, and the others in V_2, so that its length is even.

Conversely, we assume, without loss of generality, that G is connected, for otherwise we can consider the components of G separately. Take any vertex $v_1 \in V$, and let V_1 consist of v_1 and all vertices of G whose shortest paths from v_1 (in terms of the number of edges) contain an even number of edges, while $V_2 = V - V_1$. Since G has no odd cycles, every edge of G joins a vertex of V_1 with a vertex of V_2 (Fig. 1.21).

For suppose there is an edge uv joining two vertices of V_1. The length of v_1 to u is even, the length of v_1 to v is even and the union of edges from v_1 to u and from v_1 to v together with the edge uv contains an odd cycle, which is a contradiction. Hence G is bipartite. ❑

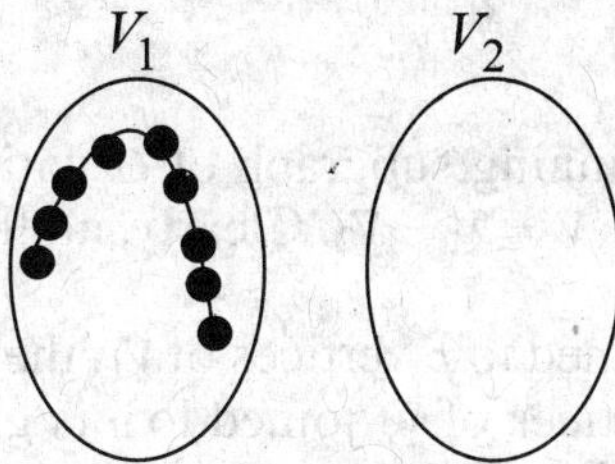

Fig. 1.21a

Theorem 1.10 A graph and its complement are not both disconnected.

Proof Let G be a disconnected graph and u, v be any two vertices of $\overline{G}$, the complement of G. If u and v belong to different components of G, then u and v are adjacent in $\overline{G}$, by definition. If u and v belong to the same component, say G_i of G, then let w be a vertex of some other component, say G_j of G. By definition both u and w, and v and w are adjacent in $\overline{G}$. In either case u is connected to v by a path in $\overline{G}$. Thus $\overline{G}$ is connected. ❑

Theorem 1.11 For any graph G with six vertices, G or $\overline{G}$ contains a triangle.

Proof Let v be a vertex of a graph G with six vertices. Since v is adjacent either in G or $\overline{G}$ to the other five vertices of G, we assume without loss of generality, that there are three vertices u_1, u_2 and u_3 adjacent to v in G. If any two of three vertices are adjacent, then they are two vertices of a triangle whose third vertex is v. If no two of them are adjacent in G, then u_1, u_2 and u_3 are the vertices of a triangle in $\overline{G}$ (Fig. 1.22). ❑

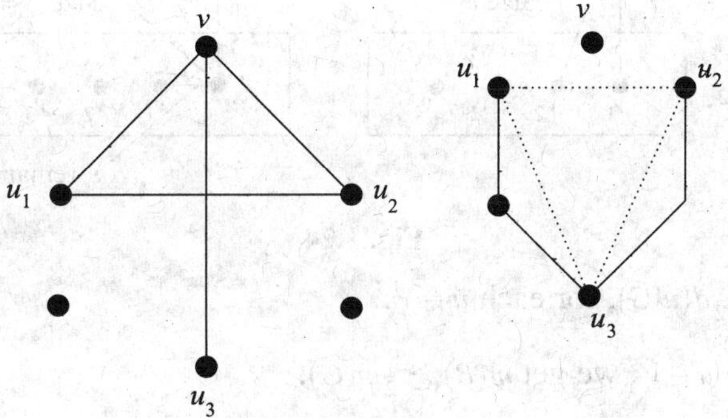

Fig. 1.22

Theorem 1.12 For any graph G of order n, $\Delta(G) \leq n - 1$.

Proof Since a vertex in a graph can be joined to at most $n-1$ other vertices, the maximum degree a vertex can have is $n-1$. So, $\Delta(G) \le n-1$. ❑

Theorem 1.13 Every graph G contains a bipartite spanning subgraph whose size is at least half the size of G.

Proof Let B be a bipartite spanning subgraph of G with B being of maximum size and the bipartition of its vertex set be $V = V_1 \cup V_2$. Clearly, all the edges of G with one end in V_1 and the other in V_2 must be in B.

Now, if any vertex $u \in V_1$ is joined to p vertices of V_1, then u is joined to at least p vertices of V_2. That is, the number of vertices of V_2 joined to u is greater or equal to the number of vertices of V_1 joined to u (Fig. 1.23).

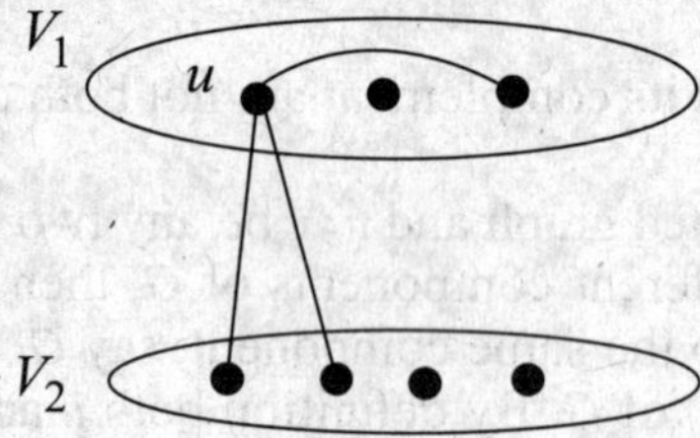

Fig. 1.23

For if $u \in V_1$ is joined to more vertices of V_1 than of V_2, then $V_1 - \{u\}$, $V_2 \cup \{u\}$ is a bipartition of V giving a bipartite subgraph of G with larger size, which is a contradiction to our assumption (Fig. 1.24).

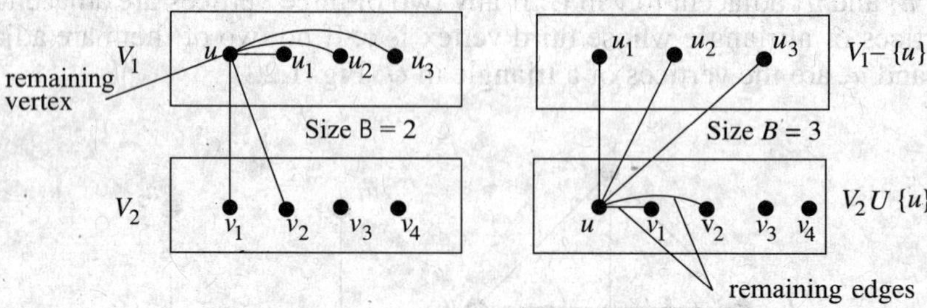

Fig. 1.24

Therefore, $d(u|B) \ge \frac{1}{2}d(u|G)$, for each $u \in V$.

Summing over all $u \in V$, we get $m(B) \ge \frac{1}{2}m(G)$. ❑

Theorem 1.14 If G is a graph with at least n_0 vertices and at least $n_0.n(G) - \binom{n_0+1}{2} + 1$ edges, then G contains a subgraph H with $\delta(H) \ge n_0 + 1$, where $n(G)$ is the number of vertices in G and $n(G) \ge n_0$.

Proof Let G_{n_0} be the set of all such graphs G with

$$G_{n_0} = \left\{ G : n(G) > n_0,\ m(G) \geq n_0.n(G) - \binom{n_0+1}{2} + 1 \right\}.$$

If $G \in G_{n_0}$, then $n(G) > n_0$, because if $n(G) = n_0$, then

$$m(G) \geq n_0.n(G) - \binom{n_0+1}{2} + 1 \text{ gives } m(G) \geq n_0.n_0 - \binom{n_0+1}{2} + 1.$$

Therefore, $m(G) \geq n_0^2 - \dfrac{(n_0+1)n_0}{2} + 1 = n_0^2 - \left\{ n_0^2 - \dfrac{n_0(n_0-1)}{2} \right\} + 1$

$$= \frac{(n_0-1)n_0}{2} + 1 = \binom{n_0}{2} + 1.$$

Thus, $m(G) \geq \binom{n_0}{2} + 1$, which is a contradiction, as the number of edges can be at most $\binom{n_0}{2}$.

Now, if $\delta(G) \leq n_0$, let u be a vertex with $d(u) \leq n_0$. Then it is easily verified that $G - u$ also belongs to G_{n_0}. By repeating this process of removing vertices with degree smaller than $n_0 + 1$ (i.e., $\leq n_0$), we arrive at a graph $H \in G_{n_0}$ with $\delta(H) \geq n_0 + 1$. ❑

Example Consider the graph G of Figure 1.25. Here $n(G) = 6$. Let $n_0 = 3$. Clearly, $m(G) \geq 3 \times 6 - \binom{4}{2} + 1 = 13$. In $G - u$, we have $n(G-u) = 5$ and again let $n_0 = 3$. Then $m(G-u) \geq 3 \times 5 - \binom{4}{2} + 1 = 10$, and thus satisfies given conditions. Hence $G - u \in G_{n_0}$.

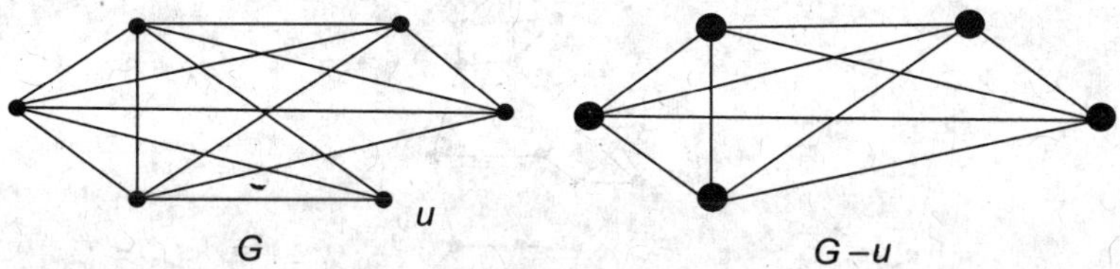

Fig. 1.25

Theorem 1.15 Any graph G has a regular supergraph H of degree $\Delta(G)$ such that G is an induced subgraph of H.

Proof We have to prove that for a graph G, there exists a graph H which is regular and the degree of every vertex of H is $\Delta(G)$, and H is the supergraph of G, $\Delta(G)$ being the maximum degree in G. If G is regular, there is nothing to prove.

Now let G be not regular and $\Delta = \Delta(G)$ be the maximum degree in G. Let d_i be the degree of the vertex v_i in G. Let $d = \sum\limits_{i=1}^{n} (\Delta - d_i)$.

Case 1 If d is even, take $\frac{d}{2}$ disjoint copies of the graph $K_{\Delta+1}-e$ (where e is an edge). For $1 \le i \le n$, join v_i to $\Delta - d_i$ different vertices from these copies having degree $\Delta - 1$. We get a graph H which is Δ-regular. Clearly, G is an induced subgraph of H.

Example Consider the graph of Figure 1.26. Here $\Delta = 2$, $d = 2-1+2-1+2-2 = 2$ (even). We take $\frac{d}{2} = \frac{2}{2} = 1$ copy of $K_{2+1} - e = K_3 - e$. Join v_i to $2 - d_i$ different vertices from this copy having degree $2 - 1 = 1$. Join v_1 to $2 - 1 = 1$ vertex of this copy having degree 1. Join v_2 to $2 - 1 = 1$ vertex.

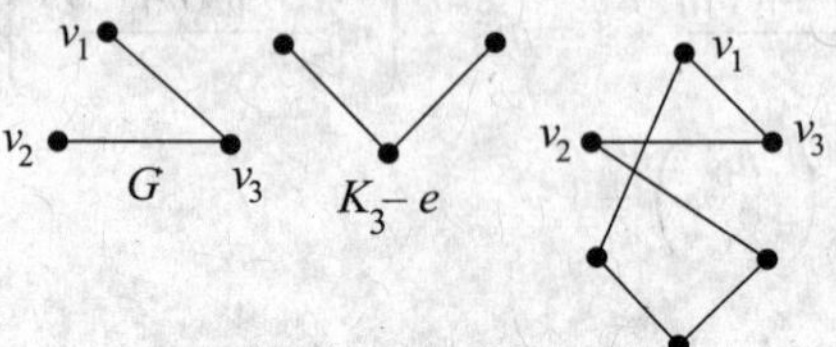

Fig. 1.26

Case 2 If d is odd, take $\frac{(d-1)}{2}$ disjoint copies of the graph $K_{\Delta+1} - e$. For $1 \le i \le n$, join v_i to $\Delta - d_i$ different vertices of degree $\Delta - 1$ from these copies. This can be done for all but one vertex of G, say v_j. Then $d(v_j) = \Delta - 1$ in the graph H_1 so constructed. Take another copy of H_1 say H_1' with $d(v_j') = \Delta - 1$. Then H is obtained by joining v_j and v_j' by an edge. Hence H is Δ – regular and G is an induced subgraph of H. ❑

Example Consider the graph G of Figure 1.27. Here $\Delta = 3$, $d = 3-1+3-1+3-1+3-2 = 2+2+2+1 = 7$, $\frac{(d-1)}{2} = \frac{(7-1)}{2} = 3$. We take 3 copies of $K_{3+1} - e = K_4 - e$.

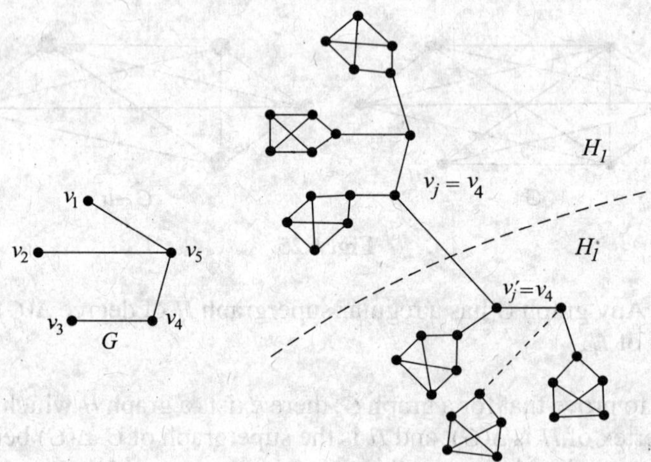

Fig. 1.27

Theorem 1.16 If $G(X, Y, E)$ is a bipartite graph with maximum degree Δ, then G has a Δ-regular bipartite supergraph $H(U, V, F)$ with $X \subseteq U, Y \subseteq V, E \subseteq F$.

Proof Let Δ be the maximum degree in $G(X, Y, E)$. Take Δ copies of G (each isomorphic to G) say $G_i(X_i, Y_i, E_i)$, $1 \le i \le \Delta$. For each $x \in X_1$ with $d(x) < \Delta$, take $r = \Delta - d(x)$ vertices say $x_1, x_2, \ldots, x_r$. Let Y_o be the set of all such vertices as x ranges over X_1 and let $V = Y_o \cup Y_1 \cup \ldots \cup Y_\Delta$. Join each vertex x_i to one vertex x $(d(x) < \Delta)$ from each of the copies X_1, $X_2, \ldots, X_\Delta$.

Similarly, for each $y \in Y_1$ with $d(y) \le \Delta$, take $s = \Delta - d(y)$ vertices say $y_1, y_2, \ldots, y_s$. Let X_o be that set of all such vertices as y ranges over Y_1 and let $U = X_0 \cup X_1 \cup \ldots \cup X_\Delta$. Join each vertex y_j to one vertex y $(d(y) < \Delta)$ from each of the copies $Y_1, Y_2, \ldots, Y_\Delta$. The resulting bipartite graph H has clearly Δ induced bipartite subgraphs G_i each isomorphic to G (Fig. 1.28). ❑

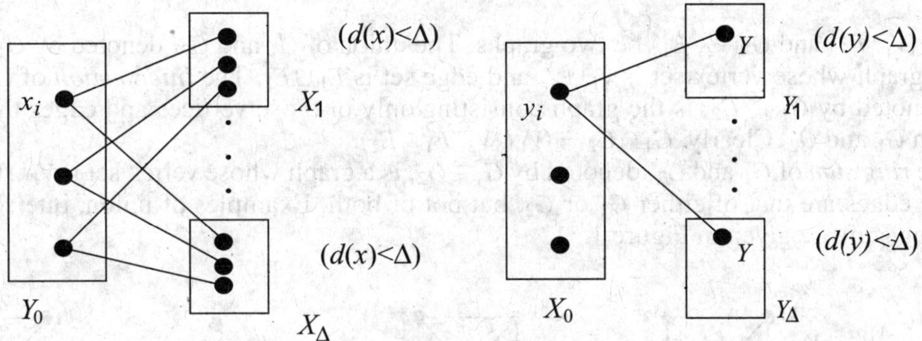

Fig. 1.28

Example 1 Consider the graph G of Figure 1.29. Here $\Delta = 3$, $d(u) = 2 < 3$, $d(x) = 2 < 3$, $d(y) = 2 < 3$, $d(z) = 1 < 3$. Now, $r = \Delta - d(u) = 3 - 2 = 1$ and $s = \Delta - d(x) + \Delta - d(y) + \Delta - d(z) = 3 - 2 + 3 - 2 + 3 - 1 = 4$.

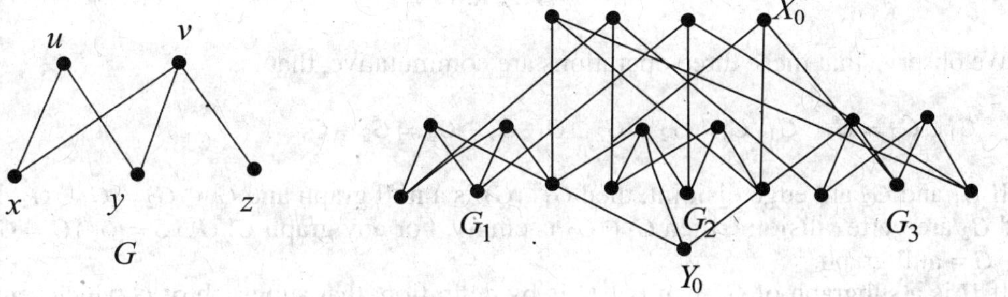

Fig. 1.29

Example 2 In the graph G of Figure 1.30, $\Delta = 2$ and $d(v) = 0 < 2$, $d(x) = 1 < 2$, $d(y) = 1 < 2$ so that $r = \Delta - d(v) = 2 - 0 = 2$ and $s = 2 - 1 + 2 - 1 = 2$.

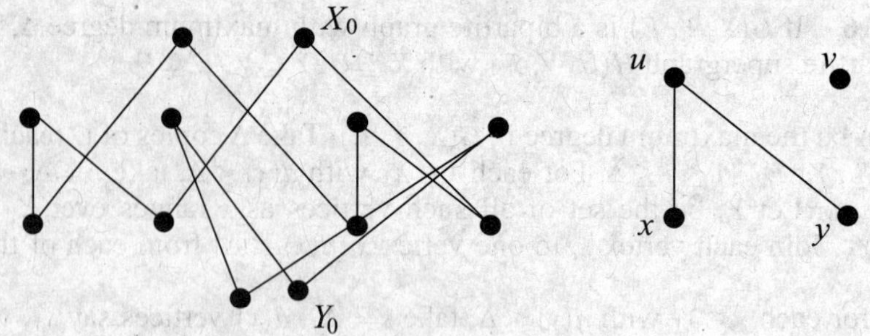

Fig. 1.30

1.7 Operations on Graphs

Let $G_1(V_1, E_1)$ and $G_2(V_2, E_2)$ be two graphs. The union of G_1 and G_2, denoted by $G_1 \cup G_2$, is the graph whose vertex set is $V_1 \cup V_2$ and edge set is $E_1 \cup E_2$. The *intersection* of G_1 and G_2, denoted by $G_1 \cap G_2$, is the graph consisting only of those vertices and edges that are both in G_1 and G_2. Clearly, $G_1 \cap G_2 = (V_1 \cap V_2,\ E_1 \cap E_2)$.

The *ring sum* of G_1 and G_2, denoted by $G_1 \oplus G_2$, is a graph whose vertex set is $V_1 \cup V_2$ and whose edges are that of either G_1 or G_2, but not of both. Examples of union, intersection and ring sum are given in Figure 1.31.

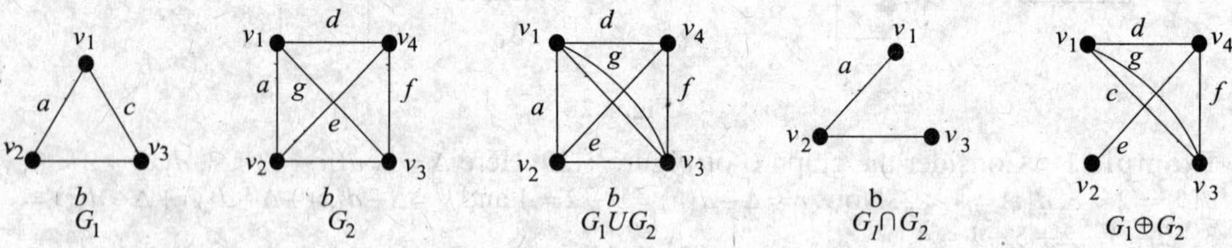

Fig. 1.31

We observe that these three operations are commutative, that is,

$$G_1 \cup G_2 = G_2 \cup G_1,\ G_1 \cap G_2 = G_2 \cap G_1,\ G_1 \oplus G_2 = G_2 \oplus G_1.$$

If G_1 and G_2 are edge disjoint, then $G_1 \cap G_2$ is a null graph and $G_1 \oplus G_2 = G_1 \cup G_2$. If G_1 and G_2 are vertex disjoint, then $G_1 \cap G_2$ is empty. For any graph G, $G \cup G = G \cap G = G$ and $G \oplus G =$ null graph.

If H is a subgraph of G, then $G \oplus H$ is by definition, that subgraph of G which remains after all the edges in H have been removed from G. We write, $G \oplus H = G - H$, whenever $H \subseteq G$. $G \oplus H = G - H$ is also called complement of H in G. Figure 1.32 illustrates this operation.

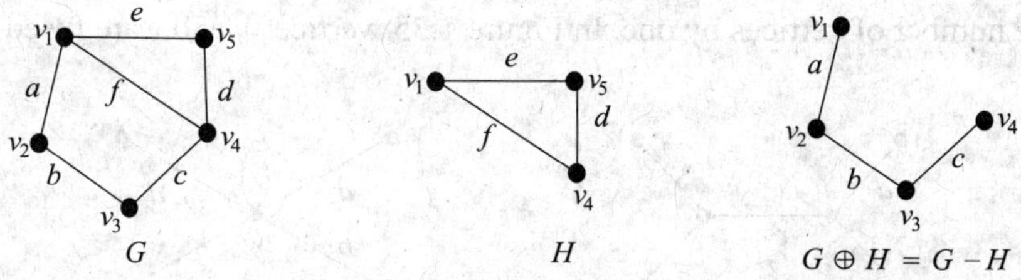

Fig. 1.32

Decomposition: A graph G is said to be decomposed into two subgraphs G_1 and G_2 if $G_1 \cup G_2 = G$ and $G_1 \cap G_2 =$ a null graph. In other words, every edge of G occurs either in G_1 or in G_2, but not in both, while as some of the vertices can occur in both G_1 and G_2. In decomposition, isolated vertices are disregarded. In Figure 1.33, graph G has been decomposed into subgraph G_1 and G_2.

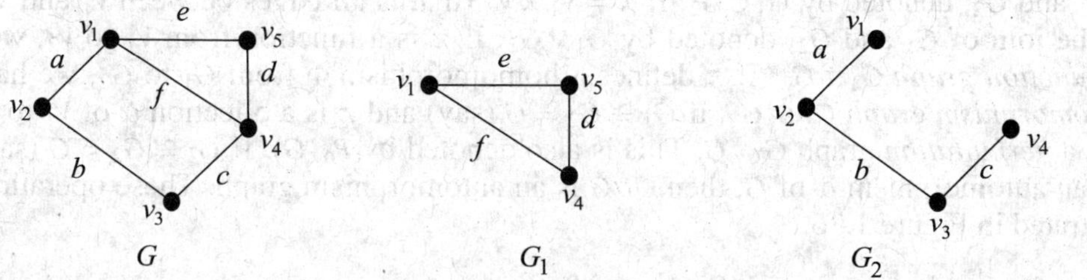

Fig. 1.33

Deletion: Let G be a graph and v be any vertex in G. Then $G - v$ denotes the subgraph of G by deleting vertex v, and all the edges of G which are incident with v. An example of deletion of a vertex is given in Figure 1.34.

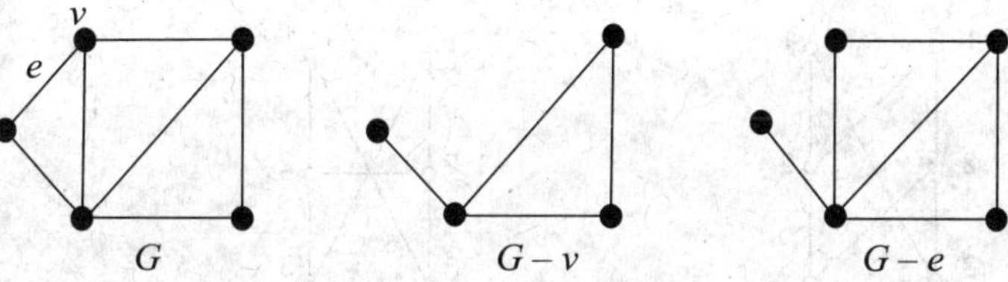

Fig. 1.34

If e is any edge of G, then $G - e$ is a subgraph of G obtained by deleting e from G (Fig. 1.34). Deletion of an edge does not imply deletion of its end vertices. Therefore $G - e = G \oplus e$.

Fusion: A pair of vertices u and v in a graph are said to be fused (merged or identified) if u and v are replaced by a single new vertex such that every edge incident on u or v is incident on this new vertex. Therefore, fusion of vertices does not alter the number of edges, but reduces the number of vertices by one. In Figure 1.35, vertices u and v are fused to a single vertex w.

Fig. 1.35

Let $G_1(V_1, E_1)$ and $G_2(V_2, E_2)$ be two graphs with $V_1 \cap V_2 = \Phi$ and $E_1 \cap E_2 = \Phi$. Let G be the compound graph whose vertex set is $V_1 \cup V_2$ and edge set is $E_1 \cup E_2 \cup E_3$, where E_3 is a subset of the set of edges $\{v_i v_j : v_i \in V_1,\ v_j \in V_2\}$. We represent E_3 by the symmetric binary relation $\pi \subseteq V_1 \times V_2$, and the compound graph G by $G_1\ \pi\ G_2$. If $\pi = \Phi$, then we get the union of G_1 and G_2, denoted by $G_1 \cup G_2$. If $\pi = V_1 \times V_2$ (that is all edges between V_1 and V_2), we get the join of G_1 and G_2, denoted by $G_1 \vee G_2$. If π is a function from V_1 to V_2, we have the *function graph* G_1 f G_2. If π defines a homomorphism Φ from G_1 to G_2, we have the *homomorphism graph* $G_1\ \Phi\ G_2$. If $G_1 \cong G_2 = G$ (say) and π is a bijection α of V_1 to V_2, we have a *permutation* graph $G\ \alpha\ G$. This is also denoted by $P_\alpha(G)$. If $G_1 \cong G_2 = G$ (say) and π is an automorphism α of G, then $G\alpha G$ is an automorphism graph. These operations are illustrated in Figure 1.36.

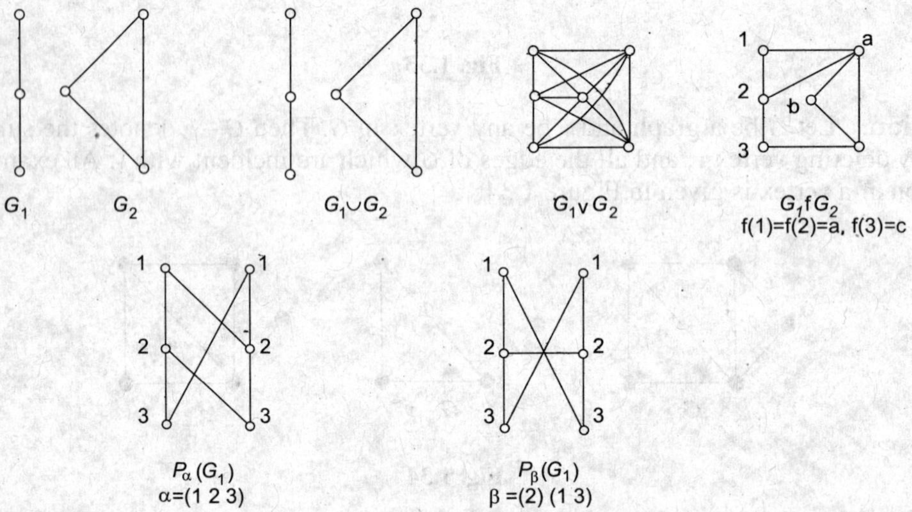

Fig. 1.36

Let G_1 (V_1, E_1) and G_2 (V_2, E_2) be two graphs, and let the vertex sets V_1 and V_2 be labelled by the same set of labels. We note here that each of V_1 and V_2 need not have all the labels.

The *sum* of G_1 and G_2, denoted by $G_1 + G_2$, is the graph $G(V, E)$, where $V = V_1 \cup V_2$ and an edge $v_iv_j \in E$ if and only if v_iv_j is an edge of G_1 or G_2 or both. The *direct sum* denoted by $G_1(+)G_2$ is the graph $G(V, E)$ with $V = V_1 \cup V_2$ and an edge $v_iv_j \in E$ if and only if v_iv_j is an edge of G_1 or G_2, but not of both. The *superposition* graph $G = G_1$ s G_2 has vertex set $V = V_1 \cup V_2$ and the edge set E contains all the edges of G_1 and G_2 with the identity of edges of G_1 and G_2 in G being preserved by assigning two different labels to these edges. So, if v_iv_j is an edge in both G_1 and G_2, then there are two edges v_iv_j in G with different labels. For illustration of these operations, see Figure 1.37. We can extend these operations to a finite number of graphs.

We form the compound graphs G from G_1 and G_2 with vertex sets $V_1 \times V_2$ as follows.

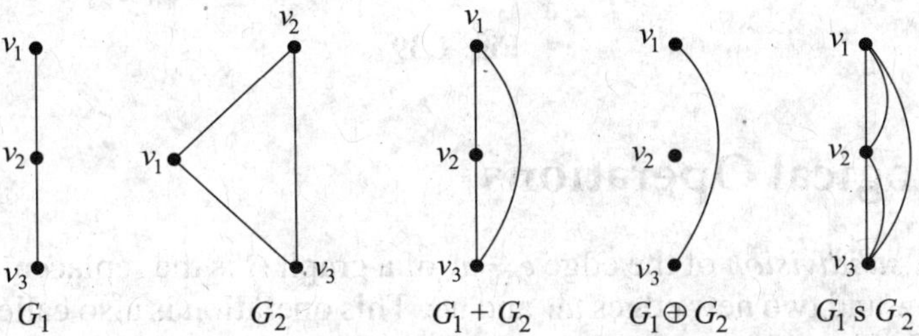

Fig. 1.37

The cartesian product of G_1 and G_2, denoted by $G = G_1 \times G_2$, is the graph whose vertex set is $V = V_1 \times V_2$ and for any two vertices $w_1 = (u_1, v_1)$ and $w_2 = (u_2, v_2)$ in V; $u_1, u_2 \in V_1$ and $v_1, v_2 \in V_2$, there is an edge $w_1w_2 \in E(G)$ if and only if either (a) $u_1 = u_2$ and $v_1v_2 \in E_2$, or (b) $v_1 = v_2$ and $u_1u_2 \in E_1$.

The *tensor product* (conjunction), denoted by $G = G_1 \wedge G_2$, is the graph with vertex set $V = V_1 \times V_2$ and for any two vertices $w_1 = (u_1, v_1)$ and $w_2 = (u_2, v_2)$ in V; $u_1, u_2 \in V_1$ and $v_1, v_2 \in V_2$, there is an edge $w_1w_2 \in E(G)$ if and only if $u_1u_2 \in E_1$ and $v_1v_2 \in E_2$.

The *normal product* (strong product), denoted by $G = G_1 \circ G_2$, is the graph with vertex set $V = V_1 \times V_2$ and for any two vertices $w_1 = (u_1, v_1)$ and $w_2 = (u_2, v_2)$ in V; $u_1, u_2 \in V_1$ and $v_1, v_2 \in V_2$, there is an edge $w_1w_2 \in E(G)$ if and only if one of the following holds:
(a) $u_1 = u_2$ and $v_1v_2 \in E_2$ (b) $v_1 = v_2$ and $u_1u_2 \in E_1$ (c) $u_1u_2 \in E_1$ and $v_1v_2 \in E_2$.

It is easy to see that $G_1 \times G_2$ and $G_1 \wedge G_2$ are spanning subgraphs of $G_1 \circ G_2$ and also $G_1 \circ G_2 = (G_1 \times G_2) \oplus (G_1 \wedge G_2)$. Figure 1.38 illustrates these operations.

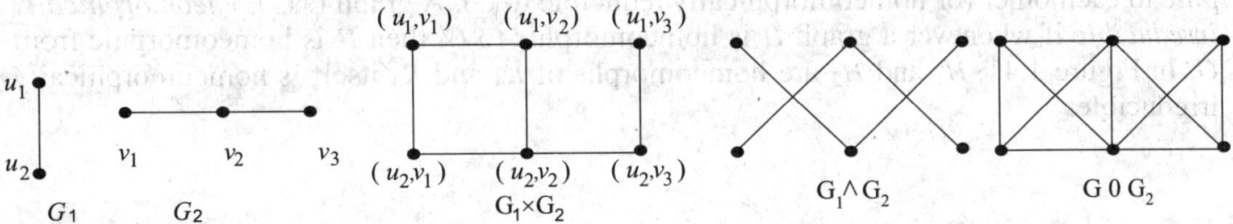

Fig. 1.38

The *composition* of G_1 and G_2, denoted by $G = G_1[G_2]$, is the graph with vertex set $V = V_1 \times V_2$, and for any two vertices $w_1 = (u_1, v_1)$ and $w_2 = (u_2, v_2)$ in V; $u_1, u_2 \in V_1$ and $v_1, v_2 \in V_2$, there is an edge $w_1w_2 \in E(G)$ if and only if either (a) $u_1u_2 \in E_1$ or (b) $u_1 = u_2$ and $v_1v_2 \in E_2$ (Fig. 1.39).

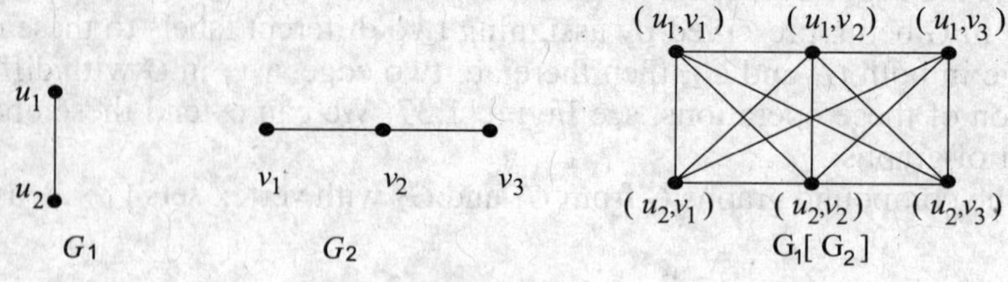

Fig. 1.39

1.8 Topological Operations

Definition: A *subdivision* of the edge $e = uv$ of a graph G is the replacement of the edge e by a new vertex w and two new edges uw and wv. This operation is also called an *elementary subdivision* of G (Fig. 1.40).

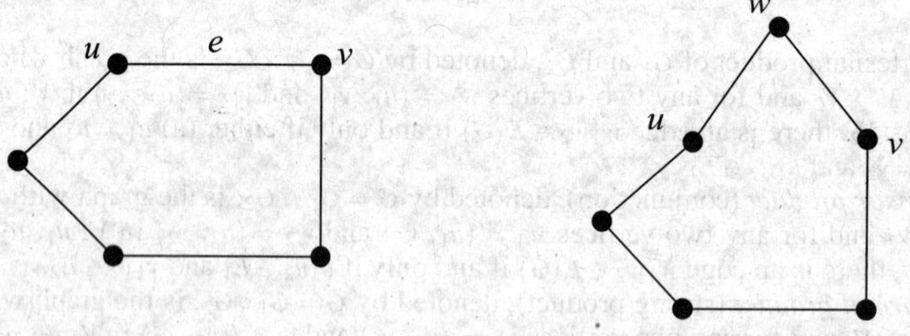

Fig. 1.40

A graph H obtained by a sequence of elementary subdivisions from a graph G is said to be a *subdivision graph* of G, or to be homeomorphic (or a homeomorph) of G. Two graphs H_1 and H_2 which are homeomorphs of the same graph G are said to be *homeomorphic* to each other (or homeomorphically reducible to G). A graph G is *homeomorphically irreducible* if whenever a graph H is homeomorphic to G, then H is homeomorphic from G. In Figure 1.41, H_1 and H_2 are homeomorphs of K_4 and K_4 itself is homeomorphically irreducible.

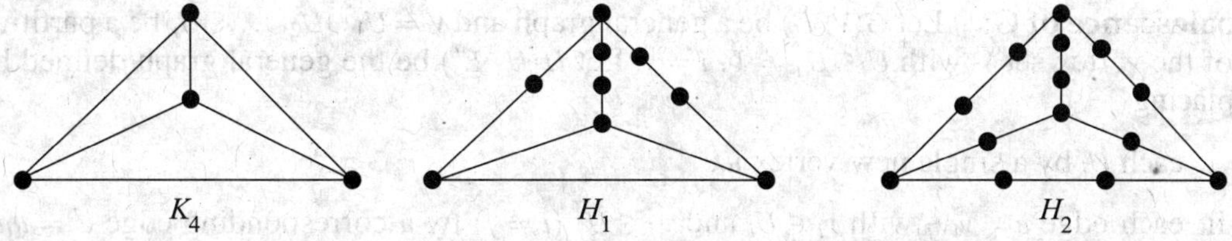

Fig. 1.41

The relation being homeomorphic to each other is an equivalence relation and each equivalence class contains a unique homeomorphically irreducible graph which is taken as the representative of the class.

Identification of the vertices: Let $G(V, E)$ be a general graph and let U be a subset of the vertex set V. Let H be the general graph obtained from G by the following operations.

i. Replace the set of vertices U by a single new vertex u.

ii. Replace the edge $e = ab$ with $a \in U$ and $b \in V - U$ by a corresponding edge $e' = ub$.

iii. Replace each edge $e = ab$ with $a, b \in U$ (b possibly being the same as a) by a loop at u.

Let K be the multigraph obtained from H by dropping all loops and L be the graph obtained from K by replacing each multiple edge by a single edge. Then H, K, L are respectively said to be obtained from G by a *general, multiple, simple identification* of the vertices of U. We write $H = G * U$, $K = G : U$, $L = G.U$. This operation is illustrated in Figure 1.42.

Remarks

1. The operation in (ii) may result in the generation of multiple edges and that in (iii), in the generation of loops even when G is a simple graph.

2. For $b \neq u$ in H, $q_H[a, b] = \sum \{q_G[a, b] : a \in U\}$.

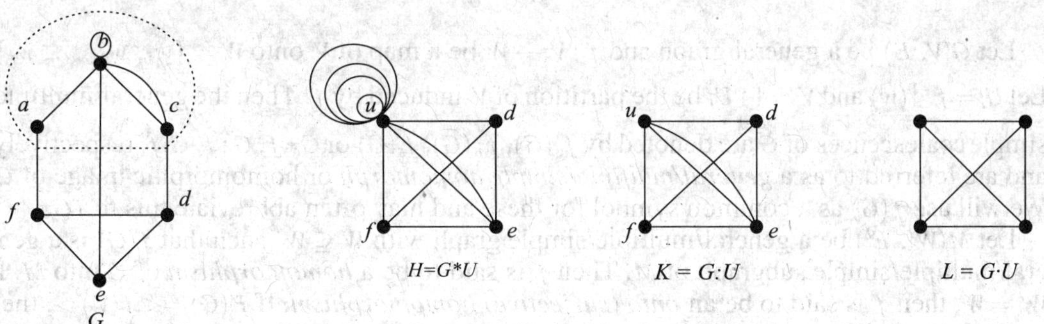

Fig. 1.42

Coalescence of G: Let $G(V, E)$ be a general graph and $V = U_1 \cup U_2 \cup \ldots \cup U_r$ be a partition π of the vertex set V with $U_i \cap U_j \neq \Phi$, $i \neq j$. Let $H(U, E')$ be the general graph defined by replacing

i. each U_i by a single new vertex u_i,

ii. each edge $e = v_i v_j$ with $v_i \in U_i$ and $v_j \in U_j$ $(i \neq j)$ by a corresponding edge $e' = u_i u_j$ and

iii. each edge $e = ab$ with $a, b \in U_i$ by a loop at u_i.

Let K be the multigraph obtained from H by dropping the loops and L be the graph obtained from K by replacing the multiple edges by single edges. Then H, K, L are respectively called the *general/multiple/simple coalescence* of G and we write $H = G * \Pi, K = G : \Pi$ and $L = G.\Pi$. Coalescence of a graph is illustrated in Figure 1.43.

Remarks

1. Clearly H is obtained from G by sequentially identifying the vertices in U_i, $1 \leq i \leq r$ in any order.

2. To coalescence a partition π_1 of a proper subset V_1 of V, we may adopt the above definition by augmenting π_1 to a partition of V by adjoining the singleton sets corresponding to the vertices in $V - V_1$.

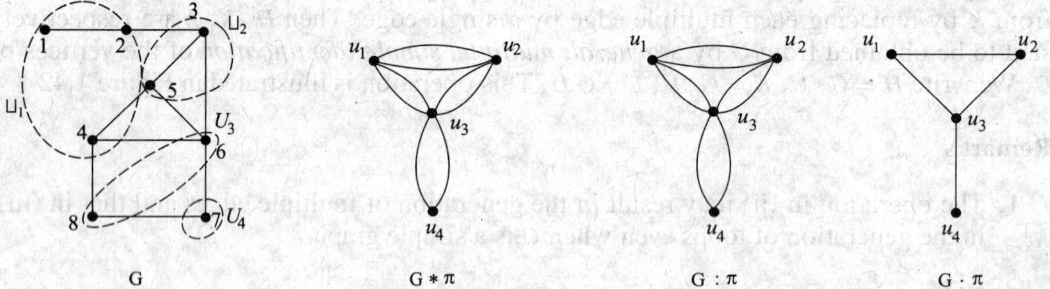

Fig. 1.43

Let $G(V, E)$ be a general graph and $f : V \to W$ be a map of V onto $W = \{w_1, w_2, \ldots, w_r\}$. Let $U_i = f^{-1}(w)$ and $V = \bigcup_{i=1}^{r} U_i$ be the partition of V induced by f. Then the general/multiple/simple coalescences of G are denoted by $f_g(G)$, $f_m(G)$, $f_s(G)$ or $G * f$, $G : f$, $G.f$, respectively, and are referred to as a *general/multiple/simple homomorph* or homomorphic image of G. We will use $f(G)$ as a common symbol for these and may often abbreviate this to fG.

Let $M(W', E')$ be a general/multiple/simple graph with $W \subseteq W'$ such that $f(G)$ is a general/multiple/simple subgraph of M. Then f is said to be a *homomorphism* of G into M. If $W' = W$, then f is said to be an *onto (surjective) homomorphism*. If $F(G) =< f(V) >$, then f is called a *full homomorphism.* In case $f(G) = M$, then f is called a *full onto homomorphism*.

Remarks

1. An injective homomorphism (i.e., f is injective) is a *monomorphism.* A full onto monomorphism is an *isomorphism.*

2. If every U_i is an independent set in G, then f is a discrete homomorphism. If $U_1 = \{u, v\}$ and other U_i's are singleton sets of V, then f is called an *elementary homomorphism*, and if $uv \notin E$, then f is a *discrete elementary homomorphism.*

3. If every $< U_i >$ is a connected subgraph of G, then f is called *connected homomorphism.* An elementary homomorphism with $uv \in E$ is called a *connected elementary homomorphism.*

4. A mapping $f : V \to W'$, where $G(V, E)$ and $M(W', E')$ are simple graphs, is a homomorphism of G into M if and only if $uv \in E$ implies that $f(u)f(v) \in E'$.

The following result is due to Ore [178].

Theorem 1.17 Any homomorphism is the product of a connected and a discrete homomorphism.

Proof Let f be a homomorphism of $G(V, E)$ into $M(W', E')$ with $f(V) = W$ (i.e., $f(V_i) = W_i$). So, $V = f^{-1}(W)$ and $V_i = f^{-1}(W_i)$. Then each $< f^{-1}(W_i) >$ can consist of a number of components (which are, in fact, connected) $C_{i_1}, C_{i_2}, \ldots, C_{i_j}, \ldots, C_{i_{n_i}}$ with vertex sets $V_{i_1}, V_{i_2}, \ldots, V_{i_j}, \ldots, V_{i_{n_i}}$.

The coalescence of $V_i = f^{-1}(W_i)$ can be done in two stages. First, we perform a multiple coalescence of $V_i = V_{i_1} \cup V_{i_2} \cup \ldots \cup V_{i_j} \cup \ldots \cup V_{i_{n_i}}$ sending vertex set V_{i_j} to a single vertex W_{i_j}. This, when done for all $V_i = f^{-1}(W_i)$'s, corresponds to a connected homomorphism Φ of G. Next, identify the vertices W_{i_j}, $1 \le j \le n_i$ of $\Phi(G)$ into a single vertex W_i for $1 \le i \le |W|$. This corresponds to a discrete homomorphism θ of $\Phi(G)$ into M. Clearly, $f(G) = \theta(\Phi(G))$. ❑

Contractions: Let $G(V, E)$ be a general graph and F be a subset of E such that the edge-induced subgraph $< F >$ is connected on the vertex subset $U = V(< F >)$. Then the general/multiple/simple graphs obtained by the identification of the vertex set U' in the general graph $G - F$ are called the *general/multiple/simple contractions* of F in G and are denoted by $G|$ þ F, $G||F$ and $G|F$ respectively. Consider the graph of Figure 1.44. The vertices of $U = \{v_1, v_2, v_3, v_4\}$ in $G - F$ have been identified.

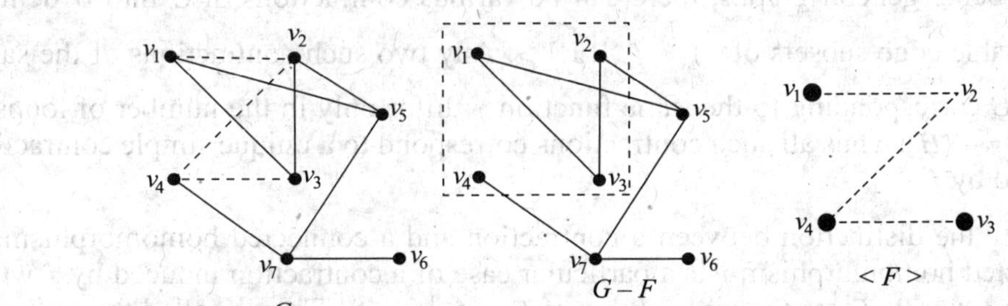

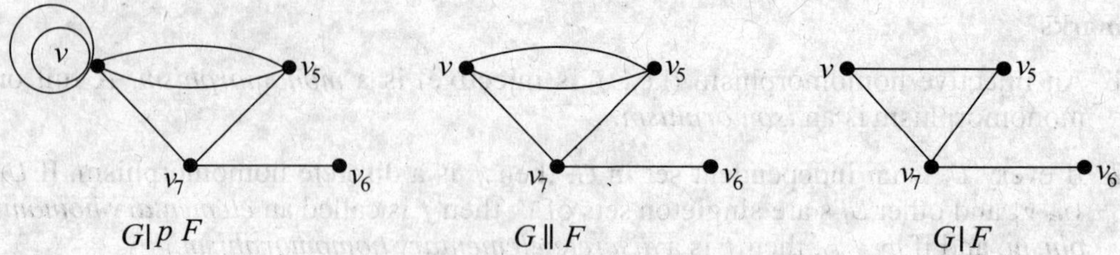

Identification of U = $\{v_1\ v_2, v_3, v_4\}$ in G–F

Fig. 1.44

Let $G(V,\ E)$ be a general graph and let F be a subset of E such that the edge-induced subgraph $< F >$ has components $< F_i >$ on vertex sets $V(< F_i >) = U_i$, $1 \leq i \leq r$. Let π be the partition of V induced by the U_i, vertices in U_i being taken as singleton sets of the partition.

The general/multiple/simple coalescences in the general graph $G - F$ are called the *general/multiple/simple contractions* of F in G and are denoted by $G|\,\text{þ}\,F$, $G||F$ and $G|F$ respectively.

Let $G(V,\ E)$ be a general graph and let $W = \{w_1,\ w_2,\ \ldots,\ w_r\}$. Suppose $f : V \rightarrow W$ is a map such that $< U_i >$ is a connected general subgraph of G, where $U_i = f^{-1}(w_i)$, $1 \leq i \leq r(f(U_i = w_i)$. Let $F_i \subseteq E(U_i)$ be such that F_i induces a spanning connected subgraph of $< U_i >$ and let $F = \bigcup_{i=1}^{r} F_i$. Then $G|\,\text{þ}\,F$, $G||F$ and $G|F$ are respectively called general/ multiple/simple contraction induced by f and F and are denoted by $f_F(G)$. Here f is called a *contraction mapping* of G.

If $f_F(G) = H$, then G is said to be $g/m/s$- contractible to H and H is called a $g/m/s$-*contraction* of G, according as H is a $g/m/s$-graph. We call *simple contractible* and *simple contraction* as *contractible* and *contraction*.

If a subgraph of G is contractible to H (equivalently, if H is a subgraph of a contraction of G), then H is called a *subcontraction* of G, and we also say that G is *subcontractible* to H. We denote this by $G\}H$.

Remarks

1. It can be observed that corresponding to every general contraction there exists a unique contraction mapping f but given a mapping f from $V(G)$ to $V(H)$, with G and H being general graphs, there can be various contractions of G into H defined by suitable edge subsets of $\bigcup_{i=1}^{k} < f^{-1}(w_i) >$. Any two such contractions of the same graph G corresponding to the same function f differ only in the number of loops at $w_i \in W = V(H)$. Thus all such contractions correspond to a unique simple contraction induced by f.

2. We note the distinction between a contraction and a connected homomorphism. A connected homomorphism f is a particular case of a contraction induced by f when the edge subsets F_i are the null subsets of $E < f^{-1}(w_i) >$. This is called the *null con-*

traction corresponding to f and is denoted by $f_0(G)$. Also, the connected homomorphism induced by f differs from any proper contraction induced by f only in the number of loops at $w_i \in W$. The contraction induced by f in which each $F_i = E < f^{-1}(w_i) >$ is called the *full contraction* induced by f.

3. If $e = uv \in E$ and $F = \{e\}$, then $G|\flat e$ is called an *elementary contraction* of G and differs from the corresponding connected elementary homomorphism $G * \{v, u\}$ by the absence of a loop at the common vertex $w = \{u, v\}$ in H.

The following result is due to Behzad and Chartrand [15].

Theorem 1.18 If a graph H is homeomorphic from a graph G, then G is a contraction of H.

Proof If $G = H$, then obviously G is the null contraction of H corresponding to the identity mapping $f : V(H) \to V(G)$.

Let $G \neq H$. Then H is obtained from G by a sequence of elementary subdivisions, say $\in_1, \in_2, \ldots, \in_k$, through the intermediate graphs $G_i = \in_i (G_{i-1})$, $G_0 = G$, $G_k = H$. Let G_i be obtained from G_{i-1} by subdividing the edge uv, introducing a new vertex w. Then G_{i-1} is obtainable from G_i by the elementary contraction with $f = \{uw\}$. That is, $G_{i-1} = G_i|uw = \Phi(G_i)$, say. Then, clearly we have $G = \Phi_1(\Phi_2 \ldots (\Phi_k(H) \ldots)$. Therefore G can be obtained from H by a sequence of elementary contractions and is thus a contraction of H. ❑

The converse of the above theorem is not true in general. To see this, consider the graphs in Fig. 1.45. Here the graph H is a contraction of the graph G by using the mapping $f(a) = f(b) = f(c) = a'$, $f(g) = g'$, $f(h) = h'$, $f(d) = f(e) = f(f) = d'$. But G is not homeomorphic from H.

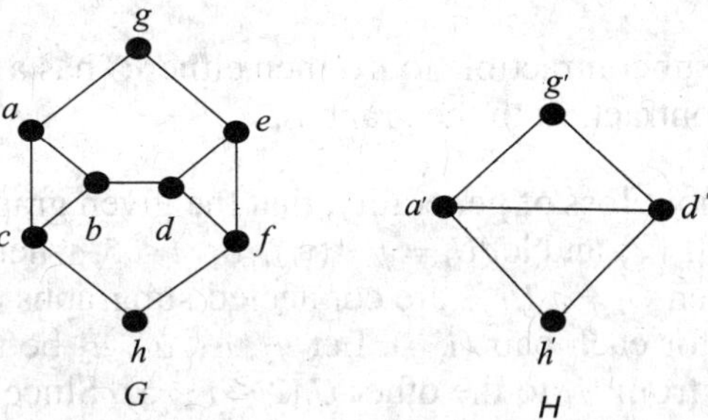

Fig. 1.45

Corollary 1.1 If a graph H contains a subgraph K homeomorphic from a non-trivial connected graph G, then G has a sub contraction of H.

The next result due to Halin can be found in Ore [172].

Theorem 1.19 If a graph G is contractible to a graph H and $\Delta(H) \leq 3$, then G has a subgraph homeomorphic from H.

Proof Let G be a graph contractible to the graph H. Hence there is a mapping $f: V(G) \to V(H)$ inducing the contraction H. Therefore, $G_i = < f^{-1}(v_i) >$ for $v_i \in V(H)$ are connected induced subgraphs of G which have been contracted to the vertices v_i of H. Let $U_i = f^{-1}(v_i)$.

As $\Delta(H) \leq 3$, for given U_1 there are at most three U_i, say U_2, U_3, U_4 such that there is an edge from U_1 to U_i. Let the end vertices in U_1 of three such edges from U_1 to U_2, U_3, U_4, respectively be u_2, u_3, u_4. Since G_1 is connected, there is $u_2 - u_3$ path P and a $u_4 - u_5$ path Q in G_1, where u_5 is the first vertex that Q has in common with P. (If there are only two vertices, we consider only the path P.) For each edge v_iv_j in H, we choose one edge between U_i and U_j in G and then the set of subgraphs PUQ in G_i. The graph H_1 so formed is a subgraph of G and clearly from the construction it is homeomorphic from H (Fig. 1.46). ❑

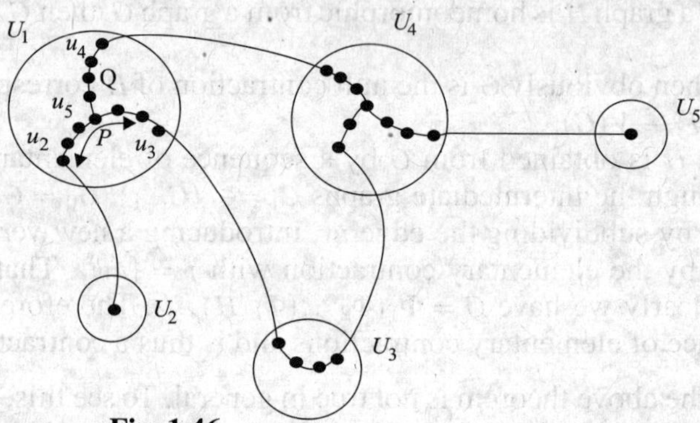

Fig. 1.46

Corollary 1.2 If the graph G has a sub contraction H with $\Delta(H) \leq 3$, then G has a subgraph homeomorphic from H.

Theorem 1.20 If G is subcontractible to K_5, then either G has a subgraph homeomorphic from K_5, or G has a subcontraction to the graph L.

Proof We assume without loss of generality, that the given graph G is contractible to K_5. Let $V(K_5) = \{v_1, v_2, v_3, v_4, v_5\}$ and let $U_i = f^{-1}(v_i)$, $1 \leq i \leq 5$, where $f: V(G) \to V(K_5)$ is the contraction mapping. Then $G_i = < U_i >$ are connected subgraphs of G and there is an edge in G between U_i and U_j for each pair (i, j). Let u_2, u_3, u_4, u_5 be the end vertices in U_1, of four such edges selected from U_1 to the other $U_i (2 \leq i \leq 5)$. Since G_1 is connected, there is a $u_2 - u_3$ path P in G, and there are $u_4 - u_4'$, $u_5 - u_5'$ paths Q and R, where u_4' and u_5' are the first vertices that these paths have in common with P.

If $u_4' \neq u_5'$, we can contract each U_i, $2 \leq i \leq 5$ to a vertex to get a K_4 and this together with the selected edges from U_1 to the U_i, and the path P, Q, R is a graph homeomorphic to L, so that G has a subcontraction to L.

If $u_4' = u_5'$, for any choice of P and for every set U_i, G has a subgraph homeomorphic from K_5. The same is the case when in each U_i, the four end vertices u_j coincide (Fig. 1.47). ❑

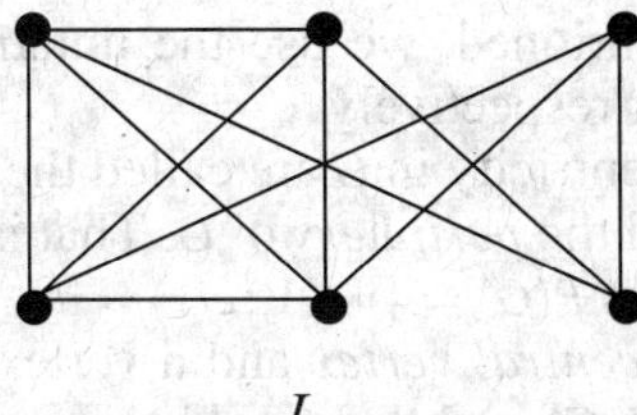

Fig. 1.47

1.9 Distance and eccentricity

Definition: Distance between two vertices u and v of a connected graph G is the length of the shortest path between u and v. It is denoted by $d(u, v)$. Clearly, by convection, $d(u, u) = 0$. The shortest path is called a $u-v$ *geodesic*, or a $u-v$ distance path.

Theorem 1.21 The distance function for a connected graph is a metric defined on its vertex set.

Proof Let G be a connected graph and $d(u, v)$ be the distance function, with u and v being vertices of G.

1. Clearly, $d(u, v) \geq 0$, with $d(u, u) = 0$.
2. Also, $d(u, v) = d(v, u)$, because the length of the shortest path from u to v is same as the length of the shortest path from v to u.
3. For any vertices u, v, w in G, we have $d(u, v) \leq d(u, w) + d(w, v)$

Thus d is a metric. ❑

Note The distance between two vertices u and v in different components of a disconnected graph is infinite and this distance function does not induce a metric on the vertex set.

Neighbourhood: Let v be any vertex of a connected graph G. The ith neighbourhood of v is $N_i(v) = \{u \in V : d(v, u) = i\}$. We set $N_0(v) = \{v\}$ and denote $N_1(v)$ simply by $N(v)$, and call $N(v)$ as the neighbourhood of v, or the neighbours of v.

The s-ball at v is $B_s(v) = \bigcup_{j=0}^{s} N_j(v)$.

Eccentricity of a vertex: Let G be a connected graph. The eccentricity of a vertex v in G is the distance of the vertex u farthest from v. It is denoted by $e(v)$. That is, $e(v) = \max\{d(u, v) : u \in V\}$.

The minimum eccentricity is called the *radius* of G and the maximum eccentricity is called the *diameter* of G. The radius is denoted by r and diameter by d.

Therefore, $r = \min\{e(v) : v \in V\}$ and $d = \max\{e(v) : v \in V\}$.

When the graph is to be mentioned, we use the notations, $e(v|G)$, $r(G)$ and $d(G)$ for eccentricity, radius and diameter respectively.

The vertices of minimum eccentricity in G are called the *centres* of G and the vertices of maximum eccentricity are called the *periphery* of G. That is, the centre of G is $C(G) = \{v \in V : e(v) = r\}$ and periphery of G is $P(G) = \{v \in V ; e(v) = d\}$.

A vertex in $C(G)$ is called a *central vertex* and a vertex in $P(G)$ is called a *peripheral vertex*. A graph having $C(G) = V(G)$ is called a *self-centered graph*.

A longest geodesic (maximum among the shortest paths between any two vertices) of a graph is called a *diametral path* of G. Note that this is not same as a longest path in G. The diameter is the length of any diametral path. A graph G is said to be *geodetic* if any two of its vertices are joined by a unique geodesic.

Theorem 1.22 The radius and diameter of a graph are related as $r \le d \le 2r$.

Proof Clearly, $r \le d$ follows from the definition of r and d. Let u and v be the ends of a diametral path and w be a central vertex. Then,

$$d = d(u, v) \le d(u, w) + d(w, v) \le r + r = 2r,$$

by using the triangle inequality of the metric and definition of r. ❑

Example Consider the graph shown in Figure 1.48. The eccentricities are 5, 4, 3, 3, 3, 4, 5, 4, 5; $r(G) = 3$, $d(G) = 5$, $C(G) = \{v_3, v_4, v_5\}$, $d(G) = \{v_1, v_7, v_9\}$. Diametral paths are $v_1v_2v_4v_5v_6v_7$, $v_1v_2v_3v_5v_6v_7$, $v_1v_2v_4v_5v_8v_9$ and $v_1v_2v_3v_5v_8v_9$.

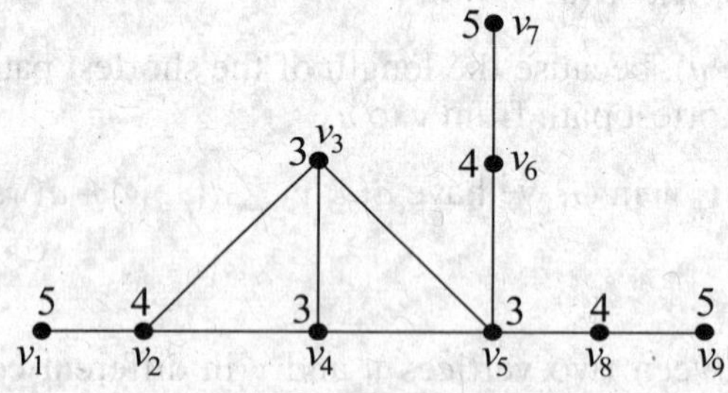

Fig. 1.48

Detours: A *detour path* between the vertices u and v in a graph G is the path of maximum length between u and v. The length of detour path is called *detour distance* and is denoted by $\partial(u, v)$.

The *detour eccentricity* of a vertex v is defined by $\partial(v) = \max\{\partial(v, u) : u \in V\}$.

The *detour diameter*, or detour number of G is defined as $\partial(G) = \max\{\partial(v) : v \in V\}$ and the *detour radius* is defined by $r_\partial(G) = \min\{\partial(v) : v \in V\}$.

A longest path in G is called a *detour path* in G and its length is $\partial(G)$. The *detour center* of G is $C_\partial(G) = \{v \in V : \partial(v) = r_\partial(G)\}$.

Theorem 1.23 If a connected graph G of order n has minimum degree δ, then

$$\partial(G) = \min(n-1, 2\delta). \quad (1.23.1)$$

Proof Clearly, $\partial(G) \leq n-1$. If $\partial(G) = n-1$, then (1.23.1) is obviously true, as min $(n-1,\ 2\delta) = 2$, or $n-1$ according as $\delta = 1$, or $\delta = n-1$. Now, let $\partial(G) < n-1$. Assume the contrary,

$$\partial(G) < \min(n-1,\ 2\delta). \quad (1.23.2)$$

Let $P = v_0v_1\ldots v_\partial$ be a path of length $\partial = \partial(G)$ and H be the subgraph induced by the vertex set of P. Then H does not contain a spanning cycle, because otherwise some vertex $v \in V(G) - V(H)$ will be adjacent to some vertex v_i of $V(H)$ giving a path of length $\partial + 1$. Thus $v_0v_\partial \notin E$, and for similar reasons v_0 and v_∂ are adjacent only to vertices in H.

Let $S = \{v_i \in V(H) : v_0v_i \in E\}$ and $T = \{v_i \in V(H) : v_{i-1}v_\partial \in E\}$.

Since H does not contain a spanning cycle, $S \cap T = \Phi$. Also, $v_0 \notin SUT$, so that $|S \cup T| \leq \partial$. Also, $|S| \geq \delta$ and $|T| \geq \delta$, therefore $\partial \geq |S \cup T| = |S| + |T| \geq \delta + \delta = 2\delta$. That is,

$$\partial \geq 2\delta. \quad (1.23.3)$$

Therefore, $2\delta \leq \partial < n-1$, so that $2\delta < n-1$.

Thus (1.23.2) gives $\partial < \min(n-1,\ 2\delta)$ implying $\partial < 2\delta$ (because min $(n-1,\ 2\delta) = 2\delta$ as $2\delta < n-1$), which contradicts (1.23.3) and so our assumption (1.23.2) is wrong.

Hence, $\partial(G) \geq \min(n-1,\ 2\delta)$. ❑

1.10 Exercises

1. If G is a graph with n vertices and m edges and if k is the smallest positive integer such that $k \geq 2m/n$, then prove G has a vertex of degree at least k.

2. If G is a graph with n vertices and if r vertices out of n have degree k and the others have degree $k+1$, then prove $r = (k+1)n - 2m$, where m is the number of edges in G.

3. If G is a k-regular graph (k being odd), prove that the number of edges in G is a multiple of k.

4. If G is a graph with n vertices and exactly $n-1$ edges, then prove that G has either a vertex of degree 1 or a vertex of degree zero.

5. If in a graph G, $\delta \geq \frac{n-1}{2}$, then show that G is connected.

6. If a graph G is not connected, then show that $\overline{G}$ is connected.

7. Show that if a self-complementary graph contains a pendant vertex, then it must have at least another pendant vertex.

8. Prove that any two connected graphs with n vertices, all of degree 2, are isomorphic.

9. Prove that if a connected graph G is decomposed into two subgraphs G_1 and G_2, there must be at least one vertex common between G_1 and G_2.

10. Prove that a connected graph G remains connected after removing an edge e from G if and only if e is in some cycle of G.

11. If the intersection of two paths is a disconnected graph, show that the union of the two paths has at least one cycle.

12. Show that the order of a self-complementary graph is of the form $4n$ or $4n+1$, where n is a positive integer.

13. Draw all the non-isomorphic self complementary graphs on four vertices.

14. Show that the bipartition of a connected graph is unique. Prove that a graph with $n(n > 1)$ vertices has at least $(n-1)([n/2])$ cycles.

15. Prove that a graph with n vertices must be connected if it has more than $(n-1)(n-2)/2$ edges.

16. Prove that a graph with n vertices $(n > 2)$ cannot be bipartite if it has more than $n^2/4$ edges.

17. Prove that every graph with n vertices is isomorphic to a subgraph of K_n.

18. Prove that if a graph has more edges than vertices then it must possesses at least one cycle.

2. Degree Sequences

The concept of degrees in graphs has provided a framework for the study of various structural properties of graphs and has therefore attracted the attention of many graph theorists. Here we deliberate on the various criteria for a non-decreasing or non-increasing sequence of non-negative integers to be a degree sequence of some graph.

2.1 Degree Sequences

Let d_i, $1 \le i \le n$, be the degrees of the vertices v_i of a graph in any order. The sequence $[d_i]_1^n$ is called the degree sequence of the graph. The non-negative sequence $[d_i]_1^n$ is called the degree sequence of the graph if it is the degree sequence of some graph, and the graph is said to realise the sequence.

The set of distinct non-negative integers occurring in a degree sequence of a graph is called its *degree set*. A set of non-negative integers is called a *degree set* if it is the degree set of some graph, and the graph is said to realise the degree set.

Two graphs with the same degree sequence are said to be *degree equivalent*. In the graph of Figure 2.1(a), the degree sequence is $D = [1,\ 2,\ 3,\ 3,\ 3,\ 4]$ or $D = [1\ 2\ 3^3\ 4]$ and its degree set is $\{1,\ 2,\ 3,\ 4\}$, while the degree sequence of the graph in Figure 2.1(b) is $[1,\ 1,\ 2,\ 3,\ 3]$ and its degree set is $\{1,\ 2,\ 3\}$.

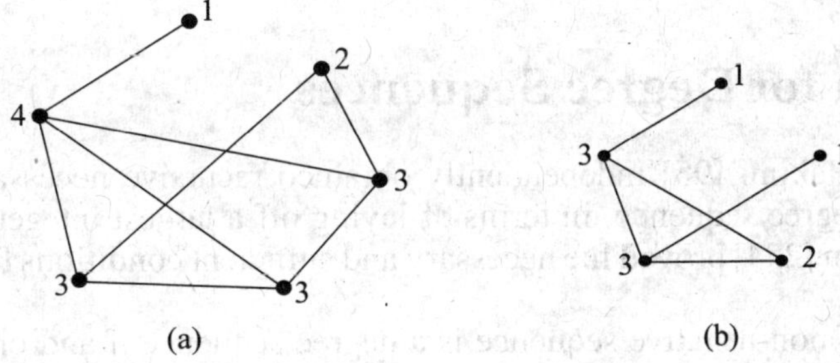

Fig. 2.1

If the degree sequence is arranged as the non-decreasing positive sequence $d_1^{n_1}$, $d_2^{n_2}, \ldots$ $d_k^{n_k}$, $(d_1 < d_2 < \ldots < d_k)$, the sequence $n_1, n_2, \ldots, n_k$ is called the *frequency sequence* of the graph.

The two necessary conditions implied by Theorem 1.1 and Theorem 1.12 are not sufficient to ensure that a non-negative sequence is a degree sequence of a graph. To see this, consider the sequence $[1, 2, 3, 4, \ldots, 4, n-1, n-1]$. The sum of the degrees is clearly even and $\Delta = n-1$. However, this is not a degree sequence, since there are two vertices with degree $n-1$, and this requires that each of the two vertices is joined to all the other vertices, and therefore $\delta \geq 2$. But the minimum number in the sequence is 1.

A degree sequence is *perfect* if no two of its elements are equal, that is, if the frequency sequence is 1, 1, ..., 1. A degree sequence is *quasi-perfect* if exactly two of its elements are same.

Definition: Let $D = [d_i]_1^n$ be a non-negative sequence and k be any integer $1 \leq k \leq n$. Let $D' = [d_i']_1^n$ be the sequence obtained from D by setting $d_k = 0$ and $d_i' = d_i - 1$ for the d_k largest elements of D other than d_k. Let H_k be the graph obtained on the vertex set $V = \{v_1, v_2, \ldots, v_n\}$ by joining v_k to the d_k vertices corresponding to the d_k elements used to obtain D'. This operation of getting D' and H_k is called *laying off* d_k and D' is called the *residual sequence*, and H_k the subgraph obtained by laying off d_k.

Example Let $D = [2, 2, 3, 3, 4, 4]$. Take $d_3 = 0$. Then $D' = [2, 2, 0, 2, 3, 3]$. The subgraph H_k in this case is shown in Figure 2.2.

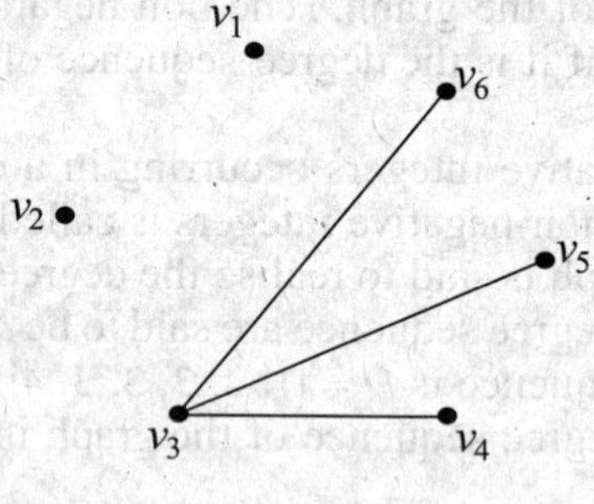

Fig. 2.2

2.2 Criteria for Degree Sequences

Havel [108] and Hakimi [95] independently obtained recursive necessary and sufficient conditions for a degree sequence, in terms of laying off a largest integer in the sequence. Wang and Kleitman [254] proved the necessary and sufficient conditions for arbitrary layoffs.

Theorem 2.1 A non-negative sequence is a degree sequence if and only if the residual sequence obtained by laying off any non-zero element of the sequence is a degree sequence.

Proof

Sufficiency Let the non-negative sequence be $[d_i]_1^n$. Suppose d_k is the non-zero element laid off and the residual sequence $[d_i']_1^n$ is a degree sequence. Then there exists a graph G'

realising $[d'_i]_1^n$ in which v_k has degree zero and some d_k vertices, say v_{i_j}, $1 \le j \le d_k$ have degree $d_{i_j} - 1$. Now, by joining v_k to these vertices we get a graph G with degree sequence $[d_i]_1^n$. (Observe that the subgraph obtained by such joining is precisely the subgraph H_k obtained by laying off d_k).

Necessity We are given that there is a graph realising $D = [d_i]_1^n$. Let d_k be the element to be laid off. First, we claim there is a graph realising D in which v_k is adjacent to all the vertices in the set S of d_k largest elements of $D - \{d_k\}$. If not, let G be a graph realising D such that v_k is adjacent to the maximum possible number of vertices in S. Then there is a vertex v_i in S to which v_k is not adjacent and hence a vertex v_j outside S to which v_k is adjacent (since $d(v_k) = |S|$). By definition of S, $d_j \le d_i$. Therefore there is a vertex v_h in $V - \{v_k\}$ adjacent to v_i, but not adjacent to v_j. Note that v_h may be in S (Fig. 2.3).

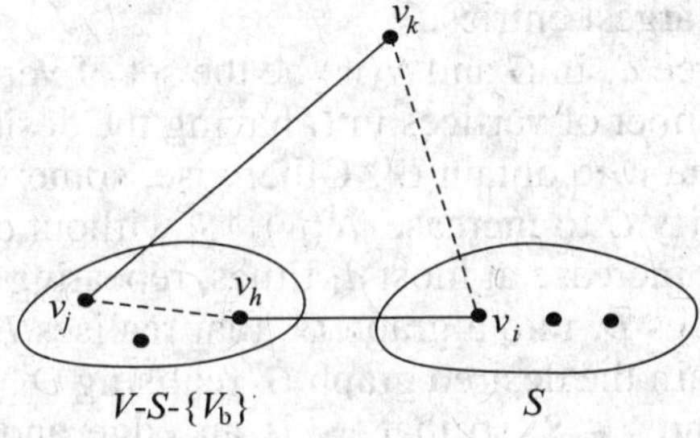

Fig. 2.3

Construct a graph H from G by deleting the edges v_jv_k and v_hv_i and adding the edges v_jv_h and v_iv_k. This operation does not change the degree sequence. Thus H is a graph realising the given sequence, in which one more vertex, namely v_i of S is adjacent to v_k, than in G. This contradicts the choice of G and establishes the claim.

To complete the proof, if G is a graph realising the given sequence and in which v_k is adjacent to all vertices of S, let G' be the graph obtained from G by removing all the edges incident at v_k. Then G' has the residual degree sequence obtained by laying off d_k. ❑

Definition: Let the subgraph H on the vertices v_i, v_j, v_r, v_s of a multigraph G contain the edges v_iv_j and v_rv_s. The operation of deleting these edges and introducing a pair of new edges v_iv_s and v_jv_r, or v_iv_r and v_jv_s is called an elementary degree preserving transformation (EDT), or simple exchange, or 2-switching, or elementary degree-invariant transformation.

Remarks

1. The result of an EDT is clearly a degree equivalent multigraph.
2. If an EDT is applied to a graph, the result will be a graph only if the latter pair of edges (v_iv_s and v_jv_r), or (v_iv_r and v_jv_s) does not exist in G.

Theorem 2.2 (Havel, Hakimi) The non-negative integer sequence $D = [d_i]_1^n$ is graphic if and only if D' is graphic, where D' is the sequence (having $n-1$ elements) obtained from D by deleting its largest element Δ and subtracting 1 from its Δ next largest elements.

Proof

Sufficiency Let $D = [d_i]_1^n$ be the non-negative sequence with $d_1 \geq d_2 \geq \ldots \geq d_n$. Let G' be the graph realising the sequence D'. We add a new vertex adjacent to vertices in G' having degrees $d_2 - 1, \ldots, d_{\Delta+1} - 1$. Those d_i are the Δ largest elements of D after Δ itself. (But the numbers $d_2 - 1, \ldots, d_{\Delta+1} - 1$ need not be the Δ largest elements in D').

Necessity Let G be a graph realising $D = [d_i]_1^n$, $d_1 \geq d_2 \geq \ldots \geq d_n$. We produce a graph G' realising D', where D' is the sequence obtained from D by deleting the largest entry d_1 and subtracting 1 from d_1 next largest entries.

Let w be a vertex of degree d_1 in G and $N(w)$ be the set of vertices which are adjacent to w. Let S be the set of d_1 number of vertices in G having the desired degrees $d_2, \ldots, d_{d_1+1}$.

If $N(w) = S$, we can delete w to obtain G'. Otherwise, some vertex of S is missing from $N(w)$. In this case, we modify G to increase $|N(w) \cap S|$ without changing the degree of any vertex. Since $|N(w) \cap S|$ can increase at most d_1 times, repeating this procedure converts an arbitrary graph G that realises D, into a graph G^* that realises D, and has $N(w) = S$. From G^*, we then delete w to obtain the desired graph G' realising D'.

If $N(w) \neq S$, let $x \in S$ and $z \notin S$, so that wz is an edge and wx is not an edge, since $d(w) = d_1 = |S|$. By this choice of S, $d(x) \geq d(z)$ (Fig. 2.4).

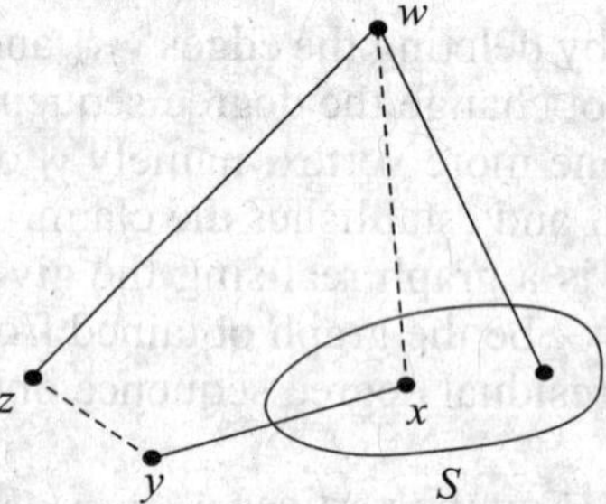

Fig. 2.4

We would like to add wx and delete wz without changing their respective degrees. It suffices to find a vertex y outside $T = \{x, z, w\}$ such that yx is an edge, while yz is not. If such a y exists, then we also delete xy and add zy. Let q be the number of copies of the edge xz (0 or 1). Now x has $d(x) - q$ neighbours outside T, and z has $d(z) - 1 - q$ neighbours outside T. Since $d(x) \geq d(z)$, the desired y outside T exists and we can perform the EDT (elementary degree preserving transformation or 2-switch). ❑

Algorithm: The above recursive conditions give an algorithm to check whether a non-negative sequence is a degree sequence and if so to construct a graph realising it.

The algorithm starts with an empty graph on vertex set $V = \{v_1, v_2, \ldots, v_n\}$ and at the kth iteration generates a subgraph H_k of G by deleting (laying off) a vertex of maximum degree in the residual sequence at that stage. If the given sequence is a degree sequence, we end up with a null degree sequence (i.e., for each i, $d_i = 0$) and the graph realising the original sequence is simply the sum of the subgraphs H_j. If not, at some stage, one of the elements of the residual sequence becomes negative, and the algorithm reports non-realisability of the sequence.

An obvious modification of the algorithm, obtained by choosing an arbitrary vertex of positive degree, gives the *Wang-Kleitman algorithm* for generating a graph with a given degree sequence.

Remarks

1. There can be many non-isomorphic graphs with the same degree sequence. The smallest example is the pair shown in Figure 2.5 on five vertices with the degree sequence [2, 2, 2, 1, 1].

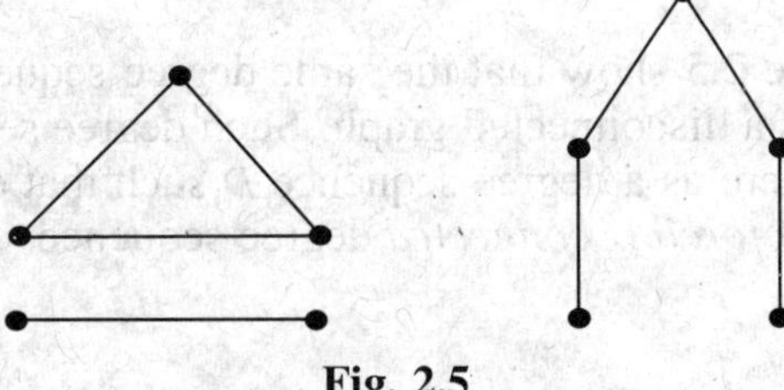

Fig. 2.5

The problem of generating all non-isomorphic graphs of given order and size involves the problem of graph isomorphism for which a good algorithm is not yet known. So also is the problem of generating all non-isomorphic graphs with given degree sequence. In fact, even the problem of finding the number of non-isomorphic graphs with given order and size, or with given degree sequence (and several other problems of similar nature) has not been satisfactorily solved.

2. The Wang-Kleitman algorithm is certainly more general than the Havel-Hakimi algorithm, as it can generate more number of non-isomorphic graphs with a given degree sequence, because of the arbitrariness of the laid-off vertex. For example, not all the five non-isomorphic graphs with the degree sequence [3, 3, 2, 2, 1, 1] can be generated by the Havel-Hakimi algorithm unlike the Wang-Kleitman algorithm.

3. Even the Wang-Kleithman algorithm cannot always generate all graphs with a given degree sequence. For example, the graph G with degree sequence [3, 3, 3, 3, 2, 2, 2, 2, 1, 1, 1, 1] shown in Figure 2.6, cannot be generated by this algorithm. For

   a. if we lay off a 3, it has to be laid off against the other 3's and will generate a graph in which a vertex with degree 3 is adjacent to three other vertices with degree 3,

   b. if we lay off a 2 it will generate a graph with a vertex of degree 2 adjacent to two vertices of degree 3,

c. if we lay off a one it will generate a graph in which a vertex of degree one is adjacent to a vertex of degree 3. None of these cases is realised in the given graph G.

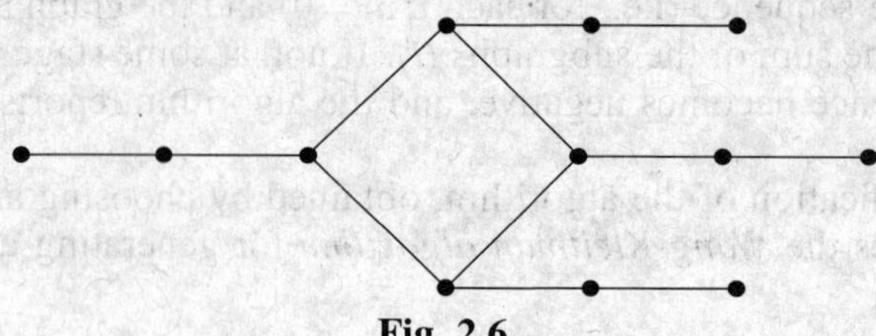

Fig. 2.6

However, there are other methods of generating all graphs realising a degree sequence D from any one graph realising D based on a theorem by Hakimi [95]. But those will also be inefficient unless some efficient isomorphism testing is developed.

4. The graphs in Figure 2.5 show that the same degree sequence may be realised by a connected as well as a disconnected graph. Such degree sequences are called *potentially connected*, where as a degree sequence D such that every graph realising D is connected is called a *forcibly connected* degree sequence.

Definition: If P is a graph property, and $D = [d_i]_1^n$ is a degree sequence, then D is said to be *potentially-P*, if at least one graph realising D is a P-graph, and it is said to be *forcibly-P* if every graph realising it is a P-graph.

Theorem 2.3 (Hakimi) If G_1 and G_2 are degree equivalent graphs, then one can be obtained from the other by a finite sequence of EDTs.

Proof Superimpose G_1 and G_2 such that each vertex of G_2 coincides with a vertex of G_1 with the same degree. Imagine the edges of G_1 are coloured blue and the edges of G_2 are coloured red. Then in the superimposed multigraph H, the number of blue edges incident equals the number of red edges incident at every vertex. We refer to this as blue-red parity. If there is a blue edge v_iv_j and a red edge v_iv_j in H, we call it a blue-red parallel pair.

Let K be the graph obtained from H by deleting all such parallel pairs. Then K is the null graph if and only if G_1 and G_2 are label-isomorphic in H and hence originally isomorphic. If this is not the case, we show that we can create more parallel pairs by a sequence of EDTs and delete them till the final resultant graph is null. This will prove the theorem.

Let B and R denote the sets of blue and red edges in K. If $v_iv_j \in B$, we show that we can produce a parallel pair at v_iv_j, so that the pair can be deleted. This would establish the claim made above.

Now, by construction, there is a blue-red degree parity at every vertex of K. So there are red edges v_iv_k, v_jv_r in K. If $v_k \neq v_r$ (Fig. 2.7(a)) an EDT in G_2 switching the red edges to v_iv_j, v_kv_r produces a blue-red parallel at v_iv_j.

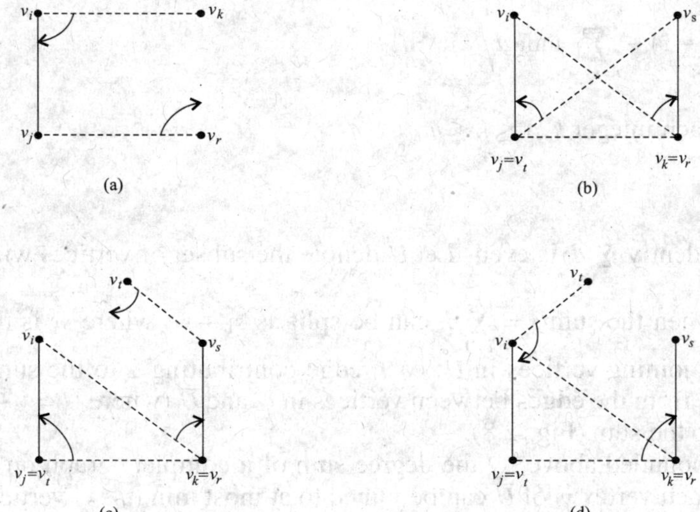

Fig. 2.7

If $v_k = v_r$, again by degree parity, at v_k there are at least two blue edges. Let $v_k v_s$ be one such blue edge. Then v_s is distinct from both v_i and v_j, for otherwise, there is a blue-red parallel pair $v_i v_k$ or $v_j v_r$. Then there is another red edge $v_s v_t$, v_t distinct from v_i or v_j.

Let $v_t \neq v_i$. The two subcases $v_t = v_j$ and $v_t \neq v_j$ are shown in Figure 2.7(b) and (c). In the case of (b), one EDT of G_2 switching $v_i v_k$ and $v_s v_t$ to positions $v_i v_j$ and $v_s v_k$ produces a blue-red pair at $v_i v_j$ and $v_k v_s$. In the case of (c), one EDT of G_2 switching $v_i v_k$ and $v_t v_s$ to positions $v_s v_k$ and $v_t v_i$ produces a blue-red parallel pair at $v_k v_s$ (which can be deleted). Another EDT of G_2 switching the blue-red pair $v_t v_i$ and $v_j v_k$ to positions $v_i v_j$ and $v_s v_k$ produces a blue-red pair $v_i v_j$.

Since in both cases we get a blue-red pair at $v_i v_j$ position, our claim is established and the proof of the theorem is complete. ❑

Remarks In the related context of a (0, 1) matrix A (that is, a matrix A whose elements are 0's or 1's), Ryser [221] defined an interchange as a transformation of the elements of A that changes a minor of type $A_1 = \begin{pmatrix} 1 & 0 \\ 0 & 1 \end{pmatrix}$ into a minor of the type $A_1 = \begin{pmatrix} 0 & 1 \\ 1 & 0 \end{pmatrix}$, or vice versa and proved an interchange theorem which can be interpreted as EDT theorem for bipartite graphs and digraphs.

The next result is a combinatorial characterisation of degree sequences, due to Erdos and Gallai [70]. Several proofs of the criterion exist; the first proof given here is due to Choudum [57] and the second one is due to Tripathi et al [239].

Theorem 2.4 (Erdos-Gallai) A non-increasing sequence $[d_i]_1^n$ of non-negative integers is a degree sequence if and only if $D = [d_i]_1^n$ is even and the inequality

$$\sum_{i=1}^{k} d_i \leq k(k-1) + \sum_{i=k+1}^{n} \min(d_i,\, k) \tag{2.4.1}$$

is satisfied for each integer k, $1 \leq k \leq n$.

Proof

Necessity Evidently $\sum_{i=1}^{n} d_i$ is even. Let U denote the subset of vertices with the k highest degrees in D. Then the sum $s = \sum_{i=1}^{k} d_i$ can be split as $s_1 + s_2$, where s_1 is the contribution to s from edges joining vertices in U, each edge contributing 2 to the sum, and s_2 is the contribution to s from the edges between vertices in U and $\overline{U}$ (where $\overline{U} = V - U$), each edge contributing 1 to the sum (Fig. 2.8).

s_1 is clearly bounded above by the degree sum of a complete graph on k-vertices, i.e., $k(k-1)$. Also, each vertex v_i of $\overline{U}$ can be joined to at most min $(d_i,\, k)$ vertices of U, so that s_2 is bounded above by $\sum_{i=k+1}^{n} \min(d_i,\, k)$. Together, we get (2.4.1).

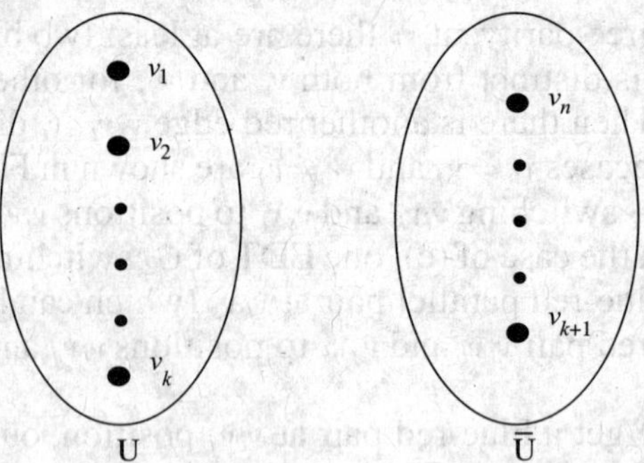

Fig. 2.8

Sufficiency We induct on the sum $s = \sum_{i=1}^{n} d_i$ and use the obvious inequality

$$\min(a,\, b) - 1 \leq \min(a-1,\, b), \tag{2.4.2}$$

for positive integers a and b.

For $s = 2$, clearly $K_2 \cup (n-2)K_1$ realises the only sequence $[1,\, 1,\, 0,\, 0,\, \ldots\, 0]$ or $[1^2 0^{n-2}]$ satisfying the conditions (2.4.1).

As induction hypothesis, let all non-increasing sequences of non-negative integers with even sum at most $s-2$ and satisfying (2.4.1) be degree sequences.

Let $D = [d_i]_1^n$ be a sequence with sum s and satisfying (2.4.1). We produce a new non-increasing sequence D' of non-negative integers by subtracting one each from two positive terms of D and verify that D' satisfies the hypothesis of the theorem. Since the trailing zeros in the non-increasing sequences of non-negative integers do not essentially affect the argument, there is no loss of generality in assuming that $d_n > 0$, and we assume this to simplify the expression.

To define D', let t be the smallest integer (≥ 1) such that $d_t > d_{t+1}$. That is, let D be $d_1 = d_2 = \ldots = d_t > d_{t+1} \geq d_{t+2} \geq \ldots \geq d_n > 0$.

If D is regular (that is, $d_i = d > 0$, for all i) then let t be $n-1$.

$$\text{Then } d_i' = \begin{cases} d_i, & for \ \ 1 \leq i \leq t-1 \ \ and \ \ t+1 \leq i \leq n-1, \\ d_t - 1, & for \ \ i = t, \\ d_n - 1, & for \ \ i = n. \end{cases}$$

Clearly, D' is a non-increasing sequence of non-negative integers and $\sum\limits_{i=1}^{n} d_i' = s-2$ is even.

We verify that D' satisfies (2.4.1) by considering several cases depending on the relative position of k and the magnitudes of d_k and d_n.

Case I Let $k = n$. Therefore, $\sum\limits_{i=1}^{k} d_i' = \sum\limits_{i=1}^{k} d_i - 2 \leq n(n-1) - 2 < n(n-1) =$ RHS of (2.4.1) for D'.

Case II Let $t \leq k \leq n-1$.

$$\text{Then } \sum_{i=1}^{k} d_i' = \sum_{i=1}^{k} d_i - 1 \leq k(k-1) + \sum_{i=k+1}^{n} \min(d_i,\, k) - 1 \text{ (since } D \text{ satisfies (2.4.1))}$$

$$= k(k-1) + \sum_{i=k+1}^{n-1} \min(d_i',\, k) + \min(d_n,\, k) - 1$$

$$\leq k(k-1) + \sum_{i=k+1}^{n-1} \min(d_i',\, k) + \min(d_n - 1,\, k) \qquad \text{by (2.4.2)}$$

$$= k(k-1) + \sum_{i=k+1}^{n-1} \min(d_i',\, k) + \min(d_n',\, k)$$

$$\text{Therefore, } \sum_{i=1}^{k} d_i' \leq k(k-1) + \sum_{i=k+1}^{n} \min(d_i',\, k).$$

Case III Let $k \leq t-1$.

Subcase III.1 Assume $d_k \leq k-1$.

$$\text{Then } \sum_{i=1}^{k} d_i' = kd_k \leq k(k-1) \leq k(k-1) + \sum_{i=k+1}^{n} \min(d_i',\, k),$$

since the second term is non-negative.

Subcase III.2 Every $d_j = k$, $1 \leq j \leq k$. We first observe that $d_{k+2} + \ldots + d_n \geq 2$.

This is obvious if $k+2 \leq n-1$, because $d_n > 0$ gives $d_n \geq 1$ and $d_{n-1} \geq 1$. When $k+2 = n$, we have $k = n-2$. As $k \leq t-1$, $t \geq k+1 = n-2+1 = n-1$. Since $t > n-1$ is not possible, $t = n-1$.

The sequence D is $[n-2, n-2, \ldots, n-2, d_n]$, or $[(n-2)^{n-1} d_n]$. Then $s = (n-1)(n-2) + d_n$. Since s is even, d_n is even and hence $d_n \geq 2$. Thus, $d_{k+2} + \ldots + d_n \geq 2$.

Therefore, $d_{k+2} + \ldots + d_n - 2 \geq 0$.

Now,

$$\sum_{i=1}^{k} d_i' = \sum_{i=1}^{k} d_i = k.k = k^2 = k^2 - k + k$$

$$= k^2 - k + d_{k+1}, \text{ (because } k \leq t-1, \text{ and } d_1 = \ldots = d_{t-1} = d_t,$$

so if $d_{t-1} = k$, then $d_t = k$, and if $d_k = k$, $d_{k+1} = k$).

Thus, $\sum_{i=1}^{k} d_i' \leq k^2 - k + d_{k+1} + (d_{k+2} + \ldots + d_n - 2) = k(k-1) + \sum_{i=k+1}^{n} \min(d_i, k) - 2,$

(because $\min(d_{k+1}, k) = d_{k+1}$, $\min(d_{k+2}, k) = k = d_{k+2}$, $\ldots$, $\min(d_t, k) = k = d_t$, $\ldots$, $\min(d_{t+1}, k) = d_{t+1}$ (as $d_{t+1} < d_t = k$), $\ldots$, $\min(d_n, k) = d_n$ (as $d_n < d_t = k$)).

Hence, $\sum_{i=1}^{k} d_i' \leq k(k-1) + \sum_{\substack{i=k+1 \\ i \neq t, n}}^{n} \min(d_i, k) + \min(d_t, k) + \min(d_n, k) - 2$

$$= k(k-1) + \sum_{\substack{i=k+1 \\ i \neq t, n}}^{n} \min(d_i', k) + \min(d_t' + 1, k) + \min(d_n' + 1, k) - 2$$

$$\leq k(k-1) + \sum_{\substack{i=k+1 \\ i \neq t, n}}^{n} \min(d_i', k) + \min(d_t', k) + 1 + \min(d_n', k) + 1 - 2$$

$$= k(k-1) + \sum_{i=k+1}^{n} \min(d_i', k).$$

Subcase III.3 Let $d_k \geq k+1$.

i. Let $d_n \geq k+1$.

Then $\sum_{i=1}^{k} d_i' = \sum_{i=1}^{k} d_i \leq k(k-1) + \sum_{i=k+1}^{n} \min(d_i, k)$ (since D satisfies (2.4.1))

$$= k(k-1) + \sum_{\substack{k+1 \\ i \neq t, n}}^{n} \min(d_i, k) + \min(d_t, k) + \min(d_n, k)$$

$$= k(k-1) + \sum_{\substack{k+1 \\ i\neq t,\, n}}^{n} \min(d_i',\, k) + \min(d_t - 1,\, k) + \min(d_n - 1,\, k),$$

(because $\min(d_t,\, k) = \min(d_t - 1,\, k) = k$, $\min(d_n,\, k) = \min(d_n - 1,\, k) = k$, as $d_t \geq k + 1$, $d_n \geq k+1$ implies that $d_t - 1 \geq k$, $d_n - 1 \geq k$).

So, $\sum_{i=1}^{k} d_i' \leq k(k-1) + \sum_{\substack{k+1 \\ i\neq t,\, n}}^{n} \min(d_i',\, k) + \min(d_t',\, k) + \min(d_n',\, k)$

$$= k(k-1) + \sum_{i=k+1}^{n} \min(d_i',\, k).$$

ii. Let $d_n \leq k$ and let r be the smallest integer such that $d_{t+r+1} \leq k$. We verify that in (2.4.1), D can not attain equality for such a choice of k. For, with equality, we have

$$\sum_{i=1}^{k} d_i = kd_k = k(k-1) + \sum_{k+1}^{t+r} \min(d_i,\, k) + \sum_{t+r+1}^{n} \min(d_i,\, k)$$

$$= k(k-1) + (t+r-k)k + \sum_{t+r+1}^{n} d_i,$$

because $\min\,(d_i, k) = \begin{cases} k, & for\, i = k+1,\, ...,\, t+r\; as\; d_i \geq k+1, \\ d_i, & for\, i = t+r+1, ..., n\; as\; d_i \leq k. \end{cases}$

So, $kd_k = k(t+r-1) + \sum_{t+r+1}^{k} d_i$.

Then $\sum_{i=1}^{k+1} d_i = (k+1)d_k = (k+1)\left\{(t+r-1) + \frac{1}{k}\sum_{t+r+1}^{n} d_i\right\}$, (using d_k from above)

$$= (k+1)(t+r-1) + \frac{k+1}{k}\sum_{t+r+1}^{n} d_i > (k+1)(t+r-1) + \sum_{t+r+1}^{n} d_i$$

$$= (k+1)k - (k+1)k + (k+1)(t+r-1) + \sum_{t+r+1}^{n} d_i$$

$$= (k+1)k + (k+1)(t+r-k-1) + \sum_{t+r+1}^{n} d_i = (k+1)k + \sum_{k+1}^{t+r}(k+1) + \sum_{t+r+1}^{n} d_i$$

$$= (k+1)k + \sum_{t+r+1}^{n} \min\,(d_i,\, k+1),$$

because $\min(d_i,\, k+1) = k+1$ for $i = k+1, \ldots, t+r$, and

$$\min(d_i,\, k+1) = d_i, \quad \text{for } i = t+r+1, \ldots, n.$$

So, $$\sum_{i=1}^{k+1} d_i > k(k+1) + \sum_{k+1}^{n} \min(d_i,\, k+1).$$

Therefore, $$\sum_{i=1}^{k+1} d_i > k(k+1) + (k+1) + \sum_{k+2}^{n} \min(d_i,\, k+1),$$

which is a contradiction to (2.4.1), for D for $k+1$. Hence D has strict inequality for k.

Therefore, $$\sum_{i=1}^{k} d'_i = \sum_{i=1}^{k} d_i < k(k-1) + \sum_{k+1}^{n} \min(d_i,\, k).$$

Thus, $$\sum_{i=1}^{k} d'_i = \sum_{i=1}^{k} d_i \leq k(k-1) + \sum_{k+1}^{n} \min(d_i,\, k) - 1$$

$$= k(k-1) + \sum_{\substack{i=k+1 \\ i \neq t}}^{n-1} \min(d_i,\, k) + \min(d_t,\, k) + \min(d_n,\, k) - 1$$

$$\leq k(k-1) + \sum_{\substack{i=k+1 \\ i \neq t}}^{n-1} \min(d'_i,\, k) + \min(d_t - 1,\, k) + \min(d_n - 1,\, k),$$

as $\min(d_n,\, k) - 1 \leq \min(d_n - 1,\, k)$, $\min(d_t,\, k) = k$ (since $d_t \geq k+1$), $\min(d_t - 1,\, k) = k$ (since $d_t - 1 \geq k$).

Therefore, $$\sum_{i=1}^{k} d'_i \leq k(k-1) + \sum_{k+1}^{n} \min(d'_i,\, k).$$

Hence in all cases D' satisfies (2.4.1).

Therefore by induction hypothesis, there is a graph G' realising D'. If $v_t v_n \notin E(G')$, then $G' + v_t v_n$ gives a realisation G of D. If $v_t v_n \in E(G')$, since $d(v_t|G') = d_t - 1 \leq n-2$, there is a vertex v_r such that $v_r v_t \notin E(G')$. Also, since $d(v_r|G') > d(v_n|G')$, there is a vertex v_s such that $v_s v_n \notin E(G')$. Making an EDT exchanging the edge pair $v_t v_n$, $v_r v_s$ for the edge pair $v_t v_r$, $v_s v_n$, we get a realisation G'' of D' with $v_t v_n \notin E(G'')$. Then $G'' + v_t v_n$ realises D.

Second Proof of Sufficiency (Tripathi et al.) Let a subrealisation of a non-increasing sequence $[d_1, d_2, \ldots, d_n]$ be a graph with vertices $v_1, v_2, \ldots, v_n$ such that $d(v_i) = d_i$ for $1 \leq i \leq n$, where $d(v_i)$ denotes the degree of v_i. Given a sequence $[d_1, d_2, \ldots, d_n]$ with an even sum that satisfies (2.4.1), we construct a realisation through successive subrealisations. The initial subrealisation has n vertices and no edges.

In a subrealisation, the *critical index* r is the largest index such that $d(v_i) = d_i$ for $1 \leq i < r$. Initially, $r = 1$ unless the sequence is all 0, in which case the process is complete. While $r \leq n$, we obtain a new subrealisation with smaller deficiency $d_r - d(v_r)$ at vertex v_r while not changing the degree of any vertex v_i with $i < r$ (the degree sequence increases lexicograpically). The process can only stop when the subrealisation is a realisation of d.

Let $S = \{v_{r+1}, \ldots, v_n\}$. We maintain the condition that S is an independent set, which certainly holds initially. Write $u_i \leftrightarrow v_j$ when $v_i v_j \in E(G)$; otherwise, $v_i \not\leftrightarrow v_j$

Case 0 $v_r \not\leftrightarrow v_i$ for some vertex v_i such that $d(v_i) < d_i$. Add the edge $u_r v_i$.

Case 1 $v_r \not\leftrightarrow v_i$ for some i with $i < r$. Since $d(v_i) = d_i \geq d_r > d(v_r)$, there exists $u \in N(u_i) - (N(v_r) \cup \{v_r\})$, where $N(z) = \{y : z \leftrightarrow y\}$. If $d_r - d(v_r) \geq 2$, then replace uv_i with $\{uv_r, v_i v_r\}$. If $d_r - d(v_r) = 1$, then since $\sum d_i - \sum d(v_i)$ is even there is an index k with $k > r$ such that $d(v_k) < d_k$. Case 0 applies unless $v_r \leftrightarrow v_k$; replace $\{v_r v_k, uv_i\}$ with $\{uv_r, v_i u_r\}$.

Case 2 $v_1, \ldots, v_{r-1} \in N(v_r)$ and $d(v_k) \neq \min\{r, d_k\}$ for some k with $k > r$. In a subrealisation, $d(v_k) \leq d_k$. Since S is independent, $d(v_k) \leq r$. Hence $d(v_k) < \min\{r, d_k\}$, and case 0 applies unless $u_k \leftrightarrow v_r$. Since $d(v_k) < r$, there exists i with $i < r$ such that $u_k \not\leftrightarrow v_i$. Since $d(v_i) > d(v_r)$, there exists $u \in N(v_i) - (N(v_r) \cup \{u_r\})$. Replace uv_i with $\{uv_r, v_i v_k\}$.

Case 3 $v_1, \ldots, v_{r-1} \notin N(v_r)$ and $v_i \leftrightarrow v_i$ for some i and j with $i < j < r$. Case 1 applies unless $v_i, v_j \in N(v_r)$. Since $d(v_i) \geq d(v_i) > d(v_r)$, there exists $u \in N(v_i) - (N(v_r) \cup \{v_r\})$ and $w \in N(v_j) - (N(v_r) \cup \{v_r\})$ (possibly $u = w$). Since $u, w \notin N(v_r)$, Case 1 applies unless $u, w \in S$. Replace $\{v_i v_j, uv_r\}$ with $\{uv_r, v, v_r\}$.

If none of these case apply, then $v_1, \ldots, v_r$ are pairwise adjacent, and $d(v_k) = \min\{r, d_k\}$ for $k > r$. Since S is independent, $\sum_{i=1}^{r} d(v_i) = r(r-1) + \sum_{k=r+1}^{n} \min\{r, d_k\}$. By (2.4.1), $\sum_{i=1}^{r} d_i$ is bounded by the right side. Hence we have already eliminated the deficiency at vertex r. Increase r by 1 and continue. ❑

Tripathi and Vijay [238] have shown that the Erdos-Gallai condition characterising graphical degree sequences of length n needs to be checked only for as many k as there are distinct terms in the sequence and not for all k, $1 \leq k \leq n$.

2.3 Degree Set of a Graph

The set of distinct non-negative integers occurring in a degree sequence of a graph is called its *degree set*. For example, let the degree sequence be $D = [2, 2, 3, 3, 4, 4]$, then degree set is $\{2, 3, 4\}$. A set of distinct non-negative integers is called a degree set if it is the degree set of some graph and the graph is said to *realise* the degree set.

Let $S = \{d_1, d_2, \ldots, d_k\}$ be the set of distinct non-negative integers. Clearly, S is the degree set as the graph

$$G = K_{d_1+1} \cup K_{d_2+1} \cup \ldots \cup K_{d_k+1},$$

realises S. This graph has $d_1 + d_2 + \ldots + d_k + k$ vertices.

Example Let $S = \{1, 3, 4\}$. Then $G = K_2 \cup K_4 \cup K_5$ (Fig. 2.9).

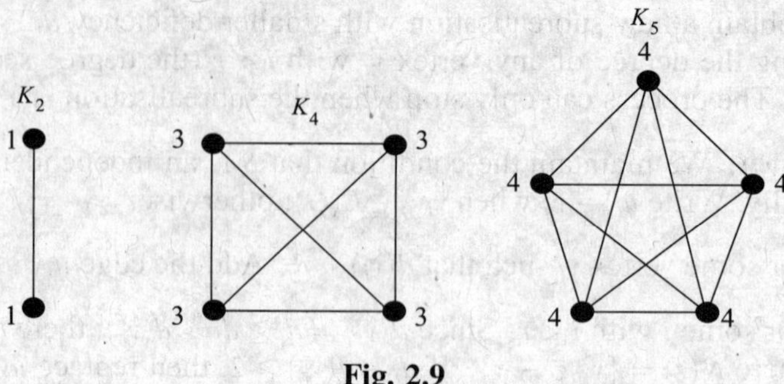

Fig. 2.9

The following result is due to Kapoor, Polimeni and Wall [122].

Theorem 2.5 Any set S of distinct positive integers is the degree set of a connected graph and the minimum order of such a graph is $M+1$, where M is the maximum integer in the set S.

Proof Let S be a degree set and $n_0(S)$ denote the minimum order of a graph G realising S. As M is the maximum integer in S, therefore in G there is a vertex adjacent to M other vertices, i.e., $n_0(S) \geq M+1$. Now, if there exists a graph of order $M+1$ with S as degree set, then $n_0(S) = M+1$. The existence of such a graph is established by induction on the number of elements p of S.

Let $S = \{a_1, a_2, \ldots, a_p\}$ with $a_1 < a_2 < \ldots < a_p$.

For $p = 1$, the complete graph K_{a_1+1} realises $\{a_1\}$ as degree set.

For $p = 2$, we have $S = \{a_1, a_2\}$. Let $G = K_{a_1} V \overline{K}_{a_2-a_1+1}$ (join of two graphs). Here every vertex of K_{a_1} has degree a_2 and every other vertex has degree a_1 and therefore G realises $\{a_1, a_2\}$ (Fig. 2.10(a)).

For $p = 3$, we have $S = \{a_1, a_2, a_3\}$. Then $G = K_{a_1} V(\overline{K}_{a_3-a_2} \cup H)$, where H is the graph realising the degree set $\{a_2 - a_1\}$ with $a_2 - a_1 + 1$ vertices, realises $\{a_1, a_2, a_3\}$ (Fig. 2.10 (b)). (Note that $d(u) = a_1 - 1 + a_3 - a_2 + a_2 - a_1 + 1 = a_3$, $d(v) = a_1$, $d(w) = a_2 - a_2 + a_1 = a_2$).

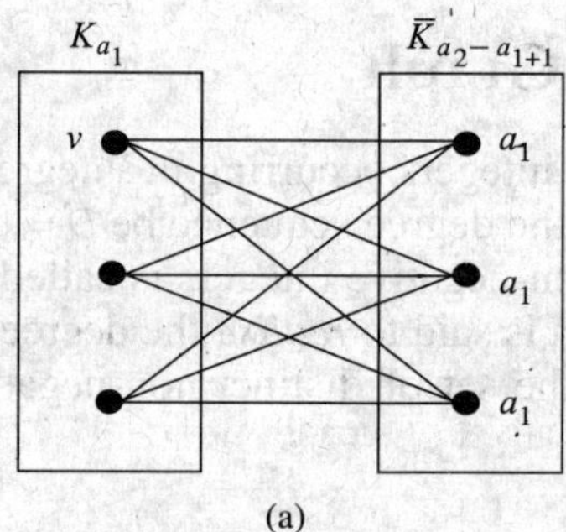

(a)

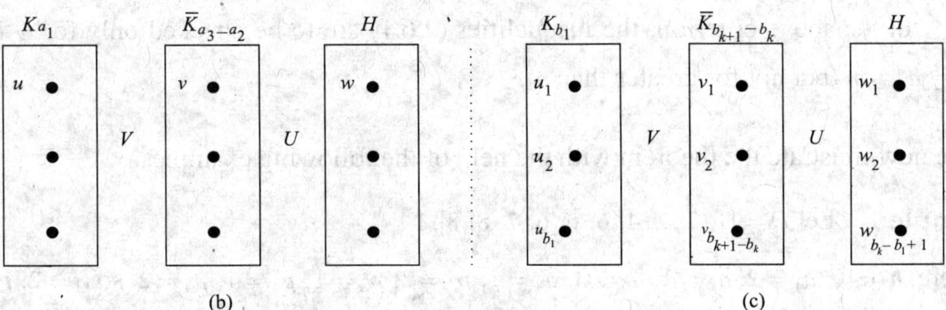

Fig. 2.10

Let every set with h positive integers, $1 \le h \le k$, be the degree set. Let $S_1 = \{b_1, b_2, \ldots, b_{k+1}\}$ be a $(k+1)$ set of positive integers arranged in increasing order. By induction hypothesis, there is a graph H realising the degree set $\{b_2 - b_1, b_3 - b_1, \ldots, b_k - b_1\}$ with order $b_k - b_1 + 1$. The graph $G = K_{b_1} V(\overline{K}_{b_{k+1}-b_k} \cup H)$, with order $b_{k+1} + 1$ realises S_1 (Fig. 2.10 (c)). Clearly by construction, all these graphs are connected.

Hence the result follows by induction. ❑

Note that $d(u_i) = b_1 - 1 + b_{k+1} - b_k + b_k - b_1 + 1 = b_k + 1$, $d(v_i) = b_1$, $d(w_i) = b_{i+1} - b_1 + b_1 = b_{i+1}$, that is $d(w_1) = b_2$, $d(w_2) = b_3$, $\ldots$, $d\left(w_{b_k - b_1 + 1}\right) = b_k - b_1 + b_1 = b_k$. Some results on degree sets in bipartite and tripartite graphs can be seen in [255].

2.4 New Criterion

We have the following notations. Let $D = [d_i]_1^n$ be a non-decreasing sequence of non-negative integers with $0 \le d_i \le n-1$ for all i. Let $n - p_1$ be the greatest integer, $n - p_1 - p_2$, the second greatest integer and $n - \sum_{r=1}^{k} p_r$, the kth greatest integer in D, $1 \le p_r \le n - (r-1)$. Let the number of times the kth greatest integer appears in D be denoted by a_k. Also, we take

$$t_k = n - \left(n - \sum_{r=1}^{k} p_r\right) = \sum_{r=1}^{k} p_r, \quad 1 \le p_r \le n - (r-1) \text{ and } j_k = 1, 2, \ldots, p_{k+1}.$$

The following result due to Pirzada and YinJian [203] is another criterion for a non-negative sequence of integers in non-decreasing order to be the degree sequence of some graph.

Theorem 2.6 A non-decreasing sequence $[d_i]_1^n$ of non-negative integers, where $\sum_{i=1}^{n} d_i$ is even and $0 \le d_i \le n-1$ for all i, is a degree sequence of a graph if and only if

$$\sum_{i=1}^{t_k + j_k - 1} d_i \ge \sum_{m=1}^{k} \{j_k + (k-m)\} a_m \tag{2.6.1}$$

for all $t_k + j_k - 1 + \sum_{m=1}^{k} a_m \le n$.

Note In the above criterion, the inequalities (2.6.1) are to be checked only for $t_k + j_k - 1 + \sum_{m=1}^{k} a_m \leq n$ (but not for greater than n).

We now illustrate the theorem with the help of the following examples.

Example 1 Let $D = [1, 2, 2, 4, 6, 6, 6, 7, 8, 8]$.

Here, $n = 10$, $a_1 = 2$, $a_2 = 1$, $a_3 = 3$, $a_4 = 1$, $p_1 = 2$, $p_2 = 1$, $p_3 = 1$, $p_4 = 2$, so $t_1 = 2$, $t_2 = 3$, $t_3 = 4$, $t_4 = 6$.

Also, $j_1 = 1$, $j_2 = 1$, $j_3 = 1$.

Now, for $j_1 = 1$, $\sum_{i=1}^{t_1+j_1-1} d_i = \sum_{i=1}^{2+1-1} d_i = \sum_{i=1}^{2} d_i = 1+2 = 3$,

and $\sum_{m=1}^{k} [j_k + (k-m)]\, a_m = \sum_{m=1}^{1} [j_1 + (1-m)]\, a_m = j_1 a_1 = 2$.

So inequalities (2.6.1) hold.

For $j_2 = 1$, $\sum_{i=1}^{t_2+j_2-1} d_i = \sum_{i=1}^{3+1-1} d_i = \sum_{i=1}^{3} d_i = 5$

and $\sum_{m=1}^{k} [j_k + (k-m)]\, a_m = \sum_{m=1}^{2} [j_2 + (2-m)]\, a_m = 2a_1 + a_2 = 4 + 1 = 5$.

So inequalities (2.6.1) hold.

For $j_3 = 1$, $\sum_{i=1}^{t_3+j_3-1} d_i = \sum_{i=1}^{4+1-1} d_i = \sum_{i=1}^{4} d_i = 9$

and $\sum_{m=1}^{3} [j_3 + (3-m)]\, a_m = \sum_{m=1}^{3} [1 + (3-m)]\, a_m = 3a_1 + 2a_2 + a_3 = 6 + 2 + 3 = 11$.

Since the inequalities (2.6.1) do not hold (as $9 > 11$ is not true), D is not the degree sequence.

Example 2 Let $D = [1, 2, 3, 4, 5, 6, 6, 7, 8, 8]$.

Here, $n = 10$, $a_1 = 2$, $a_2 = 1$, $a_3 = 2$, $a_4 = 1$, $p_1 = 2$, $p_2 = 1$, $p_3 = 1$, $p_4 = 1$, $p_5 = 1$. So $t_1 = 2$, $t_2 = 3$, $t_3 = 4$, $t_4 = 5$.

Also, $j_1 = 1$, $j_2 = 1$, $j_3 = 1$, $j_4 = 1$.

For $j_1 = 1$, $\sum_{i=1}^{t_1+j_1-1} d_i = \sum_{i=1}^{2+1-1} d_i = \sum_{i=1}^{2} d_i = 3$,

and $\sum_{m=1}^{1} [j_1 + (1-m)]\, a_m = a_1 = 2$.

Obviously the inequalities (2.6.1) hold.

For $j_2 = 1$, $\sum_{i=1}^{t_2+j_2-1} d_i = \sum_{i=1}^{3+1-1} d_i = \sum_{i=1}^{3} d_i = 6$

and $\sum_{m=1}^{2} [j_2 + (2-m)]\, a_m = \sum_{m=1}^{2} [1 + (2-m)]\, a_m = 2a_1 + a_2 = 4 + 1 = 5$.

Here again the inequalities (2.6.1) hold.

For $j_3 = 1$, $\sum_{i=1}^{t_3+j_3-1} d_i = \sum_{i=1}^{4+1-1} d_i = \sum_{i=1}^{4} d_i = 10$

and $\sum_{m=1}^{3} [j_3 + (3-m)]\, a_m = \sum_{m=1}^{3} [1 + (3-m)]\, a_m = 3a_1 + 2a_2 + a_3 = 6 + 2 + 2 = 10$.

Therefore the inequalities (2.6.1) hold.

For $j_4 = 1$, $t_4 + j_4 - 1 = 5 + 1 - 1 = 5$ and $a_1 + a_2 + a_3 + a_4 = 2 + 1 + 2 + 1 = 6$, therefore $t_4 + j_4 - 1 + \sum_{m=1}^{4} a_m = 5 + 6 = 11 > 10$ and no further verification of the inequalities is to be done.

Hence D is the degree sequence.

2.5 Equivalence of Seven Criteria

We list the seven criteria for integer sequences to be graphic.

A. The Ryser Criterion (Bondy and Murty [36] and Ryser [221]) A sequence $[a_1, \ldots, a_p;\, b_1, \ldots, b_n]$ is called bipartite-graphic if and only if there is a simple bipartite graph such that one component has degree sequence $[a_1, \ldots, a_p]$ and the other one has $[b_1, \ldots, b_n]$. Define $f = \max\{i : d_i \geq i\}$ and $\tilde{d}_1 = d_i + 1$ if $i \in \langle f \rangle (= \{1, \ldots, f\})$ and $\tilde{d}_1 = d_i$ otherwise. The criterion can be stated as follows.

The integer sequence $[\tilde{d}_1, \ldots, \tilde{d}_n;\, \tilde{d}_1, \ldots, \tilde{d}_n]$is bipartite-graphic. (A)

B. The Berge Criterion (Berge [23]) Define $[\bar{d}_1, \ldots, \bar{d}_n]$ as follows: For $i \in \langle n \rangle$, $\bar{d}_i$ is the ith column sum of the (0, 1) matrix, which has for each k and d_k leading terms in row

k equal to 1 except for the (k, k)th term that is 0 and also the remaining entries are 0. If $d_1 = 3$, $d_2 = 2$, $d_3 = 2$, $d_4 = 2$, $d_5 = 1$, then $\bar{d_1} = 4$, $\bar{d_2} = 3$, $\bar{d_3} = 2$, $\bar{d_4} = 1$, $\bar{d_5} = 0$, and the (0, 1) matrix becomes

$$\begin{bmatrix} 0 & 1 & 1 & 1 & 0 \\ 1 & 0 & 1 & 0 & 0 \\ 1 & 1 & 0 & 0 & 0 \\ 1 & 1 & 0 & 0 & 0 \\ 1 & 0 & 0 & 0 & 0 \end{bmatrix}$$

The criterion is

$$\sum_{i=1}^{k} \overline{d_i} \leq \sum_{i=1}^{k} d_i \text{ for each } k \in \langle n \rangle. \tag{B}$$

C. The Erdos-Gallai Criterion. (Bondy and Murty [36])

$$\sum_{i=1}^{k} d_i \leq (k)(k-1) + \sum_{j=k+1}^{n} \min\{k, d_j\} \text{ for each } k \in \langle n \rangle. \tag{C}$$

D. The Fulkerson-Hoffman-McAndrew Criterion (Fulkerson [80] and Grunbaum [90]

$$\sum_{i=1}^{k} d_i \leq (k)(n-m-1) + \sum_{i=n-m+1}^{n} d_i \text{ for each } k \in \langle n \rangle,\ m \geq 0 \text{ and } k+m \leq n. \tag{D}$$

E. The Bollobas Criterion (Bollabas[29]))

$$\sum_{i=1}^{k} d_i \leq \sum_{j=k+1}^{n} d_i + \sum_{i=1}^{k} \min\{d_j, k-1\} \text{ for each } k \in \langle n \rangle. \tag{E}$$

F. The Grunbaum Criterion (Grunbaum [90]).

$$\sum_{i=1}^{k} \max\{k-1, d_i\} \leq (k)(k-1) + \sum_{i=k+1}^{n} d_i \text{ for each } k \in \langle n \rangle. \tag{F}$$

G. The Hasselbarth Criterion (Hasselbarth [107]) Define $[d_i^*, \ldots, d_n']$ as follows. For $i \in \langle n \rangle$, d_i^* is the ith column sum of the (0, 1)-matrix in which the d_i leading terms in row i are 1's and the remaining entries are 0's. The criterion is

$$\sum_{i=1}^{k} d_i \leq \sum_{i=1}^{k} (d_i^* - 1) \text{ for each } k \in \langle f \rangle, \tag{G}$$

with $f = \max\{i : d_i \geq i\}$.

The following result due to Sierksma and Hoogeveen [235] gives the equivalence among the above seven criteria.

Theorem 2.7 (Sierksma and Hoogeveen [229]) Let $[d_1, \ldots, d_n]$ be a positive integer sequence with even sum. Then each of the criteria $(A)-(G)$ is equivalent to the statement that $[d_1, \ldots, d_n]$ is graphic.

Proof Refer to Ryser [221].

2.6 Signed Graphs

A signed graph is a graph in which every edge is labelled with *a*'+' or *a*'−'. An edge uv labelled with *a*'+' is called a *positive edge*, and is denoted by uv^+. An edge uv labelled with *a*'−' is called a *negative edge*, and is denoted by uv^-. In a signed graph $G(V, E)$, the *positive degree* of a vertex u is $\deg^+(u) = |\{uv : uv^+ \in E\}|$, the *negative degree* of a vertex u is $\deg^-(u) = |\{uv : uv^- \in E\}|$, the *signed degree* of u is $\text{sdeg}(u) = \deg^+(u) - \deg^-(u)$ and the *degree* of u is $\deg(u) = \deg^+(u) + \deg^-(u)$.

An integral sequence $[d_i]_1^n$ is the *signed degree sequence* of a signed graph $G(V, E)$ with $V = \{v_1, v_2, \ldots, v_n\}$ if $s\deg(v_i) = d_i$, for $1 \leq i \leq n$.

Chartrand et al. [50] have given the characterisation of signed degree sequences of signed paths, signed stars, signed double stars and complete signed graphs. An integral sequence is *s-graphical* if it is the signed degree sequence of a signed graph. An integral sequence $[d_i]_1^n$ is *standard* if $n-1 \geq d_1 \geq d_2 \geq \ldots \geq d_n$ and $d_1 \geq |d_n|$.

The following lemma shows that a signed degree sequence can be modified and rearranged into an equivalent standard form.

Lemma 2.1 If $[d_i]_1^n$ is the signed degree sequence of a signed graph G, then $[-d_i]_1^n$ is the signed degree sequence of the signed graph G' obtained from G by interchanging positive edges with negative edges.

The following necessary and sufficient condition under which an integral sequence is s-graphical is due to Chartrand et al. [50].

Theorem 2.8 A standard integral sequence $[d_i]_1^n$ is s-graphical.if and only if the sequence $[d_2 - 1, d_{d_1+s+1} - 1, d_{d_1+s+2}, \ldots, d_{n-s}, d_{n-s+1} + 1, \ldots, d_n + 1]$ is s-graphical for some $0 \leq s \leq (n-1-d_1)/2$.

Remark We note that Hakimi's theorem for degree sequences is a case of Theorem 2.8 by taking $s = 0$. This leads to an efficient algorithm for recognising the degree sequences of a graph. But the wide degree of latitude for choosing s in Theorem 2.8 makes it harder to devise an efficient algorithm implementation.

The following result due to Yan et al. [262] provides a good choice for parameter s in Theorem 2.8. It leads to a polynomial time algorithm for recognising signed degree sequences.

Theorem 2.9 A standard sequence $D = [d_i]_1^n$ is s-graphical if and only if $D_m = [d_2 - 1, d_{d_1+m+1} - 1, \ldots, d_{d_1+m+2}, \ldots, d_{n-m}, d_{n-m+1} + 1 \ldots, d_n + 1]$ is s-graphical, where m is the maximum non-negative integer such that $d_{d_1+m+1} > d_{n-m+1}$.

Proof Let D be the signed degree sequence of a signed graph $G(V, E)$ with $V = \{v_1, v_2, \ldots, v_n\}$ and $\mathrm{sdeg}(v_i) = d_i$, for $1 \leq i \leq n$. For each s, $0 \leq s \leq (n-1-d_1)/2$, consider the sequence

$$D_s = [d_2 - 1, \ldots, d_{d_1+s+1} - 1, d_{d_1+s+2}, \ldots, d_{n-s}, d_{n-s+1} + 1, \ldots, d_n + 1].$$

By Theorem 2.8, D_s is s-graphical for some s. We may choose s such that $|s-m|$ is minimum. Suppose $G'(V', E')$ is a signed graph with $V' = \{v_2, v_3, \ldots, v_n\}$ whose signed degree sequence is D_s.

If $s < m$, then $d_a > d_b$ by the choice of m, where $a = d_1 + s + 2$ and $b = n - s$. Since $d_a > d_b$, there exists some vertex v_k of G' different from v_a and v_b and satisfies one of the following conditions.

i. $v_a v_k^+$ is a positive edge and $v_b v_k^-$ is a negative edge.

ii. $v_a v_k^+$ is a positive edge and v_b is not adjacent to v_k

iii. v_a is not adjacent to v_k and $v_b v_k^-$ is a negative edge

For (i), remove $v_a v_k^+$ and $v_b\, v_k^-$ from G', and for (ii), remove $v_a v_k^+$ from G' and add a new positive edge $v_b v_k^+$ to G' and for (iii), remove $v_b v_k^-$ from G' and a new negative edge $v_a v_k^-$ to G'. These modifications result in a signed graph G'' whose signed degree sequence is D_{s+1}. This contradicts the minimality of $|s-m|$.

If $s > m$, then $d_{d_1+s+1} = d_{n-s+1}$, and therefore, $d_{d_1+s+1} - 1 < d_{n-s+1} - 1$. An argument similar to the above leads to a contradiction in the choice of s. Therefore, $s = m$ and D_m is s-graphical.

Conversely, suppose D_m is the signed degree sequence of a signed graph $G'(V', E')$ in which $V' = \{v_2, v_3, \ldots, v_n\}$. If G is the signed graph obtained from G' by adding a new vertex v_1 and new positive edges $v_1 v_i^+$ for $2 \leq i \leq d_1 + m + 1$ and new negative edges $v_1 v_j^-$ for $n - m + 1 \leq j \leq n$, then D is the signed degree sequence of G. ❑

In a signed graph $G(V, E)$ with $|V| = n$, $|E| = m$, we denote by m^+ and m^- respectively, the numbers of positive edges and negative edges of G. Further, n_+, n_0 and n_- denote respectively, the numbers of vertices with positive, zero and negative signed degrees.

The following result is due to Chartrand et al. [50].

Lemma 2.2 If $G(V, E)$ is a signed graph with $|V| = n$, $|E| = m$, then $k = \sum_{v \in V} s\deg(v) \equiv 2m (\mathrm{mod} 4)$; $m^+ = \frac{1}{4}(2m + k)$ and $m^- = \frac{1}{4}(2m - k)$.

The next result is due to Yan et al [262].

Lemma 2.3 For any signed graph $G(V, E)$ without isolated vertices, $\sum_{v\in V} |\text{sdeg}(v)| + 2n_0 \leq 2m$.

Proof First, each $|\text{sdeg}(v)| = |\deg^+(v) - \deg^-(v)| \leq \deg^+(v) + \deg^-(v)$. Since G has no isolated vertices, $2 \leq \deg^+(v) + \deg^-(v)$ when $\text{sdeg}(v) = 0$. Thus,

$$\sum_{v\in V} |\text{s deg}(v)| + 2n_0 \leq \sum_{v\in V} (\deg^+(v) + \deg^-(v)) = 2m^+ + 2m^- = 2m. \quad \square$$

Lemma 2.4 For any connected signed graph $G(V, E)$, $\sum_{v\in V} |\text{s deg}(v)| + 2 \sum_{\text{sdeg}(v)<0} |\text{sdeg}(v)| \leq 6m + 4 - 4\alpha - 4n_+ - 4n_0$, where $\alpha = 1$ if $n_+ n_- > 0$ and $\alpha = 0$ otherwise.

Proof Consider the subgraph $G'(V', E')$ of G induced by those edges incident to vertices with non-negative signed degrees. We have,

$$\sum_{\text{sdeg}(v)>0} |\text{sdeg}(v)| \leq 2 \text{ (number of positive edges in } G') - \text{(number of negative edges in } G') \leq 3m^+ - |E'|.$$

Since G is connected, each component of G' contains at least one vertex of negative signed degree except for the case of $G' - G$.

Therefore, $n_+ + n_0 - 1 + \alpha \leq |E'|$. Thus,

$$\sum_{s\deg(v).0} |s\deg(v)| + n_+ + n_0 - 1 + \alpha \leq 3m^+ = 3\left(\frac{1}{2}m + \frac{1}{4}\sum_{v\in V} s\deg(v)\right).$$

Hence, $\sum_{v\in V} |s\deg(v)| + 2 \sum_{s\deg(v)<0} |s\deg(v)| \leq 6m + 4 - 4\alpha - 4n_+ - 4n_0$. $\square$

For any integer k, k copies of $v_i v_j$ means k copies of positive edges $v_i v_j^+$ if $k > 0$, no edges if $k = 0$ and k copies of negative edges $v_i v_j^-$ if $k < 0$. The next result for signed graphs with loops or multiple edges is due to Yan et al. [262].

Theorem 2.10 An integral sequence $[d_i]_1^n$ is the signed degree sequence of a signed multigraph if and only if $\sum_{i=1}^{n} d_i$ is even.

Proof The necessity follows from Lemma 2.2.

Sufficiency Let $\sum_{i=1}^{n} d_i$ be even. Then the number of odd terms is even, say $d_i = 2e_i + 1$ for $1 \leq i \leq 2k$ and $d_i = 2e_i$ for $2k + 1 \leq i \leq p$. Then $[d_1, d_2, \ldots, d_n]$ is the signed degree sequence of the signed graph with vertex set $\{v_1, v_2, \ldots, v_n\}$ and edge set $\{-d_3 + \frac{1}{2}\sum_{i=1}^{n} d_i$ copies of $v_1v_2\} \cup \{d_2 + d_3 - \frac{1}{2}\sum_{i=1}^{n} d_i$ copies of $v_2v_3\} \cup \{d_1 + d_3 - \frac{1}{2}\sum_{i=1}^{n} d_i$ copies of $v_1v_3\} \cup \{d_i$ copies of $v_3v_i : 4 \le i \le n\}$. ❑

Various results on signed degrees in signed graphs can be found in [251], [255] and [257].

2.7 Exercises

1. Verify whether or not the following sequences are degree sequences.
   a. [1, 1, 1, 2, 3, 4, 5, 6, 7], b. [1, 1, 1, 2, 2, 2],
   c. [4, 4, 4, 4, 4, 4], d. [2, 2, 2, 2, 4, 4].
2. Show that there is no perfect degree sequence.
3. What conditions on n and k will ensure that k^n is a degree sequence?
4. Give an example of a graph that can not be generated by the Wang-Kleitman algorithm.
5. Draw the five non isomorphic graphs with degree sequence [3, 3, 2, 2, 1, 1].
6. Show that a graph and its complement have the same frequency sequence.
7. Construct a graph with a degree sequence [3, 3, 3, 3, 2, 2, 2, 2, 1, 1, 1, 1] by using Havel-Hakimi algorithm.

3. Eulerian and Hamiltonian Graphs

There are many games and puzzles which can be analysed by graph theoretic concepts. In fact, the two early discoveries which led to the existence of graphs arose from puzzles, namely, the Kõnigsberg Bridge Problem and Hamiltonian Game, and these puzzles also resulted in the special types of graphs, now called Eulerian graphs and Hamiltonian graphs. Due to the rich structure of these graphs, they find wide use both in research and application.

3.1 Euler Graphs

A closed walk in a graph G containing all the edges of G is called an *Euler line* in G. A graph containing an Euler line is called an *Euler graph*.

We know that a walk is always connected. Since the Euler line (which is a walk) contains all the edges of the graph, an Euler graph is connected except for any isolated vertices the graph may contain. As isolated vertices do not contribute anything to the understanding of an Euler graph, it is assumed now onwards that Euler graphs do not have any isolated vertices and are thus connected.

Example Consider the graph shown in Figure 3.1. Clearly, $v_1\ e_1\ v_2\ e_2\ v_3\ e_3\ v_4\ e_4\ v_5\ e_5\ v_3\ v_6\ e_7\ v_1$ in (a) is an Euler line, whereas the graph shown in (b) is non-Eulerian.

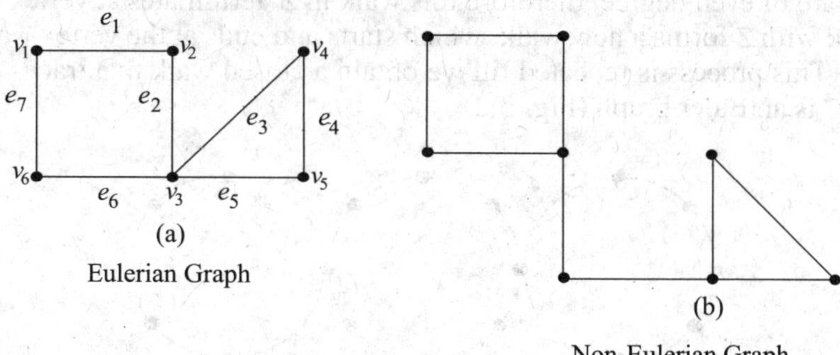

Fig. 3.1

The following theorem due to Euler [71] characterises Eulerian graphs. Euler proved the necessity part and the sufficiency part was proved by Hierholzer [111].

Theorem 3.1 (Euler) A connected graph G is an Euler graph if and only if all vertices of G are of even degree.

Proof

Necessity Let $G(V, E)$ be an Euler graph. Thus G contains an Euler line Z, which is a closed walk. Let this walk start and end at the vertex $u \in V$. Since each visit of Z to an intermediate vertex v of Z contributes two to the degree of v and since Z traverses each edge exactly once, $d(v)$ is even for every such vertex. Each intermediate visit to u contributes two to the degree of u, and also the initial and final edges of Z contribute one each to the degree of u. So the degree $d(u)$ of u is also even.

Sufficiency Let G be a connected graph and let degree of each vertex of G be even. Assume G is not Eulerian and let G contain least number of edges. Since $\delta \geq 2$, G has a cycle. Let Z be a closed walk in G of maximum length. Clearly, $G - E(Z)$ is an even degree graph. Let C_1 be one of the components of $G - E(Z)$. As C_1 has less number of edges than G, it is Eulerian and has a vertex v in common with Z. Let Z' be an Euler line in C_1. Then $Z' \cup Z$ is closed in G, starting and ending at v. Since it is longer than Z, the choice of Z is contradicted. Hence G is Eulerian.

Second proof for sufficiency Assume that all vertices of G are of even degree. We construct a walk starting at an arbitrary vertex v and going through the edges of G such that no edge of G is traced more than once. The tracing is continued as far as possible. Since every vertex is of even degree, we exit from the vertex we enter and the tracing clearly cannot stop at any vertex but v. As v is also of even degree, we reach v when the tracing comes to an end. If this closed walk Z we just traced includes all the edges of G, then G is an Euler graph. If not, we remove from G all the edges in Z and obtain a subgraph Z' of G formed by the remaining edges. Since both G and Z have all their vertices of even degree, the degrees of the vertices of Z' are also even. Also, Z' touches Z at least at one vertex say u, because G is connected. Starting from u, we again construct a new walk in Z'. As all the vertices of Z' are of even degree, therefore this walk in Z' terminates at vertex u. This walk in Z' combined with Z forms a new walk, which starts and ends at the vertex v and has more edges than Z. This process is repeated till we obtain a closed walk that traces all the edges of G. Hence G is an Euler graph (Fig. 3.2) ❑

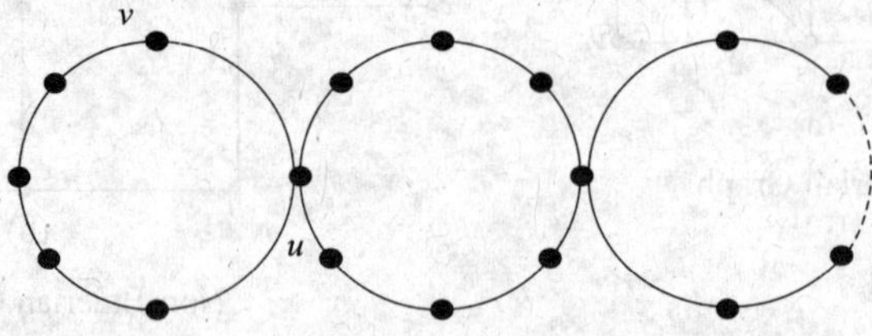

Fig. 3.2

3.2 Konigsberg Bridge Problem

Two islands *A* and *B* formed by the Pregal river (now Pregolya) in Konigsberg (then the capital of east Prussia, but now renamed Kaliningrad and in west Soviet Russia) were connected to each other and to the banks *C* and *D* with seven bridges. The problem is to start at any of the four land areas, *A*, *B*, *C*, or *D*, walk over each of the seven bridges exactly once and return to the starting point.

Euler modelled the problem representing the four land areas by four vertices, and the seven bridges by seven edges joining these vertices. This is illustrated in Figure 3.3.

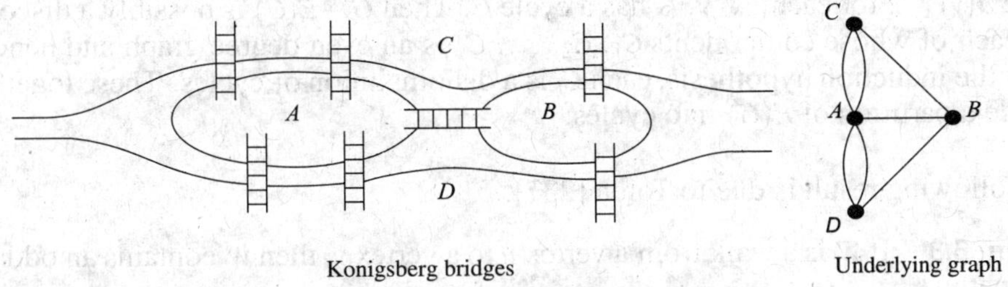

Fig. 3.3

We see from the graph *G* of the Konigsberg bridges that not all its vertices are of even degree. Thus *G* is not an Euler graph, and implies that there is no closed walk in *G* containing all the edges of *G*. Hence it is not possible to walk over each of the seven bridges exactly once and return to the starting point.

Note Suppose there are two additional bridges, one between the land areas *C* and *D* and the second between the land areas *A* and *B*. Now in the graph of Konigsberg bridge problem with nine bridges, every vertex is of even degree and the graph is thus Eulerian. Hence it is now possible to walk over each of the nine bridges exactly once and return to the starting point (Fig 3.4).

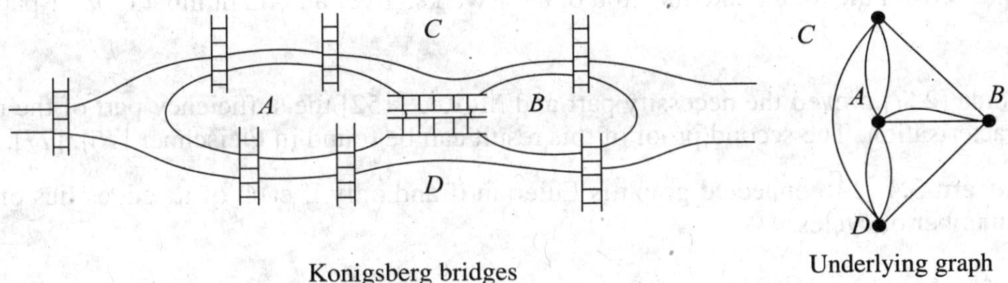

Fig. 3.4

The following characterisation of Eulerian graphs is due to Veblen [247].

Theorem 3.2 A connected graph G is Eulerian if and only if its edge set can be decomposed into cycles.

Proof Let $G(V, E)$ be a connected graph and let G be decomposed into cycles. If k of these cycles are incident at a particular vertex v, then $d(v) = 2k$. Therefore the degree of every vertex of G is even and hence G is Eulerian.

Conversely, let G be Eulerian. We show G can be decomposed into cycles. To prove this, we use induction on the number of edges.

Since $d(v) \geq 2$ for each $v \in V$, G has a cycle C. Then $G - E(C)$ is possibly a disconnected graph, each of whose components $C_1, C_2, \ldots, C_k$ is an even degree graph and hence Eulerian. By the induction hypothesis, each C_i is a disjoint union of cycles. These together with C provide a partition of $E(G)$ into cycles. ❑

The following result is due to Toida [237].

Theorem 3.3 If W is a walk from a vertex u to a vertex v, then W contains an odd number of $u - v$ paths.

Proof Let W be a walk which we consider as a graph in itself, and not as a subgraph of some other graph. Let u and v be initial and final vertices of the walk W. Clearly, $d(u|W)$ and $d(v|W)$ are odd, and $d(w|W)$ is even, for every $w \in V(W) - \{u, v\}$. We count the number of distinct $u - v$ walks in W. These walks are the subgraphs of W.

When we take a $u - v$ walk by successively selecting the edges $e_1, e_2, \ldots, e_s$, initial vertex of e_1 being u and terminal vertex of e_s being v, for each edge there are an odd number of choices. The total number of such edges is the product of these odd numbers and is therefore odd. Now from these walks, we find the $u - v$ paths. If a $u - v$ walk W_1 is not a path, then it contains one or more cycles. The traversal of these cycles in the two possible alternative directions (clockwise and anticlockwise) produces in all an even number of walks, all with the same edge set as W_1. Omitting these even number of walks which are not paths from the total odd collection of $u - v$ walks, gives an odd number of $u - v$ paths. ❑

Toida [237] proved the necessity part and McKee [152] the sufficiency part of the next characterisation. The second proof of this result can be found in Fleischner [76], [77].

Theorem 3.4 A connected graph is Eulerian if and only if each of its edges lies on an odd number of cycles.

Proof

Necessity Let G be a connected Eulerian graph and let $e = uv$ be any edge of G. Then $G - e$ is a $u - v$ walk W, and so $G - e = W$ contains an odd number of $u - v$ paths. Thus each of the odd number of $u - v$ paths in W together with e gives a cycle in G containing e and these are the only such cycles. Therefore there are an odd number of cycles in G containing e.

Sufficiency Let G be a connected graph so that each of its edges lies on an odd number of cycles. Let v be any vertex of G and $E_v = \{e_1, \ldots, e_d\}$ be the set of edges of G incident on v, then $|E_v| = d(v) = d$. For each i, $1 \le i \le d$, let k_i be the number of cycles of G containing e_i. By hypothesis, each k_i is odd. Let $c(v)$ be the number of cycles of G containing v. Then clearly $c(v) = \frac{1}{2}\sum_{i=1}^{d} k_i$ implying that $2c(v) = \sum_{i=1}^{d} k_i$. Since $2c(v)$ is even and each k_i is odd, d is even. Hence G is Eulerian. ❑

Corollary 3.1 The number of edge–disjoint paths between any two vertices of an Euler graph is even.

A consequence of Theorem 3.4 is the result of Bondy and Halberstam [37], which gives yet another characterisation of Eulerian graphs.

Corollary 3.2 A graph is Eulerian if and only if it has an odd number of cycle decompositions.

Proof In one direction, the proof is trivial. If G has an odd number of cycle decompositions, then it has at least one, and hence G is Eulerian.

Conversely, assume that G is Eulerian. Let $e \in E(G)$ and let $C_1, \ldots, C_r$ be the cycles containing e. By Theorem 3.4, r is odd. We proceed by induction on $m = |E(G)|$, with G being Eulerian.

If G is just a cycle, then the result is true. Now assume that G is not a cycle. This means that for each i, $1 \le i \le r$, by the induction assumption, $G_i = G - E(C_i)$ has an odd number, say s_i, of cycle decompositions. (If G_i is disconnected, apply the induction assumption to each of the nontrivial components of G_i). The union of each of these cycle decompositions of G_i and C_i yields a cycle decomposition of G. Hence the number of cycle decompositions of G containing C_i is s_i, $1 \le i \le r$. Let $s(G)$ denote the number of cycle decompositions of G. Then

$$s(G) \equiv \sum_{i=1}^{r} s_i \equiv r (\text{mod } 2) \qquad (\text{since } s_i \equiv 1 (\text{mod } 2))$$

$$\equiv 1 (\text{mod } 2).$$ ❑

Two examples of Euler graphs are shown in Figure 3.5.

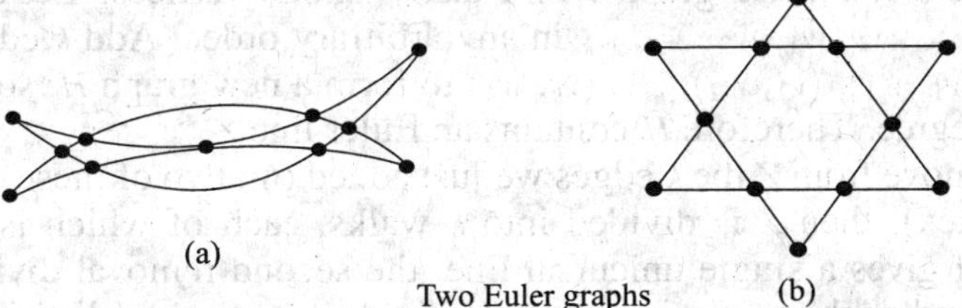

Two Euler graphs

Fig. 3.5

3.3 Unicursal Graphs

An open walk that includes (or traces) all edges of a graph without retracing any edge is called a unicursal line or open Euler line. A connected graph that has a unicursal line is called a unicursal graph. Figure 3.6 shows a unicursal graph.

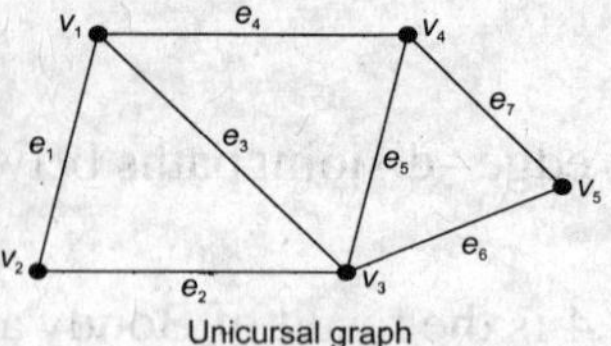

Fig. 3.6

Clearly by adding an edge between the initial and final vertices of a unicursal line, we get an Euler line.

The following characterisation of unicursal graphs can be easily derived from Theorem 3.1.

Theorem 3.5 A connected graph is unicursal if and only if it has exactly two vertices of odd degree.

Proof Let G be a connected graph and let G be unicursal. Then G has a unicursal line, say from u to v, where u and v are vertices of G. Join u and v to a new vertex w of G to get a graph H. Then H has an Euler line and therefore each vertex of H is of even degree. Now, by deleting the vertex w, the degree of vertices u and v each get reduced by one, so that u and v are of odd degree.

Conversely, let u and v be the only vertices of G with odd degree. Join u and v to a new vertex w to get the graph H. So every vertex of H is of even degree and thus H is Eulerian. Therefore, $G = H - w$ has a $u - v$ unicursal line so that G is unicursal. ❑

The following result is the generalisation of Theorem 3.5.

Theorem 3.6 In a connected graph G with exactly $2k$ odd vertices, there exists k edge disjoint subgraphs such that they together contain all edges of G and that each is a unicursal graph.

Proof Let G be a connected graph with exactly $2k$ odd vertices. Let these odd vertices be named $v_1, v_2, \ldots, v_k; w_1, w_2, \ldots, w_k$ in any arbitrary order. Add k edges to G between the vertex pairs $(v_1, w_1), (v_2, w_2), \ldots, (v_k, w_k)$ to form a new graph H, so that every vertex of H is of even degree. Therefore H contains an Euler line Z.

Now, if we remove from Z the k edges we just added (no two of these edges are incident on the same vertex), then Z is divided into k walks, each of which is a unicursal line. The first removal gives a single unicursal line, the second removal divides that into two unicursal lines, and each successive removal divides a unicursal line into two unicursal lines, until there are k of them. Hence the result. ❑

3.4 Arbitrarily Traceable Graphs

An Eulerian graph G is said to be arbitrarily traceable (or randomly Eulerian) from a vertex v if every walk with initial vertex v can be extended to an Euler line of G. A graph is said to be arbitrarily traceable if it is arbitrarily traceable from every vertex (Fig. 3.7).

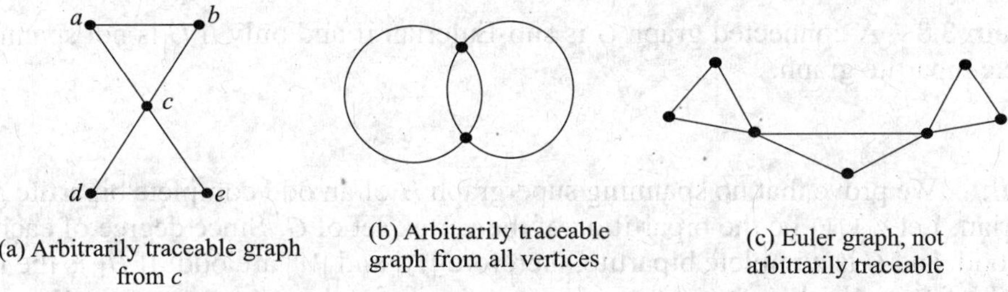

(a) Arbitrarily traceable graph from c

(b) Arbitrarily traceable graph from all vertices

(c) Euler graph, not arbitrarily traceable

Fig. 3.7

The following characterisation of arbitrarily traceable graphs is due to Ore [169]. Such graphs were also characterised by Chartrand and White [55] .

Theorem 3.7 An Eulerian graph G is arbitrarily traceable from a vertex v if and only if every cycle of G passes through v.

Proof

Necessity Let the Eulerian graph G be arbitrarily traceable from a vertex v. Assume there is a cycle C not passing through v. Let $H = G - E(C)$. Then every vertex of H has an even degree and the component of H containing v is Eulerian. This component of H can be traversed as an Euler line Z, starting and ending with v and contains all those edges of G which are incident at v. Clearly, this $v-v$ walk cannot be extended to contain the edges of C also, contradicting that G contains v. Thus every cycle in G contains v.

Sufficiency Let every cycle of the Eulerian graph G pass through the vertex v of G. We show that G is arbitrarily traceable from v. Assume, on the contrary, that G is not arbitrarily traceable from v. Then there is a $v-v$ closed walk W of G containing all the edges of G incident with v and yet not containing all the edges of G. Let one such edge be incident at a vertex u on W. So every vertex of $H = G - E(W)$ is of even degree and v is an isolated vertex of H and u is not. The component of H containing u is therefore Eulerian subgraph of G not passing through v, contradicting the assumption. Hence the result follows. ❑

Corollary 3.3 Cycles are the only arbitrarily traceable graphs.

3.5 Sub-Eulerian Graphs

A graph G is said to be *sub-Eulerian* if it is a spanning subgraph of some Eulerian graph.

The following characterisation of sub-Eulerian graphs is due to Boesch, Suffel and Tindell [28].

Theorem 3.8 A connected graph G is sub-Eulerian if and only if G is not spanned by a complete bipartite graph.

Proof

Necessity We prove that no spanning supergraph H of an odd complete bipartite graph G is Eulerian. Let $V_1 \cup V_2$ be the bipartition of the vertex set of G. Since degree of each vertex of G is odd, and G is complete bipartite, therefore $|V_1|$ and $|V_2|$ are odd. If H_1 is the induced subgraph of H on V_1, then at least one vertex, say v, of V_1 has even degree in H_1, since $|V_1|$ is odd. But then $d(v|H) = d(v|H) + |V_2|$, which is odd. Therefore H is not Eulerian.

Sufficiency Refer Boesch et. al., [28]. ❑

Super-Eulerian graphs

A non-Eulerian graph G is said to be *super-Eulerian* if it has a spanning Eulerian subgraph.

The following sufficient conditions for super-Eulerian graphs are due to Lesniak-Foster and Williams [143].

Theorem 3.9 If a graph G is such that $n \geq 6$, $\delta \geq 2$ and $d(u) + d(v) \geq n - 1$, for every pair of non-adjacent vertices u and v, then G is super-Eulerian.

The following result is due to Balakrishnan and Paulraja [12].

Theorem 3.10 If G is any connected graph and if each edge of G belongs to a triangle in G, then G has a spanning Eulerian subgraph.

Proof Since G has a triangle, G has a closed walk. Let W be the longest closed walk in G. Then W must be a spanning Eulerian subgraph of G. If not, there exists a vertex $v \notin W$ and v is adjacent to a vertex u of W. By hypothesis, uv belongs to a triangle, say uvw. If none of the edges of this triangle is in W, then $W \cup \{uv, vw, wu\}$ yields a closed walk longer than W (Fig. 3.8). If $uw \in W$, then $(W - uw) \cup \{uv, vw\}$ would be a closed walk longer than W. This contradiction proves that W is a spanning closed walk in G. ❑

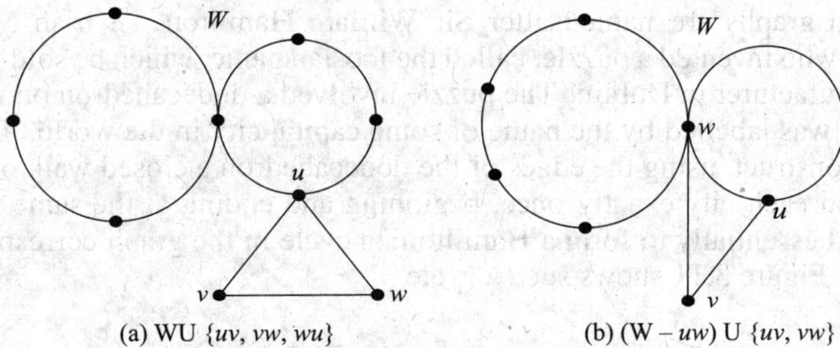

(a) WU {uv, vw, wu}   (b) (W – uw) U {uv, vw}

Fig. 3.8

3.6 Hamiltonian Graphs

A cycle passing through all the vertices of a graph is called a *Hamiltonian cycle*. A graph containing a Hamiltonian cycle is called a *Hamiltonian graph*. A path passing through all the vertices of a graph is called a *Hamiltonian path* and a graph containing a Hamiltonian path is said to be *traceable*. Examples of Hamiltonian graphs are given in Figure 3.9.

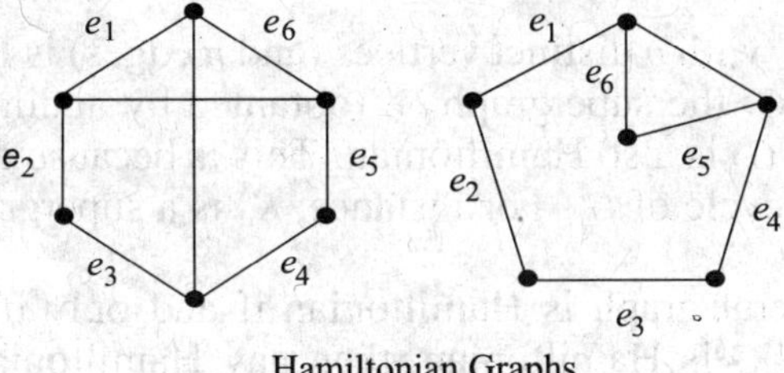

Hamiltonian Graphs

Fig. 3.9

If the last edge of a Hamiltonian cycle is dropped, we get a Hamiltonian path. However, a non-Hamiltonian graph can have a Hamiltonian path, that is, Hamiltonian paths cannot always be used to form Hamiltonian cycles. For example, in Figure 3.10, G_1 has no Hamiltonian path, and so no Hamiltonian cycle; G_2 has the Hamiltonian path $v_1v_2v_3v_4$, but has no Hamiltonian cycle, while G_3 has the Hamiltonian cycle $v_1v_2v_3v_4v_1$.

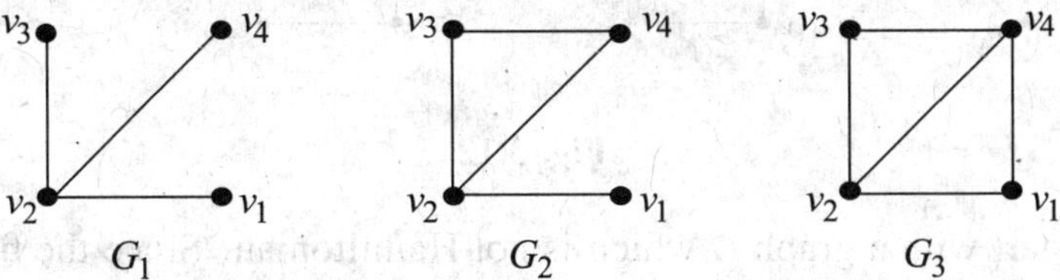

Fig. 3.10

Hamiltonian graphs are named after Sir William Hamilton, an Irish Mathematician (1805–1865), who invented a puzzle, called the Icosian game, which he sold for 25 guineas to a game manufacturer in Dublin. The puzzle involved a dodecahedron on which each of the 20 vertices was labelled by the name of some capital city in the world. The aim of the game was to construct, using the edges of the dodecahedron a closed walk of all the cities which traversed each city exactly once, beginning and ending at the same city. In other words, one had essentially to form a Hamiltonian cycle in the graph corresponding to the dodecahedron. Figure 3.11 shows such a cycle.

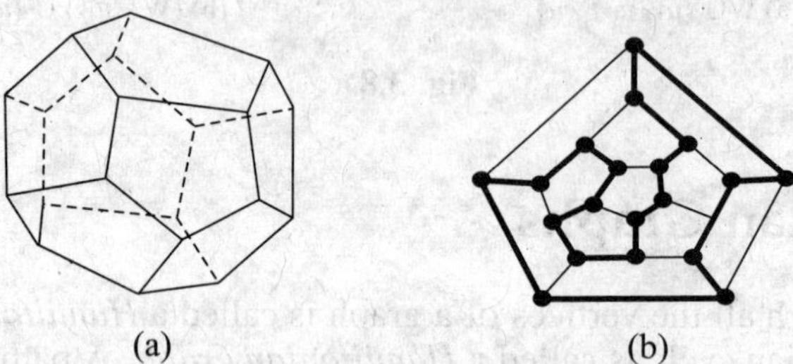

Dedecahedron and its graph shown with the Hamiltonian cycle

Fig. 3.11

Clearly, the n-cycle C_n with n distinct vertices (and n edges) is Hamiltonian. Now, given any Hamiltonian graph G, the supergraph G' (obtained by adding in new edges between non-adjacent vertices of G) is also Hamiltonian. This is because any Hamiltonian cycle in G is also a Hamiltonian cycle of G'. For instance, K_n is a supergraph of an n-cycle and so K_n is Hamiltonian.

A multigraph or general graph is Hamiltonian if and only if its underlying graph is Hamiltonian, because if G is Hamiltonian, then any Hamiltonian cycle in G remains a Hamiltonian cycle in the underlying graph of G. Conversely, if the underlying graph of a graph G is Hamiltonian, then G is also Hamiltonian.

Let G be a graph with n vertices. Clearly, G is a subgraph of the complete graph K_n. From G, we construct step by step supergraphs of G to get K_n, by adding an edge at each step between two vertices that are not already adjacent (Fig. 3.12).

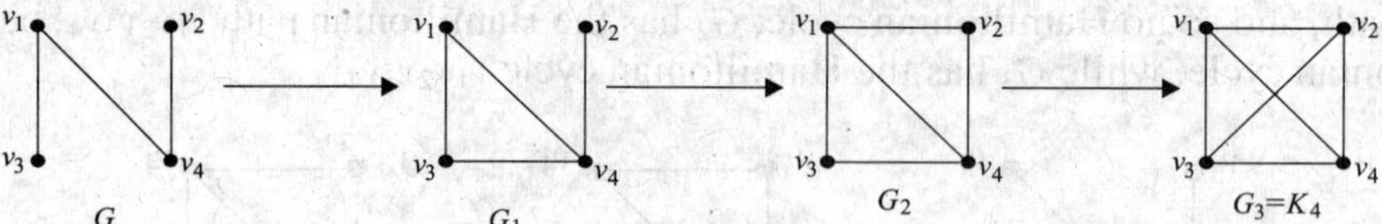

Fig. 3.12

Now, let us start with a graph G which is not Hamiltonian. Since the final outcome of the procedure is the Hamiltonian graph K_n, we change from a non-Hamiltonian graph to a Hamiltonian graph at some stage of the procedure. For example, the non-Hamiltonian graph G_1 above is followed by the Hamiltonian graph G_2. Since supergraphs of Hamiltonian graphs are Hamiltonian, once a Hamiltonian graph is reached in the procedure, all the subsequent supergraphs are Hamiltonian.

Definition: A simple graph G is called *maximal non-Hamiltonian* if it is not Hamiltonian and the addition of an edge between any two non-adjacent vertices of it forms a Hamiltonian graph. For example, G_1 above is maximal non-Hamiltonian. Figure 3.13 shows a maximal non-Hamiltonian graph.

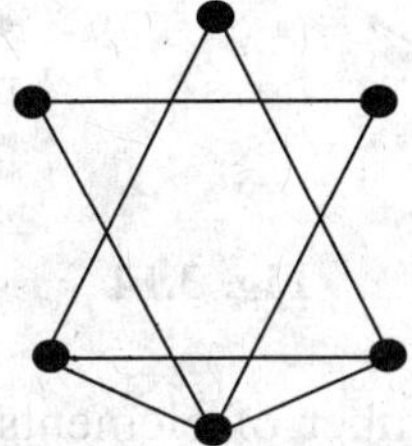

Fig. 3.13

It follows from the above procedure that any non-Hamiltonian graph with n-vertices is a subgraph of a maximal non-Hamiltonian graph with n vertices.

The above procedure is used to prove the following sufficient conditions due to Dirac [65].

Theorem 3.11 (Dirac) If G is a graph with n vertices, where $n \geq 3$ and $d(v) \geq n/2$, for every vertex v of G, then G is Hamiltonian.

Proof Assume that the result is not true. Then for some value $n \geq 3$, there is a non-Hamiltonian graph H in which $d(v) \geq n/2$, for every vertex of H. In any spanning super graph K (i.e., with the same vertex set) of H, $d(v) \geq n/2$ for every vertex of K, since any proper supergraph of this form is obtained by adding more edges. Thus there is a maximal non-Hamiltonian graph G with n vertices and $d(v) \geq n/2$ for every v in G. Using this G, we obtain a contradiction.

Clearly, $G \neq K_n$, as K_n is Hamiltonian. Therefore there are non-adjacent vertices u and v in G. Let $G+uv$ be the supergraph of G by adding an edge between u and v. Since G is maximal non-Hamiltonian, $G+uv$ is Hamiltonian. Also, if C is a Hamiltonian cycle of $G+uv$, then C contains the edge uv, since otherwise C is a Hamiltonian cycle of G, which is not possible. Let this Hamiltonian cycle C be $u = v_1, v_2, \ldots, v_n = v, u$.

Now, let $S = \{v_i \in C :$ there is an edge from u to v_{i+1} in $G\}$ and $T = \{v_j \in C :$ there is an edge from v to v_j in $G\}$.

Then $v_n \notin T$, since otherwise there is an edge from v to $v_n = v$, that is a loop, which is impossible.

Also $v_n \notin S$, (taking v_{n+1} as v_1), since otherwise we again get a loop from u to $v_1 = u$. Therefore, $v_n \notin S \cup T$ (Fig. 3.14).

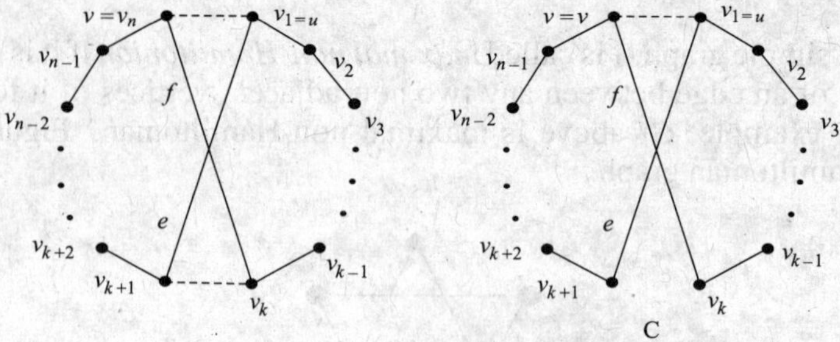

Fig. 3.14

Let $|S|$, $|T|$ and $|S \cup T|$ be the number of elements in S, T and $S \cup T$ respectively. So $|S \cup T| < n$. Also, for every edge incident with u, there corresponds one vertex v_i in S. Therefore, $|S| = d(u)$. Similarly, $|T| = d(v)$.

Now, if v_k is a vertex belonging to both S and T, there is an edge e joining u to v_{k+1} and an edge f joining v to v_k. This implies that $C' = v_1, v_{k+1}, v_{k+2}, \ldots, v_n, v_k, v_{k-1}, \ldots, v_2, v_1$ is a Hamiltonian cycle in G, which is a contradiction as G is non-Hamiltonian. This shows that there is no vertex v_k in $S \cap T$, so that $S \cap T = \Phi$.

Thus $|S \cup T| = |S| + |T| - |S \cap T|$ gives $|S| + |T| = |S \cup T|$, so that $d(u) + d(v) < n$. This is a contradiction, because $d(u) \geq n/2$ for all u in G, and so $d(u) + d(v) \geq n/2 + n/2$ giving $d(u) + d(v) \geq n$. Hence the theorem follows. ❑

The following result is due to Ore [171].

Theorem 3.12 (Ore) Let G be a graph with n vertices and let u and v be non-adjacent vertices in G such that $d(u) + d(v) \geq n$. Let $G + uv$ denote the super graph of G obtained by joining u and v by an edge. Then G is Hamiltonian if and only if $G + uv$ is Hamiltonian.

Proof Let G be a graph with n vertices and suppose u and v are non-adjacent vertices in G such that $d(u) + d(v) \geq n$. Let $G + uv$ be the super graph of G obtained by adding the edge uv. Let G be Hamiltonian. Then obviously $G + uv$ is Hamiltonian. Conversely, let $G + uv$ be Hamiltonian. We have to show that G is Hamiltonian. Then, as in Theorem 3.11, we get $d(u) + d(v) < n$, which contradicts the hypothesis that $d(u) + d(v) \geq n$. Hence G is Hamiltonian. ❑

The following is the proof of Bondy [35] of Theorem 3.12, and this proof bears a close resemblance to the proof of Dirac's theorem given by Newman [166], but is more direct.

Proof (Bondy [35]) Consider the complete graph K on the vertex set of G in which the edges of G are coloured blue and the remaining edges of K are coloured red. Let C be a

Hamiltonian cycle of K with as many blue edges as possible. We show that every edge of C is blue, in other words, that C is Hamiltonian cycle of G.

Suppose to the contrary, C has a red edge uu^- (where u^- is the successor of u on C). Consider the set S of vertices joined to u by blue edges (that is, the set of neighbours of u in G). The successor u^- of u on C must be joined by a blue edge to some vertex v^- of S^-, because if u^- is adjacent in C only to vertices $V-(S^- U\{u^-\})$, $d_G(u)+d_G(u^-)=|N_G(u)|+|N_G(u^-)| \leq |S|+(|V|-|S^-|-1)=|V(G)|-1$, contradicting the hypothesis that $d_G(u)+d_G(u^-)\geq |V(G)|$, u and u^- being non-adjacent in G. But now the cycle C obtained from C by exchanging the edges uu^- and vv^- has more blue edges than C, which is a contradiction. ❑

Definition: Let G be a graph with n vertices. If there are two non-adjacent vertices u_1 and v_1 in G such that $d(u_1)+d(v_1)\geq n$, join u_1 and v_1 by an edge to form the super graph G_1. Now, if there are two non-adjacent vertices u_2 and v_2 in G_1 such that $d(u_2)+d(v_2)\geq n$, join u_2 and v_2 by an edge to form supergraph G_2. Continue in this way, recursively joining pairs of non-adjacent vertices whose degree sum is at least n until no such pair remains. The final supergraph thus obtained is called the *closure* of G and is denoted by $c(G)$.

The example in Figure 3.15 illustrates the closure operation.

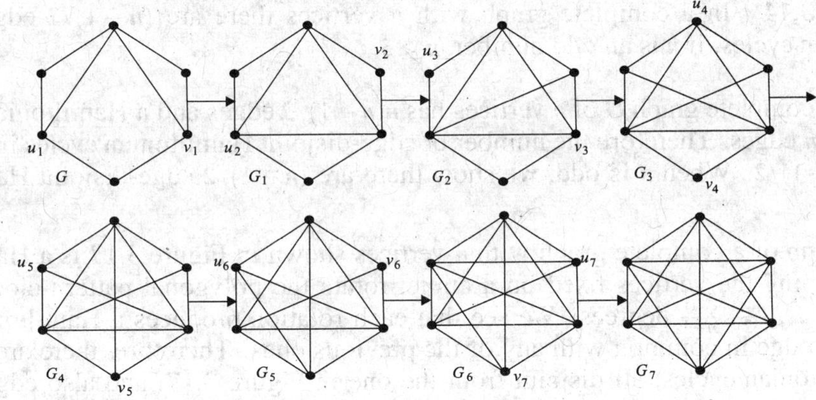

Fig. 3.15

We observe in this example that there are different choices of pairs of non-adjacent vertices u and v with $d(u)+d(v)\geq n$. Therefore the closure procedure can be carried out in several different ways and each different way gives the same result.

In the graph shown in Figure 3.16, $n=7$ and $d(u)+d(v)<7$, for any pair u, v of adjacent vertices. Therefore, $c(G)=G$.

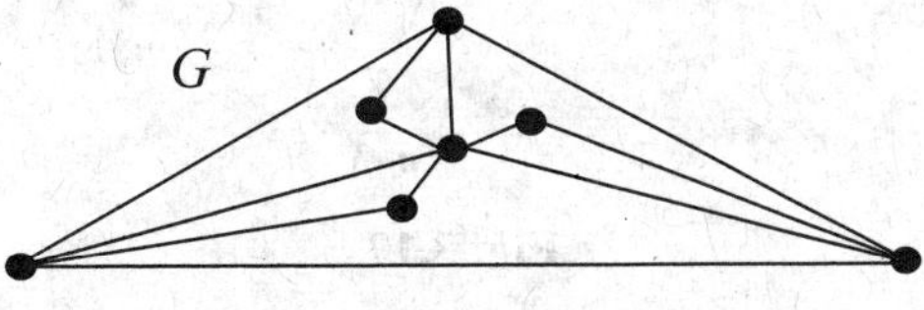

Fig. 3.16

The importance of $c(G)$ is given in the following result due to Bondy and Chvatal [36].

Theorem 3.13 A graph G is Hamiltonian if and only if its closure $c(G)$ is Hamiltonian.

Proof Let $c(G)$ be the closure of the graph G. Since $c(G)$ is a supergraph of G, therefore, if G is Hamiltonian, then $c(G)$ is also Hamiltonian.

Conversely, let $c(G)$ be Hamiltonian. Let $G, G_1, G_2, \ldots, G_{k-1}, G_k = c(G)$ be the sequence of graphs obtained by performing the closure procedure on G. Since $c(G) = G_k$ is obtained from G_{k-1} by setting $G_k = G_{k-1} + uv$, where u, v is a pair of non adjacent vertices in G_{k-1} with $d(u) + d(v) \geq n$, therefore it follows that G_{k-1} is Hamiltonian. Similarly G_{k-2}, so G_{k-3}, ..., G_1 and thus G is Hamiltonian. ❑

Corollary 3.4 Let G be a graph with n vertices with $n \geq 3$. If $c(G)$ is complete, then G is Hamiltonian.

There can be more than one Hamiltonian cycle in a given graph, but the interest lies in the edge-disjoint Hamiltonian cycles. The following result gives the number of edge-disjoint Hamiltonian cycles in a complete graph with odd number of vertices.

Theorem 3.14 In a complete graph with n vertices there are $(n-1)/2$ edge-disjoint Hamiltonian cycles, if n is an odd number, $n \geq 3$.

Proof A complete graph G of n vertices has $n(n-1)/2$ edges and a Hamiltonian cycle in G contains n edges. Therefore the number of edge-disjoint Hamiltonian cycles in G cannot exceed $(n-1)/2$. When n is odd, we show there are $(n-1)/2$ edge-disjoint Hamiltonian cycles.

The subgraph of a complete graph with n vertices shown in Figure 3.17 is a Hamiltonian cycle. Keeping the vertices fixed on a circle, rotate the polygonal pattern clockwise by $\frac{360}{n-1}, 2.\frac{360}{n-1}, \ldots, \frac{n-3}{2}.\frac{360}{n-1}$ degrees. We see that each rotation produces a Hamiltonian cycle that has no edge in common with any of the previous ones. Therefore, there are $(n-3)/2$ new Hamiltonian cycles, all disjoint from the one in Figure 3.17, and also edge-disjoint among themselves. Thus there are $(n-1)/2$ edge disjoint Hamiltonian cycles. ❑

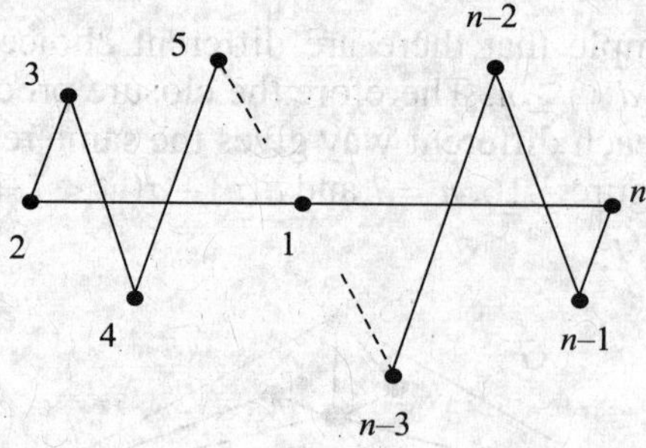

Fig. 3.17

The next result involving degrees give the sufficient conditions for a graph to be Hamiltonian.

Theorem 3.15 Let $D = [d_i]_1^n$ be a degree sequence of a graph $G(V, E)$, $d_1 \le d_2 \le \ldots \le d_n$. Each of the following gives the sufficient conditions for G to be Hamiltonian.

A. $1 \le k \le n \Rightarrow d_k \ge \frac{n}{2}$ (Dirac [65])

B. $uv \notin E \Rightarrow d(u) + d(v) \ge n$ (Ore [171]).

C. $1 \le k \le \frac{n}{2} \Rightarrow d_k > k$ (Posa [205]).

D. $j < k$, $d_j \le j$ and $d_k \le k-1 \Rightarrow d_j + d_k \ge n$ (Bondy [33])

E. $d_k \le k < \frac{n}{2} \Rightarrow d_{n-k} \ge n-k$ (Chvatal [58])

F. For every i and j with $1 \le i \le n$, $1 \le j \le n$, $i + j \ge n$, $v_iv_j \notin E$, $d(v_i) \le i$ and $d(v_j) \le j-1 \Rightarrow d(v_i) + d(v_j) \ge n$ (Las Vergnas [249].

G. $c(G)$ is complete (Bondy and Chvatal [36]).

Proof We first prove that

$$A \overset{(i)}{\Rightarrow} B \overset{(ii)}{\Rightarrow} C \overset{(iii)}{\Rightarrow} D \overset{(iv)}{\Rightarrow} E \overset{(v)}{\Rightarrow} F \overset{(vi)}{\Rightarrow} G.$$

i. This can be easily established.

ii. Assume that (C) is not true, so that there exists a k with $1 \le k < \frac{n}{2}$ and $d_k \le k$. Then the induced subgraph on the vertices $v_1, v_2, \ldots, v_k$ is a complete graph. For, if there are vertices i and j with $1 \le i < j \le k$ and $v_iv_j \notin E$, then $d_i + d_j \le 2d_k < n$, contradicting (B). Since $d_k \le k$, each v_i, $1 \le i \le k$, is adjacent to at most one v_j, $k+1 \le j \le n$. Also, $n-k > k$, because $k < \frac{n}{2}$. Therefore there is a vertex v_j, $k+1 \le j \le n$ not adjacent to any of the vertices $v_1, v_2, \ldots, v_k$. For this v_j, we have $d_j \le n-k-1$. But then $d_j + d_k \le (n-k-1) + k = n-1$. Thus there is a $v_jv_k \notin E$ with $d_j + d_k \le n-1$, contradicting (B). Hence proving (ii).

iii. Assume that (D) is not true, so that there exist j and k with $j < k$, $d_j \le j$, $d_k \le k-1$ and $d_j + d_k < n$. This gives $i = d_j < \frac{n}{2}$. But then $d_j \le j$ gives $d_{d_j} \le d_j$, since the sequence is non-decreasing. Therefore, $d_i \le d_j = i$. Thus there is an i, $1 \le i \le \frac{n}{2}$ with $d_i \le i$, contradicting (C). This proves (iii).

iv. If (E) is not true, there is a k with $d_k \le k < \frac{n}{2}$ and $d_{n-k} \le n-k-1$. Then $d_k + d_{n-k} \le n-1$. Setting $n-k = j$, we have $k < j$, $d_k \le k$, $d_j \le j-1$ and $d_j + d_k \le n-1$. This contradicts (D) and so (iv) is proved.

v. Assume that (F) is not true, so that there is a pair of vertices v_i and v_j, $i < j$ with $v_iv_j \notin E$ and violating (F). Choose i to be the least such possible integer. Then by minimality of i, $d_{i-1} > i-1$. Thus $d_i \ge d_{i-1} \ge i$ and since $d_i \le i$, we obtain $d_i = i$. If

$i \geq \frac{n}{2}$, we get $d_i + d_j \geq 2d_i \geq n$, contradicting the violation of (F). Therefore, $i < \frac{n}{2}$. Thus there is an i, $1 \leq i < \frac{n}{2}$ with $d_i = i$. Now, if (E) is satisfied, we have $d_{n-i} \geq n - i$ and since $j \geq n-i$, we obtain $d_j \geq d_{n-i} \geq n-i$. By minimality of i, $d_i = i$ and we have $d_j + d_i \geq (n-i) + i = n$, again contradicting the violation of (F). Thus negation of (F) implies negation of (E) and (V) is established.

vi. Assume that $c(G) = H$ is not complete. Let v_i and v_j be non-adjacent vertices in H such that (a) j is as large as possible and (b) i is as large as possible subject to (a). Then $i < j$, and since H is the closure of G, therefore

$$d(v_i|H) + d(v_j|H) \leq n-1, \tag{3.15.1}$$

$$d(v_i|G) + d(v_j|G) \leq n-1.$$

By the choice of j, v_i is adjacent in H to all v_k with $k > j$, so that

$$d(v_i|H) \geq n-j. \tag{3.15.2}$$

Again, by the choice of i, v_j is adjacent in H to all v_k with $k > i$, $k \neq j$, so that

$$d(v_j|H) \geq n-i-1. \tag{3.15.3}$$

From (3.15.1) and (3.15.2), we have

$$d(v_j|G) \leq d(v_j|H) \leq (n-1) - (n-j) = j-1.$$

From (3.15.1) and (3.15.3), we have

$$d(v_j|G) \leq d(v_i|H) \leq (n-1) - (n-i-1) = i.$$

From (3.15.2) and (3.15.3), we have

$$i + j \geq (2n-1) - d(v_i|H) - d(v_j|H) \geq n. \qquad \text{(using (1))}$$

Therefore i and j contradict the given conditions. Thus $H = c(G)$ is complete. This proves (vi).

By Theorem 3.13 it follows that if (G) holds, then G is Hamiltonian. ❑

The next result is due to Nash-Williams [163].

Theorem 3.16 (Nash-Williams) Every k-regular graph on $2k+1$ vertices is Hamiltonian.

Proof Let G be a k-regular graph on $2k+1$ vertices. Add a new vertex w and join it by an edge to each vertex of G. The resulting graph H on $2k+2$ vertices has $\delta = k+1$. Thus by Theorem 3.15 (A), H is Hamiltonian. Removing w from H, we get a Hamiltonian path, say $v_0 v_1 \ldots v_{2k}$.

Assume that G is not Hamiltonian, so that (a) if $v_0v_i \in E$, then $v_{i-1}v_{2k} \notin E$, (b) if $v_0v_i \notin E$, then $v_{i-1}v_{2k} \in E$, since $d(v_0) = d(v_{2k}) = k$.

The following cases arise.

Case (i) v_0 is adjacent to $v_1, v_2, \ldots, v_k$, and v_{2k} is adjacent to $v_k, v_{k+1}, \ldots, v_{2k-1}$. Then there is an i with $1 \le i \le k$ such that v_i is not adjacent to some v_j for $0 \le j \le k (j \ne i)$. But $d(v_i) = k$. So v_i is adjacent to v_j for some j with $k+1 \le j \le 2k-1$. Then the cycle C given by $v_iv_{i-1}\ldots v_0v_{i+1}\ldots v_{j-1}v_{2k}v_{2k+1}\ldots v_j$ is a Hamiltonian cycle of G (Fig 3.18).

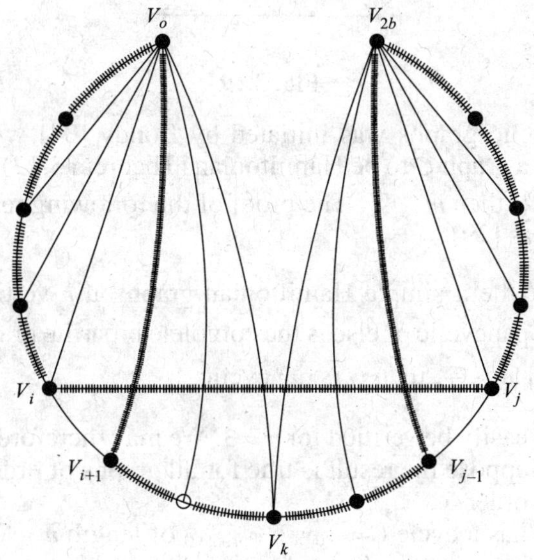

Fig. 3.18

Case (ii) There is an i with $1 \le i \le 2k-1$ such that $v_{i+1}v_0 \in E$, but $v_iv_0 \notin E$. Then by (b), $v_{i-1}v_{2k} \in E$. Thus G contains the $2k$-cycle $v_{i-1}v_{i-2}\ldots v_0v_{i+1}$. Renaming the $2k$-cycle C as $u_1u_2\ldots u_{2k}$ and let u_0 be the vertex of G not on C. Then u_0 cannot be adjacent to two consecutive vertices on C and hence u_0 is adjacent to every second vertex on C, say $u_1, u_3, \ldots, u_{2k-1}$. Replacing u_{2i} by u_0, we obtain another maximum cycle C' of G and hence u_{2i} must be adjacent to $u_1, u_3, \ldots, u_{2k-1}$. But then u_1 is adjacent to $u_0, u_2, \ldots, u_{2k}$, implying $d(u_1) \ge k+1$. This is a contradiction and hence G is Hamiltonian. ❑

3.7 Pancyclic Graphs

Definition: A graph G of order $n(\ge 3)$ is *pancyclic* if G contains all cycles of lengths from 3 to n. G is called *vertex-pancyclic* if each vertex v of G belongs to a cycle of every length ℓ, $3 \le \ell \le n$.

Example Clearly, a vertex-pancyclic graph is pancyclic. However, the converse is not true. Figure 3.19 displays a pancyclic graph that is not vertex-pancyclic.

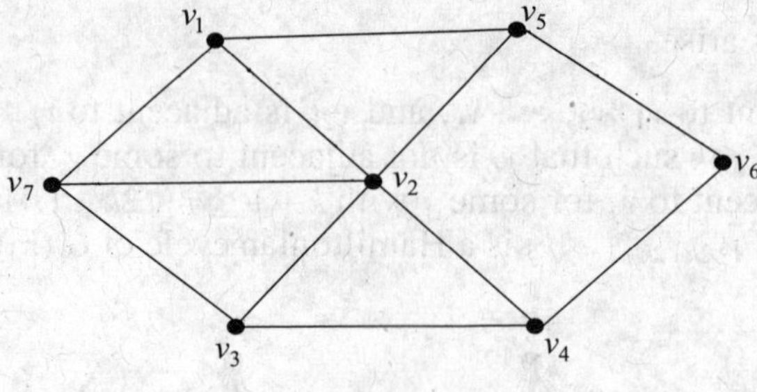

Fig. 3.19

The result of pancyclic graphs was initiated by Bondy [34], who showed that Ore's sufficient condition for a graph G to be Hamiltonian (Theorem 3.12) actually implies much more. Note that if $\delta \geq \frac{n}{2}$, then $m \geq \frac{n^2}{2}$. The proof of the following result due to Thomassen can be found in Bollobas [29].

Theorem 3.17 Let G be a simple Hamiltonian graph on n vertices with at least $\left[\frac{n^2}{2}\right]$ edges. Then G is either pancyclic or else is the complete bipartite graph $K_{\frac{n}{2},\frac{n}{2}}$. In particular, if G is Hamiltonian and $m > \frac{n^2}{4}$, then G is pancyclic.

Proof The result can easily be verified for $n = 3$. We may therefore assume that $n \geq 4$. We apply induction on n. Suppose the result is true for all graphs of order at most $n-1 (n \geq 4)$, and let G be a graph of order n.

First, assume that G has a cycle $C = v_0 v_1 \ldots v_{n-2} v_0$ of length $n-1$. Let v be the (unique) vertex of G not belonging to C. If $d(v) \geq \frac{n}{2}$, v is adjacent to two consecutive vertices on C and hence G has a cycle of length 3. Suppose for some r, $2 \leq r \leq \frac{n-1}{2}$, C has no pair of vertices u and w on C adjacent to v in G with $d_C(u, w) = r$. Then if $v_{i_1}, v_{i_2}, \ldots v_{i_{d(v)}}$ are the vertices of C that are adjacent to v in G (recall that C contains all the vertices of G except v), then $v_{i_1+r}, v_{i_2+r}, \ldots, v_{i_{d(v)}+r}$ are nonadjacent to v in G, where the suffixes are taken modulo $(n-1)$. Thus, $2d(v) \leq n-1$, a contradiction. Hence, for each r, $2 \leq r \leq \frac{n-1}{2}$, C has a pair of vertices u and w on C adjacent to v in G with $d_C(u, w) = r$. Thus for each r, $2 \leq r \leq \frac{n-1}{2}$, G has a cycle of length $r+2$ as well as a cycle of length $n-1-r+2 = n-r+1$ (Fig. 3.20). Thus G is pancyclic.

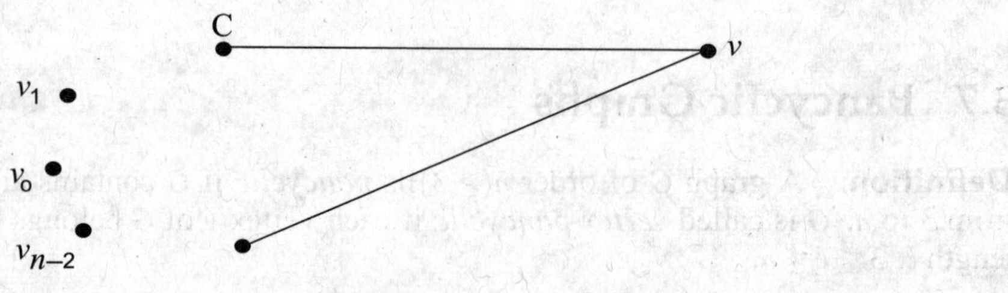

Fig. 3.20

If $d(v) \leq \frac{n-1}{2}$, then $G[V(C)]$, the subgraph of G induced by $V(C)$ has at least $\frac{n^2}{4} - \frac{n-1}{2} > \frac{(n-1)^2}{4}$ edges. So, by the induction assumption, $G[V(C)]$ is pancyclic and hence G is pancyclic. (By hypothesis, G is Hamiltonian).

Next, assume that G has no cycle of length $n-1$. Then G is not pancyclic. In this case, we show that G is $K_{\frac{n}{2},\frac{n}{2}}$.

Let $C = v_0v_1v_2\ldots v_{n-1}v_0$ be a Hamiltonian cycle of G. We claim that of the two pairs v_iv_k and $v_{i+1}v_{k+2}$ (where suffixes are taken modulo n), at most only one of them can be an edge of G. Otherwise, $v_kv_{k-1}v_{k-2}\ldots v_{i+1}v_{k+2}v_{k+3}v_{k+4}\ldots v_iv_k$ is an $(n-1)$-cycle in G, a contradiction. Hence, if $d(v_i) = r$, then there are r vertices adjacent to v_i in G and hence at least r vertices (including v_{i+1} since $v_iv_{i-1} \in E(G)$) that are nonadjacent to v_{i+1}. Thus, $d(v_{i+1}) \leq n-r$ and $d(v_i)+d(v_{i+1}) \leq n$.

Summing the last inequality over i from 0 to $n-1$, we get $4m \leq n^2$. But by hypothesis, $4m \geq n^2$. Hence, $m = \frac{n^2}{4}$ and so n must be even.

This gives $d(v_i)+d(v_{i+1}) = n$ for each i, and thus for each i and k, exactly one of v_iv_k and $v_{i+1}v_{k+2}$ is an edge of G. (3.17.1)

Thus, if $G \neq K_{\frac{n}{2},\frac{n}{2}}$, then certainly there exist i and j such that $v_iv_j \in E$ and $i \equiv j \pmod 2$. Hence for some j, there exists an even positive integer s such that $v_{j+1}v_{j+1+s} \in E$. Choose s to be the least even positive integer with the above property. Then $v_jv_{j+1+s} \notin E$. Hence, $s \geq 4$ (as $s=2$ would mean that $v_jv_{j+1} \notin E$). Again, by (3.17.1), $v_{j-1}v_{j+s-3} = v_{j-1}v_{j-1+(s-2)} \in E(G)$ contradicting the choice of s. Thus, $G = K_{\frac{n}{2},\frac{n}{2}}$. The last part follows from the fact that $|E(K_{\frac{n}{2},\frac{n}{2}})| = \frac{n^2}{4}$. ❑

Theorem 3.18 Let $G \neq K_{\frac{n}{2},\frac{n}{2}}$, be a simple graph with $n \geq 3$ vertices and let $d(u)+d(v) \geq n$ for every pair of non-adjacent vertices of G. Then G is pancyclic.

Proof By Ore's Theorem (Theorem 3.12), G is Hamiltonian. We show that G is pancyclic by first proving that $m \geq \frac{n^2}{4}$ and then invoking Theorem 3.17. This is true if $\delta \geq \frac{n}{2}$ (as $2m = \sum_{i=1}^{n} d_i \geq \delta n \geq n^2/2$). So assume that $\delta < \frac{n}{2}$.

Let S be the set of vertices of degree δ in G. For every pair (u, v) of vertices of degree δ, $d(u)+d(v) < \frac{n}{2}+\frac{n}{2} = n$. Hence by hypothesis, S induces a clique of G and $|S| \leq \delta+1$. If $|S| = \delta+1$, then G is disconnected with $G[S]$ as a component, which is impossible (as G is Hamiltonian). Thus, $|S| \leq \delta$. Further, if $v \in S$, v is nonadjacent to $n-1-\delta$ vertices of G. If u is such a vertex, $d(v)+d(u) \geq n$ implies that $d(u) \geq n-\delta$. Further, v is adjacent to at least one vertex $w \notin S$ and $d(w) \geq \delta+1$, by the choice of S. These facts give that

$$2m = \sum_{i=1}^{n} d_i \geq (n-\delta-1)(n-\delta)+\delta^2+(\delta+1),$$

where the last $(\delta+1)$ comes out of the degree of w. Thus,

$$2m \geq n^2 - n(2\delta+1)+2\delta^2+2\delta+1,$$

which implies that

$$4m \geq 2n^2 - 2n(2\delta+1) + 4\delta^2 + 4\delta + 2$$
$$= (n-(2\delta+1)^2 + n^2 + 1$$
$$\geq n^2 + 1, \text{ since } n > 2\delta.$$

Consequently, $m > \frac{n^2}{4}$, and by Theorem 3.17, G is pancyclic. ❑

3.8 Exercises

1. Prove that the wheel W_n is Hamiltonian for every $n \geq 2$, and n-cube Q_n is Hamiltonian for each $n \geq 2$.
2. If G is a k-regular graph with $2k-1$ vertices, then prove that G is Hamiltonian.
3. Show that if a cubic graph G has a spanning closed walk, then G is Hamiltonian.
4. If $G = G(X, Y)$ is a bipartite Hamiltonian graph, then show that $|X| = |Y|$.
5. Prove that for each $n \geq 1$, the complete tripartite graph $K_{n,\,2n,\,3n}$ is Hamiltonian, but $K_{n,\,2n,\,3n+1}$ is not Hamiltonian.
6. How many spanning cycles are there in the complete bipartite graphs $K_{3,\,3}$ and $K_{4,\,3}$?
7. Prove that a graph G with $n \geq 3$ vertices is arbitrarily traceable if and only if it is one of the graphs C_n, K_n or $K_{n,\,n}$ with $n = 2p$.
8. Prove that a graph G with $n \geq 3$ vertices is randomly traceable if and only if it is randomly Hamiltonian.
9. Find the closure of the graph given in Figure 3.2. Is it Hamiltonian?
10. Does there exist an Eulerian graph with
    i. an even number of vertices and an odd number of edges,
    ii. and odd number of vertices and an even number of edges.

    Draw such a graph if it exists.
11. Characterise graphs which are both Eulerian and Hamiltonian.
12. Characterise graphs which possess Hamiltonian paths but not Hamiltonian cycles.
13. Characterise graphs which are unicursal but not Eulerian.
14. Give an example of a graph which is neither pancyclic nor bipartite, but whose n-closure is complete.

4. Trees

One of the important classes of graphs is the trees. The importance of trees is evident from their applications in various areas, especially theoretical computer science and molecular evolution.

4.1 Basics

Definition: A graph having no cycles is said to be *acyclic*. A *forest* is an acyclic graph.

Definition: A *tree* is a connected graph without any cycles, or a tree is a connected acyclic graph. The edges of a tree are called *branches*. It follows immediately from the definition that a tree has to be a simple graph (because self-loops and parallel edges both form cycles). Figure 4.1(a) displays all trees with fewer than six vertices.

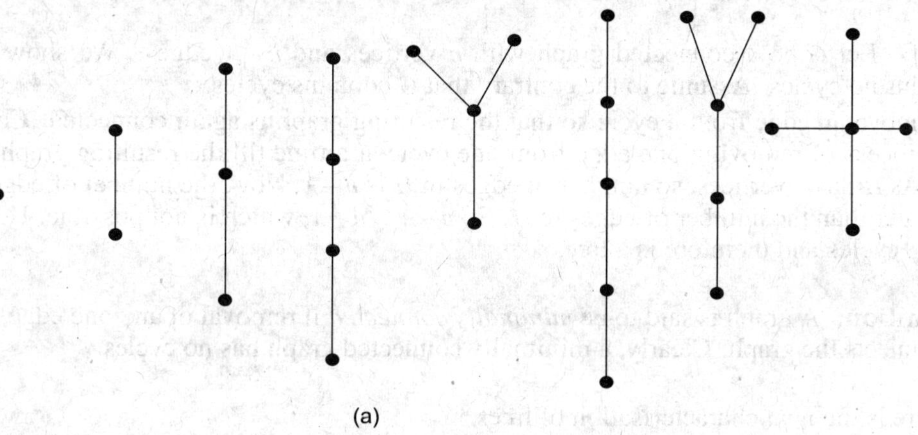

Fig. 4.1(a)

The following result characterises trees.

Theorem 4.1 A graph is a tree if and only if there is exactly one path between every pair of its vertices.

Proof Let G be a graph and let there be exactly one path between every pair of vertices in G. So G is connected. Now G has no cycles, because if G contains a cycle, say between vertices u and v, then there are two distinct paths between u and v, which is a contradiction. Thus G is connected and is without cycles, therefore it is a tree.

Conversely, let G be a tree. Since G is connected, there is at least one path between every pair of vertices in G. Let there be two distinct paths between two vertices u and v of G. The union of these two paths contains a cycle which contradicts the fact that G is a tree. Hence there is exactly one path between every pair of vertices of a tree. ❑

The next two results give alternative methods for defining trees.

Theorem 4.2 A tree with n vertices has $n-1$ edges.

Proof We prove the result by using induction on n, the number of vertices. The result is obviously true for $n = 1$, 2 and 3. Let the result be true for all trees with fewer than n vertices. Let T be a tree with n vertices and let e be an edge with end vertices u and v. So the only path between u and v is e. Therefore deletion of e from T disconnects T. Now, $T-e$ consists of exactly two components T_1 and T_2 say, and as there were no cycles to begin with, each component is a tree. Let n_1 and n_2 be the number of vertices in T_1 and T_2 respectively, so that $n_1+n_2 = n$. Also, $n_1 < n$ and $n_2 < n$. Thus, by induction hypothesis, number of edges in T_1 and T_2 are respectively n_1-1 and n_2-1. Hence the number of edges in $T = n_1-1+n_2-1+1 = n_1+n_2-1 = n-1$. ❑

Theorem 4.3 Any connected graph with n vertices and $n-1$ edges is a tree.

Proof Let G be a connected graph with n vertices and $n-1$ edges. We show that G contains no cycles. Assume to the contrary that G contains cycles.

Remove an edge from a cycle so that the resulting graph is again connected. Continue this process of removing one edge from one cycle at a time till the resulting graph H is a tree. As H has n vertices, so number of edges in H is $n-1$. Now, the number of edges in G is greater than the number of edges in H. So $n-1 > n-1$, which is not possible. Hence, G has no cycles and therefore is a tree. ❑

Definition: A graph is said to be *minimally connected* if removal of any one edge from it disconnects the graph. Clearly, a minimally connected graph has no cycles.

Here is the next characterisation of trees.

Theorem 4.4 A graph is a tree if and only if it is minimally connected.

Proof Let the graph G be minimally connected. Then G has no cycles and therefore is a tree.

Conversely, let G be a tree. Then G contains no cycles and deletion of any edge from G disconnects the graph. Hence G is minimally connected. ❑

The following results give some more properties of trees.

Theorem 4.5 A graph G with n vertices, $n-1$ edges and no cycles is connected.

Proof Let G be a graph without cycles with n vertices and $n-1$ edges. We have to prove that G is connected. Assume that G is disconnected. So G consists of two or more components and each component is also without cycles. We assume without loss of generality that G has two components, say G_1 and G_2 (Fig. 4.1(b)). Add an edge e between a vertex u in G_1 and a vertex v in G_2. Since there is no path between u and v in G, adding e did not create a cycle. Thus $G \cup e$ is a connected graph (tree) of n vertices, having n edges and no cycles. This contradicts the fact that a tree with n vertices has $n-1$ edges. Hence G is connected.

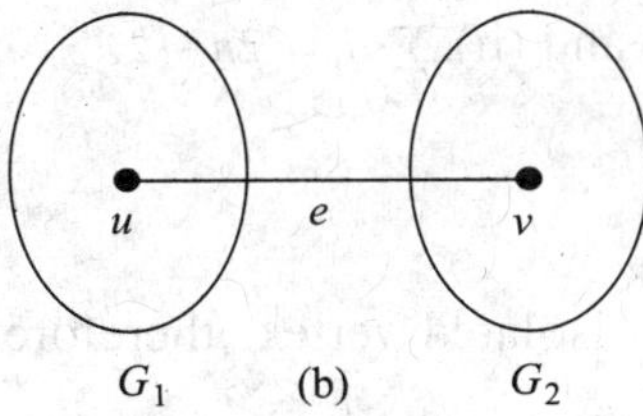

Fig. 4.1(b)

Theorem 4.6 Any tree with at least two vertices has at least two pendant vertices.

Proof Let the number of vertices in a given tree T be $n(n > 1)$. So the number of edges in T is $n-1$. Therefore the degree sum of the tree is $2(n-1)$. This degree sum is to be divided among the n vertices. Since a tree is connected it cannot have a vertex of 0 degree. Each vertex contributes at least 1 to the above sum. Thus there must be at least two vertices of degree exactly 1.

Second proof We use induction on n. The result is obviously true for all trees having fewer than n vertices. We know that T has $n-1$ edges, and if every edge of T is incident with a pendant vertex, then T has at least two pendant vertices, and the proof is complete. So let there be some edge of T that is not incident with a pendant vertex and let this edge be $e = uv$ (Fig. 4.2). Removing the edge e, we see that the graph $T-e$ consists of a pair of trees say T_1 and T_2 with each having fewer than n-vertices. Let $u \in V(T_1)$, $v \in V(T_2)$, and $|V(T_1)| = n_1$, $|V(T_2)| = n_2$. Applying induction hypothesis on both T_1 and T_2, we observe that each of T_1 and T_2 has two pendant vertices. This shows that each of T_1 and T_2 has at least one pendant vertex that is not incident with the edge e. Thus the graph $T-e+e=T$ has at least two pendant vertices.

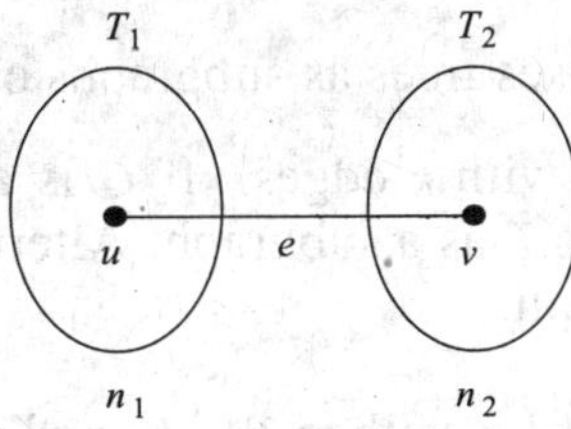

Fig. 4.2

Third proof Let T be a tree with $n(n > 1)$ vertices. The number of edges in T is $n-1$ and the sum of degrees in T is $2(n-1)$, that is, $\sum d_i = 2(n-1)$. Assume T has exactly one vertex v_1 of degree one, while all the other $n-1$ vertices have degree ≥ 2. Then sum of degrees is $d(v_1)+d(v_2)+\ldots+d(v_n) \geq 1+2+2+\ldots+2 = 1+2(n-1)$. So, $2(n-1) \geq 1+2(n-1)$, implying $0 \geq 1$, which is absurd. Hence T has at least two vertices of degree one. ❑

The following result characterises tree degree sequences.

Theorem 4.7 The sequence $[d_i]_1^n$ of positive integers is a degree sequence of a tree if and only if

$$\text{(i) } d_i \geq 1 \text{ for all } i,\ 1 \leq i \leq n \text{ and (ii) } \sum_{i=1}^{n} d_i = 2n-2.$$

Proof

Necessity Since a tree has no isolated vertex, therefore $d_i \geq 1$ for all i. Also, $\sum_{i=1}^{n} d_i = 2(n-1)$, as a tree with n vertices has $n-1$ edges.

Sufficiency We use induction on n. For $n = 2$, the sequence is $[1, 1]$ and is obviously the degree sequence of K_2. Suppose the claim is true for all positive sequences of length less than n.

Let $[d_i]_1^n$ be the non-decreasing positive sequence of n terms, satisfying conditions (i) and (ii). Then $d_1 = 1$ and $d_n > 1$ (by Theorem 4.5).

Now, consider the sequence $D' = [d_2, d_3, \ldots, d_{n-1}, d_n - 1]$, which is a sequence of length $n-1$. Obviously in D', $d_i \geq 1$ and $\sum d_i = d_2+d_3+\ldots+d_{n-1}+d_n-1 = d_1+d_2+d_3+\ldots+d_{n-1}+d_n-1-1 = 2n-2-2 = 2(n-1)-2$ (because $d_1 = 1$). So D' satisfies conditions (i) and (ii), and by induction hypothesis there is a tree T' realising D'. In T', add a new vertex and join it to the vertex having degree $d_n - 1$ to get a tree T. Therefore the degree sequence of T is $[d_1, d_2, \ldots, d_n]$.

Theorem 4.8 A forest of k trees which have a total of n vertices has $n-k$ edges.

Proof Let G be a forest and $T_1, T_2, \ldots, T_k$ be the k trees of G. Let G have n vertices and $T_1, T_2, \ldots, T_k$ have respectively $n_1, n_2, \ldots, n_k$ vertices. Then $n_1+n_2+\ldots+n_k = n$. Also, the number of edges in $T_1, T_2, \ldots, T_k$ are respectively $n_1-1, n_2-1, \ldots, n_k-1$. Thus number of edges in $G = n_1-1+n_2-1+\ldots+n_k-1 = n_1+n_2+\ldots+n_k-k = n-k$. ❑

The following result characterises trees as subgraphs of a graph.

Theorem 4.9 Let T be a tree with k edges. If G is a graph whose minimum degree satisfies $\delta(G) \geq k$, then G contains T as a subgraph. Alternatively, G contains every tree of order atmost $\delta(G)+1$ as a subgraph.

Proof We use induction on k. If $k = 0$, then $T = K_1$ and it is clear that K_1 is a subgraph of any graph. Further, if $k = 1$, then $T = K_2$ and K_2 is a subgraph of any graph whose minimum degree is one. Assume the result is true for all trees with $k-1$ edges ($k \geq 2$) and consider a tree T with exactly k edges. We know that T contains at least two pendant vertices. Let v be one of them and let w be the vertex that is adjacent to v. Consider the graph $T-v$. Since $T-v$ has $k-1$ edges, the induction hypothesis applies, so $T-v$ is a subgraph of G. We can think of $T-v$ as actually sitting inside G (meaning w is a vertex of G, too). Since G contains at least $k+1$ vertices, and $T-v$ contains k vertices, there exist vertices of G that are not a part of the subgraph $T-v$. Further, since the degree of w in G is at least k, there must be a vertex u not in $T-v$ that is adjacent to w. The subgraph $T-v$ together with u forms the tree T as a subgraph of G (Fig. 4.3). ❑

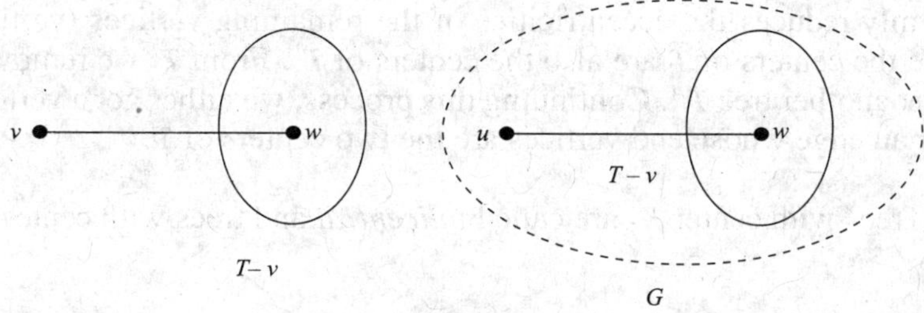

Fig. 4.3

4.2 Rooted and Binary Trees

A tree in which one vertex (called the *root*) is distinguished from all the others is called a *rooted tree*.

A *binary tree* is defined as a tree in which there is exactly one vertex of degree two and each of the remaining vertices is of degree one or three. Obviously, a binary tree has three or more vertices. Since the vertex of degree two is distinct from all other vertices, it serves as a root, and so every binary tree is a rooted tree. ❑

Below are given some properties of binary trees.

Theorem 4.10 Every binary tree has an odd number of vertices.

Proof Apart from the root, every vertex in a binary tree is of odd degree. We know that there are even number of such odd vertices. Therefore when the root (which is of even degree) is added to this number, the total number of vertices is odd.

Corollary 4.1 There are $\frac{1}{2}(n+1)$ pendant vertices in any binary tree with n vertices.

Proof Let T be a binary tree with n vertices. Let q be the number of pendant vertices in T. Therefore there are $n-q$ internal vertices in T and so $n-q-1$ vertices of degree 3. Thus the number of edges in $T = \frac{1}{2}[3(n-q-1)+2+q]$. But the number of edges in T is $n-1$.

Hence, $\frac{1}{2}[3(n-q-1)+2+q] = n-1$, so that $q = \frac{1}{2}(n+1)$. ❑

The following result is due to Jordan [118].

Theorem 4.11 (Jordan) Every tree has either one or two centers.

Proof The maximum distance, $\max d(v, v_i)$ from a given vertex v to any other vertex occurs only when v_i is a pendant vertex. With this observation, let T be a tree having more than two vertices. Tree T has two or more pendant vertices. Deleting all the pendant vertices from T, the resulting graph T' is again a tree. The removal of all pendant vertices from T uniformly reduces the eccentricities of the remaining vertices (vertices in T') by one. Therefore the centers of T are also the centers of T'. From T' we remove all pendant vertices and get another tree T''. Continuing this process, we either get a vertex, which is a center of T, or an edge whose end vertices are the two centers of T.

Definition: Trees with center K_1 are called *unicentral* and trees with center K_2 are called *bicentral trees.*

Spanning trees

A tree is said to be a spanning tree of a connected graph G, if T is a subgraph of G and T contains all vertices of G.

Example Consider the graph of Fig. 4.4, where the bold lines represent a spanning tree.

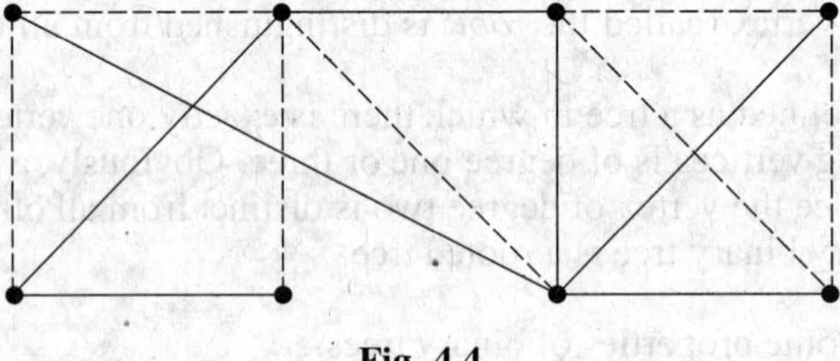

Fig. 4.4

❑

The following result shows the existence of spanning trees in connected graphs.

Theorem 4.12 Every connected graph has at least one spanning tree.

Proof Let G be a connected graph. If G has no cycles, then it is its own spanning tree. If G has cycles, then on deleting one edge from each of the cycles, the graph remains connected and cycle free containing all the vertices of G.

Definition: An edge in a spanning tree T is called a *branch* of T. An edge of G that is not in a given spanning tree T is called a *chord*. It may be noted that branches and chords are defined only with respect to a given spanning tree. An edge that is a branch of one spanning tree T_1 (in a graph G) may be a chord with respect to another spanning tree T_2. In Figure 4.5, $u_1u_2u_3u_4u_5u_6$ is a spanning tree, u_2u_4 and u_4u_6 are chords.

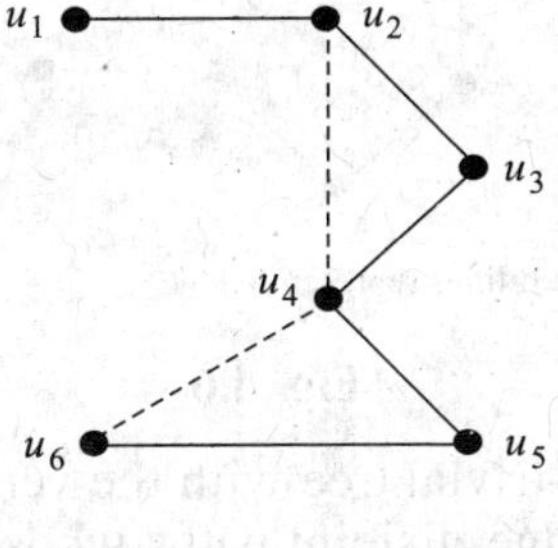

Fig. 4.5

A connected graph G can be considered as a union of two subgraphs T and $\overline{T}$, that is $G = T \cup \overline{T}$, where T is a spanning tree, $\overline{T}$ is the complement of T in G. $\overline{T}$ being the set of chords is called the *co tree*, or chord set.

The following result provides the number of chords in any graph with a spanning tree.

Theorem 4.13 With respect to any of its spanning trees, a connected graph of n vertices and m edges has $n-1$ tree branches and $m-n+1$ chords.

Proof Let G be a connected graph with n vertices and m edges. Let T be the spanning tree. Since T contains all n vertices of G, T has $n-1$ edges and thus the number of chords in G is equal to $m-(n-1) = m-n+1$. ❑

Definition: Let G be a graph with n vertices, m edges and k components. The *rank* r and *nullity* μ of G are defined as $r = n-k$ and $\mu = m-n+k$.

Clearly, the rank of a connected graph is $n-1$ and the nullity is $m-n+1$.

It can be seen that rank of G = number of branches in any spanning tree (or forest) of G. Also, nullity of G = number of chords in G. So, rank + nullity = number of edges in G.

The nullity of a graph is also called its *cyclomatic number*, or first Betti number.

Theorem 4.14 If T is a tree with $2k \geq 0$ vertices of odd degree, then $E(T)$ is the union of k pair-wise edge-disjoint paths.

Proof We prove the result for every forest G, using induction on k. If $k = 0$, then G has no pendant vertex and therefore no edge. Let $k > 0$ and let each forest with $2k-2$ vertices of odd degree has decomposition into $k-1$ paths. Since $k > 0$, some component of G is a tree with at least two vertices. This component has at least two pendant vertices. Let P be the path connecting two pendant vertices. Deleting $E(P)$ changes the parity of the vertex degree only for the end vertices of P and it makes them even. Thus $G-E(P)$ is a forest with $2k-2$ vertices of odd degree. So by the induction hypothesis, $G-E(P)$ is the union of

$k-1$ pair wise edge-disjoint paths. These $k-1$ edge-disjoint paths together with P partition $E(G)$ into k pair wise edge-disjoint paths (Fig. 4.6).

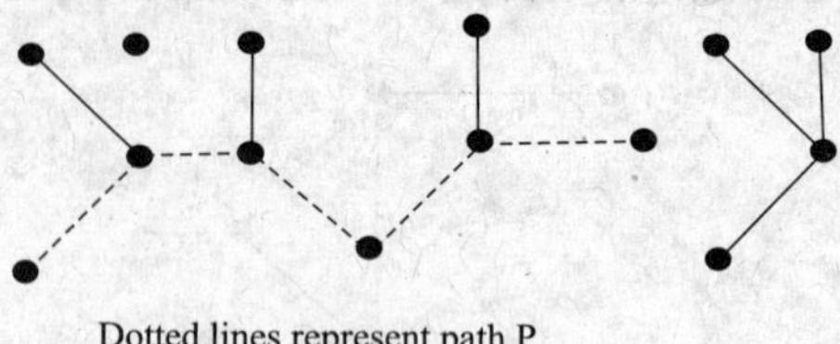

Dotted lines represent path P

Fig. 4.6

Theorem 4.15 Let T be a non-trivial tree with the vertex set S and $|S| = 2k$, $k \geq 1$. Then there exists a set of k pairwise edge-disjoint paths whose end vertices are all the vertices of S.

Proof Obviously, there exists a set of k paths in T whose end vertices are all the vertices of S. Let $P = \{P_1, P_2, \ldots, P_k\}$ be such a set of k paths and let the sum of their lengths be the minimum.

We show that the paths of P are pairwise edge-disjoint. Assume to the contrary, and let P_i and P_j, $i \neq j$, be paths having an edge in common. Then P_i and P_j have path P_{ij} of length ≥ 1 in common. Therefore, $P_i \Delta P_j$ the symmetric difference of P_i and P_j is a disjoint union of two paths, say Q_i and Q_j, with their end vertices being disjoint pairs of vertices belonging to S (Fig. 4.7).

If P_i and P_j are replaced by Q_i and Q_j in P, then the resulting set of paths has the property that their end vertices are all the vertices of S and that the sum of their lengths is less than the sum of the lengths of the paths in P. This is a contradiction to the choice of P.

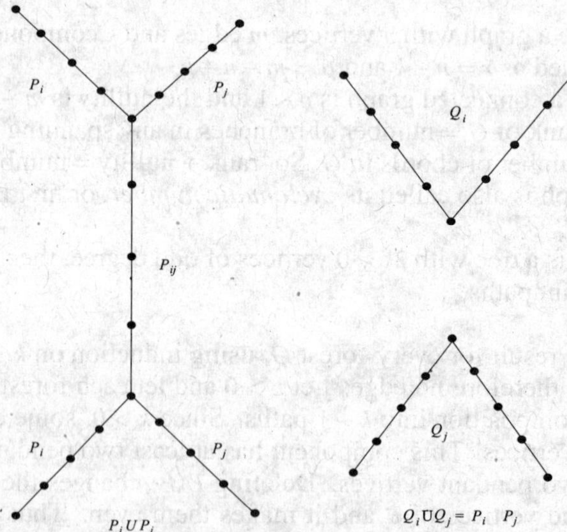

Fig. 4.7

Theorem 4.16 If u is a vertex of an n-vertex tree T, then $\sum_{v \in V(T)} d(u, v) \le \binom{n}{2}$.

Proof Let $T(V, E)$ be a tree with $|V| = n$. Let u be any vertex of T. We use induction on n. If $n = 2$, the result is trivial. Let $n > 2$. The graph $T - u$ is a forest and let the components of $T - u$ be $T_1, T_2, \ldots, T_k$, where $k \ge 1$. Since T is connected, u has a neighbour in each T_i. Also, since T has no cycles, u has exactly one neighbour v_i in each T_i. For any $v \in V(T_i)$, the unique $u - v$ path in T passes through v_i and we have $d_T(u, v) = 1 + d_{T_i}(v_i, v)$. Let $n_i = n(T_i)$ (Fig. 4.8). Then we have

$$\sum_{v \in V(T_i)} d_T(u, v) = n_i + \sum_{v \in V(T_i)} d_{T_i}(v_i, v). \tag{4.16.1}$$

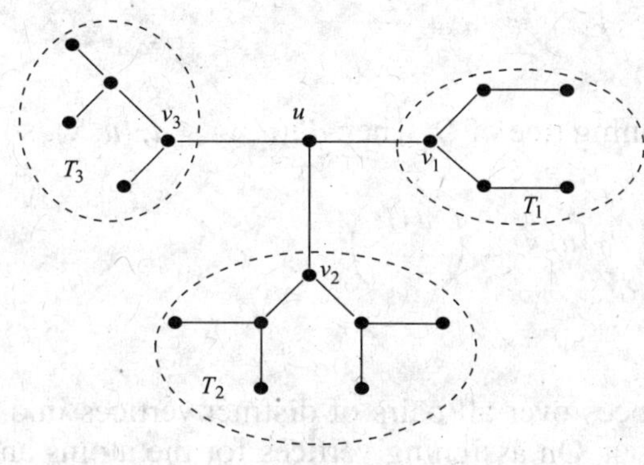

Fig. 4.8

By the induction hypothesis, we have

$$\sum_{v \in V(T_i)} d_{T_i}(v_i, v) \le \binom{n_i}{2}.$$

We now sum the formula (4.16.1) for distances from u over all the components of $T - u$ and we get

$$\sum_{v \in V(T_i)} d_T(u, v) \le (n-1) + \sum_i \binom{n_i}{2}.$$

Now, we have $\sum_i n_i = n - 1$. Clearly, $\sum_i \binom{n_i}{2} \le \binom{\sum n_i}{2}$, because the right side counts the edges in $K_{\sum n_i}$ or K_{n-1}, and the left side counts the edges in a subgraph of $K_{\sum n_i}$, the subgraph being union of disjoint cliques $K_{n_1}, K_{n_1}, \ldots, K_{n_k}$.

Thus, $\sum_{v \in V(T)} d_T(u, v) \le (n-1) + \binom{n-1}{2} = \binom{n}{2}$.

Corollary 4.2 The sum of the distances from a pendant vertex of the path P_n to all other vertices is $\sum_{i=0}^{n-1} i = \binom{n}{2}$.

Corollary 4.3 If H is a subgraph of a graph G, then $d_G(u, v) \le d_H(u, v)$.

Proof Every $u-v$ path in H appears also in G, and G may have additional $u-v$ paths that are shorter than any $u-v$ path in H.

Corollary 4.4 If u is a vertex of a connected graph G, then

$$\sum_{v \in V(G)} d(u, v) \le \binom{n(G)}{2}.$$

Proof Let T be a spanning tree of G. Then $d_G(u, v) \le d_T(u, v)$, so that

$$\sum_{v \varepsilon V(G)} d_G(u, v) \le \sum_{v \varepsilon V(G)} d_T(u, v) \le \binom{n(G)}{2}.$$ ❑

The sum of the distances over all pairs of distinct vertices in a graph G is the Wiener index $W(G) = \sum_{u, v \varepsilon V(G)} d(u, v)$. On assigning vertices for the atoms and edges for the atomic bonds, we can use graphs to study molecules. Wiener [261] originally used this to study the boiling point of paraffin.

Theorem 4.17 Let v be any vertex of a connected graph G. Then G has a spanning tree preserving the distances from v.

Proof Let G be a connected graph. We find a spanning tree T of G such that for each $u \in V = V(G) = V(T)$, $d_G(v, u) = d_T(v, u)$.

Consider the neighbourhoods of v,
$N_i(v) = \{u \in V : d_G(v, u) = i\}$, $1 \le i \le e$, where $e = e(v)$.

Let H be the graph obtained from G by removing all edges in each $< N_i(v) >$. Clearly, H is connected. Let $< B_i(v) >_H$ denote the induced subgraph of H, induced by the ball $B_i(v)$. Clearly, $< B_1(v) >_H$ does not contain any cycle. If $< B_2(v) >_H$ contains cycles, remove edges from $[N_1(v), N_2(v)]$ sequentially, one edge from each cycle, till it becomes acyclic. Proceeding successively by removing edges from $[N_i(v), N_{i+1}(v)]$ to make $< B_{i+1}(v) >_H$ acyclic for $1 \le i \le e-1$, we get a spanning tree of H and hence of G.

Since in this procedure one distance path from v to each of the other vertices remains intact, we have $d_G(v, u) = d_T(v, u)$ for each $u \in V$. ❑

Remarks The above result implies that for any vertex v of a connected graph G, there exists an image $\Phi_v(G)$ which is a spanning tree of G preserving distances from v. This is called an *isometric tree* of G at v. If there is only one such tree (upto isomorphism) at v, we say that G has a *unique isometric tree* at v. If G has the same unique isometric tree at each vertex v, then G is said to have a *unique isometric tree* (or unique distance tree). $K_{2,2}$ and the Peterson graph are examples of graphs having unique isometric trees, while $K_{3,3}$ does not have a unique isometric tree at any vertex. Every tree has a unique isometric tree.

The next result due to Chartrand and Stewart [51] gives the necessary condition for a graph to have a unique isometric tree.

Theorem 4.18 Let G be a connected graph with $d = 2r$, which has a unique isometric tree. Then the end vertices of every diametral path of G has degree 1.

Proof Let G be a connected graph with $d = 2r$ and let P be a diametral path with end vertices u and v. If possible let $d(u|G) > 1$. Let T_u be the isometric tree at u. It is easy to see that T_u can be chosen to contain P.

Since u has degree at least 2 in G, there is a vertex u_i adjacent to u and not lying in P. Clearly, $d_{T_u}(u_i, v) = 1 + d$.

Let c be a central vertex of G. Then for any two vertices w_1 and w_2 of G, we have

$$d_G(w_1, c) \le r = \tfrac{1}{2}d \text{ and } d_G(w_2, c) \le r = \tfrac{1}{2}d.$$

Therefore, $d_G(w_1, w_2) \le d(w_1, c) + d(c, w_2) \le d$.

Since T_c is isometric with G at c, we also have $d_{Tc}(w_1, w_2) \le d$.

Thus no path T_c has length greater than d, whereas there is a path in T_u of length $1 + d$. Therefore $T_c \ne T_u$ and G does not have a unique isometric tree. This contradicts the hypothesis. Hence the result follows. ❑

Remark The above condition is necessary but not sufficient. To see this, consider the graph given in Figure 4.9.

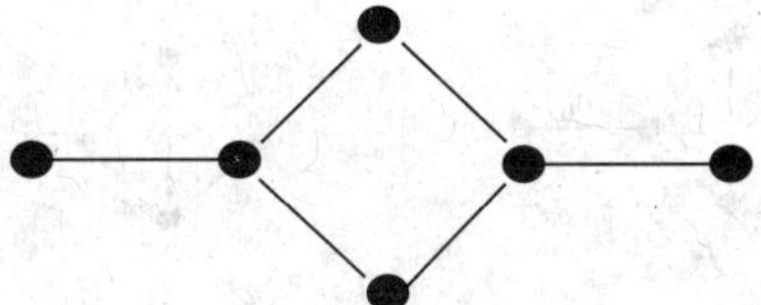

Fig. 4.9 *Graph without a unique isometric tree*

Chartrand and Schuster [53], and Kundu [138] have given some more results on the graphs with unique isometric trees.

Definition: The *complexity* $\tau(G)$ of a graph G is the number of different spanning trees of G.

The following result gives a recursive formula for $\tau(G)$.

Theorem 4.19 For any cyclic edge e of a graph G, $\tau(G) = \tau(G-e) + \tau(G|pe)$.

Proof Let S be the set of spanning trees of G and let S be partitioned as $S_1 \cup S_2$, where S_1 is the set of spanning trees of G not containing e and S_2 is the set of the spanning trees of G containing e.

Since e is a cyclic edge, $G-e$ is connected and there is a one-one correspondence between the elements of S_1 and the spanning trees of $G-e$. Also, there is a one-one correspondence between the spanning trees of $G|\text{þ}e$ and the elements of S_2.

Thus, $\tau(G) = |S_1| + |S_2| = \tau(G-e) + \tau(G|\text{þ}e)$. ❑

Remarks

1. The above recurrence relation is valid even if e is a cut edge. This is because $\tau(G-e) = 0$ and every spanning tree of G contains every cut edge.

2. The recurrence relation is valid even if G is a general graph and e is a multiple edge, but not when e is a loop.

3. The complexity of any graph G is computed by repeatedly applying the above recurrence. We observe that on applying the elementary contraction to a multiple edge, the resulting graph can have a loop and by remark (2) the procedure can be still continued. At each stage of the algorithm, only an edge belonging to the proper cycle is chosen. The algorithm starts with a given graph and produces two graphs (possibly general) at the end of the first stage. At each subsequent stage one proper cyclic edge from each graph is chosen (if it exists) for applying the recurrence. On termination of the algorithm, we get a set of graphs (or general graphs) none of which have a proper cycle. Then $\tau(G)$ is the sum of the number of these graphs. If H is any of these graphs, then $\tau(H)$ is the product of its edges, ignoring the loops.

Example Consider the graph G given in Figure 4.10.

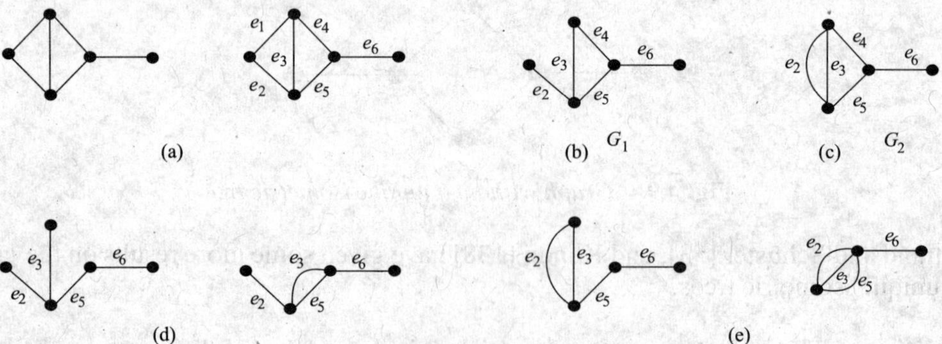

Fig. 4.10

Label the edges of G arbitrarily. Choose e_1 as the first cyclic edge. Then $\tau(G)$ is the sum of the complexities of the graphs given in Figure 4.10(b) and (c). Now, choose e_4 in both G_1 and G_2 as the next cyclic edge. Then $\tau(G)$ is the sum of the complexities of the graphs in Figure 4.10(d) and (e). Since there are no more cyclic edges, the algorithm terminates, and we have $\tau(G) = 1+2+2+3 = 8$.

4.3 Number of Labelled Trees

Let us consider the problem of constructing all simple graphs with n vertices and m edges. There are $n(n-1)/2$ unordered pairs of vertices. If the vertices are distinguishable from each other (i.e., labelled graphs), then the number of ways of selecting m edges to form the graph is $\binom{\frac{n(n-1)}{2}}{m}$.

Thus the number of simple labelled graphs with n vertices and m edges is

$$\binom{\frac{n(n-1)}{2}}{m}. \tag{A}$$

Clearly, many of these graphs can be isomorphic (that is they are same except for the labels of their vertices). Thus the number of simple, unlabelled graphs of n vertices and m edges is much smaller than that given by (A) above.

Theorem 4.20 The number of simple, labelled graphs of n vertices is $2^{\frac{n(n-1)}{2}}$.

Proof The number of simple graphs of n vertices and $0, 1, 2, \ldots, n(n-1)/2$ edges are obtained by substituting $0, 1, 2, \ldots, n(n-1)/2$ for m in (A). The sum of all such numbers is the number of all simple graphs with n vertices.

Therefore the total number of simple, labelled graphs of n vertices is

$$\binom{\frac{n(n-1)}{2}}{0} + \binom{\frac{n(n-1)}{2}}{1} + \binom{\frac{n(n-1)}{2}}{2} + \ldots + \binom{\frac{n(n-1)}{2}}{\frac{n(n-1)}{2}} = 2^{\frac{n(n-1)}{2}},$$

by using the identity $\binom{k}{0} + \binom{k}{1} + \binom{k}{2} + \ldots + \binom{k}{k} = 2^k$.

The following result was proved independently by Tutte [245] and Nash-Williams [162]. We prove the necessity and for sufficiency the reader is referred to the original papers of Tutte and Nash-Williams.

Theorem 4.21 A simple connected graph G contains k pairwise edge-disjoint spanning trees if and only if, for each partition π of $V(G)$ into p parts, the number $m(\pi)$ of edges of G joining distinct parts is at least $k(p-1)$.

Proof
Necessity Let G has k pairwise edge-disjoint spanning trees. If T is one of them, and if $\pi = \{V_1, V_2, \ldots, V_p\}$ is a partition of $V(G)$ into p parts, then identification of each part V_i into a single vertex v_i, $1 \le i \le p$, results in a connected graph G_0 (possibly with multiple edges) on $\{V_1, V_2, \ldots, V_p\}$. Clearly, G_0 contains a spanning tree with $p-1$ edges, and each such edge belongs to T, and joins distinct partite sets of π. Since this is true for each of the k edge –disjoint spanning trees of G, the number of edges joining distinct parts of π is at least $k(p-1)$. ❑

Cayley [45] in 1889 discovered the formula $\tau(K_n) = n^{n-2}$. Clearly, the number of spanning trees of K_n is same as the number of non-label-isomorphic trees on n vertices. Several proofs of this result have appeared since Cayley's discovery. Moon [159] has outlined ten such proofs, and a complete presentation of some of these can also be found in Lovasz [148]. Here we give two proofs, and the first is due to Prufer [206].

Theorem 4.22 (Cayley) There are n^{n-2} labelled trees with n vertices, $n \ge 2$.

Proof Let T be a tree with n vertices and let the vertices be labelled $1, 2, \ldots, n$. Remove the pendant vertex (and the edge incident to it) having the smallest label, say u_1. Let v_1 be the vertex adjacent to u_1. From the remaining $n-1$ vertices, let u_2 be the pendant vertex with the smallest label and let v_2 be the vertex adjacent to u_2. We remove u_2 and the edge incident on it. We repeat this operation on the remaining $n-2$ vertices, then on $n-3$ vertices, and so on. This process completes after $n-2$ steps, when only two vertices are left.

Let the vertices after each removal have labels $v_1, v_2, \ldots, v_{n-2}$. Clearly, the tree T uniquely defines the sequence

$$(v_1, v_2, \ldots, v_{n-2}). \tag{4.22.1}$$

Conversely, given a sequence of $n-2$ labels, an n-vertex tree is constructed uniquely as follows. Determine the first number in the sequence

$$1, 2, 3, \ldots, n, \tag{4.22.2}$$

that does not appear in (4.22.1). Let this number be u_1. Thus the edge (u_1, v_1) is defined. Remove v_1 from sequence (4.22.1) and u_1 from (4.22.2). In the remaining sequence of (4.22.2), find the first number which does not appear in the remaining sequence of (4.22.1). Let this be u_2 and thus the edge (u_2, v_2) is defined. The construction is continued till the sequence (4.22.1) has no element left. Finally, the last two vertices remaining in (4.22.2) are joined.

For each of the $n-2$ elements in sequence (4.22.1), we choose any one of the n numbers, thus forming n^{n-2} $(n-2)$-tuples, each defining a distinct labelled tree of n vertices. Since each tree defines one of these sequences uniquely, there is a one–one correspondence between the trees and the n^{n-2} sequences. ❑

Example Consider the tree shown in Figure 4.11. Pendant vertex with smallest label is u_1. Remove u_1. Let v_1 be adjacent to u_1 (label of v_1 is 1). Pendant vertex with smallest label is 4. Remove 4. Here 4 is adjacent to 1. Pendant vertex with smallest label is 1. Remove 1. Here 1 is adjacent to 3. Remove 3. Then 3 is adjacent to 5. Remove 6. So 6 is adjacent to 5. Remove 7. 7 is adjacent to 5. Remove 5. So 8 is adjacent to 9. Sequence $(v_1, v_2, \ldots, v_{n-2})$ is (1, 1, 3, 5, 5, 5, 9).

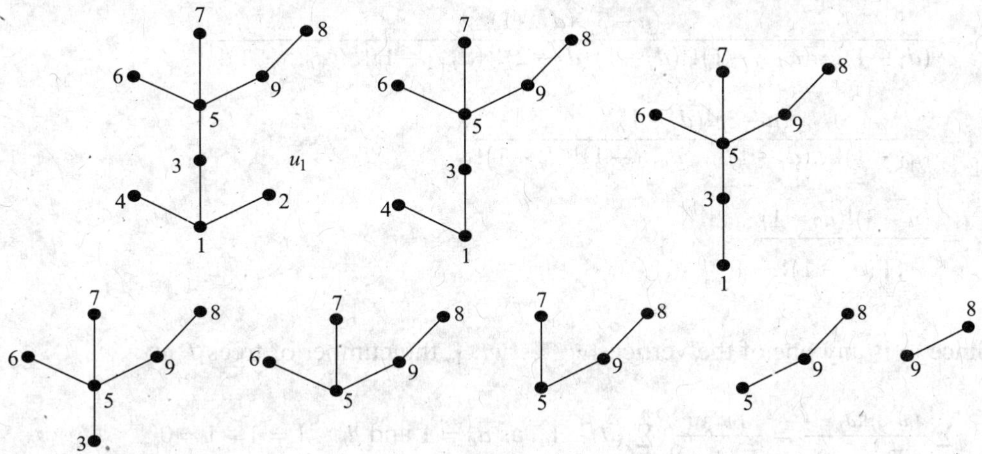

Fig. 4.11

Theorem 4.23 If $D = [d_i]_1^n$ is the degree sequence of a tree, then the number of labelled trees with this degree sequence is

$$\frac{(n-2)!}{(d_1-1)!(d_2-1)!\ldots(d_n-1)!}.$$

Proof We first observe that, when asking for all possible trees with the vertex label set $V = \{v_1, v_2, \ldots, v_n\}$ with degree sequence $D = [d_i]_1^n$, it is not necessary that $d_i = d\,(v_i)$ and it is not necessary that the sequence be monotonic non-decreasing.

Therefore we assume that $D = [d_i]_1^n$ is an integer sequence satisfying the conditions $\sum d_i = 2(n-1)$ and $d_i \geq 1$ and find all the trees on the vertex set V with $d(v_i) = d_i$. We use induction on n. The result is obvious for $n = 1, 2$. For $n = 2$, the sequence is $[d_1, d_2]$ and the only degree sequence in this case is $[1, 1]$. Clearly, there is only one labelled tree with this degree sequence.

Also, $$\frac{(n-2)!}{(d_1-1)!\ldots(d_n-1)} = \frac{(2-2)!}{(1-1)!(1-1)!} = 1.$$

Now, assume that the result is true for all sequences of length $n-1$. Let $D = [d_i]_1^n$ be an n length sequence. By assumption there is a $d_i = 1$ and let it be $d_n = 1$. Let T_n be a tree realising $D = [d_i]_1^n$. Now, removing v_n, we get a tree T_{n-1} on the vertex set $\{v_1, v_2, \ldots, v_{n-1}\}$ with degrees $d_1, \ldots, d_{j-1}, d_j - 1, d_{j+1}, \ldots, d_{n-1}$, where v_j is the vertex to which v_n is adjacent in T_n. Clearly, the converse is also true. Therefore, by induction hypothesis, the number of trees T_{n-1} is

$$\frac{(n-3)!}{(d_1-1)!\ldots(d_{j-1}-1)!(d_j-1-1)!(d_{j+1}-1)!\ldots(d_{n-1}-1)!}$$

$$= \frac{(n-3)!(d_j-1)}{(d_1-1)!\ldots(d_{j-1}-1)!\,[(d_j-1)\,(d_j-2)!]\,(d_{j+1}-1)!\ldots(d_{n-1}-1)!}$$

$$= \frac{(n-3)!(d_j-1)}{(d_1-1)!\ldots(d_j-1)!\ldots(d_{n-1}-1)!(d_n-1)!}$$

$$= \frac{(n-3)!(d_j-1)}{\prod_{j=1}^{n}(d_j-1)!}.$$

Since v_j is any one of the vertices $v_1, \ldots, v_{n-1}$, the number of trees T_n is

$$\sum_{j=1}^{n-1} \frac{(n-3)!(d_j-1)}{\prod_{j=1}^{n}(d_j-1)!} = \frac{(n-3)!}{\prod_{j=1}^{n}(d_j-1)!}\sum_{j=1}^{n}(d_j-1), \text{ as } d_n = 1 \text{ and } d_n - 1 = 1 - 1 = 0$$

$$= \frac{(n-3)!}{\prod_{j=1}^{n}(d_j-1)!}(n-2), \text{ since } \sum_{j=1}^{n}(d_j-1) = 2(n-1) - n = n-2$$

$$= \frac{(n-2)!}{\prod_{j=1}^{n}(d_j-1)!}.$$

❑

Now, we use Theorem 4.22 to obtain $\tau(K_n) = n^{n-2}$, which forms the second proof of Cayley's Theorem.

Second Proof of Theorem 4.22 We know the number of labelled trees with a given degree sequence $[d_i]_1^n$ is

$$\frac{(n-2)!}{\prod_{j=1}^{n}(d_j-1)!}.$$

The total number of labelled trees with n vertices is obtained by adding the number of labelled trees with all possible degree sequences.

Therefore, $\tau(T) = \sum_{\substack{d_i \geq 1 \\ \sum_{i=1}^{n} d_i = 2n-2}} \left[\frac{(n-2)!}{\prod_{j=1}^{n} (d_j - 1)!} \right].$

Let $d_i - 1 = k_i$. So $d_i \geq 1$ gives $d_i - 1 \geq 0$, or $k_i \geq 0$.

Also, $\sum_{i=1}^{n} k_i = \sum_{i=1}^{n} (d_i - 1) = \sum_{i=1}^{n} d_i - n = 2n - 2 - n = n - 2.$

Thus, $\tau(T) = \sum_{\substack{k_i \geq 0 \\ \sum_1^n k_i = n-2}} \frac{(n-2)!}{k_1!k_2!\ldots k_n!} = \sum_{\substack{k_i \geq 0 \\ \sum_1^n k_i = n-2}} \frac{(n-2)!}{k_1!k_2!k_n!} 1^{k_1} 1^{k_2} \ldots 1^{k_n}$

$= (1+1+\ldots+1)^{n-2}$, by multinomial theorem.

Hence, $\tau(T) = n^{n-2}$. ❑

Note The multinomial distribution is given by

$$\frac{n!}{x_1!x_2!\ldots x_k!} p_1^{x_1} p_2^{x_2} \ldots p_k^{x_k} = (p_1 + p_2 + \ldots + p_k)^n, \text{ where } \sum_{i=1}^{n} x_i = n.$$

4.4 The Fundamental Cycles

Definition: Let T be a spanning tree of a connected graph G. Let $\overline{T}$ be the spanning subgraph of G containing only the edges of G which are not in T (i.e., $\overline{T}$ is the relative complement of T in G). Then $\overline{T}$ is called the co tree of T in G. The edges of T are called branches and the edges of $\overline{T}$ are called chords of G relative to the spanning tree T.

Theorem 4.24 If T is a spanning tree of a connected graph G and f is a chord of G relative to T, then $T + f$ contains a unique cycle of G.

Proof Let $f = uv$. Then there is a unique $u - v$ path P in T. Clearly, $P + f$ is a cycle of G. Since T is acyclic, any cycle C of $T + e$ should contain e, and $C - e$ is a $u - v$ path in T. Since there is a unique path in T, $T + e$ contains a unique cycle of G. ❑

Remarks

1. If f_1 and f_2 are two distinct chords of the connected graph G relative to a spanning tree T, then there are two unique distinct cycles C_1 and C_2 of G containing respectively f_1 and f_2.
2. If $e \in E(\overline{G})$ and T is a spanning tree of G, then $T + e$ contains a unique cycle of K_n.

Definition: Let G be a connected graph with n vertices and m edges. The number of chords of G relative to a spanning tree T of G is $m-n+1=\mu$. The μ distinct cycles of a connected graph G corresponding to the distinct chords of G relative to a spanning tree T of G are said to form a set of fundamental cycles of G.

If G is a disconnected graph with k components $G_1, G_2, \ldots, G_k$ and T_i, $1 \leq i \leq k$, are a set of k spanning trees of G_i, then the union of the set of fundamental cycles of G_i with respect to T_i is a set of fundamental cycles for G. It is to be noted that different spanning trees give different sets of fundamental cycles.

The following result characterises cycles in terms of the set of all spanning trees.

Theorem 4.25 Any cycle of a connected graph G contains at least one chord of every spanning tree of G.

Proof Let C be a cycle and assume the result is not true. So there exists a spanning tree T of G such that C is contained in the edge set $E(G)-E(\overline{T})$, where $\overline{T}$ is the cotree of G corresponding to T. This means that the tree T contains the cycle C, which is a contradiction. ❑

Theorem 4.26 A set of edges C of a connected graph G is a cycle of G if and only if it is a minimal set of edges containing at least one chord of every spanning tree of G.

Proof Let C be a cycle of G. Then it contains at least one chord of every spanning tree of G. If C' is any proper subset of C, then C' does not contain a cycle and is a forest. A spanning tree T of G can therefore be constructed containing C'. Clearly, C' does not contain any chord of T. Thus no proper subset of C has the stated property, proving that C is minimal with respect to the property.

To prove sufficiency, let C be minimal set with the stated property. Then C is not acyclic. Therefore C contains at least a cycle C'. But by the necessary part, C' is minimal with respect to the property and hence $C'=C$, that is, C is a cycle. ❑

4.5 Generation of Trees

Definition: Let T_1 and T_2 be two spanning trees of a connected graph G and let there be edges $e_1 \in T_1$ and $e_2 \in T_2$ such that $T_1-e_1+e_2=T_2$ (and hence $T_2-e_2+e_1=T_1$). The transformation $T_1 \leftrightarrow T_2$ is called an *elementary tree transformation* (ETT), or a fundamental exchange. If e_1 and e_2 are adjacent in G, then the ETT is called a *neighbour transformation* (NT). If e is a pendant edge of T_1 (and hence e_2 is a pendant edge of T_2) the ETT is called a *pendant-edge transformation* (PET) or an end-line transformation.

Definition: Let I be the collection of all spanning trees of a connected graph G. Let $Tr(G)$ be the graph whose vertices t_i correspond to the elements T_i of I, and in which t_i and t_j are adjacent if and only if there is an ETT between T_i and T_j, that is, if and only if $E(T_i)\Delta E(T_j)=\{e_i, e_j\}$. Then $Tr(G)$ is called the *tree graph* of G. The distance $d(T_i,\, T_j)$

between the spanning trees T_i and T_j of G is defined to be the distance between t_i and t_j in $Tr(G)$.

Theorem 4.27 The tree graph $Tr(G)$ of a connected graph is connected.

Proof Let G be a connected graph with n vertices and let $Tr(G)$ be its tree graph. To prove that $Tr(G)$ is connected, it is enough to show that any two spanning trees of G can be obtained from each other by a finite sequence of ETT's.

Let T and T' be two distinct spanning trees of G. Then there is a set $S = \{e_1, e_2, \ldots, e_k\}$ of some k edges of T which are not in T'. Since a spanning tree has $n-1$ edges, there is a corresponding set $S' = \{e'_1, e'_2, \ldots, e'_k\}$ of edges of T' which are not in T. Thus $T + e'_1$ contains a unique fundamental cycle $T\,e'_1$. As T' is a tree, at least one edge of $T\,e'_1$ (which is a branch of T) will not be in T' and thus is a member of S. Without loss of generality, let this edge be e_1. Define $T_1 = T - e_1 + e'_1$. Then T_1 can be obtained from T by an ETT and therefore T_1 and T' have one more edge in common.

Repeating this process $k-1$ more times, we get a sequence of spanning trees $T_0 = T, T_1, T_2, \ldots, T_{k-1}, T_k = T'$ such that there is an ETT $T_i \longleftrightarrow T_{i+1}$, $0 \le i \le k-1$. ❑

Theorem 4.28 An elementary tree transformation can be obtained by a sequence of neighbour transformations.

Proof Let T and $T' = T - x + y$ be spanning trees of the graph G, where x and y are non-adjacent edges of G. Then we can choose a set of edges $e_1, e_2, \ldots, e_k$ such that $x, e_1, e_2, \ldots, e_k, y$ is a path in $T + y$. Define $T_1 = T - x + e_1$ and $T_i = T_{i-1} - e_{i-1} + e_i$, $2 \le i \le k$ and $T_{k+1} = T_k - e_k + y$. Then $T_{k+1} = T'$, and is obtained from T by a sequence of $k+1$ neighbour transformations through the intermediate trees T_i, $1 \le i \le k$. ❑

Definition: A spanning tree of a graph G corresponding to a central vertex of the tree $Tr(G)$ is called a *central tree*.

The set of diameters of the spanning trees of a connected graph G is the *tree diameter set* of G. A set of positive integers is a *feasible tree diameter set* if it is the tree diameter set of some graph. For example, the graph in Figure 4.12 has one spanning tree of diameter seven and all others of diameter five.

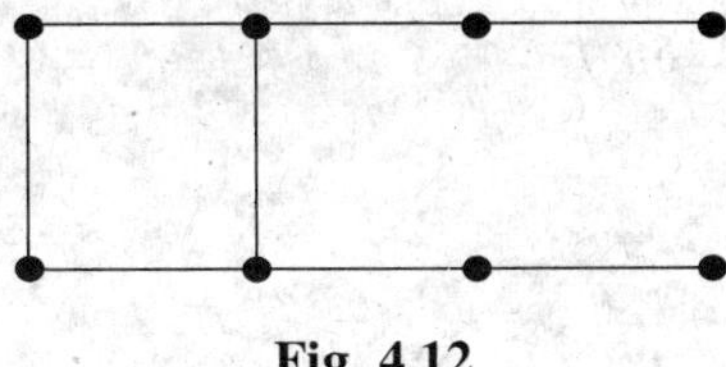

Fig. 4.12

The *girth* $g(G)$ of a graph G is the length of a smallest cycle of G. A cycle of smallest length is called a *girdle* of G. The *circumference* $c(G)$ of a graph G is the length of the longest cycle of G. A cycle of maximum length is called a *hem* of G.

Let $\underline{n}$ (δ, g) denote the minimum order (minimum vertices) of a graph with minimum degree at least δ (≥ 3) and girth at least g (≥ 2). Let $\bar{n}$ (Δ, g) denote the maximum order of a graph with degree at most Δ and girth at most g.

The following upper bound for $\underline{n}$ (δ, g) can be found in Bollobas [29].

Theorem 4.29 (Bollobas) $\underline{n}$ $(\delta, g) \leq (2\delta)^g$.

Proof Clearly, $\underline{n}$ (δ, g) denotes the minimum order of a graph with minimum degree at least δ (≥ 3) and girth at least g (≥ 2). Therefore we construct a graph with atmost $(2\delta)^g$ vertices with these properties. Let $n = (2\delta)^g$.

Consider all graphs with vertex set $V = \{1, 2, \ldots, n\}$ and having exactly δn edges.

Since there are $\binom{n}{2}$ possible positions to accommodate these δn edges, the number of such graphs

$$= \binom{\binom{n}{2}}{\delta n}.$$

Among the n available vertices, the number of ways an h-cycle can be formed is

$$= \frac{1}{2}\binom{n}{h}(h-1)!$$

Obviously, $\frac{1}{2}\binom{n}{h}(h-1)! < \frac{1}{2h}n^h$.

The number of graphs in the set which contain a given h-cycle is

$$= \binom{\binom{n}{2}-h}{\delta n-h}.$$

Hence the average number of cycles of length at most $g-1$ in these graphs

$$< \sum_{h=3}^{g-1} \frac{1}{2h} n^h \binom{\binom{n}{2}-h}{\delta n-h} \Big/ \binom{\binom{n}{2}}{\delta n}$$

$$< \sum_{h=3}^{g-1} (2\delta)^h < (2\delta)^g = n.$$

Since the average is less than n, there is an element in the set with value less than or equal to $n-1$. Thus there is a graph G on n vertices with δn edges and at most $n-1$ cycles of length at most $g-1$. Removing one edge from each of these cycles, we get a graph G_0 with girth at least g. The number of edges removed is atmost $n-1$, so that $m(G_0) \geq n\delta - (n-1) \geq n\,(\delta-1)+1$ and $n\,(G_0) = n$. Thus $G_0 \in G_{\delta-1}$, and hence G_0 contains a subgraph H with $\delta(H) \geq \delta$. By construction, $g(H) \geq g$ and $n(H) \leq n = (2\delta)^g$. Thus we have constructed a graph H with the desired properties. ❑

Note If G is a graph with at least n_0 vertices and at least $n_0 n(G) - \binom{n_0+1}{2} + 1$ edges, then G contains a subgraph H with $\delta(H) \geq n_0 + 1$.

We denote by $G_{n_o} = \left\{ G : n(G) > n_0,\ m(G) \geq n_0.n(G) - \binom{n_0+1}{2} + 1 \right\}$.

The following lower bound for $\underline{n}\,(\delta,\, g)$ is due to Tutte [241].

Theorem 4.30 (Tutte)

$$\underline{n}(\delta,\, g) \geq \begin{cases} \dfrac{\delta(\delta-1)^{\frac{g-1}{2}} - 2}{\delta - 2}, & \text{if } g \text{ is odd,} \\ \dfrac{2(\delta-1)^{\frac{g}{2}} - 1}{\delta - 2}, & \text{if } g \text{ is even.} \end{cases}$$

Proof

i. Let g be odd, say $g = 2d + 1$. Then clearly the diameter of G is at least d. Let v be a vertex with eccentricity at least d. Consider the neighbourhoods

$$N_i = N_i(V),\ 1 \leq i \leq d = (g-1)/2.$$

Obviously, no vertex of N_i is adjacent to more than one vertex of N_{i-1}, because otherwise, there will be a cycle of length $1 \leq 2i < g$. Similarly, there is no edge in $< N_i >$.

Therefore, for every $u \in N_i$, we have

$$|N(u) \cap N_{i-1}| = 1,\ |N(u) \cap N_{i+1}| = d(u) - 1 \text{ and}$$

$$|N_{i+1}| = \sum_{u \in N_i} \{d(u) - 1\} \geq (\delta - 1)\,|N_i|. \tag{4.30.1}$$

As $V \supseteq \{v\} \cup \bigcup_{i=1}^{d} N_i(v)$, therefore

$$n \geq 1 + \sum_{i=1}^{d} |N_i| \geq 1 + \delta + \delta(\delta-1) + \ldots + \delta(\delta-1)^{d-1}$$

$$= 1 + \frac{\delta}{\delta - 2}\left\{(\delta-1)^d - 1\right\} = \frac{\left\{\delta(\delta-1)^{\frac{g-1}{2}} - 2\right\}}{\delta - 2}.$$

ii. Let g be even, say $g = 2d$. Then again the diameter is at least d. Let xy be an edge of G and let

$$S_i = \{v \in V : d(x, v) = i, \text{ or } d(y, v) = i\}, \text{ for } 1 \le i \le d-1 \text{ and } S_0 = \{x, y\}.$$

The girth requirement forces that there are no edges in $< S_i >$, for $1 \le i \le d-2$, and that each vertex of S_i be adjacent to at most one vertex of S_{i-1}, for $1 \le i \le d-1$.

Thus, for each $u \in S_i$, we have $|N(u) \cap S_{i-1}| = 1$, $|N(u) \cap S_{i+1}| = d(u) - 1$ and

$$|S_{i+1}| = \sum_{u \varepsilon S_i} (d(u) - 1) \ge (\delta - 1)\,|S_i|. \tag{4.30.2}$$

Since $V \supseteq \{x, y\} \cup \bigcup_{i=1}^{d-1} S_i$,

$$n = \sum_{i=0}^{d-1} |S_i| \ge 2 \sum_{i=0}^{d-1} (\delta - 1)^i = \frac{2}{\delta - 2}\left[(\delta - 1)^{\frac{g}{2}} - 1\right].$$ ❑

By using arguments as in Theorem 4.30 and by replacing δ by Δ, we obtain the following result.

Theorem 4.31

$$\bar{n}(\Delta, g) \le \begin{cases} \dfrac{\Delta(\Delta-1)^{\frac{g-1}{2}} - 2}{\Delta - 2}, & \text{if g is odd,} \\[2ex] \dfrac{2\left[(\Delta-1)^{\frac{g}{2}} - 1\right]}{\Delta - 2}, & \text{if g is even.} \end{cases}$$

Definition: A k-regular graph with girth g and with minimum order $\underline{n}(k, g)$ is called a *(k, g)-cage*.

$$\text{The integer } n_0 = \begin{cases} \dfrac{k(k-1)^{\frac{g-1}{2}} - 2}{k-2}, & if\ g\ is\ odd, \\[2ex] \dfrac{2\left[(k-1)^{\frac{g}{2}} - 1\right]}{k-2}, & if\ g\ is\ even, \end{cases}$$

is called the *Moore bound* for a k-regular graph with g.

4.6 Helly Property

Definition: A family $\{A_i : i \in I\}$ of subsets of a set A is said to satisfy the Helly property if $J \subseteq I$, and $A_i \cap A_j \ne \phi$, for every $i,\ j \in J$, then $\bigcap_{j \in J} A_j \ne \phi$.

The following result is reported by Balakrishnan and Ranganathan [13].

Theorem 4.32 A family of subtrees of a tree satisfies the Helly property.

Proof Let $\tau = \{T_i : i \in I\}$ be a family of subtrees of a tree T. Suppose for all $i,\ j \in J \subseteq I$, $T_i \cap T_j \neq \phi$. We have to prove $\bigcap_{j \in J} T_j \neq \phi$. If some tree $T_i \in \tau$, $i \in J$, is a single vertex tree $\{v\}$ (that is, K_1), then clearly, $\bigcap_{j \in J} T_j = \{v\}$. So assume that each tree $T_i \in T$ with $i \in J$ has at least two vertices.

We induct on the number of vertices of T. Suppose the result is true for all trees with at most n vertices and let T be a tree with $(n+1)$ vertices. Let v_0 be an end vertex of T and u_0 its unique neighbour in T. Let $T_i' = T_i - v_0$, $i \in J$ and $T' = T - v_0$. By induction hypothesis, the result is true for the tree T'. Also, $T_i' \cap T_j' \neq \phi$, for any $i,\ j \in J$. In fact, if T_i and T_j have a vertex u $(\neq v_0)$ in common, then T_i' and T_j' also have u in common, whereas if T_i and T_j have v_0 in common, then T_i and T_j have u_0 also in common, and so do T_i' and T_j'. Hence by induction hypothesis, $\bigcap_{j \in J} T_j' \neq \phi$ and therefore $\bigcap_{j \in J} T_j \neq \phi$. ❑

4.7 Signed Trees

The following result by Yan et al. [264] characterises signed degree sequences in signed trees.

Theorem 4.33 Let $D = [d_i]_1^n$ be an integral sequence of $n \geq 2$ terms and let D has n_+ positive terms, n_0 zero and n_- negative terms. Let $\alpha = 1$ if $n_+ n_- > 0$, and $\alpha = 0$, otherwise. Then D is the signed degree sequence of a signed tree if and only if (i) to (iv) hold.

i. $\sum_{i=1}^{n} d_i \equiv 2n - 2 (\mathrm{mod} 4)$.

ii. $\sum_{i=1}^{n} |d_i| \leq 2n - 2 - 2n_0$.

iii. $\sum_{i=1}^{n} |d_i| + 2 \sum_{d_i < 0} |d_i| \leq 2n - 2 - 4\alpha + 4p_-$.

iv. $\sum_{i=1}^{n} |d_i| + 2 \sum_{d_i > 0} |d_i| \leq 2n - 2 - 4\alpha + 4p_+$.

Proof Note that condition (iv) for D is same as condition (iii) for $-D$. The necessity of the theorem follows from the fact that $m = n - 1$ and Lemmas 2.2, 2.3 and 2.4.

We prove the sufficiency by induction on n. For $n = 2$, by (i) and (iii), $d_1 = d_2 = 1$ or -1. Therefore D is the signed degree sequence of K_2 with positive edge or a negative edge. Assume that the theorem is true for $n - 1$. Let $n \geq 3$.

By (ii), D has at least two terms in which $|d_i| = 1$. After rearranging the terms in D or taking $-D$, we may assume without loss of generality that $d_n = 1$ and one of the following holds.

1. $|d_i| \leq 1$, for $1 \leq i \leq n$, $d_1 \geq 0$ and $d_1 = 0$, if $n_0 > 0$.
2. $d_1 \geq 2$.
3. $d_i \leq 1$ but $d_i \neq -1$ for $1 \leq i \leq n$ and $d_1 = 0$ and $\alpha = 1$.
4. $d_i = 1$ or $d_i \leq -2$, for $1 \leq i \leq n$ and $d_1 = \alpha = 1$.

For any of the above, consider the sequence $D' = [d_i']_i^{n'}$, where $n' = n-1$ and $d_i' = d_1 - 1$ and $d_i' = d_i$, for $2 \leq i \leq n-1$.

Note that $\sum_{i=1}^{n'} d_i' = \left(\sum_{i=1}^{n} d_i\right) - 2 \equiv (2n-2) - 2 \equiv 2n' - 2 (\text{mod} 4)$, that is, (i) holds for D'. We check conditions (ii) to (iv) for D' according to the four cases above.

Case 1 In this case, $|d_i'| \leq 1$, for $1 \leq i \leq n-1$, we have

$$\sum_{i=1}^{n'} |d_i'| = n_+' + n_-', \ \sum_{d_i'>0} |d_i'| = n_+', \ \sum_{d_i'<0} |d_i'| = n_-'.$$

Thus (ii) to (iv) holds for D' as $n_+' + n_-' \geq 2$.

Case 2 In this case, since $d_1 \geq 2$ and $d_n = 1$, we have

$$n' = n-1, \ n_+' = n_+ - 1, \ n_0' = n_0, \ n_-' = n_-, \ \alpha' = \alpha,$$

$$\sum_{i=1}^{n'} |d_i'| = \sum_{i=1}^{n} |d_i| - 2, \ \sum_{d_i'>0} |d_i'| = \sum_{d_i>0} |d_i| - 2, \ \sum_{d_i'<0} |d_i'| = \sum_{d_i<0} |d_i|.$$

Therefore (ii) to (iv) holding for D imply that (ii) to (iv) hold for D'.

Case 3 In this case, since $d_1 = 0$ and $d_n = 1$, we have

$$n' = n-1, \ n_+' = n_+ - 1, \ n_0' = n_0 - 1, \ n_-' = n_- + 1, \ \alpha' \leq \alpha,$$

$$\sum_{i=1}^{n'} |d_i'| = \sum_{i=1}^{n} |d_i|, \ \sum_{d_i'>0} |d_i'| = \sum_{d_i>0} |d_i| - 1, \ \sum_{d_i'<0} |d_i'| = \sum_{d_i<0} |d_i| + 1.$$

So (ii) and (iii) holding for D imply that (ii) and (iii) hold for D'. Since $d_i' \leq 1$ for $1 \leq i \leq n-1$, $\sum_{d_i'>0} |d_i'| = n_+'$. By (iii) for D and the fact that $d_i \leq -2$ when $d_i < 0$,

$$n_+ + 6n_- \leq \sum_{i=1}^{n} |d_i| + 2 \sum_{d_i<0} |d_i| \leq 2n - 2 - 4\alpha + 4n_- = 2n_+ + 2n_0 + 6n_- 6,$$

and so $6 \leq n_+ + 2n_0$. Therefore, $3 \leq n'_+ + 2n'_0$ and then $4 \leq 2n'_+ + 2n'_0$.

This together with (ii) for D' and $\sum_{d'_i>0} |d'_i| = n'_+$ implies (iv) for D'.

Case 4 In this case, since $d_1 = d_n = 1$, therefore

$$n' + n - 1,\ n'_+ = n_+ - 2,\ n'_0 = n_0 + 1 = 1,\ n'_- = n_-,\ \alpha' \leq \alpha,$$

$$\sum_{i=1}^{n'} |d'_i| = \sum_{i=1}^{n} |d_i| - 2,\ \sum_{d'_i>0} |d'_i| = \sum_{d_i>0} |d_i| - 2,\ \sum_{d'_i<0} |d'_i| = \sum_{d_i<0} |d_i|.$$

(iii) for D implies that (iii) holds for D'. As in the argument for Case 3, we have $\sum_{d'_i>0} |d'_i| = n'_+$ and $6 \leq n_+ + 2n_0$. Therefore, $4 \leq n'_+$. Adding $2 \sum_{d'_i>0} |d'_i| = 2n'_+$ to the equality in (iii) for D' and dividing the resulting equality by 3, we get (ii) for D' as $2n'_0 \leq 2n'_+$. Adding $2 \sum_{d'_i>0} |d'_i| = 2n'_+$ to the equality in (ii) for D', we get (iv) for D' as $4\alpha' \leq 2n'_0 + 2n'_+$.

From the above discussion, D' satisfies (i) to (iv). By the induction hypothesis, there exists a signed tree T' with the vertex set $\{v_1, v_2, \ldots, v_{n-1}\}$ and signed degree $T'(v_i) = d'_i$, for $1 \leq i \leq n-1$. Suppose T is the signed tree obtained from T' by adding a new vertex v_n and a new positive edge $v_1 v_n^+$, then T has a signed degree sequence D. ❑

Corollary Let $D = [d_i]_1^n$ be an integral sequence of $n \geq 3$ terms. Let D has at least two terms in which $|d_i| = 1$, $d_n = 1$ and one of the following condition holds.

1. $|d_i| \leq 1$, for $1 \leq i \leq n$, $d_i \geq 0$, and $d_1 = 0$ if $n_o > 0$.

2. $d_1 \geq 2$.

3. $d_i \leq 1$ but $d_i \neq -1$ for $1 \leq i \leq n$, and $d_1 = 0$ and $\delta = 1$

4. $d_i = 1$ or $d_i \leq -2$ for $1 \leq i \leq n$, and $d_1 = \delta = 1$.

Then D is the signed degree sequence of a signed tree if and only if $D' = [d_1 - 1, d_2, \ldots, d_{n-1}]$ is the signed degree sequence of a signed tree.

4.8 Exercises

1. Draw all unlabelled trees with seven and eight vertices.

2. Draw a tree which has radius five and diameter ten.

3. If a tree has an even number of edges, then show that it contains at least one vertex of even degree.

4. If the maximum degree of a vertex in a tree is Δ, then show that it has Δ pendant vertices.

5. If T is a tree such that every vertex adjacent to a pendant vertex has degree at least three, then prove that some pair of pendant vertices in T has a common neighbour.

6. Show that a path is its own spanning tree.

7. Prove that every tree is a bipartite graph.

8. If for a simple graph G, $m(G) \geq n(G)$, prove that G contains a cycle.

9. Show that for a unicentral tree, $d = 2r$, and for a bicentral tree, $d = 2r - 1$.

10. Prove that if $K_{r,\,s}$ is a tree, then it must be a star.

11. How many spanning trees does K_4 have?

12. Prove that each spanning tree of a connected graph G contains all the pendant edges of G.

13. Prove that each edge of a connected graph G belongs to at least one spanning tree of G.

5. Connectivity

In a connected graph there is at least one path between every pair of its vertices. If in a graph, it happens that by deleting a vertex, or by removing an edge, or performing both, the graph becomes disconnected, we can say that such vertices or edges hold the whole graph, or in other words have the property of destroying the connectedness of a graph. For example, consider a communication network which is modelled as the graph G shown in Figure 5.1, where vertices correspond to communication centers and the edges represent communication channels. Clearly, deletion of vertex v results in the breakdown of the communication. This implies that in the above communication network, the center represented by vertex v has the property of destroying the communication system and thus communication network depends on the connectivity. We start this chapter with the following definitions.

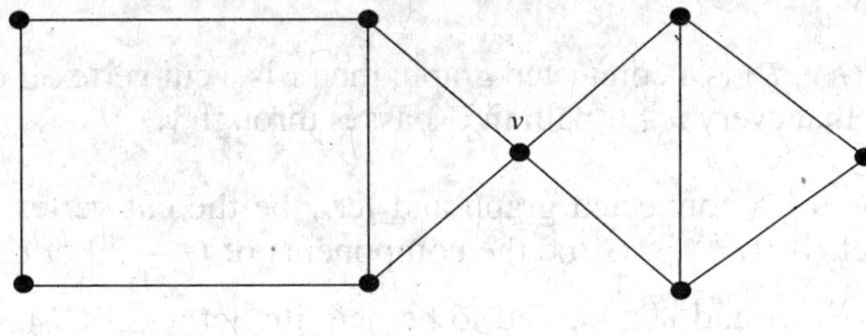

Fig. 5.1

5.1 Basic Concepts

Cut vertex: Let G be a graph with $k(G)$ components. A vertex v of G is called a cut vertex of G if $k(G-v) > k(G)$. For example, in the graph of Figure 5.2, the vertices u and v are cut vertices.

Cut edge: An edge e of a graph G is said to be a cut edge if $k(G-e) > k(G)$. In the graph of Figure 5.2, e and f are cut edges.

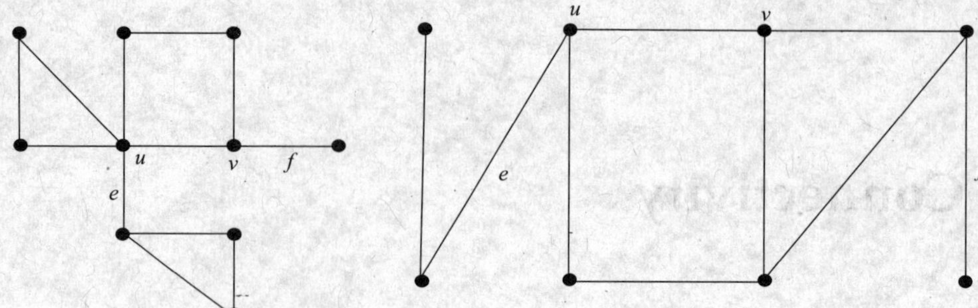

Fig. 5.2

The following observations are the immediate consequences of the definitions introduced above.

- Removal of a vertex may increase the number of components in a graph by at least one, while removal of an edge may increase the number of components by at most one.
- The end vertices of a cut edge are cut vertices if their degree is more than one.
- Every non-pendant vertex of a tree is a cut vertex.

We now give the first result which characterises cut vertices.

Theorem 5.1 If $G(V, E)$ is a connected graph, then v is a cut vertex if there exist vertices $u, w \in V - \{v\}$ such that every $u - w$ path in G passes through v.

Proof Let $G(V, E)$ be a connected graph and let v be the cut vertex of G. Then $G - v$ is disconnected. Let $G_1, G_2, \ldots, G_k$ be the components of $G - v$. Let $U = V(G_1)$ and $W = \bigcup_{i=2}^{k} V(G_i)$. Also, let $u \in U$ and $w \in W$, and to be definite, let $w \in V(G_i)$, $i \neq 1$. If there is a $u - w$ path P in G not passing through v, then P connects u and w in $G - v$ also. Therefore $G_1 \cup G_i$ is a single component in $G - v$, contradicting our assumption. Thus every $u - w$ path in G passes through v.

Conversely, let there be vertices $u, w \in V - \{v\}$ such that every $u - w$ path in G passes through v. Then there is no $u - w$ path in $G - v$. Therefore u and w belong to different components of $G - v$. Thus $G - v$ is disconnected and v is a cut vertex of G. ❑

The following result characterises cut edges.

Theorem 5.2 For a connected graph G, the following statements are equivalent.

i. e is a cut edge of G.

ii. If $e = ab$, there is a partition of the edge subset $E - \{e\}$ as $E_1 \cup E_2$ with $a \in V(< E_1 >)$ and $b \in V(< E_2 >)$ such that for any $u \in V(< E_1 >)$ and any $w \in V(< E_2 >)$, every $u - w$ path contains e.

iii. There exist vertices u and w such that every $u-w$ path in G contains e.

iv. e is not a cycle edge of G.

Proof (i) $\Rightarrow$ (ii). Let e be a cut edge of G. So $G-e$ is disconnected. Let G_1 and G_2 be two components of $G-e$ and $E_1 = E(G_1)$ and $E_2 = E(G_2)$. If $u \in V(G_1)$ and $w \in v(G_2)$ exist such that there is a $u-w$ path P in G which does not contain e, then u and w are connected in $G-e$ by the path P. This implies that $G_1 \cup G_2$, that is, $G-e$ is connected, contradicting the hypothesis. This proves (ii).
(ii) $\Rightarrow$ (iii). Obvious.
(iii) $\Rightarrow$ (iv). Suppose e lies on a cycle C. Then $C-e$ gives an $a-b$ path Q not containing e. With vertices u and w following the condition given in (iii), let P be any $u-w$ path. Without loss of generality, assume that a and b occur in that order in P. Let u_0 and w_0 be the first and last vertices that P has in common with C (the possibility of these coinciding with a, b, u or w is not ruled out). Then $P_{u,\, u_o} \cup Q_{u_0,\, w_0} \cup P_{w_0,\, w}$ is a $u-w$ path P' of G which does not contain e, contradicting (iii). (See Figure 5.3(a), where broken curves represent path Q and thick curves represent path P.)

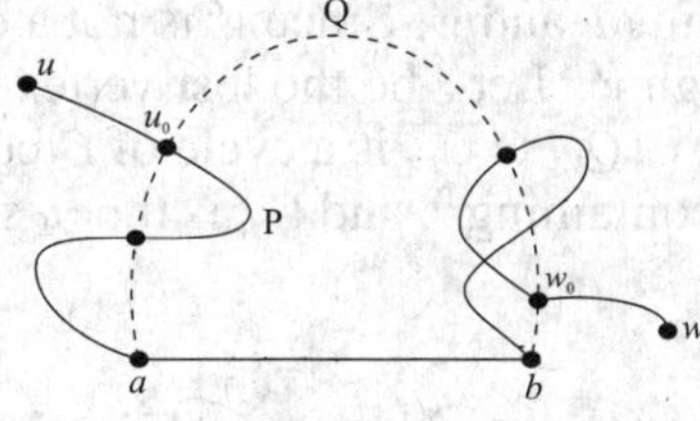

Fig. 5.3(a)

(iv) $\Rightarrow$ (i). Let e be not a cyclic edge of G. We have to prove that e is a cut edge of G, that is, $G-e$ is disconnected. Assume $G-e$ is connected. Then there is an $a-b$ path P in $G-e$. But then $P \cup e$ is a cycle containing e, which contradicts (iv). ❑

Block: A block is a connected graph which does not have any cut vertex. We observe that a block does not have any cut edge. The graph $K_2 = (\{a, b\}, e)$ does not have a cut vertex and hence is a block. However, e is a cut edge in this case. We call K_2 a *trivial block*. All other blocks are *non-trivial*.

Separable graph: A connected graph with at least one cut vertex is called a separable graph. A block of a graph G is a maximal graph H of G such that H is a block. That is, H has no cut vertex, but for any $v \in V(G) - V(H)$, $\langle V(H) \cup \{v\} \rangle$ is either a disconnected graph or a separable graph.

The next result characterises blocks.

Theorem 5.3 For a connected graph G, the following are equivalent.

i. G is a non-trivial block.

ii. Any two vertices of G lie on a cycle.

iii. Given any vertex u and any edge vw, there is a cycle of G containing both.

iv. Given any pair of edges $e = uv$ and $e' = u'v'$, there is a cycle of G containing both.

v. Given any pair of vertices u and u' and any edge $e = vw$, there is a $u - u'$ path of G containing e.

Proof

a. (i) $\Rightarrow$ (ii). The proof is by induction on the distance between the vertices. If $d(u, v) = 1$, then uv is an edge, and since G is a block, uv is not a cut edge. Hence uv is a cyclic edge, and so u and v lie on a cycle. Now, for the induction hypothesis, we assume that if u is any vertex, then any vertex v' at a distance at most $k-1$ from u lies on a cycle with u.

Let v be a vertex at a distance k from u. We prove that u and v lie on a cycle. Let P be a shortest $u - v$ path and v' the nearest vertex on P from u. By induction hypothesis there is a cycle C containing u and v'. Since v' is not a cut vertex of G, there is a $u - v$ path Q not passing through v'. Let z be the last vertex from u that Q has in common with C. Then $C_{uv'} \cup \{v'v\} \cup Q_{vz} \cup C_{zu}$ is a cycle of G containing u and v. (Here $C_{uv'}$ is the uv' segment of C not containing z, and C_{zu} is the zu segment of C not containing v') (Fig. 5.3(b)).

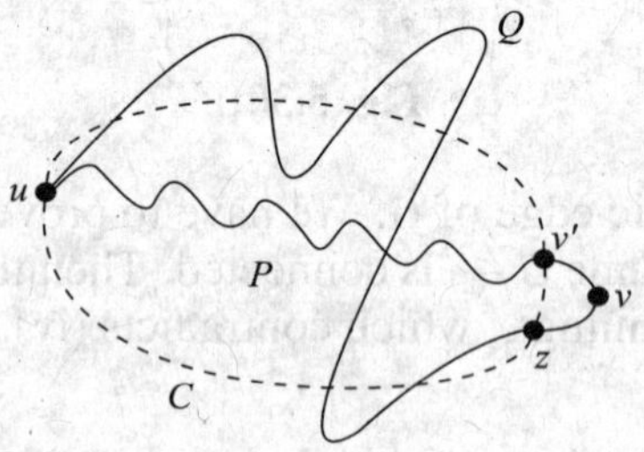

Fig. 5.3(b)

b. (ii) $\Rightarrow$ (i). Let any two vertices of G lie on a cycle. We prove that G is a non-trivial block, that is, G has no cut vertex. Assume to the contrary that G has a cut vertex u. Then there are vertices v and w such that every $v - w$ path passes through u. But then there is no cycle containing v and w, which is a contradiction. Thus G has no cut vertex.

c. (ii) $\Rightarrow$ (iii). Let any two vertices of G lie on a cycle. Let vertex u and edge vw be given. So by (b), G is a block and therefore vw is not a cut edge.

Let C be a cycle containing vw. If C contains u, the proof is complete. If not, by (ii), there is a cycle Z containing u and v. Taking any orientation of Z, let x and y be the first and last vertices from u that Z has in common with C. Then the $u - x$ segment of Z, the $x-y$ segment of C containing vw and the $y-u$ segment of Z constitute a cycle of G containing u and vw.

d. (iii) $\Rightarrow$ (ii). Let u and v be any two vertices. Since v cannot be an isolated vertex, there is an edge vw. By (iii) there is a cycle containing u and vw (Fig. 5.4).

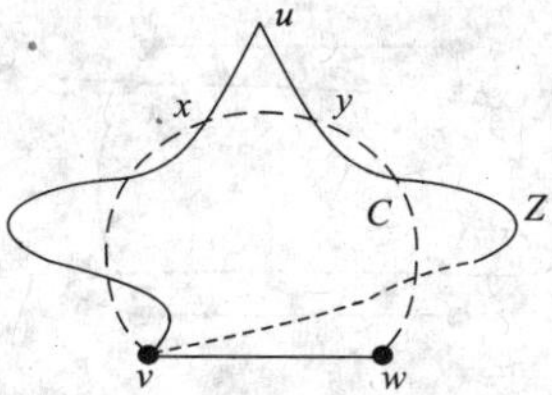

Fig. 5.4

e. (iii) $\Rightarrow$ (iv). Let uv and $u'v'$ be the given edges. By (iii) there is a cycle C through u containing $u'v'$. If it passes through v, then the $u-v$ segment of C containing $u'v'$ and the edge vu constitute a cycle as required. If not, then as the earlier implications show that G is a block, u is not a cut vertex, and hence there is a $v-v'$ path P in G not passing through u (Fig. 5.5).

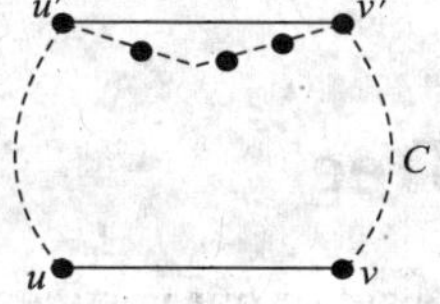

Fig. 5.5

Let w be the first vertex from v that P has in common with C. Then $v-w$ segment of P, the $w-u$ segment of C containing $u'v'$ and the edge uv constitute a cycle of G as desired (Fig. 5.6).

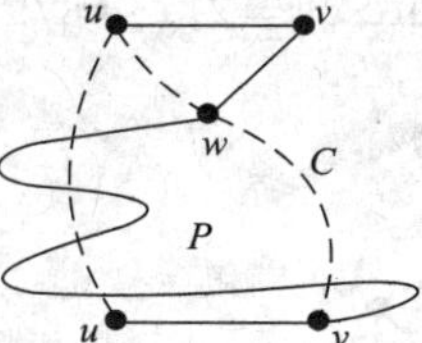

Fig. 5.6

f. (iv) $\Rightarrow$ (iii). This can be proved as in (d).

g. (iv) $\Rightarrow$ (v). Let u and u' be the vertices and vw the given edge. If uv' is also an edge, then there is nothing to prove. If not, since u is not an isolated vertex, there is an edge

uv_1 and by (iv) there is a cycle C containing uv_1 and vw. By previous implications, G is a block and hence u is not a cut vertex. Therefore there is a $u'w$ path P not passing through u. Let x be the first vertex from u' that P has in common with C. Then the $u'x$ segment of P and the xu segment of C containing vw constitute a path as desired (Fig. 5.7).

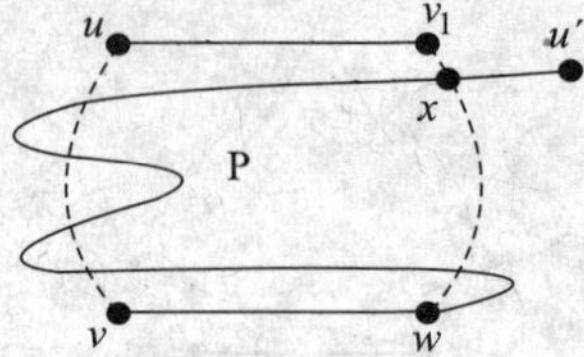

Fig. 5.7

h. (v) ⇒ (iv). Obvious. ❑

Remark Property (iv) of the above theorem can be used to define an equivalence relation on the edge set E of a graph G by $e \sim f$ if and only if e and f lie on a common cycle in G. The equivalence classes are simply the blocks of G and the edge set E is partitioned into blocks. These blocks are joined at cut vertices, two blocks having at most one vertex in common.

5.2 Block–Cut Vertex Tree

Let B be the set of blocks and C be the set of cut vertices of a separable graph G. Construct a graph H with vertex set $B \cup C$ in which adjacencies are defined as follows: $c_i \in C$ is adjacent to $b_j \in B$ if and only if the block b_j of G contains the cut vertex c_i of G. The bipartite graph H constructed above is called the *block-cut vertex tree* of G.

Example Consider the graph in Figure 5.8. The blocks are $b_1 = <1, 2>$, $b_2 = <2, 3, 4>$, $b_3 = <2, 5, 6, 7>$, $b_4 = <7, 8, 9, 10, 11>$, $b_5 = <8, 12, 13, 14, 15>$, $b_6 = <10, 16>$, $b_7 = <10, 17, 18>$ and cut vertices are $c_1 = 2$, $c_2 = 7$, $c_3 = 8$, $c_4 = 10$.

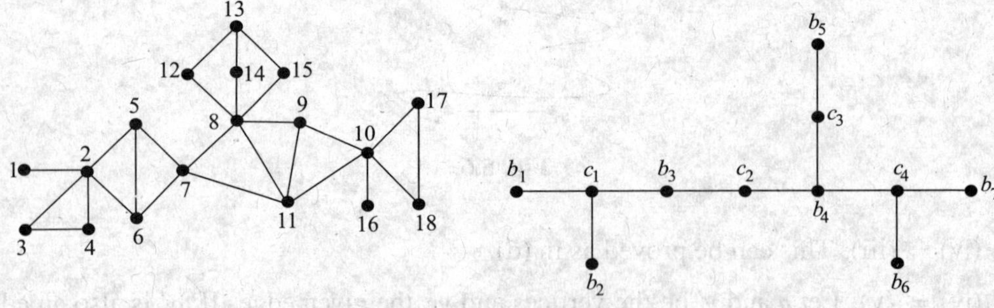

Fig. 5.8

End block: A block of a graph G containing only one cut vertex is called an *end block* of G.

We have the following result on blocks.

Theorem 5.4 Every separable graph has at least one cut vertex and therefore has at least two end blocks.

Proof A separable graph G has at least one cut vertex and therefore has at least two blocks. Thus its block-cut vertex tree T has at least three vertices. Now, for any separable graph the end blocks correspond to the pendant vertices of its block-cut vertex tree. Also, any tree with at least two vertices has two vertices of degree one. Thus the block-cut vertex tree T has at least two pendant vertices. Hence G has at least two end-blocks. ❑

The next result is due to Harary and Norman [105].

Theorem 5.5 The center of any connected graph G lies on a block of G.

Proof If not, let B_1, B_2 be blocks of G containing central vertices. If b_1, b_2 are the vertices of the block-cut vertex tree T of G corresponding to B_1 and B_2, then there is at least one vertex c in the unique $b_1 - b_2$ path of T, corresponding to a cut-vertex c of G. So there are two components G_1 and G_2 of $G - c$ such that $B_1 - c \subseteq G_1$ and $B_2 - c \subseteq G_2$. Let $\bar{c}$ be an eccentric vertex of c in G and P be a $c - \bar{c}$ path of G having length $e(c)$. Then at least one of the components G_1 and G_2, say G_2, contains no vertex of P. Let s be a central vertex in G_2 and Q be a shortest $s - c$ path in G. Then $Q \cup P$ is clearly an $s - \bar{c}$ path in G and thus $d(s, \bar{c}) = d(s, c) + e(c)$. Therefore $e(s) > e(c)$, contradicting the fact that s is a central vertex. Thus the center of G lies in a single block. Hence the center of any connected graph G lies on a block of G. ❑

Definition: If G is a separable graph and c a cut-vertex of G, then a maximal connected subgraph of G containing c in which c is not a cut-vertex is called a *branch* of G at c. The induced subgraph $\langle C \rangle$ on the central vertices of G is called the *central graph* of G. If G has a unique central vertex c, then G is said to be a *unicentric graph*. The unique block B of G to which the center c of G belongs is called the *central block* of G. This is unambiguously defined except when G is unicentric and the unique central vertex is a cut-vertex of G. When $B = \langle C \rangle = G$, then G is called a *self-centered graph*. If the unique central vertex c of G is a cut-vertex of G, the unique block of any of the branches of G at c in which c has an eccentric vertex $\bar{c}$ may be taken as the chosen central block of G.

We note that the central graph of a tree is either K_1 or K_2. Buckley, Miller and Slater [42] have studied graphs with specified central graphs. The following result is atributed to Hedetniemi and is reported in Parthasarathy [175].

Theorem 5.6 For any graph H there exists a graph G with 4 more vertices such that H is the central graph of G.

Proof Take two new vertices v and w, and join each to every vertex of H. Take two other vertices x and y, join x to v, and y to w. Then in the resulting graph G, $e(x) = e(y) = 4$, $e(v) = e(w) = 3$ and $e(u) = 2$, for every vertex $u \in V(H)$. Thus H is an induced subgraph of G and the central graph of G. ❑

5.3 Connectivity Parameters

Assume that a graph does not get disconnected by deleting a single vertex, or by removing a single edge. A natural question then arises: what is the minimum number of vertices or edges required to disconnect a graph? This and other related questions are answered in this section. Before proceeding, we have the following definitions.

Definition: Let $G = (V, E)$ be a graph. A subset S of $V \cup E$ is called a *disconnecting set* of the graph G if $k(G-S) > k(G)$, or $G-S$ is the trivial graph.

If a disconnecting set S is a subset of V, it is called a *vertex cut* of G, and if it is a subset of E it is called an *edge cut* of G. If a disconnecting set S contains vertices and edges it is called a *mixed cut*.

Example For the graph shown in Figure 5.9, $S = \{3, e_3\}$ is a mixed cut, $S = \{3\}$ is a vertex cut and $S = \{e_1, e_3\}$ is an edge cut.

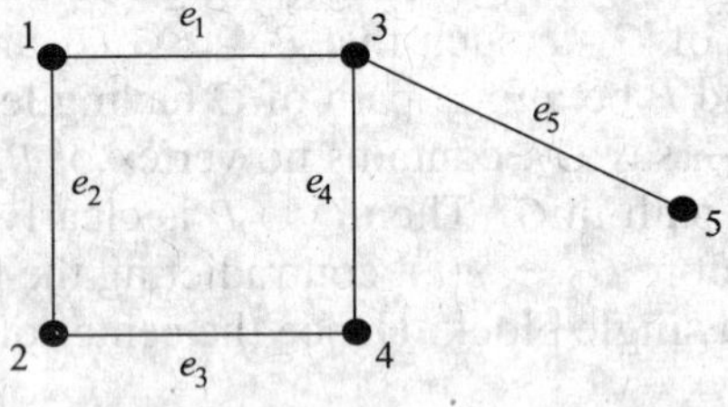

Fig. 5.9

A mixed cut/vertex cut/edge cut S is *minimal* if no proper subset of S has the same property as S. A mixed cut/vertex cut/edge cut S is *minimum* if it has least cardinality among all such minimal sets. A minimal vertex cut is called a *knot* and a minimum vertex cut is called a *clot*. The cardinality of a clot is called the *vertex-connectivity* number, or clot number of the graph G and is denoted by $\kappa(G)$.

A minimal edge cut is called a *bond* and a minimum edge cut is called a *band*. The cardinality of a band is called the *edge-connectivity* number, or band number of the graph G, and is denoted by $\lambda(G)$.

The minimum cardinality of a mixed set is denoted by $\sigma(G)$.

Let S be a disconnected set of the graph $G(V, E)$. Let vertices s and t be in the same component of G, but in different components of $G-S$. Then S is called an $s-t$ *separating* set in G. Minimal $s-t$ separating vertex cut is called an $s-t$ *knot*, and the minimum $s-t$ separating vertex cut is called an $s-t$ *clot*. Minimal $s-t$ separating edge cut is called an $s-t$ *bond*, and the minimum $s-t$ separating edge cut is called an $s-t$ *band*. The cardinality of an $s-t$ clot is called the $s-t$ *clot number* and is denoted by $\kappa(s, t)$, and the cardinality of an $s-t$ band, called the $s-t$ *band number*, is denoted by $\lambda(s, t)$. The cardinality of a minimum $s-t$ separating mixed cut is denoted by $\sigma(s, t)$. The following result gives vertex connectivity of complete graphs and an upper bound for non-complete graphs.

Theorem 5.7 $\kappa(K_n) = n-1$. If G is incomplete, then $\kappa(G) \le n-2$.

Proof

i. Clearly, K_n is a connected graph with n vertices. Deletion of a vertex v_1 keeps the graph $G - v_1$ connected. Clearly, $G - v_1$ has $n-1$ vertices. Deleting one more vertex, say v_2 from $G - v_1$, gives a graph $G - \{v_1, v_2\}$, which is again connected. Continuing this process, we observe that deleting any number of vertices i, $1 \le i \le n-1$ does not disconnect the graph, but deleting exactly $n-1$ vertices gives a trivial graph with one vertex. Thus, $\kappa(K_n) = n-1$.

ii. Let G be an incomplete graph with n vertices. Then there are at least two vertices, say v_i and v_j which are not adjacent. If there is exactly one edge $v_i v_j$ missing, then deleting the $n-2$ vertices other than v_i and v_j disconnects the graph. So in this case $\kappa(G) = n-2$. If there are more edges missing, then clearly $\kappa(G) < n-2$ (Fig. 5.10). Hence, $\kappa(G) \le n-2$. ❑

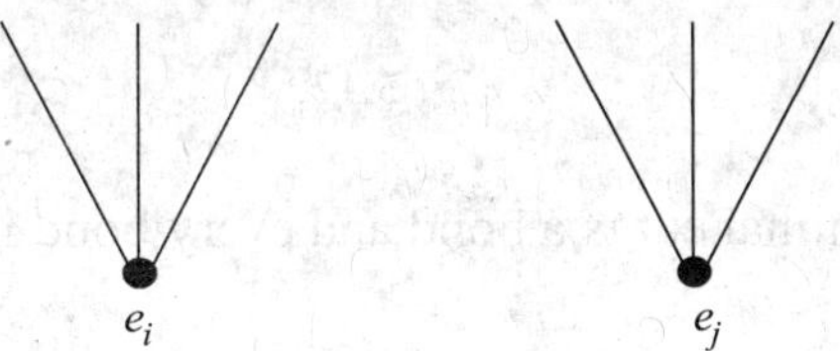

Fig. 5.10

The following result is obvious.

Theorem 5.8 $\kappa(G) = \min\limits_{\substack{s,\,t \in v \\ st \notin E}} \kappa(s, t)$, $\lambda(G) = \min\limits_{s,\,t \in v} \lambda(s, t)$, $\sigma(G) = \min\limits_{s,\,t \in v} \sigma(s, t)$.

Cut of a graph: Let $G(V, E)$ be a graph and let A be any non-empty sub-set of the vertex set V. Let $\bar{A} = V - A$. The set of all edges with one end in A and the other end in $\bar{A}$, denoted by $[A, \bar{A}]$ is called a *cut* of G. The concept of a cut of a graph is intermediate between that of an edge cut and a bond.

We note that every cut is an edge cut, but the converse is not true. Consider the graph in Figure 5.11. Here $F = \{e_1, e_2, e_3, e_4, e_5\}$ is an edge cut, but F is not a cut.

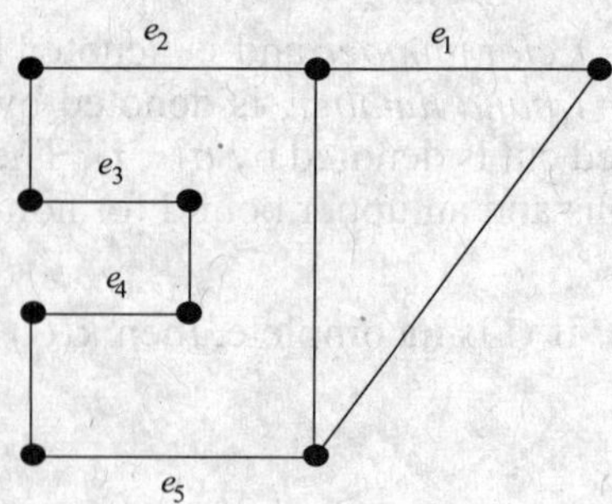

Fig. 5.11

Also, every bond is a cut, but the converse is not true. This is illustrated by the graph in Figure 5.12. Let $A = \{1, 2, 3, 4\}$. Then $\bar{A} = \{5, 6, 7, 8\}$. So $[A, \bar{A}] = \{e_1, e_2, e_3, e_4\}$. Here $[A, \bar{A}]$ is a cut but not a bond.

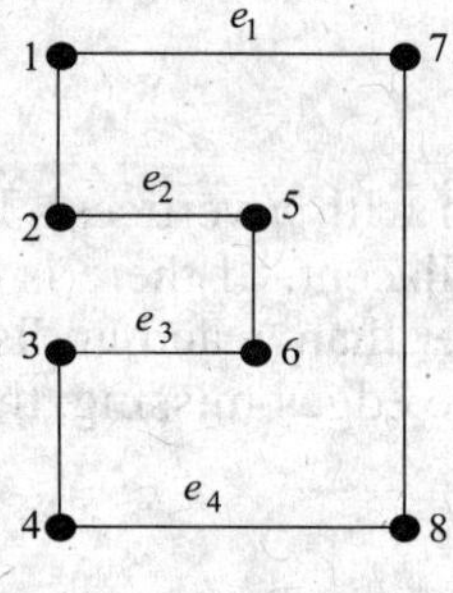

Fig. 5.12

Theorem 5.9 Every minimal cut is a bond and every bond is a minimal cut.

Proof Let $G(V, E)$ be a graph and let $C = [A, \bar{A}]$ be a cut of G. Assume C to be a minimal cut. Then no subset of the edges of C is a cut and this implies that $G - C$ has only two components $\langle A \rangle$ and $\langle \bar{A} \rangle$. Therefore C is a bond.

Conversely, let F be a bond. Then $G - F$ has only two components, say C_1 and C_2. Then $F = [V_1, V_2]$, with $V_2 = \bar{V}_1$. Thus F is a cut and hence a minimal cut. ❑

Theorem 5.10 Every cut is a disjoint union of minimal cuts.

Proof Let $G(V, E)$ be a graph and let $C = [A, \bar{A}]$ be a cut of G. Let C be not a minimal cut. Then at least one of $\langle A \rangle$; or $\langle \bar{A} \rangle$ has more than one component.

Assume $C_1, C_2, \ldots, C_r$ to be the components of $\langle A \rangle$ and $C_1', C_2', \ldots, C_s'$ be the components of $\langle \bar{A} \rangle$. (Clearly, at least one of r and s is greater than one.) Let C_i be coalesced to vertices c_i, $1 \le i \le r$ and C_i' be coalesced to vertices c_i', $1 \le i \le s$, and let H be the simple coalescence thus obtained. Obviously in H, there are no edges of the form $c_i c_j$ and $c_i' c_j'$, $i \ne j$. Thus H is a bipartite graph (because there are edges $c_i c_j'$ in H) (Fig. 5.13).

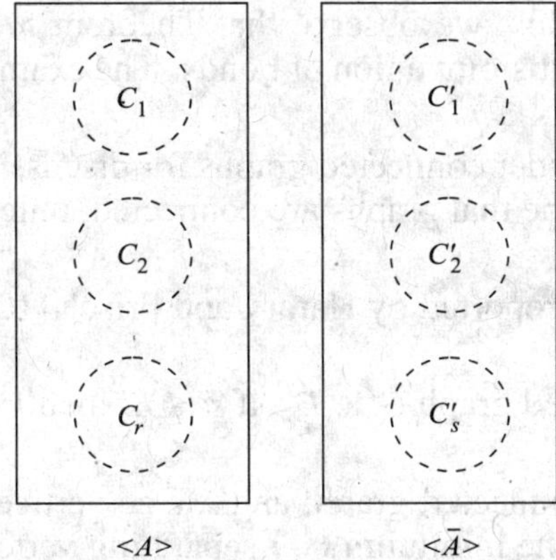

Fig. 5.13

If we can partition the edge set of H into a disjoint union of bonds of H, the edges of G corresponding to these bonds will be disjoint bonds of G whose union is C. To achieve such a partition of $E(H)$, we first take the cut edges of H as members of the partition and let F be the set of such cut edges. For the remaining members of the partition, we take the stars at the remaining (non-isolated) vertices c_i (or c_i'). This gives the required partition and hence the result follows. ❑

Illustration Consider the graph of Figure 5.14. Partition of $E(H)$ is $\{e_1\}\cup\{e_2\}\cup\{e_3, e_4\}$ $\cup\{e_5, e_6\}$. e_1 is a cut edge, e_2 is a cut edge, $\{e_3, e_4\}$ form the star $K_{1,2}$ and $\{e_5, e_6\}$ form the star $K_{1,2}$.

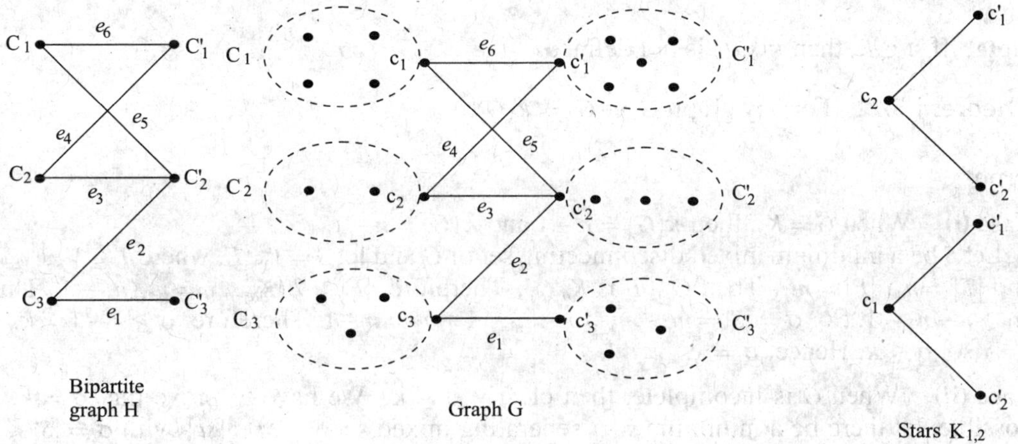

Fig. 5.14

Remark Though the equivalence of minimal edge cuts and minimal cuts is brought out by Theorem 5.10, there is an essential difference between edge cuts and cuts as already mentioned. To emphasise this, we observe that Theorem 5.10 cannot be generalised to state that every edge cut is a disjoint union of bonds. The example in Figure 5.11 illustrates this point.

Since it is enough to consider connected graphs for discussing connectivity concepts, in what follows, we shall assume that graphs are connected, unless stated otherwise.

The following results are reported by Harary and Frisck [101].

Theorem 5.11 In a connected graph $G(V, E)$, if $st \notin E$, then $\kappa(s, t) \leq \sigma(s, t)$.

Proof Let $G(V, E)$ be a connected graph, and s, t be vertices in V such that $st \notin E$. Let $\kappa(s, t)$ be the cardinality of the minimum $s-t$ separating vertex cut ($s-t$ clot). Let $\sigma(s, t)$ be the cardinality of a minimum $s-t$ separating mixed cut. We prove that from any mixed $s-t$ separating set, we can get an $s-t$ separating vertex cut with no more elements.

Let S be a minimum mixed $s-t$ separating set. If ij is an edge in S, then both i and j cannot coincide with s and t, since $st \notin E$.

If $i = s$, add i to S, and remove from S all edges with i as an end vertex. If $i \neq s$, add j to S and remove from S all edges with j as an end vertex. The resulting, possibly mixed set is clearly an $s-t$ separating set with no more elements than S.

We repeat this process and remove all edges from S and obtain a vertex cut S' with atmost $|S|$ elements.

Since $\kappa(s, t) \leq |S'| \leq |S| = \sigma(s, t)$, we have $\kappa(s, t) \leq \sigma(s, t)$. ❑

Corollary In a connected graph $G(V, E)$, if $st \notin E$, then $\kappa(s, t) \leq \lambda(s, t)$.

Note If $st \in E$, then $\kappa(s, t)$ is not defined.

Theorem 5.12 For any graph G, $\sigma(G) = \kappa(G)$.

Proof

Case (i) When $G = K_n$, then $\kappa(G) = n-1$ and $\lambda(G) = n-1$.

Let S be a minimum mixed disconnecting set of G and let $S = T \cup F$, where $T \subseteq V$, $F \subseteq E$, and $|T| = n_1$, $|F| = m_1$. Then $G-T$ is K_{n-n_1}. Therefore, $|F| \geq \lambda(K_{n-n_1}) = n-n_1-1$. Thus, $m_1 \geq n-n_1-1$. So, $\sigma = |S| = m_1+n_1 \geq n-n_1-1+n_1 = n-1$. Therefore, $\sigma \geq n-1 = \kappa$.

Also, $\sigma \leq \kappa$. Hence, $\sigma = \kappa$.

Case (ii) When G is incomplete, then clearly $\sigma \leq \kappa$. We have to prove that $\sigma = \kappa$. If possible, let there be a minimum $s-t$ separating mixed set $S = M \cup \{st\}$ with $\sigma = |S| < \kappa$. Now, M can be replaced by a set of vertices T (a subset of the vertex set of the induced subgraph $\langle M \rangle$) to provide a vertex cut of $G^* = G - st$ with cardinality at most $|M|$.

Let C_1 and C_2 be the components of $G-S$ to which s and t respectively belong. Let there be another component C_3 of $G-S$ and let v be a vertex of C_3. Then $T \cup \{s\}$ is a $v-t$ separating vertex cut of G. But then $|T \cup \{s\}| \leq |S| < \kappa$, a contradiction (Fig. 5.15).

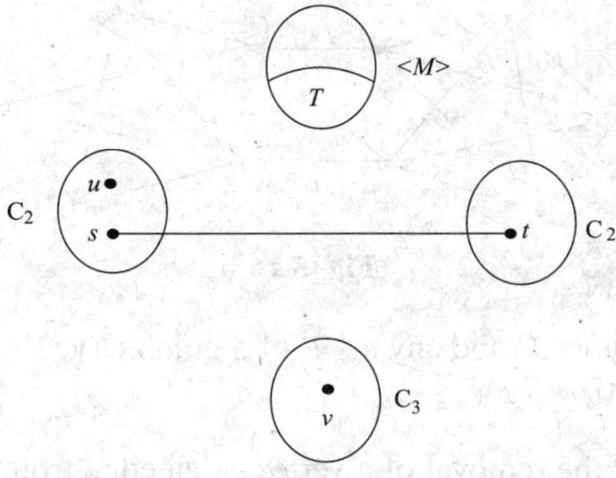

Fig. 5.15

Thus C_1 and C_2 are the only components of $G-S$. Also, if $u \in V(C_1)$, and $u \neq s$, then $T \cup \{s\}$ is a $u-t$ separating vertex cut of G, again leading to a contradiction. Thus $C_1 = \{s\}$, and similarly $C_2 = \{t\}$. So G has $|V(M)|+2$ vertices, and is incomplete. Therefore $\kappa(G) \leq n-2 = |V(M)|+2-2 = |V(M)| < \kappa$ implying $\kappa(G) < \kappa$, a contradiction. Thus $\sigma \not< \kappa$. Hence $\sigma = \kappa$. ❑

The following inequalities are due to Whitney [258].

Theorem 5.13 (Whitney) For any graph G, $\kappa(G) \leq \lambda(G) \leq \delta(G)$.

Proof We first prove $\lambda(G) \leq \delta(G)$.

If G has no edges, then $\lambda = 0$ and $\delta = 0$. If G has edges, then we get a disconnected graph, when all edges incident with a vertex of minimum degree are removed. Thus, in either case, $\lambda(G) \leq \delta(G)$.

We now prove $\kappa(G) \leq \lambda(G)$. For this, we consider the various cases. If $G = K_n$, then $\kappa(G) = \lambda(G) = n-1$. Now let G be an incomplete graph. In case G is disconnected or trivial, then obviously $\kappa = \lambda = 0$.

If G is disconnected and has a cut edge (bridge) x, then $\lambda = 1$. In this case, $\kappa = 1$, since either G has a cut vertex incident with x, or G is K_2.

Finally, let G have $\lambda \geq 2$ edges whose removal disconnects it. Clearly, the removal of $\lambda - 1$ of these edges produces a graph with a cut edge (bridge) $x = uv$. For each of these $\lambda - 1$ edges, select an incident vertex different from u or v. The removal of these vertices also removes the $\lambda - 1$ edges and quite possibly more. If the resulting graph is disconnected, then $\kappa < \lambda$. If not, x is a cut edge (bridge) and hence the removal of u or v will result in either a disconnected or a trivial graph, so that $\kappa \leq \lambda$ in every case. ❑

Illustration We illustrate this by the graph shown in Figure 5.16. Here $\kappa = 2$, $\lambda = 3$ and $\delta = 4$.

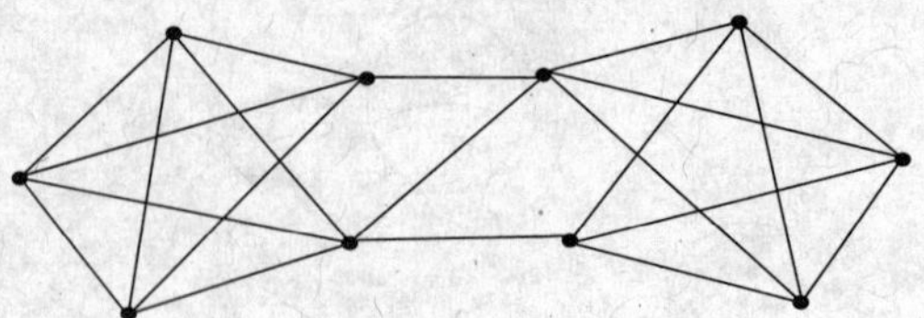

Fig. 5.16

Theorem 5.14 For any $v \in V$ and any $e \in E$ of a graph $G(V, E)$, $\kappa(G) - 1 \leq \kappa(G - v)$ and $\lambda(G) - 1 < \lambda(G - e) \leq \lambda(G)$.

Proof We observe that the removal of a vertex or an edge from a graph can bring down κ or λ by at most one, and that while κ may be increased by the removal of a vertex, λ cannot be increased by the removal of an edge. ❑

Theorem 5.15 For any three integers r, s, t with $0 < r \leq s \leq t$, there is a graph G with $\kappa = r$, $\lambda = s$ and $\delta = t$.

Proof Take two disjoint copies of K_{t+1}. Let A be a set of r vertices in one of them and B be a set of s vertices in the other. Join the vertices of A and B by s edges utilising all the vertices of B and all the vertices of A. Since A is a vertex cut and the set of these s edges is an edge cut of the resulting graph G, it is clear that $\kappa(G) = r$ and $\lambda(G) = s$. Also, there is at least one vertex which is not in $A \cup B$, and it has degree t, so that $\delta(G) = t$. ❑

Illustration Let $r = 1$, $s = 2$, $t = 3$. Take two copies of K_4. Here $\kappa(G) = 1$, $\lambda(G) = 2$, $\delta(G) = 3$ (Fig. 5.17).

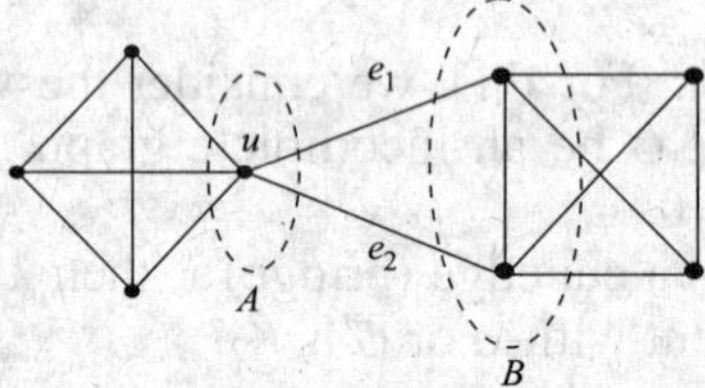

Fig. 5.17

Theorem 5.16 For a graph, $\delta \geq \frac{n}{2}$ ensures $\lambda = \delta$.

Proof Let G be a graph with $\delta \geq \frac{n}{2}$. Let $\lambda < \delta$. Let F be a set of λ edges disconnecting G. Let C_1 and C_2 be the components of $G - F$, and A_1 and A_2 be the end vertices of F in C_1 and C_2, respectively.

Suppose $|A_1| = r$, $|A_2| = s$ and also $V(C_1) = A_1$. Then each vertex of C_1 is adjacent with at least one edge of F. So the number m_1 of edges in C_1 satisfies the inequality

$$m_1 \geq \frac{1}{2}(r\delta - \lambda) > \frac{1}{2}(r\delta - \delta), \text{ since } \lambda < \delta \text{ by assumption.}$$

Therefore, $m_1 > \frac{1}{2}(r-1)\delta > \frac{1}{2}(r-1)r$, since $r \leq |F| = \lambda < \delta$.

But a graph on n vertices cannot have more than $\frac{1}{2}r(r-1)$ edges. Thus, $|V(C_1)| > |A_1|$. Similarly, $V(C_2) > |A_2|$. Thus each of C_1 and C_2 contains at least $\delta+1$ vertices.

Therefore, $n = |V(G)| \geq 2(\delta+1) \geq 2(\frac{n}{2}+1) = n+2$ or $n \geq n+2$, which is a contradiction. Hence $\lambda < \delta$ is not possible. So $\lambda = \delta$. ❑

5.4 Menger's Theorem

Harary [100] listed eighteen variations of Menger's theorem including those for digraphs. Clearly, all these are equivalent and one can be obtained from the other. Several proofs of the various forms of Menger's theorems have appeared, for example, in Dirac [64], Ford and Fulkerson [78], Lovasz [146], McCuaig [151], Menger [153], Nash-Williams and Tutte [164], O'Neil [168], Pym [207] and Wilson [262].

Let u and v be two distinct vertices of a connected graph G. Two paths joining u and v are called disjoint (vertex disjoint) if they have no vertices other than u and v (and hence no edges) in common. The maximum number of such paths between u and v is denoted by $p(u, v)$. If the graph G is to be specified, it is denoted by $p(u, v|G)$.

The following is the vertex form of Menger's theorem. The proof is due to Nash-Williams and Tutte [169].

Theorem 5.17 (Menger-vertex form) The minimum number of vertices separating two non-adjacent vertices s and t is equal to the maximum number of disjoint $s-t$ paths, that is, for any pair of non-adjacent vertices s and t, the clot number equals the maximum number of disjoint $s-t$ paths. That is, $\kappa(s, t) = p(s, t)$, for every pair $s, t \in V$ with $st \notin E$.

Proof Let $G(V, E)$ be a graph with $|E| = m$. We use induction on m, the number of edges. The result is obvious for a graph with $m = 1$ or $m = 2$. Assume that the result is true for all graphs with less than m edges. Let the result be not true for the graph G with m edges. Then we have

$$p(s, t|G) < \kappa(s, t|G) = q \text{ (say)}, \tag{5.17.1}$$

as for any graph, we obviously have $p(s, t) \leq \kappa(s, t)$.

Let $e = uv$ be an edge of G. The deletion graph $G_1 = G - e$, and the contraction graph $G_2 = G|e$ have less number of edges than G. Therefore, by induction hypothesis, we have

$$p(s, t|G_1) = \kappa(s, t|G_1) \text{ and } p(s, t|G_2) = \kappa(s, t|G_2). \tag{5.17.2}$$

Let I be an $(s, t)-$ clot in G_1 and J' be an $(s, t)-$ clot in G_2. Then we have

$|I| = \kappa(s,\, t|G_1) = p(s,\, t|G_1) \le p(s,\, t|G) < q$ and

$|J'| = \kappa(s,\, t|G_2) = p(s,\, t|G_2) \le p(s,\, t|G) < q$, by using (5.17.2) and (5.17.1).

So $|J'| < q$ and therefore $|J'| \le q-1$.

Now to J' there corresponds an $(s-t)$ vertex cut J of G such that $|J| \le |J'|+1$, since, by elementary contraction, $\kappa(s,\, t)$ can be decreased by at most one, and this decrease actually occurs when $e \in E(\langle J\rangle)$.

Thus, $|J| \le |J'|+1 \le q-1+1 = q$,

that is, $|J| \le q$. (5.17.3)

Since J is an $(s,\, t)$ vertex cut in G, $\kappa(s,\, t) \le |J|$, $q \le |J|$.

Thus, $q \le |J| \le q$, so that $|J| = q$.

Therefore, $|I| < q$ and $|J| = q$ and $u,\, v \in J$ by (5.17.3). (5.17.4)

Let

$H_s = \{w \in I \cup J$: there exists an $s-w$ path in G, vertex-disjoint from $I \cup J - \{w\}\}$ and

$H_t = \{w \in I \cup J$: there exists a $t-w$ path in G, vertex-disjoint from $I \cup J - \{w\}\}$.
Clearly, H_s and H_t are $(s-t)$ separating vertex cuts in G. Therefore,

$|H_s| \ge q$ and $|H_t| \ge q$. (5.17.5)

Obviously, $H_s \cup H_t \subseteq I \cup J$.
We claim that $H_s \cap H_t \subseteq I \cup J$. For this, let $w \in H_s \cap H_t$. Then there exists an $s-w$ path P_1 and $w-t$ path P_2 in G vertex disjoint from $I \cup J - \{w\}$. So $P_1 \cup P_2$ contains a path, say P. If $e \in P$ then we have $u,\, v \in V(P) \cap J \subseteq \{w\}$, which is impossible. Therefore $e \notin P$ and so $P \subseteq G-e$. Since I is an $(s,\, t)$ separator in $G-e$ and J is an separator in G, P has a vertex common with I and also with J. So $w \in I \cap J$. Thus, $H_s \cap H_t \subseteq I \cap J$.
Combining (5.17.4) and (5.17.5), and the above observation, we have

$$q+q \le |H_s|+|H_t| = |H_s \cup H_t| + |H_s \cap H_t| \le |I \cup J| + |I \cap J|$$

$$= |I|+|J| < q+q,$$

which is a contradiction.

Thus (5.17.1) is not true, and therefore, we have

$\kappa(s,\, t|G) = p(s,\, t|G)$. ❑

Definition: Two paths joining u and v are said to be *edge-disjoint* if they have no edges in common. The maximum number of edge-disjoint paths between u and v is denoted by $l(u, v)$.

The following is the edge form of Menger's theorem and the proof is adopted from Wilson [196].

Theorem 5.18 (Menger-edge form) For any pair of vertices s and t of a graph G, the minimum number of edges separating s and t equals the maximum number of edge-disjoint paths joining s and t, that is, $\lambda(s, t) = l(s, t)$ for every pair $s, t \in V$.

Proof Let $G(V, E)$ be a graph and let $|E| = m$. We use induction on the number of edges m of G. For $m = 1, 2$, the result is obvious. Assume the result to be true for all graphs with fewer than m edges. Let $\lambda(s, t) = k$. We have two cases to consider.

Case (i) Suppose G has an $(s-t)$ band F such that not all edges of F are incident with s, nor all edges of F are incident with t. Then $G-F$ consists of two non-trivial components C_1 and C_2 with $s \in C_1$ and $t \in C_2$. Let G_1 be the graph obtained from G by contracting the edges of C_1, and G_2 be a graph obtained from G by contracting the edges of C_2. Therefore,

$$G_1 = G||E(C_1) \text{ and } G_2 = G||E(C_2).$$

Since G_1 and G_2 have less edges than G, the induction hypothesis applies to them. Also, the edges corresponding to F provide an $(s-t)$ band in G_1 and G_2, so that $\lambda(s, t|G_1) = k$ and $\lambda(s, t|G_2) = k$. Thus, by induction hypothesis, there are k edge-disjoint paths joining s and t in G_1, and there are k edge-disjoint paths joining s and t in G_2. Thus $l(s, t|G_1) = k$ and $l(s, t|G_2) = k$.

The section of the path of the k edge-disjoint paths joining s and t in G_2 which are in C_1 and the section of the paths of the k edge-disjoint paths joining s and t in G_1 which are in C_2 can now be combined to get $k-$ edge disjoint paths between s and t in G. Hence $l(s, t|G) = k$.

Case (ii) Every $(s-t)$ band of G is such that either all its edges are incident with s, or all its edges are incident with t.

If G has an edge e which is not in any $(s-t)$ band of G, then $\lambda(s, t|G-e) = \lambda(s, t|G) = k$. Since the induction hypothesis is applicable to $G-e$, there are k edge-disjoint paths between s and t in $G-e$ and thus in G. Hence $l(s, t|G) = k$.

Now, assume that every edge of G is in at least one $(s-t)$ band of G. Then every $s-t$ path P of G is either a single edge or a pair of edges. Any such path P can therefore contain at most one edge of any $(s-t)$ band. Then $G-E(P) = G_1$ is a graph with $\lambda(s, t|G_1) = k-1$.

Appling induction hypothesis, we have $l(s, t|G_1) = k-1$. Together with P, we get $l(s, t|G) = k$. ❑

5.5 Some Properties of a Bond

We give some properties of a bond (bond is also called a cut-set). The first property follows.

Theorem 5.19 Every bond in a connected graph G connects at least one branch of every spanning tree of G.

Proof Let G be a connected graph and T be a spanning tree of G. Let S be an arbitrary bond in G. Clearly, there are edges which are common in S and T. For, if there is no edge of S which is also in T, then removal of the bond S from G will not disconnect the graph, as $G-S$ contains T and is therefore connected. Thus S and T have at least one common edge. ❑

Theorem 5.20 In a connected graph G, any minimal set of edges containing at least one branch of every spanning tree of G is a bond.

Proof Let G be a connected graph and let Q be a minimal set of edges containing at least one branch of every spanning tree of G.

Consider $G-Q$, the subgraph that remains after removing the edges in Q from G. Since $G-Q$ contains no spanning tree of G, therefore $G-Q$ is disconnected (one component of which may just consist of an isolated vertex). Also, since Q is a minimal set of edges with this property, therefore any edge e from Q returned to $G-Q$ creates at least one spanning tree. Thus the subgraph $G-Q+e$ is a connected graph. Therefore Q is a minimal set of edges whose removal from G disconnects G. This, by definition, is a bond. ❑

Theorem 5.21 Every cycle has an even number of edges in common with any bond.

Proof Let G be a graph and let S be a bond of G. Let the removal of S partition the vertices of G into two mutually disjoint subsets V_1 and V_2. Consider a cycle C in G (Fig. 5.18).

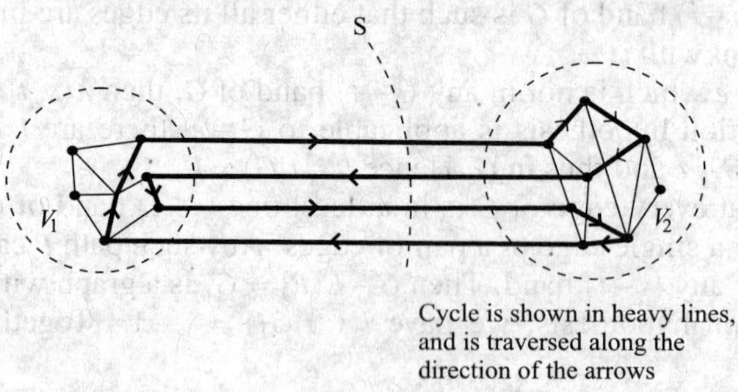

Fig. 5.18

If all the vertices in C are entirely within vertex set V_1 (or V_2), then the number of edges common to S and C is zero, which is an even number. If, on the other hand, some vertices in C are in V_1 and some in V_2, we traverse back and forth between the sets V_1 and V_2 as we traverse the cycle. Because of the closed nature of a cycle, the number of edges between V_1 and V_2 must be even. And, since every edge in S has one end in V_1 and other in V_2, and no other edge in G has the property of separating sets V_1 and V_2, the number of edges common to S and C is even. ❑

5.6 Fundamental Bonds

Consider a spanning tree T of a connected graph G. Take any branch b in T. Since $\{b\}$ is a bond in T, therefore $\{b\}$ partitions all vertices of T into two disjoint sets, one at each end of b. Consider the same partition of vertices in G and the bond S in G that corresponds to this partition. Bond S will contain only one branch b of T and the rest (if any) of the edges in S are chords with respect to T. Such a bond S containing exactly one branch of a tree T is called a *fundamental bond* with respect to T.

Theorem 5.22 The ring sum of any two bonds is either a third bond, or an edge-disjoint union of bonds.

Proof Let G be a connected graph, and S_1 and S_2 be two bonds. Let V_1 and V_2 be the unique and disjoint partitioning of the vertex set V of G corresponding to S_1. Let V_3 and V_4 be the partitioning corresponding to S_2.

Clearly, $V_1 \cup V_2 = V$, $V_1 \cap V_2 = \varphi$, $V_3 \cup V_4 = V$ and $V_3 \cap V_4 = \varphi$ (Fig. 5.19(a) and (b)).

Now, let $(V_1 \cap V_4) \cup (V_2 \cap V_3) = V_5$ and $(V_1 \cap V_3) \cup (V_2 \cap V_4) = V_6$.

Clearly, $V_5 = V_1 \oplus V_3$ and $V_6 = V_2 \oplus V_3$ (Fig. 5.19(c)).

The ring sum of two bonds $S_1 \oplus S_2$ consists only of edges that join vertices in V_5 to those in V_6. Also, there are no edges outside $S_1 \oplus S_2$ that joins vertices in V_5 to those in V_6. Thus the set of edges $S_1 \oplus S_2$ produces a partitioning of V into V_5 and V_6 such that $V_5 \cup V_6 = V$ and $V_5 \cap V_6 = \varphi$. Hence $S_1 \oplus S_2$ is a bond if the subgraphs containing V_5 and V_6 each remain connected after $S_1 \oplus S_2$ is removed from G. Otherwise, $S_1 \oplus S_2$ is an edge disjoint union of bonds. ❑

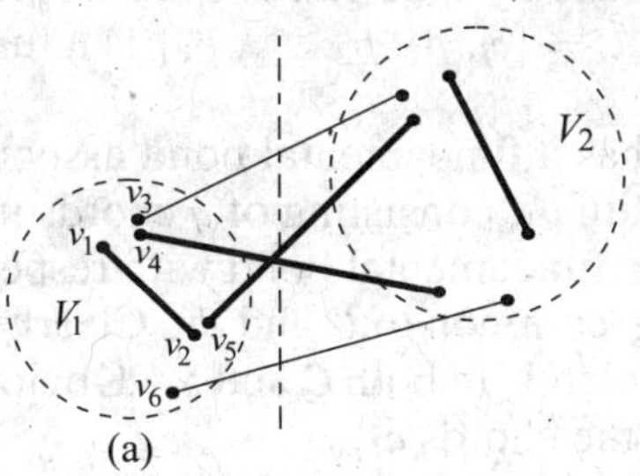

(a)

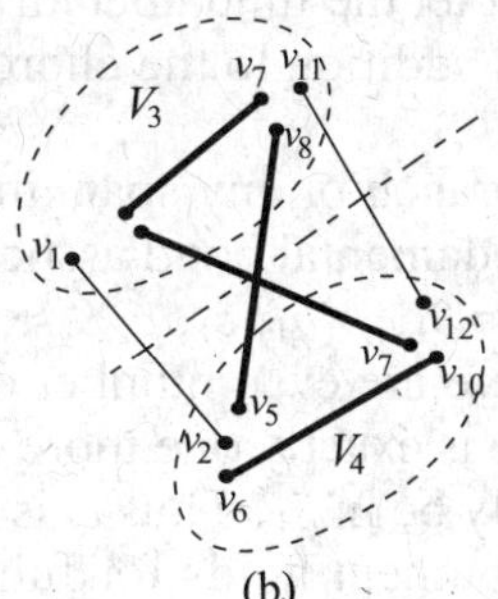

(b)

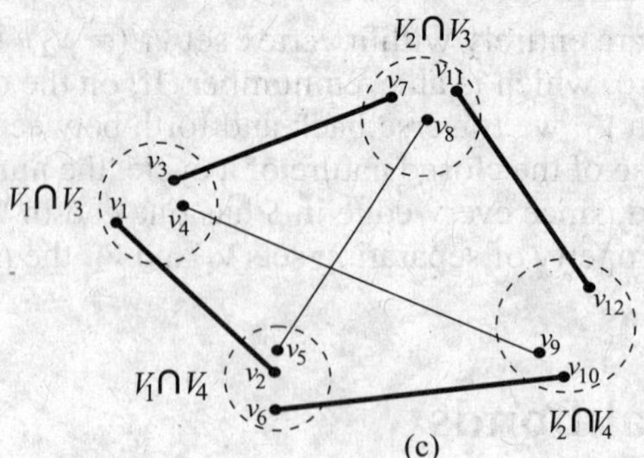

Fig. 5.19

Example Consider the graph in Figure 5.20. Here $\{d, e, f\} \oplus \{f, g, h\} = \{d, e, g, h\}$ is a bond, $\{a, b\} \oplus \{b, c, e, f\} = \{a, c, e, f\}$ is another bond and $\{d, e, g, h\} \oplus \{f, g, k\} = \{d, e, f, h, k\} = \{d, e, f\} \cup \{h, k\}$ an edge disjoint union of bonds.

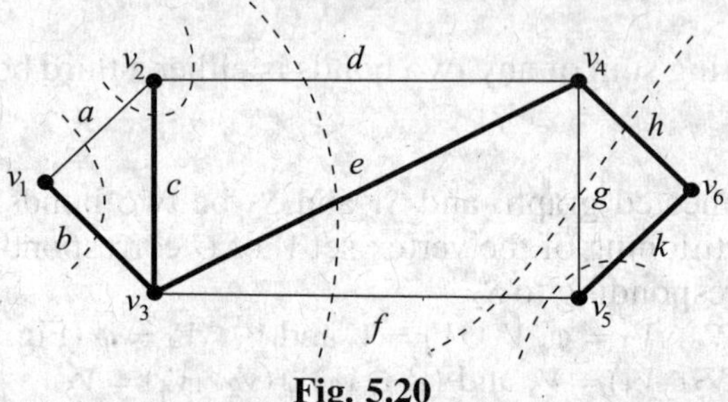

Fig. 5.20

Theorem 5.23 With respect to a given spanning tree T, a chord c_i that determines a fundamental cycle C occurs in every fundamental bond associated with the branches in C and in no other.

Proof Let G be a connected graph and T be a spanning tree of G. Let c_i be a chord with respect to T and let the fundamental cycle made by c_i be called C, consisting of k branches $b_1, b_2, \ldots, b_k$ in addition to the chord c_i. So $C = \{c_i, b_1, b_2, \ldots, b_k\}$ is a fundamental cycle with respect to T.

Now every branch of any spanning tree has a fundamental bond associated with it. So let S_1 be the fundamental bond associated with b_1, consisting of q chords in addition to the branch b_1. Thus, $S_1 = \{b_1, c_1, c_2, \ldots, c_q\}$ is a fundamental bond with respect to T.

We know there are even number of edges common to C and S_1. Clearly, b_1 is in both C and S_1. So there is exactly one more edge which is in both C and S_1. Obviously, the edge c_i in C can possibly be in S_1. Thus c_i is one of the chords $c_1, c_2, \ldots, c_q$.

The same argument holds for fundamental bonds associated with $b_2, b_3, \ldots, b_k$. Thus the chord c_i is contained in every fundamental bond associated with branches in C.

Now we show that the chord c_i is not in any other fundamental bond S' with respect to T, besides those associated with $b_1, b_2, \ldots, b_k$. Let this be possible. Then since none of the branches in C are in S', there is only one edge c_i common to S' and C, which gives a contradiction to the fact that there are even number of edges common to a fundamental bond and a cycle. ❑

Example In the graph of Figure 5.20, consider the spanning tree $\{b, c, e, h, k\}$. The fundamental cycle made by the chord f is $C = \{f, e, h, k\}$. The three fundamental bonds determined by the three branches e, h and k are as follows: (i) determined by e is $\{d, e, f\}$, (ii) determined by h is $\{f, g, h\}$ and (iii) determined by k is $\{f, g, k\}$. Clearly, chord f occurs in each of these three fundamental bonds and there is no other fundamental bond that contains f.

Theorem 5.24 With respect to a given spanning tree T, a branch b_i that determines a fundamental bond S is contained in every fundamental cycle associated with the chords in S, and in no others.

Proof Let G be a connected graph and T be a spanning tree in G. Let the fundamental bond determined by a branch b_i be $S = \{b_i, c_1, c_2, \ldots, c_p\}$.

Let C_1 be the fundamental cycle determined by chord c_1, so that

$$C_1 = \{c_1, b_1, b_2, \ldots, b_q\}.$$

We know that S and C_1 have even number of edges in common. One common edge is obviously c_1. Thus the second common edge should be b_i, so that b_i is also in C_1. Therefore b_i is one of the branches $b_1, b_2, \ldots, b_q$.

The same is true for the fundamental cycles made by the chords $c_2, c_3, \ldots, c_p$.

Now assume that b_i occurs in a fundamental cycle C_{p+1} made by a chord other than $c_1, c_2, \ldots, c_p$. Since none of the chords $c_1, c_2, \ldots, c_p$ is in C_{p+1}, there is only one edge b_i common to a cycle C_{p+1} and the bond S, which is not possible. Hence the result follows. ❑

Example Consider the graph of Figure 5.20. Consider the branch e of spanning tree $\{b, c, e, h, k\}$. The fundamental bond determined by e is $\{e, d, f\}$. The two fundamental cycles determined by chords d and f are respectively $\{d, c, e\}$ and $\{f, e, h, k\}$. Clearly, branch e is contained in both these fundamental cycles and none of the remaining three fundamental cycles contains branch e.

Theorem 5.25 Let A, B be two disjoint vertex subsets of a graph G and let any vertex subset of G which meets every $A-B$ path in G have at least k vertices. Then there are k vertex disjoint $A-B$ paths in G.

Proof Let G be a graph and let A and B be two disjoint vertex subsets of G. Let S be any vertex subset of G which meets every $A-B$ path in G and let $|S| \geq k$.

Take two new vertices s and t, and join s by an edge to each vertex of A, and join t by an edge to each vertex of B. Let G' be the resulting graph, and in G' we have $\kappa(s, t) \geq k$.

Hence by Menger's theorem, there are k vertex disjoint paths between s and t in G'. Omitting the edges incident with s and t in these paths, we get k vertex-disjoint $A-B$ paths in G. ❑

Definition: A graph G is *k-connected* if $\kappa(G) = k$, and G is *k-edge connected* if $\lambda(G) = k$. A k-connected (k-edge connected) graph is r-connected (r-edge 1-connected) for each r, $0 \leq r \leq k-1$. Clearly, a separable graph ($\kappa = 1$) is connected and not 2-connected. A separable graph without cut edge is 2-edge connected. A separable graph with cut edges is only 1-connected.

The following result is due to Whitney [258].

Theorem 5.26 A graph G with at least three vertices is 2-connected if and only if any two vertices of G are connected by at least two internally disjoint paths.

Proof Let G be 2-connected so that G contains no cut vertex. Let u and v be two distinct vertices of G. To prove the result, we induct on $d(u, v)$.

If $d(u, v) = 1$, let $e = uv$. Since G is 2-connected and $n(G) \geq 3$, therefore e cannot be a cut edge of G. For, if e is a cut edge, then at least one of u and v is a cut vertex. Now, by Theorem 5.2, e belongs to a cycle C in G. Then $C-e$ is a $u-v$ path in G, internally disjoint from the path uv.

Assume any two vertices x and y of G, such that $d(x, y) = t-1$, $t \geq 2$, are joined by two internally disjoint $x-y$ paths in G. Let $d(u, v) = t$ and let P be a $u-v$ path of length t, and w be the vertex before v on P. Then $d(u, w) = t-1$. Therefore, by induction hypothesis, there are two internally disjoint $u-w$ paths, say P_1 and P_2, in G. Since G has no cut vertex, $G-w$ is connected and therefore there exists a $u-v$ path Q in $G-w$. Clearly, Q is a $u-v$ path in G not containing w. Suppose x is the vertex of Q such that $x-v$ section of Q contains only the vertex x in common with $P_1 \cup P_2$ (Fig. 5.21). Assume x belongs to P_1. Then the union of the $u-x$ section of P_1 and $x-v$ section of Q together with $P_2 \cup \{wv\}$ are two internally disjoint $u-v$ paths in G.

Conversely, assume any two distinct vertices of G are connected by at least two internally disjoint paths. Then G is connected. Also, G has no cut vertex. For, if v is a cut vertex of G, then there exist vertices u and w such that every $u-w$ path contains v, contradicting the hypothesis. Thus G is 2-connected. ❑

The following property of 3-connected graphs is given in Thomassen [234] and is attributed to Barnette and Grunbaum [14] and Titov [236].

Theorem 5.27 If G is a 3-connected graph with at least five vertices, then G has an edge e such that $G-e$ is a subdivision of a 3-connected graph.

Proof Since G is 3-connected, $\delta \geq 3$, and so by Menger's theorem, G has a subdivision of K_4.

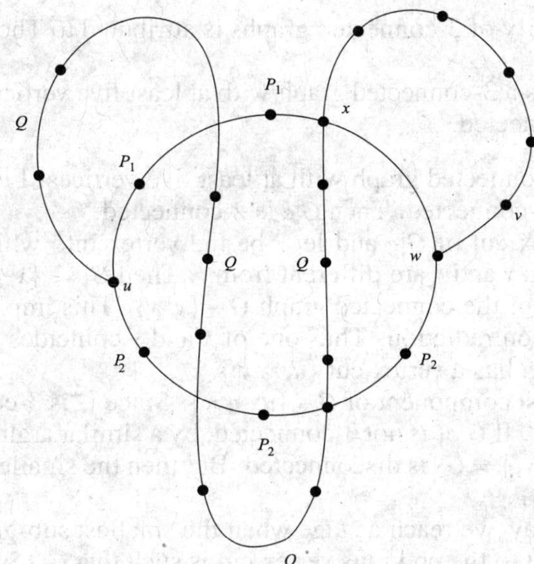

Fig. 5.21

Let H be a proper subgraph of G which is a subdivision of a 3-connected graph, and let H have maximum possible number of edges. If H is a 3-connected spanning subgraph of G, then by the maximality of H, G has an edge e such that $H = G - e$ is a subgraph of G with the desired property.

Now, let H be 3-connected but not spanning (Fig. 5.22). Then there is a vertex $v \in V(G) - V(H)$, so that there are three $v - V(H)$ paths, say P_1, P_2 and P_3 which have only vertex v in common. Let the other end vertices of these paths in $V(H)$ be v_1, v_2 and v_3. If $v_1 v_2 = e \in E(H)$, then $H + P_1 + P_2 - e$ is a subdivision of a 3-connected graph. Otherwise, $H + P_1 + P_2$ is a subdivision of a 3-connected graph. In both cases the maximality of H is contradicted.

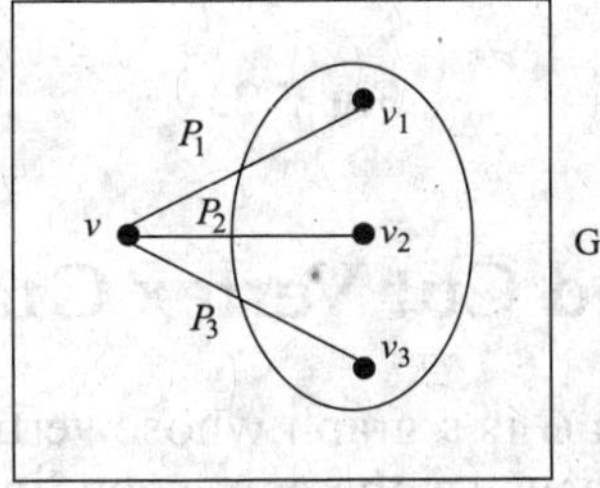

Fig. 5.22

Let H be not 3-connected. Then H has a suspended path P of length at least 2. Let u and v be the end vertices of P. Since G is 3-connected, $G - \{u, v\}$ has a path P' joining an internal vertex w of P to a vertex in $V(H) - V(P)$. But then $H \cup P'$ is a subdivision of a 3-connected graph. By the choice of H, $H \cup P' = G$ and P' consists of a single edge e'. ❑

The following property of 3-connected graphs is attributed to Thomassen [234].

Theorem 5.28 If G is a 3-connected graph with at least five vertices, then G has an edge e such that $G|e$ is 3-connected.

Proof Let G be a 3-connected graph with at least five vertices. Let $e = uv$ be an edge of G such that $G|e$ is not 3-connected. Then $G|e$ is 2-connected.

Let $\{x, y\}$ be a vertex cut of $G|e$ and let z be the vertex into which x and y have been coalesced. Assume both x and y are different from z. Then $G|e - \{x, y\}$ is a graph obtained by contracting an edge of the connected graph $G - \{x, y\}$. This implies that $G|e - \{x, y\}$ is connected, which is a contradiction. Thus one of x and y coincides with z. Renaming the other as w, we see that G has a vertex cut $\{u, v, w\}$.

Let G_1 be the smallest component of $G - \{u, v, w\}$. Since G is 3-connected, G_1 is joined to w by an edge $e_1 = wx_1$. If $G|e_1$ is not 3-connected, by a similar argument, there is a vertex y_1 such that $G - \{w, x_1, y_1\} = G_2$ is disconnected. But then the smallest component of G_2 is a proper subgraph of G_1.

Continuing in this way, we reach a stage when the smallest sub-graph is a single vertex and the edge f joining it to the previous vertex cut is such that $G|f$ is a 3-connected graph. ❑

Illustration We illustrate this in Figure 5.23, where graph G is 3-connected having vertex cut $\{u, v, w\}$. $G|e$ is 2-connected with vertex cut $\{z, w\}$ and $G|e_1$ is 3-connected. In $G - \{u, v, w\}$, we observe that the smallest subgraph is a single vertex.

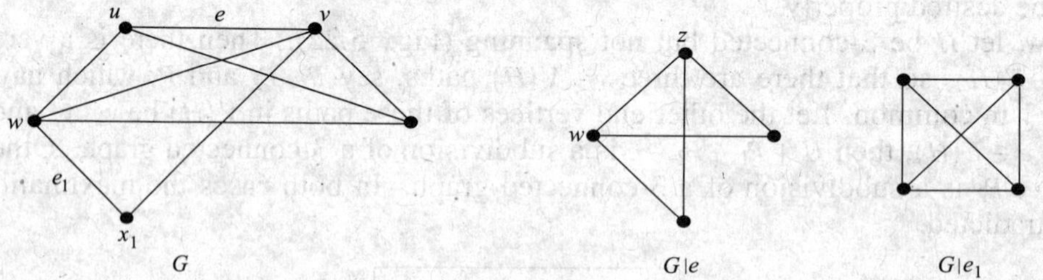

Fig. 5.23

5.7 Block Graphs and Cut Vertex Graphs

The block graph $B(G)$ of a graph G is a graph whose vertices are the blocks of G and two of these vertices are adjacent whenever the corresponding blocks contain a common cut vertex of G. The cut vertex graph $C(G)$ of a graph G has vertices as cut vertices of G and two such vertices are adjacent if the cut vertices of G to which they belong lie on a common block (Fig. 5.24).

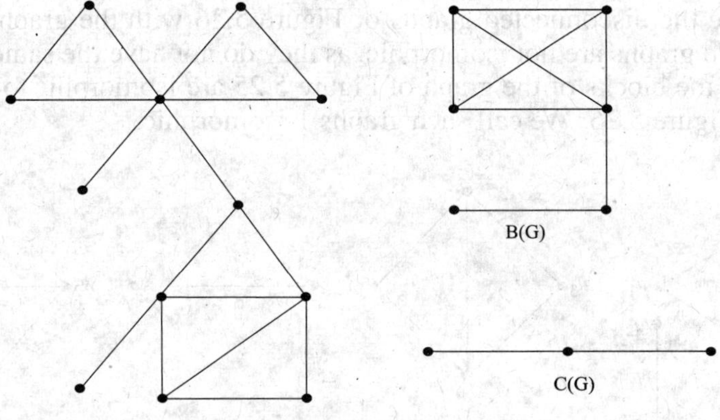

Fig. 5.24

The following characterisation of block graphs is due to Harary [99].

Theorem 5.29 A graph H is the block graph of some graph if and only if every block of H is complete.

Proof Let $H = B(G)$ and assume there is a block H_i of H which is not complete. Then there are two vertices in H_i which are non-adjacent and lie on a shortest common cycle Z of length at least 4. But the union of the blocks of G corresponding to the vertices of H_i which lie on Z is then connected and has no cut vertex, so it itself is contained in a block, contradicting the maximality property of a block of a graph.

Conversely, let H be a given graph in which every block is complete. Form $B(H)$, and then form a new graph G by adding to each vertex H_i of $B(H)$ a number of end edges equal to the number of vertices of the block H_i which are not cut vertices of H. Then it is easy to see that $B(G)$ is isomorphic to H. ❑

1-isomorphism A separable graph consists of two or more non-separable subgraphs, and each of the largest non-separable subgraph is a block. The graph in Figure 5.25 has five blocks and three cut vertices u, v and w. We note that a non-separable connected graph consists of just one block.

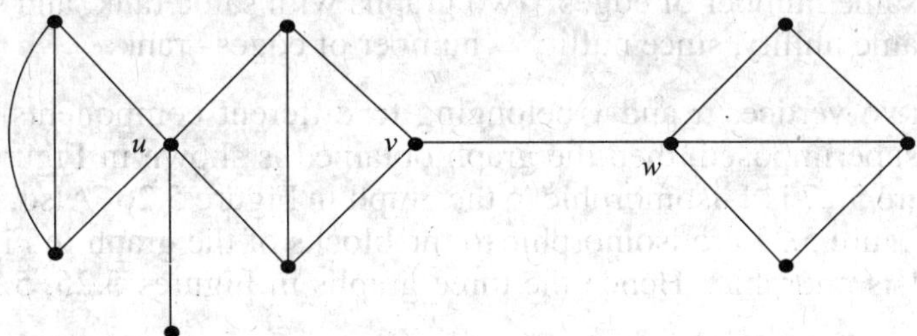

Fig. 5.25

Now, compare the disconnected graphs of Figure 5.26 with the graph of Figure 5.25. Clearly, these two graphs are not isomorphic, as they do not have the same number of vertices. Evidently, the blocks of the graph of Figure 5.25 are isomorphic to the components of the graph of Figure 5.26. We call such graphs 1-isomorphic.

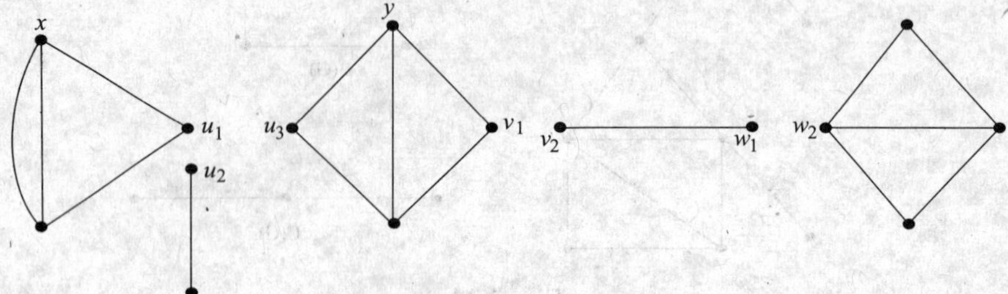

Fig. 5.26

These observations lead to the following definition.

Definition: Two graphs G_1 and G_2 are said to be *1-isomorphic* if they become isomorphic to each other under repeated application of the following operation.

Operation 1 Split a cut vertex into two vertices to produce two disjoint subgraphs.

This definition implies that two non-separable graphs are 1-isomorphic if and only if they are isomorphic.

Two 1-isomorphic graphs have the following property.

Theorem 5.30 If G_1 and G_2 are 1-isomorphic graphs, then rank G_1 = rank G_2 and nullity G_1 = nullity G_2.

Proof Under operation 1, whenever a cut vertex in a graph G is split into two vertices, the number of components in G increases by one. Therefore, rank G = number of vertices in G-number of components in G, remains invariant under operation 1.

Since no edges are destroyed or new edges created by operation 1, two 1-isomorphic graphs have the same number of edges. Two graphs with same rank, and same number of edges have the same nullity, since nullity = number of edges−rank. ❑

Suppose the two vertices x and y belonging to different components of the graph in Figure 5.26 are superimposed, then the graph obtained is shown in Figure 5.27. Clearly, the graph in Figure 5.27 is 1-isomorphic to the graph in Figure 5.26. Also, since the blocks of the graph in Figure 5.27 are isomorphic to the blocks of the graph in Figure 5.25, these two graphs are 1-isomorphic. Hence the three graphs in Figures 5.25, 5.26 and 5.27 are 1-isomorphic.

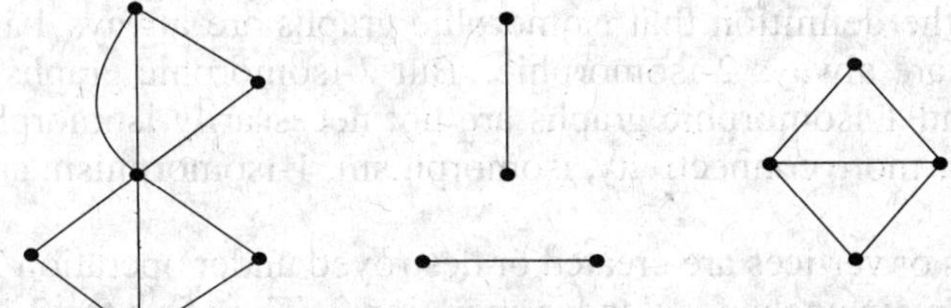

Fig. 5.27

We have seen that a graph G_1 is 1-isomorphic to a graph G_2 if the blocks of G_1 are isomorphic to the blocks of G_2. Since a non-separable graph is a block, 1-isomorphism for non-separable graphs is same as isomorphism. For separable graphs, obviously 1-isomorphism is different from isomorphism. In fact, graphs that are isomorphic are also 1-isomorphic, but the converse need not be true.

2-isomorphism In a 2-connected graph G, let x and y be a pair of vertices whose removal from G, leaves the remaining graph disconnected. That is, G consists of a subgraph H and its complement $\bar{H}$ such that H and $\bar{H}$ have exactly two vertices x and y, in common. Now, we perform the following operation on G.

Operation 2 Split the vertex x into x_1 and x_2, and the vertex y into y_1 and y_2 such that G is split into H and $\bar{H}$. Let vertices x_1 and y_1 go with H, and x_2 and y_2 with $\bar{H}$. Now, rejoin the graphs H and $\bar{H}$ by merging x_1 with y_2 and x_2 with y_1. Clearly, edges whose end vertices are x and y in G can go with H or $\bar{H}$, without affecting the final graph.

Two graphs are said to be *2-isomorphic* if they become isomorphic after undergoing operation 1, or operation 2, or both any number of times. For example, Figure 5.28 shows how the two graphs in (a) and (d) are 2-isomorphic.

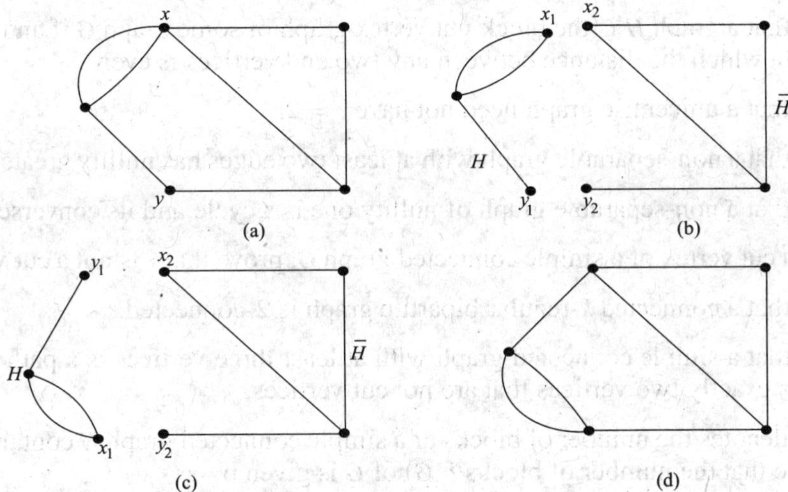

Fig. 5.28

It follows from the definition that isomorphic graphs are always 1-isomorphic and 1-isomorphic graphs are always 2-isomorphic. But 2-isomorphic graphs are not necessarily 1-isomorphic and 1-isomorphic graphs are not necessarily isomorphic. However, for graphs with three or more connectivity, isomorphism, 1-isomorphism and 2-isomorphism are same.

Clearly, no edges or vertices are created or destroyed under operation 2. So the rank and nullity of a graph remain unchanged under operation 2. Therefore the 2-isomorphic graphs are equal in rank and equal in nullity.

Cycle correspondence: Two graphs G_1 and G_2 are said to have a cycle correspondence if there is a one-one correspondence between the edges of G_1 and G_2, and a one-one correspondence between the cycles of G_1 and G_2, such that a cycle in G_1 formed by certain edges of G_1 has a corresponding cycle in G_2 formed by the corresponding edges of G_2, and vice versa. Clearly, isomorphic graphs have cycle correspondence. Since in a separable graph G, every cycle is confined to a particular block, every cycle in G retains its edges as G undergoes operation 1. Thus 1-isomorphic graphs have cycle correspondence.

The following result for 2-isomorphic graphs is due to Whitney [259].

Theorem 5.31 Two graphs are 2-isomorphic if and only if they have cycle correspondence.

5.8 Exercises

1. Prove that a vertex v of a tree is a cut vertex if and only if $d(v) > 1$.
2. Prove that a unicentric graph need not be separable.
3. Prove that a graph H is the block-cut vertex graph of some graph G if and only if it is a tree in which the distance between any two end vertices is even.
4. Prove that a unicentric graph need not have $d = 2r$.
5. Prove that a non-separable graph with at least two edges has nullity greater than zero.
6. Prove that a non-separable graph of nullity one is a cycle and its converse.
7. If v is a cut vertex of a simple connected graph G, prove that v is not a cut vertex of $\bar{G}$.
8. Prove that a connected k-regular bipartite graph is 2-connected.
9. Show that a simple connected graph with at least three vertices is a path if and only if it has exactly two vertices that are not cut vertices.
10. If $b(v)$ denotes the number of blocks of a simple connected graph G containing vertex v, prove that the number of blocks $b(G)$ of G is given by

$$b(G) = 1 + \sum_{v \in V(G)} (b(v) - 1).$$

11. Prove that if a graph G is k-connected or k-edge-connected, then $m \geq \frac{nk}{2}$.
12. Prove that a connected graph with at least two vertices contains at least two vertices that are not cut vertices.
13. Prove that a 3-regular connected graph has a cut vertex if and only if it has a cut edge.
14. Prove that the connectivity and edge connectivity of a cubic graph are equal.
15. Prove that a graph with at least three vertices is 2-connected if and only if any two vertices of G lie on a common cycle.
16. Prove that a graph is 2-connected if and only if for every pair of disjoint connected subgraphs G_1 and G_2, there exist two internally disjoint paths P_1 and P_2 of G between G_1 and G_2.
17. In a 2-connected graph G, prove that any two longest cycles have at least two vertices in common.
18. Prove that a connected graph G is 3-connected if and only if every edge of G is the exact intersection of the edge sets of two cycles of G.
19. Prove that a connected graph is Eulerian if and only if each of its blocks is Eulerian.
20. Prove that a connected graph is Eulerian if and only if each of its edge cuts has an even number of edges.

6. Planarity

Let $G(V,E)$ be a graph with $V = \{v_1,\ v_2,\ldots,\ v_n\}$ and $E = \{e_1, e_2, \ldots, e_m\}$. Let S be any surface (like the plane, sphere) and $P = \{p_1,\ p_2,\ \ldots,\ p_n\}$ be a set of n distinct points of S, p_i corresponding to v_i, $1 \le i \le n$. If $e_i = v_j v_k$, draw a Jordan arc J_i on S from p_j to p_k such that J_i does not pass through any other p_i. Then $P \cup \{J_1,\ J_2,\ldots,\ J_m\}$ is called a *drawing* of G on S, or a diagram representing G on S. The p_i are called the *points* of the diagram and J_i, the *lines* of the diagram.

An *embedding* of a graph G on a surface S is a diagram of G drawn on the surface such that the Jordan arcs representing any two edges of G do not intersect except at a point representing a vertex of G.

A graph is *planar* if it has an embedding on the plane. A graph which has no embedding on the plane is *nonplanar*. That is, a graph G is said to be planar if there exists some geometric representation of G which can be drawn on a plane such that no two of its edges intersect and a graph that cannot be drawn on a plane without a crossover between its edges is called nonplanar.

In order that a graph G is nonplanar, we have to show that of all possible geometric representations of G, none can be embedded in a plane. Equivalently, a geometric graph G is planar if there exists a graph isomorphic to G that is embedded in a plane.

An embedding of a planar graph G on a plane is called a *plane representation* of G. Figure 6.1 shows three diagrams of the same graph which is planar. The two graphs in Figure 6.2 represent the same planar graph.

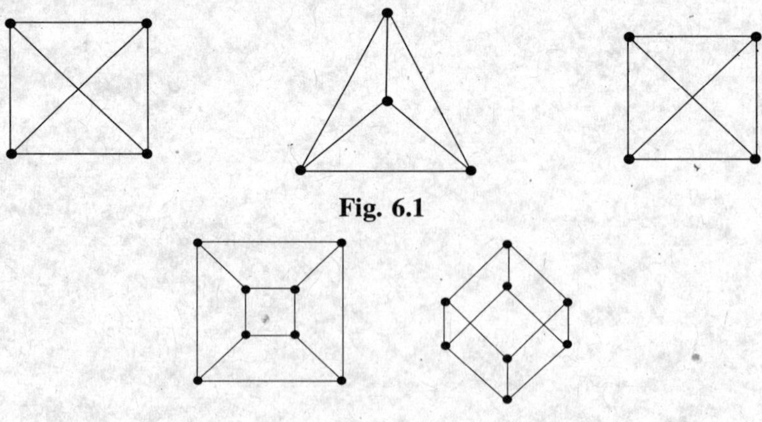

Fig. 6.1

Fig. 6.2

6.1 Kuratowski's Two Graphs

The complete graph K_5 and the complete bipartite graph $K_{3,3}$ are called Kuratowski's graphs, after the polish mathematician Kasimir Kurtatowski, who found that K_5 and $K_{3,3}$ are nonplanar.

Theorem 6.1 The complete graph K_5 with five vertices is nonplanar.

Proof Let the five vertices in the complete graph be named v_1, v_2, v_3, v_4, v_5. Since in a complete graph every vertex is joined to every other vertex by means of an edge, there is a cycle $v_1v_2v_3v_4v_5v_1$ that is a pentagon. This pentagon divides the plane of the paper into two regions, one inside and the other outside, Figure 6.3(a).

Since vertex v_1 is to be connected to v_3 by means of an edge, this edge may be drawn inside or outside the pentagon (without intersecting the five edges drawn previously). Suppose we choose to draw the line from v_1 to v_3 inside the pentagon, Figure 6.3(b). In case we choose outside, we end with the same argument. Now we have to draw an edge from v_2 to v_4 and another from v_2 to v_5. Since neither of these edges can be drawn inside the pentagon without crossing over the edge already drawn, we draw both these edges outside the pentagon, Figure 6.3(c). The edge connecting v_3 and v_5 cannot be drawn outside the pentagon without crossing the edge between v_2 and v_4. Therefore v_3 and v_5 have to be connected with an edge inside the pentagon, Figure 6.3(d). Now, we have to draw an edge between v_1 and v_4 and this cannot be placed inside or outside the pentagon without a crossover. Thus the graph cannot be embedded in a plane. ❑

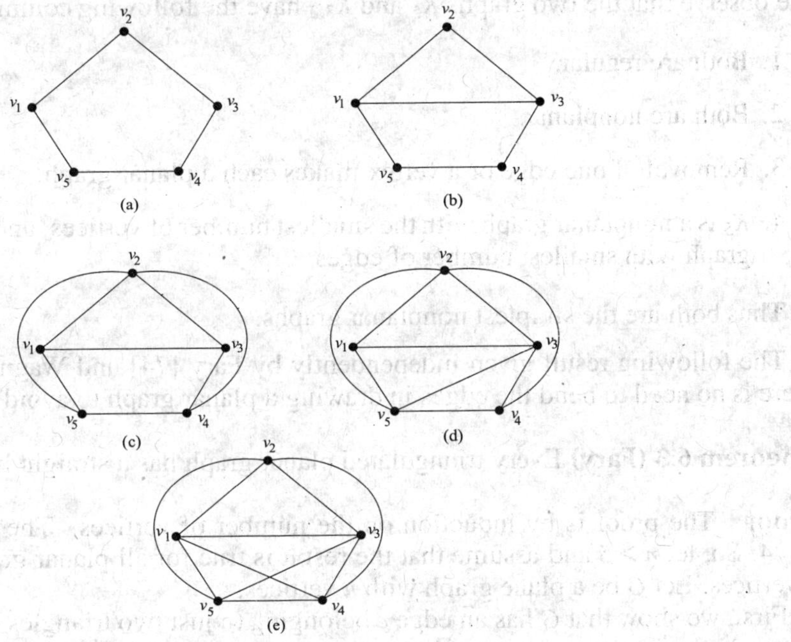

Fig. 6.3

Theorem 6.2 The complete bipartite graph $K_{3,3}$ is nonplanar.

Proof The complete bipartite graph has six vertices and nine edges. Let the vertices be u_1, u_2, u_3, v_1, v_2, v_3. We have edges from every u_i to each v_i, $1 \le i \le 3$. First we take the edges from u_1 to each v_1, v_2 and v_3. Then we take the edges between u_2 to each v_1, v_2 and v_3, Figure 6.4(a). Thus we get three regions namely I, II and III. Finally we have to draw the edges between u_3 to each v_1, v_2 and v_3. We can draw the edge between u_3 and v_3 inside the region II without any crossover, Figure 6.4(b). But the edges between u_3 and v_1, and u_3 and v_2 drawn in any region have a crossover with the previous edges. Thus the graph cannot be embedded in a plane. Hence $K_{3,3}$ is nonplanar. ❑

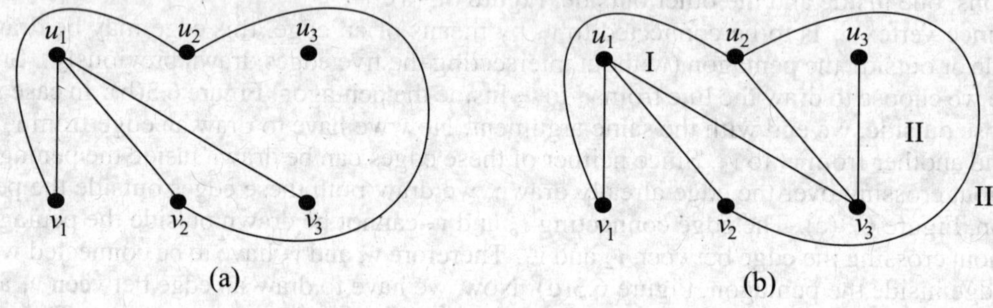

Fig. 6.4

We observe that the two graphs K_5 and $K_{3,3}$ have the following common properties.

1. Both are regular.
2. Both are nonplanar.
3. Removal of one edge or a vertex makes each a planar graph.
4. K_5 is a nonplanar graph with the smallest number of vertices, and $K_{3,3}$ is the nonplanar graph with smallest number of edges.

Thus both are the simplest nonplanar graphs.

The following result given independently by Fary [74] and Wagner [253] implies that there is no need to bend the edges in drawing a planar graph to avoid edge intersections.

Theorem 6.3 (Fary) Every triangulated planar graph has a straight line representation.

Proof The proof is by induction on the number of vertices. The result is obvious for $n = 4$. So, let $n \ge 5$ and assume that the result is true for all planar graphs with fewer than n vertices. Let G be a plane graph with n vertices.

First, we show that G has an edge e belonging to just two triangles. For this, let x be any vertex in the interior of a triangle T and choose x and T such that the number of regions inside T is minimal.

Let y be a neighbour of x, and the edge xy lies inside T, and let xy belong to three triangles xyz_1, xyz_2 and xyz_3. Then one of these triangles lies completely inside another. Assume that z_3 lies inside xyz_1. Then z_3 and xyz_1 contradict the choice of x and T (Fig. 6.5).

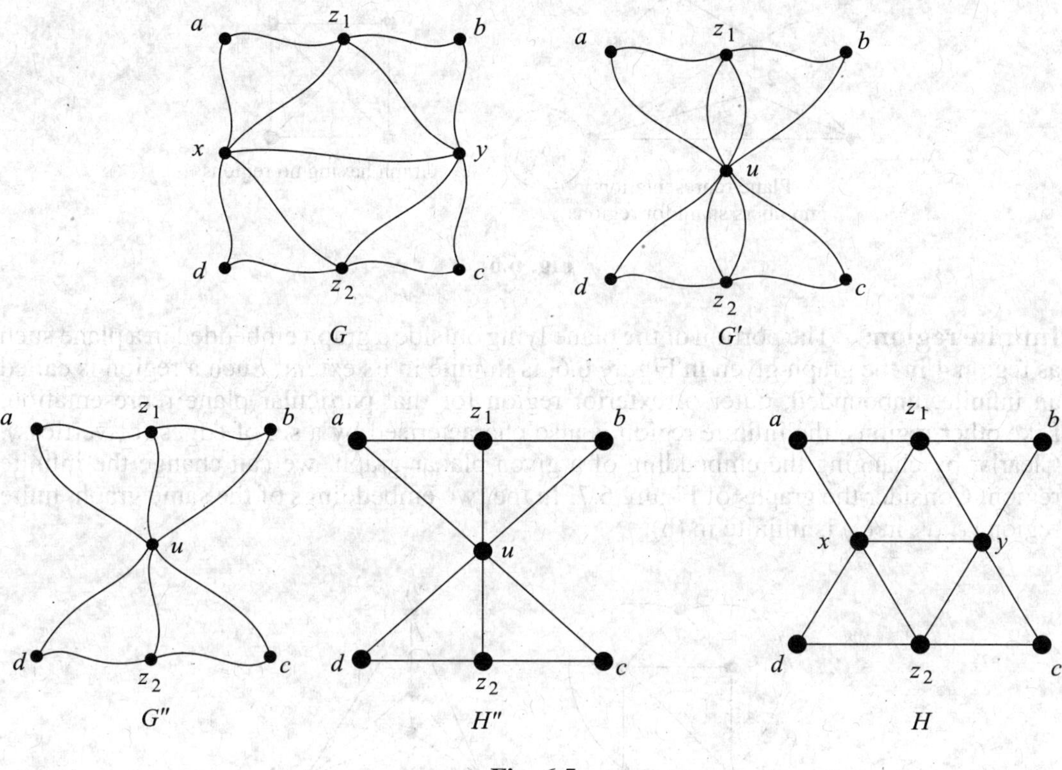

Fig. 6.5

Thus there is an edge $e = xy$ lying in just two triangles xyz_1 and xyz_2. Contracting xy to a vertex u, we get a new graph G' with a pair of double edges between u and z_1, and u and z_2. Remove one each of this pair of double edges to get a graph G'' which is a triangulated graph with $n-1$ vertices. By the induction hypothesis, it has a straight line representation H''. The edges of G'' correspond to uz_1, uz_2 in H''. Divide the angle around u into two parts in one of which the pre-images of the edges adjacent to x in G lie, and in the other, the pre-images of the edges adjacent to y in G. Thus u can be pulled apart to x and y, and the edge xy is restored by a straight line to get a straight line representation of G. ❑

6.2 Region

A plane representation of a graph divides the plane into regions (also called windows, faces or meshes). A region is characterised by the set of edges (or the set of vertices) forming its boundary. We note that a region is not defined in a nonplanar graph, or even in a planar graph not embedded in a plane. Thus a region is a property of the specific plane representation of a graph and not of an abstract graph.

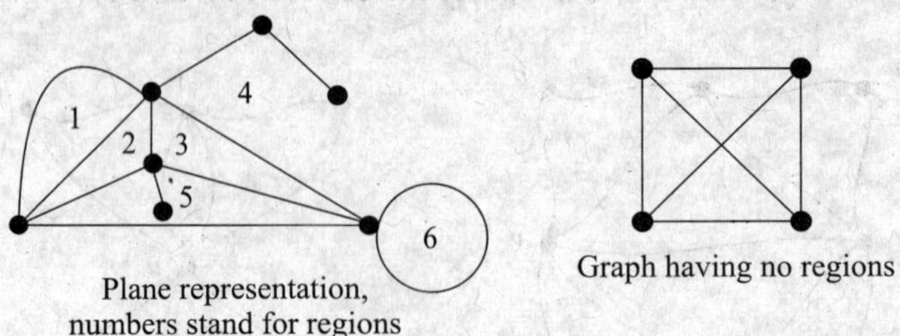

Fig. 6.6

Infinite region: The portion of the plane lying outside a graph embedded in a plane such as region 4 in the graph given in Figure 6.6, is infinite in its extent. Such a region is called an infinite, unbounded, outer or exterior region for that particular plane representation. Like other regions, the infinite region is also characterised by a set of edges (or vertices). Clearly, by changing the embedding of a given planar graph, we can change the infinite region. Consider the graphs of Figure 6.7. In the two embeddings of the same graph, finite region $v_1v_3v_5$ in (a) is infinite in (b).

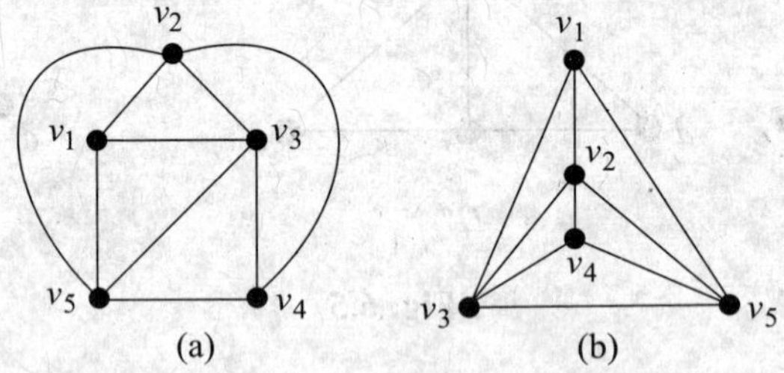

Fig. 6.7

Embedding on a sphere: A graph is spherical if it can be embedded on the surface of a sphere.

The following result implies that a planar graph can often be embedded on the surface of a sphere, so that there is no distinction between finite and infinite region.

Theorem 6.4 A graph can be embedded on the surface of a sphere if it can be embedded in a plane.

Proof Consider the stereographic projection of a sphere on the plane. Put the sphere on the plane and call the point of contact as *SP* (south-pole). At point *SP*, draw a straight line perpendicular to the plane, and let the point where this line intersects the surface of the sphere be called *NP* (north-pole).

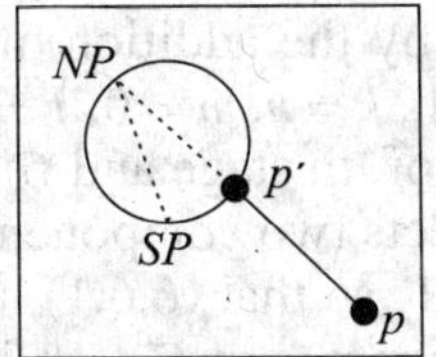

Fig. 6.8

Now, corresponding to any point p on the plane, there exists a unique point p' on the sphere, and vice versa, where p' is the point where the straight line from point p to point NP intersects the surface of the sphere. Thus there is a one-one correspondence between the points of the sphere and the finite points on the plane, and points at infinity in the plane corresponding to the point NP on the sphere.

Therefore from this construction, it is clear that any graph that can be embedded in a plane can also be embedded on the surface of the sphere, and vice versa. ❑

We now have the following result.

Theorem 6.5 A planar graph can be embedded in a plane such that any specified region, specified by the edges forming it, can be made the infinite region.

Proof A planar graph embedded on the surface of the sphere divides the surface of the sphere into different regions. Each region of the sphere is finite, the infinite region on the plane having been mapped onto the region containing the point NP. Clearly, by suitably rotating the sphere, we can make any specified region map onto the infinite region on the plane. Hence the result. ❑

Remark Thinking in terms of the regions on the sphere, we observe that there is no real difference between the infinite region and the finite regions on the plane. Therefore, when we discuss the regions in a plane representation of a graph, we include the infinite region. Also, since there is no essential difference between an embedding of a planar graph on a plane, or on a sphere (a plane can be regarded as the surface of the sphere of infinitely large radius), the term plane representation of a graph is often used to include spherical as well as plane embedding.

6.3 Euler's Theorem

The following important result due to Euler gives a relation between the number of vertices, edges, regions and the components of a planar graph.

Theorem 6.6 If G is a planar graph with n vertices, m edges, f regions and k components, then

$$n-m+f=k+1. \qquad (6.6.1)$$

Proof We construct the graph G by the addition of successive edges starting from the null graph $\overline{K_n}$. For this starting graph, $k = n$, $m = 0$, $f = 1$, so that (6.6.1) is true.

Let G_{i-1} be the graph at the start of ith stage and G_i be the graph obtained from G_{i-1} by addition of the ith edge e. If e connects two components of G_{i-1}, then f is not altered, m is increased by 1 and k is reduced by 1, so that (6.6.1) holds for G_i as it holds for G_{i-1}. If e joins two vertices of the same components of G_{i-1}, k is unaltered, m is increased by 1 and f is increased by 1, so that again (6.6.1) holds for G_i. ❑

The following relation between the number of vertices, edges and regions is the discovery of Euler [72] and is also called as Euler's formula for planar graphs.

Theorem 6.7 (Euler) In a connected planar graph with n vertices, m edges and f regions (faces), $n - m + f = 2$.

(The proof can also be deduced from Theorem 6.6 by taking $k = 1$, as the connected graph has one component.)

Proof Without loss of generality, assume that the planar graph is simple. Since any simple planar graph can have a plane representation such that each edge is a straight line, any planar graph can be drawn such that each region is a polygon (a polygon net). Let the polygon net representing the given graph consist of f regions. Let k_p be the number of p-sided regions. Since each edge is on the boundary of exactly two regions,

$$3k_3 + 4k_4 + 5k_5 + \ldots + rk_r = 2m, \tag{6.7.1}$$

where k_r is the number of polygons with r edges.

$$\text{Also, } k_3 + k_4 + k_5 + \ldots + k_r = f. \tag{6.7.2}$$

The sum of all angles subtended at each vertex in the polygon net is $2\pi n$. (6.7.3.)

Now, the sum of all interior angles of a p-sided polygon is $\pi(p-2)$ and the sum of the exterior angles is $\pi(p+2)$. The expression in (6.7.3) is the total sum of all interior angles of $f-1$ finite regions plus the sum of the exterior angles of the polygon defining the infinite region. This sum is

$$\pi(3-2)k_3 + \pi(4-2)k_4 + \ldots + \pi(r-2)k_r + 4\pi$$

$$= \pi[3k_3 + 4k_4 + \ldots + rk_r + 2(k_3 + k_4 + \ldots + k_r)] + 4\pi$$

$$= \pi(2m - 2f) + 4\pi = 2\pi(m - f + 2). \tag{6.7.4}$$

Equating (6.7.3) and (6.7.4) we get

$$2\pi(m - f + 2) = 2n\pi, \text{ so that } f = m - n - 2.$$ ❑

Definition: Let ϕ be a region of a planar graph G. We define the *degree* of ϕ, denoted by $d(\phi)$, as the number of edges on the boundary of ϕ.

Second proof of Theorem 6.7 We use induction on m, the number of edges. If $m = 0$, then G is K_1, a graph with 1 vertex and 1 region. So, $n - m + f = 1 - 0 + 1 = 2$, and the result is true. If $m = 1$, then the number of vertices in G is either one or two, the first possibility occurring when the edge is a loop. These two possibilities give rise respectively to two regions and one region.

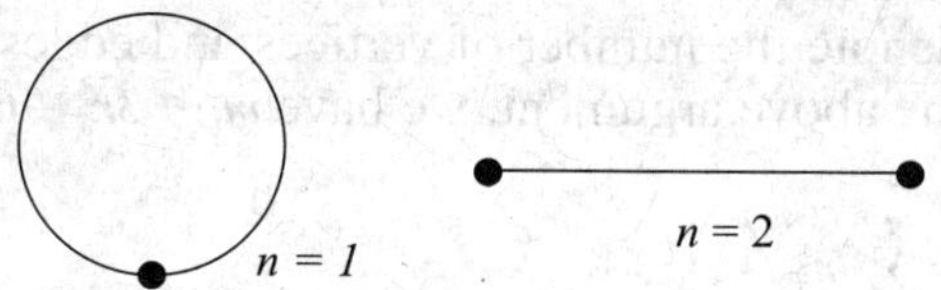

Fig. 6.9

Therefore, $n - m + f = \begin{cases} 1 - 1 + 2, & \textit{in the loop case}, \\ 2 - 1 + 1, & \textit{in the non loop case}. \end{cases}$

Thus, $n - m + f = 2$, and again the result is true.

Assume that the result is true for all connected planar graphs with fewer than m edges. Let G have m edges.

Case I Suppose G is a tree. Then $m = n - 1$ and $f = 1$, because a planar representation of a tree has only one region. Thus, $n - m + f = n - (n - 1) + 1 = 2$, and the result holds.

Case II Suppose G is not a tree. Then G has cycles. Let C be a cycle in G. Let e be an edge of C. The graph $G - e$ has one edge less than the graph G. Also the number of vertices in $G - e$ and G are same. Since removing e coalesces two regions in G into one in $G - e$, therefore $G - e$ has one region less than that in G. Thus by induction hypothesis in $G - e$, we have $n - (m - 1) + (f - 1) = 2$, so that $n - m + f = 2$. Hence the result. ❑

The next result gives an upper bound for the edges of a simple planar graph.

Theorem 6.8 Let G be a simple planar graph with n vertices and m edges, where $n \geq 3$. Then $m \leq 3n - 6$.

Proof First assume that the planar graph G is connected. If $n = 3$, then since G is simple, therefore G has at most three edges. Thus $m \leq 3$, that is, $m \leq 3 \times 3 - 6$, and the result is true.

Now, let $n \geq 4$. First let G be a tree so that $m = n - 1$. Since $n \geq 4$, obviously we have $n - 1 \leq 3n - 6$.

Now, let G be not a tree. Then G has cycles. Clearly, there is a cycle in G, all of whose edges lie on the boundary of the exterior region of G. Then, since G is simple, we have $d(\phi) \geq 3$, for each region ϕ of G.

Let $b = \sum_{\phi \in F} d(\phi)$, where F denotes the set of all regions of G.

Since each region has at least three edges on its boundary, therefore we have $b \geq 3f$, where f is the number of regions of G. However, when we sum to get b, each edge of G is counted either once or twice (twice when it occurs as a boundary edge for two regions). Therefore, $b \leq 2m$ so that $3f \leq b \leq 2m$. In particular, we have $3f \leq 2m$.

Using Euler's formula $n - m + f = 2$, we get $m \leq 3n - 6$.

Let G be not connected and let $G_1, G_2, \ldots, G_t$ be its connected components. For each i, $1 \leq i \leq t$, let n_i and m_i denote the number of vertices and edges in G_i. Since each G_i is a planar simple graph, by the above argument, we have $m_i \leq 3n_i - 6$, for each i, $1 \leq i \leq t$.

Also, $n = \sum_{i=1}^{t} n_i$ and $m = \sum_{i=1}^{t} m_i$.

Hence, $m = \sum_{i=1}^{t} m_i \leq \sum_{i=1}^{t} (3n_i - 6) = 3\sum_{i=1}^{t} n_i - 6t \leq 3n - 6$. ❑

The following result gives the existence of a vertex of degree less than six in a simple planar graph.

Theorem 6.9 If G is a simple planar graph, then G has a vertex v of degree less than 6.

Proof The result is obviously true for $n \leq 6$.

Let $n > 6$. Assume degree of every vertex in G is at least six.

Then, $\sum_{v \in V(G)} d(v) \geq 6n$.

We know $\sum_{v \in V(G)} d(v) = 2m$.

Thus, $2m \geq 6n$ so that $m \geq 3n$.

This is not possible because, by Theorem 6.8, we have $m \leq 3n - 6$. Thus we get a contradiction. Hence G has at least one vertex of degree less than 6. ❑

Corollary 6.1 K_5 is nonplanar.

Proof Here $n = 5$ and $m = 10$. So, $3n - 6 = 15 - 6 = 9$. Thus $m > 3n - 6$. Therefore K_5 is nonplanar.

Corollary 6.2 $K_{3,3}$ is nonplanar.

Proof Since $K_{3,3}$ is bipartite, it contains no odd cycles, and so no cycle of length three. It follows that every region of a plane drawing of $K_{3,3}$ if it exists, has at least four boundary edges. We have $d(\phi) \geq 4$, for each region ϕ of G.

Let $b = \sum_{\phi \in F} d(\phi)$, where F denotes the set of all regions of G. Since each region has at least four edges on its boundary, we have $b \geq 4f$, where f is the number of regions of G.

Now, when we sum up to get b, each edge of G is counted either once or twice, and so $b \leq 2m$. Thus, $4f \leq b \leq 2m$, so that $2f \leq m$.

For $K_{3,3}$, we have $m = 9$, and so $2f \leq 9$ giving $f \leq \frac{9}{2}$. But by Euler's formula, $f = m - n + 2 = 9 - 6 + 2 = 5$, a contradiction. Hence $K_{3,3}$ is nonplanar. ❑

Euler's formula gives a necessary condition for connected planar graphs.

Theorem 6.10 For a connected simple planar graph with n vertices and m edges, and girth g, we have $m \leq \frac{g(n-2)}{g-2}$.

Proof Let G be a connected simple planar graph with n vertices, m edges and girth g. Let F be the set of regions and $d(\phi)$ be the degree of the region ϕ. Then $\sum_{\phi \in F} d(\phi) = 2m$. Let f be the number of regions, that is $|F| = f$. As g is the length of the smallest cycle in G, therefore g is the smallest degree of a region. So, $\sum_{\phi \in F} d(\phi) \geq gf$. Thus, $2m \geq gf$. Now, using Euler's formula, $f = m - n + 2$, we have $2m \geq g(m - n + 2)$, so that $m \leq \frac{g(n-2)}{g-2}$.

Corollary 6.3 The Peterson graph P is nonplanar.

Proof The girth of the Peterson graph P is 5, $n(P) = 10$, and $m(P) = 15$. Thus, if P were planar, $15 = 5\left(\frac{10-2}{5-2}\right)$, which is not true. Hence P is nonplanar. ❑

Corollary 6.4 Any graph containing a homeomorph of a K_5 or $K_{3,3}$ is nonplanar. This follows from the fact that any homeomorph of a nonplanar graph is nonplanar.

The following result characterises nonplanar 3-connected graphs with minimum edges.

Theorem 6.11 A nonplanar connected graph G with minimum number of edges that contains no subdivision of K_5 or $K_{3,3}$ is simple and 3-connected.

Proof Since G has minimum number of edges, G is minimal with respect to these properties. The minimality of G ensures that it is simple. Also, a graph is planar if and only if each of its blocks is planar. This implies that a minimal nonplanar graph is a block.

Suppose such a graph has a two vertex cut $S = \{u, v\}$. Then $G - S$ is disconnected. Let G_1 be one of its components and G_2 be the union of all of its other components.

Let $H_1 = \langle V(G_1) \cup S \rangle + e$ and $H_2 = \langle V(G_2) \cup S \rangle + e$, where $e = uv$.

Clearly, these are nonempty graphs with fewer edges than G. Since G is nonplanar, at least one of H_1 and H_2 is nonplanar. If both are planar, let $\tilde{H}_1$ be a plane embedding of H_1 and let ϕ be a region of $\tilde{H}_1$ containing the edge e.

A plane embedding $\tilde{H}_2$ of H_2 inside ϕ can then be obtained with the edge e of both $\tilde{H}_1$ and $\tilde{H}_2$ coinciding. Then $\tilde{H}_1 \cup \tilde{H}_2 - e$ is a plane embedding of G, contradicting our hypothesis.

Suppose H_1 is nonplanar. Since $m(H_1) < m(G)$, therefore H_1 contains a subdivision K of either K_5 or $K_{3,3}$ according to the hypothesis. Clearly $e \in E$, since otherwise $K \subset G$, contradicting the assumption. Now, replacing e of K by a $u-v$ path in H_2, we get a homeomorph of K contained in G. This is again a contradiction and shows that G has no 2-vertex cut. Hence G is 3-connected. ❑

The following result is used in proving Kuratowski's theorem.

Theorem 6.12

a. If $G|e$ contains a subdivision of K_5, then G contains a subdivision of K_5 or $K_{3,3}$.

b. If $G|e$ contains a subdivision of $K_{3,3}$, then G contains a subdivision of $K_{3,3}$.

Proof Let $G' = G|e$ be a graph obtained by contracting the edge $e = xy$ of G. Let w be the vertex of G' obtained by contracting $e = xy$.

a. Let $G|e$ contains a subdivision of K_5, say H. If w is not a branch vertex of H, then G also contains a subdivision of K_5, obtained by expanding w back into the edge xy, if necessary (Fig. 6.10).

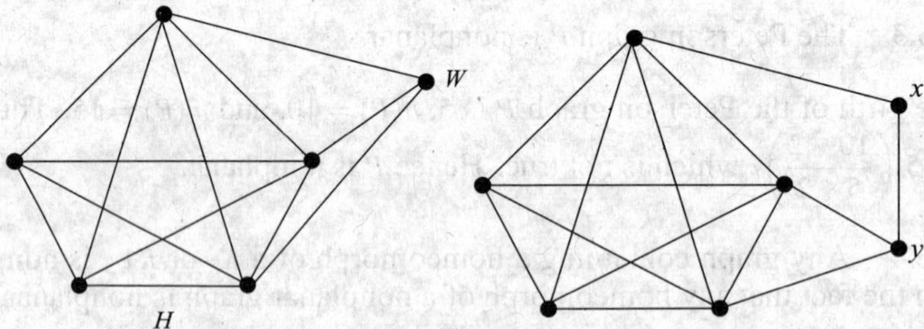

Fig. 6.10

Assume w is a branch vertex of H and each of x, y is incident in G to two of the four edges incident to w in H. Let u_1 and u_2 be the branch vertices of H that are at the other ends of the paths leaving w on edges incident to x in G. Let v_1, v_2 be the branch vertices of H that are at the other ends of the paths leaving w on edges incident to y in G (Fig. 6.11).

By deleting the $u_1 - u_2$ path and $v_1 - v_2$ path from H, we obtain a subdivision of $K_{3,3}$ in G, in which y, u_1, u_2 are branch vertices for one partite set, and x, v_1, v_2 are branch vertices of the other.

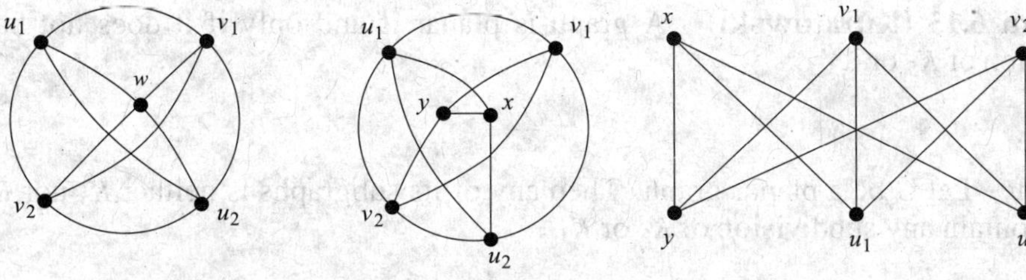

Fig. 6.11

b. Let $G|e$ contain a subdivision of $K_{3,3}$, say H. If w is not a branch vertex of H, then G also contains a subdivision of $K_{3,3}$, obtained by expanding w back into the edge xy, if necessary (Fig. 6.12).

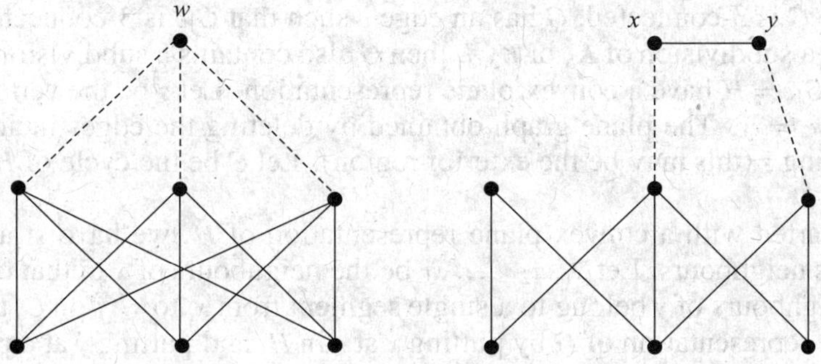

Fig. 6.12

Now, assume that w is a branch vertex in H and at most one of the edges incident to w in H is incident to x in G. Then w can be expanded into xy to lengthen that path and y becomes the corresponding branch vertex of $K_{3,3}$ in G (Fig. 6.13). ❑

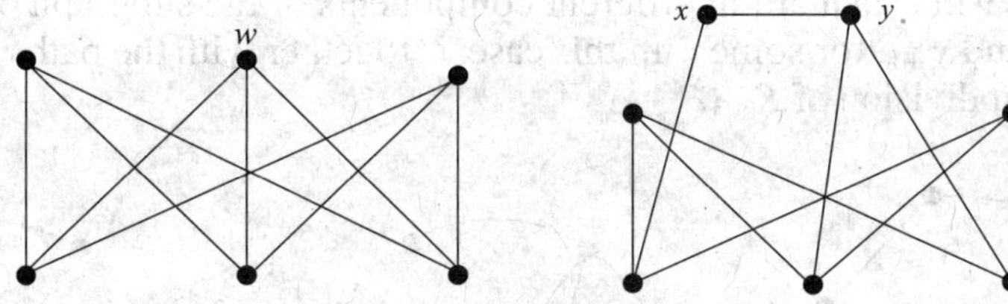

Fig. 6.13

6.4 Kuratowski's Theorem

This theorem was independently given by Kuratowski [140] and Frink and Smith. In 1954, Dirac and Schuster [66] found a proof that was slightly shorter than the original proof. The proof given here is due to Thomassen [234].

Theorem 6.13 (Kuratowski) A graph is planar if and only if it does not have any subdivision of K_5 or $K_{3,3}$.

Proof

Necessity Let G be a planar graph. Then any of its subgraphs is neither K_5 nor $K_{3,3}$ nor does it contain any subdivision of K_5 or $K_{3,3}$.

Sufficiency It is enough to prove sufficiency for 3-connected graphs. Let G be a 3-connected graph with n vertices. We prove that the 3-connected graph G either contains a subdivision of K_5 or $K_{3,3}$ or has a convex plane representation. This we prove by using induction on n. Since G is 3-connected, therefore $n \geq 4$. For $n = 4$, $G = K_4$ and clearly has a plane representation.

Now, let $n \geq 5$. Assume the result to be true for all 3-connected graphs with fewer than n vertices. Since G is 3-connected, G has an edge e such that $G|e$ is 3-connected. Let $e = xy$. If $G|e$ contains a subdivision of K_5 or $K_{3,3}$, then G also contains a subdivision of K_5 or $K_{3,3}$. Therefore, let $G|e = H$ have a convex plane representation. Let z be the vertex obtained by contraction of $e = xy$. The plane graph obtained by deleting the edges incident to z has a region containing z (this may be the exterior region). Let C be the cycle of $H - z$ bounding this region.

Since we started with a convex plane representation of H, we have straight segments from z to all its neighbours. Let $x_1, x_2, \ldots, x_k$ be the neighbours of x in that order on C.

If all the neighbours of y belong to a single segment from x_i to x_{i+1} on C, then we obtain a convex plane representation of G by putting x at z in H, and putting y at a point close to z in the wedge formed by $x\,x_i$ and $x\,x_{i+1}$.

If all the neighbours of y do not belong to any single segment $x_i\,x_{i+1}$ on C $(1 \leq i \leq k$, $x_{k+1} = x_1)$, then we have the following cases (Fig. 6.14).

a. y shares three neighbours with x. In this case C together with these six edges involving x and y form a subdivision of K_5.

b. y has two u, v in C that are in different components of the subgraph of C obtained by deleting x_i and x_{i+1}, for some i. In this case, C together with the paths uyv, $x_i\,xx_{i+1}$ and xy form a subdivision of $K_{3,3}$. ❑

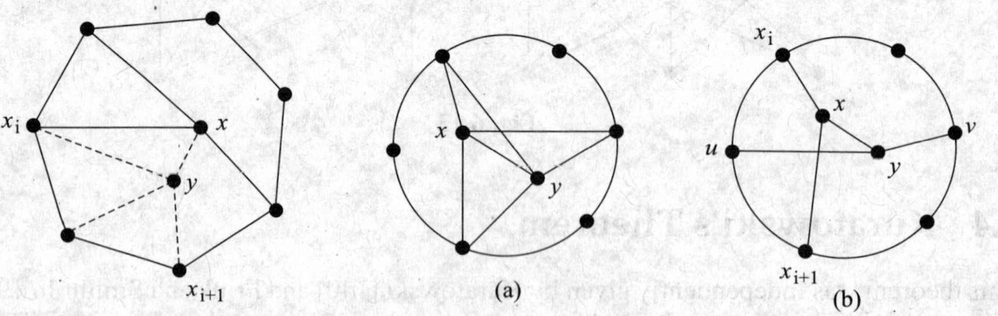

Fig. 6.14

6.5 Geometric Dual

Let G be a plane graph. The dual of G is defined to be the graph G^* constructed as follows. To each region f of G there is a corresponding vertex f^* of G^* and to each edge e of G there is corresponding edge e^* in G^* such that if the edge e occurs on the boundary of the two regions f and g, then the edge e^* joins the corresponding vertices f^* and g^* in G^*. If the edge e is a bridge, i.e., the edge e lies entirely in one region f, then the corresponding edge e^* is a loop incident with the vertex f^* in G^*. For example, consider the graph shown in Figure 6.15.

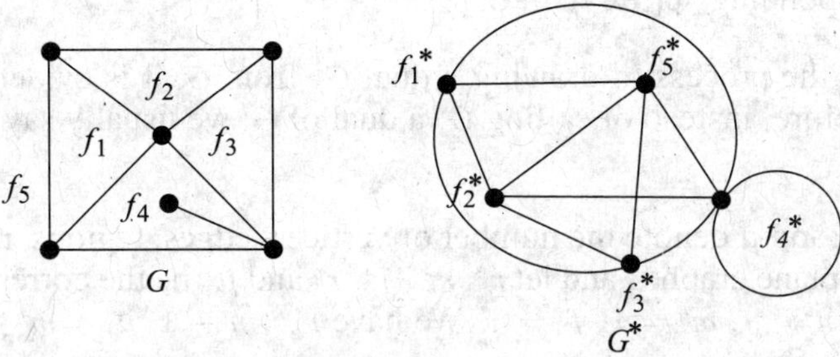

Fig. 6.15

Theorem 6.14 The dual G^* of a plane graph is planar.

Proof Let G be a plane graph and let G^* be the dual of G. The following construction of G^* shows that G^* is planar.

Place each vertex f_i^* of G^* inside its corresponding region f_i. If the edge e_i lies on the boundary of two regions f_j and f_k of G, join the two vertices f_j^* and f_k^* by the edge e_i^*, drawing so that it crosses the edge e exactly once and crosses no other edge of G (Fig. 6.16). ❑

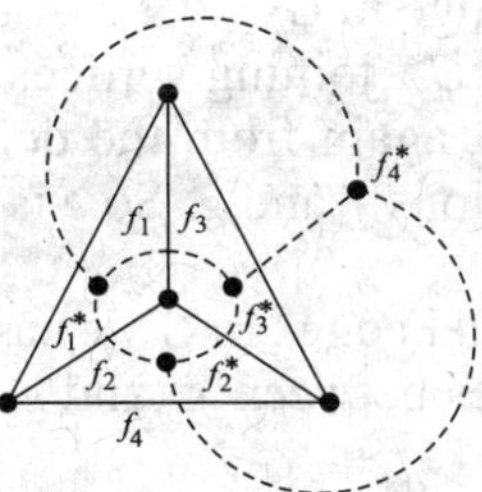

Fig. 6.16

Remarks Clearly, there is one-one correspondence between the edges of plane graph G and its dual G^* with one edge of G^* intersecting one edge of G.

1. An edge forming a self-loop in G gives a pendant edge in G^* (An edge incident on a pendant vertex is called a pendant edge).

2. A pendant edge in G gives a self loop in G^*.

3. Edges that are in series in G produce parallel edges in G^*.

4. Parallel edges in G produce edges in series in G^*.

5. The number of edges forming the boundary of a region f_i in G is equal to the degree of the corresponding vertex f_i^* in G^*.

6. Considering the process of drawing a dual G^* from G, it is evident that G is a dual of G^*. Therefore, instead of calling G^* a dual of G, we usually say that G and G^* are dual graphs.

7. Let n, m, f, r and μ denote the number of vertices, edges, regions, rank and nullity of a connected plane graph G and let n^*, m^*, f^*, r^* and μ^* be the corresponding numbers in G^*. Then $n^* = f$, $m^* = m$, $f^* = n$. We have $r^* = n^* - 1$, $\mu^* = m^* - n^* + 1$, $r = n - 1$, $\mu = m - n + 1$. So, $r^* = f - 1$, $\mu^* = m - f + 1$, $r = n - 1$, $\mu = m - n + 1$.

Using Euler's formula, $n - m + f = 2$ or $f = m - n + 2$, we have $r^* = m - n - 2 - 1 = m - n + 1 = \mu$ and $\mu^* = m - f + 1 = n + f - 2 - f + 1 = n - 1 = r$.

We now have the following result.

Theorem 6.15 The edge e is a loop in G if and only if e^* is a bridge in G^*.

Proof Let the edge e be a loop in a plane graph G. Then it is the edge on the common boundary of two regions on which, say f, lies within the area of the plane surrounded by e with the other, say g, lying outside the area. Thus, from definition of G^*, e^* is the only path from f^* to g^* in G^*. Thus $e^*$is a bridge in G^*.

Conversely, let e^* be a bridge in G^*, joining vertices f^* and g^*. Thus e^* is the only path in G^* from f^* to g^*. This implies, again from the definition of G^*, that the edge e in G completely encloses one of the regions f and g. So e is a loop in G. ❑

Remark The occurrence of parallel edges in G^* is easily described. Given two regions f and g of G, there are k parallel edges between f^* and g^* if and only if f and g have k edges on their common boundary.

Note We have defined the dual of a plane graph instead of a planar graph. The reason for this is that different plane drawings G_1 and G_2 of the same planar graph G may result in non-isomorphic duals G_1^* and G_2^*.

2-isomorphism Two graphs $G(V, E)$and $H(W, F)$ are said to be 2-isomorphic if there exists a bijection $\phi: E \to F$ such that both ϕ and ϕ^{-1} preserve cycles.

Two graphs G and H are said to be 2-isomorphic if there exists a one-onc correspondence between their edge sets such that the edges of a cycle in G correspond to the edges of a cycle in G_2 and vice versa.

Example Figure 6.17(a) shows 2-isomorphic graphs.

1-isomorphism Graphs which become isomorphic after the splitting of all of their cut vertices are said to be 1-isomorphic.

Example Figure 6.17(b) shows 1-isomorphic graphs.

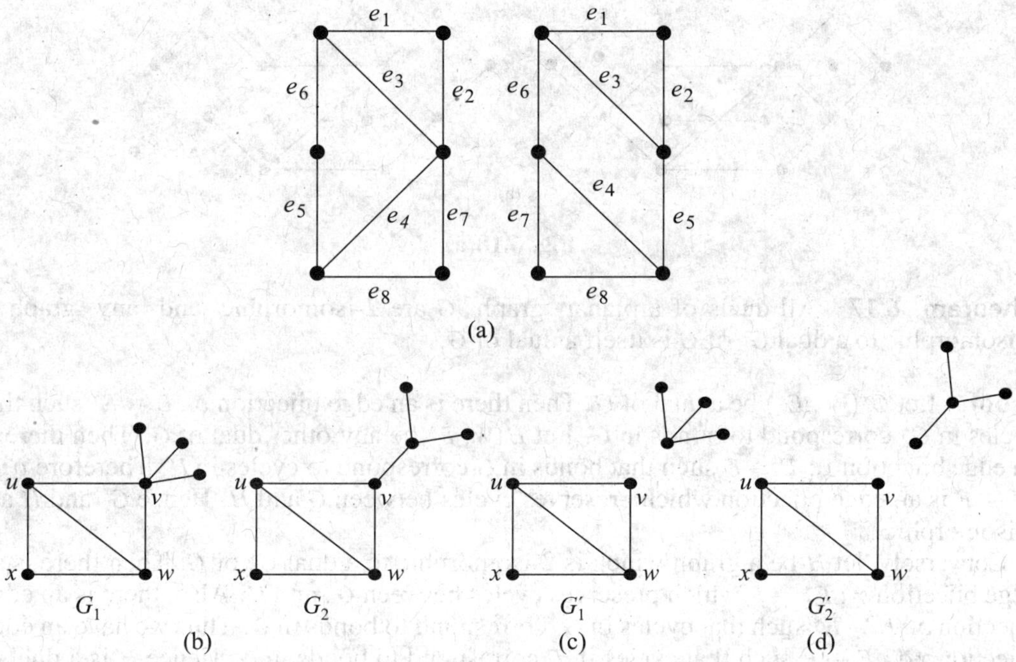

Fig. 6.17

Consider the two non-isomorphic graphs G_1 and G_2 shown in Fig. 6.17(a) and (b). They both have a single cut vertex, namely v. If this cut vertex is split into two vertices in each of G_1 and G_2, we obtain the edge disjoint graphs G_1' and G_2' as shown in (c) and (d). Clearly, G_1' and G_2' are isomorphic. Thus G_1 and G_2 are 1-isomorphic.

The next result gives a correspondence between the edges of a graph with the edges of its dual.

Theorem 6.16 Edges in a plane graph G form a cycle in G if and only if the corresponding dual edges form a bond in G^*.

Proof Let $D \subseteq E(G)$. It is sufficient to prove that D contains a cycle if and only if the set D^* of dual edges contains a bond of G^*. Now, let D contain a cycle C. Then by the Jordan Curve theorem, some region of G lies inside C and some region lies outside C. These regions correspond to vertices v^*, w^* in G^*, one drawn inside C and one outside C. A $v^* - w^*$ path in G^* crosses C and hence uses an edge of G^*, that is dual to an edge of C. Thus D^* disconnects v^* from w^* and hence D^* contains a bond (Fig. 6.18(a)).

Conversely, let D^* contain a bond. We show that D contains a cycle. Assume that D does not contain a cycle. Then D encloses no region. It remains possible to reach each region of G from every other without crossing D. Hence $G^* - D^*$ is connected, and so D^* contains no bond. This is a contradiction. Hence D contains a cycle. ❑

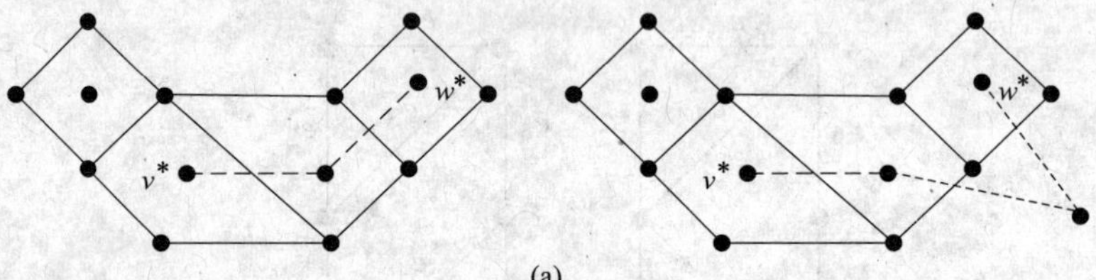

Fig. 6.18(a)

Theorem 6.17 All duals of a planar graph G are 2-isomorphic and any graph H 2-isomorphic to a dual G^* of G is itself a dual of G.

Proof Let $G^*(V^*, E^*)$ be a dual of G. Then there is an edge bijection $\phi : E \to E^*$ such that cycles in G^* correspond to bonds in G. Let $H(W, F)$ be any other dual of G. Then there is an edge bijection ψ: $E \to F$ such that bonds in G correspond to cycles in H. Therefore $\phi\psi$: $E^* \to F$ is an edge bijection which preserves cycles between G and H. Hence G^* and H are 2-isomorphic.

Conversely, let H be a graph which is 2-isomorphic to a dual G^* of G. Then there is an edge bijection $\chi : E^* \to F$ which preserves cycles between G^* and H. Also, there is an edge bijection $\phi : E \to E^*$ such that cycles in G^* correspond to bonds in G. Thus we have an edge bijection $\chi\phi : F \to E$ such that cycles in F correspond to bonds in G. Hence H is a dual of G. ❑

The following result provides the condition for two given graphs to be duals of each other.

Theorem 6.18 A necessary and sufficient condition for two planar graphs G_1 and G_2 to be the duals of each other is that there should be a one-one correspondence of the edges in G_1 with the edges in G_2 such that the subset of edges in G_1 forms a cycle if and only if the corresponding set of edges in G_2 forms a bond.

Proof

Necessity Consider a plane representation of a planar graph G_1 and let G_1^* be the dual of G_1. Let C be an arbitrary cycle in G_1.

Clearly, C will form some closed simple curve in the plane representation of G_1, dividing the plane into two areas. Thus the vertices of G_1^* are partitioned into two non-empty, mutually exclusive subsets, one inside C and the other outside. In other words, the set of edges C^* in G_1^* corresponding to the set C in G_1 is a bond in G_1^*.

Similarly, corresponding to a bond S^* in G_1^*, there is a unique cycle consisting of the corresponding edge set S in G_1 such that S is a cycle.

Sufficiency Let G be a planar graph, and let G' be a graph for which there is a one-one correspondence between the bonds of G and the cycles of G' and vice versa. Let G^* be the dual graph of G. Therefore there is a one-one correspondence between the bonds of G and cycles of G^*. So there is a one-one correspondence between the cycles of G' and G^*. Thus G' and G^* are 2-isomorphic. Hence G' is the dual of G. ❑

Let G be a plane graph and G^* be the dual of G. So to every vertex of G we have a region of G^*. Let the region ϕ of the plane graph G^* corresponding to the vertex v of G has $e_1^*, e_2^*, \ldots, e_k^*$ as its boundary edges. Then each of these edges e_i^* crosses the corresponding edge e_i of G, and these edges are all incident at the vertex v. It follows that ϕ contains the vertex v. As G^* is a plane graph, we can construct the dual of G^*, called the double dual of G and is denoted by G^{**}.

We now have the following observation.

Theorem 6.19 Let G be a plane connected graph. Then G is isomorphic to its double dual G^{**}.

Proof Let G be a plane connected graph and G^* be the dual of G. Now, any region ϕ of dual G^* contains exactly one vertex of G, namely its corresponding vertex v of G. This is because the number of the regions of G^* is same as the number of vertices of G.

Thus in the construction of G^{**}, we take the vertex v to be the vertex in G^{**} corresponding to the region ϕ of G^*. This choice gives the required isomorphism. ❑

Definition: A connected graph G is called *self-dual* if it is isomorphic to its dual G^*. For example, K_4 is self-dual.

The next result is a characterisation of bipartite graphs in terms of duality.

Theorem 6.20 A connected plane graph G is bipartite if and only if its dual graph G^* is Eulerian.

Proof Let G be a bipartite graph. Then G does not contain odd cycles. Since G is a plane, all the regions of G are of even length. So degree of every region in G is even. Let G^* be the dual graph of G. Since the vertex degrees of G^* are same as the corresponding degrees of the regions of G, degree of every vertex in G^* is even. Hence G^* is Eulerian.

Conversely, assume G^* is Eulerian. Then degree of every vertex in G^* is even. Since the degree of a vertex in G^* corresponds to the degree of the region in G, degree of every region in G is even. This shows that G contains only even cycles. Hence G is bipartite. ❑

Dual of a subgraph: Let G be a plane graph and let G^* be its dual. Let e be an edge in G and let e^* be the corresponding edge in G^*. We delete the edge e and find dual of $G-e$. If edge e is on the boundary of two regions, then removal of e merges these two regions into one.

Thus the dual $(G-e)^*$ is obtained from G^* by deleting the corresponding edge e^* and then fusing the two end vertices of e^* in G^*-e^*. On the other hand, if edge e is not on the boundary, then e^* forms a self-loop. In that case, G^*-e^* is the same as $(G-e)^*$.

Thus, if a graph G has a dual G^*, then the dual of any subgraph of G can be obtained by successive application of this procedure.

Dual of a homeomorphic graph: Let G be a plane graph and G^* be its dual. Let e be an edge in G and let e^* be the corresponding edge in G^*. We create an additional vertex in G by introducing a vertex of degree two in edge e (e now becomes two edges in series). This simply adds an edge parallel to e^* in G^*. Likewise, the reverse process of merging two edges in series will simply eliminate one of the corresponding parallel edges in G^*. Thus, by this procedure, if the graph G has dual G^*, the dual of any graph homeomorphic to G can be obtained from G^*. These are illustrated in Figure 6.18(b).

The following important result is due to Whitney [260].

Theorem 6.21 (Whitney) A graph has a dual if and only if it is planar.

Proof We have only to prove that a nonplanar graph does not have a dual. Let G be a nonplanar graph. Then according to Kuratowski's theorem, G contains K_5 or $K_{3,3}$, or a sub-division of K_5 or $K_{3,3}$.

We know that a graph G has a dual only if every subgraph H of G and every subdivision of G has a dual. Thus to prove the result, we show that neither K_5 nor $K_{3,3}$ has a dual.

a. Suppose that $K_{3,3}$ has a dual D. Then the bonds in $K_{3,3}$ correspond to cycles in D and vice-versa. Since $K_{3,3}$ has no bond consisting of two edges, D has no cycle consisting of two edges. That is, D contains no pair of parallel edges. Since every cycle in $K_{3,3}$ is of length four or six, D has no bond with less than four edges. Therefore the degree of every vertex in D is at least four. As D has no parallel edges and the degree of every vertex is at least four, D has at least five vertices each of degree four or more (≥ 4). That is, D has at least $\frac{5\times4}{2}=10$ edges. This is a contradiction to the fact that $K_{3,3}$ has nine edges. Hence $K_{3,3}$ has no dual.

b. Suppose K_5 has a dual H. We note that K_5 has

   i. 10 edges,
   ii. no pair of parallel edges,
   iii. no bond with two edges, and
   iv. bonds with only four or six edges.

   Therefore graph H has

   i. 10 edges,

ii. no vertex with degree less than three,

iii. no bond with two edges, and

iv. cycles of length four or six only.

Now graph H contains a hexagon (a cycle of length six) and no more than three edges can be added to a hexagon without creating a cycle of length three, or a pair of parallel edges. Since both of these are not present in H, and H has 10 edges, there must be at least seven vertices in H. The degree of each of these vertices is at least three. This implies that H has at least 11 edges, which is a contradiction. Hence K_5 has no dual. ❑

Definition: Two plane graphs G and G^* are said to be *duals* (or combinatorial duals) of each other if there is a one-one correspondence between the edges of G and G^* such that if H is any subgraph of G, and H^* is the corresponding subgraphs of G^*, then rank $(G^* - H^*) =$ rank $G^* -$ nullity H.

6.6 Polyhedron

A polyhedron is a solid bounded by surfaces, called *faces*, each of which is a plane. That is, a solid bounded by plane surfaces is called a polyhedron. For example, brick, window frame, tetrahedron.

A polyhedron is said to be *convex* if any two of its interior points can be joined by a straight line lying entirely within the interior. For example, a brick is convex, but a window frame is not convex.

The vertices and edges of a polyhedron, which form a skeleton of the solid, give a simple graph in three dimensional space. It can be shown that for a convex polyhedron this graph is planar.

To see this, imagine the faces of the convex polyhedron to be made of rubber, with one face, say at the base, missing. Then taking hold of the edges at the missing face, we are able to stretch out the rubber to form one plane sheet. The vertices and edges in this transformation now form a plane graph. Moreover, each face of this plane graph corresponds to a face of a solid, with the exterior face of the graph corresponding to the missing face we used in stretching process.

Clearly, the plane graph is also connected, the degree of every vertex is at least 3 and the degree of every face is also at least 3. Also, the graph is simple.

A simple connected plane graph G is called *polyhedral* if $d(v) \geq 3$, for each vertex v of G, and $d(\phi) \geq 3$, for every face ϕ of G.

The following is a simple but useful property of polyhedral graphs.

Theorem 6.22 Let P be a convex polyhedron and G be its polyhedral graph. For each $n \geq 3$, let n_i denote the number of vertices of G of degree i and let f_i denote the number of faces of G of degree i. Then

a. $\sum\limits_{i \geq 3} in_i = \sum\limits_{i \geq 3} if_i = 2m$, where m is the number of edges of G.

b. The polyhedron P, and so the graph G, has at least one face bounded by a cycle of length n for either $n = 3$, 4 or 5.

Proof

a. The expression $\sum_{i\geq 3} in_i$ is simply $\sum_{v\in V(G)} d(v)$, since $d(v) \geq 3$ for each vertex v.

We know, $\sum_{v\in V(G)} d(v) = 2m$, so that $\sum_{i\geq 3} in_i = 2m$.

For each $n \geq 3$, the expression if_i is obtained by going round the boundary of each face having a cycle of length i as its boundary, counting up the edges as we go. If we do this over all possible i, then we count each edge twice, and so $\sum_{i\geq 3} if_i = 2m$.

b. Assume to the contrary that P has no faces bounded by cycles of length 3, 4 or 5. Then $f_3 = f_4 = f_5 = 0$.

So by (a), $2m = \sum_{i\geq 6} if_i \geq \sum_{i\geq 6} 6f_i = 6\sum_{i\geq 6} f_i = 6f$, where f is the total number of faces of P. Thus, $f \leq \frac{1}{3}m$.

Also by (a), $2m = \sum_{i\geq 3} in_i \geq \sum_{i\geq 3} 3n_i = 3\sum_{i\geq 3} n_i = 3n$, where n is the total number of vertices of P. Thus, $n \leq \frac{2}{3}m$.

Now, by Euler's formula, $m = n + f - 2$ and we have

$$m \leq \frac{2}{3}m + \frac{1}{3}m - 2 = m - 2, \text{ and this implies that } 2 \leq 0,$$

which is impossible. Hence P must have a face of length 3, 4 or 5. ❑

Regular polyhedra: A polyhedron is called regular if it is convex and its faces are congruent regular polygons (so that the polyhedral angles are all equal). The regular polyhedra are also called Platonic bodies or Platonic solids.

A fact that has been known for at least 2000 years is that there are only five regular polyhedra, which is proved next by using graph theoretic argument.

Theorem 6.23 The only regular polyhedra are the tetrahedron, the cube, the octahedron, the dodecahedron and the icosahedron.

Proof Let P be a regular polyhedron and let G be its corresponding polyhedral graph. Let n, m and f denote the number of vertices, edges and faces of G. Since the faces of G are congruent to each other, each one is bounded by the same number of edges. Thus, $d(\phi) = k, k \geq 3$ for each face ϕ of G. Also, we know that there is at least one cycle of length 3, 4 or 5, therefore, $3 \leq k \leq 5$. Similarly, since the polyhedral angles are all equal to each other, the graph G is regular, say r-regular, where $r \geq 3$. Thus we have

$rn = 2m$ and $kf = 2m$, so that

$$2m = rn = kf. \tag{6.23.1}$$

Using this in Euler's formula $n - m + f = 2$, we have

$$8 = 4n - 4m + 4f = 4n - 2m + 4f - 2m = 4n - rn + 4f - kf.$$

Therefore, $8 = (4 - r)n + (4 - k)f$. (6.23.2)

Since n and f are both positive and also $3 \leq k \leq 5$ and $r \geq 3$, there are only five possible cases (Fig. 6.19).

Case 1 Let $r = 3$ and $k = 3$. Then $8 = (4 - 3)n + (4 - 3)f$, so that $8 = n + f$.

From (6.23.1.), $n = f$. So, $n + f = 8$ gives $n = 4$, $f = 4$.

Thus, $n = 4$, $m = 6$, $f = 4$, which is a tetrahedron.

Case 2 Let $r = 3$, $k = 4$. Then from (6.23.2), $8 = (4 - 3)n + (4 - 4)f$.

So, $n = 8$. Then, (6.23.1) gives $3n = 4f$, so that $f = 6$. Also, $m = 12$.

So, $n = 8$, $m = 12$, $f = 6$, and thus is a cube.

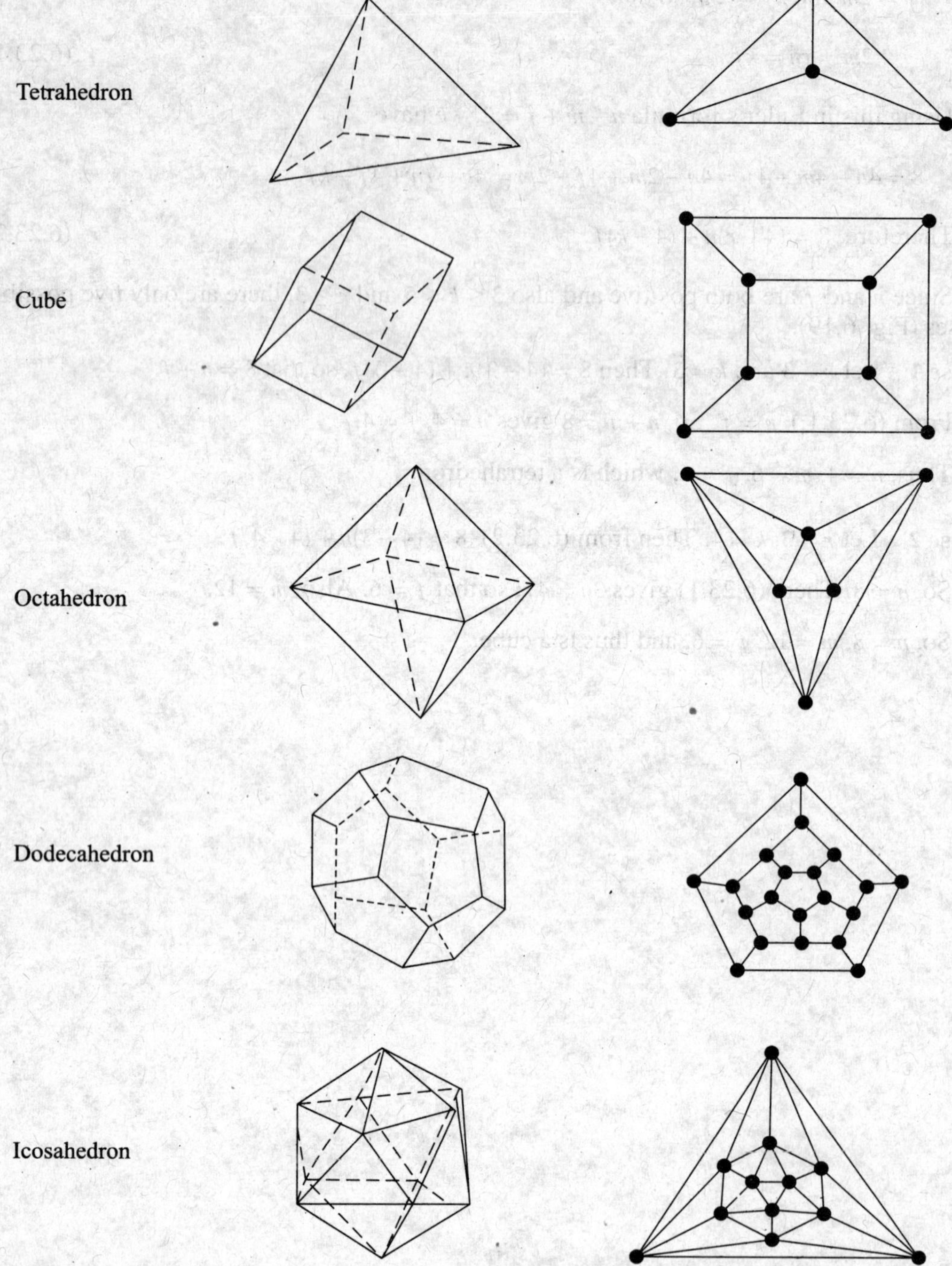

Fig. 6.19

Case 3 Let $r = 3$, $k = 5$. Then (6.23.2) gives $8 = (4-3)n + (4-5)f$, so that $8 = n - f$. From (6.23.1), $3n = 5f$. Solving $8 = n - f$ and $3n = 5f$, we get $n = 20$, $f = 12$.

Thus, $n = 20$, $m = 30$, $f = 12$, which is a dodecahedron.

Case 4 Let $r = 4$, $k = 3$. Then we get $n = 6$, $f = 8$.

So, $n = 6$, $m = 12$, $f = 8$, which is an octahedron.

Case 5 Let $r = 5$, $k = 3$. Then we have $n = 12$, $f = 20$.

Thus, $n = 12$, $m = 30$, $f = 20$, which is an icosahedron. ❑

The following is an elegant necessary condition for a plane graph to be Hamiltonian and is due to Grinberg [83].

Theorem 6.24 If G is a loopless plane graph having a Hamiltonian cycle C, then $\sum_{i=2}^{n} (i-2)(\phi_i' - \phi_i'') = 0$, where ϕ_i' and ϕ_i'' are the number of regions of G of degree i contained in interior C and exterior C respectively.

Proof Let E' and E'' denote the sets of edges of G contained in int $C$and ext C, respectively, and let $|E'| = m'$ and $|E''| = m''$. Then int C contains exactly $m'+1$ regions (Fig. 6.20) and so

$$\sum_{i=2}^{n} \phi_i' = m' + 1, \tag{6.24.1}$$

Since G is loopless, $\phi_1' = \phi_1'' = 0$.

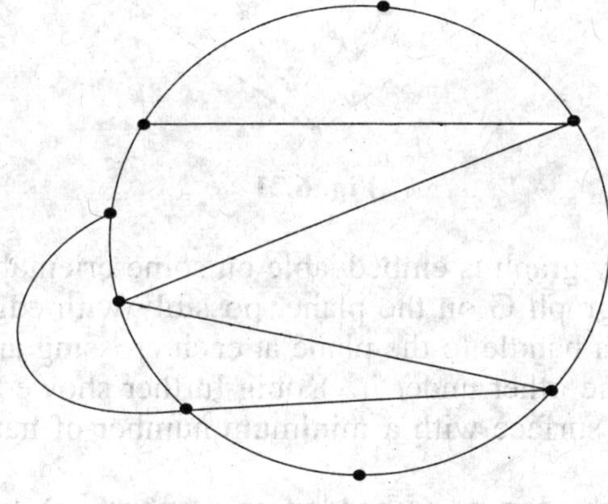

Fig. 6.20

Also, each edge in int C is on the boundary of exactly two regions in int C and each edge of C is on the boundary of exactly one region in int C. Thus, counting the edges of all the regions in int C, we obtain

$$\sum_{i=2}^{n} i\phi_i'' = 2m' + n. \tag{6.24.2}$$

Eliminating m' between (6.24.1) and (6.24.2), we get

$$\sum_{i=2}^{n} (i-2)\phi_i'' = n-2. \tag{6.24.3}$$

Similarly, $\sum_{i=2}^{n} (i-2)\phi_i'' = n-2.$ (6.24.4)

The required result follows from equation (6.24.3) and (6.24.4). ❑

Example Consider the Herschel graph G shown in Figure 6.21. Clearly, G has 9 regions and all the regions are of degree 4. Thus, if G were Hamiltonian, then $2(\phi_4' - \phi_4'') = 0$. This implies $\phi_4' = \phi_4''$, which is impossible, since $\phi_4' + \phi_4''$ = number of regions of degree 4 in $G = 9$ is odd. Hence G is non-Hamiltonian.

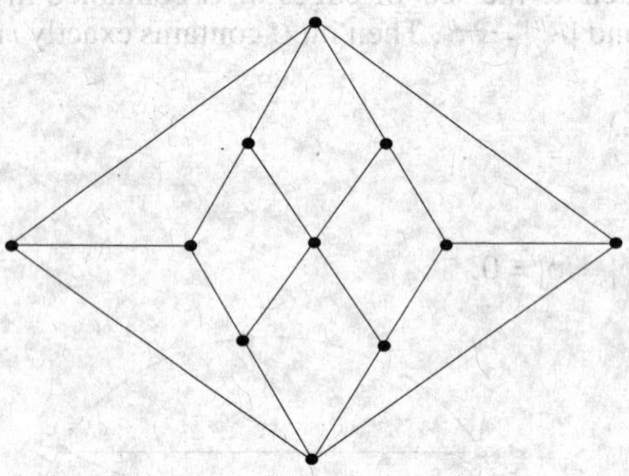

Fig. 6.21

Konig observed that every graph is embeddable on some orientable surface. This is seen by drawing an arbitrary graph G on the plane, possibly with edges that cross over each other and then attaching a handle to the plane at each crossing and allowing one edge to go over the handle and the other under it. Konig further showed that any embedding of a graph on an orientable surface with a minimum number of handles has all its regions simply connected.

Obviously, planar graphs can be embedded on a sphere. A toroidal graph is a graph embedded on a torus, for instance, K_5, $K_{3,3}$, K_7 and $K_{4,4}$.

Definition: The *genus* $\gamma(G)$of a graph G is the minimum number of handles which are added to the sphere so that G can be embedded on the resulting surface. Obviously $\gamma(G) = 0$ if and only if G is planar. The homeomorphic graphs have the same genus.

The genus of a polyhedron is the number of handles required on the sphere for a surface to contain the polyhedron.

Definition: The least number of planar subgraphs whose union is a given graph G is called the *thickness* of G. Clearly the thickness of any planar graph is 1. Also, K_5 and $K_{3,3}$ have thickness 2, while the thickness of K_9 is 3.

The *crossing number* of a graph G is the minimum number of pairwise intersections of its edges when G is drawn in the plane. Clearly, crossing number of a graph is zero if and only if G is planar.

The following result is due to Euler and the proof can be found in Courant and Robbins [60].

Theorem 6.25 For a polyhedron of genus γ with n vertices, m edges and f regions

$$n - m + f = 2 - 2\gamma.$$

We have the following observations.

If G is a connected graph of genus γ, then

$$m = \begin{cases} 3(n-2+2\gamma), & \textit{if every region in G is a triangle,} \\ 2(n-2+2\gamma), & \textit{if every region in G is a quadrilateral.} \end{cases}$$

From this, we have the following.

If G is a connected graph of genus γ, then $\gamma \geq \frac{1}{6}m - \frac{1}{2}(n-2)$, and if G has no triangles, then $\gamma \geq \frac{1}{4}m - \frac{1}{2}(n-2)$.

The proof of the following result is due to Ringel and Youngs [217] and some details can be found in Harary [100].

Theorem 6.26 For $n \geq 3$, the genus of the complete graph is

$$\gamma(K_n) = \frac{(n-3)(n-4)}{12}.$$

6.7 Decomposition of Some Planar Graphs

Schnyder [232] proved that each triangulated planar graph G can be decomposed into three edge disjoint trees. If instead triangles all faces (or regions) of G are quadrilaterals, and G is without loops and multiple edges, Petrovic [178] proved that two trees are sufficient.

The following two lemmas are used in proving Theorem 6.27.

Lemma 6.1 If G is a planar graph on $n(n \geq 4)$ vertices whose all regions are quadrilaterals, then $|E(G)| = 2n-4$.

Lemma 6.2 If G is a planar graph on $n(n \geq 4)$ vertices whose all regions are quadrilaterals, then G contains at least three vertices of degree ≤ 3.

The following result is due to Petrovic [178].

Theorem 6.27 (Petrovic) Let G be a planar graph on $n(n \geq 4)$ vertices whose all faces are quadrilaterals, and v_r and v_b any two non-adjacent vertices of G (we assume v_r is coloured red and v_b blue). Then the edges of G can be partitioned into red and blue ones so that red ones form a spanning tree T_r of $G - v_b$, and blue ones a spanning tree T_b of $G - v_r$.

Proof We call T_r the red, and T_b the blue tree. A vertex of G is red (respectively blue) if it belongs to T_r (respectively T_b). A vertex is red-blue if it belongs to both T_r and T_b. Thus v_r is the only red, and v_b is only blue vertex in G. We proceed by induction on n. For $n = 4$, the assertion is obvious. Assume that it holds for each graph on less than $n(n > 4)$ vertices, and consider a graph G on n vertices. Let u $(u \neq v_r,\ v_b)$ be a vertex of G of degree ≤ 3 existing by Lemma 6.2.

a. $d(u) = 2$. Let uv_1, uv_2 be the edges, and uv_1xv_2u, uv_1yv_2u the faces incident with u. Since $G \neq C_4$, each of vertices v_1 and v_2 has degree ≥ 3. It implies that all regions of $G-u$ are quadrilaterals. By induction hypothesis $G-u$ can be partitioned into trees T'_r and T'_b. Now, independent of the kind of vertices v_1 and v_2, (red, blue or red-blue) we can always colour the edges uv_1 and uv_2 so that the obtained trees T_r and T_b are as desired.

b. $d(u) = 3$. Let uv_1, uv_2, uv_3 be the edges and uv_1xv_2u, uv_2yv_3u, uv_3zv_1u be the faces incident with u.

First assume that all vertices x, y, z are distinct. Since no triangle can be partitioned into disjoint quadrilaterals whose vertices are vertices of the triangle and some its inner points, $xy,\ yz,\ zx \notin E(G)$. Suppose one of vertices x, y, z, is blue and there is no edge connecting it with the opposite vertex of the hexagon $v_1xv_2yv_3z$. Without loss of generality, we may assume it is x. Then $xv_3 \notin E(G)$. Denote by G'' the graph obtained from G by deleting the edges xv_1 and xv_2 and identifying vertices u and x. Since each face of G'' is a quadrilateral it can be partitioned into two trees T''_r and T''_b, where $V(T''_r) = V(G''-v_b)$ and $V(T''_b) = V(G''-v_r)$. If edges uv_1 and uv_2 are coloured differently in G'', say uv_1 red and uv_2 blue, we colour xv_1 red and xv_2 blue obtaining the required trees $T_r = T'_r + xv_1$ and $T_b = T''_b + xv_2$ in G. Therefore assume that uv_1 and uv_2 are monocoloured, say red. Then one of vertices v_1 and v_2, say v_1, is red–blue. As u is also a red-blue vertex, there is the unique blue $u - v_1$ path P in G''. If P contains uv_3, we colour xv_1 and xv_2 blue and red, respectively. If not, we colour both edges xv_1 and xv_2 red, and recolour uv_1 blue. It is routine to check that obtained trees $T_r = T''_r + xv_1$, $T_b = T''_b + xv_2$ in the first case, and $T_r = T''_r - uv_1 + xv_1 + xv_2$, $T_b = T''_b + uv_1$ in the second, are as required.

Now, assume none of the vertices x, y, z satisfy the condition above. Since at most one of edges xv_3, yv_1, zv_2 can exist, we may assume without loss of generality that x is red-blue, y is the red, z is the blue vertex, $xv_3 \in E(G)$ and $yv_1 \notin E(G)$. Then each region of the graph G''' obtained from G by deleting edges yv_2 and yv_3 and identifying y and u is a quadrilateral. By induction ypothesis, G''' can be composed into trees T_r''' and T_b''', where $V(T''') = V(G''' - z)$ and $V(T_b''') = V(G''' - y)$. Colouring all edges incident with y red, and recolouring the edge uv_3 blue, we obtain the decomposition of G into trees T_r and T_b, where $V(T_r) = V(G - z)$ and $V(T_b) = V(G - y)$.

Suppose two of vertices x, y, z, say y and z, coincide. Then $d(v_3) = 2$. If v_3 is red-blue, we finish the proof as in case (a). If x is red-blue we proceed as above. So we may assume that $\{v_3, x\} = \{v_r, v_b)$. Let $v_3 = v_r$, $x = v_b$. By induction hypothesis the graph $G^{IV} = G - v_3$ can be decomposed into trees T_r^{IV} and T_b^{IV}, where $V(T_r^{IV}) = V(G^{IV} - x)$ and $V(T_b^{IV}) = V(G^{IV} - u)$. Then edges uv_1, uv_2 are coloured red and edges xv_1, xv_2, blue. It implies that edges yv_1, yv_2 are coloured differently, yv_1, red and yv_2, blue. Now, colouring v_3u and v_3y red and recolouring uv_1 blue, we get from T_r^{IV} and T_b^{IV} the desired trees T_r and T_b, where $V(T_r) = V(T_r) = V(G - x)$ and $V(T_b) = V(G - v_3)$.

If $x = y = z$, then $v(G) = \{u, x, v_1, v_2, v_3\}$, $E(G) = \{uv_1, uv_2, uv_3, xv_1, xv_2, xv_3\}$ and the statement holds trivially. ❑

6.8 Exercises

1. If G is a connected planar graph of order less than 12, prove that $\delta(G) = 4$.
2. If G is a planar graph of order 24 and is regular of degree 3, then what is the number of regions in a planar representation of G?
3. Prove that Euler's formula fails for disconnected graphs.
4. Show that every graph with at most three cycles is planar.
5. Find a simple graph G with degree sequence [4, 4, 3, 3, 3, 3] such that
   a. G is planar,
   b. G is nonplanar.
6. Show that every simple bipartite cubic planar graph contains a C_4.
7. Prove that a simple planar graph has at least 4 vertices of degree 5 at most.
8. Let G be a planar, triangle free graph of order n. Prove that G has no more than $2n - 4$ edges.
9. Let G be of order $n = 11$. Show that at least one of G or $\overline{G}$ is non planar.
10. Show that the average degree of a planar graph is less than 6.
11. Use Kuratowski's theorem to prove that the Peterson graph is nonplanar.

12. Show that the edges forming a spanning tree in a planar graph G correspond to the edges forming a set of chords in the dual G^*.

13. Prove that the complete graph K_4 is self-dual.

7. Colourings

Colouring is one of the important branches of graph theory and has attracted the attention of almost all graph theorists, mainly because of the four colour theorem and its applications.

7.1 Vertex colouring

A vertex colouring (or simply colouring) of a graph G is a labelling $f : V(G) \to \{1, 2, \ldots\}$; the labels called *colours*, such that no two adjacent vertices get the same colour and each vertex gets one colour. A k-colouring of a graph G consists of k different colours and G is then called *k-colourable*. A 2-colourable and a 3-colourable graph are shown in Figure 7.1. It follows from this definition that the k-colouring of a graph $G(V, E)$ partitions the vertex set V into k independent sets $V_1, V_2, \ldots, V_k$ such that $V = V_1 \cup V_2 \cup \ldots \cup V_k$. The independent sets $V_1, V_2, \ldots, V_k$ are called the *colour classes* and the function $f : V(G) \to \{1, 2, \ldots, k\}$ such that $f(v) = i$ for $v \in V_i$, $1 \le i \le k$, is called the *colour function*.

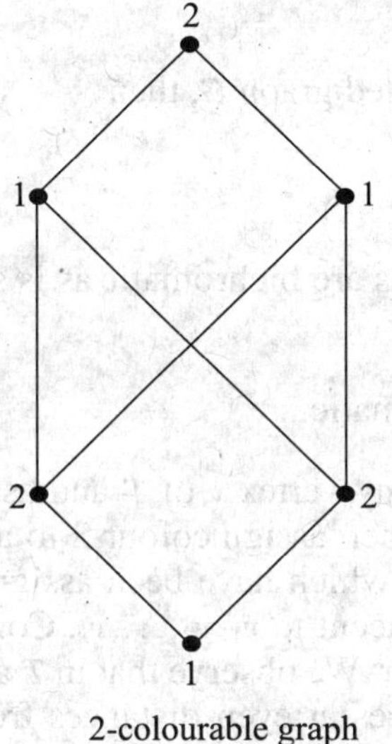
2-colourable graph

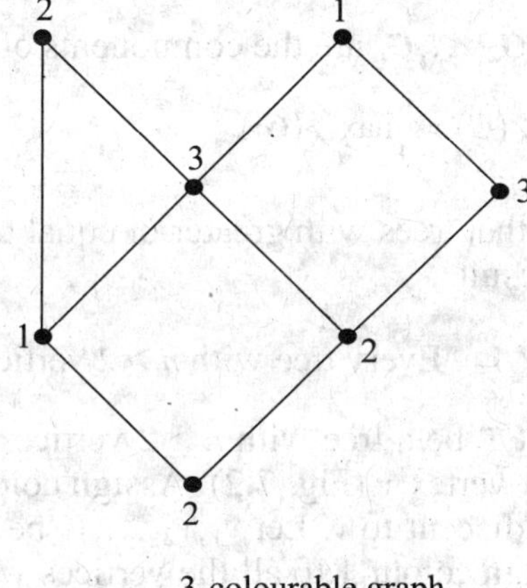
3-colourable graph

Fig. 7.1

The minimum number k for which there is a k-colouring of the graph is called the *chromatic number* (chromatic index) of G and is denoted by $\chi(G)$. If $\chi(G) = k$, the graph G is said to be *k-chromatic*.

We observe that colouring any one of the components in a disconnected graph does not affect the colouring of its other components. Also, parallel edges can be replaced by single edges, since it does not affect the adjacencies of the vertices. Thus, for colouring considerations, we opt only for simple connected graphs.

The following observations are the immediate consequences of the definitions introduced above.

1. A graph is 1-chromatic if and only if it is totally disconnected.
2. A graph having at least one edge is at least 2-chromatic (bichromatic).
3. A graph G having n vertices has $\chi(G) \leq n$.
4. If H is subgraph of a graph G, then $\chi(H) \leq \chi(G)$.
5. A complete graph with n vertices is n-chromatic, because all its vertices are adjacent. So, $\chi(K_n) = n$ and $\chi(\overline{K}_n) = 1$. Therefore we see that a graph containing a complete graph of r vertices is at least r-chromatic. For example, every graph containing a triangle is at least 3-chromatic.
6. A cycle of length $n \geq 3$ is 2-chromatic if n is even and 3-chromatic if n is odd. To see this, let the vertices of the cycle be labelled 1, 2, ..., n, and assign one colour to odd vertices and another to even. If n is even, no adjacent vertices get the same colour, if n is odd, the nth vertex and the first vertex are adjacent and have the same colour, therefore need the third colour for colouring.
7. If $G_1, G_2, \ldots, G_r$ are the components of a disconnected graph G, then

$$\chi(G) = \max_{1 \leq i \leq r} \chi(G_i).$$

We note that trees with greater or equal to two vertices are bichromatic as is seen in the following result.

Theorem 7.1 Every tree with $n \geq 2$ vertices is 2-chromatic.

Proof Let T be a tree with $n \geq 2$ vertices. Consider any vertex v of T and assume T to be rooted at vertex v (Fig. 7.2). Assign colour 1 to v. Then assign colour 2 to all vertices which are adjacent to v. Let $v_1, v_2, \ldots, v_r$ be the vertices which have been assigned colour 2. Now assign colour 1 to all the vertices which are adjacent to $v_1, v_2, \ldots, v_r$. Continue this process till every vertex in T has been assigned the colour. We observe that in T all vertices at odd distances from v have colour 2, and v and vertices at even distances from v have colour 1. Therefore along any path in T, the vertices are of alternating colours. Since there is one and only one path between any two vertices in a tree, no two adjacent vertices have the same colour. Thus T is coloured with two colours. Hence T is 2-chromatic. ❑

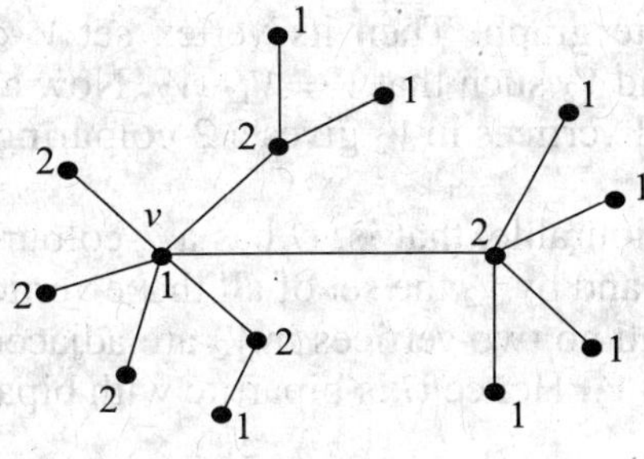

Fig. 7.2

The converse of the above theorem is not true, i. e., every 2-chromatic graph need not be a tree. To see this, consider the graph shown in Figure 7.3. Clearly, G is 2-chromatic, but is not a tree.

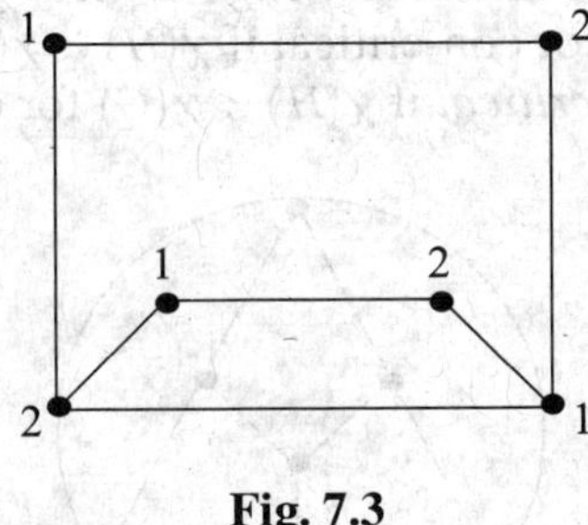

Fig. 7.3

The next result due to Konig [138] characterises 2-chromatic graphs.

Theorem 7.2 (Konig) A graph is bicolourable (2-chromatic) if and only if it has no odd cycles.

Proof Let G be a connected graph with cycles of only even length and let T be a spanning tree in G. Then, by Theorem 7.1, T can be coloured with two colours. Now add the chords to T one by one. As G contains cycles of even length only, the end vertices of every chord get different colours of T. Thus G is coloured with two colours and hence is 2-chromatic. Conversely, let G be bicolourable, that is, 2-chromatic. We prove G has even cycles only. Assume to the contrary that G has an odd cycle. Then by observation (6), G is 3-chromatic, a contradiction. Hence G has no odd cycles. ❑

Corollary 7.1 For a graph G, $\chi(G) \geq 3$ if and only if G has an odd cycle.

The following result is yet another characterisation of 2-chromatic graphs.

Theorem 7.3 A nonempty graph G is bicolourable if and only if G is bipartite.

Proof Let G be a bipartite graph. Then its vertex set V can be partitioned into two nonempty disjoint sets V_1 and V_2 such that $V = V_1 \cup V_2$. Now assigning colour 1 to all vertices in V_1 and colour 2 to all vertices in V_2 gives a 2-colouring of G. Since G is nonempty, $\chi(G) = 2$.

Conversely, let G be bicolourable, that is, G has a 2-colouring. Denote by V_1 the set of all those vertices coloured 1 and by V_2 the set of all those vertices coloured 2. Then no two vertices in V_1 are adjacent and no two vertices in V_2 are adjacent. Thus any edge in G joins a vertex in V_1 and a vertex in V_2. Hence G is bipartite with bipartition $V = V_1 \cup V_2$. ❑

7.2 Critical Graphs

If G is a k-chromatic graph and $\chi(G-v) = k-1$ for every vertex v in G, then G is called a k-critical graph. A 4-critical graph is shown in Figure 7.4. If G is k-chromatic, but $\chi(G-e) = k-1$ for each edge e of G, then G is called *k-edge-critical graph*, or k-minimal. A graph G is said to be *contraction critical* or con-critical if $\chi(H) < \chi(G)$ for every proper contraction H of G. A graph G is said to be *critical* if $\chi(H) < \chi(G)$ for every proper subgraph H of G.

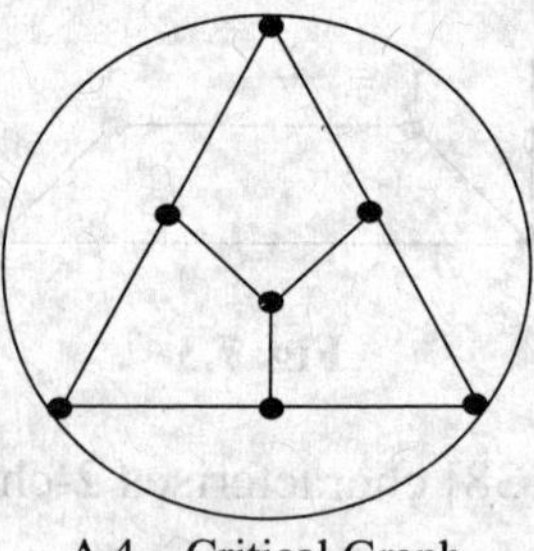

A 4 – Critical Graph

Fig. 7.4

We have the following observations.

1. Every critical or minimal graph is connected.
2. Every connected k-chromatic graph contains a critical or minimal k-chromatic graph.
3. $\chi(G) = \max\ \{\chi(B) : B \text{ is a block of } G\}$.
4. The only 1-critical or 1-minimal graph is K_1, the only 2-critical or 2-minimal graph is K_2 and the only 3-critical or 3-minimal graphs are $C_{2n+1}, n \geq 1$, that is, odd cycles.

The following result due to Dirac [63] describes some of the important properties of a k-critical graph.

Theorem 7.4 If G is a k-critical graph, then

a. G is connected,

b. $\delta(G) \geq k-1$,

c. G has no pair of subgraphs G_1 and G_2 for which $G = G_1 \cup G_2$, and $G_1 \cap G_2$ is a complete graph,

d. $G - v$ is connected for every vertex v of G, provided $k > 1$.

Proof

a. Assume G is not connected. Since $\chi(G) = k$, by observation 7, there is a component G_1 of G such that $\chi(G_1) = k$. If v is any vertex of G which is not in G_1, then G_1 is a component of the subgraph $G - v$. Therefore, $\chi(G - v) = \chi(G_1) = k$. This contradicts the fact that G is k-critical. Hence G is connected.

b. Let v be a vertex of G so that $d(v) < k-1$. Since G is k-critical, the subgraph $G - v$ has a $(k-1)$-colouring. As v has at most $k-2$ neighbours, these neighbours use at most $k-2$ colours in this $(k-1)$-colouring of $G - v$. Now, colour v with the unused colour and this gives a $(k-1)$-colouring of G. This contradicts the given assumption that $\chi(G) = k$. Hence every vertex v has degree at least $k-1$.

c. Let $G = G_1 \cup G_2$, where G_1 and G_2 are subgraphs with $G_1 \cap G_2 = K_t$. Since G is k-critical, therefore G_1 and G_2 both have chromatic number at most $k-1$. Consider a $(k-1)$-colouring of G_1 and a $(k-1)$-colouring of G_2. As $G_1 \cap G_2$ is complete, in the overlap, every vertex in $G_1 \cap G_2$ has a different colour (in each of the $(k-1)$-colourings). This implies that colours in the $(k-1)$-colouring of G_2 can be rearranged such that it assigns the same colour to each vertex in $G_1 \cap G_2$, as is given by the colouring of G_1. Combining the two colourings then produces a $(k-1)$-colouring of all of G. This is impossible, since $\chi(G) = k$. Thus no subgraphs of the type G_1 and G_2 exist.

d. Assume $G - v$ is disconnected, for some vertex v of G. Then $G - v$ has a subgraph H_1 and H_2 with $H_1 \cup H_2 = G - v$ and $H_1 \cap H_2 = \Phi$. Let G_1 and G_2 be the subgraphs of G, where G_1 is induced by H_1 and v, while G_2 is induced by H_2 and v. Then $G = G_1 \cup G_2$ and $G_1 \cap G_2 = K_1$ (with K_1 as a single vertex). This contradicts (c) and thus $G - v$ is connected. ❑

Let $S = \{u, v\}$ be a 2-vertex cut of a critical k-chromatic graph G. Since no separating set of a critical graph is a complete graph, therefore uv is not an edge of G. Let G_i be the S-component of G. G_i is said to be of type 1 if every $(k-1)$ colouring of G_i assigns the same colour to u and v, G_i is of type 2 if every $(k-1)$-colouring of G_i assigns different colours to u and v, and G_i is of type 3 if some $(k-1)$-colouring of G_i assigns same colour to u and v, while some other $(k-1)$-colouring assigns different colours to u and v.

The following characterisation of k-critical graphs with a 2-vertex cut is due to Dirac.

Theorem 7.5 If G is a minimal k-chromatic graph with a 2-vertex cut $S = \{u, v\}$, then (i) $G = G_1 \cup G_2$, where G_i is the S-component of type i, $i = 1, 2$ and (ii) both $G + uv$ and $G : uv$ are k-minimal.

Proof Let G be a minimal k-chromatic graph with a 2-vertex cut $S = \{u, v\}$. So the S-components of G are $(k-1)$-colourable. If there is no set of $(k-1)$-colourings of the S-components all of which agree on S, then G is $(k-1)$-colourable. Therefore there is a type 1 S-component G_1 and a type 2 S-component G_2. Then $G_1 \cup G_2$ is not $(k-1)$-colourable. Since G is k-critical, there is no third S-component G_3. Hence, $G = G_1 \cup G_2$.

Let $H_1 = G_1 + uv$ and $H_2 = G_2 : uv$. We prove that H_2 is k-minimal. Since G_2 is of type 2, therefore every $(k-1)$-colouring of G_2 assigns different colours to u and v. As u and v are identified to a single vertex, say w in H_2, so a k-colouring is necessary to colour H_2, that is, H_2 is k-chromatic. We further prove that $\chi(H_2 - e) = k-1$ for any edge of H_2. Any such edge e can be considered to belong to G and in the $(k-1)$-colouring of $G-e$, u and v get the same colour, since they can be considered to belong to G_1 which is a subgraph of $G-e$. The restriction of such a colouring of $G-e$ to $H_2 - e$ (with u and v identified as w with the common colour of u and v) is a $(k-1)$-colouring of $H_2 - e$. This proves the result.

That H_1 is minimal, can be proved in a similar manner. ❑

Theorem 7.6 Every k-chromatic graph can be contracted into a con-critical chromatic graph.

Proof Let G be a k-chromatic graph and let the edge e of G be contracted. Then a colouring of G can be used to give a colouring of $G|e$ except that, possibly the vertex formed by the contraction may be assigned an extra colour. Thus, $\chi(G|e) \leq \chi(G) + 1$. On the other hand, a colouring of $G|e$ can be used to get a colouring for G by using an extra colour for one of the end vertices of e. Therefore, $\chi(G) \leq \chi(G|e) + 1$. Thus the contraction of an edge changes the chromatic number by at most one. Sometimes contraction of an edge may increase the chromatic number, but by repeated contractions, the number of edges and therefore the chromatic number gets reduced. Clearly, the connected graph can be contracted to a single vertex whose chromatic number is one. In between, a stage arises where the chromatic number of the graph is the same as the original, but the contraction of any edge reduces the chromatic number by one. ❑

As noted earlier, every connected $k-$ chromatic graph contains a critical or minimal k-chromatic graph. To see this, we observe that if G is not k-critical, then $\chi(G - v) = k$, for some vertex v of G. If $G - v$ is $k-$critical, then this is the required subgraph. If not, then $G - \{v, w\} = (G - v) - w$ has chromatic number k, for some vertex w in $G - v$. If this new subgraph is k-critical, then again this is the required subgraph. If not, we continue this vertex deletion procedure, and we will clearly get a k-critical subgraph.

We have the following immediate observation.

Theorem 7.7 Any k-chromatic graph has at least k vertices of degree at least $k-1$ each.

Proof Let G be a k-chromatic graph and let H be a k-critical subgraph of G. Then, by Theorem 7.4 (b), every vertex of H has degree at least $k-1$ in H and hence in G. Since H is k-chromatic, H has at least k vertices. This completes the proof. ❑

We note that there is no easy characterisation of graphs with chromatic number greater or equal to three. The graph vertex - colouring problem is a standard NP-complete problem and no good algorithm for finding $\chi(G)$ has been discovered for the class of all graphs, though for some special classes of graphs polynomial time algorithms have been found. There are various results which give upper bounds for the chromatic number of an arbitrary graph G, provided the degrees of all the vertices of G are known. The first of these is due to Szekeres and Wilf [231].

Theorem 7.8 Let G be a graph and $k = \max\{\delta(G') : G'$ is a subgraph of $G\}$. Then $\chi(G) \leq k+1$.

Proof Let H be a k-minimal subgraph of G. Then H is subgraph of G and therefore $\delta(H) \leq k$. Using Theorem 7.4, we have, $\delta(H) \geq \chi(H) - 1 = \chi(G) - 1$. Thus, $\chi(G) \leq \delta(H) + 1 = k+1$. ❑

The next result is due to Welsh and Powell [255] and its proof is due to Bondy [32].

Theorem 7.9 Let G b a graph with degree sequence $[d_i]_1^n$ such that $d_1 \geq d_2 \geq \ldots \geq d_n$. Then, $\chi(G) \leq \max\{\min\{i,\ d_i\ +1\}\}$.

Proof Let G be k-chromatic. Then, by Theorem 7.8, G has at least k vertices of degree at least $k-1$. Therefore, $d_k \geq k-1$ and $\max\ \{\min\ \{i,\ d_i+1\}\} \geq \min\ \{k,\ d_k+1\} = k = \chi(G)$. ❑

We have the following upper bounds for chromatic number.

Theorem 7.10 For any graph G, $\chi(G) \leq \triangle(G)+1$.

Proof Let G be any graph with n vertices. To prove the result, we induct on n. For $n = 1, G = K_1$ and $\chi(G) = 1$ and $\triangle(G) = 0$. Therefore the result is true for $n = 1$.

Assume that the result is true for all graphs with $n-1$ vertices and therefore by induction hypothesis, $\chi(G) \leq \triangle(G-v)+1$. This shows that $G-v$ can be coloured by using $\triangle(G-v)+1$ colours. Since $\triangle(G)$ is the maximum degree of a vertex in G, vertex v has at most $\triangle(G)$ neighbours in G. Thus these neighbours use up at most $\triangle(G)$ colours in the colouring of $G-v$.

If $\triangle(G) = \triangle(G-v)$, then there is at least one colour not used by v's neighbours and that can be used to colour v giving a $\triangle(G)+1$ colouring for G.

In case $\triangle(G) \neq \triangle(G-v)$, then $\triangle(G-v) < \triangle(G)$. Therefore, using a new colour for v, we have a $\triangle(G-v)+2$ colouring of G and clearly, $\triangle(G-v)+2 \leq \triangle(G)+1$. Hence in both cases, it follows that $\chi(G) \leq \triangle(G)+1$. ❑

Remarks

1. Clearly, Theorem 7.10 is a simple consequence of Theorem 7.7. This is because if G is $k-$ chromatic, then Theorem 7.4 gives $\triangle \geq k-1$, that is, $\chi \leq \triangle+1$.
2. The equality in Theorem 7.10 holds if $G = C_{2n+1}$, $n \geq 1$ and if $G = K_m$.

7.3 Brook's Theorem

Greedy colouring algorithm: The greedy colouring with respect to a vertex ordering $v_1, v_2, \ldots, v_n$ of $V(G)$ is obtained by colouring vertices in the order $v_1, v_2, \ldots, v_n$ assigning to v_i the smallest – indexed colour not already used on its lower – indexed neighbours. This is reported in West [256].

The following recolouring technique as noted in Clark and Holton [59] is due to Kempe [124].

Kempe Chain argument: Let G be a graph with a colouring using at least two different colours represented by i and j. Let $H(i, j)$ denote the subgraph of G induced by all the vertices of G coloured either i or j and let K be a connected component of the subgraph $H(i, j)$. If we interchange the colours i and j on the vertices of K and keep the colours of all other vertices of G unchanged, then we get a new colouring of G, which uses the same colours with which we started. This subgraph K is called a Kempe chain and the recolouring technique is called the Kempe chain argument (Fig. 7.5).

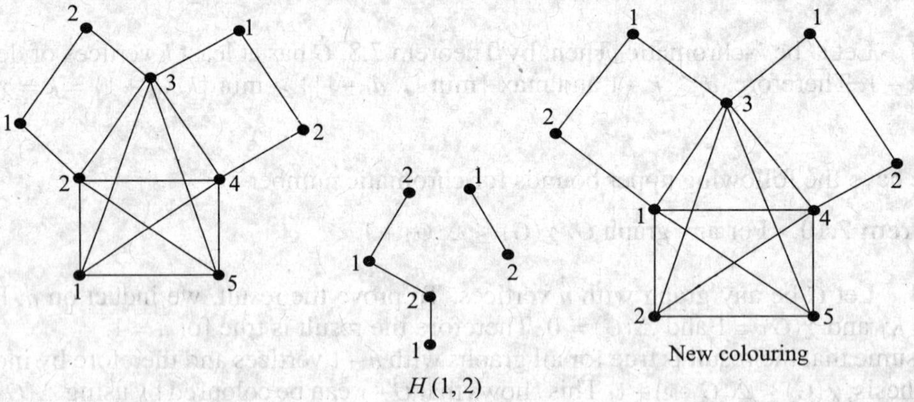

Fig. 7.5

The following result due to Brooks [39] is an improvement of the bounds obtained in Theorem 7.10. We give two proofs of Brooks theorem, the first given by Lovasz [146] uses greedy colouring, and the second proof uses Kempe chain argument.

Theorem 7.11 (Brooks) If G is a connected graph which is neither complete nor an odd cycle, then $\chi(G) \le \Delta(G)$.

Proof Let G be a connected graph with vertex set $V = \{v_1, v_2, \ldots, v_n\}$ which is neither a complete graph, nor an odd cycle and let $\Delta = k$. Since G is a complete graph for $k = 1$ and G is an odd cycle or a bipartite graph for $k = 2$, let $k \ge 3$.

Assume G is not k-regular. Then there exists a vertex say $v = v_n$ such that $d(v) < k$. Since G is connected, we form a spanning tree of G starting from v_n and whose vertices are arranged in the order $v_n, v_{n-1}, \ldots, v_1$ (Fig. 7.6).

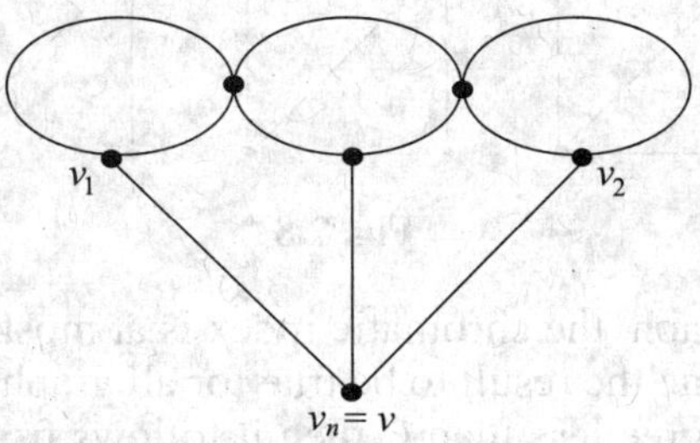

Fig. 7.6

Clearly, each vertex v_i other than v_n in the resulting order $v_n, v_{n-1}, \ldots, v_1$ has a higher indexed neighbour along the path to v_n in the tree. Therefore each vertex v_i has atmost $k-1$ lower indexed neighbours and the greedy colouring needs at most k colours (Fig. 7.7).

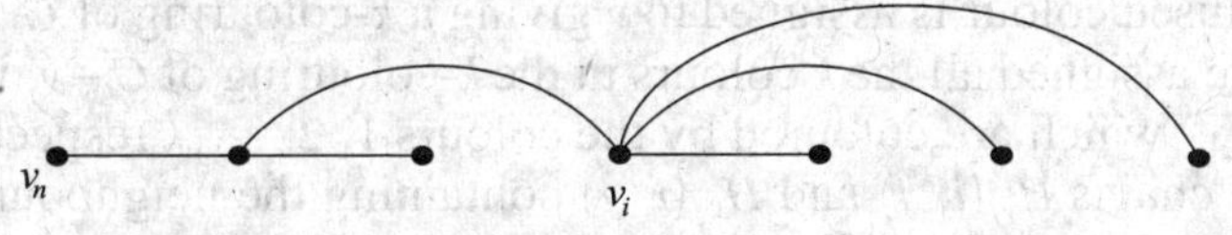

Fig. 7.7

Now, let G be k-regular. Assume G has a cut vertex say x and let G' be a subgraph containing a component of $G-x$ together with the edges of $G-x$ to x. Clearly, $d(x|G') < k$. Therefore, by using the above argument, we have a k-colouring of G'. By making use of the permutations of the colours, it can be seen that this is true for all such subgraphs. Thus G is k-colourable.

Now, let G be 2-connected. We claim that G has an induced 3-vertex path, with vertices say v_1, v_n, v_2 in order, such that $G-\{v_1, v_2\}$ is connected.

To prove the claim, let x be any vertex of G. If $k(G-x) \geq 2$, let v_1 be x and let v_2 be a vertex with distance two from x, which clearly exists, as G is regular and not a complete graph. If $k(G-x) = 1$, then x has a neighbour in every end block of $G-x$, since G has no cut vertex. Let v_1 and v_2 be the neighbours of x in two such blocks. Clearly v_1 and v_2 are non adjacent. Also, since blocks have no cut vertices, $G-\{x, v_1, v_2\}$ is connected. As $k \geq 3$, so $G-\{v_1, v_2\}$ is connected and we let $x = v_n$, proving the claim.

Now arrange the vertices of a spanning tree of $G-\{v_1, v_2\}$ as $v_3, v_4, \ldots, v_n$. As before, each vertex before n has atmost $k-1$ lower indexed neighbours. The greedy colouring uses at most $k-1$ colours on neighbours of v_n, since v_1 and v_2 get the same colour.

Second Proof (Using Kempe chain argument) Let G be a connected graph with n vertices which is neither complete nor an odd cycle. Let $\triangle(G) = k$. For $k = 1$, G is complete and for $k = 2$, G is an odd cycle or a bipartite graph. Therefore, assume $k \geq 3$.

We induct on n. Since $k \geq 3$, the induction starts from $n = 4$. As G is not complete, then for $n = 4$, G is one of the graphs given in Figure 7.8.

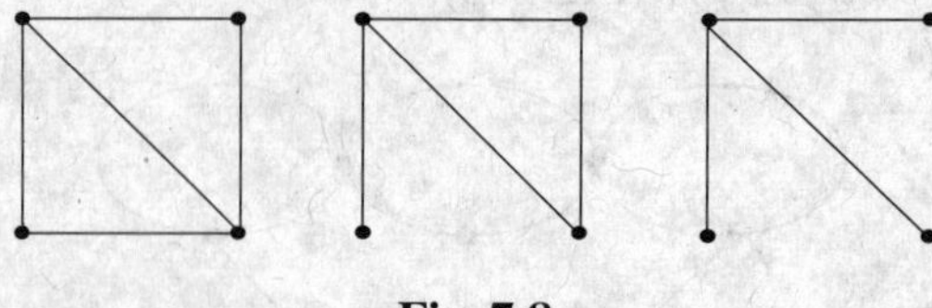

Fig. 7.8

Clearly, for each such graph, the chromatic index is at most three.

Now, let $n \geq 5$, and assume the result to be true for all graphs with fewer than n vertices.

If G has a vertex v of degree less than k, then it follows from Theorem 7.10 that G can be coloured by k colours, since the neighbours of v use up atmost $k-1$ colours. Therefore the result is true in this case.

Now assume that degree of every vertex of G is k, that is, G is k-regular. We show that G has a k-colouring.

Let v be any vertex of G. Then by induction hypothesis, the subgraph $G-v$ has a k-colouring. If the neighbours of v in G do not use all the k colours in the k-colouring of $G-v$, then any unused colour is assigned to v giving a k-colouring of G. Assume that the k neighbours of v are assigned all the k colours in the k-colouring of $G-v$. Let the neighbours of v be $v_1, v_2, \ldots, v_k$ which are coloured by the colours $1, 2, \ldots, k$ respectively.

Let the Kempe chains $H_{v_i}(i, j)$ and $H_{v_j}(i, j)$ containing the neighbours v_i and v_j be different. That is, v_i and v_j are in different components of the subgraph $H(i, j)$ induced by the colours i and j. Therefore, using Kempe chain argument, the colours in $H_{v_i}(i, j)$ are interchanged to give a k-colouring of $G-v$, where now v_i has been assigned the colour j. This implies that the neighbours of v use less than k colours and the unused colour assigned to v gives a k-colouring of G.

Now assume that for each i and j, the neighbours v_i and v_j are in the same Kempe chain, which is briefly denoted by H. If the degree of v_i in H is greater than one, then v_i is adjacent to at least two vertices coloured j. Therefore there is a third colour, say ℓ, not used in colouring the neighbours of v_i. Recolour v_i by ℓ and then colour v by i, giving the k-colouring of G. Assume that v_i and v_j both are of degree one in H. Let P be a path from v_i to v_j in H and let there be a vertex in P with degree at least three in H (Fig. 7.9). Let u be the first such vertex and coloured i. (If u is coloured j, the same argument is used as in case of i). Then at least three neighbours of u are coloured j and therefore there is a colour, say ℓ, not used by these neighbours. Recolour u by ℓ and interchange colours i and j on the vertices of P from v_i upto u, excluding u. So we get a colouring of $G-v$, where v_i and v_j are now both coloured j. This allows v to be coloured by i.

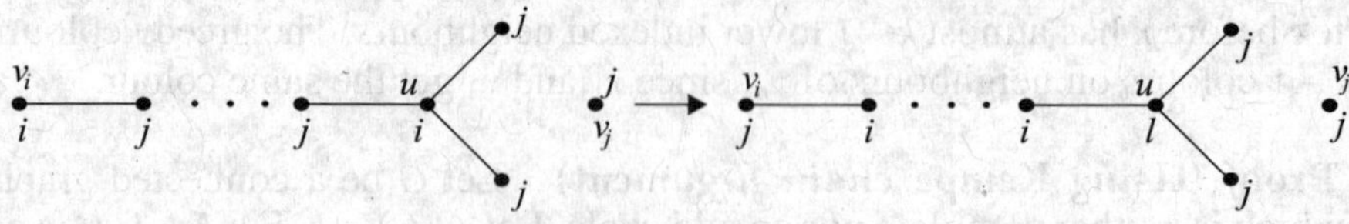

Fig. 7.9

Let all the vertices on a path v_i to v_j, excluding the end vertices v_i and v_j, be of degree two in H. Clearly H contains a single path from v_i to v_j.

Let all the Kempe chains be paths. Let H and K be such chains corresponding to v_i, v_j and v_i, v_ℓ respectively, with $j \neq \ell$. Let $w \neq v_i$ be a vertex present in both the chains (Fig. 7.10). Then w is coloured i, has two neighbours coloured j and two neighbours coloured ℓ. Therefore there is a fourth colour, say s, not used by the neighbours of w. Now colour w by s, and interchange colours ℓ and i on the vertices of K beyond w upto and including v_ℓ, we get a colouring of $G - v$, where v_i and v_ℓ are now both coloured i. This allows v to be coloured by ℓ.

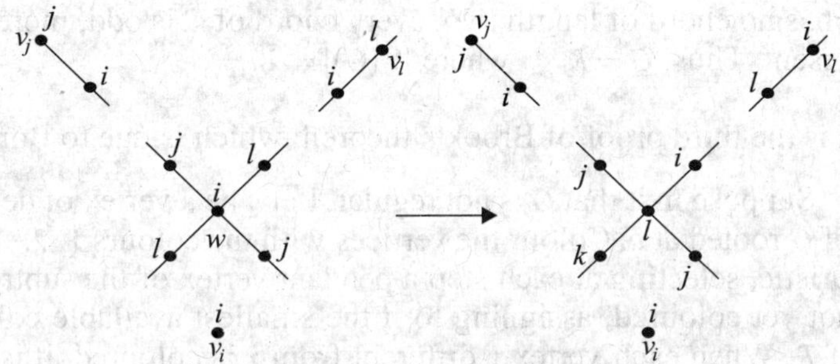

Fig. 7.10

Thus assume that two such Kempe chains meet only at their common end vertex v_i.

Let v_i and v_j be two neighbours of v which are nonadjacent and let x be the vertex coloured j, adjacent to v_i on the Kempe chain H from v_i to v_j. With $\ell \neq j$, let K denote the Kempe chain from v_i to v_j. Then by the Kempe chain argument, we interchange the colours in K, without changing the colours of the other vertices. This results in v_i coloured ℓ, and v_ℓ coloured i. Since x is adjacent to v_i, it is in the Kempe chain for colours ℓ and j. However,it is also the Kempe chain for colours i and j. This contradicts the assumption that Kempe chains have at most one vertex in common, the end vertex. This contradiction implies that any two v_i and v_j are adjacent. In other words, all neighbours of v are also neighbours of each other. This shows that G is the complete graph K_k, a contradiction to the hypothesis of G. ❑

Definition: In the depth first search tree (DFS), a search tree T is used to represent the edge examination process. In DFS a new adjacent vertex is selected, which is incident with the first edge incident with v. In other words, in DFS we leave$v$ as quickly as possible, examining only one of its incident edges and replacing v by a new vertex, which is adjacent to v.

The following result is due to Chartrand and Kronk [50].

Theorem 7.12 Let G be a connected graph every depth-first search tree of which is a Hamiltonian path. Then G is a cycle, a complete graph, or a complete bipartite graph $K_{n,n}$.

Proof Let P be a Hamiltonian path of G, with origin u. Because the path $P-u$ extends to a Hamiltonian path of G, the path P extends to a Hamiltonian cycle C of G.

When C has no chord, $G=C$ is a cycle. So let uv be a chord of C. Then u^-v^- is one too, because $u^-CvuC^{-1}v^-$ is a Hamiltonian path of G, likewise, u^-v^- is a chord of C (where u^- denotes the successor of u on C and u^{--} is the successor of u^-). And if the length of uCv is at least four, uv and u^-v^- are also chords of C, in view of the Hamiltonian path $u^{--}Cv^-u^-C^{-1}v^-u^-uv$ and the fact that $u^-v^- = (u^-)^-v^-$.

When C has a chord uw of length two, let $v = u^-(=w^-)$. Then $vw^- \in E$. Moreover, if $vw^- \in E$, then $vw^{-(-1)} \in E$ in view of the Hamiltonian path $w^{-(-1)}CuwCw^-v$. It follows that v is adjacent to every vertex of G. But then G is complete, because u^-w^- is a chord of length two for all i. If C has no chord of length two, every chord of C is odd, moreover, every odd chord must be present. Thus, $G=K_{n,\,n}$, where $|V(G)|=2n$. ❑

The following is the third proof of Brook's theorem which is due to Bondy [35].

Bondy's Proof Suppose first that G is not regular. Let u be a vertex of degree α and let T be a search tree of G rooted at u. Colour the vertices with the colours 1, 2, …, $\triangle$ according to the greedy heuristic, selecting at each step a pendant vertex of the subtree of T induced by the vertices not yet coloured, assigning to it the smallest available colour and ending with the root u of T. When each vertex v different from x is coloured, it is adjacent (in T) to at least one uncoloured vertex and so is adjacent to at most $d(v)-1<\triangle-1$ coloured vertices. It is therefore assigning one of the colours 1, 2, …, $\triangle$, because $d(u)=\alpha\leq\triangle-1$. The greedy heuristic therefore produces a $\triangle$-colouring of G.

Now, let G be regular. If G has a cut vertex u, then $G=G_1\cup G_2$, where G_1 and G_2 are connected and $G_1\cap G_2=\{u\}$. Because the degree of u in G is less than $\triangle(G)$, neither subgraph of G is regular, so $\chi(G)\leq\triangle(G_i)=\triangle(G)$, $i=1,2$ and $\chi(G)=\max\{\chi(G_1),\chi(G_2)\}\leq\triangle(G)$. Therefore we assume that G is 2-connected.

If every depth- first search tree of G is a Hamiltonian path, then G is a cycle, a complete graph, or a complete bipartite graph $K_{n,\,n}$, by Theorem 7.12. Since by hypothesis, G is neither an odd cycle nor a complete graph, $\chi(G)=2\leq\triangle(G)$. Suppose then, that T is a depth-first search tree of G, but not a path. Let u be a vertex of T with at least two children, v and w. Because G is 2-connected, both $G-v$ and $G-w$ are connected. Thus there are proper descendants of v and w, each of which is joined to an ancestor of u, and it follows that $G-\{v,\,w\}$ is connected. Consider a search tree T with root u in G. By colouring v and w with colour 1 and then the vertices of T by the greedy heuristic as above, ending with the root u, we obtain a $\triangle$-colouring of G. ❑

Brooks theorem and the observation that in a graph G containing K_n as a subgraph, $\chi(G)\geq n$, provide estimates for the chromatic number. For instance, in Figure 7.11(a) for the graph G_1, $\triangle(G_1)=8$ and G_1 has K_4 as a subgraph. Therefore, $4\leq\chi(G_1)\leq 8$. It can be easily seen that $\chi(G_1)=4$. Similarly for G_2 in Fig. 7.11(b) known as the Birkhoff diamond, $\triangle(G_2)=5$ and G_2 has K_3 as a subgraph. So, $3\leq\chi(G_2)=5$. In fact, $\chi(G_2)=4$.

Independent set: A set of vertices in a graph G is independent if no two of them are adjacent. The largest number of vertices in such a set is called the vertex independence number of G and is denoted by $\alpha_0(G)$ or α_0. Analogously, an independent set of edges of G has no two of its edges adjacent and the maximum cardinality of such a set is the edge independence number $\alpha_1(G)$ or α_1. For the complete graph K_n, $\alpha_0 = 1$, $\alpha_1 = \left[\frac{n}{2}\right]$. In the graph of Figure 7.12, $\alpha_0(G) = 2$ and $\alpha_1(G) = 3$.

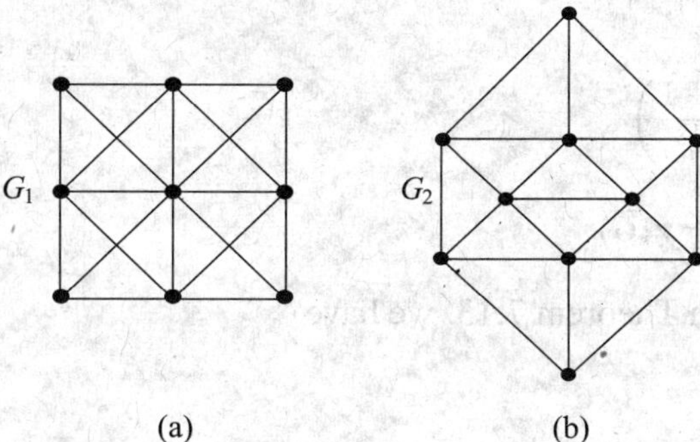

Fig. 7.11

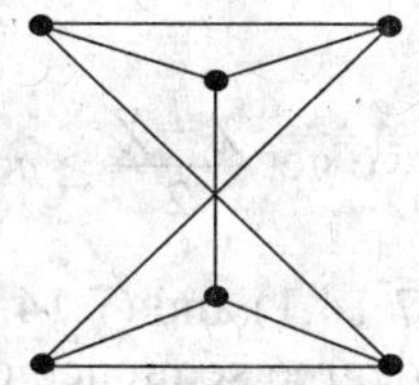

Fig. 7.12

A lower bound, noted in Berge [22] and Ore [173] and an upper bound by Harary and Hedetniemi [110] involve the vertex independent number α_0 of a graph.

Theorem 7.13 For any graph G, $\dfrac{n}{\chi(\overline{G})} \le \dfrac{n}{\alpha_o} \le \chi(G) \le n - \alpha_o + 1$.

Proof If $\chi(G) = k$, then V can be partitioned into k colour classes $V_1, V_2, \ldots, V_k$, each of which is an independent set of vertices.

If $|V_i| = n_i$, then every $n_i \le \alpha_o$, so that $n = \sum n_i \le k\alpha_o$. This proves the middle inequality.

Now, let S be a maximal independent set containing α_o vertices. Clearly, $\chi(G - S) \ge \chi(G) - 1$.

As $G - S$ has $n - \alpha_o$ vertices, $\chi(G - S) \le n - \alpha_o$, and $\chi(G) \le \chi(G - S) + 1 \le n - \alpha_o + 1$, proving the last inequality.

As $\overline{G}$ has a complete subgraph of order $\alpha_o(G)$,

$$\chi(\overline{G}) \ge \alpha_o(G), \text{ or } \frac{n}{\chi(\overline{G})} \le \frac{n}{\alpha_o(G)}, \text{ proving the first inequality.}$$ ❑

The following result due to Nordhaus and Gaddum [167] gives the bounds on the sum and product of the chromatic numbers of a graph and its complement.

Theorem 7.14 For any graph of order n,

$$2\sqrt{n} \le \chi + \overline{\chi} \le n+1, \tag{7.14.1}$$

$$\text{and } n \le \chi\overline{\chi} \le \left(\frac{n+1}{2}\right)^2, \tag{7.14.2}$$

where $\chi = \chi(G)$ and $\overline{\chi} = \chi(\overline{G})$.

Proof Evidently from Theorem 7.13, we have

$$\chi\overline{\chi} \ge n. \tag{7.14.3}$$

Since the arithmetic mean is greater than or equal to the geometric mean,

$$\frac{\chi+\overline{\chi}}{2} \ge \sqrt{\chi\overline{\chi}}. \tag{7.14.4}$$

Combining (7.14.3) and (7.14.4), we get $\dfrac{\chi+\overline{\chi}}{2} \ge n$.

Therefore the left inequalities of (7.14.1) and (7.14.2) are proved.

Now, let $d_1 \ge d_2 \ge \ldots \ge d_n$ be the degree sequence of G. Then $\overline{d}_1 \ge \overline{d}_2 \ge \ldots \ge \overline{d}_n$, where $\overline{d}_i = n-1-d_{n+1-i}$, is the degree sequence of $\overline{G}$. Then by using Theorem 7.9, we have

$$\begin{aligned}\chi(G)+\chi(\overline{G}) &\le \max_i \min\{d_i+1, i\} + \max_i \min\{n-d_{n+1-i}, i\}\\ &= \max_i \min\{d_i+1, i\} + (n+1) - \min_i \max\{d_{n+1-i}+1, n+1-i\}\\ &= \max_i \min\{d_i+1, i\} + (n+1) - \min_j \max\{d_j+1, j\}.\end{aligned}$$

Thus, $\chi(G)+\chi(\overline{G}) \le n+1$.

Also, $\dfrac{\chi(G)+\chi(\overline{G})}{2} \ge \sqrt{\chi\overline{\chi}}$. Therefore, $\sqrt{\chi\overline{\chi}} \le \dfrac{\chi+\overline{\chi}}{2} \le \dfrac{n+1}{2}$. Thus, $\chi\overline{\chi} \le \left(\dfrac{n+1}{2}\right)^2$.

Second Proof Let G be k-chromatic and let $v_1, v_2, \ldots, v_k$ be the colour classes of G, where $|V_i| = n_i$ Then $\Sigma n_i = n$ and max $n_i \ge n/k$. Since each V_i induces a complete subgraph of $\overline{G}, \overline{\chi} \ge \max n_i \ge n/k$, so that $\chi\overline{\chi} \ge n$. As the geometric mean of two positive numbers is always less or equal to their arithmetic mean, it follows that $\chi+\overline{\chi} \ge 2\sqrt{n}$.

To prove $\chi+\overline{\chi}\leq n+1$, we induct on n. Clearly, the equality holds for $n=1$. We assume that $\chi(G)+\overline{\chi}(G)\leq n$ for all graphs G having fewer than n vertices. Let H and $\overline{H}$ be complementary graphs with n vertices and let v be a vertex of H. Then $G=H-v$ and $\overline{G}=\overline{H}-v$ are complementary graphs with $n-1$ vertices. Let the degree of v in H be d, so that degree of v in $\overline{H}$ is $n-d-1$. Clearly, $\chi(H)\leq\chi(G)+1$ and $\overline{\chi}(H)\leq\overline{\chi}(G)+1$. If either $\chi(H)<\chi(G)+1$ or $\overline{\chi}(H)<\overline{\chi}$ (G) + 1, then $\chi(H)+\overline{\chi}(H)\leq n+1$. If $\chi(H)=\chi(G)+1$ and $\overline{\chi}(H)=\overline{\chi}(G)+1$, then the removal of v from H, producing G, decreases the chromatic number, so that $d\geq\chi(G)$. Similarly, $n-d-1\geq\overline{\chi}(G)$. Thus, $\chi(G)+\overline{\chi}(G)\leq n-1$. Therefore we always have $\chi(H)+\overline{\chi}(H)\leq n+1$. Applying now the inequality $4\chi\overline{\chi}\leq(\chi+\overline{\chi})^2$, we get $\chi\overline{\chi}\leq\left(\frac{n+1}{2}\right)^2$. ❑

We now have the following result.

Theorem 7.15 If a connected k-chromatic graph has exactly one vertex of degree exceeding $k-1$, then it is minimal.

Proof Let G be a connected k-chromatic graph having exactly one vertex of degree exceeding $k-1$. Let e be any edge of G. Then $\delta(G-e)\leq k-2$ (otherwise, G will have at least two vertices of degree exceeding $k-1$).

For every induced subgraph H of $G-e$, we have $\delta(H)\leq k-2$. Thus, by Theorem 7.7, $\chi(G-e)\leq k-1$ and hence $\chi(G-e)\leq k-1$. Since e is arbitrary, therefore G is minimal. ❑

We observe from Theorem 7.4(b) that the number of edges m of a k-critical graph is at least $n(k-1)/2$. Dirac extended this to the inequality $2m\geq n(k+1)-2$ for a $(k+1)$-critical graph, the proof of which can be found in Bollobas [29].

7.4 Edge colouring

An edge colouring of a nonempty graph G is a labelling $f: E(G)\rightarrow\{1, 2, \ldots\}$; the labels are called *colours*, such that adjacent edges are assigned different colours. A k-edge colouring of G is a colouring of G which consists of k different colours and in this case G is said to be *k-edge colourable*.

The definition implies that the k-edge colouring of a graph $G(V, E)$ partitions the edge set E into k independent sets $E_1, E_2, \ldots, E_k$ such that $E=E_1\cup E_2\cup\ldots\cup E_k$. The independent sets E_i, $1\leq i\leq k$ are called the *colour classes* and the function $f: E(G)\rightarrow\{1, 2, \ldots, k\}$ such that $f(e)=i$, for each $e\in E_i$, $1\leq i\leq k$, is called the *colour function*. The minimum number k for which there is a k-colouring of G is called the *edge chromatic umber* (or edge chromatic index) and is denoted by $\chi'(G)$.

We have the following observations.

1. If H is a subgraph of a graph G, then $\chi'(H)\leq\chi'(G)$.

2. For any graph $G, \chi'(G)\geq\triangle(G)$.

If v is any vertex of G with $d(v) = \triangle(G)$, then the $\triangle(G)$ edges incident with v have a different colour in any edge colouring of G.

3. $$\chi'(C_n) = \begin{cases} 2, & \text{if n is even}, \\ 3, & \text{if n is odd}. \end{cases}$$

The following is a recolouring technique for edge colouring, called *Kempe chain argument*.

Let G be a graph with an edge colouring using at least two different colours say i and j. Let $H(i, j)$ represent the subgraph of G induced by all the edges coloured either i or j. Let K be a connected component of the subgraph $H(i, j)$. It can be easily verified that K is a path whose edges are alternately coloured by i and j. If the colours on these edges are interchanged and the colours on all other edges of G are kept unchanged, the result is a new colouring of G, using the same initial colours. The component K is called Kempe chain and this recolouring method is called the Kempe chain argument.

Definition: Let i be a colour used in the edge colouring of a graph G. If there is an edge coloured i incident at the vertex v of G, we say i is *present* at v, and if there is no edge coloured i at v, we say i is *absent* from v.

The following result is due to Konig [130].

Theorem 7.16 (Konig) For a nonempty bipartite graph G, $\chi'(G) = \triangle(G)$.

Proof The proof is by induction on the number of edges of G. If G has only one edge, the result is trivial.

Let G have more than one edge and assume that the result is true for all nonempty bipartite graphs having fewer edges than G. Since $\triangle(G) \leq \chi'(G)$, it is enough to prove that G has a $\triangle(G)$-edge colouring. We let $\triangle(G) = k$. Let $e = uv$ be an edge of G. Then $G - e$ is bipartite with less edges than G. Therefore, by induction hypothesis, $G - e$ has a $\triangle(G - e)$-edge colouring. Since $\triangle(G - e) \leq \triangle(G) = k$, $G - e$ has a k-colouring. We show that the same k colours are used to colour G.

As $d(u) \leq k$ in G and the edge e is uncoloured, there is at least one of the k colours absent from u. Similarly, at least one of these colours is absent from v.

If one of the colours absent at u and v is same, we use this to colour e and we get a k-edge colouring of G.

Now take the case of a colour i present at u, but absent from v and a colour j present at v, but absent from u.

Let K be the Kempe chain containing u in the subgraph $H(i, j)$ induced by the edges coloured i or j. We claim that v does not belong to the Kempe chain K.

For if v belongs to K, then there is a path P in K from u to v. Since u and v are adjacent, they do not belong to the same bipartition subset of the bipartite graph G and therefore the length of the path P is odd. As the colour i is present at u, the first edge of P is coloured i. Since the edges of P are alternately coloured i and j, and P is of odd length, therefore the last edge of P, which is incident at v, is also coloured i. This is a contradiction, as i is absent from v, proving our claim.

Using Kempe chain argument on K, the interchanging of colours now makes i absent from u and does not affect the colours of the edges incident at v. Therefore i is absent from both u and v in this new edge colouring and colouring edge e by i gives a k-edge colouring of G. ❑

The next result gives edge chromatic number of complete graphs.

Theorem 7.17 If $G = K_n$ is a complete graph with n vertices, $n \geq 2$, then

$$\chi'(G) = \begin{cases} n-1, & \textit{if } n \textit{ is even}, \\ n, & \textit{if } n \textit{ is odd}. \end{cases}$$

Proof Let $G = K_n$ be a complete graph with n vertices.

Assume n is odd. Draw G so that its vertices form a regular polygon. Clearly, there are n edges of equal length on the boundary of the polygon. Colour the edges along the boundary using a different colour for each edge. Now, each of the remaining internal edges of G is parallel to exactly one edge on the boundary. Each such edge is coloured with the same colour as the boundary edge. So two edges have the same colour if they are parallel and therefore we have the edge colouring of G. Since it uses n colours, we have shown that $\chi'(G) \leq n$.

Let G have an $(n-1)$-colouring. From the definition of an edge colouring, the edges of one particular colour form a matching in G (set of independent edges). Since n is odd, therefore the maximum possible number of these is $(n-1)/2$. This implies that there are atmost $(n-1)(n-1)/2$ edges in G. This is a contradiction, as K_n has $n(n-1)/2$ edges. Thus G does not have an $(n-1)$ colouring. Hence, $\chi'(G) = n$.

Now, let n be even, and let v be any vertex of G. Clearly $G - v$ is complete with $n-1$ vertices. Since $n-1$ is odd, $G - v$ has an $(n-1)$-colouring. With this colouring, there is a colour absent from each vertex and different vertices having different absentees. Reform G from $G - v$ by joining each vertex w of $G - v$ to v by an edge and colour each such edge by the colour absent from w. This gives an $(n-1)$-colouring of G and therefore $\chi'(G) = n-1$. ❑

The above result is illustrated by taking K_5 and K_6 in Figure 7.13.

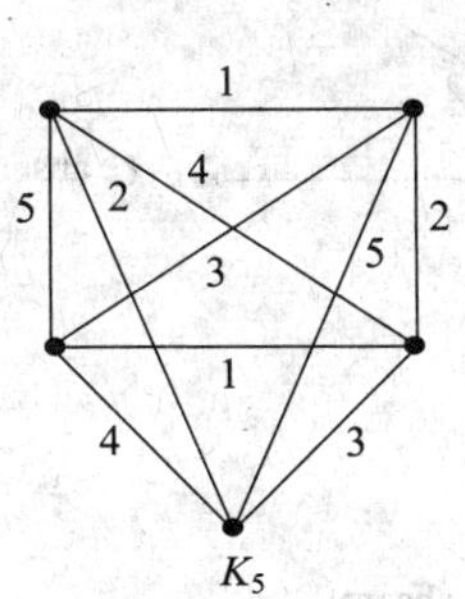

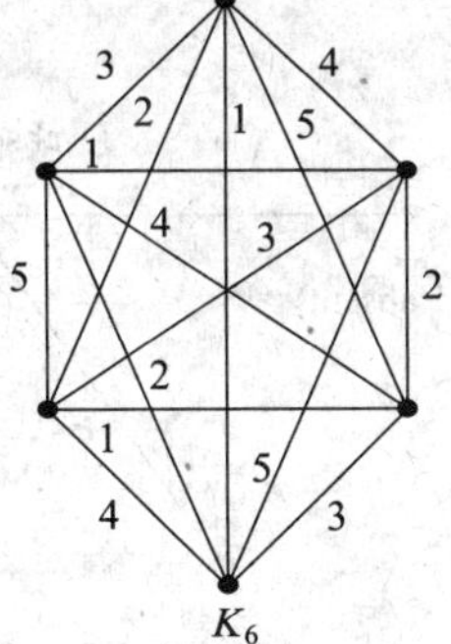

Fig. 7.13

Since $\triangle(G) = n-1$ in a complete graph, Theorem 7.17 shows that $\chi'(K_n)$ is either $\triangle(G)$ or $\triangle(G)+1$. The next result obtained by Vizing [251] and independently by Gupta [91] gives the tight bounds for edge chromatic number of a simple graph.

Theorem 7.18 (Vizing) For any graph G, $\triangle(G) \leq \chi'(G) \leq \triangle(G)+1$.

Proof Let G be a simple graph, we always have $\triangle(G) \leq \chi'(G)$.

To prove $\chi'(G) \leq \triangle(G)+1$, we use induction on the number of edges of G. Let $\triangle(G) = k$. If G has only one edge, then $k = 1 = \chi'(G)$. Therefore assume that G has more than one edge and that the result is true for all graphs having fewer edges than G.

Let $e = v_1v_2$ be an edge of G. Then by induction hypothesis the subgraph $G-e$ has $(k+1)$-edge colouring and let the colours used be 1, 2, ..., $k+1$.

Since $d(v_1) \leq k$ and $d(v_2) \leq k$, out of these $k+1$ colours at least one colour is absent from v_1 and at least one colour is absent from v_2. If there is a common colour absent from both v_1 and v_2, then we use this to colour e and get a $(k+1)$-colouring of G. Therefore in this case, $\chi'(G) \leq k+1$.

We now assume that there is a colour, say 1, absent from v_1 but present at v_2 and there is a colour, say 2, absent from v_2 but present at v_1. We start from v_1 and v_2 and construct a sequence of distinct vertices $v_1, v_2, \ldots, v_j$, where each v_i for $i \geq 2$ is adjacent to v_1. Let v_1v_3 be coloured 2. This v_3 exists, because 2 is present at v_1. We observe that not all the $k+1$ colours are present at v_3 and assume that the colour 3 is absent from v_3. But the colour 3 is present at v_1 and choose the vertex v_4 so that v_1v_4 is coloured 3. Continuing in this way, we choose a new colour i absent from v_i but present at v_1, so that v_1v_{i+1} is the edge coloured i. In this way, we get a sequence of vertices $v_1, v_2, v_3, \ldots, v_{j-1}, v_j$ such that

a. v_i is adjacent to v_1 for each $i > 1$,

b. the colour i is absent from each $i = 1, 2, \ldots, j-1$ and

c. the edge v_1v_{i+1} is coloured i for each i = 1, 2, ..., $j-1$.

This is illustrated in Figure 7.14.

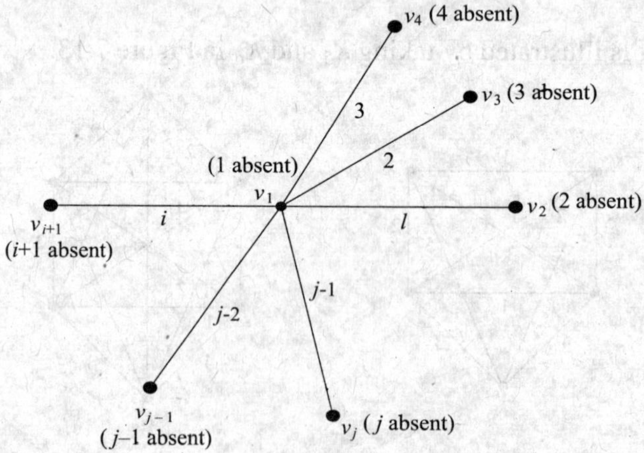

Fig. 7.14

As $d(v_1) \leq k$, (a) implies that such a sequence has at most $k+1$ terms, that is, $j \leq k+1$. Assume that $v_1, v_2, \ldots, v_j$ is a longest such sequence, that is, the sequence for which it is not possible to find a new colour j, absent from v_j, together with a new neighbour v_{j+1} of v_1 such that $v_1 v_{j+1}$ is coloured j.

We first assume that for some colour j absent from v_j there is no edge of that colour present at v_1. We colour the edge $e = v_1 v_2$ by colour 2 and then recolour the edges $v_1 v_j$ by colour i, for $i = 3, \ldots, j-1$. Since i was absent from v_i, for each $i = 2, \ldots, j-1$, this gives a $(k+1)$-colouring of the subgraph $G - v_1 v_j$. Now as the colour j is absent from both v_j and v_1, recolour $v_1 v_j$ by the colour j. This gives a $(k+1)$-colouring of G (Fig. 7.15).

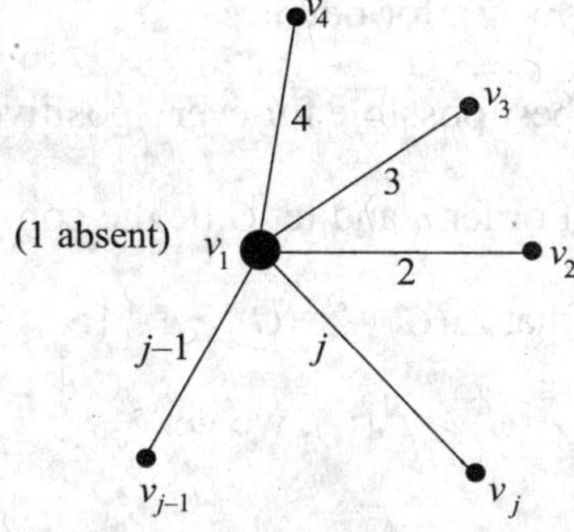

Fig. 7.15

Now assume that whenever j is absent from v_j, j is present at v_1. If v_{j+1} is a new neighbour of v_1 so that $v_1 v_{j+1}$ is coloured by j, then we have extended our sequence to $v_1, v_2, \ldots, v_j, v_{j+1}$ which is a contradiction to the assumption that $v_1, v_2, \ldots, v_j$ is the longest sequence. Thus one of the edges $v_1 v_3, \ldots, v_1 v_{j-1}$ is to be coloured by j, say $v_1 v_\ell$, with $3 \leq \ell \leq j-1$. Now colour $e = v_1 v_2$ by 2, and for $i = 3, \ldots, \ell-1$, recolour each of the edges $v_1 v_i$ by i while unaltering the colours of the edges $v_1 v_i$, for $i = \ell+1, \ldots, j$. Removing the colour j from $v_1 v_\ell$, we have a $(k+1)$-colouring of the edge deleted subgraph $G - v_1 v_\ell$.

Let $H(1, j)$ represent the subgraph of G induced by the edges coloured 1 or j in this partial colouring of G. Since the degree of every vertex in $H(1, j)$ is either 1 or 2, each component of $H(1, j)$ is either a path or a cycle. As 1 is absent from v_1 and j is absent from both v_j and v_ℓ, it follows that all these three vertices do not belong to the same connected component of $H(1, j)$. Therefore, if K and L represent the corresponding Kempe chains containing v_j and v_ℓ respectively, then either $v_1 \notin K$ or $v_1 \notin L$. Let $v_1 \notin L$. Then interchanging the colours of L, the Kempe chain argument gives a $(k+1)$-colouring of $G - v_1 v_\ell$ in which 1 is missing from both v_1 and v_ℓ. Colouring $v_1 v_\ell$ by 1 gives a $(k+1)$-colouring of G.

Now, let $v_1 \notin K$. Colour the edge $v_1 v_\ell$ by ℓ, recolour the edges $v_1 v_i$ by i, for $i = \ell, \ldots, j-1$, and remove the colour $j-1$ from $v_1 v_j$. Then, from the definition of the sequence $v_1, v_2, \ldots, v_j$, we get a $(k+1)$-colouring of $G - v_1 v_j$ without affecting two coloured subgraph $H(1, j)$. Using Kempe chain argument to interchange the colours of K, we obtain a $(k+1)$-colouring of $G - v_1 v_j$ in which 1 is absent from both v_1 and v_j. Therefore, again colouring $v_1 v_j$ by 1 gives $(k+1)$-colouring of G. ❑

The following result is due to Vizing [252] and Alavi and Behzad [2].

Theorem 7.19 Let G be a graph of order n and let $\overline{G}$ be the complement of G. Then

a. $n-1 \leq \chi'(G)+\chi'(\overline{G}) \leq 2(n-1)$,

$0 \leq \chi'(G)\chi'(\overline{G}) \leq (n-1)^2$, for even n,

b. $n \leq \chi'(G)+\chi'(\overline{G}) \leq 2n-3$,

$0 \leq \chi'(G)\chi'(\overline{G}) \leq (n-1)(n-2)$, for odd n.

Further, the bounds are the best possible for every positive integer $n (n \neq 2)$.

Proof Let G be a graph of order n and let $\overline{G}$ be the complement of G. Clearly,

$\triangle(\overline{G}) \geq n-1-\triangle(G)$, so that $\triangle(G)+\triangle(\overline{G}) \geq n-1$.

Therefore, combining with $\chi'(G) \geq \triangle(G)$, we get

$\chi'(G)+\chi'(\overline{G}) \geq n-1$.

b. If n is odd, we have $\chi'(G)+\chi'(\overline{G}) \geq n$, since $\chi'(G)+\chi'(\overline{G}) < n$ implies $\chi'(K_n) < n$, which is a contradiction.

Obviously, $\chi'(G)\chi'(\overline{G}) \geq 0$. It can be seen that the lower bounds are attained in complete graphs K_n.

We now prove that $\chi'(G)+\chi'(\overline{G}) \leq 2n-3$ and $\chi'(G)\chi'(\overline{G}) \leq (n-1)(n-2)$.

Clearly, for $n = 1, 3$, the inequalities $\chi'(G)+\chi'(\overline{G}) \leq 2n-3$ are true. So, let $n \geq 5$. If $\triangle(G)+\triangle(\overline{G}) \leq 2n-5$, then by Vizing's theorem, we get $\chi'(G)+\chi'(\overline{G}) \leq 2n-3$.

Otherwise, we have the following cases.

i. $\triangle(G) = n-1$ and $\triangle(\overline{G}) = n-2$. So G has a pendant vertex v. Then $\triangle(G-v) \geq n-2$ and $\chi'(G-v) \geq n-2$. But $\chi'(G-v) \leq \chi'(K_{n-1}) = n-2$. Therefore, $\chi'(G-v) = n-2$. Thus, $\chi'(G) = n-1$.

   As $\overline{G}$ is the disjoint union of an isolated vertex and a subgraph of K_{n-1}, $\chi'(\overline{G}) \leq n-2$. Hence, $\chi'(G)+\chi'(\overline{G}) \leq 2n-3$.

ii. $\triangle(G) = n-2$ and $\triangle(\overline{G}) = n-2$. Again, G has a pendant vertex v and as before, $\chi'(G-v) \leq n-2$ and $\chi'(G) = n-2$. Similarly, $\chi'(\overline{G}) = n-2$. Thus, $\chi'(G)+\chi'(\overline{G}) = 2n-4 < 2n-3$.

iii. $\triangle(G) = n-1$ and $\triangle(\overline{G}) = n-3$. In this case, G has a vertex v of degree two and so $\chi'(G-v) = n-2$.

Let vu and vw be the edges incident with v in G, with $d(u) = n-1$. In $(n-2)$-edge colouring of $G-v$, change the colour i of an edge $uu'(u' \neq w)$ to a new colour $n-1$, and now colour vu by i and vw by $n-1$. This gives an $(n-1)$-colouring of G. Now, by Vizing's theorem, $\chi'(\overline{G}) \leq n-2$.

Together, we get $\chi'(G)+\chi'(\overline{G}) \leq 2n-3$. Since $\chi'(G)+\chi'(\overline{G}) \leq 2n-3$, clearly we have $\chi'(G)\chi'(\overline{G}) \leq (n-1)(n-2)$. We observe that in graph $K_{1,n-1}$, the upper bounds are attained.

a. Let n be even. Then $\chi'(G)+\chi'(\overline{G}) \geq n-1$. Also, $\chi'(G)\chi'(\overline{G}) \geq 0$.

The lower bounds are attained for complete graphs.

To get the upper bounds, since G and $\overline{G}$ are subgraphs of K_n and $\chi'(K_n) = n-1$ for all even n, $\chi'(G)+\chi(\overline{G}) \leq 2(n-1)$ and $\chi'(G)\chi'(\overline{G}) \leq (n-1)^2$. These upper bounds are attained in the complete bipartite graphs $K_{1,n-1}, n \neq 2$. ❑

7.5 Region Colouring (Map Colouring)

A region colouring of a planar graph is a labeling of its regions $f : R(G) \to \{1, 2, \ldots\}$; the labels called *colours*, such that no two adjacent regions get the same colour. A k-region colouring of a planar graph G consists of k different colours and G is then called *k-region colourable*. From the definition, it follows that the k-region colouring of a planar graph G partitions the region set R into k independent sets $R_1, R_2, \ldots, R_k$, so that $R = R_1 \cup R_2 \cup \ldots \cup R_k$. The independent sets are called the *colour classes*, and the function $f : R(G) \to \{1, 2, \ldots, k\}$ such that $f(r) = i$, for each $r \in R_i$, $1 \leq i \leq k$, is called the *colour function*. The minimum number k for which there is a k-region colouring of the planar graph G is called the *region-chromatic number* of G, and is denoted by $\chi''(G)$. The colouring of regions is also called *map colouring*, because of the fact that in an atlas different countries are coloured such that countries with common boundaries are shown in different colours.

The four colour problem: Any map on a plane surface (or a sphere) can be coloured with at most four colours so that no two adjacent regions have the same colour.

Now coming to the origin of the four colour problem, there have been reports that Mobius was familiar with the problem in 1840. But the problem was introduced in 1852 by Francis Guthrie, student of Augustus DeMorgan and the problem first appeared in a letter (October 23, 1852) from DeMorgan to Sir William Hamilton. DeMorgan continued the discussion of the problem with other mathematicians and in the years that followed attempts were made to prove or disprove the problem by top mathematical minds of the world. In 1878, Cayley announced the problem to the London Mathematical Society, and in 1879, Alfred Kempe announced that he had found a proof. An error in Kempe's proof was discovered by P. J. Heawood in 1890. Kempe's idea was based on the alternating paths and Heawood used this idea to prove that five colours are sufficient. Kempe's argument did not prove the four colour problem, but did contain several ideas which formed the foundation for many later attempts at the proof, including the successful attempts by Appel and Haken. In 1976, K. Appel and W. Haken [5, 6, 7] with the help of J. Koch established what is now called four colour theorem. Their proof made use of large scale computers (using over

1000 hours of computer time) and this is the first time in the history of mathematics that a mathematical proof depended upon the external factor of the availability of a large scale computing facility. Though the Appel-Haken proof is accepted as valid, mathematicians are still in search of alternative proof. Robertson, Sanders, Seymour and Thomas [225] have given a short and clever proof, but their proof still requires a number of computer calculations. Saaty [224] presents thirteen colourful variations of four colour problem.

The following observations are immediate from the definitions introduced above.

1. A planar graph is k-vertex colourable or k-region colourable if and only if its components have this property.
2. A planar graph is k-vertex colourable or k-region colourable if and only if its blocks have this property.

These observations imply that for studying vertex colourings or region colourings, it suffices to consider the graph to be a block.

Theorem 7.20

a. A planar graph G is k-region colourable if and only if its dual G is k-vertex colourable.

b. If G is a plane connected graph without loops, then G has a k-vertex colouring if and only if its dual G^* has a k-region colouring.

Proof

a. Let the regions and edges of G be respectively denoted by $r_1, \ldots, r_t$ and $e_1, \ldots, e_m$. Let the vertices of G^* be $r_1^*, \ldots, r_t^*$ and edges be $e_1^*, \ldots, e_m^*$. Then the vertices and edges of G^* are in one-to-one correspondence with the regions and edges of G, and two vertices r^* and s^* in G^* are joined by an edge e^* if and only if the corresponding regions r and s in G have the corresponding edge e as a common edge on their boundary.

Let G be k-region colourable. We colour the vertices in G^* such that each vertex in G^* gets the same colour as assigned to the region r in G. Since the vertices r^* and s^* are only adjacent in G^* if the corresponding regions r and s are adjacent in G, G^* is k-vertex colourable.

Conversely, let G^* be k-vertex colourable. Now colour the regions of G such that the region r in G gets the samecolour as the vertex r^* in G^*. This gives a k-region colouring of G, since the regions r and s are adjacent in G only if the corresponding vertices r^* and s^* are adjacent in G^*.

b. Since G has no loops its dual G^* has no bridges, and therefore G^* is planar. Thus by (a), G^* is k-region colourable if and only if the double dual G^{**} is k-vertex colourable. Since G is connected, G is isomorphic to G^{**} and hence the result follows. ❑

Remarks A graph has a dual if and only if it is planar and this implies that colouring the regions of a planar graph G is equivalent to colouring the vertices of its dual G^* and vice versa. It also follows from Theorem 7.17 that if G^* is the dual of the planar graph G, then $\chi(G) = \chi''(G^*)$ and $\chi(G^*) = \chi''(G)$. These observations give the dual form of the four colour problem which states that, every planar graph is 4-vertex colourable.

Since loops and multiple edges are not allowed in vertex colourings, it may be assumed that no two regions have more than one boundary edge in common, for region colouring of a planar graph

As every triangulation is a planar graph (in fact, a maximal planar graph) and every planar graph is a subgraph of a triangulation, the four colour problem is true if and only if every triangulation is 4-colourable.

The following result shows that a planar graph is 6-colourable.

Theorem 7.21 Every planar graph is 6-colourable.

Proof Let G be a planar graph and H be the dual of G. Then it is sufficient to prove that H has a vertex colouring of at most 6 colours. More generally, we prove that any graph H is 6-colourable.

To prove the result, we use induction on n, the order of H. The result is trivial if H has at most six vertices. So assume $n \geq 7$.

Let all planar graphs with fewer than n vertices be 6-colourable. Obviously, H has a vertex, say v, so that $d(v) \leq 5$. Therefore v has at most five neighbours in H and these neighbours evidently need at most five colours for colouring. The vertex deleted subgraph $H - v$ is planar with $n - 1$ vertices and therefore by induction hypothesis is 6-colourable. Since at most five colours are used for colouring the neighbours of v, therefore assigning v the sixth colour not used by the its neighbours gives the 6-colouring of H. ❑

The following result is a consequence of Theorem 7.20.

Theorem 7.22 A planar graph G is 2-colourable if and only if it is an Euler graph.

Proof Let G be a planar graph which is 2-colourable. Then, if G^* is the geometric dual of G, we have $\chi(G^*) = 2$. Therefore G^* is bipartite and thus G^{**} (the dual of G^*) is an Euler graph. Since G and G^{**} are isomorphic, therefore G is an Euler graph.

Conversely, let G be an Euler graph. Then its double dual G^{**} is an Euler graph and thus G^* is bipartite. Therefore, $\chi(G^*) = 2$ and hence the planar graph G is 2-colourable. ❑

The next result due to Heawood [109] is called *five colour theorem* and Heawood used the Kempe chain argument in proving it.

Theorem 7.23 (Heawood) Every planar graph is 5-colourable.

Proof Let G be a planar graph with n vertices. We use induction on n, the order of G. The result is obvious for $n \leq 5$. So, let $n \geq 6$. Assume the result to be true for all planar graphs with fewer than n vertices.

Let G' be the graph obtained from G by deleting the vertex v and removing all the edges incident with v. The graph G' with order $n-1$ is clearly planar and by induction hypothesis is 5-colourable. Let the colours used to colour G' be c_1, c_2, c_3, c_4, c_5.

We know for a planar graph with $n \geq 6$ vertices, there exists a vertex, say v, such that $d(v) \leq 5$. Thus v has atmost five neighbours in G and all of these neighbours are the already coloured vertices in G'.

If in G' less than five colours are used to colour these neighbours, then the 5-colouring of G is obtained by using the colouring for G' on all vertices, and by colouring v with the colour not used to colour the neighbours of v (Fig. 7.16).

Let all the five colours be used in G', to colour the neighbours of v. This implies that there are exactly five neighbours of v, say u_1, u_2, u_3, u_4 and u_5. Assume without loss of generality that u_i is coloured with c_i, for each i, $1 \leq i \leq 5$.

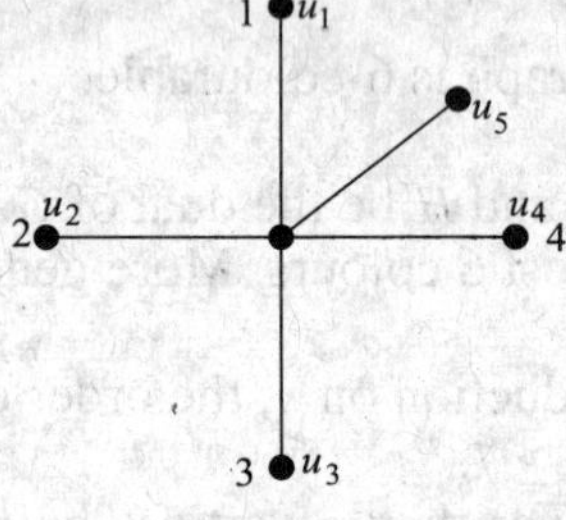

Fig. 7.16

Consider all the vertices of G' that are coloured with colour c_1 and c_3. If u_1 and u_3 are in different components of the Kempe subgraph $H(c_1, c_3)$ induced by those vertices coloured c_1 and c_3, then using the Kempe chain argument to interchange the colours c_1 and c_3 in the component containing u_1 leaves c_1 unused on the set $\{u_1, u_2, u_3, u_4, u_5\}$. We colour v by c_1 to get a 5-colouring of G.

Finally, if u_1 and u_3 are in the same component of $H(c_1, c_3)$, and u_2 and u_4 are in the same component of $H(c_2, c_4)$, then the $c_1 - c_3$ Kempe chain from u_1 to u_3 crosses the $c_2 - c_4$ Kempe chain from u_2 to u_4. This is impossible as the triangulation is a plane graph (Fig. 7.17). ❑

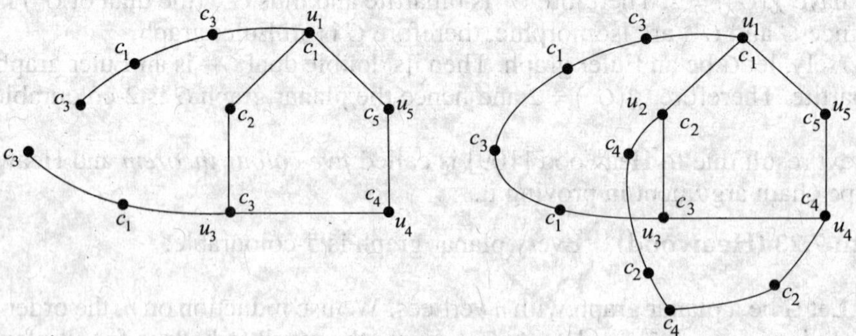

Fig. 7.17

The following result is due to Grunbaum [88].

Theorem 7.24 Every planar graph with fewer than four triangles is 3-colourable.

The next result due to Grotzsch [87] immediately follows from Theorem 7.24.

Theorem 7.25 Every planar graph without triangles is 3-colourable.

While making various attempts to solve the four colour problem, the problem got translated into several equivalent conjectures and sometimes conjectures were made which implied the four colour problem. The details of several such conjectures can be found in Saaty [223] and Saaty and Kainen [224]. Finch and Sachs [75] proved that every planar graph with at most 21 triangles is 4-colourable. Ore and Stemple [179] showed that all planar graphs with upto 39 regions are 4-colourable.

The following result is one such equivalence.

Theorem 7.26 Every planar graph is four colourable if and only if every cubic bridgeless planar graph is 4-colourable.

Proof We observe that every planar graph is four colourable if and only if every bridgeless planar graph (without cut edges) is four colourable. This is because if G has a bridge e and G' is obtained from G by contracting e, then $\chi''(G') = \chi''(G)$ (as the elementary contraction of identifying the end vertices of a bridge affects neither the number of regions in the planar graph nor the adjacency of any of the regions).

We now prove that every bridgeless planar graph is 4-colourable if and only if every cubic bridgeless planar graph is 4-colourable. If every bridgeless planar graph is 4-colourable, then evidently every cubic bridgeless planar graph is 4-colourable.

Conversely, let all cubic bridgeless planar graphs be 4-colourable. Let G be a bridgeless planar graph. We obtain G' from G by performing the following operations. In case G has a vertex v of degree two, let xv and yv be the edges incident with v. Subdivide xv at u and yv at w. Take two new vertices a and b and add the edges au, aw, bu, bw and ab. Now remove v (and uv and uw). In doing so, we have replaced v by a $K_4 - e$ and we see that each new vertex has degree three (Fig. 7.18).

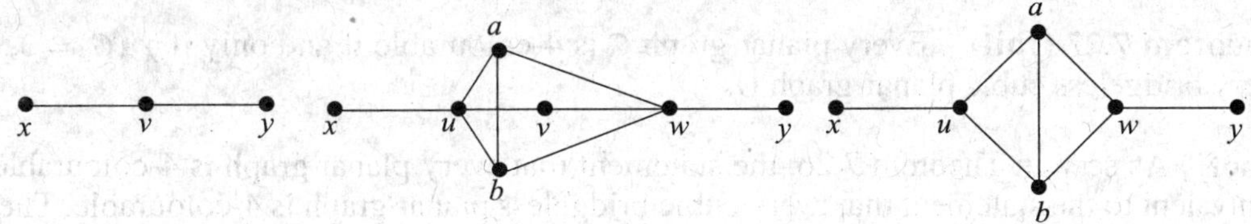

Fig. 7.18

If G has a vertex v so that $d(v) \geq 4$, let $vx_1, vx_2, \ldots, vx_d$ be the edges incident with v. Subdivide each vx_i producing a new vertex v_i, for $1 \leq i \leq d$. We then remove v and add the new edges v_1v_2, v_2v_3, ..., $v_{d-1}v_d$, v_dv_1. Here we have replaced v by C_d and again the degree of each new vertex is three (Fig. 7.19).

In both cases the graph G' formed is a bridgeless cubic graph. If these $K_4 - e$ and C_d introduced are contracted, we get the original graph G. Hence G is 4-colourable, since we have assumed that G' is 4-colourable. ❑

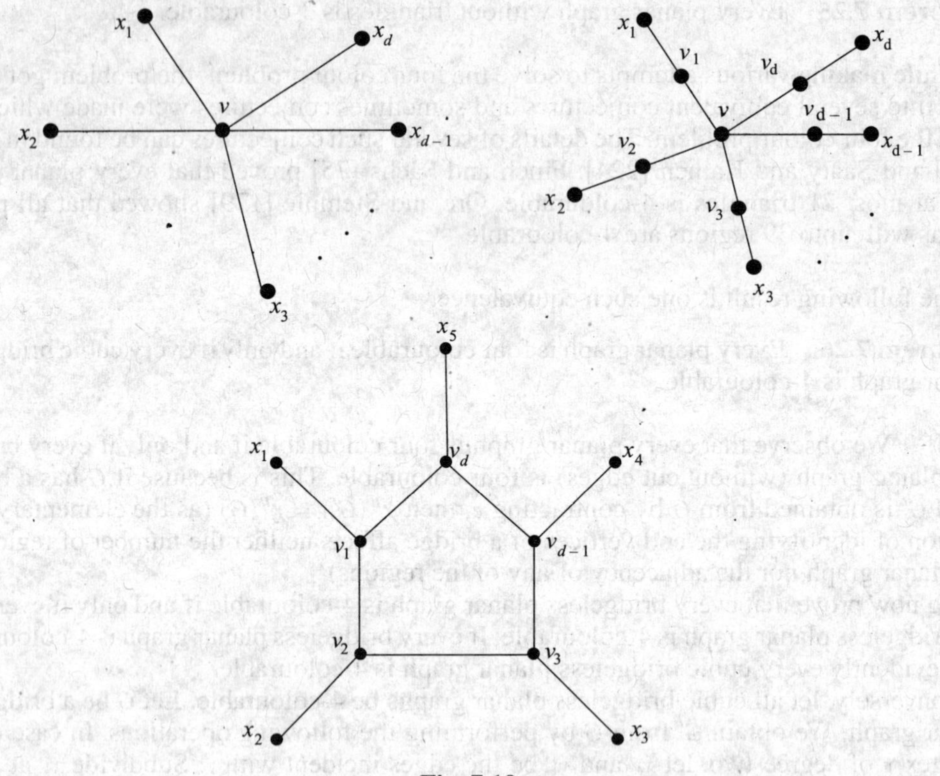

Fig. 7.19

The next result is due to Tait [232] and the details can also be found in Bondy and Chvatal [36] and Bollobas [29].

Theorem 7.27 (Tait) Every planar graph G is 4-colourable if and only if $\chi'(G) = 3$, for every bridgeless cubic planar graph G.

Proof As seen in Theorem 7.26, the statement that every planar graph is 4-colourable is equivalent to the statement that every cubic bridgeless planar graph is 4-colourable. Therefore, to prove the result, we prove that a cubic bridgeless planar graph G is 4-colourable if and only if $\chi'(G) = 3$.

Now assume that G is a bridgeless cubic planar graph which is 4-colourable. For the set of colours we choose the elements of the Klein four group $Q = \{c_0, c_1, c_2, c_3\}$, where addition in Q is defined by $c_i + c_i = c_0$ and $c_1 + c_2 = c_3$, with c_0 being the identity element.

Now, define the colour of an edge to be the sum of the colours of two distinct regions which are incident with that edge. We see that the edges are coloured with elements of the set $\{c_1, c_2, c_3\}$ and that no two adjacent edges get the same colour. Hence, $\chi'(G) = 3$.

Conversely, let G be a bridgeless cubic planar graph with $\chi'(G) = 3$ and colour its edges with the three non-zero elements of Q. Consider a region, say R_0, and give the colour c_0 to it. Let R be any other region of G and let C be any curve in the plane joining the interior of R_0 with the interior of R, so that C does not pass through a vertex of G. Then the colour of R is defined to be the sum of the colours of those edges which intersect C.

That the colours of the regions are well defined follows from the fact that the sum of the colours of the edges which intersect any simple closed curve not passing through a vertex of G is c_0. Suppose S is such a curve and assume $q_1, q_2, \ldots, q_n$ to be the colours of the edges which intersect S. Also assume $r_1, r_2, \ldots, r_m$ be the colours of those edges interior to S. If $c(v)$ denotes the sum of the colours of the three edges incident with v, then we see that $c(v) = c_0$. Thus, for all vertices v interior to S, we have $\sum c(v) = c_0$. While on the other hand, we have $\sum c(v) = q_1 + q_2 + \ldots + q_n + 2(r_1 + r_2 + \ldots + r_m) = q_1 + q_2 + \ldots + q_n$ as every element of Q is self-inverse. Thus, $q_1 + q_2 + \ldots. + q_n = c_o$. Hence we get the 4-colouring of the regions of G and the colours used are c_0, c_1, c_2, c_3. ❑

Remarks Because of Theorem 7.27, a three colouring of the edges of a cubic graph is called a *Tait colouring*.

In an attempt to solve the four colour problem, Tait considered edge colourings of bridgeless cubic planar graphs and proved that every such graph is 3-edge colourable. In 1880, Tait tried to give a proof of the four colour problem by using Theorem 7.27 and based on the wrong assumption that any bridgeless cubic planar graph is Hamiltonian. A counter example called the Tuttle graph to Tait's assumption was given by Tutte in 1946 and is shown in Figure 7.20.

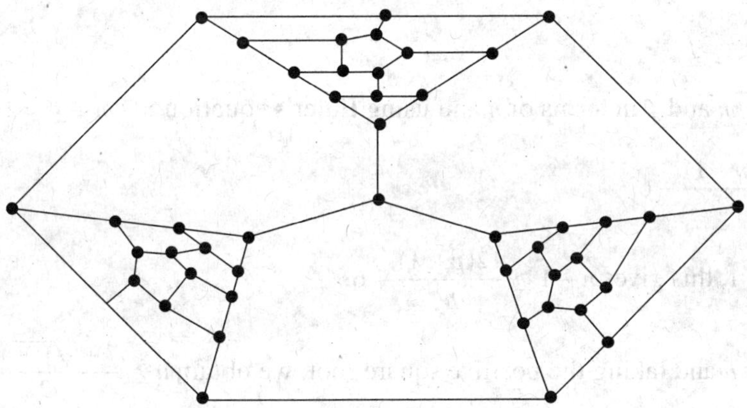

Fig. 7.20

7.6 Heawood Map-Colouring Theorem

Let S_p be the orientable surface of genus p, so that S_p is topologically equivalent to a sphere with p handles. The chromatic number of S_p, denoted by $\chi(S_p)$, is the maximum chromatic number among all graphs which can be embedded on S_p. The surface S_o is clearly the sphere. The four colour problem states that $\chi(S_0) = 4$.

Definition: The genus $\gamma(G)$ of a graph is the minimum number of handles which must be added to a sphere so that G can be embedded on the resulting surface. Clearly, $\gamma(G) = 0$ if and only if G is planar. Further, for a polyhedron, $n - m + f = 2 - 2\gamma$.

For $n \geq 3$, the genus of the complete graph K_n is

$$\gamma(K_n) = \frac{(n-3)(n-4)}{12}.$$

The following inequality is due to Heawood [109].

Theorem 7.28 The chromatic number of the orientable surface of positive genus p has the upper bound

$$\chi(S_p) \leq \frac{7 + \sqrt{1+48p}}{2}, \; p > 0.$$

Proof Let G be an (n, m) graph embedded on S_p. Since any graph can be augmented to a triangulation of the same genus by adding edges without reducing χ, we assume G to be a triangulation. Let d' be the average degree of the vertices of G. Then n, m and f (the number of regions) are related by the equations

$$d'n = 2m = 3f.$$

Solving for m and f in terms of n and using Euler's equation $n - m + f = 2 - 2\gamma$, we get

$$d' = \frac{12(p-1)}{n} + 6. \tag{7.28.1}$$

As $d' \leq n - 1$, this gives $n - 1 \geq \dfrac{12(p-1)}{n} + 6$.

Solving for n and taking the positive square root, we obtain $n \geq \dfrac{7 + \sqrt{1+48p}}{2}$.

Let $H(p) = \dfrac{7 + \sqrt{1+48p}}{2}$. Then we show that $H(p)$ colours are sufficient to colour the vertices of G. If $n = H(p)$, obviously we have sufficient colours. In case $n > H(p)$, we substitute $H(p)$ for n in (7.28.1) and obtain

$$d' < \frac{12(p-1)}{H(p)} + 6 = H(p) - 1.$$

Therefore, when $n > H(p)$, there is a vertex v of degree at most $H(p) - 2$. Identify v and any adjacent vertex by an elementary contraction to obtain a new graph G'. If $n' = n - 1 = H(p)$, then G' can be coloured in $H(p)$ colours. If $n' > H(p)$, repeat the argument and evidently we get an $H(p)$ colourable graph. It is then easy to see that the colouring of this graph induces a colouring of the preceding one in $H(p)$ colours, and so forth, so that G itself is $H(p)$–colourable. Hence the result follows. ❑

The next result is called Heawood map colouring theorem, the proof of which is due to Ringel and Youngs [217].

Theorem 7.29 (Heawood map-colouring theorem) For every positive integer p, the chromatic number of the orientable surface of genus p is given by

$$\chi(S_p) = \frac{7 + \sqrt{1+48p}}{2},\ p > 0.$$

Proof Let G be an (n, m) graph embedded on S_p. Then,

$$\chi(S_p) \leq \frac{7 + \sqrt{1+48p}}{2},\ p > 0.$$

Now, if the complete graph K_n is embedded in S_p, then

$$p \geq \gamma(K_n) = \frac{(n-3)(n-4)}{12}. \qquad (7.29.1)$$

Setting n to be the largest integer satisfying (7.29.1), we have

$$\frac{(n-3)(n-4)}{12} \leq p \leq \left[\frac{(n-2)(n-3)}{12}\right] - 1 < \frac{(n-2)(n-3)}{12}.$$

Solving for n, we get

$$\frac{5 + \sqrt{1+48p}}{2} < n \leq \frac{7 + \sqrt{1+48p}}{2}$$

Thus, $n = \dfrac{7 + \sqrt{1+48p}}{2}$.

Since $\chi(K_n) = n$, we have found a graph with genus p and chromatic number equal to $H(p)$. This shows that $H(p)$ is a lower bound for $\chi(Sp)$, completing the proof. ❑

7.7 Uniquely Colourable Graph

A graph $G(V, E)$ is said to be *uniquely k-vertex-colourable* (or uniquely k-colourable) if there is a unique k-part partition of the vertex set V into independent subsets. That is, in the uniquely k-colouring of a graph G, every k-colouring of G induces the same partition of V. The graph of Figure 7.21(a) is uniquely 3-colourable, since every 3-colouring of G has the partition $\{v_1\}$, $\{v_2, v_4\}$, $\{v_3, v_5\}$. The graph of the Figure 7.21(b) is not uniquely 3-colourable. A pentagon is not uniquely 3-colourable, as five different partitions of its vertex set are possible.

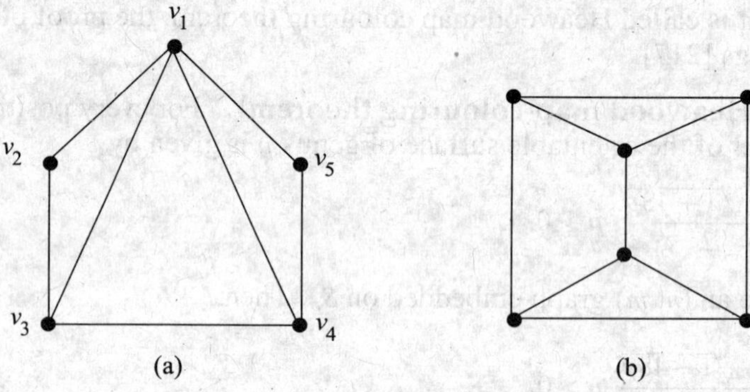

Fig. 7.21

We observe that the empty graphs $\overline{K_n}$ are the only uniquely 1-colourable graphs and the connected bipartite graphs are the only uniquely 2-colourable graphs. We note that unique k-colourability is not defined for $k > n$. Further, we see that K_n is uniquely n-colourable. These observations imply to assume $3 \leq k \leq n$, for studying uniquely k-colourable graphs.

We have the following observation.

Theorem 7.30 If G is uniquely k-colourable, then $\delta(G) \geq k-1$.

Proof Let G be a uniquely k-colourable graph. Then every vertex v of G is adjacent to at least one vertex of every colour different from that assigned to v. For otherwise, a different k-colouring of G is obtained by recolouring v. This implies that $d(v) \geq k-1$, for every v. ❑

Corollary 7.2 If G is a uniquely k-colourable graph with n vertices and m edges, then $2m \geq n(k-1)$.

The next result, due to Cartwright and Harary [44], gives a necessary condition for a graph to be uniquely colourable.

Theorem 7.31 The subgraph induced by the union of any two colour classes in a k-colouring of a uniquely k-colourable graph is connected.

Proof Let G be a uniquely k-colourable graph. Let C_1 and C_2 be two classes in the k-colouring of the graph G. Assume the subgraph S of G induced by $C_1 \cup C_2$ to be disconnected, and let S_1 and S_2 be components of S. Then each of S_1 and S_2 contain vertices of both C_1 and C_2. Now interchanging the colour of the vertices in $C_1 \cap S_1$ by the colour of the vertices in $C_2 \cap S_1$ gives a different k-colouring of G. This contradicts the hypothesis that G is uniquely k-colourable. Hence S is connected. ❑

The converse of Theorem 7.31 is not true. To see this, consider the 3-chromatic graph G of Fig. 7.21(b). The graph G has the property that in any 3-colouring, the subgraph induced by the union of any 2 colour classes is connected. But G is not uniquely colourable. It follows from Theorem 7.30 that every uniquely k-colourable graph, $k \geq 2$, is connected.

The following stronger result is due to Chartrand and Geller [48].

Theorem 7.32 Any uniquely k-colourable graph is $(k-1)$-connected.

Proof Let G be a uniquely k-colourable graph. In case G is K_k, then it is $(k-1)$-connected. Now assume G to be an incomplete graph which is not $(k-1)$–connected. Therefore there exists a set U of $k-2$ vertices whose removal disconnects G. Then in any k-colouring of G, there are at least two distinct colours, say c_1 and c_2, not assigned to any vertex of U. By Theorem 7.30, a vertex coloured c_1 is connected to any vertex coloured c_2 by a path all of whose vertices are coloured c_1 or c_2. Therefore the set of vertices of G coloured c_1 or c_2 lies within the same component of $G-U$, say G_1. Another k-colouring of G can thus be obtained by taking any vertex of $G-U$ which is not in G_1 and recolouring it with either c_1 or c_2. This contradicts the hypothesis that G is uniquely k-colourable. Hence G is $(k-1)$-connected. ❑

Corollary 7.3 In any k-colouring of uniquely k-colouring graph, the subgraph induced by the union of any h colour classes, $2 \leq h \leq k$, is $(h-1)$-connected.

The following result due to Bollobas [30] gives a sufficient lower bound for uniquely colourable graphs.

Theorem 7.33 If G is a k-colourable graph of order $n(k \geq 2)$ with $\delta(G) > n(3k-5)/(3k-2)$, then G is uniquely k-colourable.

The following result is due to Harary, Hedetniemi and Robinson [103].

Theorem 7.34 For all $k \geq 3$, there is a uniquely k-colourable graph which contains no subgraph isomorphic to K_k.

Clearly, a graph is uniquely 1-colourable if and only if it is 1-colourable, that is, totally disconnected. Also, a graph is uniquely 2-colourable if and only if G is 2-chromatic and connected. Chartrand and Geller observed that if a 2-connected 3-chromatic planar graph G has at most one region which is not a triangle, then G is uniquely 3-colourable.

The converse of the above statement is not true. This is because a uniquely 3-colourable planar graph may have more than one region which is not a triangle, as shown in Figure

7.22.

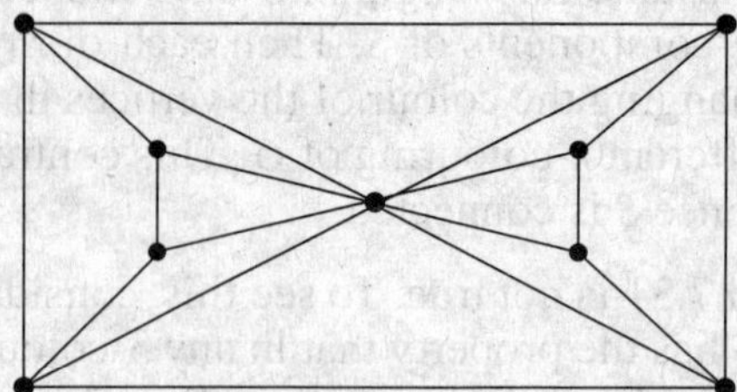

Fig. 7.22 *Uniquely 3-colourable planar graph*

Theorem 7.35 If G is a uniquely 3-colourable planar graph with at least four vertices, then G contains at least two triangles.

Theorem 7.36 Every uniquely 4-colourable planar graph is maximal planar.

Proof Let a 4-colouring be given to uniquely 4-colourable planar graph G with the colour classes denoted by $V_i, 1 \leq i \leq 4$, where $|V_i| = n_i$. Since the subgraph induced by $V_i \cup V_j, i \neq j$, is connected, G has at least $\sum(n_i + n_j - 1)$ edges, $1 \leq i < j \leq 4$. Clearly, $\sum(n_i + n_j - 1) = n_1 + n_2 - 1 + n_1 + n_3 - 1 + n_1 + n_4 - 1 + n_2 + n_3 - 1 + n_2 + n_4 - 1 + n_3 + n_4 - 1 = 3(n_1 + n_2 + n_3 + n_4) - 6 = 3n - 6$. Therefore, $m \geq 3n - 6$. Hence G is maximal planar. ❑

The next result for uniquely 5-colourable graphs is due to Hedetniemi [110].

Theorem 7.37 No planar graph is uniquely 5-colourable.

Theorem 7.38 A necessary and sufficient condition that a connected planar graph is 4-colourable is that G be the sum of three subgraphs G_1, G_2 and G_3 such that for each vertex v, the number of edges of each G_i incident with v are all even or odd.

The following equivalence is due to Whitney [257].

Theorem 7.39 The four colour problem holds if and only if every Hamiltonian planar graph is 4-colourable.

7.8 Hajos Conjecture

Hajos [97] made the following conjecture.

If a graph is k-chromatic, then it contains a subdivision of K_k.

When $k = 1$, or 2, the conjecture trivially holds. As for $k = 3$, every chromatic graph contains an odd cycle which is a subdivision of K_3, therefore proving the validity of the conjecture. The validity of the conjecture for $k = 4$, as noted in Parthasarthy [175] is due to Dirac [63].

Theorem 7.40 Hajos conjecture is true for $k = 4$.

Proof Assume without loss of generality that G is a 4-minimal graph. So G is a block and $\delta = 3$. In case $n = 4$, G is K_4 and the result is obvious. Therefore assume $n \geq 5$. We induct on n.

Let G have a 2-vertex cut $S = \{u, v\}$. Then by Theorem 7.5, $G = G_1 \cup G_2$, where G_1 is of type 1, and G_2 is of type 2 and $G_1 + uv$ is 4-minimal. By induction hypothesis, $G_1 + uv$ contains a subdivision of K_4. Here we replace uv by a $u - v$ path P in G_2 and so $G_1 \cup P$ contains a subdivision of K_4. Thus G also contains a subdivision of K_4. Now, let G be 3-connected. Since $\delta(G) \geq 3$, therefore it has a cycle C of length at least 4. If u and v are any two non-consecutive vertices on C, then $G - \{u, v\}$ is still connected and therefore there exist vertices x, y on C, and an $x - y$ path P in $G - \{u, v\}$. Similarly, there exists a $u - v$ path Q in $G - \{x, y\}$. If P and Q have no vertices in common, then $C \cup P \cup Q$ is a subdivision of K_4 in G. Otherwise, let w be the first vertex of P on Q, then $C \cup P_{xw} \cup Q$ is a subdivision of K_4 in G.

Hence in all cases G contains a subdivision of K_4. ❑

For $k \geq 5$, Hajos conjecture implies four colour problem. This is because if G is a planar graph which is not colourable by 4 colours, its chromatic number is at least 5 and thus contains a subdivision of K_5, and so cannot be planar, a contradiction. The four colour theorem implies that a 5-chromatic graph contains a homeomorph of K_5 or $K_{3,3}$. For $k = 5$, Hajos conjecture makes the stronger assertion that it contains a homeomorph of K_5. For $k = 5$, or 6, the conjecture has not been settled, but for $k = 7$, it is disproved by Catlin. The counter example of Catlin is the graph $H = L(3C_5) - \{v_1, v_2\}$, where $3C_5$ is the multigraph obtained from C_5 by replacing each edge by three edges, L represents the edge graph, and v_1 and v_2 are any two non-adjacent vertices of $L(3C_5)$ (Fig. 7.23).

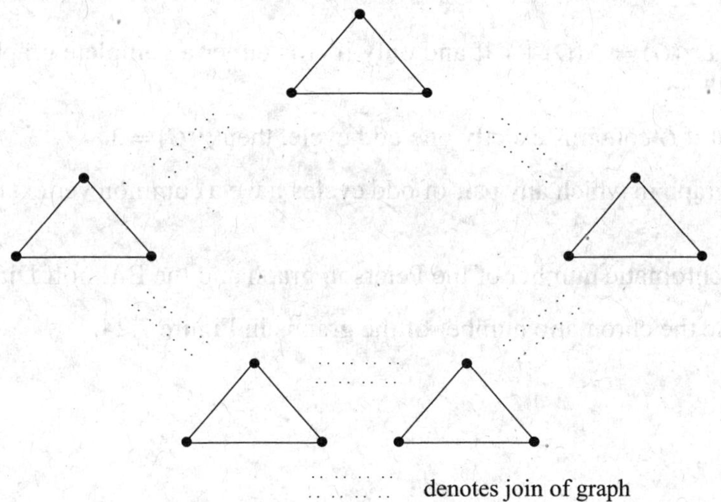

Fig. 7.23

The largest integer for which a given graph G contains a TK_n is called the subdivision number (or topological clique number or Hajos number) of G and is denoted by $tw(G)$. With this, Hajos conjecture is equivalent to $tw(G) \geq \chi(G)$. In the above example, we see that H contains a K_6 and from any vertex outside this K_6 there are no six internally disjoint paths to the vertices of the K_6. Therefore, $tw(H) = 6$. A maximum independent set of H has cardinality two, so that $\chi(H) \geq \left\lceil \frac{13}{2} \right\rceil = 7$ and a 7-colouring of H is shown in the Fig. 7.23. Thus, $\chi(H) = 7$ and hence H is a counter example for Hajos conjecture. We now observe that if G is a counter example for Hajos conjecture for k, then $G+v$ is a counter example for Hajos conjecture for $k+1$. This can be seen from the fact that $tw(G+v) = tw(G)+1$ and $\chi(G+v) = \chi(G)+1$. Hence Hajos conjecture is false for all $k = 7$. Erdos and Fajtlowicz [69] proved that almost every graph is a counter example to Hajos conjecture. Bollobas and Catlin [31] proved that $tw(G)$ is approximately $2\sqrt{n}$ for n-vertex graphs.

The following conjecture involving contractions is due to Hadwiger [92].

Hadwiger's conjecture [95] Every k-chromatic graph contains K_k as a subcontraction.

Hadwiger's conjecture is trivially true for $k = 1$. Since 2-chromatic graphs are the bipartite graphs and 3-chromatic graphs contain an odd cycle, contractible to K_3, the conjecture is true for $k = 2$ and 3. Dirac [63] proved the conjecture for $k = 4$. For $k = 5$, this conjecture states that every 5-chromatic graph is contractible to K_5 and therefore every such graph is non-planar. Thus Hadwiger's conjecture for $k = 5$ implies the four colour problem. The converse of this is given by Wagner.

7.9 Exercises

1. Prove that $\chi(G) = \triangle(G)+1$ if and only if G is either a complete graph or a cycle of odd length.
2. Show that if G contains exactly one odd cycle, then $\chi(G) = 3$.
3. If G is a graph in which any pair of odd cycles have a common vertex, then prove that $\chi(G) \leq 5$.
4. Find the chromatic number of the Peterson graph and the Birkhoff Diamond.
5. Determine the chromatic number of the graphs in Figure 7.24.

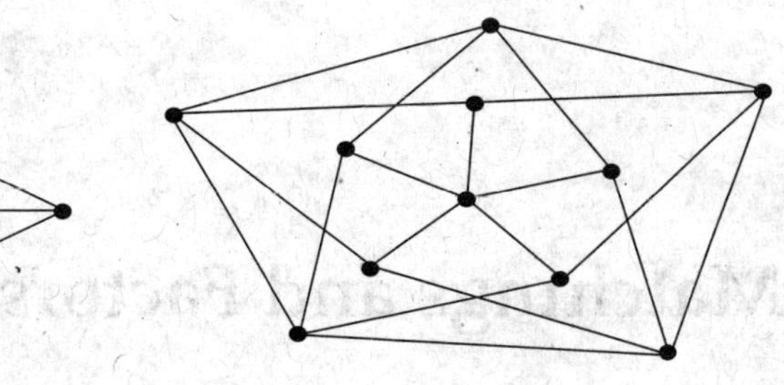

Herschel graph

Grotsch graph

Fig. 7.24

6. If G is k-regular, prove that $\chi(G) \geq \dfrac{n}{n-k}$.

7. If G is connected and $m \leq n$, show that $\chi(G) \leq 3$.

8. Prove that the 3-critical graphs are the odd cycles C_{2n+1}.

9. Prove that the wheel W_{2n-1} is a 4-critical graph for each $n \geq 2$.

10. Prove that the wheel W_{2n} is a 4-critical graph for each $n \geq 2$.

11. Prove that the Peterson graph has edge chromatic number 4.

12. If $m(G)$ is the number of edges in a longest path of G, prove that $\chi(G) \leq 1 + m(G)$.

13. Show that if G is 3-regular Hamiltonian graph, then $\chi'(G) = 3$.

14. Show that a triangulation with a vertex of degree 2 or 3 can be coloured with five colours.

15. Prove that for every $k \geq 1$ there is a k-chromatic graph M_k with no triangle subgraphs. (Mycielski, 1955).

16. If G is a graph in which no set of four vertices induces P_4 as a subgraph, then prove that $\chi(G) = cl(G)$ (Seinsche, 1974).

17. Obtain proofs of Theorems 2.24 and 2.25.

18. Show that a uniquely 3-colourable graph contains three Hamiltonian cycles.

8. Matchings and Factors

Consider the formation of an executive council by the parliament committee. Each committee needs to designate one of its members as an official representative to sit on the council, and council policy states that no senator can be the official representative for more than one committee. For example, let there be five committees 1, 2, 3, 4 and 5. Let A, C, D, E be members of committee 1; B, C, D be members of committee 2; A, B, E, F be members of committee 3; and A, F be members of committee 5. Here the executive council can be formed by members A, C, B, F and E, representing committees 1, 2, 3, 4 and 5 respectively. The problem of formation of the executive council and many related problems can be solved using the concept of matchings in graphs.

8.1 Matchings

Definition: A *matching* in a graph is a set of independent edges. That is, a subset M of the edge set E of a graph $G(V, E)$ is a matching if no two edges of M have a common vertex. A matching M is said to be *maximal* if there is no matching M' strictly containing M, that is, M is *maximal* if it cannot be enlarged. A matching M is said to be *maximum* if it has the largest possible cardinality. That is, M is maximum if there is no matching M' such that $|M'| > |M|$.

Consider the graph G shown in Figure 8.1. The examples of matchings in G are $M_1 = \{v_1v_5,\ v_2v_6,\ v_3v_4,\ v_7v_8\}$, $M_2 = \{v_1v_5,\ v_2v_6,\ v_3v_4,\ v_7v_9\}$, $M_3 = \{v_1v_5,\ v_2v_6,\ v_3v_4,\ v_7v_{10}\}$, $M_4 = \{v_1v_5,\ v_2v_6,\ v_3v_4\}$ and $M_5 = \{v_4v_7,\ v_1v_6,\ v_2v_3\}$. Clearly, M_1 is a maximum matching, whereas M_5 is maximal but not maximum.

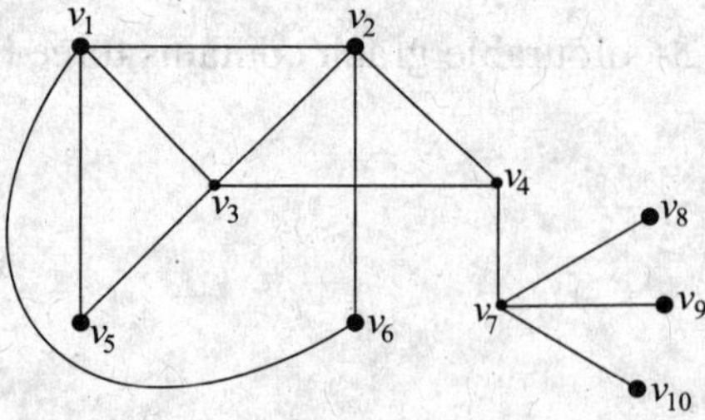

Fig. 8.1

The cardinality of a maximum matching is denoted by $\alpha_1(G)$ and is called the *matching number* of G (or the edge-independence number of G).

Definition: Let M bc a matching in a graph G. A vertex v in G is said to be *M-saturated* (or saturated by M) if there is an edge $e \in M$ incident with v. A vertex which is not incident with any edge of M is said to be *M-unsaturated.* In other words, given a matching M in a graph G, the vertices belonging to the edges of M are M-saturated and the vertices not belonging to the edges of M are M-unsaturated. Consider the graph shown in Figure 8.2. Clearly, $M = \{v_1v_2,\ v_3v_7,\ v_4v_5\}$ is a matching and the vertices v_1, v_2, v_3, v_4, v_5, v_7 are M-saturated but v_6 is M-unsaturated.

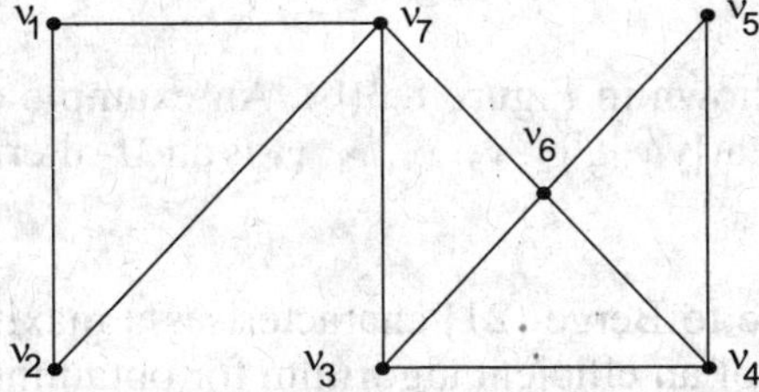

Fig. 8.2

Definition: A matching M in a graph G is said to be a *perfect matching* if M saturates every vertex of G. In Figure 8.3(a), G_1 has a perfect matching $M = \{v_1v_2,\ v_3v_6,\ v_4v_5\}$, but G_2 has no perfect matching.

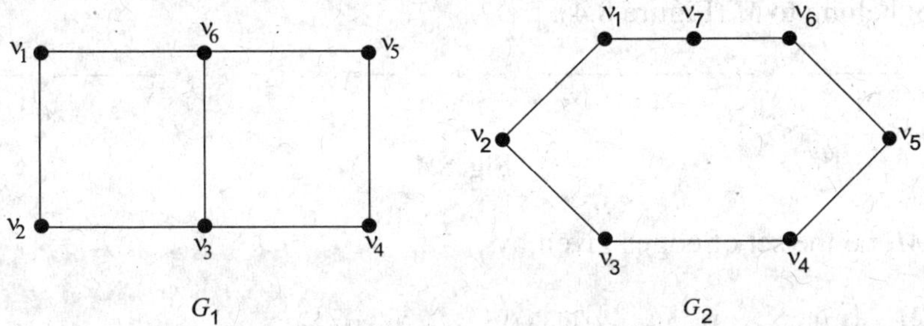

Fig. 8.3(a)

Definition: If G is a bipartite graph with bipartition $V = V_1 \cup V_2$ and $|V_1| = n_1$, $|V_2| = n_2$, then a matching M of G saturating all the vertices in V_1 is called a *complete matching* (or V_1 matched into V_2).

Definition: Let H be a subgraph of a graph G. An H-alternating path (cycle) in G is a path (cycle) whose edges are alternately in $E(G) - E(H)$ and $E(H)$.

If M is matching in a graph G, then an *M-alternating path* (cycle) in G is a path (cycle) whose edges are alternately in $E(G) - M$ and M. That is, in an M-alternating path, the edges alternate between M-edges and non-M-edges. An M-alternating path whose end vertices are M-unsaturated is said to be an *M-augmenting path.*

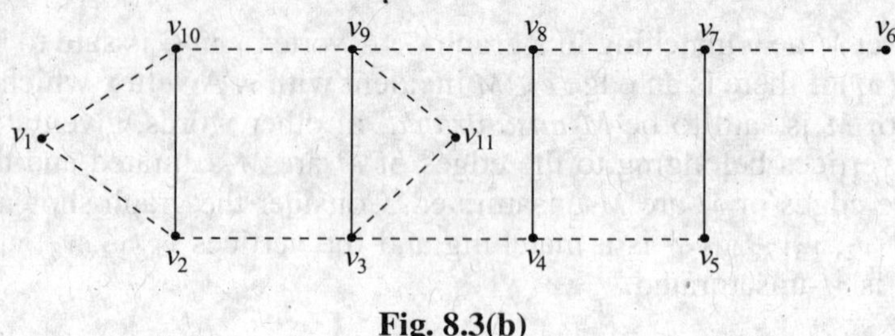

Fig. 8.3(b)

Consider the graph G shown in Figure 8.3(b). An example of a matching in G is $M = \{v_2v_{10}, v_3v_9, v_4v_8, v_5v_7\}$. Clearly $v_{10}, v_2, v_3, v_9, v_8, v_4$ is an M-alternating path and $v_1, v_{10}, v_2, v_9, v_3, v_{11}$ is an M-augmenting path.

The following result due to Berge [21] characterises a maximum matching in a graph. This forms the foundation of an efficient algorithm for obtaining a maximum matching.

Theorem 8.1 (Berge) A matching M of a graph G is maximum if and only if G contains no M-augmenting paths.

Proof Let M be a maximum matching in a graph G. Assume $P = v_1v_2 \ldots v_k$ is an M-augmenting path in G. Due to the alternating nature of M-augmenting path, we observe that k is even and the edges $v_2v_3, v_4v_5, \ldots, v_{k-2}v_{k-1}$ belong to M. Also the edges $v_1v_2, v_3v_4, \ldots, v_{k-1}v_k$ do not belong to M (Figure 8.4).

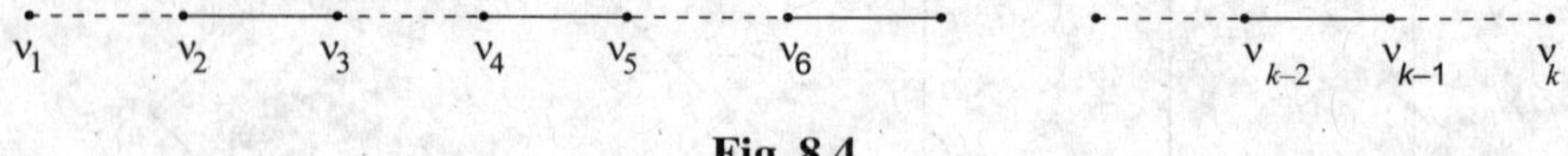

Fig. 8.4

Now, let M_1 be the set of edges given by

$$M_1 = [M - \{v_2v_3, \ldots, v_{k-2}v_{k-1}\}] \cup \{v_1v_2, \ldots, v_{k-1}v_k\}.$$

Then M_1 is a matching and clearly M_1 contains one more edge than M. This contradicts the assumption that M is maximum. Thus G contains no M-augmenting paths.

Conversely, assume that G has no M-augmenting paths. Let M' be a matching such that $|M'| > |M|$. Let H be a subgraph of G with $V(H) = V(G)$ and $E(H)$ be the set of edges of G that appear in exactly one of M and M'. Since every vertex of G lies on at most one edge from M and at most one edge from M', therefore degree (in H) of each vertex of H is at most 2. This implies that each connected component of H is either a single vertex, or a path, or a cycle (Fig. 8.5). If a component is a cycle, then it is an even cycle, because the edges alternate between M-edges and M'-edges. Since $|M'| > |M|$, there is at least one component in H that is a path which begins and ends with edges from M'. Clearly, this path is an M-

augmenting path, contradicting the assumption. Thus no such matching M' can exist and hence M is maximum. □

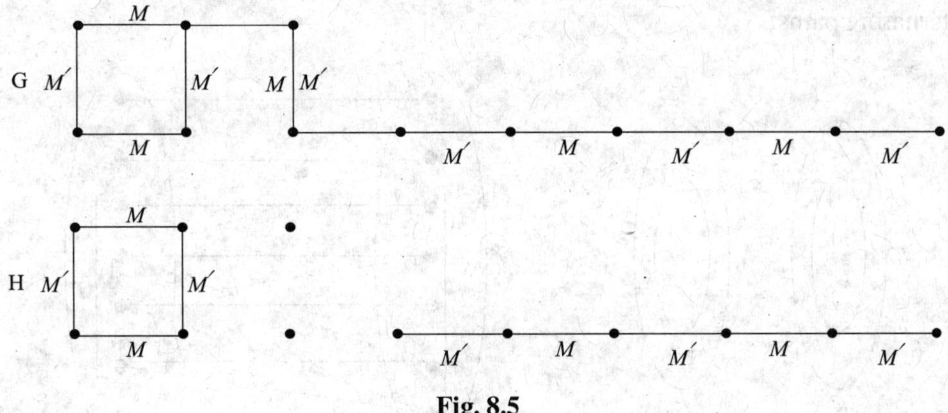

Fig. 8.5

Definition: The *neighbourhood* of a set of vertices S, denoted by $N(S)$, is the union of the neighbourhood of the vertices of S.

The following classic result due to Hall [101] characterises a complete matching in a bipartite graph.

Theorem 8.2 (Hall) If $G(V_1, V_2, E)$ is a bipartite graph with $|V_1| \le |V_2|$, then G has a matching saturating every vertex of V_1, if and only if $|N(S)| \ge |S|$, for every subset $S \subseteq V_1$.

Proof Let G have a complete matching M that saturates all the vertices of V_1 and let S be any subset of V_1. Then every vertex in S is matched by M into a different vertex in $N(S)$, so that $|S| \le |N(S)|$ (Fig. 8.6 (a)).

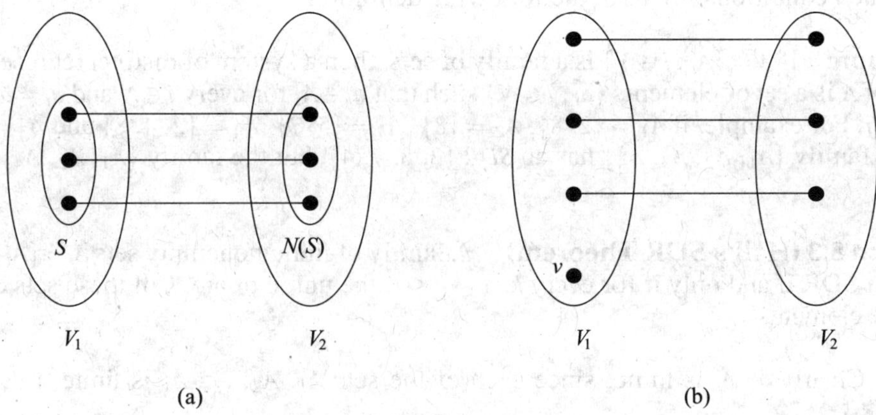

Fig. 8.6

Conversely, let $|N(S)| \geq |S|$ for all subsets S of V_1 and let M be a maximum matching. Assume G has no complete matching. Then there exists a vertex, say $v \in V_1$, which is M-unsaturated (Fig. 8.6(b)). Let Z be the set of vertices of G that can be joined to v by M-alternating paths.

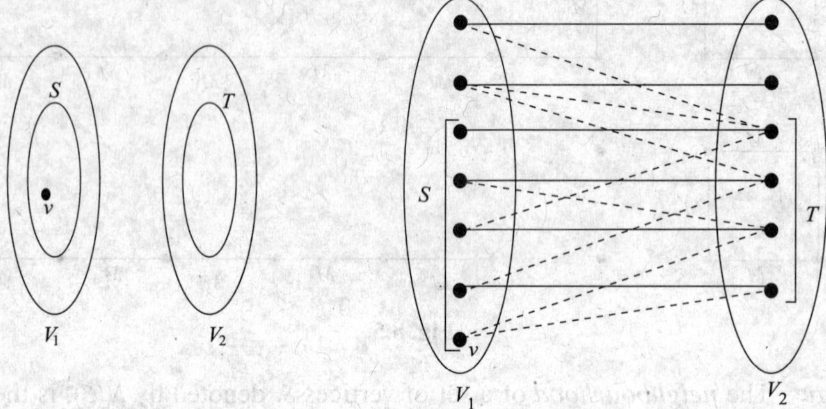

Fig. 8.7

Since M is a maximum matching, by Theorem 8.1, G has no M-augmenting path. This implies that v is the only vertex of Z that is M-unsaturated. Let $S = Z \cap V_1$ and $T = Z \cap V_2$ (Fig. 8.7). Then every vertex of T is matched under M to some vertex of $S - \{v\}$ and conversely and $N(S) = T$. Since $|T| = |S| - 1$, therefore $|N(S)| = |T| = |S| - 1 < |S|$, contradicting the given assumption. Hence G has a complete matching. ❑

The aim of the above theorem was basically to obtain the conditions for the existence of a system of distinct representatives (SDR) for a collection of subsets of a given set. Before giving such conditions, we have the following definition.

Definition: If $A = \{A_i : i \in N\}$ is a family of sets, then a system of distinct representatives (SDR) of A is a set of elements $\{a_i : i \in N\}$ such that $a_i \in A_i$ for every $i \in N$ and $a_i \neq a_j$ whenever $i \neq j$. For example, if $A_1 = \{2, 8\}$, $A_2 = \{8\}$, $A_3 = \{5, 7\}$, $A_4 = \{2, 4, 8\}$ and $A_5 = \{2, 4\}$, then the family $\{A_1, A_2, A_3, A_4\}$ has an *SDR* $\{2, 8, 7, 4\}$, but the family $\{A_1, A_2, A_4, A_5\}$ has no SDR.

Theorem 8.3 (Hall's SDR Theorem) A family of finite nonempty sets $A = \{A_i : 1 \leq i \leq r\}$ has an SDR if and only if for every k, $1 \leq k \leq r$, the union of any k of these sets contains at least k elements.

Proof Clearly $\bigcup_{i=1}^{r} A_i$ is finite, since each of the sets $A_1, A_2, \ldots, A_r$ is finite. Let $\bigcup_{i=1}^{r} A_i = \{a_1, a_2, \ldots, a_n\}$.

Construct a bipartite graph G with partite sets $X = \{A_1, \ldots, A_r\}$ and $Y = \{a_1, \ldots, a_n\}$, as shown in Figure 8.8. We take an edge between A_i and a_j if and only if $a_j \in A_i$.

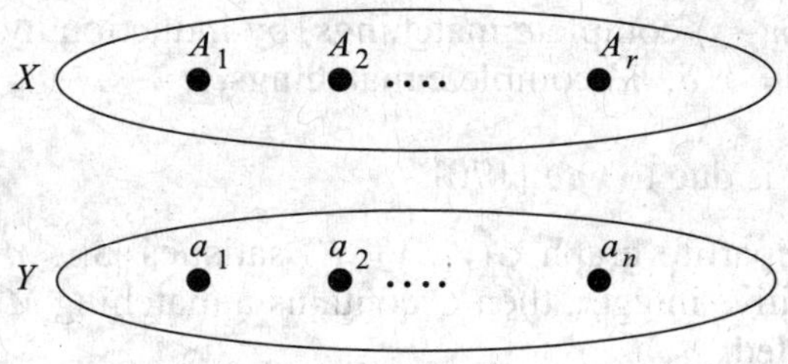

Fig. 8.8

Clearly, A has an *SDR* if and only if G has a matching that saturates all the vertices of X. Now, Theorem 8.2 implies that G has such a matching if and only if $|S| \leq |N(S)|$ for all subsets S of X, that is, if and only if $|S| \leq |\bigcup_{a_i \in S} A_i|$ proving the result. ❑

Remarks

1. Hall's theorem is often referred to as Hall's marriage theorem.
2. Since Hall's theorem, there has been remarkable progress in the theory of SDR; and besides other references the reader can refer to the book of Mirsky [156].

The following result due to M. Hall [97] counts the number of complete matchings.

Theorem 8.4 If $G(V_1, V_2, E)$ is a bipartite graph with $|V_1| = n_1 \leq n_2 = |V_2|$ and satisfying Hall's condition $|S| \leq |N(S)|$ for all $S \subseteq V_1$, then G has at least

$$r(\delta, n_1) = \prod_{1 \leq i \leq \min(\delta,\, n_1)} (\delta + 1 - i)$$

complete matchings, where $\delta = \min\{d(u) : u \in V_1\}$.

Proof Induct on n_1. The result is trivial for $n_1 = 1$. Assume the result to be true for all values of $n_1 \leq m - 1$ and let G be a bipartite graph satisfying the given conditions and $|V_1| = m$.

Case 1 For each nonempty proper subset S of V_1, $|S| < |N(S)|$. Now, for a given $u \in V_1$, choose $v \in N(u)$. This v can be chosen in at least δ ways, since $\delta = \min\{d(u) : u \in V_1\}$. Obviously, $G - \{u, v\}$ is a bipartite graph with $|V_1| = m - 1$, and $\min\{d(x) : x \in V_1\} \geq \delta - 1$. Therefore by induction hypothesis, $G - \{u, v\}$ has at least $r(\delta - 1, m - 1) = \prod_{1 \leq i \leq \min(\delta - 1, m-1)} (\delta - i)$ complete matchings. These together with uv, give at least

$$\delta[r(\delta - 1, m - 1)] = \prod_{1 \leq i \leq \min(\delta - 1,\, m-1)} (\delta - i) = \prod_{1 \leq i \leq \min(\delta,\, m)} (\delta + 1 - i) = r(\delta, m)$$

complete matchings in G.

Case 2 There is a non empty proper subset S of V_1 with $|S| = |N(S)|$. Let $|S| = s$, and $G_1 = <S \cup N(S)>$ and $G_2 = G - <S \cup N(S)>$. Then the values of n_1 and δ in G_1 are s and δ, and in G_2 are $m-s$ and $\delta_2 = \max\{\delta - s, 1\}$. Therefore G_1 and G_2 are disjoint graphs with at least $r(\delta, s)$ and $r(\delta_2, m-s)$ complete matchings, by induction hypothesis. Thus G has at least $r(\delta, s)\, r(\delta_2, m-s) = r(\delta, m)$ complete matchings. ❑

The following result is due to Ore [170].

Theorem 8.5 If a bipartite graph $G(V_1, V_2, E)$ satisfies $|S| \le d + |N(S)|$ for all $S \subseteq V_1$, where d is a given positive integer, then G contains a matching M with at most d vertices of V_1 being M-unsaturated.

Proof Let $H(V_1, U_2, E')$ be the bipartite graph with $U_2 = V_2 \cup W_2$, $|W_2| = d$ and $E' = E \cup [V_1, W_2]$. Then the given condition of G implies Hall's condition for H and so H has a complete matching M. Obviously, at most d of the edges of M can be in $E' - E$, proving the result. ❑

The following observation is an immediate consequence of Theorem 8.5.

Corollary 8.1 For a bipartite graph $G(V_1, V_2, E)$, with $|V_1| = n_1$, $\alpha_1(G) = n_1 - \max\{|S| - |N(S)| : S \subseteq V_1\} = \min\{|V_1 - S| + |N(S)| : S \subseteq V_1\}$.

The following result is a consequence of Hall's theorem.

Theorem 8.6 A $k(\ge 1)$ regular bipartite graph has a perfect matching.

Proof Let G be a k regular bipartite graph with partite sets V_1 and V_2. Then $E(G)$ is equal to the set of edges incident to the vertices of V_1 and also $E(G)$ is equal to the set of edges incident to the vertices of V_2. Therefore, $k|V_1| = k|V_2| = E(G)$ and thus $|V_1| = |V_2|$. If $S \subseteq V_1$, then $N(S) \subseteq V_2$ and thus $N(N(S))$ contains S. Let E_1 and E_2 be the sets of edges of G incident respectively to S and $N(S)$. Then $E_1 \subseteq E_2$, $|E_1| = k|S|$ and $|E_2| \ge k|N(S)|$. Since $|E_2| \ge |E_1|, |N(S)| \ge |S|$. Thus by Theorem 8.2, G has a matching that saturates all the vertices of V_1, that is G has a complete matching M. Now deleting the edges of M from G gives a $(k-1)$-regular bipartite graph G', with $V(G) = V(G')$. By the same argument, G' has a complete matching M'. Deletion of the edges of M' from G' results in a $(k-2)$-regular bipartite graph. Repeating this process $k-1$ times, we arrive at a 1-regular bipartite graph G^* such that $|V(G^*)| = |V(G)|$. Clearly G^* has a perfect matching. ❑

Definition: A set C of vertices in a graph G is said to *cover* the edges of G if every edge of G is incident with at least one vertex of C. Such a set C is called a *covering* of G. Consider the graphs G_1 and G_2 shown in Figure 8.9. Clearly, $\{v_1, v_2, v_4, v_5\}$ and $\{v_1, v_5, v_6\}$ are coverings of G_1. Also, we observe that there is no covering of G_1 with fewer than three vertices. In G_2, each of $\{v_1, v_2, v_6\}$ and $\{v_1, v_2, v_3, v_4, v_5, v_6\}$ is a covering.

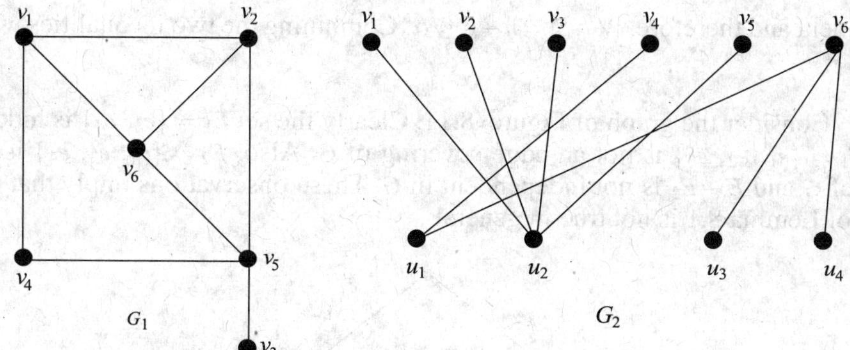

Fig. 8.9

The number of vertices in a minimum covering of G is called the *covering number* of G and is denoted by $\beta(G)$.

Definition: An *edge covering* of a graph G is a subset L of E such that every vertex of G is incident to some edge of L. Clearly, an edge covering of G exists if and only if $\delta > 0$. The cardinality of a minimum edge covering of G is denoted by $\beta_1(G)$. For example, in the wheel W_5 of Figure 8.10, the set $\{v_1v_5,\ v_2v_3,\ v_4v_6\}$ is a minimum edge covering.

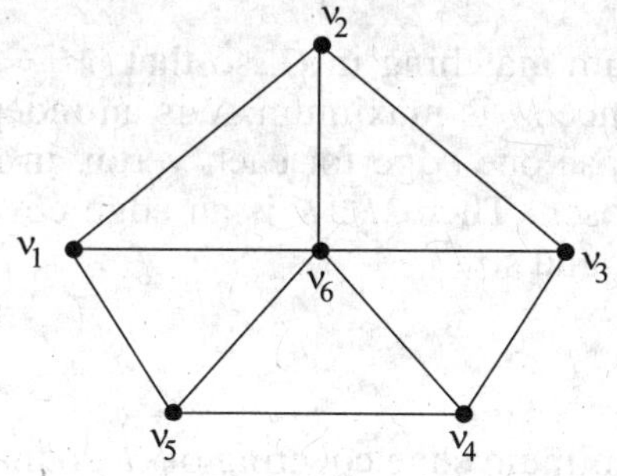

Fig. 8.10

The following results are immediate.

Lemma 8.1 A subset S of V is independent if and only if $V-S$ is a covering of G.

Proof Clearly, S is independent if and only if no two vertices in S are adjacent in G. Thus every edge of G is incident to a vertex of $V-S$. This is possible if and only if $V-S$ is a covering of G. ❑

Lemma 8.2 For any graph G, $\alpha+\beta=n$.

Proof If S is a maximum independent set of G, then by Lemma 8.1, $V-S$ is a covering of G. Therefore, $|V-S| = n-\alpha \geq \beta$. Similarly, if C is a minimum covering of G, then $V-C$

is independent and therefore, $|V-S| = n-\beta \leq \alpha$. Combining the two inequalities, we obtain $\alpha+\beta = n$. ❑

Remark Consider the graph of Figure. 8.11. Clearly the set $E_1 = \{e_3, e_4\}$ is independent and $E - E_1 = \{e_1, e_2, e_5\}$ is not an edge covering of G. Also, $E_2 = \{e_1, e_3, e_4\}$ is an edge covering of G and $E - E_2$ is not independent in G. These observations imply that the edge analogue of Lemma 8.1 is not true in general.

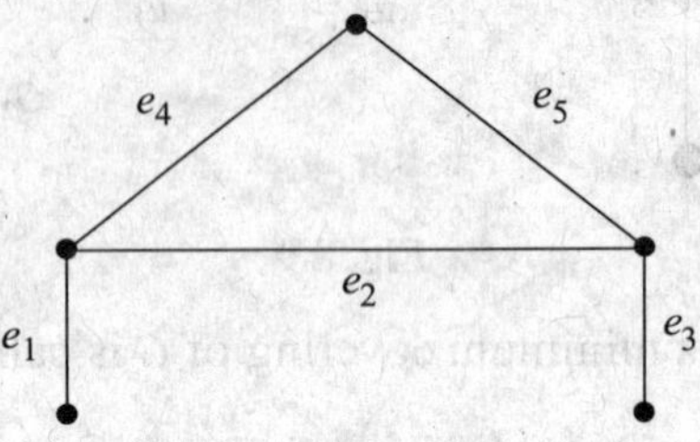

Fig. 8.11

The following result gives the relation between α_1 and β_1 of a graph G.

Theorem 8.7(a) In a graph G with n vertices and $\delta > 0$, $\alpha_1 + \beta_1 = n$.

Proof Let M be a maximum matching in G, so that $|M| = \alpha_1$. Let X be the set of M-unsaturated vertices in G. Since M is maximum, X is an independent set of vertices with $|X| = n - 2\alpha_1$. As $\delta > 0$, choose one edge for each vertex in X incident with it and let F be the set of these edges chosen. Then $M \cup F$ is an edge covering of G. Thus, $|M \cup F| = |M| + |F| = \alpha_1 + n - 2\,\alpha_1 \geq \beta_1$, and so

$$n \geq \alpha_1 + \beta_1. \tag{8.7.1}$$

Now assume that L is a minimum edge covering of G, so that $|L| = \beta_1$. Let $H = G(L)$, the edge subgraph of G defined by L and let M_H be a maximum matching in H. Let the set of M_H-unsaturated vertices in H be denoted by X. Since L is an edge covering of G, therefore, H is a spanning subgraph of G. Thus, $|L| - |M_H| = |L - M_H| \geq |X| = n - 2|M_H|$, and therefore $|L| + |M_H| \geq n$. Since M_H is a matching in G, so $|M_H| \leq \alpha_1$, and hence

$$n \leq \beta_1 + \alpha_1. \tag{8.7.2}$$

Combining (8.7.1) and (8.7.2), we obtain $\alpha_1 + \beta_1 = n$. ❑

Let M be any matching of a graph G and C be any vertex covering of G. Then in order to cover each edge of M, at least one vertex of C is to be chosen. Thus, $|M| \leq |C|$. In case, M' is a maximum matching and C' is a minimum covering of G, then $|M'| \leq |C'|$.

We have the following obvious result.

Lemma 8.3 If C is any covering and M any matching of a graph G with $|C| = |M|$, then C is a minimum covering and M is a maximum matching.

Proof Let M' be a maximum matching and C' be a minimum covering of G. Then $|M| \leq |M'|$ and $|C| \geq |C'|$. Therefore, $|M| \leq |M'| \leq |C'| \leq |C|$. As $|M| = |C|$ we have $|M| = |M'| = |C'| = |C|$, and the proof is complete. ❑

The next result is due to Konig [134].

Theorem 8.7(b) (Konig) In a loopless bipartite graph G, the maximum number of edges in a matching of G is equal to the minimum number of vertices in an edge cover of G, that is, $\alpha_1 = \beta$.

Proof Let G be a bipartite graph with partite sets V_1 and V_2 and let M be a matching of G. Let X be the set of all M-unsaturated vertices of V_1, so that $|M| = |V_1| - |X|$ (Fig. 8.12).

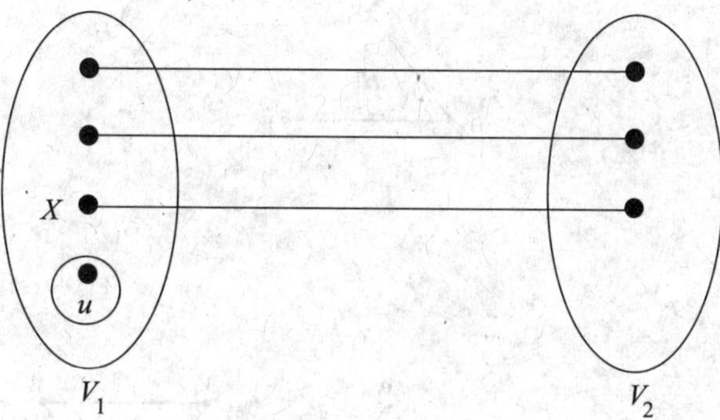

Fig. 8.12

Let A be the set of those vertices of G which are connected to some vertex of X by an M-alternating path. Further, let $S = A \cap V_1$ and $T = A \cap V_2$. Obviously, $N(S) = T$ and $S - X$ is matched to T so that $|X| = |S| - |T|$. Clearly, $C = (V_1 - S) \cup T$ is a covering of G, because if there is an edge e not incident to any vertex in C, then one of the end vertices of e is in S and the other in $V_2 - T$, which contradicts the fact that $N(S) = T$. Now, $|C| = |V_1| - |S| + |T| = |V_1| - |X| = |M|$. Then by Lemma 8.3, M is a maximum matching and C is a minimum covering of G. ❑

The following is a new proof of Konig's theorem due to Rizzi [218].

Second proof of Theorem 8.7 (Rizzi [218]) Let G be a minimal counter-example. Then G is connected but is not a cycle, nor is a path. Therefore G has a vertex of degree at least three. Let u be such a vertex and v one of its neighbours. If $\alpha_1(G - v) < \alpha_1(G)$, then by minimality, $G - v$ has a cover W' with $|W'| < \alpha_1(G)$. Thus $W' \cup \{v\}$ is a cover of G with cardinality at most $\alpha_1(G)$. Therefore assume there exists a maximum matching M of G having no edge incident at v. Let f be an edge of $G - M$ incident at u but not at v. Let W'

be a cover of $G-f$ with $|W'| = \alpha_1(G)$. Since no edge of M is incident at v, it follows that W' does not contain v. Therefore W' contains u and is a cover of G. ❑

8.2 Factors

We start this section with the following definitions.

Definition: A *factor* F of a graph G is a spanning subgraph of G. A factor F is said to be an *F–factor* if the components of F are some graphs in a given collection $F = \{H_1, H_2, \ldots, H_k\}$ of subgraphs of G. If F contains a single graph H, then F is called an *H-factor*. Consider the graph G shown in Figure 8.13. Clearly G_1 is a spanning subgraph whose components belong to the set $F = \{H_1, H_2, H_3\}$ and therefore is an F-factor. Each of the components of the spanning subgraph G_2 is a graph K_3 and so G_2 is a K_3-factor.

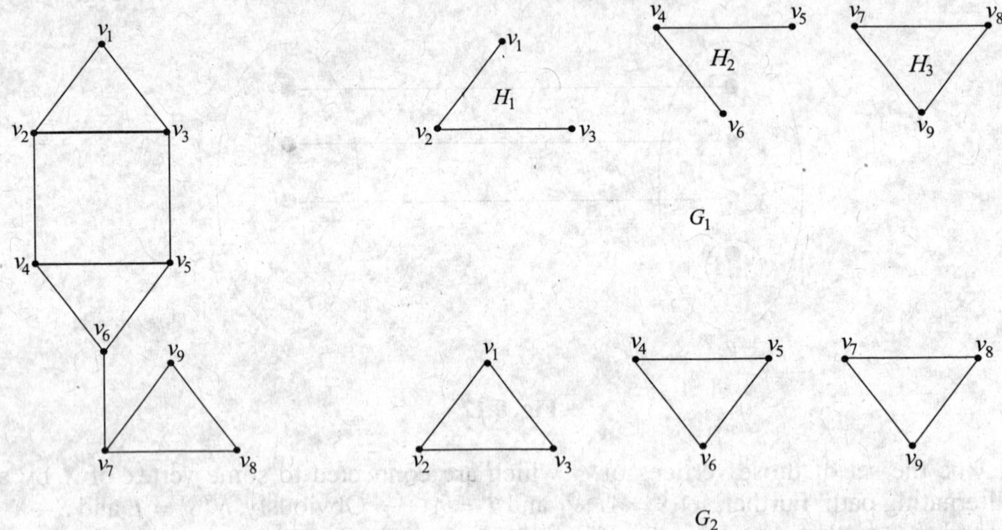

Fig. 8.13

We observe that a perfect matching is a K_2-factor, since each of the components in a perfect matching is a graph K_2.

A *vertex function* of a graph $G(V, E)$ is a function $f : V \to N_o$ (N_o being the set of non-negative integers).

Definition: A spanning subgraph F of a graph $G(V, E)$ is called an *f-factor* of G if for a vertex function f on V, $d(v|F) = f(v)$ for all $v \in V$. For example, consider the graph G shown in Figure 8.14. Define $f : V \to N_0$ by $f(v_i) = 1$ or 2, for all $v \in V$ in G. Then the f-factor of G is given by graph H.

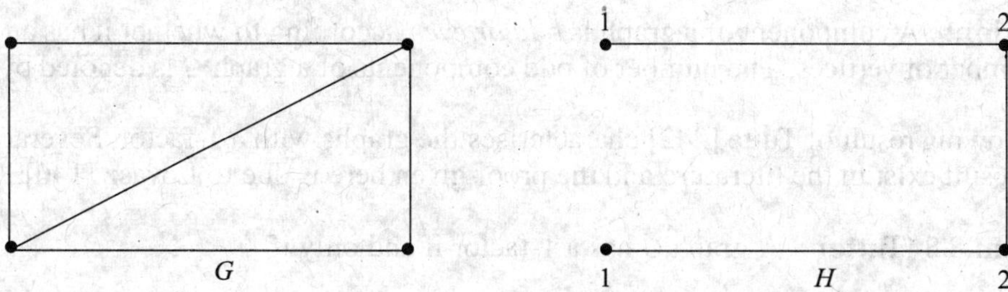

Figure 8.14

Further, F is said to be a *partial f–factor* (or f-matching) if $d(v|F) \leq f(v)$, for all $v \in V$ and F is said to be a covering f-factor of G if $d(v|F) \geq f(v)$, for all $v \in V$. Some of the details of this can be seen in Graver and Jurkat [85]. We note that an f-factor exists only if $\sum_{v \in V} f(v)$ is even.

Definition: A *k-factor* of a graph G is a factor of G that is k-regular. Clearly, a 1-factor is a perfect matching and exists only for graphs with an even number of vertices. A 2-factor of G is a factor of G that is a disjoint union of cycles of G and connected 2-factor is a Hamiltonian cycle.

Definition: If the edge set of a graph G is partitioned by the edge sets of a set of factors $F_1, F_2, \ldots, F_q$ of G, then these factors are said to constitute a *factorisation* or decomposition of G and we write $G = F_1 \cup F_2 \cup \ldots \cup F_q$. If each factor F_i in the factorisation is isomorphic to the same spanning subgraph F of G, then the factorisation is called an *isomorphic factorisation* or an F-decomposition of G.

The factorisation is called an *f-factorisation* or *k-factorisation* according as each factor f_i of a factorisation is an f-factor or k-factor. A graph G is f-factorable or k-factorable if G has respectively f-factorisation or k-factorisation.

Example In Figure 8.15, the three distinct 1-factors of G_1 are $< e_1, e_6 >$, $< e_2, e_4 >$ and $< e_3, e_5 >$. The two distinct 2-factors of G_2 are $< e_1, e_2, e_3, e_4, e_5 >$ and $< e_6, e_7, e_8, e_9, e_{10} >$.

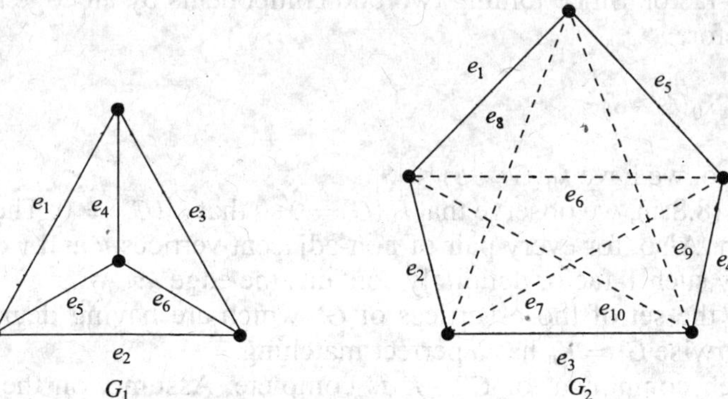

Fig. 8.15

Definition: A component of a graph is *odd or even* according to whether it has an odd or even number of vertices. The number of odd components of a graph G is denoted by $k_0(G)$.

The following result of Tutte [242] characterises the graphs with a 1-factor. Several proofs of this result exist in the literature and the proof given here is due to Lovasz [146].

Theorem 8.8 (Tutte) A graph G has a 1-factor if and only if

$$k_0(G-S) \leq |S|, \text{ for all } S \subseteq V. \tag{8.8.1}$$

Proof Let G be a graph having 1-factor M. Let S be an arbitrary subset of V and let O_1, $O_2, \ldots, O_k$ be the odd components of $G-S$. For each i, the vertices in O_i can be adjacent only to other vertices in O_i and to vertices in S. Since G has a 1-factor (perfect matching), at least one vertex from each O_i is to be matched with a different vertex in S. Thus the number of vertices in S is at least k, the number of odd components. Hence $|S| \geq k$, so that $k_0(G-S)$ $\leq |S|$ (Fig. 8.16).

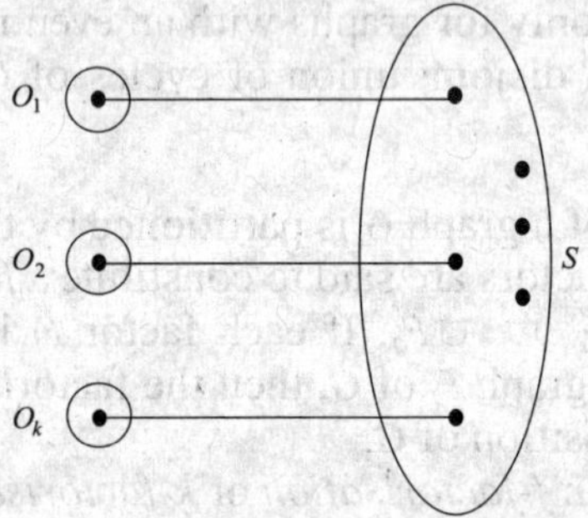

Fig. 8.16

Conversely, assume that the condition (8.8.1) holds. Let G have no 1-factor. Join pairs of non-adjacent vertices of G and continue this process till we get a maximal super graph G^* of G having no 1-factor. Since joining two odd components by an edge results in an even component, therefore

$$k_0(G^*-S) \leq k_0(G-S). \tag{8.8.2}$$

Thus for G^* also, we have $k_0(G^*-S) \leq |S|$.

When $S = \phi$ in (8.8.1), we observe that $k_0(G) = 0$ so that $k_0(G^*) = 0$. Therefore, $|V(G^*)| = |V(G)| = n$ is even. Also, for every pair of non-adjacent vertices u and v of G^*, G^*+uv has a 1-factor and any such 1-factor definitely contains the edge uv.

Now, let K be the set of those vertices of G^* which are having degree $n-1$. Clearly, $K \neq V$, since otherwise $G^* = K_n$ has a perfect matching.

Claim that each component of G^*-K is complete. Assume, on the contrary, that in G^*-K, there exists a component G_1 which is not complete. Then in G_1, there are vertices

x, y and z such that $xy, yz \in E(G^*)$ and $xy \notin E(G^*)$. Also, $y \in V(G_1)$ so that $d(y|G^*) < n-1$ and thus there exists a vertex w of G^* with $yw \notin E(G^*)$. Evidently, $w \notin K$ (Fig. 8.17).

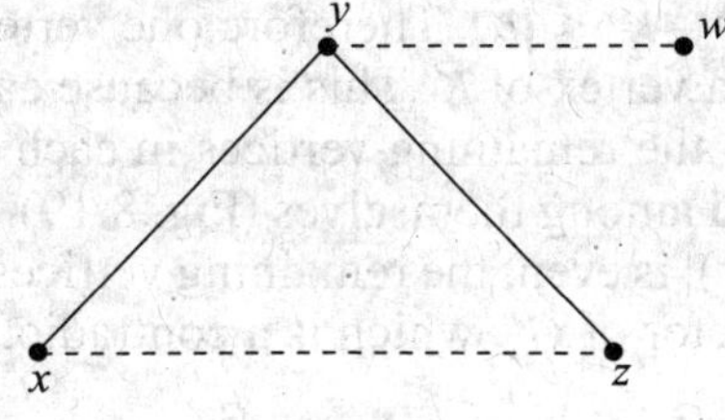

Fig. 8.17

Now, by the choice of G^*, both $G^* + xz$ and $G^* + yw$ have 1-factors, say M_1 and M_2 respectively. Clearly, $xz \in M_1$ and $yw \in M_2$. Let H be the subgraph of $G^* + \{xz, yw\}$ induced by the edges that are in M_1 and M_2 but not in both (that is, in the symmetric difference of M_1 and M_2). Since M_1 and M_2 are 1-factors, each vertex of G^* is saturated by both M_1 and M_2, and H is a disjoint union of even cycles in which the edges alternate between M_1 and M_2. We have two cases to consider.

Case 1 Let xz and yw belong to different components of H, as shown in Figure 8.18 (a). If yw belongs to the cycle C, then the edge of M_1 in C together with the edges of M_2 not belonging to C form a 1-factor of G^*, contradicting the choice of G^*.

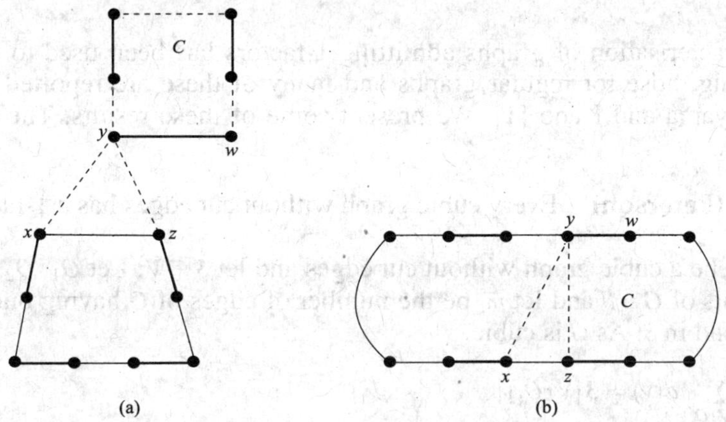

Ordinary lines correspond to the edges of M_1 and bold lines to the edges of M_2

Fig. 8.18

Case 2 Let xz and yw belong to the same component C of H. Since each component of H is a cycle, C is a cycle (Fig. 8.18 (b)). By symmetry of x and z, it can be assumed that the vertices x, y, w and z appear in that order on C. Then the edges of M_1 belonging to the

$yw\ldots z$ section of C, together with the edge yz, and the edges of M_2 not in the $yw\ldots z$ section of C form a 1-factor of G^*, again contradicting the choice of G^*.

Thus each component of $G^* - K$ is complete.

By conditions (8.8.2), $k_0(G^* - K) \le |K|$. Therefore one vertex of each of the odd components of $G^* - K$ is matched to a vertex of K. This is because each vertex of K is adjacent to every other vertex of G^*. Also the remaining vertices in each of the odd and even components of $G^* - K$ can be matched among themselves (Fig. 8.19). The total number of vertices thus matched is even. As $|V(G^*)|$ is even, the remaining vertices of K can be matched among themselves, thus giving a 1-factor of G^*, which is a contradiction. ❑

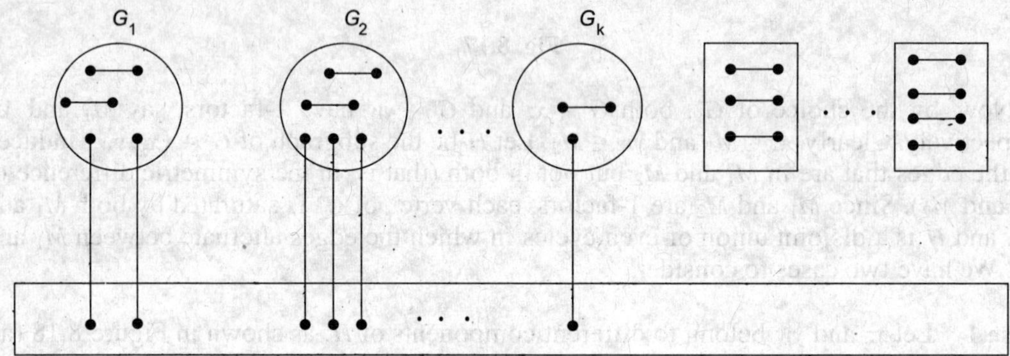

Fig. 8.19

Remark Among the various proofs of Theorem 8.8, one proof due to Anderson [4] uses Hall's theorem.

Tutte's characterisation of graphs admitting 1-factors has been used to obtain several results including those for regular graphs and many of these are reported in the review article by Akiyama and Kano [1]. We present some of these results. The first is due to Peterson [176].

Theorem 8.9 (Peterson) Every cubic graph without cut edges has a 1-factor.

Proof Let G be a cubic graph without cut edges and let $S \subseteq V$. Let $O_1, O_2, \ldots, O_k$ be the odd components of $G - S$ and let m_i be the number of edges of G having one end in $V(O_i)$ and the other end in S. As G is cubic,

therefore, $$\sum_{v \in V(O_i)} d(v) = 3|V(O_i)| \tag{8.9.1}$$

and $$\sum_{v \in S} d(v) = 3|S|. \tag{8.9.2}$$

Now, $E(O_i) = [V(O_i), V(O_i) \cup S] - [V(O_i), S]$, where [A, B] denotes the set of edges having one end in A and the other end in B, $A \subseteq V$, $B \subseteq V$. Thus, $m_i = |[V(O_i), S]| = \sum_{v \in V(O_i)} d(v) - 2|E(O_i)|$. Since $d(v) = 3$ for each v and $V(O_i)$ is odd component, m_i is odd for each i. Also, since G has no cut edges, $m_i \geq 3$. Therefore, $k_0(G-S) = k \leq \frac{1}{3} \sum_{v \in S} d(v) < \frac{1}{3} 3|S| = |S|$. Hence by Theorem 8.8, G has a 1-factor. ❑

Remark A cubic graph with cut edges may not have a 1-factor. To see this, consider the graph G_1 of Figure 8.20 (a). If we take $S = \{v\}$, then $k_0(G-S) = 3 > 1 = |S|$ and hence G_1 has no 1-factor.

Also, a cubic graph with a 1-factor may have cut edges. Consider the graph G_2 of Figure 8.20 (b). Clearly, $< e_1, e_2, e_3, e_4, e_5 >$ is a 1-factor and e_3 is a cut edge of G_2.

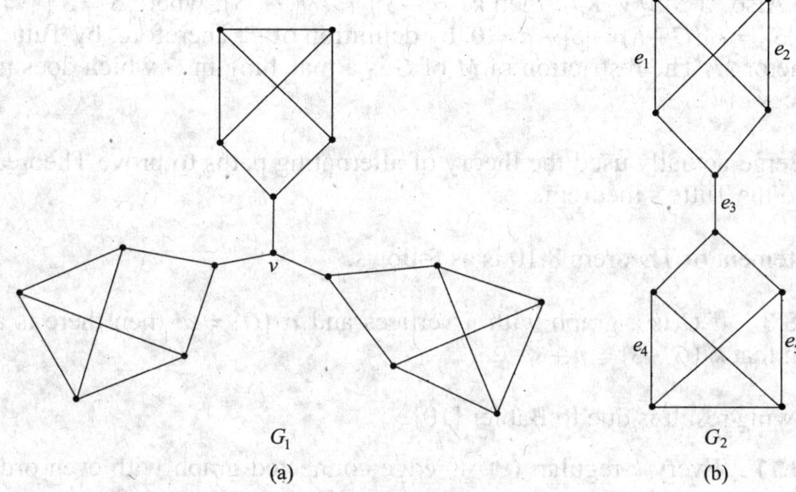

Fig. 8.20

The next result is due to Cunningham [61].

Corollary 8.2 The edge set of a simple 2-edge-connected cubic graph G can be partitioned into paths of length three.

Proof By Theorem 8.9, G is a union of a 1-factor and 2-factor. Orient the edges of each cycle of the 2-factor in any manner so that each cycle becomes a directed cycle. Then, if e is any edge of the 1-factor and f_1, f_2 are the two arcs of G having their tails at the end vertices of e, then $\{e, f_1, f_2\}$ forms a typical 3-path of the edge partition of G (Fig. 8.21). ❑

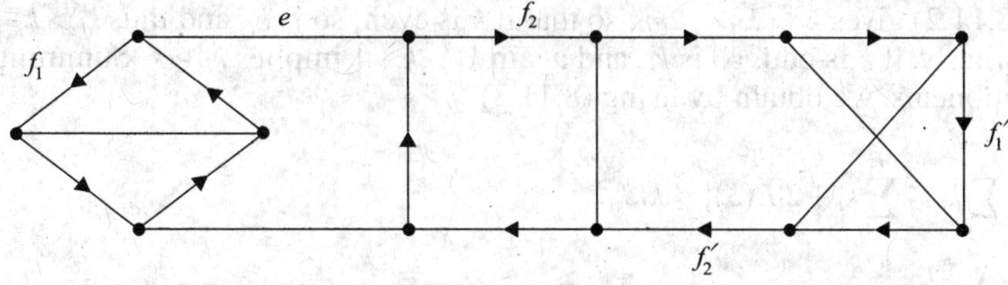

Fig. 8.21

Berge [23] obtained the following estimate for $\alpha_1(G)$ of a graph G, the proof of which is given by Bollobas [29].

Theorem 8.10 For any simple graph G, $\alpha_1(G) = (n-d)/2$, where $d = \max\{k_0(G-S) - |S| : S \subseteq V\}$.

Proof Clearly at most $n-d$ vertices can be saturated in any matching of G. In order to show that this bound is attained, we use the following construction. Let $H = GVK_d$. Then H satisfies Tutte's condition. For if S' is any subset of $V(H)$, then $k_0(H-S') = 0$ or 1 if $S' \not\supseteq V(K_d)$. Also, if $S' \supseteq V(K_d)$, then $k_0(H-S') = k_0(G-S)$, where $S = S' \cap V(G)$, so that $k_0(H-S') - |S'| = k_0(G-S) - |S| - d = 0$, by definition of d. Therefore, by Tutte's theorem, H has a 1-factor M. The restriction of M of G is a matching in G which does not cover at most d vertices of G. ❑

Remark Berge actually used the theory of alternating paths to prove Theorem 8.10 and then deduced the Tutte's theorem.

The restatement of Theorem 8.10 is as follows.

Corollary 8.3 If G is a graph with n vertices and $\alpha_1(G) = a$, then there is a set S of s vertices such that $k_0(G-S) = n+s-2a$.

The following result is due to Babler [10].

Theorem 8.11 Every k-regular, $(k-1)$-edge-connected graph with even order has a 1-factor.

Proof Let G be a k-regular, $(k-1)$-edge-connected graph with even order and let S be any subset of V. Let $O_1, O_2, \ldots, O_r$ be the odd components of $G-S$ with order n_i and size m_i, and let k_i edges join O_i to S, for $1 \le i \le r$. Then $k_i \ge k-1$, (8.11.1)

$$\sum_{v \in V(O_i)} d(v) = kn_i = 2m_i + k_i \quad (8.11.2)$$

and $\sum_{v \in S} d(v) = k|S| \ge \sum_1^r k_i + 2|E(S)|$. (8.11.3)

Now, (8.11.2) gives $k_i = kn_i - 2m_i$, so that if k is even, so is k_i, and thus $k_i > k-1$ implies $k_i \ge k$. Similarly, if k is odd, so is k_i, and again $k_i > k-1$ implies $k_i \ge k$. Summing this over r odd components, we obtain by using (8.11.3)

$$rk \le \sum_{i=1}^{r} k_i \le \sum_{i=1}^{r} k_i + 2|E(S)| \le k|S| .$$

Therefore, $k_0(G-S) = r \le |S|$ and by Tutte's theorem, G has a 1-factor. ❑

8.3 Antifactor Sets

Definition: A subset $S \subseteq V$ of a graph $G(V, E)$ such that $k_0(G-S) > |S|$ is called an *antifactor* set. An antifactor set S such that no proper subset of S is an antifactor set is called a *minimal antifactor set*. For example, in the graph of Figure 8.20(a), $\{v\}$ is an antifactor set.

Definition: A vertex $v \in V$ is a *claw centre* if and only if at least three vertices of G adjacent to v form an independent set. Clearly, vertex v is a claw centre in the graph of Figure 8.20(a).

Now assume that G is a graph of even order n and let S be an antifactor set of G. Let $k_0(G-S) = k$ and $O_1, O_2, \ldots, O_k$ be the odd components of $G-S$. Since n is even, $|S|$ and k have the same parity. Choose a vertex $u_i \in V(O_i)$, $1 \le i \le k$. Then $|S \cup \{u_1, u_2, \ldots, u_k\}|$ is even, that is, $k + |S| \equiv 0 \pmod 2$. This implies that $k \equiv |S| \pmod 2$ and therefore $k_0(G-S) \equiv |S| \pmod 2$. Thus we have the following result.

Lemma 8.4 If S is an antifactor set of a graph G of even order, then $k_0(G-S) \ge |S| + 2$.

Tutte's theorem implies that a graph G has either a 1-factor or an antifactor set. It is necessary to mention here that the computational complexity is high in the verification of Tutte's condition for every subset S of V. In order to reduce the computations, the antifactor sets are of great significance. The following result on antifactors is due to Sumner [230].

Lemma 8.5 If S is a minimal antifactor set of a connected graph G of even order and having no 1-factor, and if $k_0(G-S) = r$ and $|S| = s$, then

i. $r \ge s+2$,

ii. each vertex of S is adjacent to vertices in at least $r-s+1$ distinct odd components of $G-S$,

iii. every vertex of S is a claw centre.

Proof

i. Already established (Lemma 8.4).

ii. If $v \in S$ is adjacent to h distinct odd components say $O_1, O_2, \ldots, O_h$ with $h \le r-s$, then $G - \{S - \{v\}\}$ has the odd components $O_{h+1}, O_{h+2}, \ldots, O_r$. Then, if h is odd, $k_0(G-S') = r-h \ge s > s-1 = |S'|$, and if h is even, then $\{O_1 \cup O_2 \cup \ldots \cup O_h\} \cup \{v\}$ is also an odd component of $G-S'$ so that $k_0(G-S') = r-h+1 \ge s+1 > s-1 = |S'|$, where $S' = S - \{v\}$. That is, S' is an antifactor set, contradicting the minimality of S. Thus, $h \ge r-s+1$.

iii. Since any $v \in S$ is adjacent to at least $r-s+1 \ge 3$ (by (i)) distinct odd components, v is a claw centre, by definition. ❑

Remark The above observations imply that Tutte's theorem is equivalent to the following.

A graph G has a 1-factor if and only if G does not have a set S of claw centres such that $k_0(G-S) > |S|$. Obviously, this form of Tutte's theorem decreases the number of subsets S of V to be verified in Tutte's condition.

An improvement of Theorem 8.11 is due to Plesnik [204].

Theorem 8.12 If G is a k-regular, $(k-1)$-edge-connected graph of even order and G_1 is obtained from G by removing any $k-1$ edges, then G_1 has a 1-factor.

Proof Assume G_1 has no 1-factor. Then G_1 has an antifactor set S with $k_0(G_1-S) > |S|$. Therefore by Lemma 8.4,

$$k_0(G_1-S) \geq |S|+2. \tag{8.12.1}$$

Let $O_1, O_2, \ldots, O_r$ be the odd components and $O_{r+1}, O_{r+2}, \ldots, O_{r+s}$ be the even components of G_1-S. For a component O_i, let a_i and m_i be the number of edges respectively of $E(G)-E(G_1)$ and $E(G_1)$ joining it to S and b_i be the number of edges of $E(G)-E(G_1)$ joining it to the other O_j's. Then the total number of edges going out of O_i is $a_i+b_i+m_i$. Since G is $(k-1)$-edge-connected, $a_i+b_i+m_i \geq k-1$. By the argument used in Theorem 8.11, this implies that $a_i+b_i+m_i \geq k$, for an odd component O_i. Summing over the r odd components, we obtain

$$\sum_{i=1}^{r} a_i + \sum_{i=1}^{r} b_i + \sum_{i=1}^{r} m_i \geq rk. \tag{8.12.2}$$

The number of edges between the O_i's, and between O_i's and S, removed from G is $\sum_{i=1}^{t} a_i + \left(\frac{1}{2}\right) \sum_{i=1}^{t} b_i$, where $t=r+s$. As this is at most $k-1$, we have

$$2\sum_{i=1}^{t} a_i + \sum_{i=1}^{t} b_i \leq 2(k-1). \tag{8.12.3}$$

Also, $\sum_{i=1}^{t} a_i + \sum_{i=1}^{t} m_i \leq \sum_{v\in S} d(v) = k|S|$. (8.12.4)

Adding (8.12.3) and (8.12.4), we get

$$3\sum_{i=1}^{t} a_i + \sum_{i=1}^{t} b_i + \sum_{i=1}^{t} m_i \leq k(|S|+2)-2. \tag{8.12.5}$$

As the sum on the left of (8.12.2) is less than the sum on the left of (8.12.5), we have

$rk \leq k(|S|+2)-2 < k(|S|+2)$, giving r $< |S|+2$, which contradicts (8.12.1). ❑

We now have the following observation.

Corollary 8.4 A $(k-1)$-regular simple graph on $2k$ vertices has a 1-factor.

Proof Assume G is a $(k-1)$-regular simple graph with $2k$ vertices having no 1-factor. Then G has an antifactor set S and by Lemma 8.4, $k_0(G-S) \geq |S|+2$. Therefore, $|S|+(|S|+2) \leq 2k$ and so $|S| \leq k-1$. Let $|S| = k-r$. Then $r \neq 1$. For if $r = 1$, then $|S| = k-1$ and therefore $k_0(G-S) = k+1$. Thus each odd component of $G-S$ is a singleton and therefore each such vertex is adjacent to all the $k-1$ vertices of S, as G is $(k-1)$ regular. This implies that every vertex of S is of degree at least $k+1$, a contradiction. Thus, $|S| = k-r$, $2 \leq r \leq k-1$. If G_1 is any component of $G-S$ and $v \in V(G_1)$, then v can be adjacent to at most $|S|$ vertices of S. Since G is $(k-1)$-regular, v is adjacent to at least $(k-1)-(k-r) = r-1$ vertices of G_1. So, $|V(G_1)| \geq r$. Counting the vertices of S, we obtain $(|S|+2)r + |S| = 2k$, or $(k-r+2)r + (k-r) \leq 2k$. This gives $(r-1)(r-k) \geq 0$, violating the condition on r. ❑

The next result is due to Sumner [230].

Theorem 8.13 If G is a connected graph of even order n and claw-free (that is, contains no $K_{1,3}$ as an induced subgraph), then G has a 1-factor.

Proof If G has no 1-factor, then G contains a minimal antifactor set S of G. Also, there is an edge between S and each odd component of $G-S$. If $v \in S$ and vx, vy and vz are edges of G with x, y and z belonging to distinct odd components of $G-S$, then a $K_{1,3}$ is induced in G. This is not possible, by hypothesis.

Since $k_0(G-S) > |S|$, there exists a vertex v of S and edges vu and vw of G, with u and w in distinct odd components of $G-S$. Assume O_u and O_w to be the odd components containing u and w respectively. Then $< O_u \cup O_w \cup \{v\} >$ is an odd component of $G-S_1$, where $S_1 = S - \{v\}$. Also, $k_0(G-S_1) = k_0(G-S) - 1 > |S| - 1 = |S_1|$ and therefore S_1 is an antifactor set of G with $|S_1| = |S|-1$, a contradiction to the choice of S. So G has a 1-factor. (Clearly, by Lemma 8.4, the case $|S| = 1$ and $k_0(G-S) = 2$ does not exist). ❑

The following results are immediate, as each type of graph in these cases does not contain $K_{1,3}$ as an induced subgraph.

Corollary 8.5 Every connected even order edge graph has a 1-factor.

Corollary 8.6 If G is a connected graph of even order, then G^2 has a 1-factor.

Corollary 8.7 Every connected total graph of even order has a 1-factor.

Corollary 8.8 Every connected cubic graph in which every vertex lies on a triangle has a 1-factor.

Corollary 8.9 If a connected even order graph G has less than $\kappa(G)$ claw centres, then G has a 1-factor.

The following result is the generalisation of Theorem 8.13.

Theorem 8.14 If G is n-connected even order graph with no induced $K_{1,\,n+1}$, then G has a 1-factor.

Proof Assume G has no 1-factor. Then G has a minimal antifactor set S. Let $|S| = s$ and let the odd components of $G-S$ be $O_1, O_2, \ldots, O_k$. If $S_i' = \{v \in S : v$ is adjacent to some vertex to $O_i\}$, then S_i' is a vertex cut of G and therefore $|S_i'| \geq n$. Thus there are at least n edges from O_i incident with n distinct vertices of S. The number of such edges as i ranges from 1 to k is at least nk and this is greater or equal to $n(s+2)$, by Lemma 8.4. Thus at least one vertex v of S is incident with at least $n+1$ of these edges. But then, v is the centre of an induced $K_{1,\,n+1}$, contradicting the assumption. ❑

It can be observed that a graph can have more than one 1-factors and different 1-factors can either have no edge in common or have some edges in common. Depending on the nature of edges, we have the following definition.

Definition: In a given graph, two 1-factors are said to be *disjoint* if they have no edge in common and two 1-factors are said to be *distinct* if they have at least one different edge. For example, in the graph of Figure 8.22, the 1-factors $\{e_1, e_2, e_3\}$ and $\{e_4, e_5, e_6\}$ are disjoint, while as the 1-factors $\{e_1, e_2, e_3\}$ and $\{e_1, e_7, e_5\}$ are distinct.

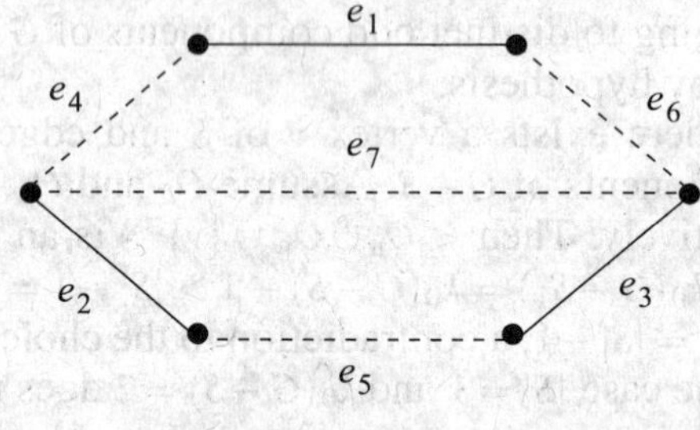

Fig. 8.22

Consider maximal sets S which satisfy Tutte's condition in graphs admitting a 1-factor. If such a graph is connected, then definitely there exist subsets S such that $k_0(G-S) = |S|$. For such a graph will have a vertex v which is not a cut vertex, and $G-v$ being connected and of odd order, $k_0(G-v) = 1 = |v|$. The maximal subsets S for which $k_0(G-S) = |S|$ holds is called a maximal factor set.

A result on counting distinct 1-factors for bipartite graphs is given by Theorem 8.4. The next result as reported in Bollobas [29] gives the bounds for distinct 1-factors in a graph..

Theorem 8.15 Let G be a graph admitting a 1-factor and let S_0 be a maximal factor set of G with $|S_0| = m$ and $O_1, O_2, \ldots, O_m$ be the odd components of $G-S_0$. Further, let $d = \min \{|N(O_i) \cap S_o| : 1 \leq i \leq m\}$ and d' be the minimum number of edges joining O_i to S_0, $1 \leq i \leq m$. Then the number $F(G)$ of 1-factors of G satisfies

i. $F(G) \geq r(d,m) = \prod_{i=1}^{\min(d,m)} \cdot (d+1-i)$ and

ii. $F(G) \geq \tilde{r}\ (d',m)$, where $\tilde{r}\ (d',m)$ is the minimum number of 1-factors in a bipartite multigraph with m vertices in each class, in which d' is the minimum degree in the first vertex class.

Proof Let S_0 be a maximal factor set of G so that $k_0(G-S_0) = |S_0|$.

Using Hall's theorem for a complete matching in a bipartite graph, we can show that $|S_0|$ odd components of $G-S_0$ can be paired with the vertices of S_0. The sufficient condition is that any k such odd components should be joined in G to at least k vertices in S_0. Clearly, this is satisfied here. For if some set of k odd components are joined in G only to a subset T of S_0 with h vertices, $h < k$, then $k_0(G-T) \geq k > h = |T|$, contradicting the hypothesis. Therefore one vertex each of $|S_0|$ odd components can be matched to one vertex of S_0. Let O be an odd component of which a vertex a has been matched with a corresponding vertex s of S_0. Clearly, $O' = O - a$ is a graph on an even number of vertices. Now we verify Tutte's condition on O'. If there is a $T \subseteq V' = V(O')$ such that $k_0(O'-T) > |T|$, then $k_0(O'-T) > |T|+2$. Let $S = S_0 \cup T \cup \{a\}$. Then $k_0(G-S) = k_0(O'-T) + k_0(G-S_0) - 1 = k_0(O'-T) + |S_0| - 1 > |T| + |S_0| + 1 = |S|$, contradicting the choice of S_0. Thus Tutte's condition is satisfied for O' and O' has a 1-factor.

If $G-S_0$ has an even component C and $a \in V(C)$, then $G-(S_0 \cup \{a\})$ has at least one more odd component than $G-S_0$, contradicting the choice of S_0 or the Tutte condition. Thus $G-S_0$ has no even components.

Therefore we have seen that for each $o_i \in O_i$ such that there is an $s_i \in S_0$ with $o_i s_i \in E$, each $O_i - o_i$ has a 1-factor forming part of a 1-factor of G. The number of such choices of m independent edges $o_i s_i$ equals the number of 1-factors in a bipartite graph $H(V_1 \cup V_2,\ E)$, where V_1 has m vertices, one corresponding to each odd component O_i of $G-S_0$ and V_2 has the m vertices of S_0. If we take the edge set E to be such that whenever $s_j \in N(O_i) \cap S_0$, we take exactly one $o_i s_i \in E$, then we get an ordinary bipartite graph for H in which the minimum degree in V_1 is $d = \min\{|N(O_i) \cap S_0|\}$ and then (i) follows from Theorem 8.4. However, if we take E to be such that for each edge joining O_i to s_j we take an edge $o_i s_j$, then we get a bipartite multigraph for H in which the least degree of a vertex in V_i is d' as defined and then (ii) follows. ❑

The following observations can be seen immediately.

Corollary 8.10 For a k-edge-connected graph with a unique 1-factor, $F(G) \geq k$.

Corollary 8.11 If G is a connected graph with a unique 1-factor, then G has a cut edge which belongs to a 1-factor.

The details of the following results can be found in Bollobas [29].

Theorem 8.16 If $\delta\,(n)$ is the minimum degree of a graph of order $2n$ with exactly one 1-factor, then $\delta(n) \leq [\log 2(n+1)]$.

Theorem 8.17 If $e(n)$ is the maximum size of a graph of order $2n$ with exactly one 1-factor, then $e(n) = n^2$.

8.4 The f-factor Theorem

The f-factor Theorem gives a set of necessary and sufficient conditions for the existence of an f-factor in a general graph. This result was proved by Tutte [243] for loopless graphs, using the theory of alternating paths, and later again by Tutte [244], using the 1-factor Theorem.

First of all, we have the following definitions.

Definition: A *vertex function* for a general graph $G(V, E)$ is a function $f : V \to N_0$ such that $0 \le f(v) \le d(v)$, for every $v \in V$.

For any function $f : V \to N_0$ and for any $U \subseteq V$, we set $f(U) = \sum_{v \in U} f(v)$.

Definition: Three pair-wise disjoint (possibly empty) subsets S, T and U of the vertex set V of a general graph G, such that $V = S \cup T \cup U$, is called a *decomposition* $D = (S, T, U)$ of G. The components, say $C_1, C_2, \ldots, C_k$, of the vertex-induced subgraph $< U >$ of G are called the components of U. For each C_i, let $h_i = f(C_i) + q_G[T, C_i]$, where f is a given vertex function of G, and $q_G[T, C_i]$ denotes the number of edges of G, whose one end is in T and the other end is in C_i. Then C_i is said to be an odd or even component of U, depending upon h_i being odd or even, and the number of odd components of U is denoted by $k_0'(D, f)$.

The *f-deficiency* of D for the given G is defined as

$$\delta(D, f) = k_0'(D, f) - f(S) + f(T) - d(T) + q[S, T].$$

The decomposition D is defined to be an *f-barrier* of G if $\delta(D, f) > 0$.

The term decomposition is used by Graver and Jurkat [85], and Tutte calls it a *G-triple*. These decompositions play the same role as the antifactor sets in the theory of 1-factors.

Before going into the details, we first state the f-factor Theorem.

Theorem 8.18 If f is a vertex function for a graph G, then either G has an f-factor or an f-barrier but not both.

It can be seen that both the statement and the proof of the f-factor Theorem as in Tutte [246] definitely have similarities to those of the 1-factor Theorem. Since there are few complications in the constructions involved which make the proof given by Tutte [246] some what lengthy, we follow here the earlier proof by Tutte [244].

Tutte [243] defines an ordinary graph G' corresponding to a given graph G such that G has an f-factor if and only if G' has a 1-factor and shows that the 1-factor condition corresponds to the f-factor condition, and derives the f-factor Theorem as a consequence of the 1-factor Theorem. Berge [23] uses the same graph construction to derive the maximum

f-matching Theorem. Since we have general graphs under consideration, we construct G' with suitable changes as reported by Parthasarthy [175], and then find that the proof still holds.

Let G be a general graph with the vertex function f. This defines for each vertex v_i, its degree $d_i = d(v_i|G)$, $f_i = f(v_i)$ and $k_i = d_i - f_i$. For each vertex v_i of G, take two subsets X_i and Y_i of vertices of G', where $|X_i| = d_i$ and $|Y_i| = k_i$. Let the vertices of Y_i be labelled y^i_j, $1 \le j \le k_i$, arbitrarily. Now, label the vertices of X_i in the following manner.

Label the edges of G arbitrarily as 1, 2, ..., m. Since $|X_i|$ = number of link edges l_i incident with v_i plus twice the number of loops ℓ^0_i incident with v_i, a vertex $x^i_j \in X_i$ is taken corresponding to each link edge j incident with v_i and two vertices x^i_h, $x^i_{h'}$ are taken corresponding to each loop h incident at v_i. As for edges, if link j joins v_i and v_k, then $x^i_j x^k_j$ is made an edge. Corresponding to loop h incident with x^i_h the edge $x^i_h\, x^i_{h'}$ is taken. In addition, all the edges of the complete bipartite subgraph with vertex partition $\{X_i, Y_i\}$ are taken for each i. These constitute the graph G'. The induced subgraph $< X_i \cup Y_i >$ of G is called the *star graph* at i and is denoted by $St(i)$. For multi graph G, it is a complete bipartite graph, but for general graphs it will contain edges in $< X_i >$ which we call *loop edges*. The other edges of $St(i)$ are called *star edges* and the remaining edges of G' are called as *link edges*.

This construction is illustrated in Figure 8.23. In the general graph G, $d(v_1) = 5$, $d(v_2) = 3$ and $d(v_3) = 2$. Let $f = (3, 2, 1)$ be the vertex function, so that $f(v_1) = 3$, $f(v_2) = 2$ and $f(v_3) = 1$. Therefore, $k_1 = 2$, $k_2 = 1$ and $k_3 = 1$. Here $|X_1| = 5$, $|X_2| = 3$ and $|X_3| = 2$, and $|Y_1| = 2$, $|Y_2| = 1$ and $|Y_3| = 1$.

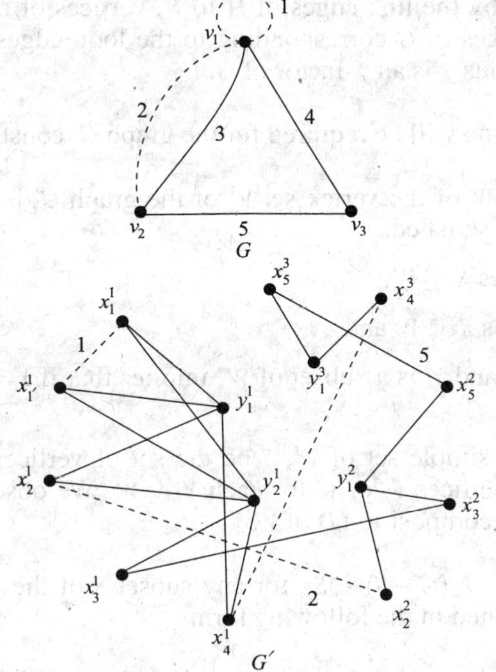

Fig. 8.23

Label the edges of G as 1, 2, 3, 4 and 5 as shown. Then $Y_1 = \{y_1^1, y_2^1\}$, $Y_2 = \{y_1^2\}$ and $Y_3 = \{y_1^3\}$, and we have $X_1 = \{x_1^1, x_{1'}^1, x_2^1, x_3^1, x_4^1\}$, $X_2 = \{x_2^2, x_3^2, x_5^2\}$ and $X_3 = \{x_4^3, x_5^3\}$. The vertex set of G' is $X_i \cup Y_i$, $1 \le i \le 3$. The edges of G' are $x_1^1x_{1'}^1$, $x_2^1x_2^2$, $x_3^1x_3^2$, $x_4^1x_4^3$, $x_5^2x_5^3$ (shown by dotted lines) and the star edges (shown by bold lines). The dotted lines in G form an f-factor with $f = (3, 2, 1)$.

The following result gives a relation between f-factors of G and the 1-factors of G'.

Theorem 8.18 A general graph G has an f-factor if and only if G' has a 1-factor.

Proof First, assume G has an f-factor F with link edges L and loop edges L^0. Let F have g_i link edges and f_i^o loop edges at the vertex v_i. Then $f_i = g_i + 2f_i^0$, $|X_i| = d_i = l_i + 2l_i^0$ and $|Y_i| = k_i = d_i - f_i = (l_i + 2l_i^0) - (g_i + 2f_i^0) = (l_i - g_i) + 2(2l_i^0 - f_i^0)$, where l_i is the number of link edges incident with v_i and l_i^0 is the number of loops incident with v_i. Let L' and $(L^0)'$ be the set of corresponding set of link and loop edges in G'. The matching consisting of these edges, keeps unsaturated all the vertices of Y_i and a set of $l_i - g_i + 2(l_i^o - f_i^o) = k_i$ vertices of X_i, for $1 \le i \le n$. Now match the vertices of Y_i with these unsaturated vertices of X_i using the star edges $St(i)$ and let S' be this set of edges. Clearly $L'U(L^0)' \cup S'$ is a 1-factor in G'.

Conversely, assume G' has a 1-factor H. As the vertices in Y_i are matched only to vertices in X_i, there are exactly $d_i - (d_i - f_i) = f_i = g_i + 2f_i^0$ vertices of X_i which are not matched by H to vertices in Y_i. Clearly, $2f_i^0$ vertices from these unmatched vertices of X_i correspond to loop edges of $< X_i >$ and thus are matched in pairs amongst themselves. The remaining g_i vertices are matched by the link edges of H to X_j vertices of other star graphs $St(i)$ of G'. If F is the set of edges of G corresponding to the loop edges and link edges, then d $(v_i| < F >) = g_i + 2f_i^0$. Thus f is an f-factor of G. ❑

The following definition will be required for the graph G' constructed as above.

Definition: A subset W of the vertex set V' of the graph G' is said to be *simple* if the following conditions get satisfied.

i. $(X_i \cap W) \ne \varphi$ implies $X_i \subseteq W$,

ii. $(Y_i \cap W) \ne \varphi$ implies $X_i \subseteq W$ and

iii. At most one of X_i and Y_i is a subset of W, implies that if $Y_i = \varphi$, then $Y_i \subseteq W$, that is $X_i \cap W = \varphi$.

Now assume W be a simple set of V', S be the set of vertices v_i of G, for each $X_i \subseteq W$ and T be the set of vertices v_j of G for each $Y_j \subseteq W$. We observe that $S \cap T = \varphi$, and $S \cup T \cup (V - S - T)$ is a decomposition D of V.

Denoting by $d(G, S) = k_0(G - S) - |S|$, for any subset S of the vertex set V of a graph, Theorem 8.8 can be restated in the following form.

Theorem 8.19 A simple graph G has a 1-factor if and only if it has no subset $S \subseteq V$ with $d(G, S) > 0$.

Theorem 8.20 If W is a simple subset of V' and D is the corresponding decomposition of V, then $d(G', W) = \delta(D, f)$.

Proof Since W is a simple subset of V' and D is the corresponding decomposition of V,

$$|W| = \sum_{v_j \in S} |X_j| + \sum_{v_j \in T} |Y_j| = \sum_{v_j \in S} d_j + \sum_{v_j \in T} (d_j - f_j) = d(S) + d(T) - f(T). \qquad (8.20.1)$$

Thus, $d(G', W) = k_0(G' - W) - d(S) - d(T) + f(T)$.

We proceed to find $k_0(G' - W)$ and in doing so we consider the components K of $G' - W$. We have the following possibilities.

i. The component K contains a single vertex of the form x_r^i. This is possible when $Y_i \subseteq W$ and the edge r is a link edge whose other end is in $Y_j \subseteq W$. Thus, in this case, K is an odd component, and the number of such odd components is equal to the number of such link edges and equals $q[S, T]$.

ii. The component K contains a single vertex of the form y_α^i, and this is possible when $X_i \subseteq W$. This again is an odd component and the number of such odd components is equal to

$$\sum_{i \in S} |Y_i| = \sum_{i \in S} (d_i - f_i) = d(S) - f(S).$$

iii. K contains a single edge of the form $x_\alpha^i\ x_\alpha$ corresponding to a loop of G at α. This is possible when $Y_i \subseteq W$, Clearly, this is an even component of $G' - W$.

iv. K contains a single edge of the form $x_r^i x_r^j$, where r is the link edge of G joining vertices v_i and v_j. Clearly, this happens when $Y_i \subseteq W$ and $Y_j \subseteq W$. This also is an even component.

v. K contains more than one edge and we call such components large components. Clearly, they have one star graph $St(i)$ as a subgraph. If K contains more than one such star graph as a proper subgraph, it will also contain all edges of G' between such star graphs. The other edges of K are of the form $x_r^i x_r^j$, where r is an edge of G joining v_i and v_j, and $St(i) \subseteq K$ and $Y_j \subseteq T$. Let $v_{i_1}, v_{i_2}, \ldots, v_{i_k}$ be the vertices of G corresponding to the star graphs $St(i_j)$, $1 \leq j \leq k$, which are subgraphs of K. Let C be the induced subgraph $< v_{i_1}, v_{i_2}, \ldots, v_{i_k} >$ of G. Then C is a component of $G - S - T$ and therefore the number of vertices of the large component K is given by

$$n(K) = |V(K)| = \sum_{v_i \in C} |V(St(i))| + q[C, T]$$

$$= \sum_{v_i \in C} (d_i + d_i - f_i) + q[C, T]$$

$$= \sum_{v_i \in C} f_i + q[C, T] \pmod 2$$

$$= f(C) + q[C, T] \pmod 2.$$

Therefore K is an odd component of $G' - W$ if and only if C is an odd component of $G - S - T$. So the number of large odd components of $G' - W$ is $k_0'(D, f)$.

Combining the above results, we observe that the number of odd components of $G' - W$ is given by

$$k_0(G' - W) = q[S, T] + d(S) - f(S) + k_0'(D, f). \tag{8.20.2}$$

Now, $\delta(D, f) = k_0'(D, f) - f(S) + f(T) - d(T) + q[S, T]$

$$= k_0(G' - W) - d(S) + f(T) - d(T), \quad \text{(by using (8.20.2))}$$

$$= d(G', W). \quad \text{(by using (8.20.1))} \quad \square$$

Now, we have the following main result.

Theorem 8.21 A general graph G has an f-factor if and only if it has no decomposition D with $\delta(D, f) > 0$.

Proof

Necessity Assume there are decompositions D for which $\delta(D, f) > 0$ and choose one such decomposition for which $|S|$ is least. Claim that for each $v_i \in S$, $f(v_i) < d(v_i)$. If not, there is a $v \in S$ such that $f(v) = d(v)$. Consider the decomposition $D' = (S', T', U')$, where $S' = S - \{v\}$, $T' = T \cup \{v\}$ and $U' = U$. Then the components of $< V - S' - T' >$ are the same as those of $< V - S - T >$. Also, for such a component C, $f(C)$ is unchanged, but $q[C, T'] = q[C, T] + q[C, v]$. Therefore at most $q[v, U]$ components can change from odd to even. That is, $k_0'(G - S' - T') \geq k_0'(G - S - T) - q[v, U]$.

Thus, $\delta(D', f) = k_0'(G - S' - T') + f(T') - f(S') - d(T') + q[S', T']$

$$= k_0'(G - S' - T') + f(T) + f(v) - f(S) + f(v) - d(T) - d(v) +$$

$$q[S, T] - q[v, T] + q[v, S]$$

$$= k_0'(G - S' - T') + f(T) - f(S) - d(T) + q[S, T] + 2f(v) - d(v)$$

$$- q[v, T] + q[v, S]$$

$$\geq k_0'(G - S - T) - q[v, U] + f(T) - f(S) - d(T) + q[S, T] + d(v)$$

$$-q[v, T] + q[v, S] \quad (\text{as } d(v) = f(v))$$

$$= \delta(D, f) + d(v) - q[v, U] - q[v, T] + q[v, S]$$

$$= \delta(D, f) + 2q[v, S] > \delta(D, f) > 0.$$

This contradicts the choice of D and thus the claim is established.

Now, suppose $W = \{X_i : v_i \in S\} \cup \{Y_j : v_j \in T\}$.

Then W is simple, as S and T are disjoint. Therefore by Theorem 8.20, $d\,(G', W) = \delta(D, f) > 0$ and G' has no 1-factor. Thus by Theorem 8.18, G has no f-factor.

Sufficiency Assume that G has no f-factor, so that G' has no 1-factor. Therefore, by Theorem 8.19, there is a subset W of V' with $d(G', W) > 0$. We choose such a W with least cardinality and prove that W is simple.

Claim 1 $Y_j \cap W \neq \varphi$ and $Y_j \subseteq W$.

If this is not true, then there is a Y_j such that $Y_j \cap W \neq \varphi$, and $Y_j \cap (V' - W) \neq \varphi$. Define $Q = W - (Y_j \cap W)$ (Fig. 8.24).

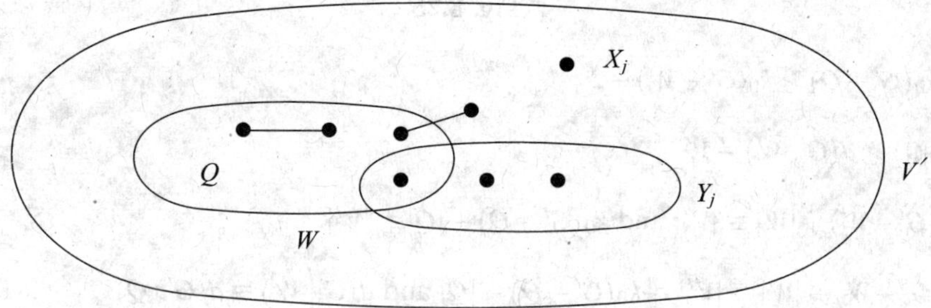

Fig. 8.24

If $X_j \nsubseteq W$, then $G' - W$ and $G' - Q$ differ in one component only, the component star edges.

If $X_j \subseteq W$, then each component of $G' - W$ is also a component of $G' - Q$.

In either case, $k_0(G' - Q) \geq k_0(G' - W) - 1$ and $|Q| \leq |W| - 1$. Therefore, $d(G', Q) > 0$, contradicting the choice of W.

Claim 2 $X_i \cap W \neq \varphi$ implies $Y_i \subseteq W$.

If this is not true, then there is an i such that $X_i \cap W \neq \varphi$ and $Y_i \subseteq W$. Let $a \in X_i \cap W$ and define $Q = W - \{a\}$. Then $G' - W$ can have at most one component with a vertex belonging to Y_i which is adjacent to a in G. Thus,

$$k_0(G' - W) \leq k_0(G' - Q) + 1 \text{ and } |Q| = |W| - 1.$$

Therefore, $d(G', Q) \geq d(G', W)$, contradicting the choice of W.

Now claim (1) and claim (2) together imply that both X_i and Y_i are not subsets of W.

Claim 3 $X_i \cap W \neq \varphi$ implies $X_i \subseteq W$.

If not, there is an i such that $X_i \cap W \neq \varphi$ and $X_i \cap (V' - W) \neq \varphi$. Let a $\in X_i \cap W$ and define $Q = W - \{a\}$. By claims (2) and (1), $Y_i \subseteq G' - W$, so that all vertices of Y_i belong to a single component of $G' - W$. Also there is at most one component of $G' - Q$ which has a vertex not belonging to Y_i which is adjacent to an a in G' (Fig. 8.25). Therefore $G' - W$ and $G' - Q$ differ in at most two components.

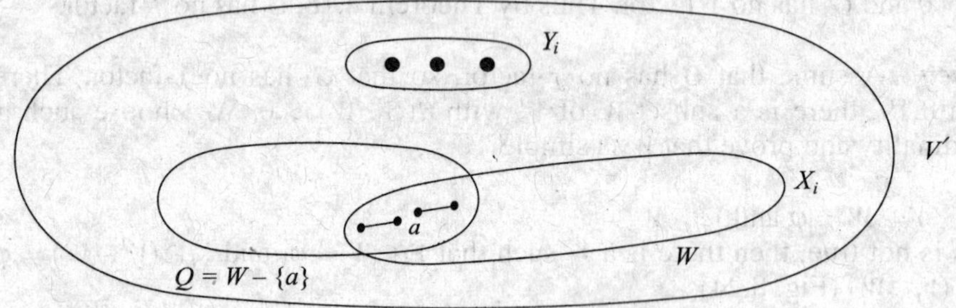

Fig. 8.25

Thus, $k_0(G' - Q) \geq k_0(G' - W) - 2$

and $d(G', Q) \geq d(G', W) - 1$. (8.21.1)

But $k_0(G' - W) + |W| \equiv |V'|$ and $k_0(G' - Q) + |Q| \equiv |V'|$.

So, $k_0(G' - W) - |W| \equiv |V'| \equiv k_0(G' - Q) - |Q|$ and $d(G', W) \equiv d(G', Q)$.

Therefore, (8.21.1) becomes $d(G', Q) \geq d(G', W) > 0$, contradicting the choice of W.

Hence we have proved that W is a simple set and by Theorem 8.20, for the corresponding decomposition D of G, $\delta(D, f) > 0$. ❑

Remark Theorem 8.21 shows that the 1-factor Theorem implies the f-factor Theorem. The converse is also true as can be seen in Theorem 8.22. Before that we have the following definition.

Definition: Suppose $D = (S, T, U)$ is a decomposition of V and $x \in S$, $y \in T$. The decomposition $D_1 = (S - \{x\}, T, U \cup \{x\})$ is said to be obtained by an x-transfer from S and the decomposition $D_2 = (S, T - \{y\}, U \cup \{y\}$ is said to be obtained by y-transfer from T.

The following result is an immediate consequence of the above definition and can be easily established.

Lemma 8.6 An x-transfer from S does not reduce the deficiency of D if $f(x) = d(x)$ or $d(x) - 1$ and a y-transfer does not reduce the deficiency of D if $f(y) = 0$ or 1.

Theorem 8.22 The f-factor Theorem implies the 1-factor Theorem.

Proof Clearly, by the f-factor Theorem with $f(v) = 1$, for all $v \in V$, G has a 1-factor if and only if it has a 1-barrier $D = (S, T, U)$. But by Lemma 8.6, $D_1 = (S, \varphi, V - S)$ has no less deficiency than D (by y-transfer from T). Therefore G has no 1-factor if and only if there is a 1-barrier of the form D_1. But $\delta(D_1, f) = k_0(G-S) - f(S) - d(T) + f(T) + q[S, T] = k_0(G-S) - |S|$ and D_1 is a 1-barrier if and only if $\delta(D_1, f) > 0$, that is $k_0(G-S) > |S|$. Hence the 1-factor Theorem. ❑

Corollary 8.12 The Erdos-Gallai Theorem 2.4 on degree sequences follows from the f-factor Theorem.

Proof Theorem 2.4 gives a necessary and sufficient condition for a non-increasing sequence $d = [d_i]_1^n$ of non-negative integers to be the degree sequence of a simple graph. In order to get this condition, we observe that d is graphic if and only if the complete graph K_n has a d-factor, where $d(v_i) = d_i$, given $\sum_{i=1}^{n} d_i = 2m$.

By the f-factor Theorem, d fails to be graphic if and only if K_n has a d-barrier $D = (S, T, U)$. Since for K_n, U can have at most one component, $k_0(D, d) = 0$ or 1, further $\delta(D, d) > 0$ is even, as $d(K_n) = \sum d_i = 2m$ is even. Therefore the condition $\delta(D, d) > 0$ becomes

$$q_{k_n} - [S, T] - d(S) - (n-1)|T| + d(T) > 0. \qquad (8.12.1)$$

Now transfer of elements t from T to U, or elements s from S to U does not decrease the deficiency $\delta(D, d)$. So elements $t \in T$ with $d(t) < |T| + |U|$ and elements $s \in S$ with $d(s) > |T|$ in S can be transferred to U without decreasing the deficiency. Also it can be seen that elements $u \in U$ with $d(u) \geq |T| + |U|$ can be transferred to S without decreasing the deficiency. Therefore the f-barrier can be made such that $d(t) > |T| + |U|$ for all $t \in T$, $|T| < d(u) < |T| + |U|$ for all $u \in U$ and $d(s) \leq |T|$ for all $s \in S$, and d is non-graphical if and only if K_n has such a d-barrier D. But for such a D, $q[S, T] = r(n - r - |U|)$, where $|T| = r$, $d(T) = \sum_1^r d_i$, and thus condition (8.12.1) becomes

$$r(n - r - |U|) - d(S) - r(n-1) + d(T) > 0.$$

That is, $\displaystyle\sum_1^r d_i > r(n-1) + d(S) - r(n - r - |U|)$

$$= r(r-1) + r(n-r) + d(S) - r(n - r - |U|)$$

$$= r(r-1) + r|U| + d(S)$$

$$> r(r-1) + \sum_{i=r+1}^{n} \min\{r,\, d_i\},$$

which is the Erdos-Gallai condition. ❑

8.5 Degree Factors

Let $d = [d_i]_1^n$ and $r = [d_i - k_i]_1^n$ be graphical sequences. The problem we consider here is the existence of a graph G realising d with a spanning subgraph (factor) realising $k = [k_i]_1^n$. This problem was asked by Rao and Rao [209] as k-factor conjecture, when $k \le k_i \le k+1$ for each i, and solved by Kundu [139]. An improvement of this was due to Kleitman and Wang [125] and further improvement by Kundu [137]. For $k_i = 1$, $1 \le i \le n$, the problem was earlier posed by Grunbaum [90] and proved by Lovasz [145], and this proof also applies when $k_i = k$, $1 \le i \le n$.

Theorem 8.23 (k-factor Theorem [90]) If $[d_i]_1^n$ is a graphical sequence such that $[d_i - k]_1^n$ is also graphical, then there is a realisation of $[d_i]_1^n$ with a k-factor.

Proof Let G_1 and G_2 be two graphs on $V = \{v_1, v_2, \ldots, v_n\}$ such that $d(v_i|G_1) = d_i$ and $d(v_i|G_2) = d_i - k$. Assume that G_1 and G_2 are chosen such that G_2 has maximum edges common with G_1. We show that all edges of G_2 are in G_1. Let $E_1 = E(G_1)$ and $E_2 = E(G_2)$.

Claim

If $v_iv_j \in E_2 - E_1$ and $v_iv_k,\, v_jv_r \in E_1 - E_2$ ($i,\, j,\, k,\, r$ being distinct), then $v_kv_r \in E_1 - E_2$.

If $v_kv_r \in E_2$, then an EDT in G_2 switching the pair v_iv_j, v_kv_r to the positions v_iv_k, v_jv_r gives a graph degree-equivalent to G_2 with more edges common with G_1, contradicting the choice of G_1 and G_2. If $v_kv_r \notin E_1$, then an EDT in G_1 switching the pair v_iv_k, v_jv_r to the positions v_iv_j, v_kv_r gives a graph degree-equivalent to G_1, such that G_2 has more common edges with this graph, again a contradiction. Thus, the claim is established.

Let G_2 has some edges which are not in G_1 and let v_1 be a vertex with a maximum number t of edges of $E_2 - E_1$ incident with it. By the degree stipulation on G_1 and G_2, there are $t+k$ vertices $v_2, v_3, \ldots, v_{t+k+1}$ which are adjacent to v_1 in G_1, but not in G_2. Assume $v_1v_k \in E_2 - E_1$ and $v_kv \in E_1 - E_2$, and consider the following two cases.

Case 1 Let $v \ne v_i$ for i, $2 \le i \le t+k+1$. Then by the above claim, $vv_i \in E_1 - E_2$ for $2 \le i \le t+k+1$, so that there are $t+k+1$ edges in $E_1 - E_2$ adjacent with v. By the degree-stipulation on G_1 and G_2, there are $t+1$ edges in $E_2 - E_1$ incident with v, contradicting the choice of v.

Case 2 Let $v = v_i$ for some i, $2 \le i \le t+k+1$, and without loss of generality, take $v = v_2$. Then again, by the above claim, $vv_i \in E_1 - E_2$ for $3 \le i \le t+k+1$. Also, vv_1, $vv_k \in E_1 - E_2$. Therefore there are $t+k+1$ edges in $E_1 - E_2$ incident with v, again a contradiction.

Hence G_2 has no edges which are not in G_1. But then $< E(G_1) - E(G_2) >$ is a k-factor of G_1. ❑

Lemma 8.7 If $[k_i]_1^n$ is a sequence of non-negative integers such that $k \le k_i \le k+1$ for $1 \le i \le n$ and for some k, $0 \le k \le n-2$, and $\sum_1^n k_i$ is even, then $[k_i]_1^n$ is a graphical sequence.

Proof Induct on $S = \sum_1^n k_i$. Clearly, the result is trivial for $S = 0$. Assume it is true for all values of $\sum_1^n k_i < S-1$ and let $[k_i]_1^n$ be a sequence with $\sum_1^n k_i = S$ (even). Then by Theorem 2.1, $[k_i]_1^n$ is graphical if and only if $[k_2 - 1, k_3 - 1, \ldots, k_{k_1+1} - 1, k_{k_1+2}, \ldots, k_n]$ is graphical, where $k_1 \ge k_2 \ge \ldots \ge k_n$. But the sum of the terms in this sequence is $S - 2k_1$, which is even, and by induction hypothesis is graphical. Hence by Theorem 2.1, $[k_i]_1^n$ is graphical. ❑

The proof given here of the following k-factor Theorem of Kundu, is due to Chen [56].

Theorem 8.24 If $[d_i]_1^n$ and $[d_i - k_i]_1^n$ are two graphical sequences satisfying $k \le k_i \le k+1$, for $1 \le i \le n$ and some $k > 0$, then there is a graph realising $[d_i]_1^n$ and having a k-factor $k = [k_i]_1^n$.

Proof Since $[d_i]_1^n$ and $[d_i - k_i]_1^n$ are both graphical, $[k_i]_1^n$ is also graphical by Lemma 8.7.

Clearly, there exists a graph with degree sequence $[d_i]_1^n$ containing a k-factor $k = [k_i]_1^n$ if and only if there exists a graph with degree sequence $[n-1-k_i]_1^n$ containing a k'-factor $k' = [n-1-d_i]_1^n$. This can be easily established by taking the complementary graphs. Thus, the conditions can be shifted from k_i's to d_i's, so that it is enough to prove that if $[d_i]_1^n$ and $[d_i - k_i]_1^n$ are graphical with $k \le d_i \le k+1$ for $1 \le i \le n$ and the k_i's unrestricted, then there is a graph with degree sequence $[d_i]_1^n$ and a k-factor $k = [k_i]_1^n$.

Let G_1 and G_2 be graphs with degree sequences $[k_i]_1^n$ and $[d_i - k_i]_1^n$ respectively, such that the multigraph G, obtained by superimposing G_1 and G_2 has a minimum number of multiple edges. Obviously, in the superimposed graph, there are at most two edges between any pair of vertices, one of G_1 and one of G_2. If there are no such multiple edges, then G_1 is a factor of G.

Assume there are multiple edges in G and let uv be one such multiple edge. Since $d(u|G) = d(u|G_1) + d(u|G_2) \le n-1$ and uv is a multiple edge, there is a vertex w not adjacent to u in G. Let V be the common vertex set of G_1, G_2 and G. If for every $x \in V - u$, $q[v, x] \ge q[w, x]$, then $d(v|G) - 2 \ge d(w|G)$, contradicting the choice that each d_i is k or $k+1$. Therefore there is a vertex $x \in V - u$ such that $q[v, x] < q[w, x]$ (Fig. 8.26).

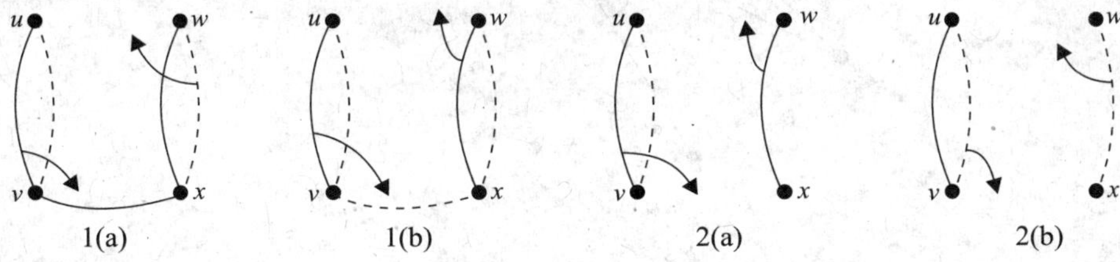

Fig. 8.26

The following two cases arise:

1. $q[v, x] = 1$ and $q[w, x] = 2$,
2. $q[v, x] = 0$ and $q[w, x] = 0$.

In case 1, we have either $1(a)$ $vx \in G_1$, or $1(b)$ $vx \in G_2$, and in case 2, either 2(a) $wx \in G_1$, or $2(b)$ $wx \in G_2$. For all these cases, make an EDT switching the pair of edges vu, wx to the positions vx, uw. In 1(a) and 2(b), this is done in G_2 to obtain a graph G_2' degree-equivalent to G_2 and with less number of multiple edges in $G_1 \cup G_2'$. In 1(b) and 2(a), this is done in G_1 to get a graph G_1' degree-equivalent to G_1 and with less multiple edges in $G_1' \cup G_2$. This contradicts the choice of G_1 and G_2. ❑

Remark If d_i's and k_i's being allowed to be arbitrary with $[d_i]_1^n$, $[d_i - k_i]_1^n$ are graphical, and so $[k_i]_1^n$ is graphical, then $[d_i]_1^n$ need not be realised with a k-factor. To see this, consider the following example of Lovasz [145].

Let $d = [8, 8, 3, 2, 2, 2, 2, 2, 3]$ and $k = [4, 4, 0, 0, 0, 1, 2, 2, 3]$ so that $d - k = [4, 4, 3, 2, 2, 1, 0, 0, 0]$. Then d and $d - k$ are graphical, realised by graphs G_1 and G_2 of Figure 8.27, and evidently k is same as $d - k$ with a different labeling. Now, it is easy to see that any realisation of $k = d - k$ needs an edge joining the two vertices of degree 4 in it. But if this uv is an edge in G_2, it will not be an edge in $G_1 - G_2$, so that there is no realisation of d with a k-factor.

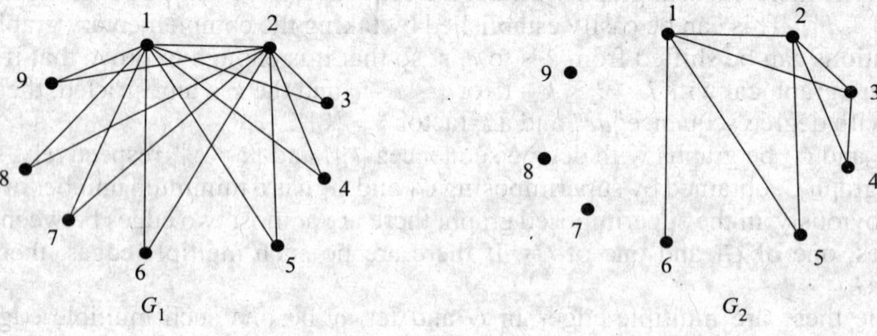

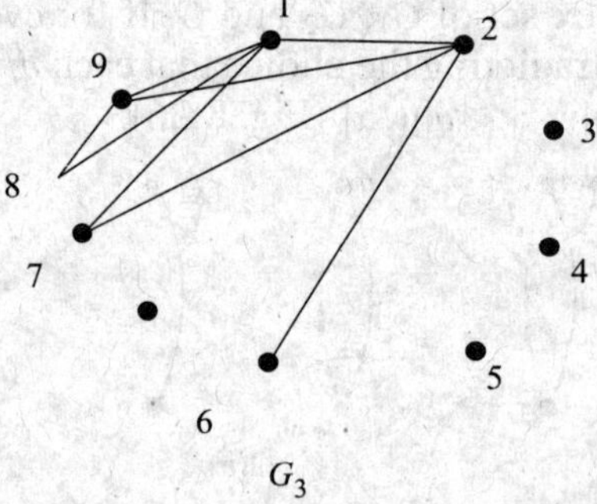

Fig. 8.27

8.6 (g, f) and [a, b]-factors

In this section, we give a brief description of (g, f) and $[a, b]$ factors in a graph.

Definition: If f and g are two vertex functions of a graph G such that $g(v) \le f(v)$ for all $v \in V$ and F is a factor of G such that $g(v) \le d(v|F) \le f(v)$ for all $v \in V$, then F is called a *(g, f)-factor* of G.

If H is a (g, f)-factor of G, its *f-deficiency* is defined as $\Delta_H(G, f) = f(V) - d(H)$, where $d(H) = \sum_{v \in V} d(v|H)$. Clearly, $\Delta_H(G, f) \equiv f(V)(\text{mod}2)$.

If $D = (S, T, U)$ is a decomposition of G, then $k''(D, f, g)$ denotes the number of odd components of U with respect to D and f for which $f(c) = g(c)$, for every vertex c of the component.

We now state the (g, f)-factor Theorem of Lovasz [144].

Theorem 8.25 If f and g are vertex functions of a graph G (V, E) such that $0 \le g(v) \le f(v) \le d(v|G)$ for all $v \in V$, then either G has a (g, f)-factor or it has a decomposition $D = (S, T, U)$ satisfying $k''(D, f, g) > f(S) + d(T) - g(T) - q[S, T]$, but not both, where $k''(D, f, g)$ is the number of odd components of $< U >_G$ with $f(v) = g(v)$ for every vertex v of the component.

Next, we state the (g, f)-factor Theorem due to Las Vergnas [248].

Theorem 8.26 Let g, f be vertex functions for a graph $G(V, E)$ such that $0 \le g(v) \le 1 \le f(v) \le d(v|G)$ for all $v \in V$. For $S \subseteq V$, let $k'(G-S)$ be the number of odd components C of $G-S$ which are such that either $C = \{v\}$ and $g(v) = 1$ or $< V(C) >$ is odd and at least 3, with $g(v) = f(v) = 1$ for all $v \in V(C)$. Then G has a (g, f)-factor if and only if $f(S) \ge k'(G-S)$ for all $S \subseteq V$.

The following variation of the (g, f)-factor Theorem is due to Kano and Saito [120].

Theorem 8.27 If g and f are vertex functions of a graph $G(V, E)$ and θ a real number such that $0 \le \theta \le 1$, and if $g(v) < f(v)$, $g(v) \le d(v|G) \le f(v)$ for all $v \in V$, then G has a (g, f)-factor.

Definition: If a and b are non-negative integers with $a \le b$ and F is a factor of G such that $a \le d(v|F) \le b$ for all $v \in V$, then F is called an *[a, b]-factor* of G. We note that an $[a, b]$-factor is a (g, f)-factor for constant vertex functions $g(v) = a$ for all $v \in V$ and $f(v) = b$ for all $v \in V$.

The following $[a, b]$-factor Theorem can easily be derived from the (g, f)-factor Theorem.

Theorem 8.28 If $G(V, E)$ is a graph, and a and b are distinct integers with $a < b$, then either G has an $[a, b]$-factor H or a decomposition $D = (S, T, U)$ such that $q[S, T] > d(T) + b|S| - a|T|$, but not both.

The following result is due to Las Vergnas [248].

Theorem 8.29 If G is a graph and $k(\geq 2)$ an integer, then G has a $[1, k]$-factor if and only if $k|N(S)| \geq |S|$, for all independent sets S of G.

The next result can be found in Kano and Saito [121].

Theorem 8.30 If k, r, s and t are integers such that $0 \leq k \leq r$, $s \geq 0$, $t \geq 1$ and $ks \leq rt$, then every $[r, r+s]$-graph has a $[k, k+1]$-factor.

The following result on the existence of $[a, b]$-factors is given by Kouider and Long [139].

Theorem 8.31 Let $b \geq a+1$ and let G be a graph with minimum degree 8.

$$\text{If} \quad a(G) \leq \begin{cases} \dfrac{4b(\delta - a+1)}{(a+1)^2}, & \text{for } a \text{ odd} \\ \dfrac{4b(\delta - a+1)}{a(a+2)}, & \text{for } a \text{ odd} \end{cases}$$

then G has an $[a, b]$-factor.

8.7 Exercises

1. Prove that a tree can have at most one perfect matching.

2. Give an example of a cubic graph having no 1-factor.

3. Show that $K_{n,n}$ and K_{2n} are 1-factorable, and further show that the number of 1-factors of $K_{n,n}$ and K_{2n} are respectively $n!$ and $\dfrac{(2n)!}{2^n n!}$.

4. Prove that the Peterson graph is not 1-factorable.

5. Let $G = (V_1, V_2, E)$ be a bipartite graph with $|V_1| = n_1$ and $|V_2| = n_2$, and the vertices $x_i \in V_1$ and $y_j \in V_2$ indexed such that $d(x_1) \leq d(x_2) \leq \ldots \leq d(x_n)$ and $d(y_1) \leq d(y_2) \leq \ldots \leq d(y_n)$. Then show that a sufficient condition for V_1 to be matched into V_2 is that $n_1 \leq n_2$, $d(x_1) > 0$ and $\sum_{i=1}^{k} d(x_i) > \sum_{i=1}^{k-1} d(y_j)$, $2 \leq k \leq n_1$.

6. Prove that a bipartite graph $G = (V_1, V_2, E)$ has a matching saturating all the vertices of maximum degree.

7. Show that the following statements are equivalent for a bipartite graph $G = (V_1, V_2, E)$.

   a. G is connected and each edge of G is contained in a 1-factor.

b. $|V_1| = |V_2|$ and for each non-empty subset S of V_1, $|S| < |N(S)|$.

c. For each $u \in V_1$ and $v \in V_2$, $G - u - v$ has a 1-factor.

8. Show that a tree T has a perfect matching if and only if $k_0(T - v) = 1$ for every vertex v of T.

9. If G is a cubic graph without cut edges or with all cut edges on a single suspended path, then prove that G has a 1-factor.

10. Prove directly that if G is a connected graph with no induced subgraph isomorphic to $K_{1,\,3}$, then G has an edge uv such that $G - \{u, v\}$ is connected.

11. If M and N are matchings in a graph G and $|M| > |N|$, then prove that there exist matchings M' and N' in G such that $|M'| = |M| - 1$, $|N'| = |N| + 1$ and M' and N' have the same union and intersection (as edge sets) as M and N.

12. Prove that deleting any perfect matching from the Peterson graph leaves the subgraph $C_5 + C_5$.

13. Determine the minimum size of a maximal matching in the cycle C_n.

14. If $G = (V_1, V_2, E)$ is a bipartite graph that has a matching of V_1 into V_2, then prove that G has at most $\binom{|V_1|}{2}$ edges belonging to no matching of V_1 into V_2.

15. Describe complete tripartite graphs of the form $K_{n,\,n,\,n}$ that have perfect matching.

16. For what values of $n \geq 4$ does the wheel W_n have a perfect matching?

17. Prove that a graph has an f-factor if and only if it has an f'-factor, where $f'(v) = d(v) - f(v)$ for every $v \in V$.

18. Show that a k-regular, $(k-1)$-edge connected graph of even order has a 1-factor.

19. If G is a connected graph of even order, then show that G^2 has a 1-factor.

20. If G is a connected cubic graph without a 1-factor and S is a minimal antifactor set, then prove that S is an independent set of claw centers and $G - S$ has exactly $|S| + 2$ odd components and no even components.

9. Edge Graphs and Eccentricity Sequences

Many authors discovered edge graphs independently and gave it a different name, for example, interchange graph by Ore [172], derivative by Sabidussi [231], derived graphs by Beineke [18], edge-to-vertex dual by Seshu and Reed [227], covering graph by Kasteleyn [123] and adjoint by Menon [154].

9.1 Edge Graphs

Definition: Let $G(V, E)$ be a graph with $V = \{v_1, v_2, \ldots, v_n\}$ and $E = \{e_1, e_2, \ldots, e_m\}$. The *edge graph* $L(G)$ of G has the vertex set E and two vertices e_i and e_j are adjacent in $L(G)$ if and only if the corresponding edges e_i and e_j of G are adjacent in G. For example, in Figure 9.1, $L(G)$ is the edge graph of G. A graph G is an edge graph if it is isomorphic to the edge graph $L(H)$ of some graph H.

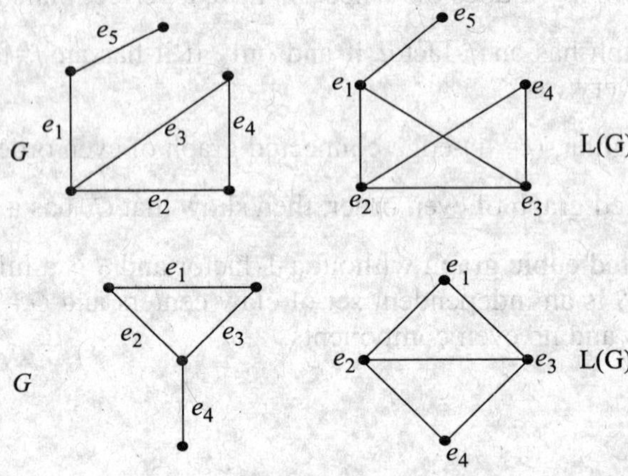

Fig. 9.1

Since isolated vertices do not contribute anything to the study of edge graphs, we assume that the graphs contain no isolated vertices. Besides this, the graphs under consideration will be without loops. We have the following observations about edge graphs.

1. A graph G is connected if and only if $L(G)$ is connected.
2. If H is a subgraph of G, then $L(H)$ is a subgraph of $L(G)$.
3. The edges incident at a vertex of G form a maximal complete subgraph of $L(G)$.
4. In G, if $e = uv$ is an edge, then the degree of e in $L(G)$ is the number of edges of G adjacent to e in G. Clearly, $d_{L(G)}(e) = d_G(u) + d_G(v) - 2$.
5. For $n > 1$, $L^n(G) = L(L^{n-1}(G))$ and $L^0(G) = G$.

The following result determines the number of edges in an edge graph.

Theorem 9.1 The number of edges m' in $L(G)$ when G has degree sequence $[d_i]_1^n$ is given by

$$m' = \frac{1}{2}\left(\sum_{i=1}^{n} d_i^2\right) - m.$$

Proof Let $[d_i]_1^n$ be the degree sequence of the graph G and let $L(G)$ the edge graph of G, have m' edges.

As the degree of the vertex v_i in G is d_i, there are d_i edges incident on v_i. From these d_i edges, any two are adjacent at v_i in G. Hence the number of edges contributed by v_i to $L(G)$ is $\binom{d_i}{2}$.

$$\text{Thus,} \quad m' = \sum_{i=1}^{n}\binom{d_i}{2} = \sum_{i=1}^{n}\frac{d_i(d_i-1)}{2} = \frac{1}{2}\sum_{i=1}^{n}(d_i^2 - d_i)$$

$$= \frac{1}{2}\sum_{i=1}^{n} d_i^2 - \frac{1}{2}\sum_{i=1}^{n} d_i$$

$$= \frac{1}{2}\left(\sum_{i=1}^{n} d_i^2\right) - m. \qquad \square$$

The following observation is immediate.

Theorem 9.2 The edge graph of a graph G is a path if and only if G is a path.

Proof Let G be a graph with n vertices. Assume G is a path P_n. Then $L(G)$ is the path P_{n-1} with $n-1$ vertices.

Conversely, let $L(G)$ be a path. Then no vertex of G has degree greater than two. For, if G has a vertex v of degree greater than two, the edges incident to v form a complete subgraph of $L(G)$ with at least three vertices. Therefore G is either a cycle or a path. But G cannot be a cycle, since the edge graph of a cycle is a cycle. ❑

We now have the following stronger result.

Theorem 9.3 A connected graph is isomorphic to its edge graph if and only if it is a cycle.

Proof Let G be a connected graph with n vertices, m edges and with degree sequence $[d_i]_1^n$. Let $L(G)$ be the edge graph of G. The number of vertices in $L(G)$ is m. The number of edges m' in $L(G)$ is given by

$$m' = \frac{1}{2}\left(\sum_{i=1}^{n} d_i^2\right) - m.$$

Clearly, $L(G)$ is connected and $L(C_n) = C_n$.

Conversely, let $G \cong L(G)$.

Then G and $L(G)$ have the same number of vertices and edges.

So, $n = m$ and $m = \frac{1}{2}\left(\sum_{i=1}^{n} d_i^2\right) - m$.

Therefore, $n = m$ and $\sum_{i=1}^{n} d_i^2 = 4m$.

Thus, variance

$$\{[d_i]\} = \frac{1}{n}\sum_{i=1}^{n} d_i^2 - \left(\frac{1}{n}\sum_{i=1}^{n} d_i\right)^2$$

$$\left[\text{Because } Var = \frac{1}{N}\sum_i f_i x_i^2 - \left(\frac{1}{N}\sum_i f_i x_i\right)^2 \text{ and we have } f_i = 1\right]$$

$$= \frac{1}{n}4m - \frac{1}{n^2}(2m)^2 = \frac{4m}{m} - \frac{4m^2}{m^2} = 4 - 4 = 0.$$

Therefore the d_i's are equal and G is regular of degree d, say.

So $nd = 2m$ implies that $d = \frac{2m}{n} = \frac{2m}{m} = 2$.

Thus G is a 2-regular connected graph, that is, C_n. ❑

The next result is about the isomorphism of edge graphs.

Theorem 9.4 If the graphs G_1 and G_2 are isomorphic, then $L(G_1)$ and $L(G_2)$ are also isomorphic.

Proof Assume (ϕ, θ) to be an isomorphism of G_1 onto G_2. Then θ is a bijection of $E(G_1)$ onto $E(G_2)$. We show that θ is an isomorphism of $L(G_1)$ to $L(G_2)$ by showing that θ preserves adjacency. Let e_i and e_j be two adjacent vertices of $L(G_1)$. So there exists a vertex v of G_1 incident to both e_i and e_j, and therefore $\phi(v)$ is a vertex incident to both $\theta(e_i)$ and $\theta(e_j)$. Thus $\theta(e_i)$ and $\theta(e_j)$ are adjacent vertices in $L(G_2)$.

Let $\theta(e_i)$ and $\theta(e_j)$ be adjacent vertices in $L(G_2)$. Then they are adjacent edges in G_2 and therefore there exists a vertex v' of G_2 incident to both $\theta(e_i)$ and $\theta(e_j)$. Then $\phi^{-1}(v')$ is a vertex of G_1 incident to both e_i and e_j, and thus e_i and e_j are adjacent vertices of $L(G_1)$.

Therefore e_i and e_j are adjacent vertices of $L(G_1)$ if and only if $\theta(e_i)$ and $\theta(e_j)$ are adjacent vertices of $L(G_2)$. Hence θ is an isomorphism of $L(G_1)$ onto $L(G_2)$. ❑

The converse of Theorem 9.4 is not true. To see this, consider the graphs $K_{1,3}$ and K_3 whose edge graphs are K_3. But $K_{1,3}$ is not isomorphic to K_3, since there is a vertex of degree three in $K_{1,3}$ while there is no such vertex in K_3. However, it was shown by Whitney [258] that the converse holds unless one is $K_{1,3}$ and the other is K_3. The proof of this result is due to Jung [119].

Theorem 9.5 Let G and G' be connected graphs with isomorphic edge graphs. Then G and G' are isomorphic unless one is K_3 and the other is $K_{1,3}$.

Proof First suppose that $n(G)$ and $n(G')$ are less than or equal to 4. A necessary condition for $L(G)$ and $L(G')$ to be isomorphic is that $m(G) = m(G')$. The only nonisomorphic connected graphs on at most four vertices are those shown in Figure 9.2.

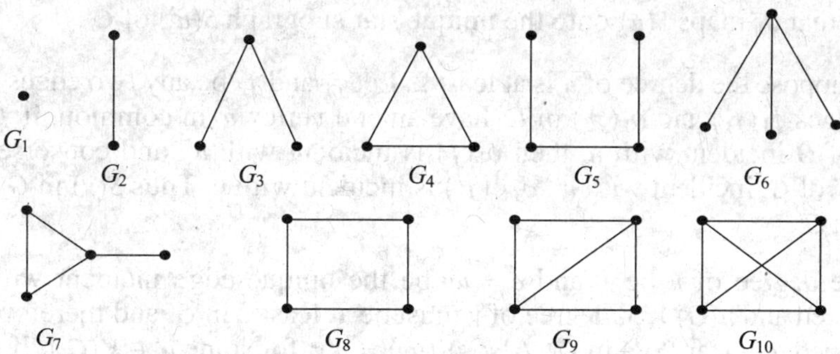

Fig. 9.2

In Figure 9.2, graphs G_4, G_5 and G_6 are the three graphs having three edges each. We know that G_4 and G_6 have isomorphic edge graphs, namely K_3. The edge graph of G_5 is a path of length 2 and hence $L(G_5)$ cannot be isomorphic to $L(G_4)$ or $L(G_6)$. Further, G_7 and G_8 are the only two graphs in the list having four edges each.

Clearly, $L(G_8) \cong G_8$ and $L(G_7)$ is isomorphic to G_9. Thus the edge graphs of G_7 and G_8 are not isomorphic. No two of the remaining graphs have the same number of edges. Hence the only non-isomorphic graphs with at most four vertices having isomorphic edge graphs are G_4 and G_6.

Now suppose that either G or G', say G, has at least five vertices and that $L(G)$ and $L(G')$ are isomorphic under an isomorphism ϕ_1. So ϕ_1 is a bijection from the edge set of G onto the edge set of G'.

We now prove that ϕ_1 transforms an induced $K_{1,3}$ subgraph of G onto a $K_{1,3}$ subgraph of G'. Let $e_1 = uv_1$, $e_2 = uv_2$ and $e_3 = uv_3$ be the edges of an induced $K_{1,3}$ subgraph of G. As G has at least five vertices and is connected, there exists an edge e adjacent to only one or all three of edges e_1, e_2 and e_3, as illustrated in Figure 9.3.

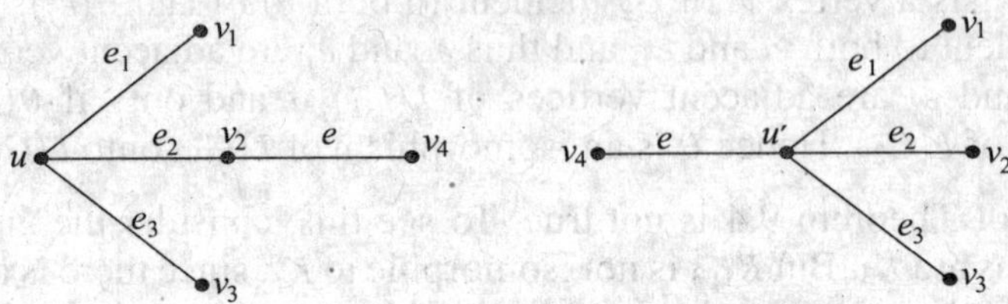

Fig. 9.3

Clearly, $\phi_1(e_1)$, $\phi_1(e_2)$ and $\phi_1(e_3)$ form either a $K_{1,3}$ subgraph or a triangle in G'. If $\phi_1(e_1)$, $\phi_1(e_2)$ and $\phi_1(e_3)$ form a triangle in G', $\phi_1(e)$ can be adjacent to precisely two of $\phi_1(e_1)$, $\phi_1(e_2)$ and $\phi_1(e_3)$ (since $L(G')$ is simple), whereas $\phi_1(e)$ must be adjacent to only one or all the three. This contradiction shows that $\{\phi_1(e_1), \phi_1(e_2), \phi_1(e_3)\}$ is not a triangle in G' and therefore forms a $K_{1,3}$ in G'.

It is clear that a similar result holds as well for ϕ_1^{-1}, since it is an isomorphism on $L(G')$ onto $L(G)$.

Let $S(u)$ denote the star subgraph of G formed by the edges of G incident at a vertex u of G. We show that ϕ_1 maps $S(u)$ onto the unique star subgraph $S(u')$ of G'.

i. First suppose the degree of u is at least 2. Let f_1 and f_2 be any two edges incident at u. The edges $\phi_1(f_1)$ and $\phi_1(f_2)$ of G' have an end vertex u' in common. If f is any other edge of G incident with u, then $\phi_1(f)$ is incident with u', and conversely, for every edge f' of G' incident with u', $\phi_1^{-1}(f')$ is incident with u. Thus $S(u)$ in G is mapped to $S(u')$ in G'.

ii. Let the degree of u be 1 and $e = uv$ be the unique edge incident with u. As G is connected and $n(G) \geq 5$, degree of v must be at least 2 in G, and therefore, by (i), $S(v)$ is mapped to a star $S(v')$ in G'. Also $\phi_1(uv) = u'v'$ for some $u' \in V(G')$. If the degree of u' is greater than 1, by (i), the star at u' in G' is transformed by ϕ_1^{-1} either to the star at u in G or to the star at v in G. But as the star at v in G is mapped to the star at v' in

G' by ϕ_1, ϕ_1^{-1} should map the star at u' to the star at u only. As ϕ_1^{-1} is $1-1$, this means that deg $u \geq 2$, a contradiction. Therefore, deg $u' = 1$ and so $S(u)$ in G is mapped to $S(u')$ in G'.

Define $\phi : V(G) \to V(G')$ by setting $\phi(u) = u'$ if $\phi_1(S(u)) = S(u')$. Since $S(u) = S(v)$ only when $u = v$ $(G \neq K_2, G' \neq K_2)$, ϕ is $1-1$. ϕ is also onto since, for v' in G', $\phi_1^{-1}(S(v')) = S(v)$ for some $v \in V(G)$, and by the definition of ϕ, $\phi(v) = v'$. Finally, if uv is an edge of G, then $\phi_1(uv)$ belongs to both $S(u')$ and $S(v')$, where $\phi_1(S(u)) = S(u')$ and $\phi_1(S(v)) = S(v')$. This means $u'v'$ is an edge of G'. But $u' = \phi(u)$ and $v' = \phi(v)$. Consequently, $\phi(u)\,\phi(v)$ is an edge of G'. If u and v are nonadjacent in G, $\phi(u)\,\phi(v)$ must be nonadjacent in G'. Otherwise, $\phi(u)\,\phi(v)$ belongs to both $S(\phi(u))$ and $S(\phi(v))$ and hence $\phi_1^{-1}(\phi(u)\phi(v)) = uv \in E(G)$, a contradiction. Thus G and G' are isomorphic under ϕ. ❑

The following result shows that $K_{1,3}$ is not an edge graph and thus $K_{1,3}$ is of great significance in studying edge graphs as will be seen in further discussions.

Lemma 9.1 The star $K_{1,3}$ is not an edge graph.

Proof Assume that $K_{1,3}$ is an edge graph. Then $K_{1,3} = L(H)$ for some graph H. Since $K_{1,3}$ has four vertices, therefore H has four edges. Also H is connected. All the connected graphs with four edges are given in Figure 9.4.

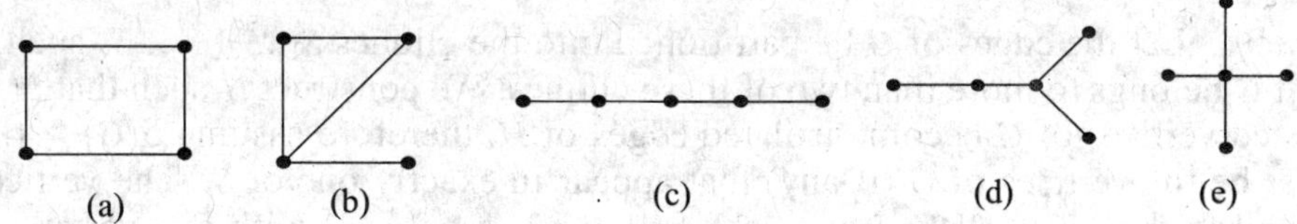

Fig. 9.4

H is neither graph (a) nor (b), because $L(C_4) = C_4$ and $L(K_{1,3}+x) = K_4 - x$. These are shown in Figure 9.5.

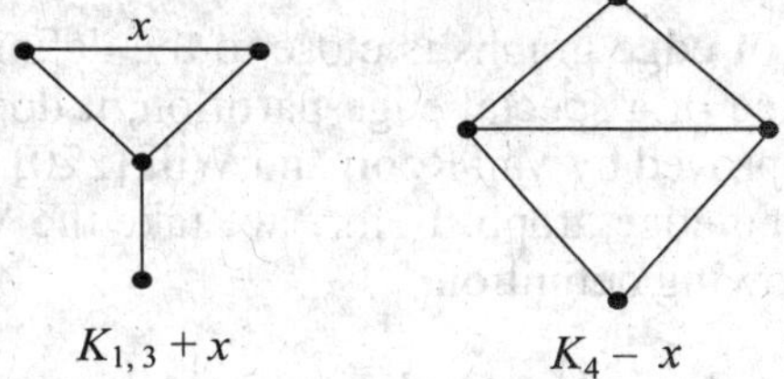

Fig. 9.5

Thus H is one of the three trees as given in (c), (d) and (e). But the edge graphs of these trees are the path P_4, the graphs K_3. K_2 and K_4, given in Figure 9.6.

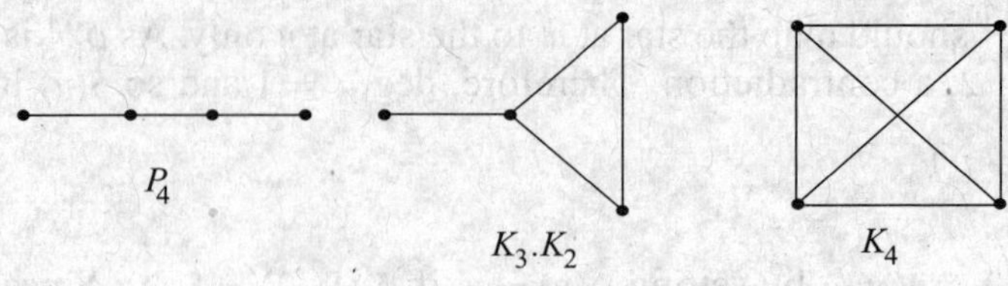

Fig. 9.6

This shows that H is none of the trees (c), (d) or (e). Hence it follows that $K_{1,3}$ is not an edge graph. ❑

Now, we proceed to give a characterisation of edge graphs which is due to Krausz [136].

Theorem 9.6 (Krausz) A graph G is the edge graph of some graph if and only if the edges of G can be partitioned into cliques such that no vertex appears in more than two cliques.

Proof

Necessity Let G be an edge graph of a graph H. Assume without loss of generality that H has no isolated vertices. Then the edges in the star $K_{1,3}$ at each vertex of H induce a clique of G and every edge of H belongs to the stars of exactly two vertices of H, therefore no vertex of G is in more than two of these cliques.

Sufficiency Let the edges of G be partitioned into the cliques $S_1, S_2, \ldots, S_k$ such that no vertex of G belongs to more than two of these cliques. We construct H such that $L(H) = G$. As isolated vertices of G become isolated edges of H, therefore assume $\delta(G) \geq 1$. Let $v_1, v_2, \ldots, v_\ell$ be the vertices of G (if any) that appear in exactly one of S_i. The vertices of H correspond to the set $S = \{S_1, S_2, \ldots, S_k, \{v_1\}, \{v_2\}, \ldots, \{v_\ell\}\}$, with one vertex for each member of S. Any two of these vertices are adjacent whenever their corresponding sets intersect. Each vertex of G appears in exactly two sets in S and no two vertices appear in the same pair of sets. Thus H is a simple graph with one edge for each vertex of G. If vertices are adjacent in G, they appear together in some S_i and the corresponding edges of H share the vertex corresponding to S_i. Hence, $G = L(H)$. ❑

Krausz characterisation of edge graphs is close to the definition. Since it characterises edge graphs by the existence of a special edge partition, it does not directly give an efficient test. This has been improved by Van Rooij and Wilf [220] by describing the structural criterion for a graph to be an edge graph. Before we take the Van Rooij and Wilf characterisation, we have the following definition.

Definition: An *induced subgraph* is a subgraph which is maximal on its vertex set. A triangle T of a graph G is said to be *odd*, if there is a vertex of G adjacent to an odd number of vertices of T, otherwise T is said to be *even*. That is, T is odd if $|V(T) \cap N(v)|$ is odd, for some $v \in V(G)$, and T is even if $|V(T) \cap N(v)|$ is even, for every $v \in V(G)$. An induced copy of $K_4 - e$ is a double triangle and clearly has two triangles with a common edge.

The following is the Van Rooij and Wilf characterisation.

Theorem 9.7 A graph G is the edge graph of some graph if and only if G does not contain an induced subgraph $K_{1,3}$ and no double triangle of G has two odd triangles.

Proof

Necessity Let $G = L(H)$. Clearly, G does not contain an induced subgraph $K_{1,3}$, since $K_{1,3}$ itself is not an edge graph. Now we observe that the vertices of a double triangle in G correspond to the edges of a $K_{1,3}+e$ in H. In particular, one of these double triangles in G is generated by a triangle in H. Obviously a triangle in G generated by a triangle in H is even, since an edge incident to a triangle in H intersects exactly two edges of the triangle in H (Fig. 9.7).

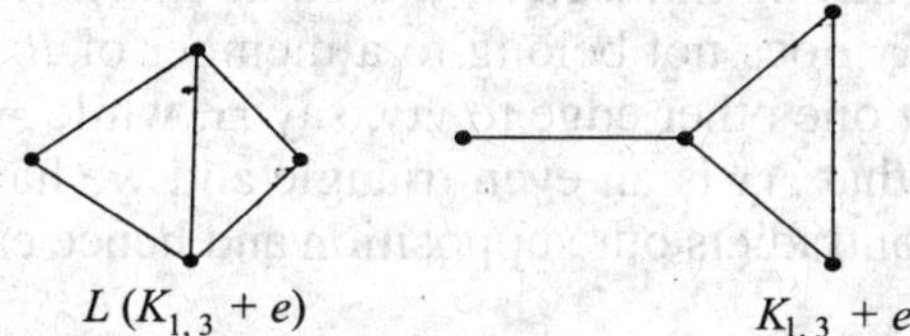

Fig. 9.7

Sufficiency Let G does not contain an induced subgraph $K_{1,3}$ and let no double triangle of G have two odd triangles. Assume G is connected, for otherwise, we apply the construction to each component. In case G is $K_{1,3}-$free and has a double triangle with both triangles even, then G is one of the graphs given in Figure 9.8.

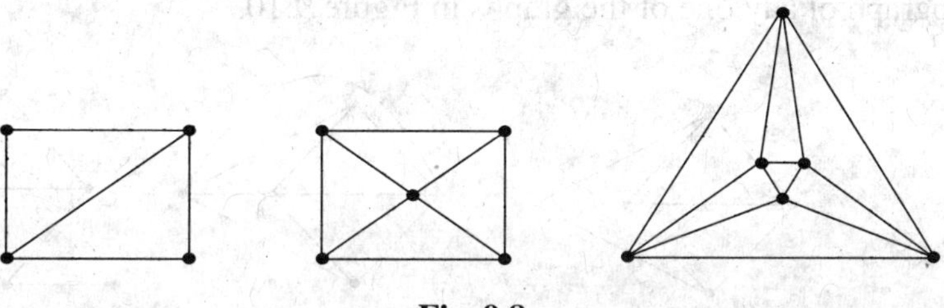

Fig. 9.8

Thus we consider the case when every double triangle of G has exactly one odd triangle. To prove the result, it suffices by Theorem 9.6, to partition $E(G)$ into cliques that cover each vertex at most twice. Now, let $S_1, S_2, \ldots, S_k$ be the maximal cliques of G that are not even triangles and let $T_1, T_2, \ldots, T_\ell$ be the edges that belong to one even triangle and no odd triangle. We claim that $B = \{S_i\} \cup \{T_j\}$ partitions $E(G)$ into cliques using each vertex at most twice.

Now, every edge appears in a maximal clique, but every triangle in a clique with more than three vertices is odd. Therefore T_j is not in any clique S_i. Also S_i and $S_{i'}$ have no common edge, because G has no double triangles with both triangles odd. Thus the cliques in B are edge-disjoint. If $e \in E(G)$, then e belongs to some S_i unless the only maximal clique containing e is an even triangle. In this case e is a T_j, since the double triangles do not have both triangles even (Fig. 9.9).

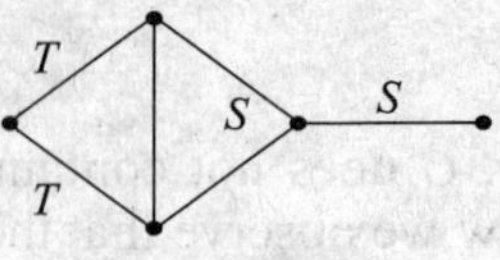

Fig. 9.9

We now show that each $v \in G$ appears at most twice in B. Assume v belongs to B_1, B_2, $B_3 \in B$. Edge-disjointness implies that v has neighbours x, y, z with each belonging to only one of B_1, B_2, B_3. Since G has no induced $K_{1,3}$, assume that xy is an edge. Now by edge-disjointness, the triangle vxy does not belong to a member of B. Therefore vxy is an even triangle. Thus z has exactly one other edge to vxy, say zx, while zy is not an edge. But now the same argument shows that zvx is an even triangle and we have a double triangle with both triangles even. This contradicts our supposition and hence each $v \in G$ appears at most twice in B. ❑

The next characterisation due to Beineke [18] displays those subgraphs which are not present in edge graphs. These subgraphs other than $K_{1,3}$ are vertex-minimal $K_{1,3}$-free graphs containing a double triangle with both triangles odd. Each such graph has a double triangle and one or two additional vertices that make the triangles odd by having one or three neighbours in the triangle.

Theorem 9.8 A graph G is an edge graph of some graph if and only if G does not contain an induced subgraph of any one of the graphs in Figure 9.10.

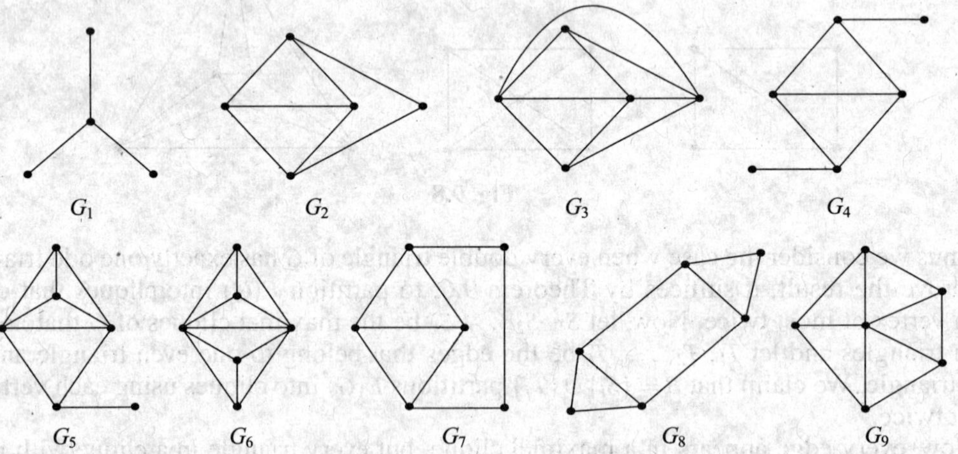

Fig. 9.10

Proof

Necessity Let G be the edge graph of some graph H so that $G = L(H)$. Then by Theorem 9.6, the edges of G can be partitioned into cliques such that every vertex appears in at most two cliques. We observe that none of these nine graphs have such a partition. Since every induced subgraph of an edge graph is itself an edge graph, G does not contain an induced subgraph of any one of the nine graphs, in Figure 9.10.

Sufficiency Let G does not contain an induced subgraph of any one of these nine graphs. We prove that no double triangle of G has two odd triangles. Assume to the contrary that G has a double triangle both of which are odd. Let these triangles be abc and abd with c and d non adjacent. We discuss two cases, one in which there is a vertex v adjacent to an odd number of vertices of both odd triangles and second when there is no such vertex.

Case 1 Assume there is a vertex v which is adjacent to an odd number of vertices in each of the triangles abc and abd. Now two possibilities arise; either v is adjacent to exactly one vertex of each of these triangles, or it is adjacent to more than one vertex of one of them. If v is adjacent to exactly one vertex of each of these triangles, then either v is adjacent to a or b giving G_1, or to both c and d giving G_2. If v is adjacent to more than one vertex of one of the triangles, then v is adjacent to all four vertices of the two triangles, giving G_3 as an induced subgraph of G (Fig. 9.11).

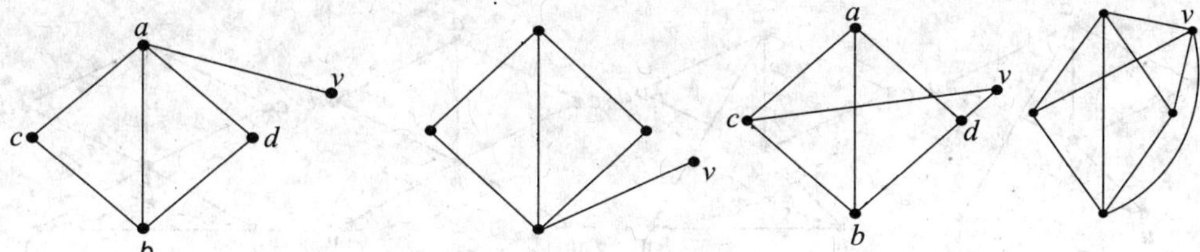

Fig. 9.11

Case 2 Now, let there be no vertex adjacent to an odd number of vertices of both triangles. Assume that the vertex u is adjacent to an odd number of vertices of triangle abc and the vertex v is adjacent to an odd number of vertices of triangle abd. We consider three subcases.

Case 2.1 u is adjacent to exactly one vertex of abc and v is adjacent to exactly one vertex of abd.

Case 2.2 One of u or v is adjacent to all three vertices of its triangle and the other to only one vertex of its triangle.

Case 2.3 u is adjacent to all three vertices of abc and v is adjacent to all three vertices of abd.

We observe that if u or v is adjacent to a or b, then it is also adjacent to c or to d, since otherwise G_1 is an induced subgraph. Also, neither u nor v is adjacent to both c and d, since otherwise G_2 or G_3 is induced.

Case 2.1 Let uc, $vd \in G$. Then for $uv \in G$, G_4 is induced, and for $uv \notin G$, G_7 is induced. Now, let ub, $vd \in G$. Then it follows from the above observations that $ud \in G$ while $vc \notin G$. Therefore for $uv \notin G$, the vertices a, d, u, v induce G_1 and for $uv \in G$, the vertices a, b, c, d, u, v induce G_8. Next, let ub, $va \in G$, then clearly ud, $vc \in G$. So, when $uv \notin G$, G_8 is induced, and when $uv \in G$, G_2 is induced. Finally, let ub, $vb \in G$, then again ud, $vc \in G$. Therefore, when $uv \in G$, G_9 is induced, and when $uv \notin G$, G_1 is induced (Fig. 9.12, Case 2.1).

Case 2.2 Let ua, ub, $uc \in G$. If $ud \in G$, then G_3 is induced. Take $ud \notin G$. Then either $vd \in G$ or $vb \in G$. If $vd \in G$, then for $uv \in G$, G_2 is induced, and for $uv \notin G$, G_5 is induced. If $vb \in G$, then G_3 or G_1 is induced depending on whether or not v is adjacent to both c and u (Fig. 9.12, Case 2.2).

Case 2.3 If ud, vc or $uv \in G$, then G_3 is induced. The only other possibility gives G_6 (Fig. 9.12, Case 2.3). ❑

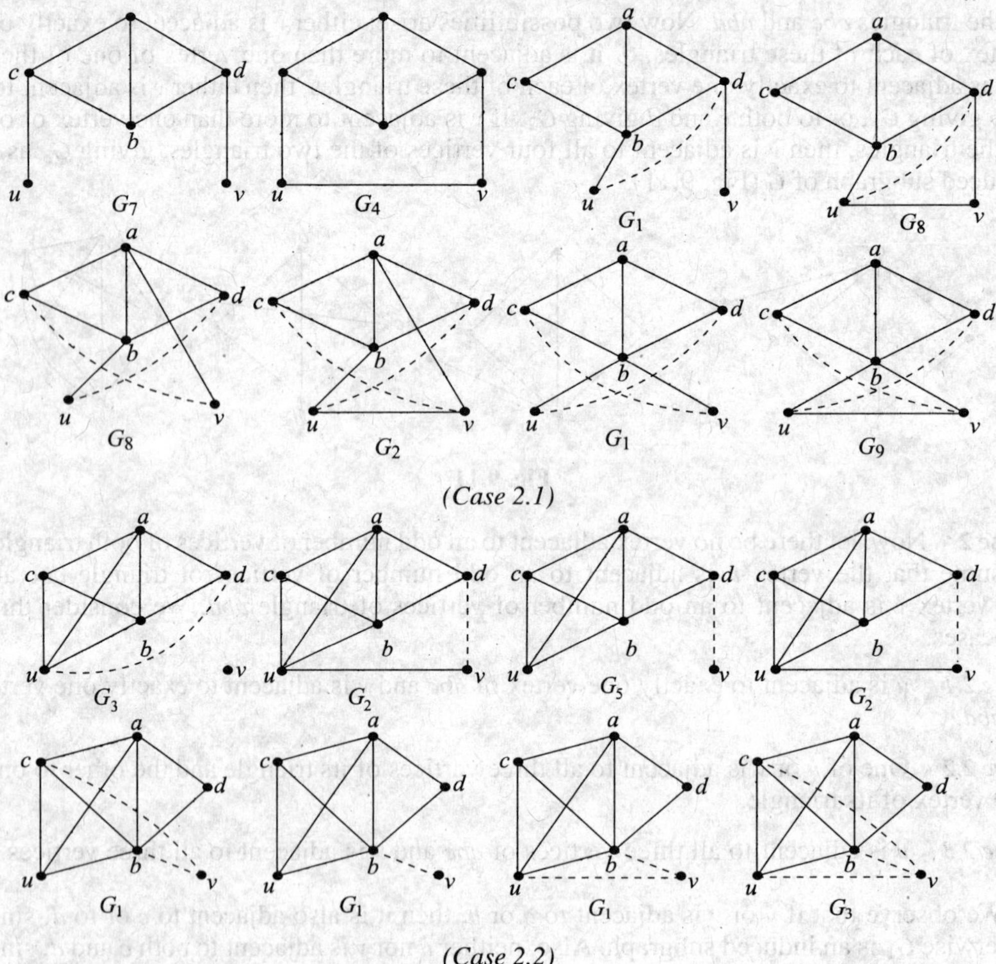

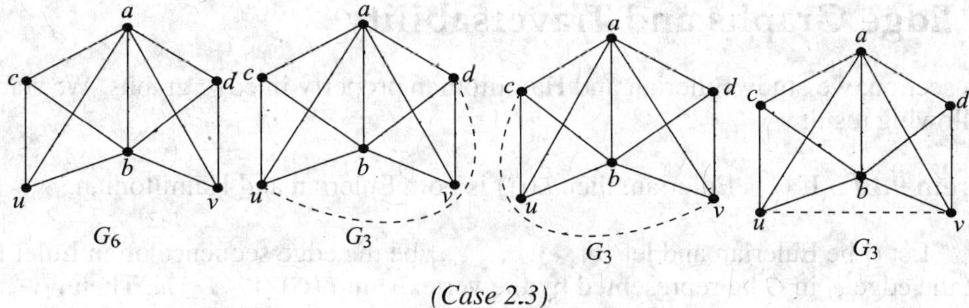

Fig. 9.12

The following result due to Chartrand [52] characterises the edge graphs of a tree.

Theorem 9.9 (Chartrand [52]) A graph is the edge graph of a tree if and only if it is a connected block graph in which each cut vertex is on exactly two blocks.

Proof

Necessity Let T be any tree and let $G = L(T)$. Then G is also $B(T)$ since the edges and blocks of a tree coincide. Each cut vertex w of G corresponds to a bridge uv of T and is on exactly those two blocks of G which correspond to the stars at u and v.

Sufficiency Let G be a block graph in which each cut vertex is on exactly two blocks. Since each block of a block graph is complete, there exists a graph H such that $L(H) = G$, by Theorem 9.6. If $G = K_3$, we can take $H = K_{1,3}$. If G is any other block graph, then we show that H is a tree. Assume H is not a tree, so that it contains a cycle. If H is itself a cycle, then by Theorem 9.3, $L(H) = H$, but the only cycle which is a block graph is K_3, a case not under consideration. Thus H properly contains a cycle, implying that H has a cycle Z and an edge e adjacent to two edges of Z, but not adjacent to some edge f in Z. The vertices e and f of $L(H)$ lie on a cycle of $L(H)$ and they are not adjacent. This contradicts the fact that $L(H)$ is a block graph. Hence H is a tree. ❑

Consider the block graph G of Figure 9.13(a) in which each cut vertex lies on just two blocks. Figure 9.13(b) shows the tree T of which G is the edge graph, is constructed by first forming the block graph $B(G)$ and then adding new vertices for the non-cut vertices of G, and the edges joining each block with its non-cut vertices.

The edge graphs of complete graphs were independently characterised by Chang [46] and Hoffman [112, 113], while the edge graphs of complete bipartite graphs were characterised by Moon [158] and Hoffman [114].

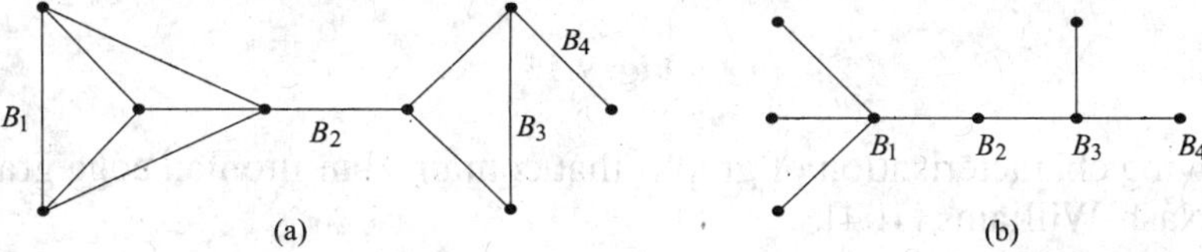

Fig. 9.13

9.2 Edge Graphs and Traversability

In this section, we study Eulerian and Hamiltonian property in edge graphs. We start with the following result.

Theorem 9.10 If G is Eulerian, then $L(G)$ is both Eulerian and Hamiltonian.

Proof Let G be Eulerian and let $\{e_1, e_2, \ldots, e_m\}$ be the edge sequence of an Euler line in G. Let the edge e_i in G be represented by the vertex v_i in $L(G)$, $1 \leq i \leq m$. Then $v_1 v_2 \ldots v_m v_1$ is a Hamiltonian cycle of $L(G)$. Now, if $e = u_i u_j \in E(G)$ and the vertex v in $L(G)$ represents the edge e, then $d_{L(G)}(v) = d_G(u_i) + d_G(u_j) - 2$, which is obviously even and greater than or equal to two, since both $d_G(u_i)$ and $d_G(u_j)$ are even (and ≥ 2). Thus in $L(G)$ every vertex is of even degree (≥ 2). Hence $L(G)$ is Eulerian. ❑

The converse of Theorem 9.11 is not true. To see this, consider the graph G shown in Figure 9.14. Clearly $L(G)$ is both Eulerian and Hamiltonian, but G is not Eulerian.

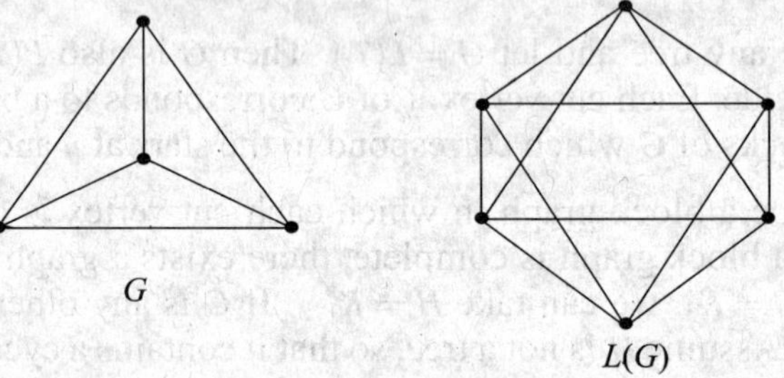

Fig. 9.14

Definition: A *dominating walk* of a graph G is a closed walk W in G (which can be just a single vertex) such that every edge of G not in W is incident with W. For example, the walk $v_1\ v_2\ v_3\ v_4$ in the graph of Figure 9.15 is a dominating walk.

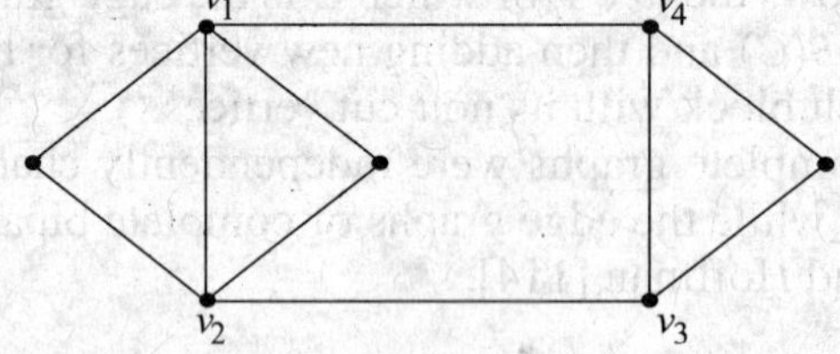

Fig. 9.15

The following characterisation of graphs that contain Hamiltonian edge graphs is due to Harary and Nash-Williams [104].

Theorem 9.11 The edge graph of a graph G with at least three edges is Hamiltonian if and only if G has a dominating walk.

Proof Let W be a dominating walk of G which is represented by the edge sequence $\{e_1, e_2, \ldots, e_k\}$. Let e_1 and e_2 be incident at v_1. Replace the subsequence $\{e_1, e_2\}$ by the sequence $\{e_1, e_{11}, e_{12}, \ldots, e_{1r_1}, e_2\}$, where $e_{11}, e_{12}, \ldots, e_{1r_1}$ are the edges other than e_1 and e_2 incident at v_1. Continuing this process for all subsequences $\{e_i, e_{i+1}\}$, $1 \le i \le k$ with $e_{k+1} = e_1$, we obtain a sequence of edges $e_1 e_{11} e_{12} \ldots e_{1r_1} e_2 e_{21} e_{22} \ldots e_{2r_2} e_3 \ldots e_k e_{k1} e_{k2} \ldots e_{kr_k} e_1$. This clearly gives the Hamiltonian cycle $u_1 u_{11} u_{12} \ldots u_{1r_1} u_2 u_{21} u_{22} \ldots u_{2r_2} u_3 \ldots u_k u_{k1} u_{k2} \ldots u_{kr_k} u_1$ in $L(G)$, with u_1 being the vertex of $L(G)$ that corresponds to the edge e_1 of G, and so on.

Conversely, let $L(G)$ contain a Hamiltonian cycle $C = u_1 u_2 \ldots u_m u_1$ and let e_i be the edge of G corresponding to the vertex u_i of $L(G)$. Let W_0 be the edge sequence $e_1 e_2 \ldots e_m e_1$. We delete edges from W_0 in succession in the following way. If $e_i e_j e_k$ are the first three distinct consecutive edges of W_0 that have a common vertex, then delete e_j, and let $W_0' = W_0 - e_j = e_1 e_2 \ldots e_i e_k \ldots e_m e_1$. Now starting with W_0', apply the same process as is applied in W, to get W_0. Continue in this way, till no such three consecutive edges exist. Clearly, the resulting subsequence of W_0 is a dominating walk or a pair of adjacent edges incident at a vertex, say v_0. In the later case, all the edges of G are incident at v_0 and hence v_0 is the dominating walk of G. ❑

The following results are simple consequences of Theorem 9.11.

Corollary 9.1 The edge graph of a Hamiltonian graph is Hamiltonian.

Proof Let G be a Hamiltonian graph with Hamiltonian cycle C. Then C is a dominating walk of G, and hence, $L(G)$ is Hamiltonian. ❑

We note that the converse of Corollary 9.1 is not true in general. To see this, consider the graph G as shown in Figure 9.16. Clearly $L(G)$ is Hamiltonian but G is not.

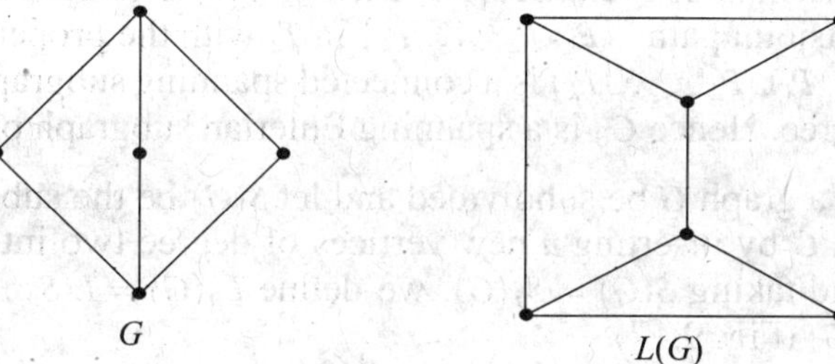

Fig. 9.16

Corollary 9.2 If G is a connected graph and each edge of G belongs to a triangle, then $L(G)$ is Hamiltonian.

Proof This follows from Theorem 9.11. ❑

The following result is due to Chartrand and Wall [54].

Theorem 9.12 If G is connected and $\delta(G) \geq 3$, then $L^2(G)$ is Hamiltonian.

Proof Since $\delta(G) \geq 3$, each vertex of $L(G)$ belongs to a clique of size at least three and hence each edge of $L(G)$ belongs to a triangle. Then the result follows by applying Corollary 9.2. ❑

The next result is due to Nebesky [165].

Theorem 9.13 If G is a connected graph with at least three vertices, then $L(G^2)$ is Hamiltonian.

Proof Since G is a connected graph with at least three vertices, every edge of G^2 belongs to a triangle. Hence by Corollary 9.2, $L(G^2)$ is Hamiltonian. ❑

Theorem 9.14 Let G be a connected graph in which every edge belongs to a triangle. If e_1 and e_2 are edges of G such that $G - \{e_1, e_2\}$ is connected, then there exists a spanning walk of G with e_1 and e_2 as its initial and terminal edges.

Proof Consider the longest walk W of G with e_1 and e_2 as its initial and terminal edges. Then proceed as in Theorem 9.11. ❑

The following result is due to Jaeger [117].

Theorem 9.15 The edge graph of a 4-connected graph is Hamiltonian.

Proof Let G be a 4-edge connected graph. By Theorem 9.11, it suffices to show that G contains a spanning Eulerian subgraph.

Now, G contains two edge-disjoint spanning trees T_1 and T_2. Let S be the set of vertices of odd degree in T_1. Then $|S|$ is even. Let $|S| = 2k$, $k \geq 1$. By Theorem 9.12, there exists a set of k pairwise edge-disjoint paths $\{P_1, P_2, \ldots, P_k\}$ in T_2 with the property stated in Theorem 9.12. Then $G_0 = T_1 U\ (P_1 \cup P_2 \cup \ldots \cup P_k)$ is a connected spanning subgraph of G in which each vertex is of even degree. Hence G_0 is a spanning Eulerian subgraph of G. ❑

Let every edge in a graph G be subdivided and let $S(G)$ be the subdivision graph. If the graph obtained from G by inserting n new vertices of degree two into every edge of G be denoted by $S_n(G)$ and taking $S(G) = S_1(G)$, we define $L_n(G) = L(S_{n-1}(G))$. We see that in general $L_n(G) \ncong L^n(G)$ (Fig. 9.17).

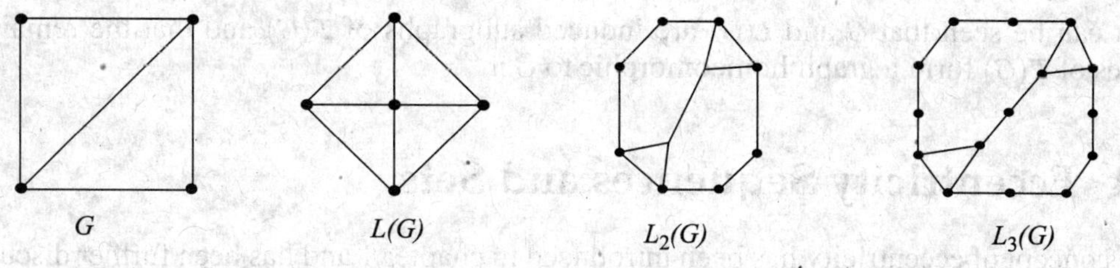

Fig. 9.17

An improvement of Theorem 9.13 is seen in the following result of Harary and Nash-Williams [104].

Theorem 9.16 A sufficient condition for $L_2(G)$ to be Hamiltonian is that G be Hamiltonian and a necessary condition is that $L(G)$ be Hamiltonian.

Now, we have the following consequence.

Corollary 9.3 A graph G is Eulerian if and only if $L_3(G)$ is Hamiltonian.

The following result is due to Chartrand [47].

Theorem 9.17 If G is a non-trivial connected graph with n vertices which is not a path, then $L^k(G)$ is Hamiltonian for all $k \geq n-3$.

9.3 Total Graphs

Let $G(V, E)$ be a graph. The total graph $T(G)$ of G has vertex set $V \cup E$ and two vertices of $T(G)$ are adjacent if and only if one of the following is true.

i. the vertices are v_i, $v_j \in V$ and v_iv_j is an edge in E.

ii. one vertex is $v \in V$ and the other $e \in E$ and the edge e of G is incident with the vertex v of G.

iii. the edges are e_i, $e_j \in E$ and the edges e_i and e_j have a vertex in common in G.

Example The total graph of a graph G is shown in Figure 9.18.

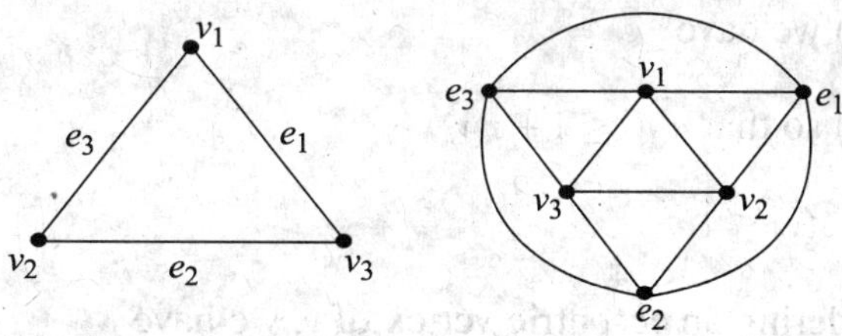

Fig. 9.18

It can be seen that G and $L(G)$ are induced subgraphs of $T(G)$ and that the remaining edges of $T(G)$ form a graph homeomorphic to G.

9.4 Eccentricity Sequences and Sets

The concept of eccentricity has been introduced in chapter 1 and has been further discussed in chapter 4. Now, we study eccentricity sequences in graphs.

Definition: A positive sequence $[e_i]_1^n$ is called an *eccentricity sequence* if it is an eccentricity sequence of some graph. The graph is said to realise the sequence. A set of positive integers is called an *eccentricity set* if it is an eccentricity set of some graph. The graph is said to realise the set. (The set of distinct eccentricities in a graph is called the eccentricity set of that graph.)

When eccentricity set is written in the increasing order $\{e_1, e_2, \ldots, e_k\}$ with $e_1 < e_2 < \ldots < e_k$, the eccentricity sequence is then expressed as $[e_1^{n_1}, e_2^{n_2}, \ldots, e_k^{n_k}]$, where $n_1, n_2, \ldots, n_k$ are respectively the number of occurrences of $e_1, e_2, \ldots, e_k$, the sequence $n_1, n_2, \ldots, n_k$ is called the *eccentricity frequency sequence* of the graph.

Here it can be noted that $e_1 = r$ (radius) and $e_k = d$ (diameter) of the graph.

Therefore, $r \leq d \leq 2r$ gives $e_1 \leq e_k \leq 2e_1$, which is a necessary condition for a positive sequence to be an eccentricity sequence.

Now, we have the following observation.

Theorem 9.18 If uv is an edge of a connected graph G, then $|e(u) - e(v)| \leq 1$.

Proof Let w be an eccentric vertex of u (i.e., w is the farthest vertex from u). Then by the triangle inequality for the metric d (distance), we have

$$d(u, w) \leq d(u, v) + d(v, w)$$

so that $e(u) \leq d(u, v) + d(v, w)$. (9.18.1)

But u and v are adjacent, therefore $d(u, v) = 1$.

Also, $e(v) \geq d(v, w)$ so that $d(v, w) \leq e(v)$.

Thus, from (9.18.1) we have

$$e(u) \leq 1 + d(v, w) \text{ so that } e(u) \leq 1 + e(v).$$

Therefore, $e(u) - e(v) \leq 1$. (9.18.2)

Similarly, by considering an eccentric vertex of v, we have

$$e(v) - e(u) \leq 1. \tag{9.18.3}$$

From (9.18.2) and (9.18.3) it follows that

$$|e(u) - e(v)| \leq 1.$$ ❑

Note The above result shows that the eccentricities of two adjacent vertices are either equal or differ by 1 as $|e(u) - e(v)| \leq 1$ gives $|e(u) - e(v)| = 0$ or $|e(u) - e(v)| = 1$.

An important consequence of Theorem 9.18 is as follows.

Corollary 9.4 If $u_0\, u_1\, u_2 \ldots u_m$ is a path in a connected graph and $e(u_0) < e(u_m)$ and k is any integer such that $e(u_0) < k < e(u_m)$, then there exists an integer j $(0 \leq j \leq m)$ such that $e(u_j) = k$.

Proof We know the difference of eccentricities of any two adjacent vertices along the path $u_0\, u_1\, u_2 \ldots u_m$ is always less or equal to 1. Therefore every integer between $e(u_0)$ and $e(u_m)$ occurs as the eccentricity of some vertex in this path. This can also be seen in the following way.

Assume, $e(u_0) < e(u_1) < \ldots < e(u_{j-1})$,

and let $j = 1 + \max\{i : e(u_i) < k\}$, that is, $j - 1 = \max\{i : e(u_i) < k\}$.

Thus, $e(u_{j-1}) < k$.

Therefore, $|e(u_j) - e(u_{j-1})| \leq 1$ gives

$$e(u_j) \leq e(u_{j-1}) + 1 < k + 1,$$

so that $e(u_j) \leq k$. (9.4.1)

But by the choice of j, we have $e(u_j) \geq k$. (9.4.2)

Hence from (9.4.1) and (9.4.2), we get $e(u_j) = k$. ❑

The following necessary condition for a positive sequence to be an eccentricity sequence is due to Lesniak [142].

Theorem 9.19 (Lesniak) If a non decreasing sequence $[e_i]_1^n$ of positive integers is an eccentric sequence then

i. $2e_1 \leq n$,

ii. $e_n \leq \min\{n - 1, 2e_1\}$ and

iii. for every integer k such that $e_1 < k \leq e_n$, there exists an integer i $(2 \leq i \leq n - 1)$ such that $e_i = e_{i+1} = k$.

Proof

i. Let the vertices of G be labelled as $v_1, v_2, \ldots, v_n$ such that $e(v_i) = e_i$. Then G has a spanning tree T which preserves the distance from v_1. This gives

$$e_G(v_1) = e_T(v_1) \text{ and } e_G(v_i) \leq e_T(v_i),$$

for $2 \leq i \leq n$ (since removal of edges cannot reduce distances)

Thus, if $[a_1, a_2, \ldots, a_n]$ is the eccentricity sequence of T, we have $a_1 = e_1$. So it is enough to prove that $2a_1 \leq n$. We prove this for any tree T.

Now let T be any tree with eccentricity sequence $[a_1, a_2, \ldots, a_n]$.

If $n = 2$, then $a_1 = a_2 = 1$, and the result is true. So assume $n \geq 3$.

Let u be a central vertex of T. Then $e(u) = a_1$. Also u is a cut vertex of T.

Suppose $a_1 = e(u) \geq \frac{n+1}{2}$. $\quad [2a_1 \geq n+1]$

Since an eccentric vertex $\bar{u}$ of u should lie in a component of $T-u$, there is at least one component C of $T-u$ with $|V(C)| \geq \frac{n+1}{2}$.

Now, let v be the vertex adjacent to u in C. Then for any vertex w in C, we have $d(v, w) = d(u, w) - 1$. So, $d(v, w) < e(u)$, because $d(u, w) \leq e(u)$ and so $d(u, w) - 1 < e(u)$.

For every vertex w in $V(T) - V(C)$, we have $d(v, w) - d(u, w) = 1$,

so that $d(v, w) = d(u, w) + 1$.

Total vertices in T is n, $|V(C)| \geq \frac{n+1}{2}$, therefore number of vertices in $V(T) - V(C)$

$$\leq n - \left(\frac{n+1}{2}\right) = \frac{n-1}{2}.$$

That is, $|V(T) - V(C)| \leq \frac{n-1}{2}$. Therefore, $d(u, w) \leq \frac{n-1}{2} - 1 = \frac{n-3}{2}$.

Thus, $d(v, w) \leq \frac{n-3}{2} + 1 = \frac{n-1}{2}$. So, $d(v, w) < e(u)$.

Hence for all vertices w, we have $d(v, w) < e(u)$, and thus $e(v) < e(u)$, so that $e(v) < a_1$, which is a contradiction as a_1 is the least eccentricity of a vertex of T. Thus,

$a_1 \geq \frac{n+1}{2}$ is wrong and so, $a_1 \leq \frac{n}{2}$.

ii. The maximum distance possible in an $n-$vertex graph is $n-1$. So, $e_n \leq n-1$. Also, $e_n \leq 2e_1$, $[r \leq d \leq 2r$, and here $d = e_n$, $r = e_1]$. Hence, $e_n \leq \min\{(n-1), 2e_1\}$.

iii. We have to prove that each integer between e_1 and e_n (e_n inclusive) occurs at least twice in the sequence. Let u_1 be the central vertex and u_k be the peripheral vertex of G. Then $e(u_1) = e_1$ and $e(u_k) = e_n$. Since G is connected, there exists a $u_1 - u_k$ path. Now by Corollary 9.4, if k is any integer between e_1 and e_k, there exists a vertex u_j in this path with $e(u_j) = k$. This gives the existence of a vertex whose eccentricity is k.

If $e(w) > e_1$, we show there is a vertex u other than w such that $e(u) = e(w)$. Let $\overline{w}$ be an eccentric vertex of w, that is, $d(w, \overline{w}) = e(w) = k$, say. As we have assumed that u_1 is the central vertex of G, let $P = u_1 \ldots u_m (u_m = \overline{w})$ be a $u_1 - \overline{w}$ distance path in G. Since $e(u_1) = e_1 < e(w) = d(\overline{w}, w) \leq e(\overline{w})$, applying Corollary 9.4, there is a vertex u_j in this path such that $e(u_j) = k$. But $d(\overline{w}, u_j) \leq m-1 = d(u_1, \overline{w}) \leq e(u_1) = e_1 < e(w) = d(\overline{w}, w)$. Therefore, $d(\overline{w}, u_j) < d(\overline{w}\, w)$. Thus, $u_j \neq w$ and the result is proved. ❑

The following characterisation of eccentricity sequences of trees is again due to Lesniak [142].

Theorem 9.20 (Lesniak) A non-decreasing sequence $[e_i]_1^n$ of positive integers is the eccentric sequence of a tree if and only if

i. For each integer k with $e_1 < k \leq e_n$, we have

$$e_i = e_{i+1} = k, \text{ for some } i,\ 2 \leq i \leq n-1,$$

ii. Either $e_1 = \frac{e_n}{2}$ and $e_1 \neq e_2$, or $e_1 = \frac{e_n+1}{2}$, $e_1 = e_2$ and $e_2 \neq e_3$.

Proof

Necessity Let the nondecreasing sequence $[e_i]_1^n$ of positive integers be the eccentric sequence of a tree. Then (i) follows from condition (iii) of the previous result.

Let r be the radius and d the diameter of the tree, so that $e_1 = r$ and $e_n = d$. Since a tree is either unicentral or bicentral, we have $d = 2r$ for unicentral,

and $d = 2r-1$ for bicentral.

In case the tree is unicentral, then the eccentricity of the center v_1 is e_1 and $e_1 \neq e_2$. Thus, $e_n = 2e_1$ which implies that $e_1 = \frac{e_n}{2}$ and $e_1 \neq e_2$.

In case the tree is bicentral, then $e_1 = e_2$ and $d = 2r-1$ gives $e_n = 2e_1 - 1$, so that $e_1 = \frac{e_n+1}{2}$ with $e_2 \neq e_3$.

Sufficiency Let the nondecreasing sequence $[e_i]_1^n$ of positive integers satisfy conditions (i) and (ii). We construct a tree with eccentric sequence $[e_i]_1^n$ in the following way.

Let P be a path of length $e_n = d$. Then eccentric sequence of P is

$$S_1 = \frac{d}{2}, \left(\frac{d}{2}+1\right)^2, \left(\frac{d}{2}+2\right)^2, \ldots, \left(\frac{d}{2}+\frac{d}{2}\right)^2, \qquad \text{if } d \text{ is even,}$$

$$\text{or} \quad S_2 = \left(\frac{d+1}{2}\right)^2, \left(\frac{d+1}{2}+1\right)^2, \ldots, \left(\frac{d+1}{2}+\frac{d+1}{2}-1\right)^2, \qquad \text{if } d \text{ is odd,}$$

that is, $S_1 = r, (r+1)^2, (r+2)^2, \ldots, (r+r)^2$, where $r = \dfrac{d}{2}$,

or $S_2 = r^2, (r+1)^2, (r+2)^2, \ldots, (r+r-1)^2$, where $r = \dfrac{d+1}{2}$,

where powers denote repetition of eccentricity.

Let the given sequence $[e_i]_1^n$ be written in power notation $\pi = r^{i_1}(r+1)^{i_2} \ldots d^{i_k}$, where $i_1 = 1$ or 2, according as d is even or odd. If $i_j > 2$ for any j, $1 < j \leq k$, we attach $i_j - 2$ vertices to any vertex with eccentricity $r+j-2$ in the path P. This does not alter the eccentricities of the vertices of P and the resulting tree T has eccentric sequence $[e_i]_1^n$. ❑

Example Construct a tree with eccentric sequence $[4^2, 5^4, 6^3, 7^4]$.

First draw a path P say $u_0\, u_1 u_2\, u_3\, u_4\, u_5\, u_6\, u_7$ of length 7. Then the eccentricities of these vertices are 7, 6, 5, 4, 4, 5, 6, 7.

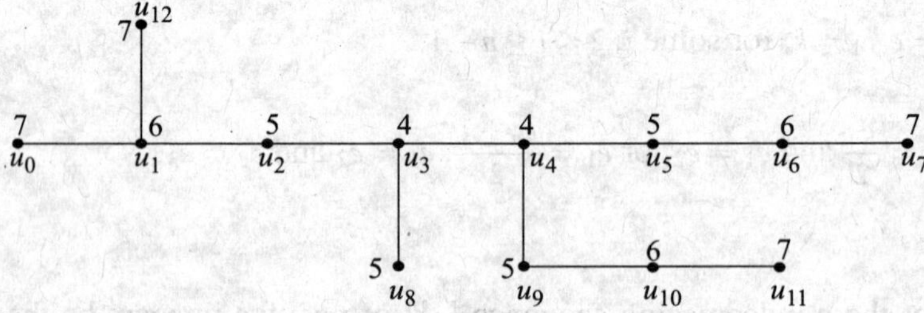

Fig. 9.19

To get two more vertices of eccentricities 5, attach a new vertex each to u_3 and u_4. Let these new vertices be u_8 and u_9. (Here $i_2 = 4 > 2$, and $i_2 - 2 = 4 - 2 = 2$). So 2 vertices one each are attached to the vertices of eccentricities $r+j-2 = r+2-2 = 4+2-2 = 4$, i.e., u_3 and u_4). Now $i_3 = 3 > 2$ and $i_3 - 2 = 3 - 2 = 1$. So one vertex is to be attached to the vertex of eccentricity $r+j-2 = 4+3-2 = 5$, i.e., the vertex u_2 or u_8 or u_9 or u_5. Let this new vertex u_{10} be attached to u_9 say. Now $i_4 = 4 > 2$ and $i_4 - 2 = 4 - 2 = 2$. So two new vertices are to be attached, one each among the vertices with eccentricities $r+j-2 = 4+4-2 = 6$, i.e., to the vertices u_1, u_6, u_{10}. Let these new vertices be u_{11} attached to u_{10} and u_{12} attached to u_1. The resulting tree is shown in Figure 9.19.

Remark Clearly there are many trees realising this eccentric sequence.

Neighbourhood Let v be any vertex of a connected graph G. The ith *neighbourhood* of v denoted by $N_i(v)$ is the set of all those vertices in V whose distance from v is i.

i.e., $N_i(v) = \{u \in V : d(v, u) = i\}$.

We denote $N_1(v)$ by $N(v)$ and call it the *neighbourhood* of v.

Example Consider the graph in Figure 9.20.

We have $N_1(v) = N(v) = \{u_1, u_2, u_3, u_4, u_5, u_6\}$.

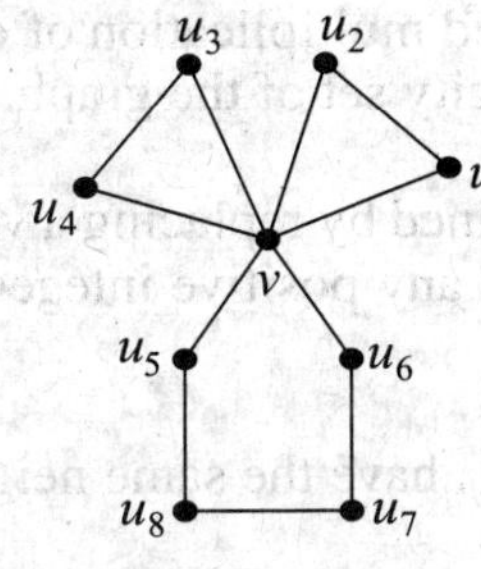

Fig. 9.20

We have the following observations.

Lemma 9.2 Any two vertices with the same neighbourhood in a graph have the same eccentricity.

Proof Let u and v be two vertices with the same neighbourhood. So $N(u) = N(v)$. Therefore the path lengths from u and v to the other vertices of the graph are equal. Clearly, u and v are not adjacent. ❑

Lemma 9.3 If u and v are adjacent in G and $N(u) - \{v\} = N(v) - \{u\}$, then u and v have the same eccentricity in G.

Proof Let G be a graph in which $uv = e$ and $N(u) - \{v\} = N(v) - \{u\}$.

Let $H = G - e$. Then u and v are not adjacent in H so that u and v have the same neighbourhood in H.

Therefore, $e(u|H) = e(v|H)$ where ($e(u|H)$ means eccentricity of vertex u in graph H). If $e(u|G) = 1$, then $e(v|G) = 1$ also. If not, then $e(u|G) = e(u|H) = e(v|H) = e(v|G)$. ❑

Definition: Let v be a vertex of a graph G and let H be a graph obtained from $G - v$ by adding edge to each vertex of a new graph K_p (or $\overline{K}_p$) to every vertex of $G - v$ to which v was adjacent in G. Then H is said to be obtained from G by replacing v by K_p (or $\overline{K}_p$). This operation is illustrated in Figure 9.21.

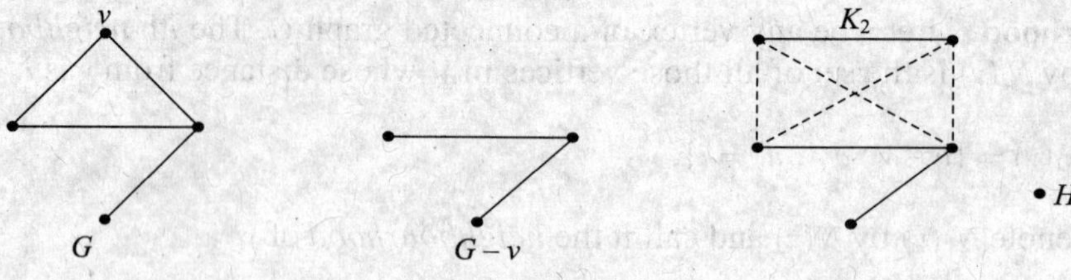

Fig. 9.21

The operation of replacing v in G by $\overline{K}_p$ is called *multiplication* of the vertex in G. The operation of replacing v in G by K_p is called the *linked multiplication* of v in G. Lesniak observed that multiplication or linked multiplication of one or more vertices of a graph is an operation preserving the eccentricity set of the graph.

Lemma 9.4 If H is the graph obtained by replacing a vertex v of a graph G with diameter greater than one, by a K_p or $\overline{K}_p$ (for any positive integer p), then G and H have the same eccentricity sets.

Proof Since v and any vertex of $\overline{K}_p$ have the same neighbourhood in H,

$$e(u|H) = e(v|G), \text{ for every } u \in \overline{K}_p.$$

For replacement by K_p, we have for any two adjacent vertices u_i and u_j in K_p,

$$N(u_i) - \{u_j\} = N(u_j) - \{u_i\}.$$

Therefore, $e(u_i|H) = e(u_j|H)$. So, $e(v|H) = e(u|G)$, for every $u \in K_p$.

Thus, $e(u|H) = e(v|G)$, for every $u \in K_p$ ($\overline{K}_p$) and obviously

$$e(w|H) = e(w|G), \text{ for all other vertices.}$$ ❑

The above result is illustrated in Figure 9.22, where we choose K_2 and $\overline{K}_2$

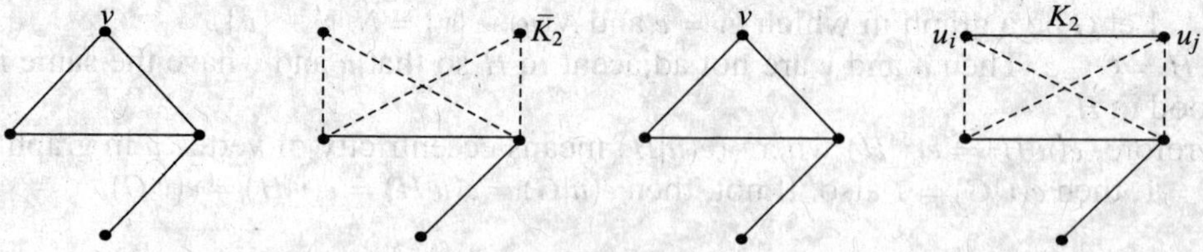

Fig. 9.22

The next gives the necessary and sufficient conditions for an eccentricity sequence of a graph, due to Lesniak [142].

Theorem 9.21 (Lesniak) A nondecreasing sequence of positive integers $[e_1^{r_1}, e_2^{r_2}, \ldots, e_k^{r_k}]$ is an eccentricity sequence if and only if some of its subsequence $[e_1^{s_1}, e_2^{s_2}, \ldots, e_k^{s_k}]$ with $s_i \le r_i$ and no $s_i = 0$ for $1 \le i \le k$, is an eccentricity sequence.

Proof

Necessity Since every sequence is its own subsequence, necessity follows.

Sufficiency Let $[e_1^{s_1}, e_2^{s_2}, \ldots, e_k^{s_k}]$ be the eccentricity sequence of a graph G. Let v_i be a vertex of G with $e(v_i) = e_i$, $1 \le i \le k$. Let $n_1 = r_1 - s_1 + 1$ so that $r_1 = n_1 + s_1 - 1$.

Now let G_1 be obtained from G by replacing v_1 by K_{n_1} or $\overline{K}_{n_1}$. Then every one of the vertices of this K_{n_1} or $\overline{K}_{n_1}$ has eccentricity $e(v_1|G)$ and the eccentricities of the vertices of G are unaltered in G_1. Thus G_1 has eccentricity sequence $[e_1^{r_1}, e_2^{s_2}, \ldots, e_k^{s_k}]$.

Let G_2 be obtained from G_1 by replacing v_2 by K_{n_2} or $\overline{K}_{n_2}$. Then by similar argument, G_2 has eccentricity sequence $[e_1^{r_1}, e_2^{r_2}, \ldots, e_k^{s_k}]$.

Proceeding in this way, by successively replacing $v_3, v_4, \ldots, v_k$ by K_{n_3} $(\overline{K}_{n_3})$, K_{n_4} $(\overline{K}_{n_4})$, $\ldots, K_{n_k}$ $(\overline{K}_{n_k})$, we get a graph G_k with eccentricity sequence $[e_1^{r_1}, e_2^{r_2}, \ldots, e_k^{r_k}]$. ❑

Remarks

1. It is assumed that $e_k > 1$.

2. The construction of G_k is not unique.

3. This result keeps unsolved the problem of characterising minimal eccentricity sequences, that is, those eccentricity sequences which have no proper eccentric subsequences.

The next result characterises eccentricity sets and is due to Behzad and Simpson [16].

Theorem 9.22 A non-empty set $S = \{e_1, e_2, \ldots, e_k\}$ of positive integers arranged in increasing order is an eccentricity set if and only if $k \le e_1 + 1$ and $e_{i+1} = e_i + 1$ for $1 \le i \le k-1$.

Proof

Necessity Let S be an eccentricity set. Then by (iii) of Theorem 4.24, $e_{i+1} = e_i + 1$ for each i, $1 \le i \le k-1$. This gives $e_k = e_1 + k - 1$. Since $e_k \le 2e_1$, we get $k \le e_1 + 1$.

Sufficiency If $e_1 = 1$, then $k = 1$ or 2 and $S = \{1\}$ or $\{1, 2\}$. In this case, K_2 and $K_{1,n}$ realise the sets.

For $e_1 > 1$, let G be the graph obtained by identifying a vertex of a cycle C_{2e_1} with an end vertex of a path P_k. Let $e_1 - k + 1 = d$. Then $d \ge 0$, and the eccentricity sequence of G is easily verified to be $[e_1^{2d+1}, (e_1+1)^3, (e_1+2)^3, \ldots, (e_1+k-2)^3, (e_1+k-1)^3]$. Hence S is the eccentricity set. ❑

9.5 Distance Degree Regular and Distance Regular Graphs

Let G be a connected graph and let v be any vertex of G. Let e be the eccentricity of vertex v and $N_j(v)$ be the jth neighbourhood of v. Assume, $n_j(v) = |N_j(v)|$, for $0 \leq j \leq e$. The sequence $D(G, v) = [n_0(v), n_1(v), \ldots, n_e(v)]$ is called the *distance degree sequence* (DDS) of v in G. If all the vertices of G have the same distance degree sequence $D(G) = [n_0, n_1, \ldots, n_d]$, then G is said to be *distance degree regular*.

If G is not distance degree regular, the n vectors $D(G, v_i)$, $1 \leq i \leq n$, arranged lexicographically in an array with variable row sizes is called the *distance degree array* of G (DDA(G)).

The *distance* of vertex v is defined by

$$D(v) = \sum_{j=1}^{e(v)} n_j(v).$$

Let D_i be the distance of the vertex v_i. The sequence $DS(G) = [D_1, D_2, \ldots, D_n]$ in non-decreasing order is called the *distance sequence* of the graph.

A vertex v with minimum distance $D(v)$ is called a *median* of G and the subgraph induced by the set M of median vertices of G is called the *median subgraph* of G.

Clearly, if G is distance degree regular, then all vertices in G have the same eccentricity, and G is a *self-centered graph*. Also, $n_0 = 1$ and $n_1 = |N_1(v)|$ for every $v \in G$, so that G is n_1-regular.

Randic [208] conjectured that two trees are isomorphic if and only if they have same DDA and Slater [187] disproved this giving the counter example as shown in Figure 9.23.

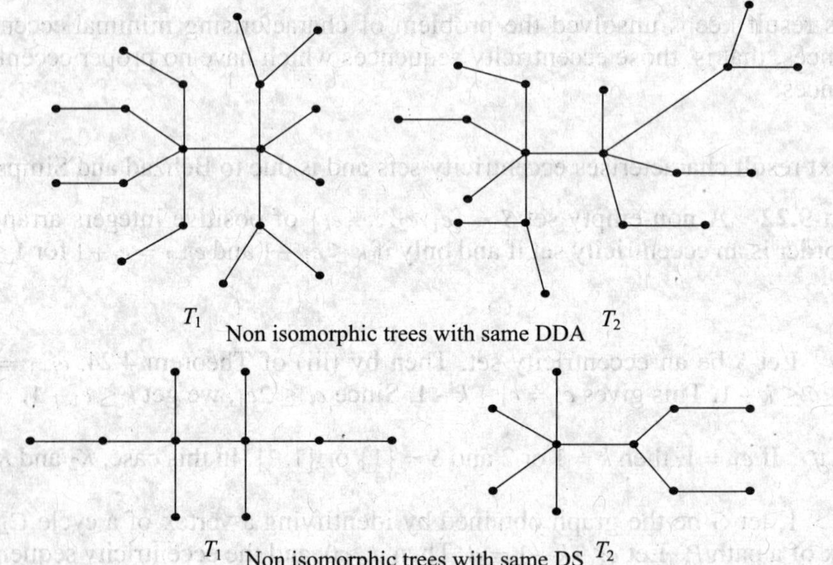

Fig. 9.23

Definition: Let G be a connected graph with diameter d and let $k = b_0, b_1, \ldots, b_{d-1}$; $l = c_1, c_2, \ldots, c_d$ be $2d$ non-negative integers. Then G is said to be *distance regular* (DR) if for every pair of vertices u, v in G with $d(u, v) = j$, we have, (i) the number of vertices in $N_{j-1}(v)$ adjacent to u is c_j, $1 \le j \le d$ and (ii) the number of vertices in $N_{j+1}(v)$ adjacent to u is b_j, $0 \le j \le d-1$.

The sequence $[b_0, b_1, \ldots, b_{d-1}, c_1, c_2, \ldots, c_d]$ is called the *intersection array* of G.

Clearly, DR graphs are k-regular and self-centered. The examples of distance regular graphs are K_n, $K_{n,\,n}$ and the cubes Q_n.

A graph G is said to be *strongly regular* (SR) with parameters (n, k, λ, μ) if it is a k-regular graph of order n in which every pair of adjacent vertices are mutually adjacent to λ vertices and every pair of non-adjacent vertices are mutually adjacent to μ vertices.

The Petersen graph is strongly regular with parameters (10, 3, 0, 1), that is $n = 10$, $k = 3$, $\lambda = 0$, $\mu = 1$ (Fig. 9.24).

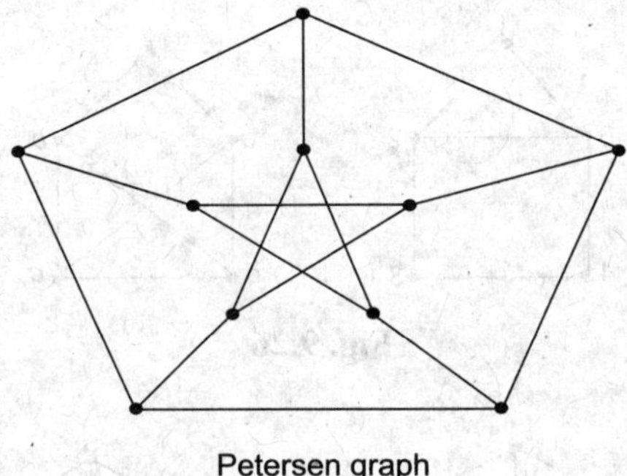

Petersen graph

Fig. 9.24

9.6 Isometry

The concept of isometry as in Chartrand and Stewart [51] is as follows.

Let G_1 and G_2 be connected graphs with vertex sets V_1 and V_2 respectively. Then G_2 is said to be *isometric* from G_1 if for each $v \in V_1$, there is a one-one map $\phi_v : V_1 \to V_2$ such that ϕ_v preserves distances from v, that is $d_{G_2}(u, v) = d_{G_1}(\phi_v(v), \phi_v(u))$ for every $u \in V_1$.

Two graphs G_1 and G_2 are said to be *isometric* if they are isometric from each other.

Example Consider the graphs shown in Figure 9.25, we have

$$\phi_1 = \phi_4 = \phi_5\,(1 \to a,\ 2 \to b,\ 3 \to c,\ 4 \to d,\ 5 \to e),$$

$$\phi_2 = (2 \to e,\ 1 \to a,\ 3 \to d,\ 4 \to c,\ 5 \to b),\ \phi_3 = (3 \to e,\ 4 \to a,\ 2 \to d,\ 1 \to b,\ 5 \to c).$$

Here G_2 is isometric from G_1.

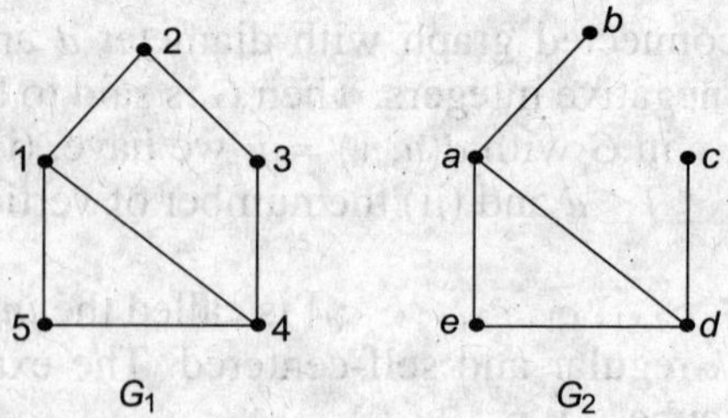

Fig. 9.25

Remarks Isometry between graphs as defined above does not imply isomorphism (Fig. 9.26). A pair of isometric graphs may even have same degree sequence and yet be non-isomorphic (Fig. 9.27).

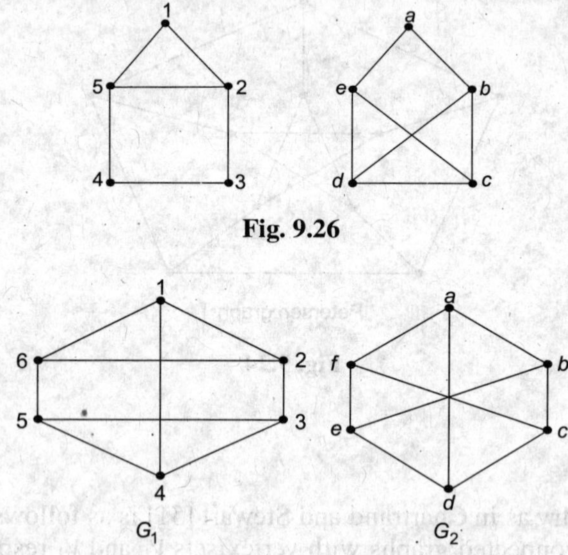

Fig. 9.26

Fig. 9.27

We now have the following results.

Theorem 9.23 If G_1 and G_2 are k-regular graphs of order n, where $k \geq n - 1/2$, then G_1 and G_2 are isometric.

Proof Since G_1 is a k-regular graph with $k \geq n - 1/2$, $d(G_1) \leq 2$.
Let $u \in V(G_1)$ and $v \in V(G_2)$ be any two vertices and define

$$\phi_u : V(G_1) \rightarrow V(G_2) \text{ by } \phi_u(u) = v.$$

For $i = 1, 2, \ldots, k$, let $u_i \in N_1(u)$ and $v_i \in N_1(v)$ and define $\phi_u(u_i) = v_i$.

For $i = k+1, \ldots, n-1$, let $u_i \in N_2(u)$ and $v_i \in N_2(v)$ and again let $\phi_u(u_i) = v_i$.

The neighbourhoods are in the appropriate graphs. Then ϕ_u is an isometry of G_2 from G_1 at u. Since u and v are arbitrary, it is easily seen that G_2 is isometric from G_1, and G_1 is isometric from G_2. ❑

Theorem 9.24 A necessary condition for two graphs to be isometric is that they have the same degree set and the same eccentricity set.

Proof Let $G_1(V_1, E_1)$ and $G_2(V_2, E_2)$ be isometric graphs. As G_2 is isometric from G_1, let ϕ_v be the one-one mapping from $V(G_1)$ to $V(G_2)$. Therefore, $d(v|G_1) = d(\Phi_v(v)|G_2)$. Also ϕ_v has the property of preserving distance, therefore $e(v|G_1) = e(\phi_v(v)|G_2)$. So the eccentricity set of G_1 is included in the eccentricity set of G_2.

Again, as G_1 is isometric from G_2, therefore, the degree set and eccentricity set of G_2 are included respectively in the degree set and eccentricity set of G_1.

Hence the degree sets are equal in G_1 and G_2 and the eccentricity sets are equal in G_1 and G_2. ❑

9.7 Exercises

1. Show that the edge graph of $K_{1,\,n}$ is K_n.
2. Show that the edge graph of K_5 is the complement of the Petersen graph.
3. Show that if $L(G)$ is connected and regular, then either G is regular or G is a bipartite graph in which vertices of the same partite set have the same degree.
4. If G is k-edge-connected, then prove that $L(G)$ is k-connected and $(2k-2)$-edge-connected.
5. Show that the graph $L_2(G)$ is Hamiltonian if and only if G has a closed spanning walk.
6. Show that the graph $L_2(G)$ is Hamiltonian if and only if there is a closed walk in G which includes at least one vertex incident with each edge of G.
7. Prove that $T(K_n) \cong L(K_{n+1})$.
8. If G is Hamiltonian, then prove that $T(G)$ is Hamiltonian.
9. If G is Eulerian, then prove that $T(G)$ is both Eulerian and Hamiltonian.
10. Prove that $T(G)$ of every nontrivial connected graph G contains a spanning Eulerian subgraph.
11. Show that the edge graph of a graph G has a Hamiltonian path if and only if G has a walk W such that every edge of G not in W is incident with W.

12. If G is any connected graph with $\delta(G) \geq 4$, then prove that $L^2(G)$ is Hamiltonian-connected.

13. Construct graphs with eccentricity sequence

$$[2,\, 3^3,\, 4^3].$$

14. If G is a connected graph with diameter 3 and $e(u|G) = 3$, then show that $e(u|\overline{G}) = 2$.

15. If $[e_1, e_2, \ldots, e_n]$ with $e_n < 2e_1 - 1$ is an eccentricity sequence, then show that each central vertex lies on a cycle.

16. If $[e_i]_1^n$ is the eccentricity sequence of an (n, m) graph, show that

$$m \leq \frac{1}{2}\left(n^2 - \sum_{i=1}^{n} e_i\right).$$

17. For a distance regular graph, prove the following

a. If $1 \leq i \leq \frac{1}{2d}$, then $b_i \geq c_i$.

b. If $1 \leq i \leq \frac{1}{d-1}$, then $b_1 \geq c_i$.

c. $c_2 \geq k - 2b_1$.

10. Graph Matrices

Since a graph is completely determined by specifying either its adjacency structure or its incidence structure, these specifications provide far more efficient ways of representing a large or complicated graph than a pictorial representation. As computers are more adept at manipulating numbers than at recognising pictures, it is standard practice to communicate the specification of a graph to a computer in matrix form. In this chapter, we study various types of matrices associated with a graph, and our study is based on Narsing Deo [62], Foulds [79], Harary [100] and Parthasarathy [175].

10.1 Incidence Matrix

Let G be a graph with n vertices, m edges and without self-loops. The incidence matrix A of G is an $n \times m$ matrix $A = [a_{ij}]$ whose n rows correspond to the n vertices and the m columns correspond to m edges such that

$$a_{ij} = \begin{cases} 1, & \textit{if jth edge } m_j \textit{ is incident on the ith vertex} \\ 0, & \textit{otherwise.} \end{cases}$$

It is also called *vertex-edge incidence matrix* and is denoted by $A(G)$.

Example Consider the graphs given in Figure 10.1. The incidence matrix of G_1 is

$$A(G_1) = \begin{matrix} & e_1 & e_2 & e_3 & e_4 & e_5 & e_6 & e_7 & e_8 \\ v_1 & 0 & 0 & 0 & 1 & 0 & 1 & 0 & 0 \\ v_2 & 0 & 0 & 0 & 0 & 1 & 1 & 1 & 1 \\ v_3 & 0 & 0 & 0 & 0 & 0 & 0 & 0 & 1 \\ v_4 & 1 & 1 & 1 & 0 & 1 & 0 & 0 & 0 \\ v_5 & 0 & 0 & 1 & 1 & 0 & 0 & 1 & 0 \\ v_6 & 1 & 1 & 0 & 0 & 0 & 0 & 0 & 0 \end{matrix}.$$

The incidence matrix of G_2 is

$$A(G_2) = \begin{array}{c} \\ v_1 \\ v_2 \\ v_3 \\ v_4 \end{array} \begin{array}{c} e_1 \; e_2 \; e_3 \; e_4 \; e_5 \\ \begin{bmatrix} 1 & 1 & 0 & 0 & 0 \\ 1 & 0 & 0 & 1 & 1 \\ 0 & 1 & 1 & 1 & 1 \\ 0 & 0 & 1 & 0 & 0 \end{bmatrix} \end{array}.$$

The incidence matrix of G_3 is

$$A(G_3) = \begin{array}{c} \\ v_1 \\ v_2 \\ v_3 \\ v_4 \end{array} \begin{array}{c} e_1 \; e_2 \; e_3 \; e_4 \; e_5 \\ \begin{bmatrix} 1 & 1 & 0 & 0 & 1 \\ 1 & 1 & 1 & 0 & 0 \\ 0 & 0 & 0 & 1 & 0 \\ 0 & 0 & 1 & 1 & 1 \end{bmatrix} \end{array}.$$

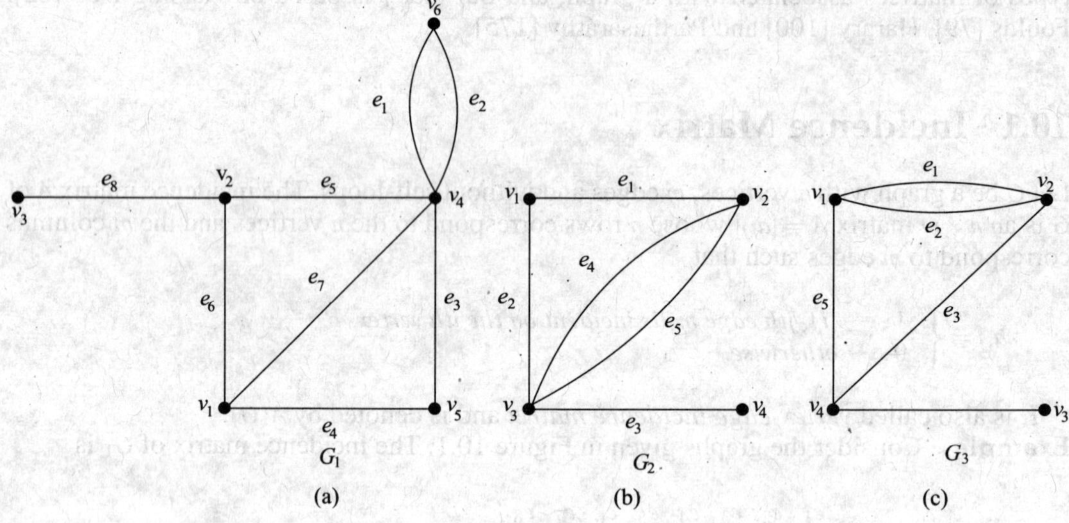

Fig. 10.1

The incidence matrix contains only two types of elements, 0 and 1. This clearly is a binary matrix or a (0, 1)-matrix.

We have the following observations about the incidence matrix A.

1. Since every edge is incident on exactly two vertices, each column of A has exactly two one's.

2. The number of one's in each row equals the degree of the corresponding vertex.

3. A row with all zeros represents an isolated vertex.

4. Parallel edges in a graph produce identical columns in its incidence matrix.

5. If a graph is disconnected and consists of two components G_1 and G_2, the incidence matrix $A(G)$ of graph G can be written in a block diagonal form as

$$A(G) = \begin{bmatrix} A(G_1) & 0 \\ 0 & A(G_2) \end{bmatrix},$$

where $A(G_1)$ and $A(G_2)$ are the incidence matrices of components G_1 and G_2. This observation results from the fact that no edge in G_1 is incident on vertices of G_2 and vice versa. Obviously, this is also true for a disconnected graph with any number of components.

6. Permutation of any two rows or columns in an incidence matrix simply corresponds to relabeling the vertices and edges of the same graph.

Note The matrix A has been defined over a field, Galois field modulo 2 or $GF(2)$, that is, the set $\{0,1\}$ with operation addition modulo 2 written as + such that $0+0=0$, $1+0=1$, $1+1=0$ and multiplication modulo 2 written as"." such that $0.0=0$, $1.0=0=0.1$, $1.1=1$.

The following result is an immediate consequence of the above observations.

Theorem 10.1 Two graphs G_1 and G_2 are isomorphic if and only if their incidence matrices $A(G_1)$ and $A(G_2)$ differ only by permutation of rows and columns.

Proof Let the graphs G_1 and G_2 be isomorphic. Then there is a one-one correspondence between the vertices and edges in G_1 and G_2 such that the incidence relation is preserved. Thus $A(G_1)$ and $A(G_2)$ are either same or differ only by permutation of rows and columns.

The converse follows, since permutation of any two rows or columns in an incidence matrix simply corresponds to relabeling the vertices and edges of the same graph. ❑

Rank of the incidence matrix

Let G be a graph and let $A(G)$ be its incidence matrix. Now each row in $A(G)$ is a vector over $GF(2)$ in the vector space of graph G. Let the row vectors be denoted by $A_1, A_2, \ldots, A_n$. Then,

$$A(G) = \begin{bmatrix} A_1 \\ A_2 \\ \vdots \\ \vdots \\ A_n \end{bmatrix}.$$

Since there are exactly two ones in every column of A, the sum of all these vectors is 0 (this being a modulo 2 sum of the corresponding entries).

Thus vectors $A_1, A_2, \ldots, A_n$ are linearly dependent. Therefore, rank $A < n$.

Hence, rank $A \leq n-1$.

From the above observations, we have the following result.

Theorem 10.2 If $A(G)$ is an incidence matrix of a connected graph G with n vertices, then rank of $A(G)$ is $n-1$.

Proof Let G be a connected graph with n vertices and let the number of edges in G be m. Let $A(G)$ be the incidence matrix and let $A_1, A_2, \ldots, A_n$ be the row vector of $A(G)$.

$$\text{Then, } A(G) = \begin{bmatrix} A_1 \\ A_2 \\ \cdot \\ \cdot \\ \cdot \\ A_n \end{bmatrix}. \tag{10.2.1}$$

$$\text{Clearly, rank } A(G) \leq n-1. \tag{10.2.2}$$

Consider the sum of any m of these row vectors, $m \leq n-1$. Since G is connected, $A(G)$ cannot be partitioned in the form

$$A(G) = \begin{bmatrix} A(G_1) & 0 \\ 0 & A(G_2) \end{bmatrix}$$

such that $A(G_1)$ has m_1 rows and $A(G_2)$ has $n-m$ rows.

Thus there exists no $m \times m$ submatrix of $A(G)$ for $m \leq n-1$, such that the modulo 2 sum of these m_1 rows is equal to zero.

As there are only two elements 0 and 1 in this field, the additions of all vectors taken m_1 at a time for $m = 1, 2, \ldots, n-1$ gives all possible linear combinations of $n-1$ row vectors.

Thus no linear combinations of m_1 row vectors of A, for $m \leq n-1$, is zero.

$$\text{Therefore, rank } A(G) \leq n-1. \tag{10.2.3}$$

Combining (10.2.2) and (10.2.3), it follows that rank $A(G) = n-1$. ❑

Remark If G is a disconnected graph with k components, then it follows from the above theorem that rank of $A(G)$ is $n-k$.

Let G be a connected graph with n vertices and m edges. Then the order of the incidence matrix $A(G)$ is $n \times m$. Now, if we remove any one row from $A(G)$, the remaining $(n-1)$ by m submatrix is of rank $(n-1)$. Thus the remaining $(n-1)$ row vectors are linearly independent. This shows that only $(n-1)$ rows of an incidence matrix are required to specify the corresponding graph completely, because $(n-1)$ rows contain the same information as the entire matrix. This follows from the fact that given $(n-1)$ rows, we can construct the nth row, as each column in the matrix has exactly two ones. Such an $(n-1) \times m$ matrix of A is called a *reduced incidence matrix* and is denoted by A_f. The vertex corresponding to the deleted row in A_f is called the *reference vertex*. Obviously, any vertex of a connected graph can be treated as the reference vertex.

The following result gives the nature of the incidence matrix of a tree.

Theorem 10.3 The reduced incidence matrix of a tree is non-singular.

Proof A tree with n vertices has $n-1$ edges and also a tree is connected. Therefore, the reduced incidence matrix is a square matrix of order $n-1$, with rank $n-1$. Thus the result follows.

Now a graph G with n vertices and $n-1$ edges which is not a tree is obviously disconnected. Therefore the rank of the incidence matrix of G is less than $(n-1)$. Hence the $(n-1) \times (n-1)$ reduced incidence matrix of a graph is non-singular if and only if the graph is a tree. ❑

10.2 Submatrices of A(G)

Let H be a subgraph of a graph G, and let $A(H)$ and $A(G)$ be the incidence matrices of H and G respectively. Clearly, $A(H)$ is a submatrix of $A(G)$, possibly with rows or columns permuted. We observe that there is a one-one correspondence between each $n \times k$ submatrix of $A(G)$ and a subgraph of G with k edges, k being a positive integer, $k < m$ and n being the number of vertices in G.

The following is a property of the submatrices of $A(G)$.

Theorem 10.4 Let $A(G)$ be the incidence matrix of a connected graph G with n vertices. An $(n-1) \times (n-1)$ submatrix of $A(G)$ is non-singular if and only if the $n-1$ edges corresponding to the $n-1$ columns of this matrix constitutes a spanning tree in G.

Proof Let G be a connected graph with n vertices and m edges. So, $m \geq n-1$.

Let $A(G)$ be the incidence matrix of G, so that $A(G)$ has n rows and m columns $(m \geq n-1)$.

We know every square submatrix of order $(n-1) \times (n-1)$ in $A(G)$ is the reduced incidence matrix of some subgraph H in G with $n-1$ edges, and vice versa. We also know that a square submatrix of $A(G)$ is non-singular if and only if the corresponding subgraph is a tree.

Obviously, the tree is a spanning tree because it contains $n-1$ edges of the n-vertex graph.

Hence $(n-1) \times (n-1)$ submatrix of $A(G)$ is non-singular if and only if $n-1$ edges corresponding to $n-1$ columns of this matrix forms a spanning tree. ❑

The following is another form of incidence matrix.

Definition: The matrix $F = [f_{ij}]$ of the graph $G(V, E)$ with $V = \{v_1, v_2, \ldots, v_n\}$ and $E = \{e_1, e_2, \ldots, e_m\}$, is the $n \times m$ matrix associated with a chosen orientation of the edges of G in which for each $e = (v_i, v_j)$, one of v_i or v_j is taken as positive end and the other as negative end, and is defined by

$$f_{ij} = \begin{cases} 1, & if\ v_i\ is\ the\ positive\ end\ of\ e_j, \\ -1, & if\ v_i\ is\ the\ negative\ end\ of\ e_j, \\ 0, & if\ v_i\ is\ not\ incident\ with\ e_j. \end{cases}$$

This matrix F can also be obtained from the incidence matrix A by changing either of the two 1s to -1 in each column.

The above arguments amount to arbitrarily orienting the edges of G, and F is then the incidence matrix of the oriented graph.

The matrix F is then the modified definition of the incidence matrix A.

Example Consider the graph G shown in Figure 10.2, with $V = \{v_1, v_2, v_3, v_4\}$ and $E = \{e_1, e_2, e_3, e_4, e_5\}$.

The incidence matrix is given by

$$A = \begin{array}{c} \\ v_1 \\ v_2 \\ v_3 \\ v_4 \end{array} \begin{array}{c} \begin{array}{ccccc} e_1 & e_2 & e_3 & e_4 & e_5 \end{array} \\ \begin{bmatrix} 1 & 0 & 0 & 1 & 0 \\ 1 & 1 & 0 & 0 & 1 \\ 0 & 1 & 1 & 0 & 0 \\ 0 & 0 & 1 & 1 & 1 \end{bmatrix} \end{array}.$$

Therefore,

$$F = \begin{array}{c} \\ v_1 \\ v_2 \\ v_3 \\ v_4 \end{array} \begin{array}{c} \begin{array}{ccccc} e_1 & e_2 & e_3 & e_4 & e_5 \end{array} \\ \begin{bmatrix} 1 & 0 & 0 & 1 & 0 \\ -1 & 1 & 0 & 0 & 1 \\ 0 & -1 & 1 & 0 & 0 \\ 0 & 0 & -1 & -1 & -1 \end{bmatrix} \end{array}.$$

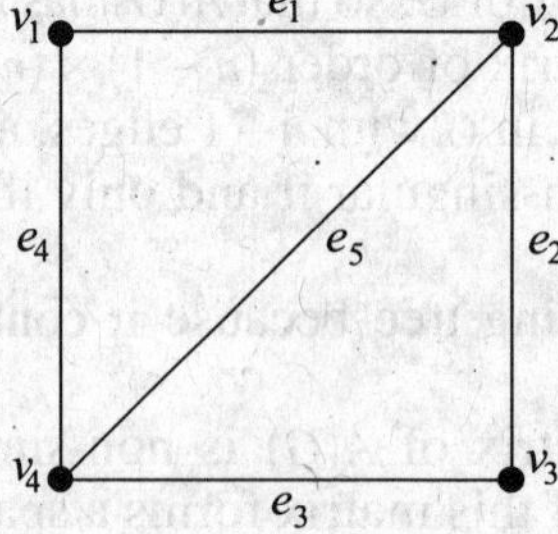

Fig. 10.2

Theorem 10.5 If G is a connected graph with n vertices, then rank $F = n-1$.

Proof Let G be a connected graph with $V = \{v_1, v_2, \ldots, v_n\}$ and $E = \{e_1, e_2, \ldots, e_m\}$. Then the matrix $F = [f_{ij}]_{n\times m}$ is given by

$$f_{ij} = \begin{cases} 1, & \textit{if } v_i \textit{ is the positive end of } e_j, \\ -1, & \textit{if } v_i \textit{ is the negative end of } e_j, \\ 0, & \textit{if } v_i \textit{ is not incident with } e_j. \end{cases}$$

Let R_j be the jth row of F. Since each column of F has only one $+1$ and one -1, as non-zero entries, rank $F < n$. Thus, rank $F \le n-1$.

Now, let $\sum_1^n c_j R_j = 0$ be any other linear dependence relation of $R_1, R_2, \ldots, R_n$ with at least one c_j non-zero.

If $c_r \neq 0$, then the row R_r has non-zero entries in those columns which correspond to edges incident with v_r. For each such column there is just one row, say R_s, at which there is a non-zero entry (with opposite sign to the non-zero entry in R_r). The dependence relation thus requires $c_s = c_r$, for all s corresponding to vertices adjacent to v_r. Since G is connected, we have $c_j = c$, for all $j = 1, 2, \ldots, n$. Therefore the dependence relation is $c\left(\sum_1^n R_j\right) = 0$, which is same as the first one. Hence, rank $F = n-1$.

Alternative Proof Let $R_1, R_2 \ldots, \ldots, R_n$ be the row matrix of F.

Then

$$F = \begin{bmatrix} R_1 \\ R_2 \\ \vdots \\ R_n \end{bmatrix}. \tag{10.5.1}$$

Since each column of F has only one +1 and one -1 as non-zero entries, $\sum_{j=1}^{n} R_j = 0$. Thus, rank $F \le n-1$. (10.5.2)

Consider the sum of any m of these row vectors, $m \le n-1$. As G is connected, F cannot be partitioned in the form $F = \begin{bmatrix} F_1 & 0 \\ 0 & F_2 \end{bmatrix}$, such that F_1 has m_1 rows and F_2 as $n-m$ rows. Therefore there exists no $m \times m$ submatrix of F for $m \le n-1$, such that the sum of these m_1 rows is equal to zero. Therefore,

$$\sum_{j=1}^{m} R_j \neq 0. \tag{10.5.3}$$

Also, there is no linear combination of $m(m \leq n-1)$ vectors of F, which is zero. For, if $\sum_{j=1}^{m} c_j R_j = 0$ is a linear combination, with at least one c_j non-zero, say $c_r \neq 0$, then the row R_r has non-zero entries in those columns which correspond to edges incident with v_r. So for each such column there is just one row, say R_s at which there is a non-zero entry with opposite sign to the non-zero entry in R_r. The linear combination thus requires $c_s = c_r$ for all s corresponding to vertices adjacent to v_r. As G is connected, we have $c_j = c$, for all $j = 1, \ldots, m$. Therefore the linear combination becomes $c(\sum_{j=1}^{m} R_j) = 0$, or $\sum_{j=1}^{m} R_j = 0$, which contradicts (10.5.3).

Hence, rank $F = n-1$. ❑

Theorem 10.6 If G is a disconnected graph with k components, then rank $F = n-k$.

Proof Since G has k components, F can be partitioned as

$$F = \begin{bmatrix} F_1 & 0 & 0 & \cdots & 0 \\ 0 & F_2 & 0 & \cdots & 0 \\ 0 & 0 & F_3 & \cdots & 0 \\ \vdots & & & & \\ 0 & 0 & 0 & \cdots & F_k \end{bmatrix},$$

where F_i is the matrix of the ith component G_i of G. We have proved that rank $F_i = n_i - 1$, where n_i is the number of vertices in G_i.

Thus, rank $F = n_1 - 1 + n_2 - 1 + \ldots + n_k - 1 = n_1 + n_2 + \ldots + n_k - k = n - k$,

as the number of vertices in G is $n_1 + n_2 + \ldots + n_k = n$. ❑

Corollary 10.1 A basis for the row space of F is obtained by taking for each i, $1 \leq i \leq k$, any $n_i - 1$ rows of F_i.

Theorem 10.7 The determinant of any square submatrix of the matrix F of a graph G has value 1, -1, or zero.

Proof Let N be the square submatrix of F such that N has both non-zero entries $+1$ and -1 in each column. Then row sum of N is zero and hence $|N| = 0$. Clearly if N has no non-zero entries, then $|N| = 0$.

Now let some column of N have only one non-zero entry. Then expanding $|N|$ with the help of this column, we get $|N| = \pm|N'|$, where N' is a matrix obtained by omitting a row and column of N. Continuing in this way, we either get a matrix whose determinant is zero, or end up with a single non-zero entry of N, in which case $|N| = \pm 1$. ❑

Theorem 10.8 Let X be any set of $n-1$ edges of the connected graph $G(V, E)$ and F_x the $(n-1) \times (n-1)$ submatrix of the matrix F of G, determined by any $n-1$ rows and those columns which correspond to the edges of X. Then F_x is non-singular if and only if the edge induced subgraph $< X >$ of G is a spanning tree of G.

Proof Let F' be the matrix corresponding to $< X >$. If $< X >$ is a spanning tree of G, then F_x consists of $n-1$ rows of F'. Since $< X >$ is connected, therefore rank $F_x = n-1$. Hence F_x is non-singular.

Conversely, let F_x be non-singular. Then F' contains an $(n-1) \times (n-1)$ non singular submatrix. Therefore, rank $F' = n-1$. Since rank + nullity $= m$, for any graph G, and $m(< X >) = n-1$ and rank $(< X >) = n-1$, therefore, nullity $(< X >) = 0$. Thus $< X >$ is acyclic and connected and so is a spanning tree of G. ❑

10.3 Cycle Matrix

Let the graph G have m edges and let q be the number of different cycles in G. The cycle matrix $B = [b_{ij}]_{q \times m}$ of G is a (0, 1)– matrix of order $q \times m$, with $b_{ij} = 1$, if the ith cycle includes jth edge and $b_{ij} = 0$, otherwise. The cycle matrix B of a graph G is denoted by $B(G)$.

Example Consider the graph G_1 given in Figure 10.3.

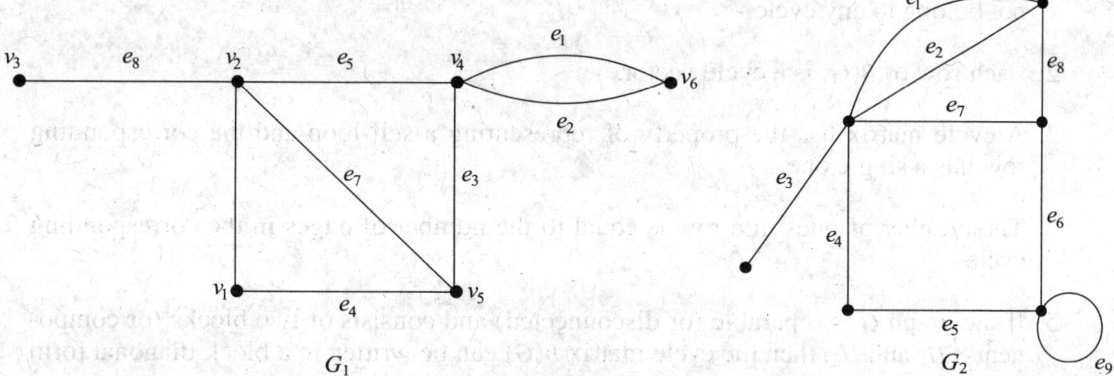

Fig. 10.3

The graph G_1 has four different cycles $Z_1 = \{e_1, e_2\}$, $Z_2 = \{e_3, e_5, e_7\}$, $Z_3 = \{e_4, e_6, e_7\}$ and $Z_4 = \{e_3, e_4, e_6, e_5\}$.

The cycle matrix is

$$B(G_1) = \begin{array}{c} \\ z_1 \\ z_2 \\ z_3 \\ z_4 \end{array} \begin{array}{c} \begin{array}{cccccccc} e_1 & e_2 & e_3 & e_4 & e_5 & e_6 & e_7 & e_8 \end{array} \\ \begin{bmatrix} 1 & 1 & 0 & 0 & 0 & 0 & 0 & 0 \\ 0 & 0 & 1 & 0 & 1 & 0 & 1 & 0 \\ 0 & 0 & 0 & 1 & 0 & 1 & 1 & 0 \\ 0 & 0 & 1 & 1 & 1 & 1 & 0 & 0 \end{bmatrix} \end{array}.$$

The graph G_2 of Figure 10.3 has seven different cycles, namely, $Z_1 = \{e_1, e_2\}$, $Z_2 = \{e_2, e_7, e_8\}$, $Z_3 = \{e_1, e_7, e_8\}$, $Z_4 = \{e_4, e_5, e_6, e_7\}$, $Z_5 = \{e_2, e_4, e_5, e_6, e_8\}$, $Z_6 = \{e_1, e_4, e_5, e_6, e_8\}$ and $Z_7 = \{e_9\}$. The cycle matrix is given by

$$B(G_2) = \begin{array}{c} \\ z_1 \\ z_2 \\ z_3 \\ z_4 \\ z_5 \\ z_6 \\ z_7 \end{array} \begin{array}{c} \begin{array}{ccccccccc} e_1 & e_2 & e_3 & e_4 & e_5 & e_6 & e_7 & e_8 & e_9 \end{array} \\ \begin{bmatrix} 1 & 1 & 0 & 0 & 0 & 0 & 0 & 0 & 0 \\ 0 & 1 & 0 & 0 & 0 & 0 & 1 & 1 & 0 \\ 1 & 0 & 0 & 0 & 0 & 0 & 1 & 1 & 0 \\ 0 & 0 & 0 & 1 & 1 & 1 & 1 & 0 & 0 \\ 0 & 1 & 0 & 1 & 1 & 1 & 0 & 1 & 0 \\ 1 & 0 & 0 & 1 & 1 & 1 & 0 & 1 & 0 \\ 0 & 0 & 0 & 0 & 0 & 0 & 0 & 0 & 1 \end{bmatrix} \end{array}.$$

We have the following observations regarding the cycle matrix $B(G)$ of a graph G.

1. A column of all zeros corresponds to a non cycle edge, that is, an edge which does not belong to any cycle.

2. Each row of $B(G)$ is a cycle vector.

3. A cycle matrix has the property of representing a self-loop and the corresponding row has a single one.

4. The number of ones in a row is equal to the number of edges in the corresponding cycle.

5. If the graph G is separable (or disconnected) and consists of two blocks (or components) H_1 and H_2, then the cycle matrix $B(G)$ can be written in a block-diagonal form as

$$B(G) = \begin{bmatrix} B(H_1) & 0 \\ 0 & B(H_2) \end{bmatrix},$$

where $B(H_1)$ and $B(H_2)$ are the cycle matrices of H_1 and H_2. This follows from the fact that cycles in H_1 have no edges belonging to H_2 and vice versa.

6. Permutation of any two rows or columns in a cycle matrix corresponds to relabeling the cycles and the edges.

7. We know two graphs G_1 and G_2 are 2-isomorphic if and only if they have cycle correspondence. Thus two graphs G_1 and G_2 have the same cycle matrix if and only if G_1 and G_2 are 2-isomorphic. This implies that the cycle matrix does not specify a graph completely, but only specifies the graph within 2-isomorphism.

For example, the two graphs given in Figure 10.4 have the same cycle matrix. They are 2-isomorphic, but are not isomorphic.

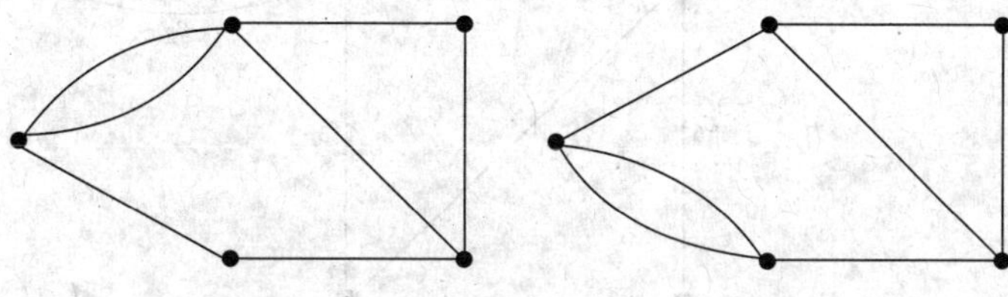

Fig. 10.4

The following result relates the incidence and cycle matrix of a graph without self-loops.

Theorem 10.9 If G is a graph without self-loops, with incidence matrix A and cycle matrix B whose columns are arranged using the same order of edges, then every row of B is orthogonal to every row of A, that is $AB^T = BA^T \equiv 0 \pmod 2$, where A^T and B^T are the transposes of A and B respectively.

Proof Let G be a graph without self-loops, and let A and B, respectively, be the incidence and cycle matrix of G.

We know that in G for any vertex v_i and for any cycle Z_j, either $v_i \in Z_j$ or $v_i \notin Z_j$.

In case $v_i \notin Z_j$, then there is no edge of Z_j which is incident on v_i and if $v_i \in Z_j$, then there are exactly two edges of Z_j which are incident on v_i.

Now, consider the ith row of A and the jth row of B (which is the jth column of B^T).

Since the edges are arranged in the same order, the rth entries in these two rows are both non-zero if and only if the edge e_r is incident on the ith vertex v_i and is also in the jth cycle Z_j.

We have $[AB^T]_{ij} = \Sigma[A]_{ir}[B^T]_{rj} = \Sigma[A]_{ir}[B]_{jr} = \Sigma a_{ir}b_{jr}$.

For each e_r of G, we have one of the following cases.

i. e_r is incident on v_i and $e_r \notin Z_j$. Here $a_{ir} = 1$, $b_{jr} = 0$.

ii. e_r is not incident on v_i and $e_r \in Z_j$. In this case, $a_{ir} = 0$, $b_{jr} = 1$.

iii. e_r is not incident on v_i and $e_r \notin Z_j$, so that $a_{ir} = 0$, $b_{jr} = 0$.

All these cases imply that the ith vertex v_i is not in the jth cycle Z_j and we have $[AB^T]_{ij} = 0 \equiv 0 \pmod 2$.

iv. e_r is incident on v_i and $e_r \in Z_j$.

Here we have exactly two edges, say e_r and e_t incident on v_i so that $a_{ir} = 1$, $a_{it} = 1$, $b_{jr} = 1$, $b_{jt} = 1$. Therefore, $[AB^T]_{ij} = \sum a_{ir} b_{jr} = 1 + 1 \equiv 0 \pmod 2$. ❑

We illustrate the above Theorem with the following example (Fig. 10.5).

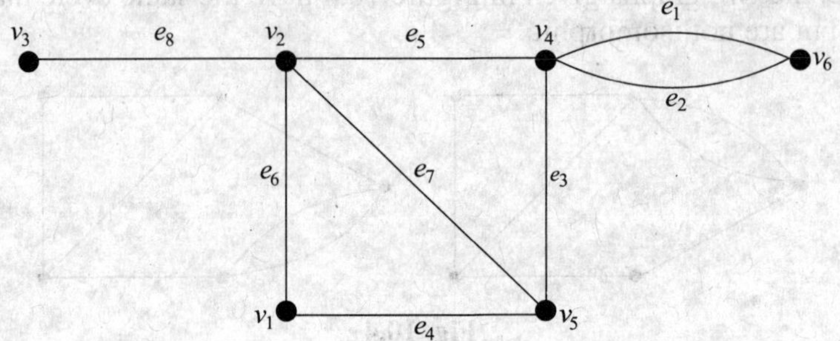

Fig. 10.5

Clearly,

$$AB^T = \begin{bmatrix} 0 & 0 & 0 & 1 & 0 & 1 & 0 & 0 \\ 0 & 0 & 0 & 0 & 1 & 1 & 1 & 1 \\ 0 & 0 & 0 & 0 & 0 & 0 & 0 & 1 \\ 1 & 1 & 1 & 0 & 1 & 0 & 0 & 0 \\ 0 & 0 & 1 & 1 & 0 & 0 & 1 & 0 \\ 1 & 1 & 0 & 0 & 0 & 0 & 0 & 0 \end{bmatrix} \begin{bmatrix} 1 & 0 & 0 & 0 \\ 1 & 0 & 0 & 0 \\ 0 & 1 & 0 & 1 \\ 0 & 0 & 1 & 1 \\ 0 & 1 & 0 & 1 \\ 0 & 0 & 1 & 1 \\ 0 & 1 & 1 & 0 \\ 0 & 0 & 0 & 0 \end{bmatrix}$$

$$= \begin{bmatrix} 0 & 0 & 2 & 2 \\ 0 & 2 & 2 & 2 \\ 0 & 0 & 0 & 0 \\ 2 & 2 & 0 & 2 \\ 0 & 2 & 2 & 2 \\ 2 & 0 & 0 & 0 \end{bmatrix} \equiv 0 \pmod 2.$$

We know that a set of fundamental cycles (or basic cycles) with respect to any spanning tree in a connected graph are the only independent cycles in a graph. The remaining cycles can be obtained as ring sums (i.e., linear combinations) of these cycles. Thus, in a cycle matrix, if we take only those rows that correspond to a set of fundamental cycles and remove all other rows, we do not lose any information. The removed rows can be formed from the rows corresponding to the set of fundamental cycles. For example, in the cycle matrix of the graph given in Figure 10.6, the fourth row is simply the mod 2 sum of the second and the third rows. Fundamental cycles are

$Z_1 = \{e_1, e_2, e_4, e_7\}$
$Z_2 = \{e_3, e_4, e_7\}$
$Z_3 = \{e_5, e_6, e_7\}$

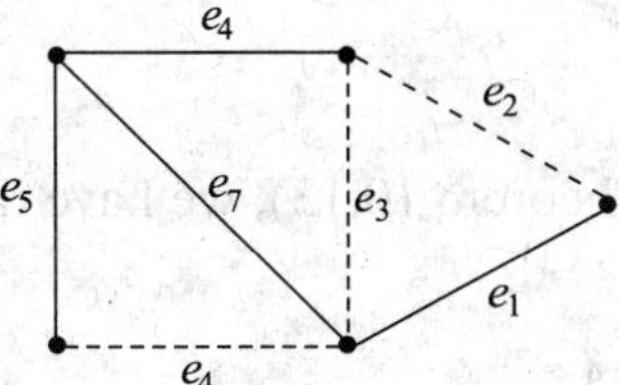

Fig. 10.6

$$\begin{array}{c} \\ Z_1 \\ Z_2 \\ Z_3 \end{array} \begin{array}{c} \begin{array}{ccccccc} e_2 & e_3 & e_6 & & e_1 & e_4 & e_5 & e_7 \end{array} \\ \left[\begin{array}{ccc:cccc} 1 & 0 & 0 & 1 & 1 & 0 & 1 \\ 0 & 1 & 0 & 0 & 1 & 0 & 1 \\ 0 & 0 & 1 & 0 & 0 & 1 & 1 \end{array}\right]. \end{array}$$

A submatrix of a cycle matrix in which all rows correspond to a set of fundamental cycles is called a *fundamental cycle matrix* B_f.

The permutation of rows and/or columns do not affect B_f. If n is the number of vertices, m the number of edges in a connected graph G, then B_f is an $(m-n+1) \times m$ matrix because the number of fundamental cycles is $m-n+1$, each fundamental cycle being produced by one chord.

Now, arranging the columns in B_f such that all the $m-n+1$ chords correspond to the first $m-n+1$ columns and rearranging the rows such that the first row corresponds to the fundamental cycle made by the chord in the first column, the second row to the fundamental cycle made by the second, and so on. This arrangement is done for the above fundamental cycle matrix.

A matrix B_f thus arranged has the form

$$B_f = [I_\mu : B_t],$$

where I_μ is an identity matrix of order $\mu = m-n+1$ and B_t is the remaining $\mu \times (n-1)$ submatrix, corresponding to the branches of the spanning tree.

From equation $B_f = [I_\mu : B_t]$, we have rank $B_f = \mu = m-n+1$.

Since B_f is a submatrix of the cycle matrix B, therefore, rank $B \geq$ rank B_f and thus,

$$\text{rank } B \geq m-n+1.$$

The following result gives the rank of the cycle matrix.

Theorem 10.10 If B is a cycle matrix of a connected graph G with n vertices and m edges, then rank $B = m - n + 1$.

Proof Let A be the incidence matrix of the connected graph G.

Then $AB^T \equiv 0(\text{mod}2)$.

Using Sylvester's theorem (Theorem 10.13), we have rank $A+$ rank $B^T \le m$ so that rank $A+$ rank $B \le m$.

Therefore, rank $B \le m-$ rank A.

As rank $A = n-1$, we get rank $B \le m-(n-1) = m-n+1$.

But, rank $B \ge m-n+1$.

Combining, we get rank $B = m-n+1$. ❑

Theorem 10.10 can be generalised in the following form.

Theorem 10.11 If B is a cycle matrix of a disconnected graph G with n vertices, m edges and k components, then rank $B = m-n+k$.

Proof Let B be the cycle matrix of the disconnected graph G with n vertices, m edges and k components. Let the k components be $G_1, G_2, ..., G_k$ with $n_1, n_2, ..., n_k$ vertices and $m_1, m_2, \ldots, m_k$ edges respectively.

Then $n_1 + n_2 + \ldots + n_k = n$ and $m_1 + m_2 + ... + m_k = m$.

Let $B_1, B_2, \ldots, B_k$ be the cycle matrices of $G_1, G_2, \ldots, G_k$.

$$\text{Then } B(G) = \begin{bmatrix} B_1(G_1) & 0 & 0 & \cdots & 0 \\ 0 & B_2(G_2) & 0 & \cdots & 0 \\ 0 & 0 & B_3(G_3) & \cdots & 0 \\ \vdots & & & & \\ 0 & 0 & 0 & \cdots & B_k(G_k) \end{bmatrix}.$$

We know rank $B_i = m_i - n_i + 1$, for $1 \le i \le k$.

Therefore, rank $B =$ rank $B_1 + \ldots +$ rank B_k

$$= (m_1 - n_1 + 1) + \ldots + (m_k - n_k + 1)$$

$$= (m_1 + \ldots + m_k) - (n_1 + \ldots + n_k) + k = m - n + k.$$ ❑

Definition: Let A be a matrix of order $k \times m$, with $k < m$. The *major determinant* of A is the determinant of the largest square submatrix of A, formed by taking any k columns of A. That is, the determinant of any $k \times k$ square submatrix is called the major determinant of A.

Let A and B be matrices of orders $k \times m$ and $m \times k$ respectively $(k < m)$. If columns $i_1, i_2, \ldots, i_k$ of B are chosen for a particular major of B, then the corresponding major in A consists of the rows $i_1, i_2, \ldots, i_k$ in A.

If A is a square matrix of order n, then $AX = 0$ has a non trivial solution $X \neq 0$ if and only if A is singular, that is $|A| = 0$. The set of all vectors X that satisfy $AX = 0$ forms a vector space called the null space of matrix A. The rank of the null space is called the nullity of A. Further more,

$$\text{rank } A + nullity A = n.$$

These definitions and the above equation also hold when A is a matrix of order $k \times n$, $k < n$.

We now give Binet-Cauchy and Sylvester theorems which will be used in the further discussions.

Theorem 10.12 (Binet–Cauchy) If A and B are two matrices of the order $k \times m$ and $m \times k$ respectively $(k < m)$, then $|AB| =$ sum of the products of corresponding major determinants of A and B.

Proof We multiply two $(m+k) \times (m+k)$ partitioned matrices to get

$$\begin{bmatrix} I_k & A \\ O & I_m \end{bmatrix} \begin{bmatrix} A & O \\ -I_m & B \end{bmatrix} = \begin{bmatrix} O & AB \\ -I_m & B \end{bmatrix},$$

where I_m and I_k are identity matrices of order m and k respectively.

Therefore, $\det \begin{bmatrix} A & O \\ -I_m & B \end{bmatrix} = \det \begin{bmatrix} O & AB \\ -I_m & B \end{bmatrix}.$

$$\text{Thus, } \det(AB) = \det \begin{bmatrix} A & O \\ -I_m & B \end{bmatrix}. \qquad (10.12.1)$$

Now apply Cauchy's expansion method to the right side of (10.12.1) and observe that the only non-zero minors of any order in $-I_m$ are its principal minors of that order. Therefore, we see that the Cauchy expansion consists of these minors of order $m-k$ multiplied by their cofactors of order k in A and B together. ❑

Theorem 10.13 (Sylvester) If A and B are matrices of order $k \times m$ and $n \times p$ respectively, then nullity $AB \leq$ nullity $A+$ nullity B.

Proof Since every vector X satisfying $BX = 0$ also satisfies $ABX = 0$, therefore we have

$$\text{nullity } AB \geq \text{nullity } B \geq 0. \qquad (10.13.1)$$

Let nullity $B = s$. So there exists a set of s linearly independent vectors $\{x_1, x_2, \ldots, x_s\}$ forming a basis of the null space of B. Therefore,

$$BX_i = 0, \text{ for } i = 1, 2, \ldots, s. \qquad (10.13.2)$$

Now let nullity $AB = s+t$. Thus there exists a set of t linearly independent vectors $[X_{s+1}, X_{s+2}, \ldots, X_{s+t}]$ such that the set $\{X_1, X_2, \ldots, X_s, X_{s+1}, \ldots, X_{s+t}\}$ forms a basis for the null space of AB. Therefore,

$$ABX_i = 0, \text{ for } i = 1, 2, \ldots, s, s+1, \ldots, s+t. \qquad (10.13.3)$$

This implies that out of the $s+t$ vectors X_i forming a basis of the null space of AB, the first s vectors are made zero by B and the remaining non-zero BX_i'$s, i = s+1, \ldots, s+t$ are made zero by A.

Clearly, the vectors $BX_{s+1}, \ldots, BX_{s+t}$ are linearly independent. For if

$$b_1BX_{s+1} + b_2BX_{s+2} + \ldots + b_tBX_{s+t} = 0,$$

i.e., if $B(b_1X_{s+1} + b_2X_{s+2} + \ldots + b_tX_{s+t}) = 0,$

then the vector $b_1X_{s+1} + b_2X_{s+2} + \ldots + b_tX_{s+t}$ is the null space of B, which is possible only if $b_1 = b_2 = \ldots = b_t = 0$.

Thus we have seen that there are at least t linearly independent vectors which are made zero by A. So, nullity $A \geq t$.

Since $t = (s+t) - s$, therefore $t =$ nullity AB – nullity B

Therefore, nullity AB– nullity $B \leq$ nullity A, and so

$$\text{nullity } AB \leq \text{nullity } A + \text{nullity } B. \qquad (10.13.4)$$

❑

Corollary 10.2 We know, rank A + nullity $A = n$, and using this in (10.13.4), we get

$$n- \text{ rank } AB \leq n- \text{ rank } A + n- \text{ rank } B.$$

Therefore, rank $AB \geq$ rank A+ rank $B - n$.

If in above, $AB = 0$, then rank A + rank $B \leq n$.

10.4 Cut-Set Matrix

Let G be a graph with m edges and q cutsets. The cut-set matrix $C = [c_{ij}]_{q\times m}$ of G is a (0, 1)-matrix with

$$c_{ij} = \begin{cases} 1, & \textit{if ith cutset contains jth edge}, \\ 0, & \textit{otherwise}. \end{cases}$$

Example Consider the graphs shown in Figure 10. 7.

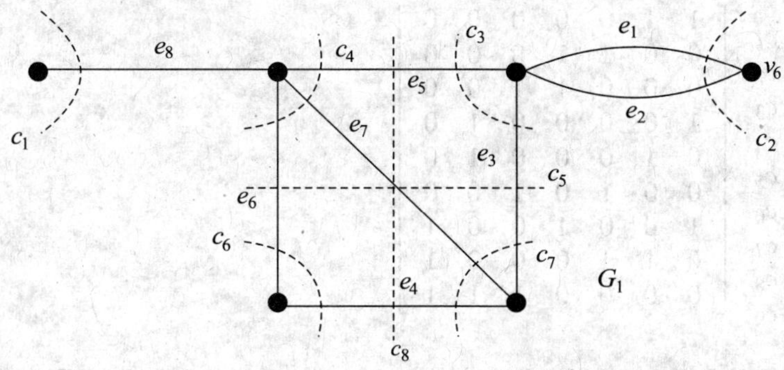

Fig. 10.7(a)

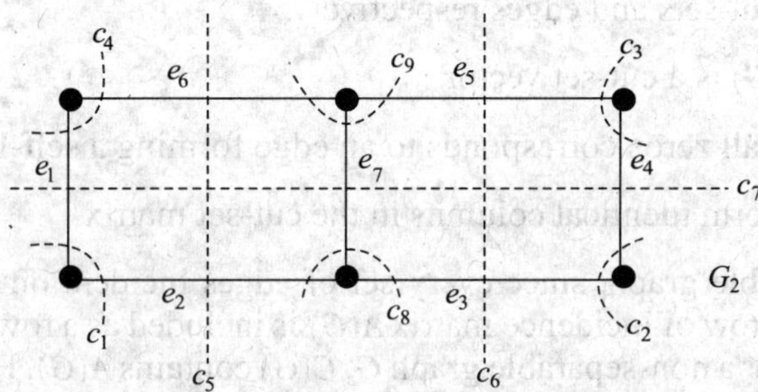

Fig. 10.7(b)

In the graph G_1, $E = \{e_1, e_2, e_3, e_4, e_5, e_6, e_7, e_8\}$.

The cut-sets are $c_1 = \{e_8\}$, $c_2 = \{e_1, e_2\}$, $c_3 = \{e_3, e_5\}$, $c_4 = \{e_5, e_6, e_7\}$, $c_5 = \{e_3, e_6, e_7\}$, $c_6 = \{e_4, e_6\}$, $c_7 = \{e_3, e_4, e_7\}$ and $c_8 = \{e_4, e_5, e_7\}$.

The cut-sets for the graph G_2 are $c_1 = \{e_1, e_2\}$, $c_2 = \{e_3, e_4\}$, $c_3 = \{e_4, e_5\}$, $c_4 = \{e_1, e_6\}$, $c_5 = \{e_2, e_6\}$, $c_6 = \{e_3, e_5\}$, $c_7 = \{e_1, e_4, c_7\}$, $c_8 = \{e_2, e_3, e_7\}$ and $c_9 = \{e_5, e_6, e_7\}$.

Thus the cut-set matrices are given by

$$C(G_1) = \begin{array}{c} \\ c_1 \\ c_2 \\ c_3 \\ c_4 \\ c_5 \\ c_6 \\ c_7 \\ c_8 \end{array} \begin{array}{c} \begin{array}{cccccccc} e_1 & e_2 & e_3 & e_4 & e_5 & e_6 & e_7 & e_8 \end{array} \\ \begin{bmatrix} 0 & 0 & 0 & 0 & 0 & 0 & 0 & 1 \\ 1 & 1 & 0 & 0 & 0 & 0 & 0 & 0 \\ 0 & 0 & 1 & 0 & 1 & 0 & 0 & 0 \\ 0 & 0 & 0 & 0 & 1 & 1 & 1 & 0 \\ 0 & 0 & 1 & 0 & 0 & 1 & 1 & 0 \\ 0 & 0 & 0 & 1 & 0 & 1 & 0 & 0 \\ 0 & 0 & 1 & 1 & 0 & 0 & 1 & 0 \\ 0 & 0 & 0 & 1 & 1 & 0 & 1 & 0 \end{bmatrix} \end{array}, \text{ and}$$

$$C(G_2) = \begin{array}{c} \\ c_1 \\ c_2 \\ c_3 \\ c_4 \\ c_5 \\ c_6 \\ c_7 \\ c_8 \\ c_9 \end{array} \begin{array}{c} \begin{array}{ccccccc} e_1 & e_2 & e_3 & e_4 & e_5 & e_6 & e_7 \end{array} \\ \begin{bmatrix} 1 & 1 & 0 & 0 & 0 & 0 & 0 \\ 0 & 0 & 1 & 1 & 0 & 0 & 0 \\ 0 & 0 & 0 & 1 & 1 & 0 & 0 \\ 1 & 0 & 0 & 0 & 0 & 1 & 0 \\ 0 & 1 & 0 & 0 & 0 & 1 & 0 \\ 0 & 0 & 1 & 0 & 1 & 0 & 0 \\ 1 & 0 & 0 & 1 & 0 & 0 & 1 \\ 0 & 1 & 1 & 0 & 0 & 0 & 1 \\ 0 & 0 & 0 & 0 & 1 & 1 & 1 \end{bmatrix} \end{array}.$$

We have the following observations about the cut-set matrix $C(G)$ of a graph G.

1. The permutation of rows or columns in a cut-set matrix corresponds simply to renaming of the cut-sets and edges respectively.
2. Each row in $C(G)$ is a cut-set vector.
3. A column with all zeros corresponds to an edge forming a self-loop.
4. Parallel edges form identical columns in the cut-set matrix.
5. In a non-separable graph, since every set of edges incident on a vertex is a cut-set, therefore every row of incidence matrix $A(G)$ is included as a row in the cut-set matrix $C(G)$. That is, for a non-separable graph G, $C(G)$ contains $A(G)$. For a separable graph, the incidence matrix of each block is contained in the cut-set matrix. For example, in the graph G_1 of Figure 10.7, the incidence matrix of the block $\{e_3, e_4, e_5, e_6, e_7\}$ is the 4×5 submatrix of C, left after deleting rows c_1, c_2, c_5, c_8 and columns e_1, e_2, e_8.
6. It follows from observation 5, that rank $C(G) \geq$ rank $A(G)$. Therefore, for a connected graph with n vertices, rank $C(G) \geq n-1$.

The following result for connected graphs shows that cutset matrix, incidence matrix and the corresponding graph matrix have the same rank.

Theorem 10.14 If G is a connected graph, then the rank of a cut-set matrix $C(G)$ is equal to the rank of incidence matrix $A(G)$, which equals the rank of graph G.

Proof Let $A(G)$, $B(G)$ and $C(G)$ be the incidence, cycle and cut-set matrix of the connected graph G. Then we have

$$\text{rank } C(G) \geq n-1. \qquad (10.14.1)$$

Since the number of edges common to a cut-set and a cycle is always even, every row in C is orthogonal to every row in B, provided the edges in both B and C are arranged in the same order.

Thus, $BC^T = CB^T \equiv 0 \pmod 2$. (10.14.2)

Now, applying Sylvester's theorem to equation (10.14.2), we have

rank $B+$ rank $C \leq m$.

For a connected graph, we have rank $B = m - n + 1$.

Therefore, rank $C \leq m-$ rank $B = m - (m - n + 1) = n - 1$.

So, rank $C \leq n - 1$. (10.14.3)

It follows from (10.14.1) and (10.14.3) that rank $C = n - 1$. ❑

10.5 Fundamental Cut-Set Matrix

Let G be a connected graph with n vertices and m edges. The fundamental cut-set matrix C_f of G is an $(n-1) \times m$ submatrix of C such that the rows correspond to the set of fundamental cut-sets with respect to some spanning tree. Clearly, a fundamental cut-set matrix C_f can be partitioned into two submatrices, one of which is an identity matrix I_{n-1} of order $n - 1$. We have

$$C_f = [C_c : I_{n-1}],$$

where the last $n - 1$ columns forming the identity matrix correspond to the $n - 1$ branches of the spanning tree and the first $m - n + 1$ columns forming C_c correspond to the chords.

Example Consider the connected graphs G_1 and G_2 given in Figure 10.8. The spanning tree is shown with bold lines. The fundamental cut-sets of G_1 are c_1, c_2, c_3, c_6 and c_7 while the fundamental cut-sets of G_2 are c_1, c_2, c_3, c_4 and c_7.

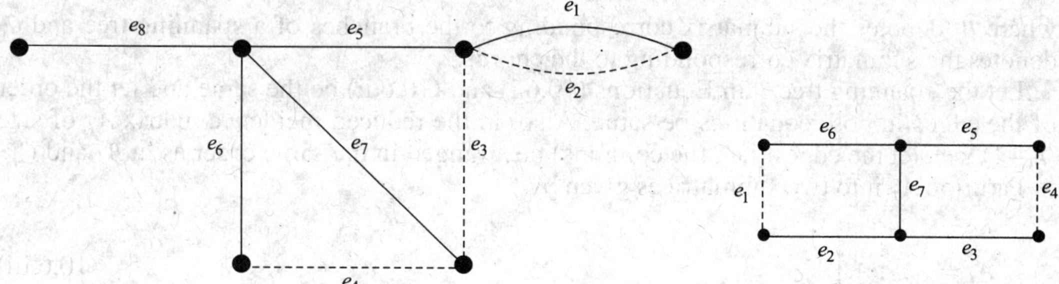

Fig. 10.8

The fundamental cut-set matrix of G_1 and G_2, respectively are given by

$$C_f = \begin{array}{c} \\ \end{array}\begin{bmatrix} 1 & 0 & 0 & \vdots & 1 & 0 & 0 & 0 & 0 \\ 0 & 1 & 0 & \vdots & 0 & 1 & 0 & 0 & 0 \\ 0 & 0 & 1 & \vdots & 0 & 0 & 1 & 0 & 0 \\ 0 & 1 & 1 & \vdots & 0 & 0 & 0 & 1 & 0 \\ 0 & 0 & 0 & \vdots & 0 & 0 & 0 & 0 & 1 \end{bmatrix} \quad \text{(columns } e_2\ e_3\ e_4 \ \vdots\ e_1\ e_5\ e_6\ e_7\ e_8\text{)}$$ and

$$C_f = \begin{matrix} c_1 \\ c_2 \\ c_3 \\ c_4 \\ c_7 \end{matrix}\begin{bmatrix} 1 & 0 & \vdots & 1 & 0 & 0 & 0 & 0 \\ 0 & 1 & \vdots & 0 & 1 & 0 & 0 & 0 \\ 0 & 1 & \vdots & 0 & 0 & 1 & 0 & 0 \\ 1 & 0 & \vdots & 0 & 0 & 0 & 1 & 0 \\ 1 & 1 & \vdots & 0 & 0 & 0 & 0 & 1 \end{bmatrix} \quad \text{(columns } e_1\ e_4 \ \vdots\ e_2\ e_3\ e_5\ e_6\ e_7\text{)}$$

10.6 Relations between A_f, B_f and C_f

Let G be a connected graph and A_f, B_f and C_f be respectively the reduced incidence matrix, the fundamental cycle matrix, and the fundamental cut-set matrix of G.

We have shown that

$$B_f = \left[I_\mu \vdots B_t \right] \tag{10.6.i}$$

and $$C_f = \left[C_c \vdots I_{n-1} \right], \tag{10.6.ii}$$

where B_t denotes the submatrix corresponding to the branches of a spanning tree and C_c denotes the submatrix corresponding to the chords.

Let the spanning tree T in Equations (10.6.i) and (10.6.ii) be the same and let the order of the edges in both equations be same. Also, in the reduced incidence matrix A_f of size $(n-1) \times m$, let the edges (i.e., the columns) be arranged in the same order as in B_f and C_f.

Partition A_f into two submatrices given by

$$A_f = \left[A_c \vdots A_t \right], \tag{10.6.iii}$$

where A_t consists of $n-1$ columns corresponding to the branches of the spanning tree T and A_c is the spanning submatrix corresponding to the $m-n+1$ chords.

Since the columns in A_f and B_f are arranged in the same order, the equation $AB^T = BA^T = 0(\text{mod } 2)$ gives

$$A_f B_f^T \equiv 0(\text{mod } 2),$$

$$\text{or} \quad \begin{bmatrix} A_c \vdots A_t \end{bmatrix} \begin{bmatrix} I_\mu \\ \vdots \\ B_t^T \end{bmatrix} \equiv 0(\text{mod } 2),$$

$$\text{or} \quad A_c + A_t B_f^T \equiv 0(\text{mod } 2). \tag{10.6.iv}$$

Since A_t is non singular, A_t^{-1} exists. Now, premultiplying both sides of equation (10.6.iv) by A_t^{-1}, we have

$$A_t^{-1} A_c + A_t^{-1} A_t B_t^T \equiv 0(\text{mod } 2),$$

$$\text{or} \quad A_t^{-1} A_c + B_t^T \equiv 0(\text{mod } 2).$$

Therefore, $A_t^{-1} A_c = -B_t^T$.

Since in mod 2 arithmetic $-1 = 1$,

$$B_t^T = A_t^{-1} A_c. \tag{10.6.v}$$

Now as the columns in B_f and C_f are arranged in the same order, therefore (in mod 2 arithmetic) $C_f . B_f^T \equiv 0(\text{mod } 2)$ in mod 2 arithmetic gives $C_f . B_f^T = 0$.

Therefore, $\begin{bmatrix} C_c \vdots I_{n-1} \end{bmatrix} \begin{bmatrix} I_\mu \\ \vdots \\ B_t^T \end{bmatrix} = 0$, so that $C_c + B_t^T = 0$, that is, $C_c = -B_t^T$.

Thus, $C_c = B_t^T$ (as $-1 = 1$ in mod 2 arithmetic).

Hence, $C_c = A_t^{-1} A_c$ from (10.6.v).

Remarks We make the following observations from the above relations.

1. If A or A_f is given, we can construct B_f and C_f starting from an arbitrary spanning tree and its submatrix A_t in A_f.
2. If either B_f or C_f is given, we can construct the other. Therefore, since B_f determines a graph within 2-isomorphism, so does C_f.
3. If either B_f and C_f is given, then A_f in general cannot be determined completely.

Example Consider the graph G of Figure 10.9.

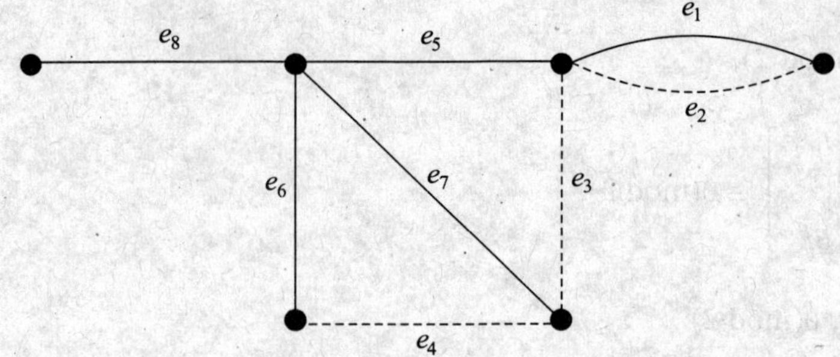

Fig. 10.9

Let $\{e_1, e_5, e_6, e_7, e_8\}$ be the spanning tree.

$$\text{We have, } A = \begin{array}{c} \begin{matrix} e_1 & e_2 & e_3 & e_4 & e_5 & e_6 & e_7 & e_8 \end{matrix} \\ \begin{bmatrix} 0 & 0 & 0 & 1 & 0 & 1 & 0 & 0 \\ 0 & 0 & 0 & 0 & 1 & 1 & 1 & 1 \\ 0 & 0 & 0 & 0 & 0 & 0 & 0 & 1 \\ 1 & 1 & 1 & 0 & 1 & 0 & 0 & 0 \\ 0 & 0 & 1 & 1 & 0 & 0 & 1 & 0 \\ 1 & 1 & 0 & 0 & 0 & 0 & 0 & 0 \end{bmatrix} \end{array}.$$

Dropping the sixth row in A, we get

$$A_f = \begin{array}{c} \begin{matrix} e_2 & e_3 & e_4 & & e_1 & e_5 & e_6 & e_7 & e_8 \end{matrix} \\ \begin{bmatrix} 0 & 0 & 1 & : & 0 & 0 & 1 & 0 & 0 \\ 0 & 0 & 0 & : & 0 & 1 & 1 & 1 & 1 \\ 0 & 0 & 0 & : & 0 & 0 & 0 & 0 & 1 \\ 1 & 1 & 0 & : & 1 & 1 & 0 & 0 & 0 \\ 0 & 1 & 1 & : & 0 & 0 & 0 & 1 & 0 \end{bmatrix} \end{array} = [A_c : A_t].$$

$$B_f = \begin{array}{c} \begin{matrix} e_2 & e_3 & e_4 & & e_1 & e_5 & e_6 & e_7 & e_8 \end{matrix} \\ \begin{bmatrix} 1 & 0 & 0 & : & 1 & 0 & 0 & 0 & 0 \\ 0 & 1 & 0 & : & 0 & 1 & 0 & 1 & 0 \\ 0 & 0 & 1 & : & 0 & 0 & 1 & 1 & 0 \end{bmatrix} \end{array} = [I_3 : B_t] \text{ and}$$

$$C_f = \begin{array}{c} \begin{array}{cccccccc} e_2 & e_3 & e_4 & e_1 & e_5 & e_6 & e_7 & e_8 \end{array} \\ \left[\begin{array}{cccccccc} 1 & 0 & 0 & 1 & 0 & 0 & 0 & 0 \\ 0 & 1 & 0 & 0 & 1 & 0 & 0 & 0 \\ 0 & 0 & 1 & 0 & 0 & 1 & 0 & 0 \\ 0 & 1 & 1 & 0 & 0 & 0 & 1 & 0 \\ 0 & 0 & 0 & 0 & 0 & 0 & 0 & 1 \end{array}\right] \end{array} = [C_c : I_5].$$

Clearly, $B_t^T = C_c$.

We verify $A_t^{-1} A_c = B_t^T$.

Now,

$$A_t = \begin{bmatrix} 0 & 0 & 1 & 0 & 0 \\ 0 & 1 & 1 & 1 & 1 \\ 0 & 0 & 0 & 0 & 1 \\ 1 & 1 & 0 & 0 & 0 \\ 0 & 0 & 0 & 1 & 0 \end{bmatrix}, B_t = \begin{bmatrix} 1 & 0 & 0 & 0 & 0 \\ 0 & 1 & 0 & 1 & 0 \\ 0 & 0 & 1 & 1 & 0 \end{bmatrix}$$

Therefore, $A_t^{-1} Ac = \begin{bmatrix} 1 & 0 & 0 \\ 0 & 1 & 0 \\ 0 & 0 & 1 \\ 0 & 1 & 1 \\ 0 & 0 & 0 \end{bmatrix}$. Hence, $A_t^{-1} A_c = B_t^T$.

10.7 Path Matrix

Let G be a graph with m edges, and u and v be any two vertices in G. The path matrix for vertices u and v denoted by $P(u, v) = [p_{ij}]_{q \times m}$, where q is the number of different paths between u and v, is defined as

$$p_{ij} = \begin{cases} 1, & if\ jth\ edge\ lies\ in\ the\ ith\ path, \\ 0, & otherwise. \end{cases}$$

Clearly, a path matrix is defined for a particular pair of vertices, the rows in $P(u, v)$ correspond to different paths between u and v, and the columns correspond to different edges in G. For example, consider the graph in Figure 10.10.

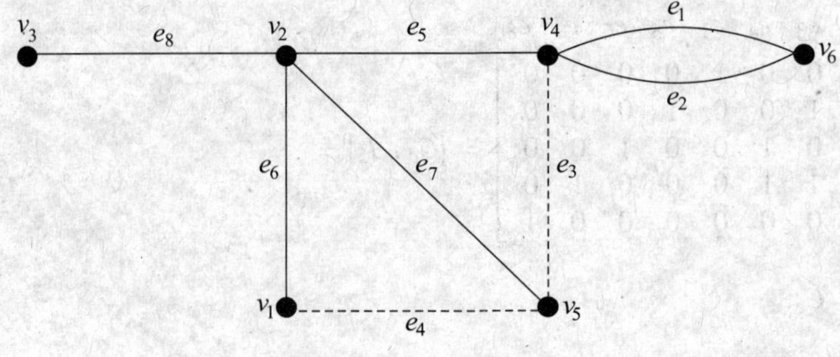

Fig. 10.10

The different paths between the vertices v_3 and v_4 are

$$p_1 = \{e_8, e_5\},\ p_2 = \{e_8, e_7, e_3\} \text{ and } p_3 = \{e_8, e_6, e_4, e_3\}.$$

The path matrix for v_3, v_4 is given by

$$P(v_3, v_4) = \begin{array}{c} \begin{matrix} e_1 & e_2 & e_3 & e_4 & e_5 & e_6 & e_7 & e_8 \end{matrix} \\ \begin{bmatrix} 0 & 0 & 0 & 0 & 1 & 0 & 0 & 1 \\ 0 & 0 & 1 & 0 & 0 & 0 & 1 & 1 \\ 0 & 0 & 1 & 1 & 0 & 1 & 0 & 1 \end{bmatrix} \end{array}.$$

We have the following observations about the path matrix.

1. A column of all zeros corresponds to an edge that does not lie in any path between u and v.
2. A column of all ones corresponds to an edge that lies in every path between u and v.
3. There is no row with all zeros.
4. The ring sum of any two rows in $P(u, v)$ corresponds to a cycle or an edge-disjoint union of cycles.

The next result gives a relation between incidence and path matrix of a graph.

Theorem 10.15 If the columns of the incidence matrix A and the path matrix $P(u, v)$ of a connected graph are arranged in the same order, then under the product (mod 2).

$$AP^T(u, v) = M,$$

where M is a matrix having ones in two rows u and v, and the zeros in the remaining $n-2$ rows.

Proof Let G be a connected graph and let $v_k = u$ and $v_t = v$ be any two vertices of G. Let A be the incidence matrix and $P(u, v)$ be the path matrix of (u, v) in G.

Now for any vertex v_i in G and for any $u-v$ path p_j in G, either $v_i \in p_j$ or $v_i \notin p_j$.
If $v_i \notin p_j$, then there is no edge of p_j which is incident on v_i.
If $v_i \in p_j$, then either v_i is an intermediate vertex of p_j, or $v_i = v_k$ or v_t. In case v_i is an intermediate vertex of p_j, then there are exactly two edges of p_j which are incident on v_i and in case $v_i = v_k$ or v_t, there is exactly one edge of p_j which is incident on v_i.
Now consider the ith row of A and the jth row of P (which is the jth column of $P^T(u, v)$).

As the edges are arranged in the same order, the rth entries in these two rows are both non zero if and only if the edge e_r is incident on the ith vertex v_i and is also on the jth path p_j. Let $AP^T(u, v) = M = [m_{ij}]$.

We have, $[AP^T]_{ij} = \sum_{r=1}^{m} [A]_{ir}[P^T]_{rj}$.

Therefore, $m_{ij} = \sum_{r=1}^{m} a_{ir} p_{jr}$.

For each edge e_r of G, we have one of the following cases.

i. e_r is incident on v_i and $e_r \notin p_j$. Here $a_{ir} = 1, b_{jr} = 0$.

ii. e_r is not incident on v_i and $e_r \in p_j$. Here $a_{ir} = 0, b_{jr} = 1$.

iii. e_r is not incident on v_i and $e_r \notin p_j$. Here $a_{ir} = 0, b_{jr} = 0$.

All these cases imply that the ith vertex v_i is not in jth path p_j and we have $M_{ij} = 0 \equiv 0 \pmod 2$. (Fig. 10.11(a)).

iv. e_r is incident on v_i and $e_r \in p_j$ (Fig. 10.11(b)).

If v_i is an intermediate vertex of p_j, then there are exactly two edges say e_r and e_t incident on v_i so that $a_{ir} = 1$, $a_{it} = 1$, $p_{jr} = 1$, $p_{jt} = 1$.

Therefore, $m_{ij} = 1 + 1 = 0 \pmod 2$.
If $v_i = v_k$ or v_t then the edge e_r is incident on either v_k or v_t. So, $a_{kr} = 1, p_{jr} = 1$, or $a_{tr} = 1, p_{jr} = 1$.

Thus, $m_{kj} = \Sigma a_{ir} p_{jr} = 1.1 \equiv 1 \pmod 2$, and

$$m_{tj} = \Sigma a_{ir} p_{jr} = 1.1 \equiv 1 \pmod 2.$$

Hence $M = [m_{ij}]$ is a matrix, such that under modulo 2,

$$m_{ij} = \begin{cases} 1, & for\ i = k, t, \\ 0, & otherwise. \end{cases}$$ ❑

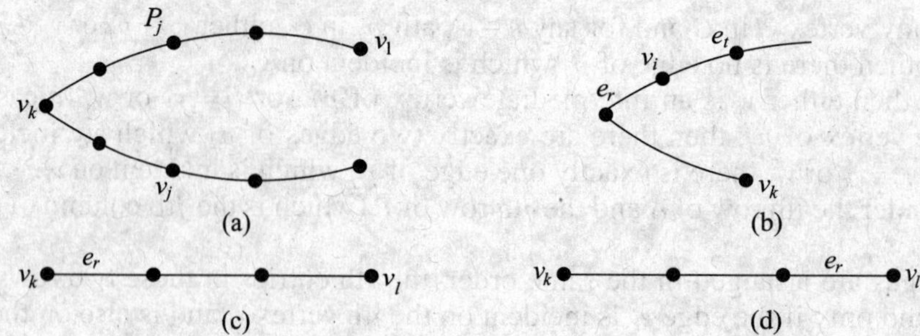

Fig. 10.11

Example In the graph of Figure 10.10, we have

$$AP^T(v_3, v_4) = \begin{bmatrix} 0&0&0&1&0&1&0&0 \\ 0&0&0&0&1&1&1&1 \\ 0&0&0&0&0&0&0&1 \\ 1&1&1&0&1&0&0&0 \\ 0&0&1&1&0&0&1&0 \\ 1&1&0&0&0&0&0&0 \end{bmatrix} \begin{bmatrix} 0&0&0 \\ 0&0&0 \\ 0&1&1 \\ 0&0&1 \\ 1&0&0 \\ 0&0&1 \\ 0&1&0 \\ 1&1&1 \end{bmatrix} = \begin{matrix} v_1 \\ v_2 \\ v_3 \\ v_4 \\ v_5 \\ v_6 \end{matrix} \begin{bmatrix} 0&0&0 \\ 0&0&0 \\ 1&1&1 \\ 1&1&1 \\ 0&0&0 \\ 0&0&0 \end{bmatrix} \pmod 2.$$

10.8 Adjacency Matrix

Let $G(V, E)$ be a graph with $V = \{v_1, v_2, \ldots, v_n\}$, $E = \{e_1, e_2, \ldots, e_m\}$ and without parallel edges. The adjacency matrix of G is an $n \times n$ symmetric binary matrix $X = [x_{ij}]$ defined over the ring of integers such that

$$x_{ij} = \begin{cases} 1, & if\ v_iv_j \in E, \\ 0, & otherwise. \end{cases}$$

Example Consider the graph G given in Figure 10.12.

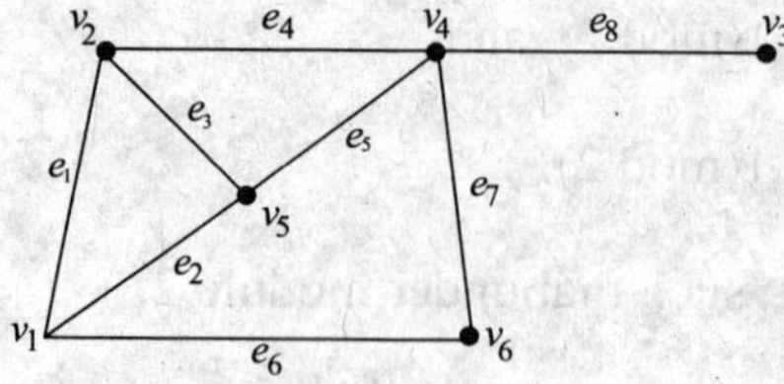

Fig. 10.12

The adjacency matrix of G is given by

$$X = \begin{array}{c} v_1 \\ v_2 \\ v_3 \\ v_4 \\ v_5 \\ v_6 \end{array} \begin{array}{c} \begin{array}{cccccc} v_1 & v_2 & v_3 & v_4 & v_5 & v_6 \end{array} \\ \begin{bmatrix} 0 & 1 & 0 & 0 & 1 & 1 \\ 1 & 0 & 0 & 1 & 1 & 0 \\ 0 & 0 & 0 & 1 & 0 & 0 \\ 0 & 1 & 1 & 0 & 1 & 0 \\ 1 & 1 & 0 & 1 & 0 & 0 \\ 1 & 0 & 0 & 1 & 0 & 0 \end{bmatrix} \end{array}.$$

We have the following observations about the adjacency matrix X of a graph G.

1. The entries along the principal diagonal of X are all zeros if and only if the graph has no self-loops. However, a self-loop at the ith vertex corresponds to $x_{ii} = 1$.

2. If the graph has no self-loops, the degree of a vertex equals the number of ones in the corresponding row or column of X.

3. Permutation of rows and the corresponding columns imply reordering the vertices. We note that the rows and columns are arranged in the same order. Therefore, when two rows are interchanged in X, the corresponding columns are also interchanged. Thus two graphs G_1 and G_2 without parallel edges are isomorphic if and only if their adjacency matrices $X(G_1)$ and $X(G_2)$ are related by

   $$X(G_2) = R^{-1}X(G_1)R,$$

   where R is a permutation matrix.

4. A graph G is disconnected having components G_1 and G_2 if and only if the adjacency matrix $X(G)$ is partitioned as

   $$X(G) = \begin{bmatrix} X(G_1) & \vdots & O \\ \cdots & \vdots & \cdots \\ O & \vdots & X(G_2) \end{bmatrix},$$

   where $X(G_1)$ and $X(G_2)$ are respectively the adjacency matrices of the components G_1 and G_2. Obviously, the above partitioning implies that there are no edges between vertices in G_1 and vertices in G_2.

5. If any square, symmetric and binary matrix Q of order n is given, then there exists a graph G with n vertices and without parallel edges whose adjacency matrix is Q.

Definition: An *edge sequence* is a sequence of edges in which each edge, except the first and the last, has one vertex in common with the edge preceding it and one vertex in common with the edge following it. A walk and a path are the examples of an edge sequence. An edge can appear more than once in an edge sequence. In the graph of Figure 10.13, $v_1e_1v_2e_2v_3e_3v_4e_4v_2e_2v_3e_5v_5$, or $e_1e_2e_3e_4e_2e_5$ is an edge sequence.

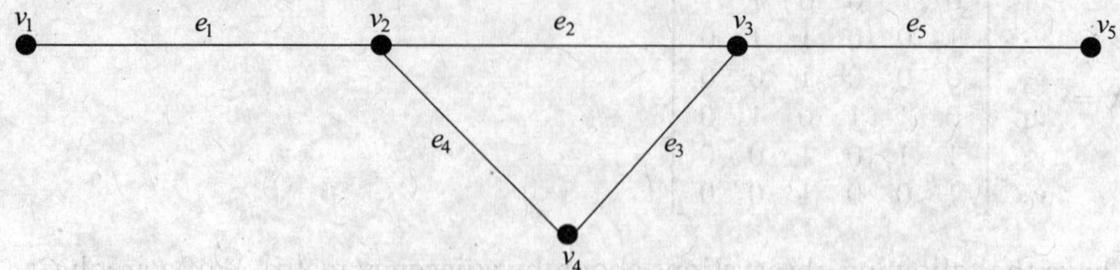

Fig. 10.13

We now have the following result.

Theorem 10.16 If $X = [x_{ij}]$ is the adjacency matrix of a simple graph G, then $[X^k]_{ij}$ is the number of different edge sequences of length k between vertices v_i and v_j.

Proof We prove the result by using induction on k. The result is trivial for $k = 0$ and 1. Since $X^2 = X.X$, X^2 is a symmetric matrix, as product of symmetric matrices is also symmetric.

For $k = 2, i \neq j$, we have

$[X^2]_{ij}$ = number of ones in the product of ith row and jth column (or jth row) of X

= number of positions in which both ith and jth rows of X have ones

= number of vertices that are adjacent to both ith and jth vertices

= number of different paths of length two between ith and jth vertices

Also, $[X^2]_{ii}$ = number of ones in the ith row (or column) of X

= degree of the corresponding vertex.

This shows that $[X^2]_{ij}$ is the number of different paths and therefore different edge sequences of length 2 between the vertices v_i and v_j. Thus the result is true for $k = 2$. Assume the result to be true for k, so that

$[X^k]_{ij}$= number of different edge sequences of length k between v_i and v_j.

We have, $[X^{k+1}]_{ij} = [X^kX]_{ij} = \sum\limits_{r=1}^{n} [X^k]_{ir}[X]_{r_j} = \sum\limits_{r=1}^{n} [X^k]_{i_r}x_{r_j}$.

Now, every $v_i - v_j$ edge sequence of length $k+1$ consists of a $v_i - v_r$ edge sequence of length k, followed by an edge $v_r v_j$. Since there are $[X^k]_{ir}$ such edge sequences of length k and x_{rj} such edges for each vertex v_r, the total number of all $v_i - v_j$ edge sequences of length $k+1$ is $\sum_{r=1}^{n} [X^k]_{ir} x_{rj}$. This proves the result for $k+1$ also. ❑

We have the following observation about connectedness and adjacency matrix.

Theorem 10.17 Let G be a graph with $V = \{v_1, v_2, \ldots, v_n\}$ and let X be the adjacency matrix of G. Let $Y = [y_{ij}]$ be the matrix $Y = X + X^2 + \ldots + X^{n-1}$.

Then G is connected if and only if for all distinct i, j, $y_{ij} \neq 0$. That is, if and only if Y has no zero entries off the main diagonal.

Proof We have, $y_{ij} = [Y]_{ij} = [X]_{ij} + [X^2]_{ij} + \ldots + [X^{n-1}]_{ij}$.

Since $[X^k]_{ij}$ denotes the number of distinct edge-sequences of length k from v_i to v_j,

$$
\begin{aligned}
y_{ij} = {} & \text{number of different } v_i - v_j \text{ edge sequence of length } 1 \\
& + \text{number of different } v_i - v_j \text{ edge sequences of length } 2 + \ldots \\
& + \text{number of different } v_i - v_j \text{ edge sequences of length } n-1.
\end{aligned}
$$

Therefore, y_{ij} = number of different $v_i - v_j$ edge sequence of length less than n.

Now let G be connected. Then for every pair of distinct i, j there is a path from v_i to v_j. Since G has n vertices, this path passes through atmost n vertices and so has length less than n. Thus, $y_{ij} \neq 0$ for each i, j with $i \neq j$.

Conversely, for each distinct pair i, j we have $y_{ij} \neq 0$. Then from above, there is at least one edge sequence of length less than n from v_i to v_j. This implies that v_i is connected to v_j. Since the distinct pair i, j is chosen arbitrarily, G is connected. ❑

The next result is useful in determining the distances between different pairs of vertices.

Theorem 10.18 In a connected graph, the distance between two vertices v_i and v_j is k if and only if k is the smallest integer for which $[X^k]_{ij} \neq 0$.

Proof Let G be a connected graph and let $X = [x_{ij}]$ be the adjacency matrix of G. Let v_i and v_j be vertices in G such that

$$d(v_i, v_j) = k.$$

Then the length of the shortest path between v_i and v_j is k.

This implies that there are no paths of length $1, 2, \ldots, k-1$ and so no edge sequences of length $1, 2, \ldots, k-1$ between v_i and v_j.

Therefore, $[X]_{ij}=0,\ [X^2]_{ij}=0,\ \ldots,\ [X^{k-1}]_{ij}=0$.

Hence k is the smallest integer such that $[X^k]_{ij}\neq 0$.

Conversely, suppose that k is the smallest integer such that $[X^k]_{ij}\neq 0$.

Therefore, there are no edge sequences of length 1, 2, ..., $k-1$ and in fact no paths of length 1, 2, ..., $k-1$ between vertices v_i and v_j.

Thus the shortest path between v_i and v_j is of length k, so that $d(v_i,\ v_j)=k$. ❑

Definition: Let G be a graph and let d_i be the degree of the vertex v_i in G. The degree matrix $H=[h_{ij}]$ of G is defined by

$$h_{ij}=\begin{cases}0, & for\ i\neq j,\\ d_i, & for\ i=j.\end{cases}$$

The following result gives a relation between the matrices F, X and H.

Theorem 10.19 Let F be the modified incidence matrix, X the adjacency matrix and H the degree matrix of a graph G. Then

$$FF^T=H-X.$$

Proof We have $(i,\ j)$th element of FF^T,

$$[FF^T]_{ij}=\sum_{r=1}^{m}[F]_{ir}[F^T]_{rj}=\sum_{r=1}^{m}[F]_{ir}[F]_{jr}.$$

Now, $[F]_{ir}$ and $[F]_{rj}$ are non-zero if and only if the edge $e_r=v_iv_j$. Then for $i\neq j$,

$$\sum_{r=1}^{m}[F]_{ir}[F]_{jr}=\begin{cases}-1, & if\ e_r=v_iv_j\ is\ an\ edge,\\ 0, & if\ e_r=v_iv_j\ is\ not\ an\ edge.\end{cases}$$

For $i=j$, $[F]_{ir}[F]_{jr}=1$ whenever $[F]_{ik}=\pm 1$, and this occurs d_i times corresponding to the number of edges incident on v_i. Thus,

$$\sum_{r=1}^{m}[F]_{ir}[F]_{jr}=d_i,\ \text{for } i=j.$$

Therefore,

$$[FF^T]_{ij}=\begin{cases}-1\ or\ 0, & according\ to\ whether\ for\ i\neq j,\ v_iv_j\ is\ an\ edge\ or\ not,\\ d_i, & for\ i=j.\end{cases}$$

Also, $[H-X]_{ij} = [H]_{ij} - [X]_{ij}$

$$= \begin{cases} d_i - 0, & \textit{for } i = j, \\ 0 - (1 \textit{ or } 0), & \textit{according as for } i \neq j, \ v_i v_j \textit{ is an edge, or } v_i v_j \textit{ is not an edge.} \end{cases}$$

$$= \begin{cases} d_i, & \textit{for } i = j, \\ -1 \textit{ or } 0, & \textit{according as for } i \neq j, \ v_i v_j \textit{ is an edge, or } v_i v_j \textit{ is not an edge.} \end{cases}$$

Hence $FF^T = H - X$. ❑

Corollary 10.3 The matrix $Q = FF^T$ is independent of the orientation used for the edges of G in getting F.

Theorem 10.20 Let X, F and H be the adjacency, modified incidence and degree matrices of the graph G, and $Q = FF^T = H - X$. Then the matrix of cofactors of Q denoted by adj Q is a multiple of the all ones $n \times n$ matrix J.

Proof If G is disconnected, then rank Q =rank $FF^T < n-1$ and so every cofactor of Q is zero. Therefore, adj $Q = O = O.J$, where $J = [J_{ij}]_{n \times n}$ with $J_{ij} = 1$ for all i, j.

Now let G be connected. Then rank $Q = n-1$ and therefore $|Q| = 0$ This implies that every column of adj Q belongs to the kernel (null space) of Q.

But nullity $Q = 1$ (as rank $Q+$ nullity $Q = n$). So, if u is the n-vector of ones, then

$$(H - X)u = 0.$$

and therefore u is in the null space of Q.

Thus every other vector in the null space of Q and in particular every column of adj Q is a multiple of u.

Since Q and so adj Q are symmetric, the multiplying factor for all columns of adj Q are same.

Hence, adj $Q = cJ$, where c is a constant. ❑

The next result called Matrix-tree theorem can be used in finding the complexity of a connected graph.

Theorem 10.21 (Matrix-tree theorem) If X, F and H are the adjacency, modified incidence and degree matrices of the connected graph G, and $Q = FF^T$, J is the $n \times n$ matrix of ones and $\tau(G)$ is the complexity of G, then adj $Q = \tau(G).J$.

Proof Let X, F and H be the adjacency, modified incidence and degree matrix of a connected graph G. We have $Q = FF^T$ and adj $Q =$ matrix of the cofactors of Q. Also $\tau(G)J$ is a matrix whose every entry is $\tau(G)$ as J is a matrix whose every entry is unity.

Therefore, to prove adj $Q = \tau(G)J$, it is enough to prove that $\tau(G) =$ any one cofactor of Q.

Let F_0 be the matrix obtained by dropping the last row from F. Then clearly, $|F_o F_o^T|$ is a cofactor of Q.

Using Binet-Cauchy theorem of matrix theory, we have

$$|F_0 F_0^T| = \sum_{X \subseteq E} |F_x|\,|F_x^T|, \tag{10.21.1}$$

where F_x is the square submatrix of F_o whose $n-1$ columns correspond to $n-1$ edges in the subset X of E, the summation running over all possible such subsets.

We know $|F_x| \neq 0$ if and only if $< X >$ is a spanning tree of G and $|Fx| = \pm 1$.

But, $|F_x^T| = |F_x|$.

Therefore each $X \subseteq E$ such that $< X >$ is a spanning tree of G contributes one to the sum on the right of (10.21.1) and all other contributions are zero.

Hence $|F_o F_o^T| = \tau(G)$, proving the theorem. ❑

Corollary 10.4 Prove $\tau(K_n) = n^{n-2}$.

Proof Here, $Q = H - X = (n-1)I - (J - I) = nI - J$. Therefore,

$$Q = \begin{bmatrix} n & 0 & 0 & .. & 0 \\ 0 & n & 0 & .. & 0 \\ 0 & 0 & n & .. & 0 \\ \vdots & & & & \\ 0 & 0 & 0 & .. & n \end{bmatrix} - \begin{bmatrix} 1 & 1 & 1 & .. & 1 \\ 1 & 1 & 1 & .. & 1 \\ 1 & 1 & 1 & .. & 1 \\ \vdots & & & & \\ 1 & 1 & 1 & .. & 1 \end{bmatrix}$$

$$= \begin{bmatrix} n-1 & -1 & -1 & .. & -1 \\ -1 & n-1 & -1 & .. & -1 \\ -1 & -1 & n-1 & .. & -1 \\ \vdots & & & & \\ -1 & -1 & -1 & .. & n-1 \end{bmatrix}.$$

The cofactor of q_{11} is the $(n-1)\times(n-1)$ determinant given by

$$\text{cofactor of } q_{11} = \begin{vmatrix} n-1 & -1 & .. & -1 \\ -1 & n-1 & .. & -1 \\ \vdots & & & \\ -1 & -1 & .. & n-1 \end{vmatrix}.$$

Subtracting the first row from each of the others and then adding the last $n-2$ columns to the first, we get

$$\text{cofactor of } q_{11} = \begin{vmatrix} 1 & -1 & -1 & .. & -1 \\ 0 & n & 0 & .. & 0 \\ 0 & 0 & n & .. & 0 \\ \vdots & & & & \\ 0 & 0 & 0 & .. & n \end{vmatrix}.$$

Expanding with the help of the first column, we have cofactor of $q_{11} = n^{n-2}$. Thus,

$$\tau(k_n) = n^{n-2}.$$ ❑

10.9 Exercises

1. Characterise A_f, B_f, C_f and X of the complete graph of n vertices.
2. Characterise simple, self-dual graphs in terms of their cycle and cut-set matrices.
3. Show that each diagonal entry in X^3 equals twice the number of triangles passing through the corresponding vertex.
4. Characterise the adjacency matrix of a bipartite graph.
5. Prove that a graph is bipartite if and only if for all odd k, every diagonal entry of A^k is zero.
6. Similar to the cycle or cut-set matrix, define a spanning tree matrix for a connected graph, and observe some of its properties.
7. If X is the adjacency matrix of a graph G and L is the adjacency matrix of its edge graph $L(G)$ and A and H are the incidence and degree matrices, show that $X = AA^T - H$ and $L = A^T A - 2I$.
8. Use the matrix tree theorem to calculate $\tau(K_4 - e)$.
9. Prove that $\tau(G) = \frac{1}{n^2}\det(J+Q)$.

11. Digraphs

The concept of digraphs (or directed graphs) is one of the richest theories in graph theory, mainly because of their applications to physical problems. For example, flow networks with valves in the pipes and electrical networks are represented by digraphs. They are applied in abstract representations of computer programs and are an invaluable tools in the study of sequential machines. They are also used for systems analysis in control theory. Most of the concepts and terminology of undirected graphs are also applicable to digraphs, and hence in this chapter more emphasis will be given to those properties of digraphs that are not found in undirected graphs.

There are two different treatments of digraphs—one can be found in the book by Harray, Norman and Cartwright [106] and the other in the book by Berge [18]. The former discusses the application of digraphs to sociological problems, and the latter gives a comprehensive mathematical treatment. One can also refer to the books by N. Deo [62], Harary [100], Behzad, Chartrand and Lesniak-Foster [16], and Buckley and Harary [41].

11.1 Basic Definitions

Digraphs (Directed graphs): A digraph D is a pair (V, A), where V is a nonempty set whose elements are called the *vertices* and A is the subset of the set of ordered pairs of distinct elements of V. The elements of A are called the *arcs* of D (Fig. 11.1(a)).

Multidigraphs: A multidigraph D is a pair (V, A), where V is a nonempty set of vertices and A is a multiset of arcs, which is a multisubset of the set of ordered pairs of distinct elements of V. The number of times an arc occurs in D is called its *multiplicity* and arcs with multiplicity greater than one are called *multiple arcs* of D (Fig. 11.1(b)).

General digraphs: A general digraph D is a pair (V, A), where V is a nonempty set of vertices, and A is a multiset of arcs, which is a multisubset of the cartesian product of V with itself. An arc of the form uu is called a *loop* of D and arcs which are not loops are called *proper arcs* of D. The number of times an arc occurs is called its multiplicity. A loop with multiplicity greater than one is called a *multiple loop* (Fig. 11.1(c)).

Oriented graph: A digraph containing no symmetric pair of arcs is called an oriented graph (Fig. 11.1(d)).

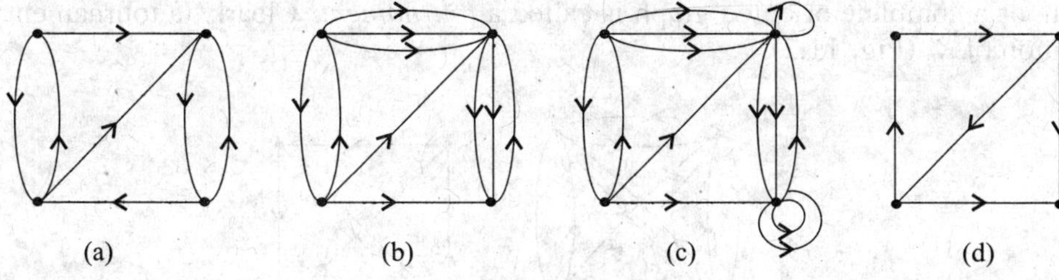

(a) (b) (c) (d)

Fig. 11.1

For $u, v \in V$, an arc $a = (u, v) \in A$ is denoted by uv and implies that a is directed from u to v. Here, u is the *initial* vertex (tail) and v is the *terminal* vertex (head). Also we say that a joins u to v; a is incident with u and v; a is incident from u and a is incident to v; and u is adjacent to v and v is adjacent from u. In case both uv and vu belong to A, then uv and vu are called a *symmetric pair of arcs*. For any $v \in V$, the number of arcs incident to v is the *indegree* of v and is denoted by $d^-(v)$. The number of arcs incident from v is called the *outdegree* of v and is denoted by $d^+(v)$. Berge calls indegree and outdegree as *inner* and *outer-demi degrees*. The *total degree* (or simply degree) of v is $d(v) = d^-(v) + d^+(v)$.

We define $N^+(v)$ and $N^-(v)$ by

$$N^+(v) = \{u \in V : vu \in A\} \text{ and } N^-(v) = \{u \in V : uv \in A\}.$$

If $d(v) = k$ for every $v \in V$, then D is said to be a *k-regular* digraph. If for every $v \in V$, $d^-(v) = d^+(v)$, the digraph is said to be an *isograph* or a *balanced digraph*. We note that an isograph is an even degree digraph, but not necessarily regular. Also, every symmetric digraph is an isograph. Edmonds and Johnson [67] call isographs as asymmetric digraphs and Berge [23] calls them pseudo-symmetric graphs. Kotzig [133, 134] calls an anti-symmetric isograph as oriented-in-equilibrium or a ρ-graph.

A vertex v for which $d^+(v) = d^-(v) = 0$ is called an *isolate*. A vertex v is called a *transmitter* or a *receiver* according as $d^+(v) > 0$, $d^-(v) = 0$ or $d^+(v) = 0$, $d^-(v) > 0$. A vertex v is called a *carrier* if $d^+(v) = d^-(v) = 1$.

Underlying graph of a digraph:

Let $D(V, A)$ be a digraph. The graph $G(V, E)$, where $uv \in E$ if and only if uv or vu or both are in A, is called the *underlying graph* of D. This is also called the *covering graph* $C(D)$ of D. Here we denote $C(D)$ by $G(D)$ or simply by G.

In case G (V, E) is a graph, the digraph with vertex set V and a symmetric uv whenever $uv \in E$, is called the *digraph corresponding* to G, and is denoted by $D(G)$, or D. Clearly, $D(G)$ is a symmetric digraph. An oriented graph obtained from the graph $G(V, E)$ by replacing each edge $uv \in E$ by an arc uv or vu, but not both is called an *orientation* of G and is denoted by $O(G)$ or O.

Complete symmetric digraph:
A digraph $D = (V, A)$ is said to be *complete* if both uv and $vu \in A$, for all $u, v \in V$. Obviously this corresponds to K_n, where $|V| = n$, and is denoted by K_n^*. A complete antisymmetric digraph, or a complete oriented graph is called a *tournament*. Clearly, a tournament is an orientation of K_n (Fig. 11.2).

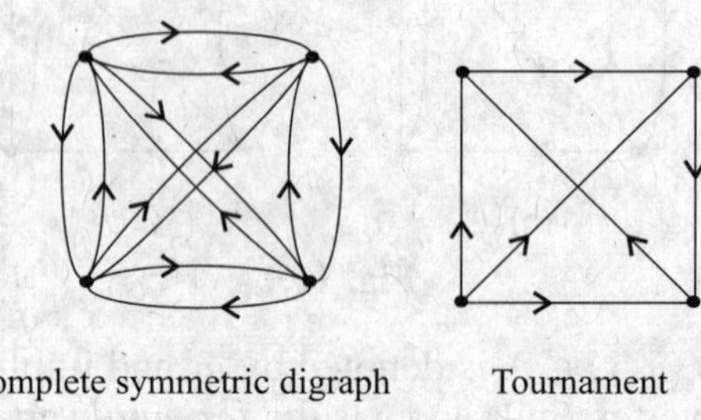

Complete symmetric digraph Tournament

Fig. 11.2

We note that the number of arcs in K_n^* is $n\,(n-1)$ and the number of arcs in a tournament is $\frac{n(n-1)}{2}$.

11.2 Digraphs and Binary Relations

Let A and B be nonempty sets. A *(binary) relation* R from A to B is a subset of $A \times B$. If $R \subseteq A \times B$ and $(a, b) \in R$, where $a \in A$, $b \in B$, we say a "is related to" b by R, and we write aRb. If a is not related to b by R, we write $a \not R\, b$. A relation R defined on a set X is a subset of $X \times X$. For example, less than, greater than and equality are the relations in the set of real numbers. The property "is congruent to" defines a relation in the set of all triangles in a plane. Also, parallelism defines a relation in the set of all lines in a plane.

Let R define a relation on a nonempty set X. If R relates every element of X to itself, the relation R is said to be *reflexive*. A relation R is said to be *symmetric* if for all $x_i\, x_j \in X$, $x_i\, R\, x_j$ implies $x_j\, R\, x_i$. A relation R is said to be *transitive* if for any three elements x_i, x_j and x_k in X, $x_i R x_j$ and $x_j\, R\, x_k$ imply $x_i\, R\, x_k$. A binary relation is called an *equivalence relation* if it is reflexive, symmetric and transitive.

A binary relation R on a set X can always be represented by a digraph. In such a representation, each $x_i \in X$ is represented by a vertex x_i and whenever there is a relation R from x_i to x_j, an arc is drawn from x_i to x_j, for every pair (x_i, x_j). The digraph in Figure 11.3 represents the relation is less than, on a set consisting of four numbers 2, 3, 4, 6.

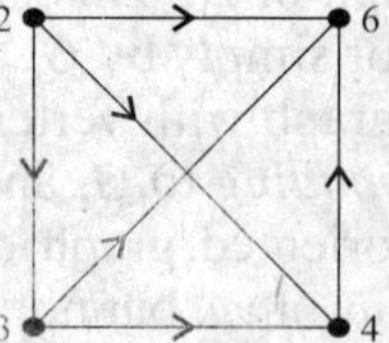

Fig. 11.3

We note that every binary relation on a finite set can be represented by a digraph without parallel edges and vice versa.

Clearly, the digraph of a reflexive relation contains a loop at every vertex (Fig. 11.4). A digraph representing a reflexive binary relation is called a reflexive digraph.

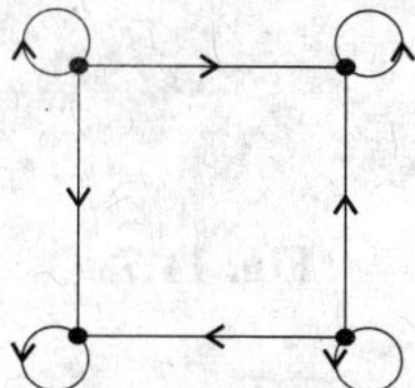

Fig 11.4

The digraph of a symmetric relation is a symmetric digraph because for every arc from x_i to x_j, there is an arc from x_j to x_i. Figure 11.5 shows the digraph of an irreflexive and symmetric relation on a set of three elements.

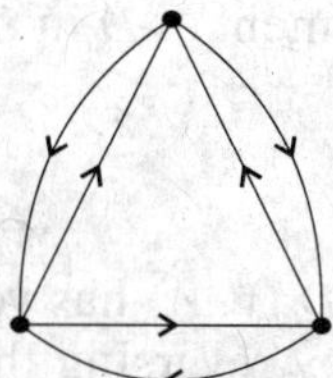

Fig. 11.5

A digraph representing a transitive relation on its vertex set is called a *transitive digraph*. Figure 11.6 shows the digraph of a transitive, which is neither reflexive, nor symmetric.

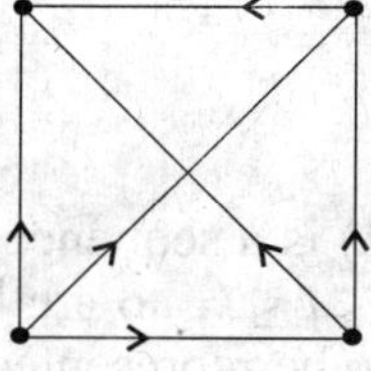

Fig. 11.6

A binary relation R on a set M can also be represented by a matrix, called a relation matrix. This is a (0, 1), $n \times n$ matrix $M_R = [m_{ij}]$, where n is the number of elements in M, and is defined by

$$m_{ij} = \begin{cases} 1 & if\ x_i\ R\ x_j\ is\ true, \\ 0, & otherwise. \end{cases}$$

Isomorphic digraphs: Two digraphs are said to be isomorphic if their underlying graphs are isomorphic and the direction of the corresponding arcs are same. Two non-isomorphic digraphs are shown in Figure 11.7.

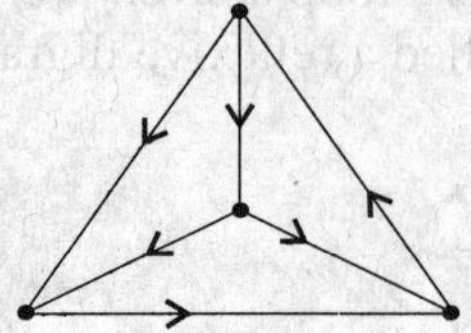
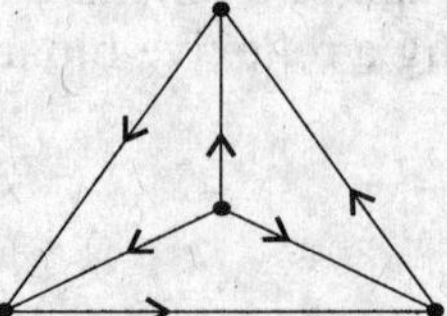

Fig. 11.7

Subdigraph: Let D (V, A) be a digraph. A digraph H (U, B) is the *subdigraph* of D whenever $U \subseteq V$ and $B \subseteq A$. If $U = V$, the subdigraph is said to be *spanning*.

Complement of a digraph:

The *complement* $\overline{D}$ $(V, \overline{A})$ of the digraph D (V, A) has vertex set V and $a \in \overline{A}$ if and only if $a \notin A$. That is, $\overline{D}$ is the relative complement of D in K_n^*, where $|V| = n$.

Converse digraph:

The *converse* $D'(V, A')$ of the digraph D (V, A) has vertex set V and $a = uv \in A'$ if and only if $a' = vu \in A$. That is, A' is obtained by reversing the direction of each arc of D. Clearly, $(D')' = D'' = D$.

A digraph D is *self-complementary* if $D \cong \overline{D}$ and D is said to be *self-converse* if $D \cong D'$. A digraph D is said to be *self-dual* if $D \cong \overline{D} \cong D'$.

11.3 Directed Paths and Connectedness

Directed walks:

A *(directed) walk* in a digraph D $(V\ A)$ is a sequence $v_0\ a_1\ v_1\ a_2\ \ldots\ a_k\ v_k$, where $v_i \in V$ and $a_i \in A$ are such that $a_i = v_{i-1}\ v_i$ for $1 \leq i \leq k$, no arc being repeated. As there is only one arc of the form $v_i\ v_j$, the walk can also be represented by the vertex sequence $v_0 v_1 \ldots v_k$. A vertex may appear more than once in a walk. Clearly, the length of the walk is k. If $v_0 \neq v_k$, the walk is *open*, and if $v_0 = v_k$, the walk is *closed*. A walk is *spanning* if $V = \{v_0, \ldots, v_k\}$.

A *(directed) path* is an open walk in which no vertex is repeated. A *(directed) cycle* is a closed walk in which no vertex is repeated. A digraph is *acyclic* if it has no cycles.

A *semiwalk* is a sequence $v_0 a_1 v_1 a_2 \ldots a_k v_k$ with $v_i \in V$ and $a_i \in A$ such that either $a_i = v_{i-1} v_i$ or $a_i = v_i v_{i-1}$ and no arc is repeated. The length of the semiwalk is k. If $v_0 \neq v_k$, the semiwalk is *open*, and if $v_o = v_k$, the semiwalk is *closed.* If no vertex is repeated in an open (closed) semiwalk, it is called a *semi path (semicycle).*

A spanning path of a digraph is called a Hamiltonian path and a spanning cycle is called a Hamiltonian cycle. A digraph with a Hamiltonian cycle is said to be Hamiltonian.

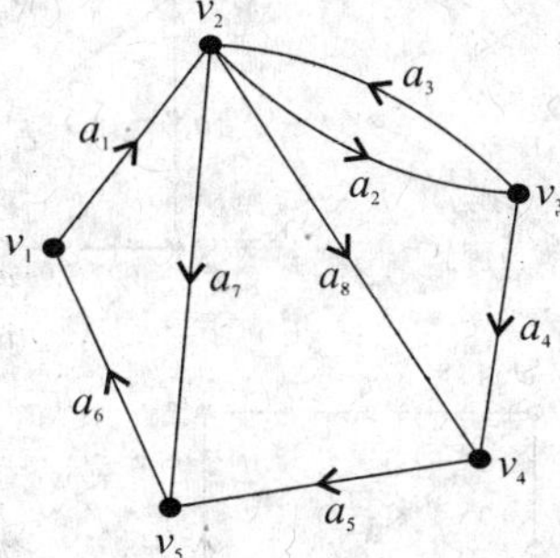

Fig. 11.8

In Figure 11.8, $v_1\ a_1\ v_2\ a_2\ v_3\ a_4\ v_4$ is an open walk, $v_1\ a_1\ v_2\ a_3\ v_3\ a_4\ v_4$ is semiwalk, $v_1\ a_1\ v_2\ a_8\ v_4\ a_5\ v_5$ is a path and $v_1\ a_1\ v_2\ a_8\ v_4\ a_5\ v_5\ a_6\ v_1$ is a cycle.

In a digraph $D\ (V, A)$, a vertex u is said to be *joined* to a vertex v, if there is a semipath from u to v. We note that the relation 'is joined to' is reflexive, symmetric and transitive, and therefore is an equivalence relation on V. A vertex u is said to be *reachable* from a vertex v, if there is a path from v to u. The relation 'is reachable from' is reflexive and transitive, but not symmetric, since there may or may not be a path from u to v. A vertex v is called a *source* of D if every vertex of D is reachable from v, and v is called a *sink* of D, if v is reachable from every other vertex.

Principle of duality for digraphs

While changing a digraph D to its converse D', we observe that the properties about D get changed to the corresponding properties about D'. When D' is changed to $D'' = D$, the original properties of D are obtained. Such type of a pair of properties are called *dual properties*, (transmitter, receiver), (source, sink), (indegree, outdegree), (isolate, isolate) and (carrier, carrier). The dual of a statement P about a digraph is the statement P' obtained from P by changing every concept in P to its dual. For any statements P and Q for digraphs, $P \Rightarrow Q$ in D is true if and only if $P' \Rightarrow Q'$ in D' and for any digraph D there is a converse D'. Therefore for every result in digraphs we get a dual result by changing every property to its dual. This is called the *principle of duality* for digraphs.

Definition:

A digraph is said to be *strongly connected* or strong, if every two of its distinct vertices u and v are such that u is reachable from v and v is reachable from u. A digraph is *unilaterally connected* or unilateral, if either u is reachable from v or v is reachable from u and is *weakly connected* or weak, if u and v are joined by a semipath.

In Figure 11.9, (a) shows a strong digraph, (b) a unilateral digraph and (c) a weak digraph.

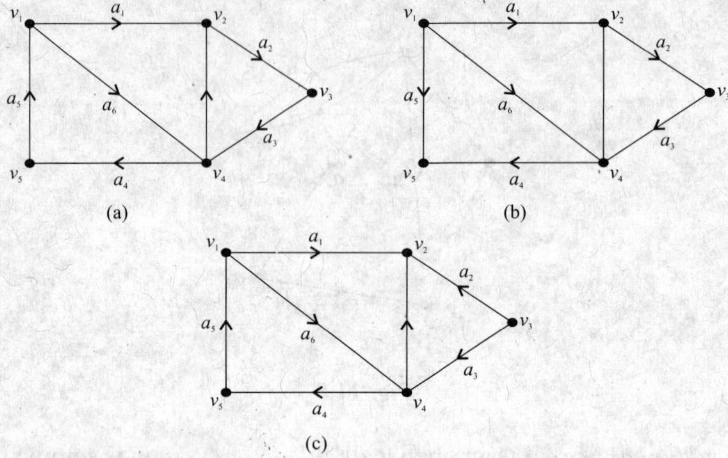

Fig. 11.9

A digraph is said to be *disconnected* if it is not even weak. A digraph is said to be *strictly weak* if it is weak, but not unilateral. It is *strictly unilateral*, if it is unilateral but not strong. Two vertices of a digraph D are said to be

i. 0-connected if there is no semipath joining them,

ii. 1-connected if there is a semipath joining them, but there is no $u-v$ path or $v-u$ path,

iii. 2-connected if there is a $u-v$ or a $v-u$ path, but not both,

iv. 3-connected if there is $u-v$ path and a $v-u$ path.

Definition:
An *arc sequence* in a digraph D is an alternating sequence of vertices and arcs of D.

The following results characterise various types of connectivity in digraphs.

Theorem 11.1 A digraph is strong if and only if it has a spanning closed arc sequence.

Proof

Necessity Let $D(V, A)$ be a strong digraph with $V = \{v_1, v_2, \ldots, v_n\}$. Then there is an arc sequence from each vertex in V to every other vertex in V. Therefore, there exists in D, arc sequences $Q_1, Q_2, \ldots, Q_{n-1}$ such that the first vertex of Q_i is v_i and the last vertex of Q_i is v_{i+1}, for $i = 1, 2, \ldots, n-1$. Also, there exists an arc sequence, say Q_n, with first vertex v_n and the last vertex v_1. Then the arc sequence obtained by traversing the arc sequences $Q_1, Q_2, \ldots, Q_n$ in succession is a spanning closed arc sequence of D.

Sufficiency Let u and v be two distinct vertices of V. If v follows u in any spanning closed arc sequence, say Q of D, then there exists a sequence of the arcs of Q forming an arc sequence from u to v. If u follows v in Q, then there is an arc sequence from u to the last vertex of Q and an arc sequence from that vertex to v. An arc sequence from u to v is then obtained by traversing these two arc sequences in succession. ❑

Theorem 11.2 A digraph D is unilateral if and only if it has a spanning arc sequence.

Proof

Necessity Assume D is unilateral. Let Q be an arc sequence in D which contains maximum number of vertices and let Q begin at the vertex v_1 of D and end at the vertex v_2 of D. If Q is a spanning arc sequence, there is nothing to prove. Assume that Q is not a spanning arc sequence. Then there exists a vertex, say u of D that is not in Q. Also in D, there is neither an arc sequence from u to v_1, nor from v_2 to u. Since D is unilateral and does not contain an arc sequence from u to v_1, D contains an arc sequence from v_1 to u.

Let $w(\neq v_2)$ be the last vertex of Q from which an arc sequence from w to u exists in D. Let Q_1 be an arc sequence from w to u in D. Let z be the vertex in D which is the immediate successor of the last appearance of w in Q. Clearly, D does not contain an arc sequence from z to u. Since D is unilateral, there is an arc sequence, say Q_2 from u to z in D. Traversing Q from v_1 to the last appearance of w, then traversing u, then traversing Q_2 to vertex z and finally traversing Q to v_2, we obtain an arc sequence from v_1 to v_2 which has more distinct vertices than Q. This is a contradiction and thus Q is a spanning arc sequence in D (Fig. 11.10).

The sufficiency follows from the definition. ❑

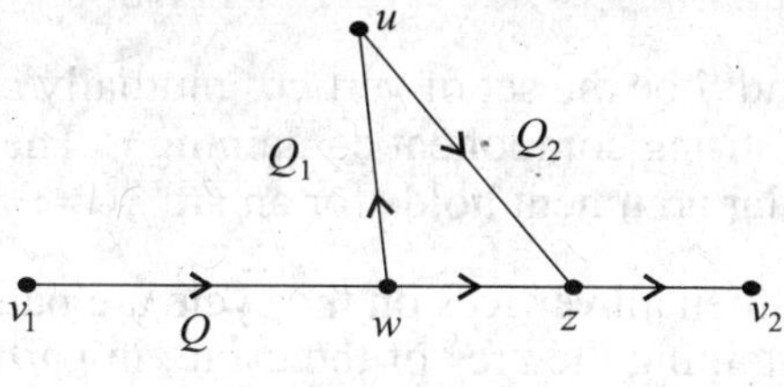

Fig. 11.10

Theorem 11.3 A digraph is weak if and only if it has a spanning semi arc sequence.

Proof Let D (V, A) be a weak digraph with $V = \{v_1, v_2, \ldots, v_n\}$. Since D is weak, there is a semi arc sequence, say Q_i from v_i to v_{i+1} in D for $i = 1, 2, \ldots, n-1$. The semi arc sequence obtained by traversing the semi arc sequences $Q_1, Q_2, \ldots, Q_n$ in succession is a spanning semi arc sequence of D.

Conversely, let D be a digraph containing a spanning semi arc sequence, say Q. Let v_1 and v_2 be two distinct vertices of D. Clearly, v_1 and v_2 are in Q, since Q is spanning. The part of Q which begins at any appearance of v_1 (v_2) and ends at any appearance of v_2 (v_1) represents a semi arc sequence from v_1 to v_2 (from v_2 to v_1) in D. Thus there is either a semi arc sequence from v_1 to v_2, or from v_2 to v_1 in D. Hence D is weak.

Definition: In a digraph D, a *strong component* is a maximal strong subdigraph of D. A *unilateral component* is a maximal unilateral subdigraph of D and a *weak component* is a maximal weak subdigraph of D. In Figure 11.1(b), the digraph has a strong component induced by the vertex set $\{v_2, v_3, v_4\}$. In Figure 11.1(c), the digraph has a unilateral component induced by the vertex set $\{v_1, v_4, v_2\}$ and a weak component which is the digraph itself.

Theorem 11.4

i. Every vertex and every arc of a digraph D belongs to a unique weak component.

ii. Every vertex and every arc of a digraph of D belongs to at least one unilateral component.

iii. Every vertex of a digraph belongs to a unique strong component. Every arc is contained in at most one strong component and it is in a strong component if and only if it is in a cycle.

Proof

i. If a vertex v lies in two weak components W_1 and W_2, let v_1 and v_2 be any two vertices of $W_1 - W_2$ and $W_2 - W_1$. Then there is a vv_1 and vv_2 semi-path. Also there is a $v_1\ v_2$ semipath, so that W_1 and W_2 are in the same weak component. Similar argument holds for an arc.

ii. Since each vertex and each arc is a unilateral subdigraph, the result follows.

iii. Let v be any vertex and S be the set of vertices mutually reachable with v including v itself. Then $\langle S \rangle$ is a strong component containing v. The uniqueness of this follows as in (i). Also, a similar argument holds for an arc.

If an arc uv is in a cycle, then all vertices on the cycle are pairwise reachable and belong to a strong component containing the arcs of the cycle, in particular uv. Conversely, if uv is in a strong component, u and v are mutually reachable and hence there is vu path, which together with uv gives a cycle. ❑

We note that the vertex sets of the weak components of a digraph give a partition π_w of its vertex set V and is called a *weak partition*. Similarly, the vertex sets of the strong components of a digraph give a partition π_s of V, which is a refinement of the partition π_w. This π_s is called the *strong partition*.

Definition: Let $V = S_1 \cup S_2 \cup \ldots \cup S_k$ be a partition π of the vertex set V of the digraph D (V, A). Consider a digraph D_π with vertex set $V_\pi = \{S_1, S_2, \ldots, S_k\}$ which has an arc S_iS_j if and only if in D there is at least one arc from a vertex of S_i to a vertex of S_j. Then D_π is called the *contraction* of D with respect to the partition π.

The contraction of a digraph D with respect to its strong partition π_S is called the *condensation* D^* of D.

Definition: The symmetrisation D^S of a digraph D is obtained from D by adding uv to A whenever $uv \notin A$, but $vu \in A$. Equivalently, $D^S = D(G(D))$, which is the digraph corresponding to the underlying graph of D.

Figure 11.11 illustrates these operations.

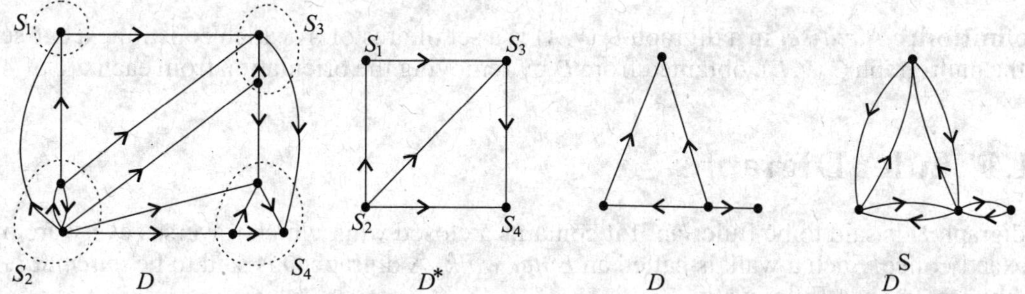

Fig. 11.11

We note from the definition of the condensation that a digraph D and its condensation have the same kind of connectedness.

Theorem 11.5 If S_1 and S_2 are two strong components of digraph D, and $v_1 \in S_1$ and $v_2 \in S_2$, then there is a $v_1 - v_2$ path in D if and only if there is an $S_1 - S_2$ path in D^*.

Proof Let there be a $v_1 - v_2$ path P in D. If length of P is one, then there is an $S_1 - S_2$ arc in D^*. We induct on the length of P. Let the result hold for any path of length $n-1$ in D. Assume that $P = v_1 u_1 u_2 \ldots u_{n-1} v_2$ is of length n. Let $S(u_{n-1})$ be the strong component containing u_{n-1}. Then by induction hypothesis, there is a path P^* from S_1 to $S(u_{n-1})$ in D^*. If $u_{n-1} \in S_2$, this path serves as an $S_1 - S_2$ path. If not, since $u_{n-1} v_2 \in A$, there is an arc from $S(u_{n-1})$ to S_2 in D^*, and thus an $S_1 - S_2$ path.

Conversely, let $S_1 S_3 S_4 \ldots S_2$ be an $S_1 - S_2$ path in D^*. Then there are arcs $u_1 u_3$, $u'_3\, u_4$, $u'_4\, u_5$, ..., $u'_n u_2$ in D, u_i, $u'_i \in S_i$. Since the S_i's are strong components, there are $v_1 - u_1$, $u_3 - u'_3$, $\ldots, u_n - u'_n, u_2 - v_2$ paths in D. These along with the arcs given above form a $v_1 - v_2$ path in D. ❑

The following result can be easily established.

Theorem 11.6 If v_1, v_2 are vertices in different strong components S_1, S_2 of a digraph D, then there is a strict semipath but no path joining v_1 to v_2 if and only if there is a strict semipath and no path from S_1 to S_2 in D^*.

Now we have the following result.

Theorem 11.7 The condensation D^* of any digraph is acyclic.

Proof If D^* contains a cycle, let $S_1 S_2$ be an arc in this cycle. By Theorem 11.1, $S_1 S_2$ lies on a strong component of D^*. Therefore S_1 and S_2 are mutually reachable in D^*, and by Theorem 11.5, there are vertices $v_1 \in S_1$ and $v_2 \in S_2$ which are mutually reachable in D. Thus v_1 and v_2 belong to the same strong component S of D. So, $S_1 = S_2 = S$, and S_1S_2 is not an arc in D^*, contradicting the assumption. ❑

We note that a digraph D is strong if and only if D^* consists of a single vertex.

Definition: A *cut-set* in a digraph $D\,(V,A)$ is a set of arcs of A, which constitute a cut-set in the multigraph $G\,(V,E)$, obtained from D by removing the orientation from each arc of A.

11.4 Euler Digraphs

A digraph D is said to be Eulerian if it contains a closed walk which traverses every arc of D exactly once. Such a walk is called an *Euler walk.* A digraph D is said to be *unicursal* if it contains an open Euler walk.

The following result characterises Eulerian digraphs.

Theorem 11.8 A digraph $D(V,A)$ is Eulerian if and only if D is connected and for each of its vertices v, $d^-(v) = d^+(v)$.

Proof

Necessity Let D be an Eulerian digraph. Therefore, it contains an Eulerian walk, say W. In traversing W, every time a vertex v is encountered we pass along an arc incident towards v and then an arc incident away from v. This is true for all the vertices of W, including the initial vertex of W, say v, because we began W by traversing an arc incident away from v and ended W by traversing an arc incident towards v.

Sufficiency Let for every vertex v in D, $d^-(v) = d^+(v)$. For any arbitrary vertex v in D, we identify a walk, starting at v and traversing the arcs of D at most once each. This traversing is continued till it is impossible to traverse further. Since every vertex has the same number of arcs incident towards it as away from it, we can leave any vertex that we enter along the walk and the traversal then stops at v. Let the walk traversed so far be denoted by W. If W includes all arcs of A, then the result follows. If not, we remove from D all the arcs of W and consider the remainder of A. By assumption, each vertex in the remaining digraph, say D_1, is such that the number of arcs directed towards it equals the number of arcs directed away from it. Further, W and D_1 have a vertex, say u in common, since D is connected. Starting at u, we repeat the process of tracing a walk in D_1. If this walk does not contain all the arcs of D_1, the process is repeated until a closed walk that traverses each of the arcs of D exactly once is obtained. Hence D is Eulerian. ❑

Theorem 11.9 A weakly connected digraph $D(V,A)$ is unicursal if and only if D contains vertices u and v such that $d^+(u) = d^-(u)+1, d^-(v) = d^+(v)+1$ and $d^+(w) = d^-(w)$, for all $w \in V$, where $w \neq u, v$. In this case, the open Euler walk begins at u and ends at v.

Proof Let D be unicursal. Then D has an Euler walk W that begins at u and ends at v. Therefore, as in Theorem 11.8, for every vertex w different from both u and v, we have $d^+(w) = d^-(w)$. Also, the first arc of W contributes one to the outdegree of u while every other occurrence of u in W contributes one each to the outdegree of u. Thus, $d^+(u) = d^-(u) + 1$.

Similarly, $d^-(v) = d^+(v) + 1$.

Conversely, let D be a weakly connected digraph containing vertices u and v such that $d^+(u) = d^-(u) + 1$, $d^-(v) = d^+(v) + 1$ and for each $w \neq u$, v, $d^+(w) = d^-(w)$. In D, add a new arc a joining u and v. Now, we get a digraph D_1 in which the new outdegree of v is one more than its old outdegree, so that $d^-(v) = d^+(v)$. Similarly, $d^-(u) = d^+(u)$, and for every other vertex w, $d^-(w) = d^+(w)$. Also, D_1 is weakly connected, and since $d^-(z) = d^+(z)$ for every vertex z in D_1, it follows from Theorem 11.8 that D_1 is Eulerian. Let W be an Euler walk in D_1. Clearly, D_1 contains all the arcs of D together with the added arc a. Deleting the arc a produces an open Euler walk in D. Hence D is unicursal. ❑

Theorem 11.10 A non-trivial weak digraph is an isograph if and only if it is the union of arc-disjoint cycles.

Proof If the weak digraph D is a union of arc-disjoint cycles, each cycle contributes one to the indegree and one to the outdegree of each vertex on it. Thus, $d^+(v) = d^-(v)$, for all $v \in V$.

Conversely, let D be a non-trivial weak isograph. Then each vertex has positive outdegree and therefore D has a cycle, say Z. Removing the edges of Z from D, we get a digraph D_1 whose weak components are isographs. By using an induction argument, each such non-trivial weak component is a union of arc-disjoint cycles. These cycles together with Z provide a decomposition of the arc set of D into cycles. ❑

Corollary 11.1 Every weak isograph is strong.

Proof If u and v are any two vertices of the weak isograph D, there is a semi path P joining u and v, and each arc of this lies on some cycle of D. The union of these cycles provides a closed walk containing u and v. Thus u and v are mutually reachable. ❑

11.5 Hamiltonian digraphs

Definition: A spanning path of a digraph is called a Hamiltonian path and a spanning cycle a Hamiltonian cycle. A digraph containing a Hamiltonian cycle is said to be Hamiltonian.

Regarding the results on Hamiltonian digraphs, there are surveys by Bermond and Thomassen [24], and by Jackson. There are a number of results that are analogous to those proved for Hamiltonian graphs in Chapter 3. Two early results on sufficient conditions are due to Ghouila-Houri [84] and Woodall [263]. But now we have a more general result due to Meyniel [155]. The proof of Meyniel's result given here is due to Bondy and Thomassen [38].

First, we have the following observations.

Lemma 11.1 Let $P = v_1 v_2 \ldots v_k$ be a path in the digraph D and v be any vertex in $V - V(P)$. If there is no $v_1 - v_k$ path with vertex set $V(P) \cup \{v\}$, then $|\{v, V(P)\}| \leq k+1$, where $\{v, V(P)\}$ is the set of all arcs in D with one end in v or $V(P)$ and the other end in $V(P)$ or v, respectively.

Proof By the assumption on P, for any $v \in V - V(P)$, there is no path $v_i\ v\ v_{i+1}$ in D. Therefore for each i, $1 \leq i \leq k-1$, $|(v_i,\ v)| + |(v,\ v_{i+1})| \leq 1$.

$$\text{Hence, } |\{v,\ V(P)\}| = \sum_{i=1}^{k-1} (|v_i\ ,v)| + |v,\ v_{i+1}| + |(v,\ v_1)| + |(v_k,\ v)|$$

$$\leq (k-1)1 + 2 = k+1.$$ ❑

Let in a digraph $D(V, A)$, S be a proper subset of V. A $u - v$ path of length at least two with only u and v in S is called an *S-path*.

Theorem 11.11 Let D be a strong non-Hamiltonian digraph and $C = v_1 v_2 \ldots v_k v_1$ be a cycle of D such that there is no cycle of D whose vertex set properly contains $V(C) = C$, say. Then there exists a $v \in V - C$, and integers p and $q (1 \leq p,\ q \leq k)$ such that (*i*) $v_p v \in A$, (ii) $v v_{p+i} \notin A$ for i, $1 \leq i \leq q$ and (iii) $d(v) + d(v_{p+q}) \leq 2n - 1 - q$.

Proof

Case 1 *D* has no *C*-path. Since *D* is strong and *C* is a proper subset of *V*, there is a vertex in *C* joined to some vertex of $V - C$ by a path and joined from some vertex of $V - C$ by a path. By the assumption on *C*, there is a cycle C' having only one vertex, say v_p, common with *C*. Let v be the successor of v_p on C' (Fig. 11.12(a)). If v is adjacent to or from any vertex of *C* other than v_p, *D* has a *C*-path. Therefore, $|\{v, C\}| \leq 2$. Clearly, $|\{v_{p+1}, C\}| \leq 2(k-1)$. For any $u \in V - C$, if $v u v_{p+1}$ or $v_{p+1} u v$ is a 2-path, then these are C-paths in *D*. Thus, such adjacencies are not possible. Therefore, $|\{u,\ \{v,\ v_{p+1}\}\}| \leq 2$ for such u. Putting these together, we have

$$d(v) + d(v_{p+1}) \leq 2 + 2(k-1) + 2(n-k-1) = 2n-2,$$

and this verifies the statements with $q = 1$.

Case 2 *D* has a *C*-path, say $P = v_p\ u_1 u_2 \ldots u_s v_{p+r}$, where $u_i \in V - C$. Choose *P* such that r is least. By the assumption on *C*, $r > 1$. Let $v = u_1$.

i. By the assumption on *C* and the minimality of r, v is not adjacent to any v_{p+i}, $1 \leq i \leq r-1$. Therefore the path $Q = v_{p+r}\ v_{p+r+1} \ldots v_k \ldots v_1 \ldots v_p$ and v satisfy the hypothesis of Lemma 11.1 and we have

$$|\{v, V(Q)\}| = |\{v, C\}| \le k-r+2. \tag{11.11.1}$$

ii. By the minimality of r, we observe that for any $u \in V-C$, vuv_{p+i} or $v_{p+i}\ uv$ are not possible paths in D, for $1 \le i \le r-1$ (Fig. 11.12(b)). Thus, for any $u \in V-C$,

$$|\{u, \{v, v_{p+i}\}\}| = 2, \text{ for any such } i. \tag{11.11.2}$$

iii. Since D is strong, there are $v_p - v_{p+r}$ and $v_{p+r} - v_p$ paths in D. Clearly, $v_{p+r}v_{p+r+1}\ldots v_kv_1v_2\ldots v_p$ is such a $v_{p+r} - v_p$ path. It is possible that there are other $v_{p+r} - v_p$ paths containing all these vertices and some more, say $v_{p+1}\ v_{p+2}\ldots.v_{p+i-1}$. Let q be the largest integer i, $1 \le i \le r$ such that there is a $v_{p+r} - v_p$ path with vertex set $S = \{v_{p+r}, v_{p+r+1}, \ldots, v_1, v_2, \ldots, v_{p-1}, v_{p+1}, \ldots, v_{p+q-2}, v_{p+q-1}, v_p\}$ and let P' be such a path. By the assumption on C, S cannot contain all the vertices of C, since $P \cup P'$ is a cycle. Therefore, $q < r$. It is possible that $q = 1$ (Fig. 11.12 (c)). Now the lemma is applicable for v_{p+q} and P'. Therefore,

$$|\{V_{p+q}, V(P')\}| \le k-r+q+1. \tag{11.11.3}$$

Using (11.11.2) with $i = q$, we have

$$|\{u, \{v, v_{p+q}\}\}| \le 2, \text{ for each } u \in V-C. \tag{11.11.4}$$

Also, v_{p+q} can be joined to and from any of the other $r-q-1$ vertices among

$$\{v_{p+q+1}, \ldots, v_{p+r-1}\}. \tag{11.11.5}$$

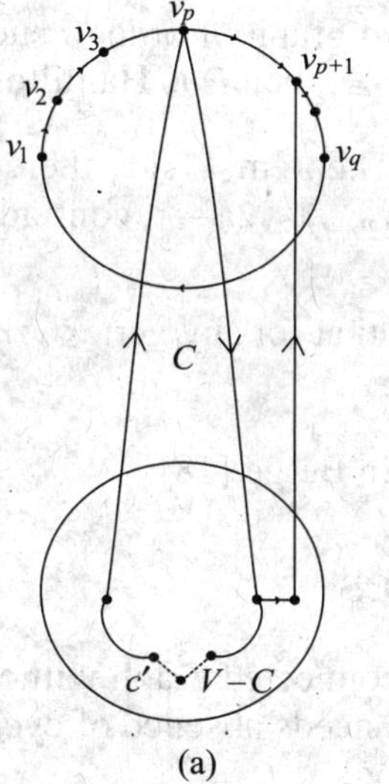

(a)

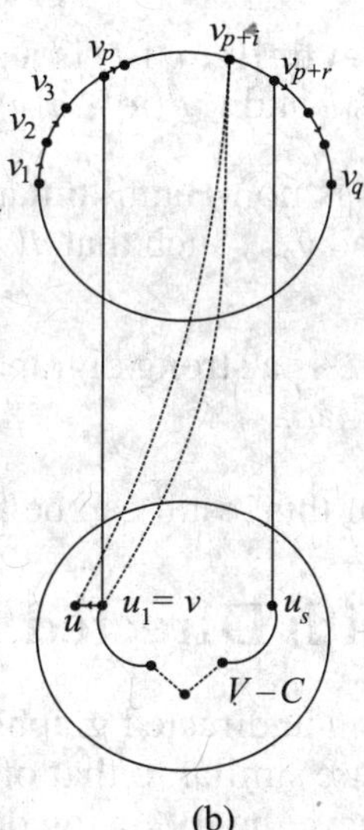

(b)

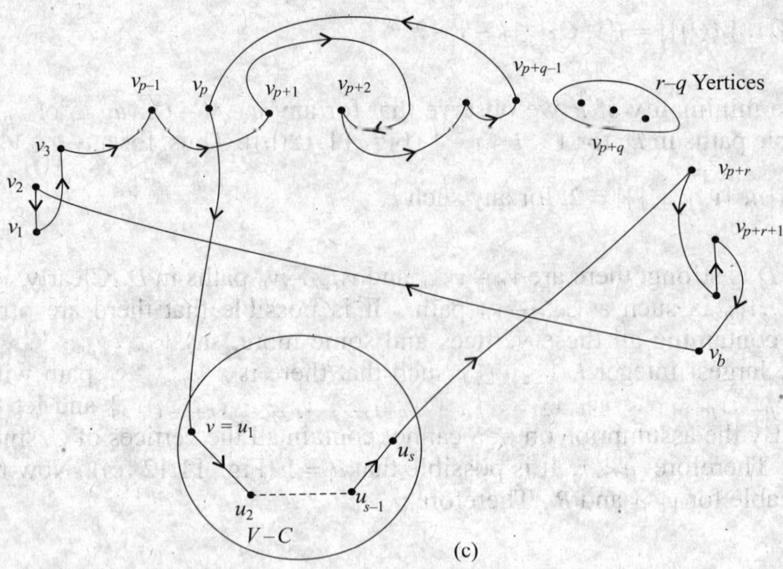

Fig. 11.12

Combining all these, we get

$$\begin{aligned}
d(v)+d(v_{p+q}) &= |\{v,C\}|+|\{v_{p+q},V(P')\}|+|\{v_{p+q},\{v_{p+q+1},\ldots,v_{p+r-1}\}\}| \\
&\quad + \sum_{u\in V-C} |\{u,\{v,v_{p+q}\}\}| \\
&\leq (k-r+2)+(k-r+q+1)+2(r-q-1)+2(n-k-1) \\
&= 2n-q-1.
\end{aligned}$$

❑

Theorem 11.12 (Meyneil) If D is a strong digraph of order n such that for any pair of non-adjacent vertices u and v, $d(u)+d(v)\geq 2n-1$, then D is Hamiltonian.

Proof If such a D is non-Hamiltonian, by Theorem 11.11, there exists a pair of non-adjacent vertices v and v_{p+q} such that $d(v)+d(v_{p+q})<2n-1$, contradicting the hypothesis. ❑

Corollary 11.2 If D is a strong digraph such that for any vertex v, $d(v)=d^+(v)+d^-(v)\geq n$, then D is Hamiltonian.

The direct proof of this result can be found in Berge [18].

11.6 Trees with Directed Edges

We know that a tree in undirected graphs is a connected graph without cycles. But in case of digraphs, a structure similar to that of a tree needs absence of cycles as well as absence of semi cycles. We have the following definition.

A *(directed) tree* is a connected digraph without cycles, neither directed cycles nor semi cycles. We observe that a tree with n vertices has $n-1$ directed edges, and has properties analogous to those of trees with undirected edges. A digraph whose weak components are trees is called a *forest*. For example, Figure 11.13 shows a tree.

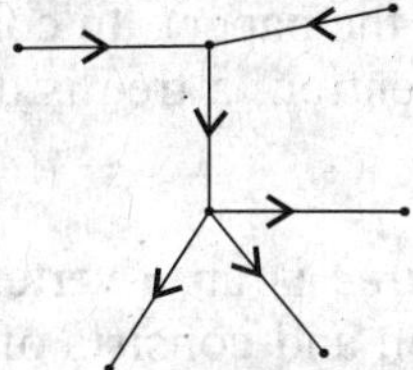

Fig. 11.13

Arborescence: A (directed) tree is said to be an *arborescence* if it contains exactly one vertex, called the *root*, with no arcs directed towards it and if all the arcs on any semipath are directed away from the root. For example, the tree in Figure 11.14 is an arborescence. That is, every vertex other than the root has indegree exactly one. Arborescence is also called an *out-tree*. If the direction of every arc in an arborescence is reversed, we get a tree called an *in-tree*.

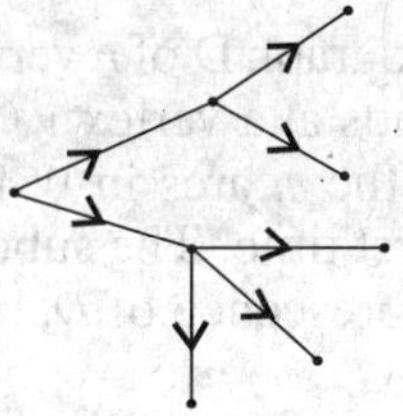

Fig. 11.14

Theorem 11.13 In an arborescence, there is a directed path from the root v to every other vertex. Conversely, a digraph D without cycles is an arborescence if there is a vertex v in D such that every other vertex is reachable from v and v is not reachable from any other vertex.

Proof In an arborescence, consider a directed path P starting from the root v and continuing as far as possible. Clearly, P can end only at a pendant vertex, since otherwise, we get a vertex whose indegree is two or more, which is a contradiction. Since an arborescence is connected, every vertex lies on some directed path from the root v to each of the pendant vertices.

Conversely, since every vertex in D is reachable from v and D has no cycle, D is a tree. Further, since v is not reachable from any other vertex, $d^-(v) = 0$. Every other vertex is reachable from v and therefore indegree of each of these vertices is at least one. The indegree is not greater than one, because there are only $n-1$ arcs in D, n being the number of vertices of D. ❑

Ordered trees: A tree in which the relative order of subtrees meeting at each vertex is preserved is called an *ordered tree* or a planar tree (because the tree can be visualised as rigidly embedded in the plane of the paper). In computer science, the term tree usually means an ordered tree and by convention, a tree is drawn hanging down with the root at the top.

Spanning trees: A *spanning tree* is an n-vertex connected digraph analogous to a spanning tree in an undirected graph and consists of $n-1$ directed arcs. A *spanning arborescence* in a connected digraph is a spanning tree that is an arborescence. For example, $\{a, b, c, g\}$ is a spanning arborescence in Figure 11.15.

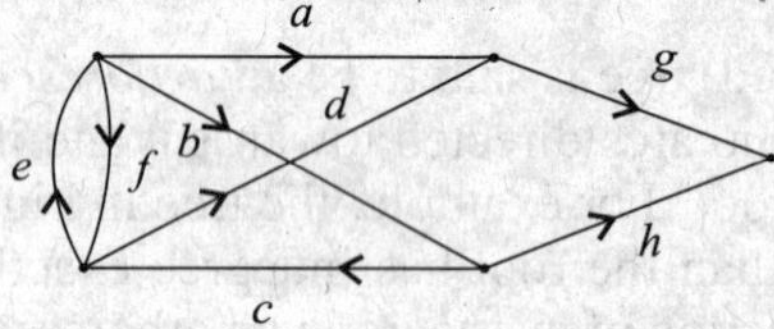

Fig. 11.15

Theorem 11.14 In a connected isograph D of n vertices and m arcs, let $W = (a_1, a_2, \ldots, a_m)$ be an Euler line, which starts and ends at a vertex v (that is, v is the initial vertex of a_1 and the terminal vertex of a_m). Among the m arcs in W there are $n-1$ arcs that enter each of $n-1$ vertices, other than v, for the first time. The subdigraph D_1 of these $n-1$ arcs together with the n vertices is a spanning arborescence of D, rooted at vertex v.

Proof In the subdigraph D_1, vertex v is of indegree zero, and every other vertex is of indegree one, for D_1 includes exactly one arc going to each of the $n-1$ vertices and no arc going to v. Further, the way D_1 is defined in W, implies that D_1 is connected and contains $n-1$ arcs. Therefore D_1 is a spanning arborescence in D and is rooted at v. ❑

Illustration: In Figure 11.16, $W = (b\ d\ c\ e\ f\ g\ h\ a)$ is an Euler line, starting and ending at vertex 2. The subdigraph $\{b, d, f\}$ is a spanning arborescence rooted at vertex 2.

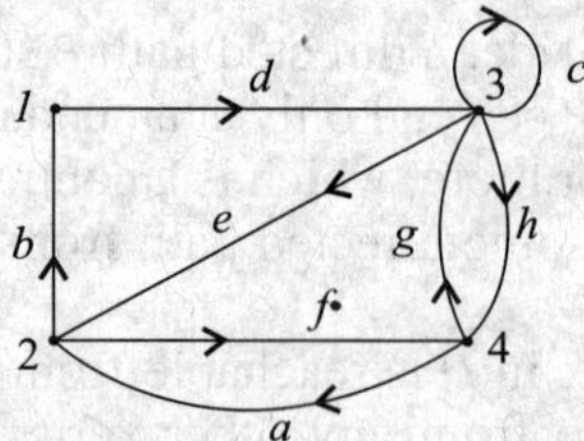

Fig. 11.16

The following result is due to Van Aardenne-Ehrenfest and N.G. de Bruijn [257].

Theorem 11.15 Let D be an Euler digraph and T be a spanning in-tree in D, rooted at a vertex v. Let a_1 be an arc in D incident out of the vertex v. Then a directed walk $W = (a_1, a_2, \ldots, a_m)$ is a directed Euler line, if it is constructed as follows.

i. No arc is included in W more than once.

ii. In exiting a vertex the one arc belonging to T is not used until all other outgoing arcs have been traversed.

iii. The walk is terminated only when a vertex is reached from which there is no arc left on which to exit.

Proof The walk W terminates at v, since all vertices have been entered as often as they have been left (because D is an isograph). Now assume there is an arc a in D that has not been included in W. Let u be the terminal vertex of a. Since D is an isograph, u is also the initial vertex of some arc b not included in W. Arc b going out of vertex u is in T, according to (i). This omitted arc leads to another omitted arc c in T, and so on. Finally we arrive at v and find an outgoing arc not included in W. This contradicts (iii). ❑

Theorem 11.14 provides a method of obtaining a spanning arborescence rooted at any specified vertex, provided the digraph is Eulerian. Conversely, given a spanning arborescence in an Euler digraph, an Euler line can be constructed using Theorem 11.15.

The number of distinct Euler lines formed from a given in-tree T and starting with arc a_1 at v, can be computed by considering all the choices available at each vertex, after starting with a_1. Since there is exactly one outgoing arc in T at each vertex and this arc is to be selected last ((ii), Theorem 11.15), the remaining $d^+(v_i) - 1$ arcs at vertex v_i can be chosen in $(d^+(v_i) - 1)!$ ways. Since these are independent choices, we have altogether $\prod_{i=1}^{n} (d^+(v_i) - 1)!$ different Euler lines that meet (i), (ii) and (iii) of Theorem 11.15.

Illustration: Consider Figure 11.17. We apply (i), (ii) and (iii) of Theorem 11.15 to obtain different Euler lines from the in-tree $\{a_2, a_3, a_7, a_{10}, a_{11}\}$, starting with arc a_1. The two Euler lines obtained are $(a_1\, a_{12}\, a_5\, a_6\, a_7\, a_8\, a_9\, a_{10}\, a_{11}\, a_2\, a_4\, a_3)$ and $(a_1\, a_{12}\, a_8\, a_9\, a_{10}\, a_{11}\, a_5\, a_6\, a_7\, a_2\, a_4\, a_3)$.

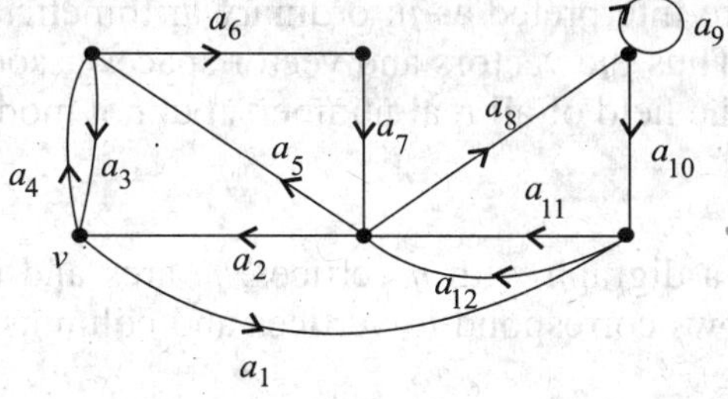

Fig. 11.17

Here, $\prod_{i=1}^{n}(d^+(v_i)-1)! = 2$.

Note that these are not all the Euler lines in the digraph, but only those that are generated by the specific in-tree in accordance with (i), (ii) and (iii) of Theorem 11.15.

Fundamental cycles in digraphs:

The arcs of a connected digraph not included in a specified spanning tree T are called the *chords* with respect to T. As in undirected graphs, every chord c_i added to the spanning tree T produces a fundamental cycle, which is a directed cycle or a semi cycle.

A *cut-set* in a connected digraph D induces a partitioning of the vertices of D into two disjoint subsets V_1 and V_2 such that the cut-set consists of all those arcs that have one end vertex in V_1 and the other in V_2. All arcs in the cut-set can be directed from V_1 to V_2, or from V_2 to V_1, or some arcs can be directed from V_1 to V_2 and others from V_2 to V_1. A cut-set in which all arcs are oriented in the same direction is called a *directed cut-set*.

Consider the digraph of Figure 11.18. A spanning tree $T = \{a, d, f, h, k\}$ is shown by bold lines. Here, rank $= 5$, nullity $= 4$. The chord set with respect to T is $\{b, c, e, g\}$. Fundamental cycles with respect to T are dfe (semi cycle), $dkhc$ (semi cycle), khg (semi cycle) and $adkhb$ (directed cycle). The fundamental cut-sets with respect to T are ab, $bcde$, ef, $bcgk$ and $bcgh$.

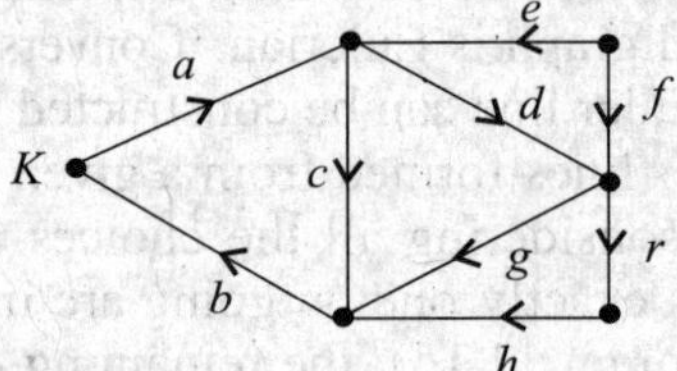

Fig. 11.18

11.7 Matrices A, B and C of Digraphs

The matrices associated with a digraph are almost similar to those discussed for an undirected graph, with the difference that in matrices of digraphs consist of 1, 0, −1 instead of only 0 and 1 for undirected graphs. The numbers 1, 0, −1 are real numbers and their addition and multiplication are interpreted as in ordinary arithmetic, not modulo 2 arithmetic as in undirected graphs. Thus the vectors and vector spaces associated with a digraph and its subdigraphs are over the field of all real numbers, but not modulo 2.

Incidence matrix:

The incidence matrix of a digraph with n vertices, m arcs and no self-loops is an $n \times m$ matrix $A = [a_{ij}]$, whose rows correspond to vertices and columns correspond to arcs, such that

$$a_{ij} = \begin{cases} 1, & if\ jth\ arc\ is\ incident\ out\ of\ ith\ vertex\,, \\ -1, & if\ jth\ arc\ is\ incident\ into\ ith\ vertex\,, \\ 0, & if\ jth\ arc\ is\ not\ incident\ on\ ith\ vertex\,. \end{cases}$$

For example, consider the digraph of Figure 11.19.

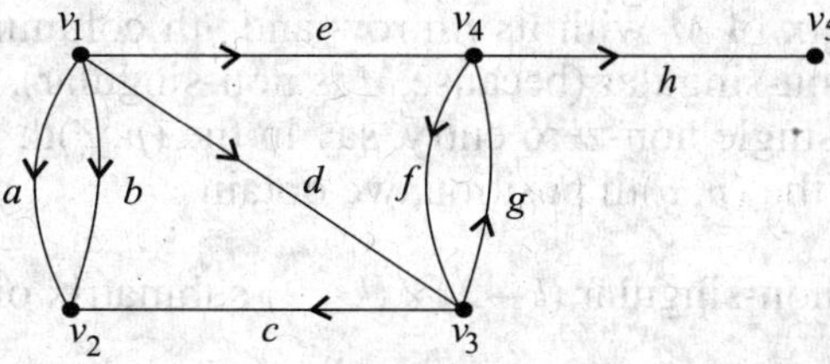

Fig. 11.19

The incidence matrix is given by

$$A = \begin{matrix} \\ v_1 \\ v_2 \\ v_3 \\ v_4 \\ v_5 \end{matrix} \begin{matrix} \begin{matrix} a & b & c & d & e & f & g & h \end{matrix} \\ \begin{bmatrix} 1 & 1 & 0 & 1 & 1 & 0 & 0 & 0 \\ -1 & -1 & -1 & 0 & 0 & 0 & 0 & 0 \\ 0 & 0 & 1 & -1 & 0 & -1 & 1 & 0 \\ 0 & 0 & 0 & 0 & -1 & 1 & -1 & 1 \\ 0 & 0 & 0 & 0 & 0 & 0 & 0 & -1 \end{bmatrix} \end{matrix}$$

Now, since the sum of each column is zero, the rank of the incidence matrix of a digraph of n vertices is less than n. The proof of the following result is almost similar to the result in undirected graphs.

Theorem 11.16 If $A(D)$ is the incidence matrix of a connected digraph of n vertices, then rank of $A(D) = n-1$.

We further note that after deleting any row from A, we get A_f, the $(n-1)\times m$ reduced incidence matrix. The vertex corresponding to the deleted row is called the reference vertex.

We now have the following result.

Theorem 11.17 The determinant of every square submatrix of A, which is the incidence matrix of a digraph, is -1, or 1, or 0.

Proof Consider a $k \times k$ submatrix M of A. If M has any column or row consisting of all zeros, then clearly $\det M = 0$. Also, $\det M = 0$, if every column of M contains the two non-zero entries, 1 and -1.

Now let $\det M \neq 0$. Then the sum of entries in each column of M is not zero. Therefore M has a column in which there is a single non-zero element that is either 1 or -1. Let this single element be in the (i, j)th position in M. Thus,

$$\det M = \pm 1 \det M_{ij},$$

where M_{ij} is the submatrix of M with its ith row and jth column deleted. The $(k-1)\times(k-1)$ submatrix M_{ij} is non-singular (because M is non-singular), therefore M_{ij} also has at least one column with a single non-zero entry, say in the (p, q)th position. Expanding det M_{ij} about this element in the (p, q)th position, we obtain

$$\det M_{ij} = \pm\,[\text{det of non-singular } (k-2)\times(k-2) \text{ submatrix of } M].$$

Repeated application of this procedure gives

$$\det M = \pm 1.$$ ❑

Unimodular matrix: A matrix is said to be unimodular if the determinant of its every square submatrix is 1, -1, or 0.

Cycle matrix of a digraph: Let D be a digraph with m arcs and q cycles (directed cycles or semi cycles). An arbitrary orientation (clockwise or counter clockwise) is assigned to each of the q cycles. Then a cycle matrix $B = [b_{ij}]$ of the digraph G is a $q \times m$ matrix defined by

$$b_{ij} = \begin{cases} 1, & \textit{if the ith cycle includes the jth arc, and the orientations of the arc} \\ & \textit{and cycle coincide}, \\ -1, & \textit{if the ith cycle includes the jth arc, and the orientations of the two} \\ & \textit{are opposite}, \\ 0, & \textit{if the ith cycle does not include the jth arc}. \end{cases}$$

Example Consider the digraph D given in Figure 11.20. The cycle matrix of D is

$$B = \begin{array}{c} \begin{matrix} a & b & c & d & e & f & g & h \end{matrix} \\ \begin{bmatrix} 0 & 0 & 0 & 1 & 0 & 1 & 1 & 0 \\ 0 & 0 & 1 & 0 & -1 & 0 & 1 & 0 \\ 0 & 0 & 1 & -1 & -1 & -1 & 0 & 0 \\ -1 & 1 & 0 & 0 & 0 & 0 & 0 & 0 \end{bmatrix} \end{array}.$$

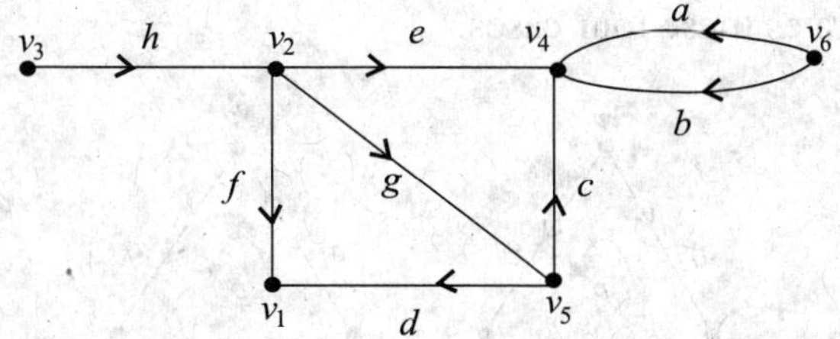

Fig. 11.20

We note that the orientation assigned to each of the four cycles is arbitrary. The cycle in the first row is assigned clockwise orientation, in the second row counter-clockwise, in the third counter-clockwise, and in the fourth clockwise. Changing the orientation of any cycle will simply change the sign of every non-zero entry in the corresponding row. Also we observe that if first row is subtracted from second, the third is obtained. Thus the rows are not all linearly independent (in the real field).

The next result gives the relation between incidence matrix and cycle matrix.

Theorem 11.18 Let B and A be respectively, the cycle matrix and the incidence matrix of a digraph (without loops) such that the columns are arranged using the same order of arcs. Then,

$$AB^T = BA^T = 0,$$

where T denotes the transposed matrix.

Proof Consider the pth row of A and the rth row of B. The rth cycle, say Z_r, either (a) does not, or (b) does possess an arc incident with vertex, say v_p, represented by the pth row of A. If (a), the product of the two rows is zero. If (b), there are exactly two arcs, say a_i and a_j, of the rth cycle incident with v_p.

We have the following four possibilities.

i. a_i and a_j are both incident towards v_p,

ii. a_i and a_j are both incident away from v_p,

iii. the directions of both a_i and a_j coincide with the orientation of Z_r and

iv. the directions of both a_i and a_j do not coincide with the orientation of Z_r.

It can be easily verified that in all these four cases, the product of the pth row of A and the rth row of B is zero. ❑

Figure 11.21 illustrates these four cases.

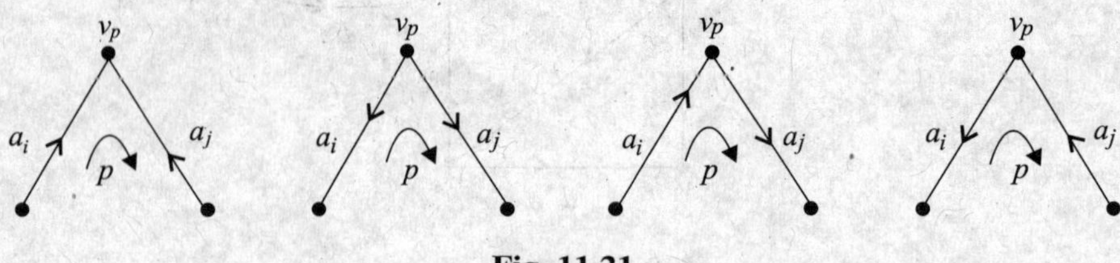

Fig. 11.21

Now, using Sylvester's theorem and Theorem 11.18, we can show that

rank $B+$ rank $A = m$.

If the digraph is connected, then rank $A = n - 1$.

Therefore, rank $B = m - n + 1$.

The following two results can be easily established.

Theorem 11.19 The non-singular submatrices of order $n-1$ of A are in one-one correspondence with spanning trees of a connected digraph of n vertices.

Theorem 11.20 The non-singular submatrices of B of order $\mu = m - n + 1$ are in one-one correspondence with the chord set (complement of the spanning tree) of the connected digraph of n vertices and m edges.

Sign of a spanning tree: For a digraph, the determinant of the non-singular submatrix of A corresponding to a spanning tree T has a value either 1 or -1. This is referred to as the sign of T.

We note that the sign of a spanned tree is defined only for a particular ordering of vertices and arcs in A, because interchanging two rows or columns in a matrix changes the sign of its determinant. Thus the sign of a spanning tree is relative. Once the sign of one spanning tree is arbitrarily chosen, the sign of every other spanning tree is determined as positive or negative with respect to this spanning tree.

Number of spanning trees: The following result determines the number of spanning trees in a connected digraph.

Theorem 11.21 If A_f is the reduced incidence matrix of a connected digraph, then the number of spanning trees in the graph is equal to det $(A_f \cdot A_f^T)$.

Proof According to Binet-Cauchy theorem,

$$\det(A_f \,.\, A_f^T) = \text{sum of the products of all corresponding majors of } A_f \text{ and } A_f^T.$$

Every major of A_f or A_f^T is zero unless it corresponds to a spanning tree, in which case its value is 1 or − 1. Since both majors of A_f and A_f^T have the same value 1 or −1, the product is 1 for each spanning tree. ❑

Fundamental cycle matrix: The μ fundamental cycles each formed by a chord with respect to some specified spanning tree, define a fundamental cycle matrix B_f for a digraph. The orientation assigned to each of the fundamental cycles is chosen to coincide with that of the chord. Therefore B_f, a $\mu \times m$ matrix can be expressed exactly in the same form as in the case of an undirected graph,

$$B_f = [I_\mu : B_t],$$

where I_μ is the identity matrix of order μ and the columns of B_t correspond to the arcs in a spanning tree. This is illustrated in Figure 11.22.

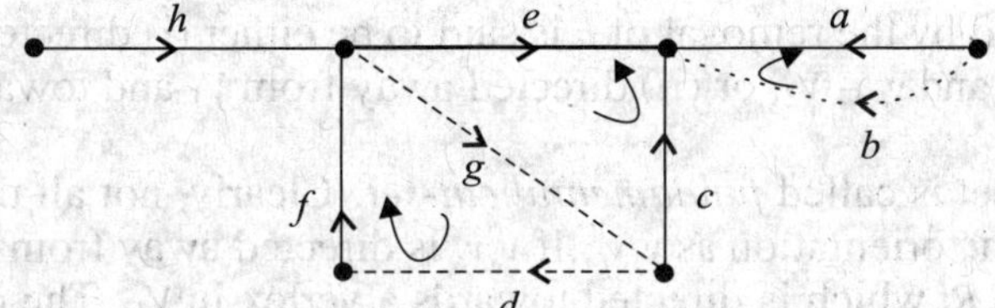

Fig. 11.22

$$\text{Here } B_f = \begin{array}{c} \begin{matrix} b & d & g & a & c & e & f & h \end{matrix} \\ \begin{bmatrix} 1 & 0 & 0 & -1 & 0 & 0 & 0 & 0 \\ 0 & 1 & 0 & 0 & -1 & 1 & 1 & 0 \\ 0 & 0 & 1 & 0 & 1 & -1 & 0 & 0 \end{bmatrix} \end{array} = [I_\mu : B_t].$$

Cut-set matrix: Let $D(V, A)$ be a connected digraph with q cut-sets. The cut-set matrix $C = [c_{ij}]$ of D is a $q \times m$ matrix in which the rows correspond to the cut-sets of D and the columns to the arcs of D. Each cut-set is given an arbitrary orientation. Let R_i be the ith cut-set of D and let R_i partition V into nonempty vertex sets V_i' and V_i''. The orientation can be defined to be either from V_i' to V_i'' or from V_i'' to V_i'. Suppose that the orientation is chosen to be from V_i' to V_i''. Then the orientation of an arc a_j of cut-set R_i is said to be the same as that of R_i if a_j is of the form $v_a\, v_b$, where $v_a \in V_i'$ and $v_b \in V_i''$ and opposite, otherwise. Then,

$$c_{ij} = \begin{cases} 1, & \textit{if arc } a_j \textit{ of cut} - \textit{set } R_i \textit{ has the same orientation as } R_i\,, \\ -1, & \textit{if arc } a_j \textit{ has the opposite orientation to } R_i\,; \\ 0, & \textit{otherwise}\,. \end{cases}$$

We have the following observations.

1. A permutation of the rows or columns corresponds to a relabelling of the cut-sets and arcs of D respectively.
2. Rank $C \geq$ rank A.
3. Rank $C \geq n-1$, by observation 2.
4. If the arcs of D are arranged in the same column order in B and C, then $BC^T = CB^T = 0$.
5. Rank $B+$ rank $C \leq m$.
6. If D is weak, rank $B = m-n+1$ and rank $C \leq n-1$.
7. Rank $C = n-1$, because of (3) and (4).

We observe that the removal of an arc, say $a = v_s v_t$ (also called a branch) of a spanning directed tree of D, partitions the vertices of a digraph D into two disjoint sets, say V_1 and V_2.

The cut-set created by the removal of a is said to be either (i) directed away from V_1 and towards V_2 if $v_s \in V_1$ and $v_t \in V_2$, or (ii) directed away from V_1 and towards V_2 if $v_s \in V_2$ and $v_t \in V_1$.

This type of cut-set is called *fundamental cut-set.* Clearly, not all the chords in R_i necessarily have the same orientation as $v_s v_t$. If $v_s v_t$ is directed away from a vertex in V_1, there may exist a chord in R_i which is directed towards a vertex in V_1. The orientation of a cut-set on the basis of the direction of the branch giving rise to it constitutes a natural way of orienting cut-sets. If all the chords of R_i are oriented as is $v_s v_t$, then R_i is said to be *directed.* Consider the graph shown in Figure 11.23 with T shown by bold lines. The fundamental cut-sets with respect to T are

branch	cut-set
a_3	$\{a_3, a_2\}$
a_5	$\{a_5, a_4\}$
a_6	$\{a_6, a_1, a_4\}$
a_7	$\{a_7, a_1, a_2\}$

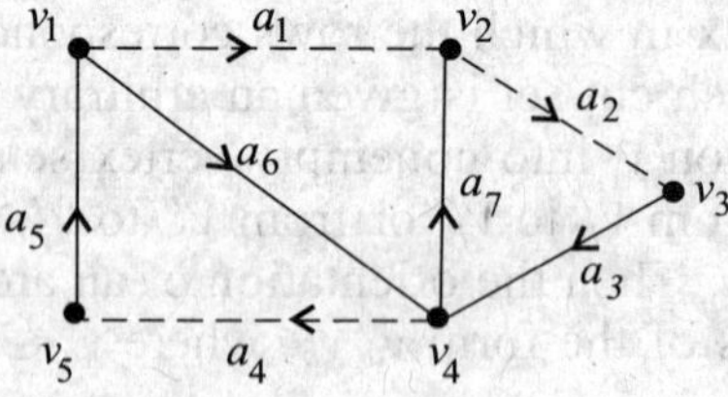

Fig. 11.23

A fundamental cut-set is created from C, the cut-set matrix of a connected digraph with the given directed spanning tree T, by deleting from C, all rows which do not correspond to fundamental cut-sets with respect to T. Therefore C_f is an $(n-1) \times m$ submatrix of C such that each row represents a unique fundamental cut-set with respect to T.

The rows of any fundamental cut-set C_f can be permuted to create a matrix of the form $C_f = [C_c : I_{n-1}]$, where C_c is an $(n-1) \times (m-n+1)$ matrix whose columns correspond to the chords of T and I_{n-1} is the identity matrix of order $n-1$ whose columns correspond to the branches of T.

Relation between $\mathbf{B}_f$, $\mathbf{C}_f$ and $\mathbf{A}_r$ A_r is the reduced incidence matrix in which an arbitrary row has been removed in order to make its rows linearly independent.

We have $B_f = [I_\mu : B_t]$ (11.7.i)

and $C_f = [C_c : I_{n-1}]$, (11.7.ii)

where t corresponds to the branches of T and c to the chords of T. Let the arcs be arranged in the same order in (11.7.i) and (11.7.ii) and in A_r. Partition A_r as

$$A_r = [A_c : A_t],$$

where A_c is an $(n-1) \times (m-n+1)$ submatrix whose columns correspond to the chords of T and A_t is an $(n-1) \times (n-1)$ submatrix whose columns correspond to the branches of T.

Since $AB^T = 0$, therefore $A_r\, B_f^T = 0$.

Thus, $[A_c : A_t] \begin{bmatrix} I_\mu \\ .. \\ B_t^T \end{bmatrix} = 0$, so that $A_c + A_t B_t^T = 0$.

Since A_t is non-singular, we have $A_t^{-1}[A_c + A_t B_t^T] = 0$.

Therefore, $A_t^{-1}A_c + B_t^T = 0$ and so $A_t^{-1}A_c = -B_t^T$. Also, $C_f B_f^T = 0$.

Therefore, $[C_c : I_{n-1}] \begin{bmatrix} I_\mu \\ .. \\ B_t^T \end{bmatrix} = 0$, and so $C_c + B_t^T = 0$.

Thus, $C_c = -B_t^T$ and so $C_c = A_t^{-1}A_c$.

Example Consider the digraph given in Figure 11.24, with spanning tree shown in bold lines.

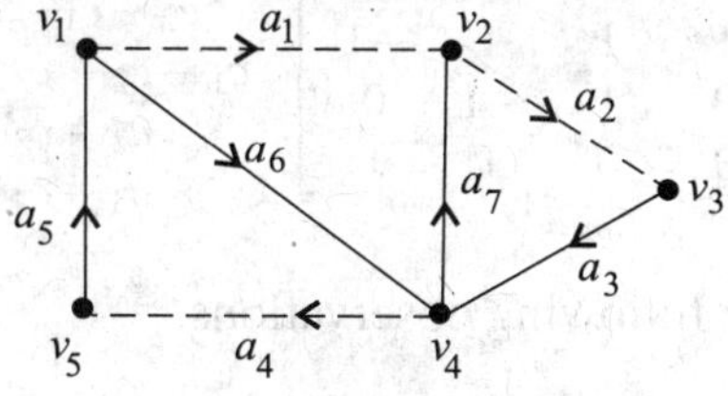

Fig. 11.24

We have

$$A_r = [A_c : At] = \begin{array}{c} \begin{matrix} a_1 & a_4 & a_2 & & a_5 & a_6 & a_7 & a_3 \end{matrix} \\ \left[\begin{matrix} -1 & 0 & 0 & \vdots & -1 & 1 & 0 & 0 \\ -1 & 0 & 0 & \vdots & 0 & 0 & -1 & 0 \\ 0 & 0 & -1 & \vdots & 0 & 0 & 0 & 1 \\ 0 & 1 & 0 & & 0 & -1 & 1 & -1 \end{matrix}\right] \end{array}$$

$$B_f = [I_3 : B_t] = \begin{array}{c} \begin{matrix} a_1 & a_4 & a_2 & & a_5 & a_6 & a_7 & a_3 \end{matrix} \\ \left[\begin{matrix} 1 & 0 & 0 & \vdots & 0 & -1 & -1 & 0 \\ 0 & 1 & 0 & \vdots & 1 & 1 & 0 & 0 \\ 0 & 0 & 1 & \vdots & 0 & 0 & 1 & 1 \end{matrix}\right] \end{array}$$

$$C_f = [C_c : I_4] = \begin{array}{c} \begin{matrix} a_1 & a_4 & a_2 & & a_5 & a_6 & a_7 & a_3 \end{matrix} \\ \left[\begin{matrix} 0 & -1 & 0 & \vdots & 1 & 0 & 0 & 0 \\ 1 & -1 & 0 & \vdots & 0 & 1 & 0 & 0 \\ 1 & 0 & -1 & \vdots & 0 & 0 & 1 & 0 \\ 0 & 0 & -1 & \vdots & 0 & 0 & 0 & 1 \end{matrix}\right] \end{array}$$

Note that the last row of A, corresponding to vertex v_5, has been removed to form A_f. We form linear combinations of the rows of C_f to create 10 rows of C, representing all of the cut-sets of the digraph in Figure 11.24.

$$C = \begin{array}{c} \begin{matrix} a_1 & a_4 & a_2 & a_5 & a_6 & a_7 & a_3 \end{matrix} \\ \left[\begin{matrix} 0 & -1 & 0 & 1 & 0 & 0 & 0 \\ 1 & -1 & 0 & 0 & 1 & 0 & 0 \\ 1 & 0 & -1 & 0 & 0 & 1 & 0 \\ 0 & 0 & -1 & 0 & 0 & 0 & 1 \\ -1 & 0 & 0 & 1 & -1 & 0 & 0 \\ 0 & -1 & 0 & 0 & 1 & -1 & 1 \\ 0 & 0 & 1 & -1 & 1 & -1 & 0 \\ 0 & 0 & 0 & 1 & 1 & 1 & -1 \\ 0 & -1 & 1 & 0 & 1 & -1 & 0 \\ 1 & 0 & 0 & 0 & 0 & 1 & 1 \end{matrix}\right] \end{array} \begin{matrix} c_1 \\ c_2 \\ c_3 \\ c_4 \\ c_1 - c_2 \\ c_2 - c_3 + c_4 \\ c_2 - c_1 - c_3 \\ c_1 - c_2 + c_3 - c_4 \\ c_2 - c_3 \\ c_3 - c_4 \end{matrix}$$

The above facts lead to the following observations.

1. Given A_r, we can construct B_f and C_f.

2. Given B_r, we can construct C_f.

3. Given C_f, we can construct B_f.

Semipath matrix: The semipath matrix $P(u, v) = [p_{ij}]$, of a digraph $D(V, A)$, where $u, v \in V$, is the matrix with each row representing a distinct semipath from u to v and the columns representing the arcs of D, in which $p_{ij} = 1$, if the ith semipath contains the jth arc, $p_{ij} = -1$ if the ith semipath contains the converse of the jth arc, and $p_{ij} = 0$ otherwise.

The matrix $P(v_3, v_5)$ for the digraph of Figure 11.25 is

$$P(v_3, v_5) = \begin{array}{c} \begin{matrix} a_1 & a_2 & a_3 & a_4 & a_5 & a_6 \end{matrix} \\ \begin{bmatrix} 0 & 0 & 1 & 0 & 0 & 0 \\ 0 & 1 & 0 & 0 & -1 & 0 \\ 1 & 0 & 0 & 1 & 0 & 1 \end{bmatrix} \end{array}$$

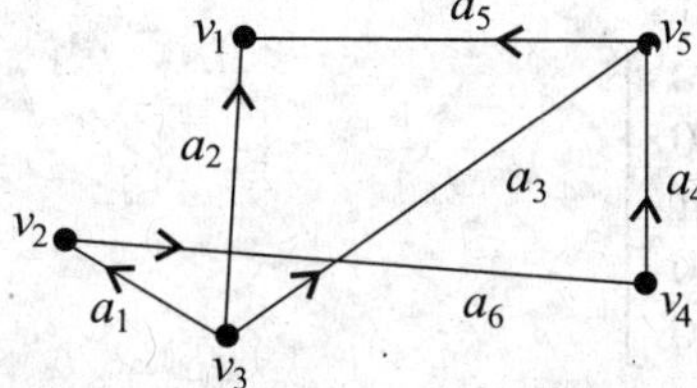

Fig. 11.25

We have the following observations about P.

1. If $P(u, v)$ contains a column of all zeros, then the vertex that it represents does not belong to any of the semipaths between u and v.

2. If $P(u, v)$ contains a column of all unit entries, then the vertex that it represents belongs to every semipath between u and v.

3. The number of non-zero entries in any row of $P(u, v)$ equals the number of arcs in the semipath represented by the row.

Adjacency matrix of a digraph: Let G be a digraph with n vertices and with no parallel arcs. The adjacency matrix $X = [x_{ij}]$ of the digraph G is an $n \times n$ (0, 1)-matrix defined by

$$x_{ij} = \begin{cases} 1, & \textit{if there is an arc directed from ith vertex to jth vertex}, \\ 0, & \textit{otherwise}. \end{cases}$$

Example Consider the digraph D of Figure 11.26.

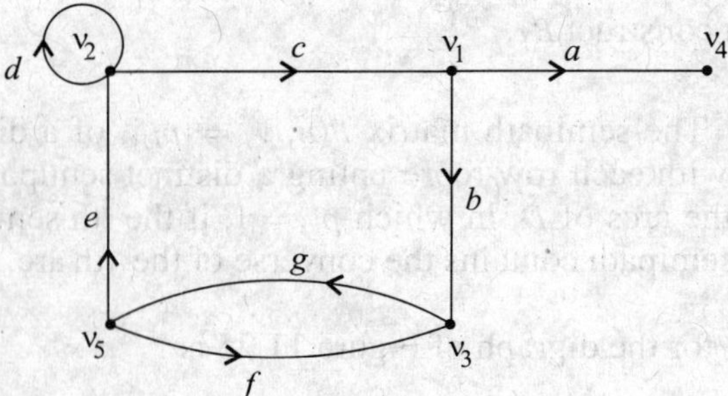

Fig. 11.26

The adjacency matrix of D is

$$X = \begin{array}{c} \\ v_1 \\ v_2 \\ v_3 \\ v_4 \\ v_5 \end{array} \begin{array}{c} \begin{array}{ccccc} v_1 & v_2 & v_3 & v_4 & v_5 \end{array} \\ \begin{bmatrix} 0 & 0 & 1 & 1 & 0 \\ 1 & 1 & 0 & 0 & 0 \\ 0 & 0 & 0 & 0 & 1 \\ 0 & 0 & 0 & 0 & 0 \\ 0 & 1 & 1 & 0 & 0 \end{bmatrix} \end{array}$$

We have the following observations about the adjacency matrix X of a digraph D.

1. X is a symmetric matrix if and only if D is a symmetric digraph.

2. Every non-zero element on the main diagonal element represents a loop at the corresponding vertex.

3. The parallel arcs cannot be represented by X and therefore X is defined only for a digraph without parallel arcs.

4. The sum of each row equals the outdegree of the corresponding vertex and the sum of each column equals the indegree of the corresponding vertex. The number of non-zero entries of X equals the number of arcs in D.

5. Permutation of any rows together with a permutation of the corresponding columns does not alter the digraph and thus the permutation corresponds to a reordering of the vertices. Therefore two digraphs are isomorphic if and only if their adjacency matrices differ only by such permutations.

6. If X is the adjacency matrix of a digraph D, then the transposed matrix X^T is the adjacency matrix of a digraph D^* obtained by reversing the direction of every arc in D.

7. For any $(0-1)$-matrix Q of order n, there exists a unique digraph D of n vertices such that Q is the adjacency matrix of D.

Connectedness and adjacency matrix: A digraph is disconnected if and only if its vertices can be ordered in such a way that its adjacency matrix X can be expressed as the direct sum of two square submatrices X_1 and X_2 as

$$X = \begin{bmatrix} X_1 & : & O \\ .. & : & .. \\ O & : & X_2 \end{bmatrix}. \tag{11.7.iii}$$

This partitioning is possible if and only if the vertices in the submatrix X_1 have no arc going to or coming from the vertex of X_2.

Similarly, a digraph is weakly connected if and only if its vertices can be ordered in such a way that its adjacency matrix can be expressed as

$$X = \begin{bmatrix} X_1 & : & O \\ .. & : & .. \\ X_{21} & : & X_2 \end{bmatrix} \tag{11.7.iv}$$

$$\text{or} \quad X = \begin{bmatrix} X_1 & : & X_{12} \\ .. & : & .. \\ O & : & X_2 \end{bmatrix}, \tag{11.7.v}$$

where X_1 and X_2 are square submatrices.

Form (11.7.iv) represents the case when there is no arc going from the subdigraph corresponding to X_1 to the one corresponding to X_2. Form (11.7.v) represents the case when there is no arc going from the subdigraph corresponding to X_2 to the subdigraph corresponding to X_1.

Since a strongly connected digraph is neither disconnected nor weakly connected, a digraph is strongly connected if and only if the vertices of D cannot be ordered such that its adjacency matrix X is expressible in the form (11.7.iii), or (11.7.iv), or (11.7.v).

Theorem 11.22 $[X^k]_{ij}$ is the number of different arc sequences of k arcs from the ith vertex to the jth vertex.

Proof Induct on k. The result is trivially true for $k = 1$. Assume the result holds for $[X^{k-1}]_{ij}$. Now,

$$[X^k]_{ij} = [X^{k-1}X]_{ij} = \sum_{r=1}^{n} [X^{k-1}]_{ir}[X]_{rj} = \sum_{r=1}^{n} [X^{k-1}]_{ir}x_{rj} \tag{11.22.1}$$

$$= \sum_{r=1}^{n} (\text{number of all directed arc sequences of length } k-1 \text{ from vertex } i \text{ to } r)\ x_{rj},$$

by induction hypothesis.

In (11.22.1), $x_{rj} = 1$ or 0, according as there is an arc from r to j. Therefore a term in the sum (11.22.1) is non zero if and only if there is an arc sequence of length k from i to j, whose last arc is from r to j. If the term is non-zero, its value equals the number of such arc sequences from i to j through r. This holds for every vertex r, $1 \le r \le n$. Thus (11.22.1) is equal to the number of all possible arc sequences from i to j. ❑

It is to be noted that $[X^k]_{ij}$ gives the number of all arc sequences from vertex i to j and these arc sequences can be of the following types.

1. Directed paths from i to j, that is, those arc sequences in which no vertex is traversed more than once.
2. Directed walks from i to j, that is, those directed arc sequences in which a vertex may be traversed more than once, but no arc is traversed more than once.
3. Those arc sequences in which an arc may also be traversed more than once.

11.8 Number of Arborescences

We now give a formula for counting the number of spanning arborescences in a labeled, connected digraph (which of course is simple). First, we have the following definition.

Kirchoff matrix: For a digraph (simple) D of n vertices, the Kirchoff matrix is an $n \times n$ matrix $K(D) = [k_{ij}]$ defined by

$$k_{ij} = \begin{cases} d^{-}(v_i), & i = j, \text{ in degree } of\ the\ ith\ vertex, \\ -x_{ij}, & i \neq j \quad (i,\ j)th\ entry\ in\ the\ adjacency\ matrix,\ with\ a\ negative\ sign\,. \end{cases}$$

Example Consider the digraph D given in Figure 11.27.

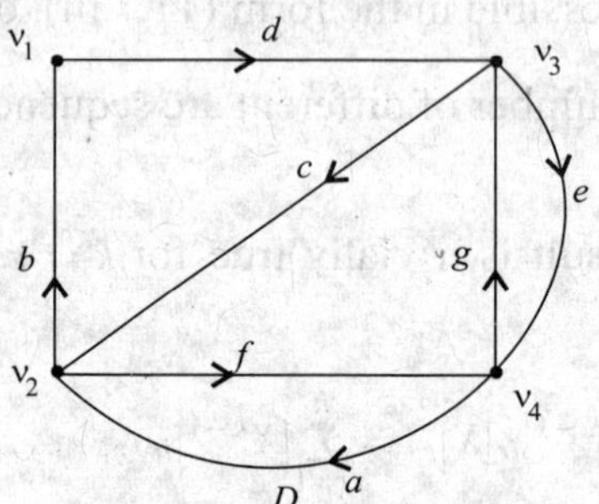

Fig. 11.27

The Kirchoff matrix of D is

$$K(D) = \begin{array}{c} \\ v_1 \\ v_2 \\ v_3 \\ v_4 \end{array} \begin{array}{c} \begin{array}{cccc} v_1 & v_2 & v_3 & v_4 \end{array} \\ \begin{bmatrix} 1 & 0 & -1 & 0 \\ -1 & 2 & 0 & -1 \\ 0 & -1 & 2 & -1 \\ 0 & -1 & -1 & 2 \end{bmatrix} \end{array}$$

Clearly, the sum of the entries in each column in K is equal to zero, so that the n rows are linearly independent. Thus, $\det K = 0$.

Theorem 11.23 A digraph (simple) D of n vertices and $n-1$ arcs is an arborescence rooted at v_1 if and only if the (1, 1) cofactor of $K(D)$ is equal to 1.

Proof

a. Let D be an arborescence with n vertices and rooted at vertex v_1. Relabel the vertices as $v_1, v_2, \ldots, v_n$ such that vertices along every path from the root v_1 have increasing indices. Permute the rows and columns of $K(D)$ to conform with this relabelling.

Since the indegree of v_1 equals zero, the first column contains only zeros. Other entries in $K(D)$ are

$$k_{ij} = \begin{cases} 0, & i > j, \\ -x_{ij}, & i < j, \\ 1, & i = j,\ i > 1. \end{cases}$$

Then the K matrix of an arborescence rooted at v_1 is of the form

$$K(D) = \begin{bmatrix} 0 & -x_{12} & -x_{13} & -x_{14} & \cdots & -x_{1n} \\ 0 & 1 & -x_{23} & -x_{24} & \cdots & -x_{2n} \\ 0 & 0 & 1 & -x_{34} & \cdots & -x_{3n} \\ 0 & 0 & 0 & 1 & \cdots & \\ \vdots & & & & \cdots & \\ 0 & 0 & 0 & 0 & \cdots & 1 \end{bmatrix}.$$

Clearly, the cofactor of the (1, 1) entry is 1, that is, $\det K_{11} = 1$.

b. Conversely, let D be a digraph of n vertices and $n-1$ arcs, and let (1, 1) cofactor of its K matrix be equal to 1, that is, $\det K_{11} = 1$.

Since $\det K_{11} \neq 0$, every column in K_{11} has at least one non-zero entry. Therefore,

$$d^-(v_i) \geq 1, \text{ for } i = 2, 3, \ldots, n.$$

There are only $n-1$ arcs to go around, therefore

$$d^-(v_i) = 1, \text{ for } i = 2, 3, \ldots, n, \text{ and } d^-(v_1) = 0.$$

Since no vertex in D has an indegree of more than one, if D can have any cycle at all, it has to be a directed cycle. Suppose that such a directed cycle exists, which passes through vertices $v_{i_1}, v_{i_2}, ..., v_{i_r}$. Then the sum of the columns $i_1, i_2, \ldots, i_r$ in K_{11} is zero. This is because each of these columns contains exactly two non-zero entries, as 1 on the main diagonal and -1 for the incoming arc from the vertex preceding it in the directed cycle. Thus the r columns in K_{11} are linearly dependent. So, det $K_{11} = 0$, a contradiction. Therefore, D has no cycles.

If D has $n-1$ arcs and no cycles, it must be a tree. Since in this tree $d^-(v_1) = 0$ and $d^-(v_i) = 1$, for $i = 2, 3, \ldots, n$, D is an arborescence rooted at vertex v_1.

The arguments in (a) and (b) are valid for an arborescence rooted at any vertex v_q. Any reordering of the vertices in D corresponds to identical permutations of rows and columns in $K(D)$. Such permutations do not alter the value or sign of the determinant. ❑

Theorem 11.24 If $K(D)$ is the Kirchoff matrix of a (simple) digraph D, then the value of the (q, q) cofactor of $K(D)$ is equal to the number of arborescences in D rooted at the vertex v_q.

Proof The proof depends on the result of Theorem 11.23 and on the fact that the determinant of a square matrix is a linear function of its columns. In particular, if P is a square matrix consisting of n column vectors, each of dimension n, that is

$$P = [p_1, p_2, \ldots, (p_i + p_i'), \ldots, p_n],$$

$$\text{then det } P = \text{det } [p_1, p_2, \ldots, p_i, \ldots, p_n] + \text{det } [p_1, p_2, \ldots, p_i', \ldots, p_n]. \quad (11.24.1)$$

In digraph D, suppose that vertex v_j has indegree d_j. The jth column of $K(D)$ can be regarded as the sum of d_j different columns, each corresponding to a digraph in which v_j has indegree one. And then (11.24.1) can be repeatedly applied. After this, splitting of columns can be carried out for each j, $j \neq q$ and det $K_{qq}(D)$ can be expressed as a sum of determinants of subdigraphs, that is

$$\det K_{qq}(D) = \sum_{D'} \det K_{qq}(D'), \quad (11.24.2)$$

where D' is a subdigraph of D with the following properties.

1. Every vertex in D' has an indegree of exactly one except v_q.
2. D' has $n-1$ vertices and hence $n-1$ arcs.

From Theorem 11.23,

$$\det K_{qq}(D') = \begin{cases} 1, & \textit{if and only if } D' \textit{ is an arborescence rooted at } q, \\ 0, & \textit{otherwise}. \end{cases}$$

Thus the summation in (11.24.2) carried over all D''s equals the number of arborescences rooted at v_q. ❑

11.9 Tournaments

A tournament is an orientation of a complete graph. Therefore in a tournament each pair of distinct vertices v_i and v_j is joined by one and only one of the oriented arcs (v_i, v_j) or (v_j, v_i). If the arc (v_i, v_j) is in T, then we say v_i dominates v_j and is denoted by $v_i \to v_j$. The relation of dominance thus defined is a complete, irreflexive, antisymmetric binary relation. Figure 11.28 displays all tournaments on three and four vertices.

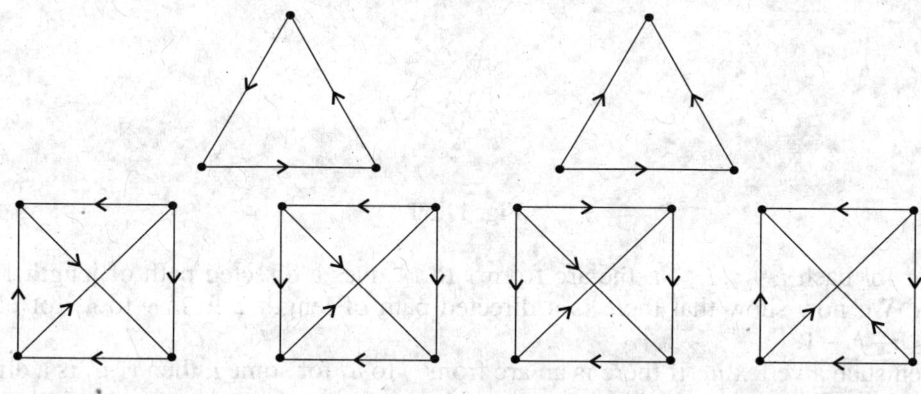

Fig. 11.28

Definition: A *triple* in a tournament T is the subdigraph induced by any three vertices. A triple (u, v, w) in T is said to be *transitive* if whenever $(u, v) \in A(T)$ and $(v, w) \in A(T)$, then $(u, w) \in A(T)$. That is, whenever $u \to v$ and $v \to w$, then $u \to w$.

Definition: A *bipartite tournament* is an orientation of a complete bipartite graph. A *k-partite tournament* is an orientation of a complete k-partite graph. Figure 11.29 displays a bipartite and a tripartite tournament.

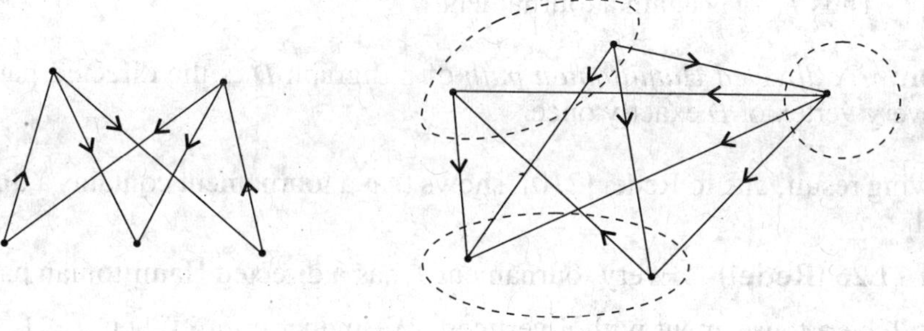

Fig. 11.29

Theorem 11.25 If v is a vertex having maximum outdegree in the tournament T, then for every vertex w of T there is a directed path from v to w of length at most 2.

Proof Let T be a tournament with n vertices and let v be a vertex of maximum outdegree in T. Let $d^+(v) = m$ and let $v_1, v_2, \ldots, v_m$ be the vertices in T such that there are arcs from v to v_i, $1 \le i \le m$. Since T is a tournament, there are arcs from the remaining $n-m-1$ vertices, say $u_1, u_2, \ldots, u_{n-m-1}$ to v. That is, there are arcs from u_j to v, $1 \le j \le n-m-1$ (Fig. 11.30).

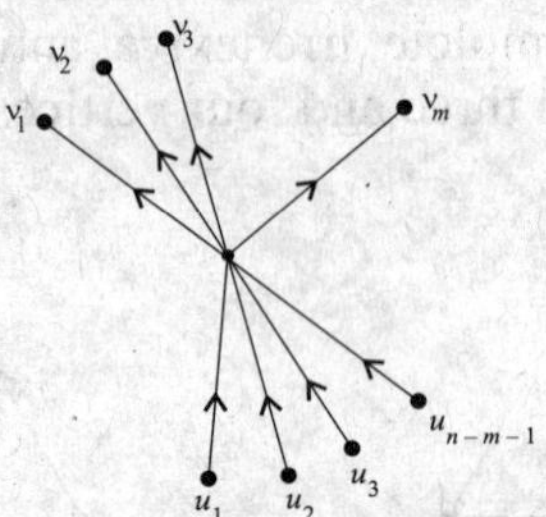

Fig. 11.30

Then for each i, $1 \le i \le m$, the arc from v to v_i gives a directed path of length 1 from v to v_i. We now show that there is a directed path of length 2 from v to u_j for each j, $1 \le j \le n-m-1$.

Given such a vertex u_j, if there is an arc from v_i to u_j for some i, then vv_iu_j is a directed path of length 2 from v to u_j. Now, let there be a vertex u_k, $1 \le k \le n-m-1$, such that no vertex $v_i, 1 \le i \le m$, has an arc from v_i to u_k. Since T is tournament, there is an arc from u_k to each of the m vertices v_i. Also, there is an arc from u_k to v and therefore $d^+(u_k) \ge m+1$. This contradicts the fact that v has maximum outdegree with $d^+(v) = m$. Thus each u_j must have an arc joining it from some v_i and the proof is complete by using the directed path vv_iu_j. ❑

Let T be a tournament with n vertices and let v be any vertex of T. Then $T - v$ is the digraph obtained from T by removing v and all arcs incident with v. Clearly, any two vertices of $T - v$ are joined by exactly one arc, since these two vertices are joined by exactly one arc in T. Thus $T - v$ is again a tournament.

Definition: A *directed Hamiltonian path* of a digraph D is the directed path in D that includes every vertex of D exactly once.

The following result, due to Redei [210], shows that a tournament contains a direct Hamiltonian path.

Theorem 11.26 (Redei) Every tournament T has a directed Hamiltonian path.

Proof Let T be a tournament with n vertices. We induct on n. When $n = 1$, 2, or 3, the result is trivially true (Fig. 11.31).

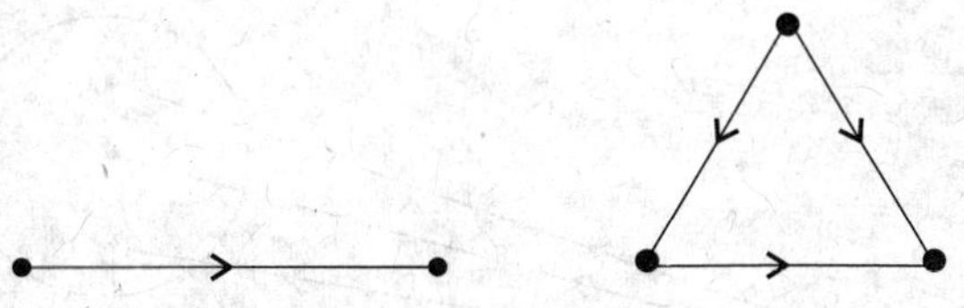

Fig. 11.31

Let $n \geq 4$. Assume that the result is true for all tournaments with fewer than n vertices. Let v be any vertex of T. Then $T - v$ is a tournament with $n - 1$ vertices and by induction hypothesis has a directed Hamiltonian path, say $P = v_1 v_2 \ldots v_{n-1}$.

In case there is an arc from v to v_1, then $P_1 = v v_1\, v_2 \ldots v_{n-1}$ is a directed Hamiltonian path in T. Similarly if there is an arc from v_{n-1} to v, then $P_2 = v_1\, v_2 \ldots v_{n-1} v$ is a directed Hamiltonian path in T.

Now, assume there is no arc from v to v_1 and no arc from v_{n-1} to v. Then there is at least one vertex w on the path P with the property that there is an arc from w to v and w is not v_{n-1}. Let v_i be the last vertex on P having this property, so that the next vertex v_{i+1} does not have this property. Then there is an arc from v_i to v and an arc from v to v_{i+1}, as shown in Figure 11.32. Thus $Q = v_1 v_2 \ldots v_i v\, v_{i+1}\, v_{i+2} \ldots v_{n-1}$ is a directed Hamiltonian path in T. ❑

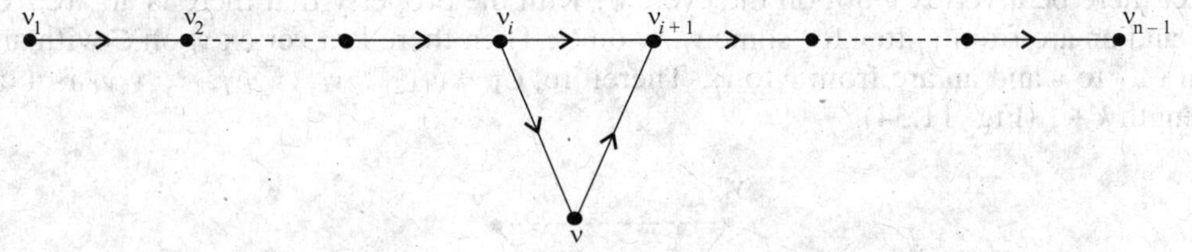

Fig. 11.32

Definition: A *directed Hamiltonian cycle* in a digraph D is a directed cycle which includes every vertex of D. If D contains such a cycle, then D is called *Hamiltonian*.

The next two results are due to Camion [43].

Theorem 11.27 (Camion) A strongly connected tournament T on n vertices contains cycles of length 3, 4,..., n.

Proof First we show that T contains a cycle of length three. Let v be any vertex of T. Let W denote the set of all vertices w of T for which there is an arc from v to w. Let Z denote the set of all vertices z of T for which there is an arc from z to v. We note that $W \cap Z = \varphi$, since T is a tournament.

Since T is strongly connected, W and Z are both nonempty. For, if W is empty, then there is no arc going out of v, which is impossible because T is strongly connected and the same argument can be used for Z. Again, because T is strongly connected, there is an arc in T going from some w in W to some z in Z. This gives the directed cycle $v\, w\, z\, v$ of length 3 (Fig. 11.33).

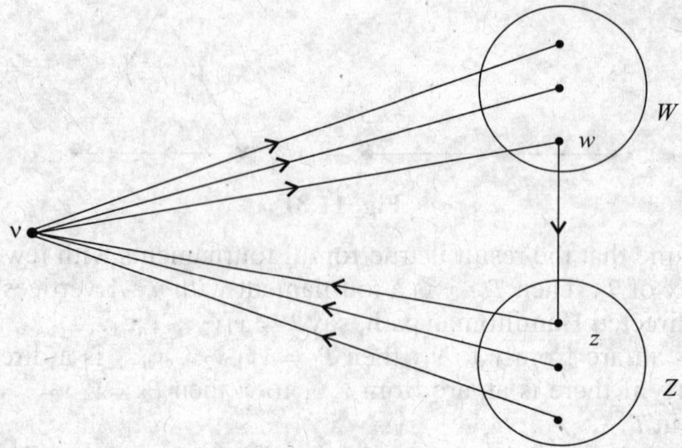

Fig. 11.33

Now induct on n. Assume T has a cycle C of length k, where $k < n$ and $k \geq 3$ and let this cycle be $v_1 v_2 \ldots v_k v_1$. We show that T has a cycle of length $k+1$.

Let there be a vertex v not on the cycle C, with the property that there is an arc from v to v_i and an arc from v_j to v for some v_i, v_j on C. Then there is a vertex v_i on C with an arc from v_{i-1} to v and an arc from v to v_i. Therefore, $C_1 = v_1 v_2 \ldots v_{i-1} v v_i v_{i+1} \ldots v_k v_1$ is a cycle of length $k+1$ (Fig. 11.34).

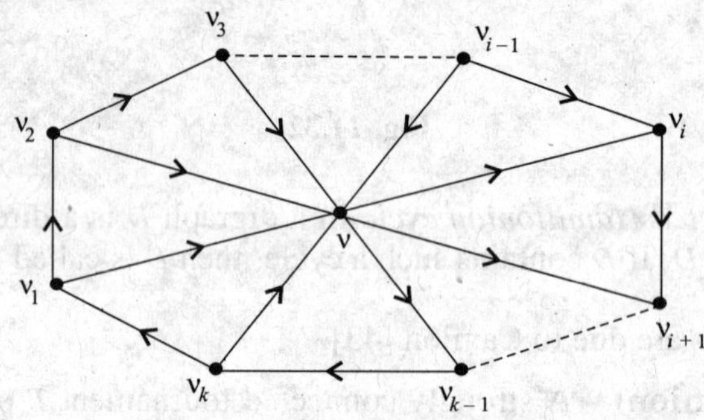

Fig. 11.34

If no vertex exists with the above property, then the set of vertices not contained in the cycle can be divided into two distinct sets W and Z, where W is the set of vertices w such that for each i, $1 \leq i \leq k$, there is an arc from v_i to w and Z is the set of vertices z such that for each i, $1 \leq i \leq k$, there is an arc from z to v_i. If W is empty then the vertices of C, and the vertices of Z together make up all the vertices in T. But, by definition of Z, there is no arc from a vertex on C to a vertex in Z, a contradiction, because T is strongly connected. Thus W is nonempty. A similar argument shows that Z is nonempty. Again, since T is strongly connected, there is an arc from some w in W to some z in Z. Then $C_1 = v_1 w z v_3 v_4 \ldots v_k v_1$ is a cycle of length $k+1$ (Fig. 11.35). This completes the proof. ❑

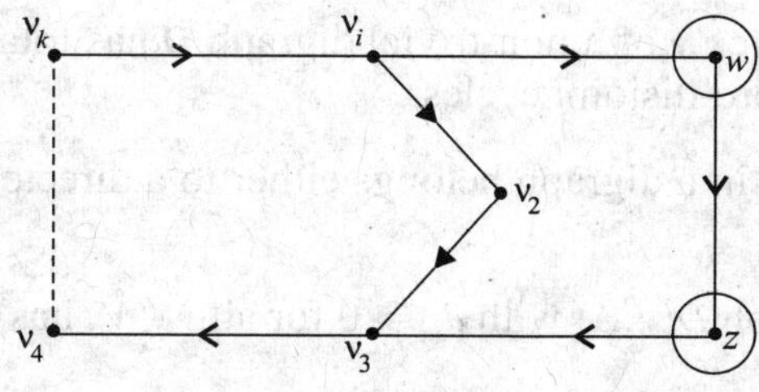

Fig. 11.35

Theorem 11.28 (Camion) A tournament T is Hamiltonian if and only if it is strongly connected.

Proof Let T have n vertices. If T is strongly connected, then by Theorem 11.27, T has a cycle of length n. Such a cycle is a Hamiltonian cycle, since it includes every vertex of T. Hence T is Hamiltonian.

Conversely, let T be Hamiltonian with Hamiltonian cycle $C = v_1 v_2 \ldots v_n v_1$. Then given any v_i, v_j with $i \geq j$, in the vertex set of T, $v_j v_{j+1} \ldots v_i$ is a path P_1 from v_j to v_i while $v_i v_{i+1} \ldots v_{n-1} v_n v_1 \ldots v_{j-1} v_j$ is a path P_2 from v_i to v_j (Fig. 11.36). Thus each vertex is reachable from any other vertex and so T is strongly connected. ❑

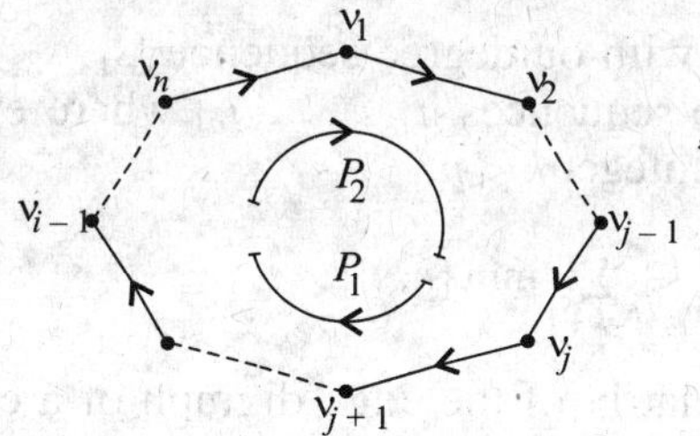

Fig. 11.36

11.10 Exercises

1. Prove that the converse of a strong digraph is also strong.

2. Show that D^*, the condensation of any digraph D, is cyclic.

3. Prove that the converse of a unilateral digraph is unilateral.

4. Show that the transmitters, receivers and isolates of a digraph D retain their properties in D^*.

5. Prove that the only acyclic digraph is $K_1 \cong K_1^*$.

6. Prove that an acyclic digraph without isolates has a transmitter and a receiver.

7. Show that every vertex v of a non-trivial digraph D has total even degree if and only if D is the union of arc-disjoint cycles.

8. Prove that every arc in a digraph belongs either to a directed cycle or a directed cut-set.

9. Prove that the digraph $D(V,A)$ with $d_v^+ > 0$ for all $v \in V$, has a cycle.

10. Prove that the digraph distance satisfies the triangle inequality.

11. Prove that every Eulerian digraph is strong. Is the converse true?

12. If $E|G|$ is the number of Euler lines in an n-vertex Euler digraph D, show that $2^{n-1}.E|G|$ is the number of Euler lines in $L(D)$.

13. If D is a digraph with an odd number of vertices and if each vertex of D has an odd outdegree, prove that there is an odd number of vertices of D with odd indegree.

14. Prove by induction on n that for each $n \geq 1$, there is a simple digraph D with n vertices $v_1, v_2, \ldots, v_n$ such that $d_{v_i}^+ = i-1$ and $d_{v_i}^- = n-i$ for each $i = 1, 2, \ldots, n$.

15. Prove that no strictly weak digraph contains a vertex whose removal results in a strong digraph.

16. There exists a digraph with outdegree sequence $[s_1, s_2, \ldots, s_n]$, where $n-1 \geq s_1 \geq s_2 \geq \ldots \geq s_n$ and indegree sequences $[t_1, t_2, \ldots, t_n]$ where every $t_j \leq n-1$ if and only if $\sum s_i = \sum t_i$ and for each integer $k < n$,

$$\sum_{i=1}^{k} s_i \leq \sum_{i=1}^{k} \min\{k-1,\, t_i\} + \sum_{i=k+1}^{n} \min\{k,\, t_i\}.$$

17. If X is the adjacency matrix of the edge digraph of a complete symmetric digraph, then $X^2 + X$ has all entries 1.

18. Let T be any tournament. Prove that the converse of T and the complement of T are isomorphic.

19. Prove that a tournament is transitive if and only if it has a unique Hamiltonian path.

20. Prove that if a simple digraph D has a cycle of length three, then it is not transitive.

21. Prove that a tournament is transitive if and only if it has no directed cycles.

12. Score Structure in Digraphs

Landau [141] associated with each tournament an ordered sequence of non-negative integers, its score structure, formed by listing the vertex outdegrees in non-decreasing order. Since then the concept of score structure has been extended to various other classes of digraphs, namely oriented graphs and semicomplete graphs.The score structure property has been used in the study of some structural properties of digraphs.

12.1 Score Sequences in Tournaments

Definition: In a tournament T, the score $s(v_i)$, or simply s_i of a vertex v_i is the number of arcs directed away from v_i and the score sequence $S(T)$ is formed by listing the vertex scores in non-decreasing order. Clearly, $0 \le s_i \le n-1$. Further, no two scores can be zero and no two scores can be $n-1$. Tournament score sequences have also been called score structures [141], score vectors [160] and score lists [29].

One interpretation of a tournament is as a competition where n participants play each other once in a match that cannot end in a tie and score one point for each win. Player v is represented in the tournament by vertex v and an arc from u to v means that u defeats v. Then player v obtains a total of d_v^+ points in the competition and the vertex scores can be ordered to obtain the score sequence of the tournament. We use $u \to v$ to denote the both, an arc from u to v and the fact that u dominates v. A result of Ryser [221] states that an n-tournament can be obtained from any other having the same score sequence by a sequence of arc reversals of 3-cycles.

Now, we give the characterisation of score sequences of tournaments which is due to Landau [141].This result has attracted quite a bit of attention as nearly a dozen different proofs appear in the literature.Early proofs tested the readers patience with special choices of subscripts, but eventually such gymnastics were replaced by more elegant arguments. Many of the existing proofs are discussed in a survey by Reid [215] and the proof we give here is due to Thomassen [235]. Further, two new proofs can be found in [86].

Theorem 12.1 (Landau) A sequence of non-negative integers $S=[s_i]_1^n$ in non-decreasing order is a score sequence of a tournament if and only if for each subset $I \subseteq [n] = \{1, 2, \ldots, n\}$,

$$\sum_{i\in I} s_i \geq \binom{|I|}{2}, \tag{12.1.2}$$

with equality when $|I| = n$.

Because of the monotonicity assumption $s_1 \leq s_2 \leq \ldots \leq s_n$, the inequalities (12.1.2), known as the Landau inequalities, are equivalent to

$$\sum_{i=1}^{k} s_i \geq \binom{k}{2},$$

for $1 \leq k \leq n$, with equality for $k = n$.

Proof

Necessity If a sequence of non-negative integers $[s_i]_1^n$ in the non-decreasing order is the score sequence of an n-tournament T, then the sum of the first k scores in the sequence counts exactly one each arc in the subtournamnent W induced by $\{v_1, v_2, \ldots, v_k\}$ plus each arc from W to $T - W$. Therefore the sum is at least $\frac{k(k-1)}{2}$, the number of arcs in W. Also, since the sum of the scores of the vertices counts each arc of the tournament exactly once, the sum of the scores is the total number of arcs, that is, $\frac{n(n-1)}{2}$.

Sufficiency (Thomassen) Let n be the smallest integer for which there is a non-decreasing sequence S of non-negative integers satisfying Landau's conditions (12.1.2), but for which there is no n-tournament with score sequence S. Among all such S, pick one for which s_1 is as small as possible.

First consider the case where for some $k < n$,

$$\sum_{i=1}^{k} s_i = \binom{k}{2}.$$

By the minimality of n, the sequence $S_1 = [s_1, s_2, \ldots, s_k]$ is the score sequence of some tournament T_1. Further,

$$\sum_{i=1}^{m} (s_{k+i} - k) = \sum_{i=1}^{m+k} s_i - \binom{k}{2} - mk \geq \binom{m+k}{2} - \binom{k}{2} - mk = \binom{m}{2},$$

for each m, $1 \leq m \leq n-k$, with the equality when $m = n-k$. Therefore, by the minimality of n, the sequence $S_2 = [s_{k+1} - k, s_{k+2} - k, \ldots, s_n - k]$ is the score sequence of some tournament T_2. By forming the disjoint union of T_1 and T_2, and adding all arcs from T_2 to T_1, we obtain a tournament with score sequence S.

Now, consider the case where each inequality in 12.1.2 is strict when $k < n$ (in particular $s_1 > 0$). Then the sequence $S_3 = [s_1 - 1, s_2, \ldots, s_{n-1}, s_n + 1]$ satisfies (12.1.2) and by the minimality of s_1, S_3 is the score sequence of some tournament T_3. Let u and v be the vertices with scores $s_n + 1$ and $s_1 - 1$ respectively. Since the score of u is larger than that of v, T_3 has a path P from u to v of length ≤ 2. By reversing the arcs of P, we obtain a tournament with score sequence S, a contradiction. ❑

Landau's theorem is the tournament analog of the Erdos-Gallai theorem for graphical sequences. A tournament analog of the Havel-Hakimi theorem for graphical sequences is the following result, the proof of which can be found in Reid and Beineke [212].

Theorem 12.2 A non-decreasing sequence $[s_i]_1^n$ of non-negative integers, $n \geq 2$, is the score sequence of an n-tournament if and only if the new sequence

$$[s_1, s_2, \ldots, s_m, s_{m+1} - 1, \ldots, s_{n-1} - 1]$$

where $m = s_n$, when arranged in non-decreasing order, is the score sequence of some $(n-1)$-tournament.

Definition: A tournament is strongly connected or strong if for every two vertices u and v there is a path from u to v and a path from v to u. A *strong component* of a tournament is a maximal strong subtournament.

The following extension of Theorem 12.1, characterises strong components. The proof is straightforward and consequently omitted.

Theorem 12.3 A non-decreasing sequence $[s_i]_1^n$ of non-negative integers is the score sequence of a strong n-tournament if and only if

$$\sum_{i=1}^{k} s_i > \binom{k}{2}, \ 1 \leq k \leq n, \text{ and } \sum_{i=1}^{n} s_i = \binom{n}{2}.$$

We have the following observation from Theorem 12.3. Let $S = [s_i]_1^n$ be a score sequence of an n-tournament T with vertex set $V = \{1, 2, \ldots, n\}$. Let $\sum_{i=1}^{p} s_i = \binom{p}{2}$, $\sum_{i=1}^{q} s_i = \binom{q}{2}$ and $\sum_{i=1}^{k} s_i > \binom{k}{2}$, for $p+1 \leq k \leq q-1$, where $0 \leq p < q \leq n$.

Then the subtournament induced by $\{p+1, \ldots, q\}$ is a strong component of T with score sequence $[s_{p+1} - p, s_{p+2} - p, \ldots, s_q - p]$.

We say that S is strong if T is strong and the strong components of S are the score sequences of the strong components of T. Theorem 12.3 shows that the strong components of S are determined by the successive values of k for which

$$\sum_{i=1}^{k} s_i = \binom{k}{2},$$

that is, the successive values of k for which equality holds in condition (12.1.2).

For example, consider the score sequence

$$S = [1, 1, 1, 4, 4, 5, 5, 7, 9, 9, 10, 11, 11],$$

$$\sum_{i=1}^{k} s_i = \binom{k}{2} \text{ for } k = 3, 7, 8, \text{ and } 13.$$

Therefore the strong components of S are, in ascending order,

$$[1, 1, 1], [1, 1, 2, 2], [0], \text{ and } [1, 1, 2, 3, 3].$$

The next result due to Brualdi and Shen [40] shows that the score sequence of an n-tournament satisfies inequalities (12.4.1) below, which are individually stronger than the inequalities (12.1.1), although collectively the two sets of inequalities are equivalent.

Theorem 12.4 (Brualdi and Shen) A sequence $S = [s_i]_1^n$ of non-negative integers in non-decreasing order is a score sequence of a tournament if and only if for every subset $I \subseteq [n]$,

$$\sum_{i \in I} s_i \geq \frac{1}{2}\sum_{i \in I}(i-1) + \frac{1}{2}\binom{|I|}{2}, \tag{12.4.1}$$

with equality when $|I| = n$.

Proof The sufficiency (12.4.1) imply the inequalities (12.1.1).

We prove that the score sequence S of a tournament satisfies (12.4.1). For any subset $I \subseteq [n]$, define

$$f(I) = \sum_{i \in I} s_i - \frac{1}{2}\sum_{i \in I}(i-1) - \frac{1}{2}\binom{|I|}{2}.$$

Choose I firstly to have $f(I)$ minimum and secondly to have $|I|$ minimum.

Claim that $I = \{i : 1 \leq i \leq |I|\}$.

Otherwise, there exists $i \notin I$ and $j \in I$ such that $j = i+1$. Then $s_i \leq s_j$. Since

$$s_j - \frac{1}{2}(j + |I| - 2) = f(I) - f(I - \{j\}) < 0$$

and $s_i - \frac{1}{2}(i + |I| - 1) = f(I \cup \{i\}) - f(I) \geq 0$, therefore

$$\frac{1}{2}(i+|I|-1) \le s_i \le s_j < \frac{1}{2}(j+|I|-2) = \frac{1}{2}(i+|I|-1),$$

which is a contradiction. This proves the claim.

Thus, $f(I) = \sum_{i=1}^{|I|} s_i - \frac{1}{2}\sum_{i=1}^{|I|}(i-1) - \frac{1}{2}\binom{|I|}{2} = \sum_{i=1}^{|I|} s_i - \binom{|I|}{2} \ge 0,$

where the inequality follows from 12.1. By the choice of the subset I, Theorem 12.4 follows. ❑

Remark Clearly, the equality can occur often in (12.4.1). For example, equality holds for regular tournaments of odd order n (with score sequence $\left[\frac{n-1}{2}, \ldots, \frac{n-1}{2}\right]$), whenever $|I| = k$, and $I = \{n-k+1, \ldots, n\}$.

Further, Theorem 12.4 is best possible in the sense that, for any real $\in > 0$, the inequality

$$\sum_{i \in I} s_i \ge \left(\frac{1}{2} + \in\right)\sum_{i \in I}(i-1) + \left(\frac{1}{2} - \in\right)\binom{|I|}{2}$$

fails for some I and some tournaments (for example, regular tournaments).

The following set of upper bounds for $\sum_{i \in I} s_i$ is equivalent to the set of lower bounds for $\sum_{i \in I} s_i$ in Theorem 12.4.

Corollary 12.1 A sequence $S = [s_i]_1^n$ of non-negative integers in non-decreasing order is a score sequence of a tournament if and only if for any subset $I \subseteq [n]$,

$$\sum_{i \in I} s_i \le \frac{1}{2}\sum_{i \in I}(i-1) + \frac{1}{4}|I|\,(2n - |I| - 1),$$

with equality when $|I| = n$.

Proof Let $J = [n] - I$. Then,

$$\sum_{i \in I} s_i = \frac{1}{2}\sum_{i \in I}(i-1) + \frac{1}{4}|I|\,(2n - |I| - 1),$$

with equality when $|I| = n$, if and only if

$$\sum_{i \in J} s_i = \binom{n}{2} - \sum_{i \in I} s_i \ge \frac{1}{2}\sum_{i \in J}(i-1) + \frac{1}{2}\binom{|J|}{2},$$

with equality when $|J| = n$. Therefore Corollary 12.1 follows from Theorem 12.4. ❑

Corollary 12.2 If $S=[s_i]_1^n$ is a score sequence of a tournament, then for each i, $\frac{i-1}{2}\le s_i \le \frac{n+i-2}{2}$.

Proof Choose $I=\{i\}$. Then the result follows immediately from Theorem 12.4 and Corollary 12.1. ❑

The next result by Brualdi and Shen [40] shows that when equality occurs in the inequalities (12.4.1), there are implications concerning the strong connectedness and regularity of every tournament with score sequence S. For any integers r and s with $r\le s$, $[r,\ s]$ denotes the set of all integers between r and s.

Theorem 12.5 If $S=[s_i]_1^n$ is a tournament score sequence and if

$$\sum_{i\in I} s_i=\frac{1}{2}\sum_{i\in I}(i-1)+\frac{1}{2}\binom{|I|}{2}$$

for some $I\subseteq[n]$, then one of the following holds.

i. $I=[1,\ |I|]$ and $\sum_{i=1}^{|I|} s_i=\binom{|I|}{2}$.

ii. $I=[t,\ t+|I|-1]$ for some t, $2\le t\le n-|I|+1$,

$$\sum_{i=1}^{t+|I|-1} s_i=\binom{t+|I|-1}{2} \text{ and } s_i=(t+|I|-2)/2, \text{ for all } i\le t+|I|-1.$$

iii. $I=[1,\ r]\cup[r+t,\ t+|I|-1]$, for some r and t such that $1\le r\le |I|-1$ and $2\le t\le n-|I|+1$,

$$\sum_{i=1}^{t+|I|-1} s_i=\binom{t+|I|-1}{2}$$

and $s_i=(r+t+|I|-2)/2$ for all i, $r+1\le i\le t+|I|-1$.

Remark Conditions (i), (ii) and (iii) of Theorem 12.5 are equivalent to the assertion that every tournament with the score sequence S has one of the three structures shown in Figure 12.1. The notation T_r is used to denote a subtournament on r vertices and the double arrows mean that all the arcs between the two parts go in that direction.

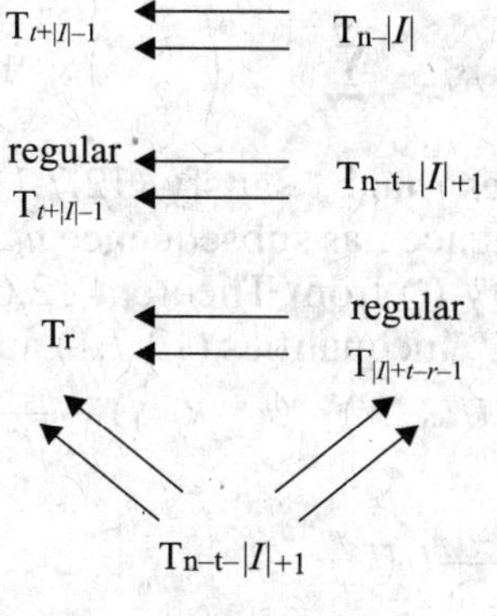

Fig. 12.1

The next result due to Bjelica [26] gives a criterion for score segments and subsequences with arbitrary positions of scores.

Theorem 12.6 If $[t_i]_1^m$ is a sequence of non-negative integers in non-decreasing order and $[s_i]_1^n$ is a score sequence of an n-tournament T with $m < n$, then the following properties are equivalent.

i. $\sum_{i=1}^{j} t_i \geq \binom{j}{2}$, $\quad 1 \leq j \leq m$,

ii. $t_j = s_j$, $\quad 1 \leq j \leq m$, for some T,

iii. $t_j = s_{k+j}$, $\quad 1 \leq j \leq m$, for some T and k,

iv. $t_j = s_{k_j}$, $\quad 1 \leq j \leq m$, for some T and $k_1 < k_2 < \ldots < k_m$.

The following result due to Bjelica and Lakic [27] gives the conditions for a set of integers to be the subset of scores with prescribed positions in some score sequence.

Denote $b(x) = \binom{x}{2}$, $X(k) = \sum_{i=1}^{k} x_i$.

Theorem 12.7 Let $0 \leq t_1 \leq t_2 \leq \ldots \leq t_m$ and $0 < k_1 < k_2 < \ldots < k_m$ be two sequences of integers. Then there exists an n-tournament T with score sequence $s_1 \leq s_2 \leq \ldots \leq s_n$ such that $t_j = s_{k_j}$, $1 \leq j \leq m$, if and only if

$$\sum_{i=1}^{j} (k_i - k_{i-1}) t_i \geq \binom{k_j}{2}, \quad 1 \leq j \leq m, \ k_0 = 0. \qquad (12.7.1)$$

The size of the tournament can be k_m if and only if in (12.7.1) the equality holds for $j = m$.

Proof

Necessity If, for some tournament, we have $t_j = s_{k_j}$, where $1 \leq j \leq m$, then monotonicity of the score sequence and the Landau theorem give

$$\sum_{i=1}^{j}(k_i-k_{i-1})t_i=\sum_{i=1}^{j}(k_i-k_{i-1})s_{k_i}\geq\sum_{i=1}^{k_j}s_i\geq\binom{k_j}{2},\quad 1\leq j\leq m.$$

Sufficiency Let some sequences t and k satisfy (12.7.1). Define the sequence $u_1 \leq u_2 \leq \ldots \leq u_{k_m}$ which includes the sequence t as subsequence $u_k = t_j$, $k_{j-1} < k < k_j$, $1 \leq j \leq m$, and we prove that it satisfies property (i) from Theorem 12.6. In the following minorisation, we apply piecewise linearity of U, inequalities (12.7.1) and convexity of binomial function $bU(k) = U(k_{j-1}) + (k-k_{j-1})t_{k_j} = U(k_{j-1}) + (k-k_{j-1})\frac{U(k_j)-U(k_{j-1})}{k_j-k_{j-1}}$

$$= \frac{k_j-k}{k_j-k_{j-1}}U(k_{j-1}) + \frac{k-k_{j-1}}{k_j-k_{j-1}}U(k_j)$$

$$\geq \frac{k_j-k}{k_j-k_{j-1}}b(k_{j-1}) + \frac{k-k_{j-1}}{k_j-k_{j-1}}b(k_j)$$

$$\geq b\left(\frac{k_j-k}{k_j-k_{j-1}}k_{j-1} + \frac{k-k_{j-1}}{k_j-k_{j-1}}k_j\right) = b(k).$$

By property (ii) from Theorem 12.6, there exists an n-tournament T with beginning score segment u. Hence scores from the sequence t appear on the prescribed positions k. ❑

12.2 Frequency Sets in Tournaments

Definition: The number of times that a particular score occurs in a score sequence of a tournament is called the *frequency* of that score. A set of distinct positive integers $F = \{f_1, f_2, \ldots, f_k\}$ is a *frequency set* if there exists a tournament T such that the set of frequencies of the scores in T is exactly F. Note that in such a case T has order at least $f_1 + f_2 + \ldots + f_k$. For example, the reversal of the orientation of three vertex disjoint arcs in a regular 7-tournament results in a 7-tournament with score sequence [2, 2 , 2, 3, 4, 4, 4] and frequency set $F = \{1, 3\}$.

Define $N(F)$ to be the smallest m such that there exists a tournament on m vertices with frequency set F. Clearly, $N(f_1, f_2, \ldots, f_n) \geq \sum_{i=1}^{n} f_i$. An almost regular tournament is an even order tournament in which the scores of the vertices are all as nearly equal as possible.

We have the following observations due to Alspach and Reid [3].

Lemma 12.1 If $f_1 < f_2 < \ldots < f_n$, $n \geq 2$, are positive integers, f_k is odd, and $N(f_1, f_2, \ldots, f_{k-1}, f_{k+1}, \ldots, f_n) = \left(\sum_{i=1}^{n} f_i\right) - f_k$, then

$$N(f_1, f_2, \ldots, f_n) = \left(\sum_{i=1}^{n} f_i\right).$$

Proof Let R be a tournament on $\left(\sum_{i=1}^{n} f_i\right) - f_k$ vertices with frequency set $\{f_1, f_2, \ldots, f_{k-1}, f_{k+1}, \ldots, f_n\}$. Let Q be a regular tournament on f_k vertices. Let T be the tournament obtained from disjoint copies of Q and R and in which every vertex of Q dominates every vertex of R. It is clear that T has $\left(\sum_{i=1}^{n} f_i\right)$ vertices and frequency set $\{f_1, f_2, \ldots, fn\}$. ❑

Lemma 12.2 Let R be a regular tournament of order r and let $Q_1, Q_2, \ldots, Q_k$ be almost regular tournaments of orders $q_1 < q_2 < \ldots < q_k$. Then there exists a tournament T of order $r + \sum_{i=1}^{k} q_i$ containing disjoint copies of $R, Q_1, Q_2, \ldots, Q_k$ as subtournaments such that $< R \cup Q_i >$ is regular of order $r + q_i$ and each vertex of Q_i dominates each vertex of Q_j when $i > j$.

The following constructive criterion due to Alspach and Reid [3] shows that every set F of positive integers is the frequency set of some tournament and determines the least order $N(F)$ of such a tournament. The proof is omitted as it is lengthy and can be found in [3].

Theorem 12.8 Let $f_1 < f_2 < \ldots < f_n$ be positive integers, at least one of which is odd. Then

$$N(f_1, f_2, \ldots, f_n) = \sum_{i=1}^{n} f_i \qquad (12.8.1)$$

unless either

i. $n = 2$, $f_1 \not\equiv f_2 \pmod 2$, $\gcd\{f_1, f_2\} = 1$, and $f_2 \neq 2$, in which case $N(f_1, f_2) = 2f_1 + f_2$ (12.8.2)

or

ii. $n = 2$, $f_1 = 1$, $f_2 = 2$, in which case

$N(1, 2) = 5$. (12.8.3)

Definition: Given the set of even integers $F = \{f_1, f_2, \ldots, f_n\}$, $e(F)$ denotes the largest power of 2 that divides every f_i, i.e., $e(F) = 2^m$ if $2^m / f_i$, $i = 1, 2, \ldots, n$, but $2^{m+1} \times f_j$ for some j.

Lemma 12.3: If T is a tournament with r vertices and frequency set $\{f_1, f_2, \ldots, f_n\}$, then for each $k \geq 1$ there is a tournament with kr vertices and frequency set $\{kf_1, kf_2, \ldots, kf_n\}$.

Proof For each i, $1 \leq i \leq k$, let T_i be a copy of T with vertices $u_{i1}, u_{i2}, \ldots, u_{ir}$. Orient the arcs between T_i and $T_j, i < j$, so that u_{ik} exactly dominates the $r/2$ vertices $u_{j,k+1}, u_{j,k+2}, \ldots, u_{j,(k+r)/2}$ where the second subscripts are interpreted modulo r. Every vertex has had its scores increased by $r(k-1)/2$ and since we started with k copies of T, the resulting tournament has kr vertices and frequency set $\{kf_1, kf_2, \ldots, kf_n\}$. ❑

The following result is also due to Alspach and Reid [3].

Theorem 12.9 Let $f_1 < f_2 < \ldots < f_n$ be even positive integers, let $e(f_1, f_2, \ldots, f_n) = 2^m$ and let $f_i = 2^m k_i$, $1 \le i \le n$. Then

i. if an even number of the $k_i's$ is odd, then
$N(f_1, f_2, \ldots, f_n) = \sum_{i=1}^{n} f_i$ and

ii. if an odd number of the $k_i's$ is odd and j is the smallest index for which k_i is odd, then
$N(f_1, f_2, \ldots, f_n) = f_j + \sum_{i=1}^{n} f_i$.

Proof Since 2^m is the highest power of 2 which is a factor of all the $f_i's$, at least one of the $k_i's$ is odd. Hence, in case (i) there are at least two odd $k_i's$ and $n \ge 2$. By Theorem 12.8, there is a tournament T on $\sum_{i=1}^{n} k_i$ vertices with frequency set $\{k_1, k_2, \ldots, k_n\}$. By Lemma 12.3 with $k = 2^m$, there is a tournament on $\sum_{i=1}^{n} f_i$ vertices and frequency set $\{f_1, f_2, \ldots, f_n\}$. This proves (i).

Now, consider Case (ii) with $(k_1, k_2) \ne (1, 2)$. First, we show that $N(f_1, f_2, \ldots, f_n) = \sum_{i=1}^{n} f_i$ is impossible. Let α_i be the score occurring with frequency f_i. Then

$$\sum_{i=1}^{n} \alpha_i f_i = \binom{f_1 + f_2 + \ldots + f_n}{2} = \frac{(f_1 + f_2 + \ldots + f_n)(f_1 + f_2 + \ldots + f_n - 1)}{2}.$$

Clearly, the left hand side is divisible by 2^m, while the right hand side is not. Thus, $N(f_1, f_2, \ldots, f_n) > \sum_{i=1}^{n} f_i$. Also, $N(f_1, f_2, \ldots, f_n) > f_k + \sum_{i=1}^{n} f_i$, for $k < j$, because of the same problem regarding divisibility by 2^m. Thus,

$$N(f_1, f_2, \ldots, f_n) \ge f_j + \sum_{i=1}^{n} f_i.$$

If $n \ge 3$, by Theorem 12.8, there is a tournament on $\sum_{i=1}^{n} k_i$ vertices with frequency set $K = \{k_1, k_2, \ldots, k_n\}$. As k_j is odd, by Lemma 12.3 there is a tournament on $k_j + \sum_{i=1}^{n} k_i$ vertices with frequency set K. If $n = 2$ and k_1 is odd, there is a tournament on $k_1 + k_1 + k_2$ vertices with frequency set K (use Lemma 12.1 if $gcd\{k_1, k_2\} > 1$). If k_1 is even and k_2 is odd, again there is a tournament with $k_1 + k_2 + k_2$ vertices and frequency set K by application of Theorem 12.8 and Lemma 12.1 if $gcd\ \{k_1, k_2\} > 1$, or by Lemma 12.2 if $gcd\ \{k_1, k_2\} = 1$. In case $n = 1$ and k_1 is odd, then an almost regular tournament of order $2k_1$ has frequency set F. In all of the above cases employ Lemma 12.3 with $k = 2^m$ to obtain the result in (ii).

Finally, let $F = \{2^m, 2^{m+1}\}, m \ge 1$. As above, $N(2^m, 2^{m+1}) \ge 2^{m+2}$. Any tournament with 2^m scores of $2^{m+1} - 2$, 2^m scores of $2^{m+1} + 2$ and 2^{m+1} scores of 2^{m+1} shows that $N(2^m, 2^{m+1}) = 2^{m+2}$ as required in (ii). ❑

12.3 Score Sets in Tournaments

Definition: The set of distinct scores in a tournament T is called the score set of T.

It is easy to see that every singleton set $\{k\}$, $k \geq 0$, is a score set. Reid [211] showed that a nonempty set S of non-negative integers is a score set whenever $|S| = 1, 2, 3$ or whenever S is either an arithmetic or geometric progression. Reid conjectured that any nonempty set S of non-negative integers is a score set. Hager [93] proved the conjecture for $|S| = 4, 5$. This problem proved to be more resistant than that of frequency set discussed above.

If the set $\{x_1, x_2, \ldots, x_k\}$ is the score set of some n-tournament T, then there are multiplicities $m_1, m_2, \ldots, m_k$ (positive integers) such that x_i occurs as a score exactly m_i times in T. These m_i are not necessarily distinct, so they are not the frequencies discussed above. We note that [115, 116] contain constructive solution of the problem of finding such a directed multigraph which has arbitary non-negative sequence as its score sequence, the maximal number of arcs between two vertices is the smallest possible and the minimal number of arcs between two vertices is the largest possible. For example, Theorem 12.1(Landau) and theorem on the multitournaments (Moon) are special cases of this result. Therefore, by Landau's Theorem, $\{x_1, x_2, \ldots, x_k\}$ is the score set of some n-tournament T if and only if there exist positive integers $m_1, m_2, \ldots, m_k$ such that

$$\sum_{i=1}^{j} m_i x_i \geq \binom{\sum_{i=1}^{j} m_i}{2}, \text{ for } 1 \leq j \leq k, \text{ with equality for } j = k.$$

Consequently, the connection to tournaments is removed, and Reid's conjecture becomes strictly an arithmetical supposition. Yan [264] proved the conjecture by pure arithmetical analysis.

Pirzada and Naikoo [200] proved by construction that if $s_1, s_2, \ldots, s_p$ are p non-negative integers with $s_1 < s_2 < \ldots < s_p$, then there exists a tournament with score set $S = \left\{ s_1, \sum_{i=1}^{2} s_i, \ldots, \sum_{i=1}^{p} s_i \right\}$. More results on score sets in tournaments can be found in [192, 193, 195]. The concept of scores in hyper tournament can be found in Zhou et at. [266]. The literature on kings in tournaments can be found in [126, 127, 128, 129, 150, 177, 179, 213, 214].

12.4 Lexicographic Enumeration and Tournament Construction

Definition: Let $[s_i]_1^n$ be any sequence of integers. The (transitive) deviation sequence of $[s_i]_1^n$ is defined to be the sequence $[d(i)] = [s_i - i + 1]$ and $d(i)$ is called the *deviation* of s_i. It is easy to see that $[s_i]_1^n$ is non-decreasing if and only if $d(i) - d(i+1) \leq 1$ for each $i < n$. Also, for each $k = 1, 2, \ldots, n$, $\sum_{i=1}^{k} d(i) = \sum_{i=1}^{k} s_i - \binom{k}{2}$. From this, it follows that a sequence

$[s_i]_1^n$ of non-negative integers in non-decreasing order is a score sequence if and only if its deviation sequence $[d(i)]_1^n$ satisfies $\sum_{i=1}^{k} d(i) \geq 0$ for $k = 1, 2, \ldots, n$ with equality for $k = n$.

Let $[s_i]_1^n$ and $[s_i']_1^n$ be score sequences of length n. Then, say that $[s_i]_1^n$ precedes $[s_i']_1^n$ if there exists a positive integer $k \leq n$ such that $s_i = s_i'$ for each $1 \leq i \leq k$ and $s_k < s_k'$. They are equal if equality holds for all i. In symbols, $[s_i] \leq [s_i']$ means $[s_i]$ proceeds $[s_i']$. Further, $[s_i']$ is the successor of $[s_i]$ if they are distinct; $[s_i] \leq [s_i']$ and $[s_i'] \leq [s_i'']$ whenever $[s_i] \leq [s_i'']$. An enumeration of all score sequences of a given length with the property that the successor of any score sequence follows it immediately in the list is called a *lexicographic enumeration*. Clearly, $[0, 1, 2, \ldots, n-1]$ is not the successor of any score sequence of length n and thus it is always the first in the lexicographic enumeration. Also, $[s_i]$ has no successor if and only if $s_n - s_1 \leq 1$.

If we know the first sequence in a lexicographic enumeration, then we can complete the work provided we know how to get the successor of any given sequence. The following algorithm due to Gervacio [82] gives the successor $[s_i']$ of $[s_i]$, if it exists.

Algorithm

1. Determine the maximum k such that $s_n - s_k \geq 2$.
2. Let $s_i' = s_i$ for all $i < k$.
3. Let $s_k' = s_k + 1$.
4. Let $s_j' = s_k + 1$ until $\sum_{i=1}^{j} s_i' < \binom{j}{2}$.
5. Let t be the minimum j such that $\sum_{i=1}^{j} s_i' < \binom{j}{2}$, set $s_t' = \binom{t}{2} - \sum_{i=1}^{t-1} s_i'$.
6. Let $s_i' = i - 1$ for all i, $t < i \leq n$.

Constructing a tournament: One method of constructing a tournament with a given score sequence can be found in [16]. The method we give here is due to Gervacio [82]. First, we have the following observations.

Lemma 12.4 Let $[s_i]_1^n$ be a score sequence with deviation sequence $[d(i)]$.

a. If max $\{d(i)\} = M > 0$, then for each $1 \leq k \leq M$, there exists a vertex u such that $d(u) = k$.

b. If min $\{d(i)\} = m < 0$, then for each $-1 \geq k \geq m$, there exists a vertex u such that $d(u) = k$.

Proof

a. Clearly, the result is true for $k = M$. Now, we show that it is true for all $1 \leq k \leq M$ by induction on k. Assume the result to be true for $k+1$, i. e., there exists a vertex u such that $d(u) = k+1$. Since $d(n) \leq 0$, there exists $t > u$ such that $d(u) = d(t) > d(t+1)$. Since $d(t) \leq d(t+1)+1, d(t+1) = d(u)-1 = k$. Hence (a) holds.

b. This can be proved by using the argument as in (a).

Lemma 12.5 Let $[s_i]_1^n$ be a score sequence with deviation sequence $[d(i)]$. If c is the number of negative terms, then $c \geq max\{d(i)\}$.

Proof Let $p = \max\ \{d(i)\}$. If $p = 0$, then $c = 0$ and the result holds. For $p > 0$, we have the following cases.

Case 1 There exists a vertex k such that $d(k) < 0$ and $|d(k)| \geq p$. By Lemma 12.4, $c \geq |d(k)| \geq p$.

Case 2 For each non-negative deviation $d(k)$, $|d(k)| < p$.

Let $q = \max\{|d(i)| : d(i) < 0\}$ and let $c < p$. Then using Lemma 12.4, $\sum\limits_{d(i)<0} |d(i)| \leq 1+2+\ldots+q$ $+(p-q)q$. But $\sum\limits_{d(i)<0} |d(i)| = \sum\limits_{d(i)>0} |d(i)|$, and by Lemma 12.4, $\sum\limits_{d(i)>0} |d(i)| \geq 1+2+\ldots+p$.

Hence, $\dfrac{q(q+1)}{2+(p-q)q} > \dfrac{p(p+1)}{2}$.

This gives the quadratic inequality $p^2-(2q-1)+q(q-1) < 0$ and this implies that $q-1 < p < q$, which is absurd, since p and q are integers. Hence, $c \geq p$. ❑

Now, we describe and validate the above algorithm.

Construction algorithm

Let $[s_i]_1^n$ be a score sequence with deviation sequence $[d(i)]_1^n$. First take n vertices arranged horizontally and labelled $1, 2, \ldots, n$ from left to right.

Step 1 Subdivide $[d(i)]$ into maximal non-increasing segments and denote by p the number of segments in the subdivision. Let n_i be the number of negative deviations in the ith segment, counting from left to right.

Step 2 Let j be the last integer such that $d(j) > 0$. If no such j exists, go to step 6. Else, determine the least integer q such that $\sum\limits_{i \leq q} n_i \geq d(j)$. For each i in the segments to the left of the qth segment such that $d(i) < 0$, let $d'(i) = d(i)+1$ and draw the arc ji.

Step 3 Let $\sigma = d(j) - \sum\limits_{i<q} n_i$ and choose a smallest (negatively largest) deviations $d(i)$ in the qth segment. For each such $d(i)$, let $d'(i) = d(i)+1$ and draw the arc ji. Let $d'(j) = 0$.

Step 4 For all other deviations $d(i)$ not changed in the preceding steps, let $d'(i) = d(i)$.

Step 5 If $[d'(i)] \neq [0]$, go to step 1 using $[d'(i)]$ in place of $[d(i)]$.

Step 6 Whenever $u < v$ and there is no arc between u and v, draw the arc vu.

Step 7 The resulting digraph is a tournament with score sequence $[s_i]_1^n$.

Now, we analyse the algorithm to verify its validity. Clearly, step 1 can always be carried out. Step 2 can be done in view of Lemma 12.5. Step 3 can be implemented because of step 2. Obviously, step 4 can be done, and after this step, $[d'(i)]$ satisfies $d'(i) - d'(i+1) \leq 1$ for all $1 \leq i \leq n$. Let D be the digraph formed when $[d'(i)] = [0]$. Then for each vertex i in D,

$$d_i^+(D) = \begin{cases} d(i), & if\ d(i) \geq 0 \\ 0, & if\ d(i) < 0 \end{cases}$$

and $$d_i^-(D) = \begin{cases} d(i), & if\ d(i) \geq 0 \\ d_i^-(D), & if\ d(i) < 0 \end{cases}$$

Let T be the tournament formed after step 6 and let i be any vertex of T. If $d(i) \geq 0$, then $s_i = d_i^+ = d_i^+(D) + i - 1 = s_i$. If $d(i) < 0$, then $d_i^- = d_i^-(D) + n - i = -d(i) + n - i$, and thus $s_i = d_i^+ = (n-1) - d_i^- = d(i) + i - 1 = s_i$.

Example Let $[s_i] = [1, 1, 2, 2]$. Then $[d(i)] = [1, 0, 0, -1]$.

The resulting digraph after using above algorithm upto $[d'(i)] = [0]$ is shown in Figure 12.2. To get the tournament, add all arcs ij $(i > j)$.

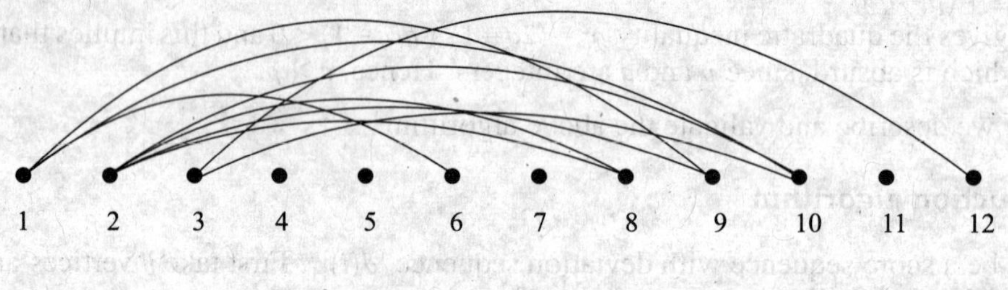

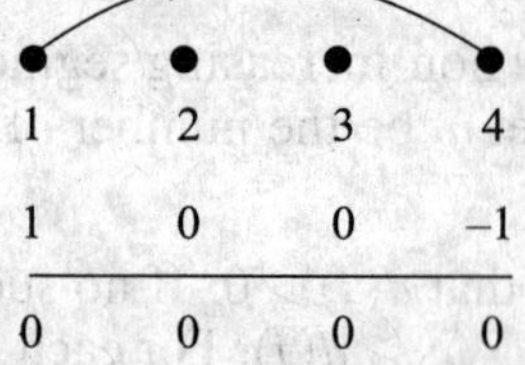

Fig. 12.2

12.5 Simple Score Sequences in Tournaments

Definition: A score sequence is simple (uniquely realisable) if it belongs to exactly one tournament. Every score sequence of tournaments with fewer than five vertices is simple, but the score sequence [1, 2, 3, 3, 3] is not simple, since the tournaments in Figure 12.3 are not isomorphic.

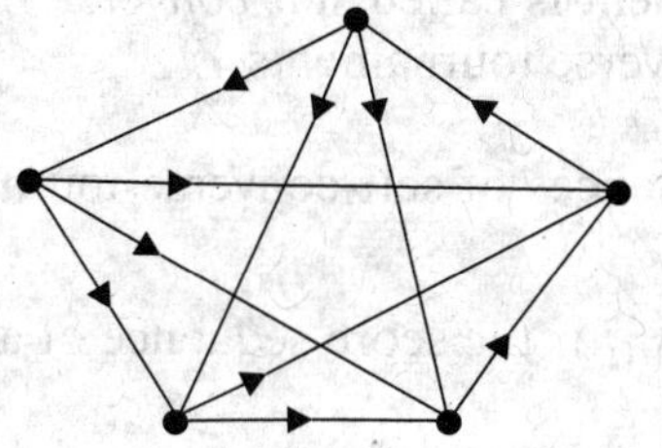
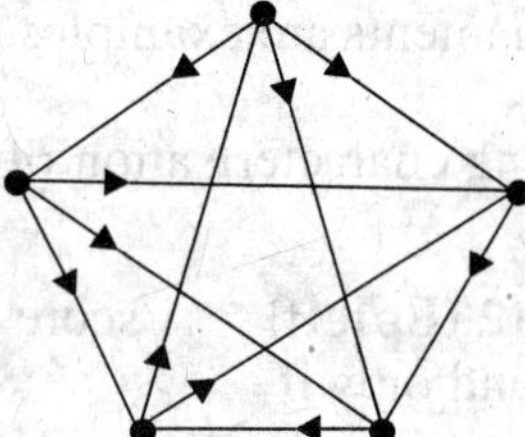

Fig. 12.3

We have the following observations.

Lemma 12.6 A score sequence S is simple if and only if every strong component of S is simple.

The following result due to Avery [8] gives a condition for determining simple score sequence in tournaments.

Theorem 12.10 (Avery) A strong score sequence is simple if it is one of [0], [1, 1, 1], [1, 1, 2, 2] or [2, 2, 2, 2, 2].

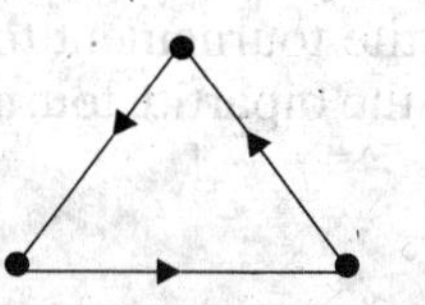
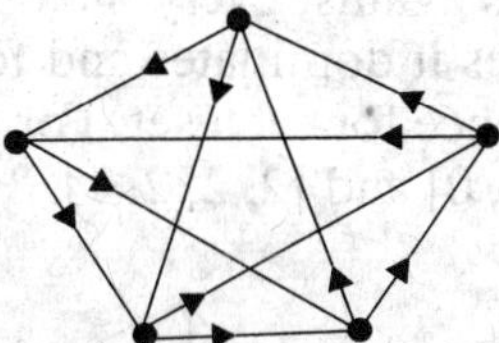

Fig. 12.4

Corollary 12.3 The score sequence S is simple if and only if every strong component of S is one of [0], [1, 1, 1] , [1, 1, 2, 2] or [2, 2, 2, 2, 2].

Hence it is possible to decide whether a given score sequence S is simple by using Theorem 12.10 to determine the strong components of S and then applying Corollary 12.3.

Let $s(n)$ denote the number of simple score sequences of order n. It is easy to show that $s(n)$ satisfies the following recurrence relation, which can be used to evaluate $s(n)$.

Theorem 12.11 $s(n) = s(n-1) + s(n-3) + s(n-4) + s(n-5)$, where $s(k) = 0$ if $k < 0$, and $s(0) = 1$.

12.6 Score Sequences of Self-Converse Tournaments

We know, the converse of an n-tournament T_n is the tournament T_n' obtained by reversing the orientation of all the arcs in T_n. A tournament is called *self-converse* if $T_n \cong T_n'$. The transitive tournaments are examples of self-converse tournaments.

The following characterisation of score sequences of self-converse tournaments is due to Eplett [68].

Theorem 12.12 (Eplett) A score sequence $[s_i]_1^n$ is the score sequence of a self-converse tournament if and only if

$$s_i + s_{n+1-i} = n - 1, \tag{12.12.1}$$

for $1 \le i \le n$.

12.7 Score Sequences of Bipartite Tournaments

A *bipartite tournament* T is an orientation of a complete bipartite graph. Clearly, the vertex set of T is the union of two disjoint nonempty sets X and Y, and arc set of T comprises exactly one of the pairs (x, y) or (y, x) for each $x \in X$ and each $y \in Y$. If the orders of X and Y are m and n respectively, T is said to be an $m \times n$ bipartite tournament.

A bipartite tournament may be used to represent competition between two teams and each player competes against everyone on the opposing team. The *score* s_v of vertex v is the number of vertices it dominates and for a bipartite tournament there is a pair of score sequences, one sequence for each set. For example, the bipartite tournament in Figure 12.5 has sequence [4, 3, 2, 0] and [2, 2, 2, 1].

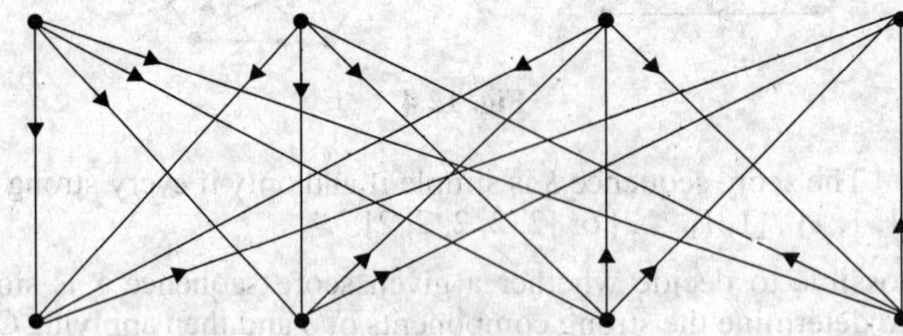

Fig. 12.5

Definition A bipartite tournament is *reducible* if there is a nonempty proper subset of its vertex set to which there are no arcs from the other vertices, otherwise irreducible. A *component* is a maximal irreducible sub-bipartite tournament. A *non-trival component* contains at least two vertices one from each partite set.

A bipartite tournament is consistent if it contains no directed cycles. It can be easily seen that a bipartite tournament is consistent if and only if, for v and w in the same partite set, v dominates every vertex which w dominates if its score is at least that of w.

The *converse* of a bipartite tournament is obtained by reversing the direction of all its arcs and a bipartite tournament is *self-converse* if it is isomorphic to its converse.

Now, assume that the partite sets of bipartite tournaments have a fixed ordering with X first and Y second. Then a given bipartite tournament T has associated with it two bipartite graphs (on the same sets of vertices) in a natural way, one graph containing those edges corresponding to the arcs directed from X to Y, the other from Y to X . For example, two graphs of the bipartite tournament T are shown in Figure 12.6. The two graphs are relative complements as bipartite graphs.

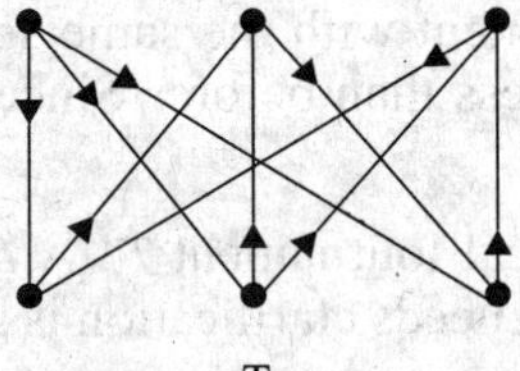

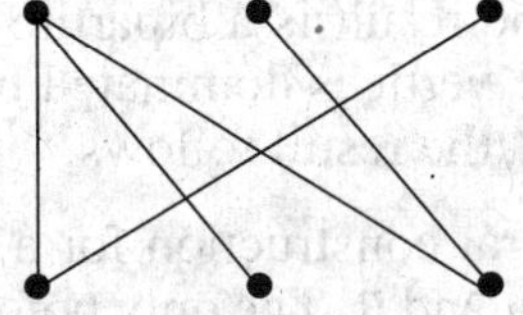

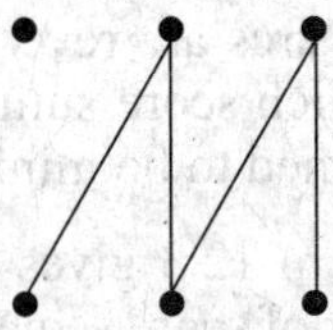

Fig. 12.6

Clearly, the pairs of score sequences of bipartite tournaments and pairs of degree sequences of bipartite graphs are equivalent.

Lemma 12.7 Let $A = [a_1, \ldots, a_m]$ and $B = [b_1, \ldots, b_n]$ be sequences of integers and let $\overline{A} = [n-a_1, \ldots, n-a_m]$ and $\overline{B} = [m-b_1, \ldots, m-b_n]$. Then the following are equivalent.

1. A and B are the score sequences of a bipartite tournament.
2. $\overline{A}$ and $\overline{B}$ are the score sequences of a bipartite tournament.
3. A and $\overline{B}$ are the degree sequences of a bipartite graph.
4. $\overline{A}$ and B are the degree sequences of a bipartite graph.

The following observation can be easily established.

Lemma 12.8 If v and v' are vertices in the same partite set of a bipartite tournament T, if $s_v \le s'_v$, and if there is a vertex w which is dominated by v and which dominates v', then there is another vertex w' which is dominated by v' and which dominates v, that is, $v \to w \to v' \to w' \to v$ is a 4-cycle.

The following result is due to Gale [81].

Theorem 12.13 (Gale) If $A = [a_1, \ldots, a_m]$ and $B = [b_1, \ldots, b_n]$ are sequences of non-negative integers in non–decreasing order, then A and B are the score sequences of some bipartite tournament if and only if the sequences $A' = [a_1, \ldots, a_{m-1}]$ and $B' = [b_1, \ldots, b_{a_m}, b_{a_m+1} - 1, \ldots, b_n - 1]$ are.

Proof First assume that A' and B' are the score sequences of a bipartite tournament T'. To the first partite set of T', add a new vertex v with arcs directed from it to vertices (in the second set) with scores $b_1, \ldots, b_{a_m}$, and to it from the others. The result is a bipartite tournament with score sequences A and B.

For the converse, it is sufficient to show that if A and B are the score sequences of a bipartite tournament, then in one realisation, a vertex (in the first set) of score a_m dominates vertices of scores $b_1, \ldots, b_{a_m}$. Among the bipartite tournament realisations of A and B, let T be the one in which a vertex x of score a_m is such that the sum S of the scores of the vertices it dominates is as small as possible. Let $S > \sum_{j=1}^{a_m} b_j$. Then there exist vertices y and y' such that $x \to y'$, $y \to x$ and $s_y < s'_y$. By Lemma 12.8, T has a 4-cycle $x \to y' \to x' \to y \to x$, and if its arcs are reversed, the result is a bipartite tournament with the same sequences, but in which score sum of the vertices dominated by x is less than before. Since the sum was assumed to be minimised, the result follows. ❑

Theorem 12.3 gives a natural construction for a canonical tournament $T^*(A, B)$ from a given pair of score sequences A and B. The only point which needs clarification is getting B' into non-decreasing order, i.e., we must specify dominance when a vertex v_i must dominate some but not all vertices y with a particular score. This is done by forming B' as follows. Let h and k denote the smallest and largest integers j for which $b_j = b_{a_m}$. Let $A' = [a_1, \ldots, a_{m-1}]$, and $B' = [b'_1, \ldots, b'_n]$ with

$$b'_j = \begin{cases} b_j, & for\ 1 \le j < h\ \ and\ \ h+k-a_m \le j \le k, \\ b_j - 1, & otherwise \end{cases}$$

This reduction and the resulting construction is illustrated by the following example, starting with sequences $A = [1, 1, 3, 5, 5]$ and $B = [1, 1, 2, 3, 4, 4]$.

$A = [1, 1, 3, 5, 5]$ $\quad B = [1, 1, 2, 3, 4, 4]$

$A_1 = [1, 1, 3, 5]$ $\quad B_1 = [1, 1, 2, 3, 3, 4]$

(x_5 dominates y_1, y_2, y_3, y_4, y_6)

$A_2 = [1, 1, 3]$ $\quad B_2 = [1, 1, 2, 3, 3, 3]$

(x_4 dominates y_1, y_2, y_3, y_4, y_5)

$A_3 = [1, 1]$ $\quad B_3 = [1, 1, 2, 2, 2, 2]$

(x_3 dominates y_1, y_2, y_3)

$A_4 = [1]$ $B_4 = [0, 1, 1, 1, 1, 1]$

(x_2 dominates y_2)

$A_5 = \varphi$ $B_5 = [0, 0, 0, 0, 0, 0]$

(x_1 dominates y_1)

Figure 12.7 shows the X to Y arcs resulting from this construction.

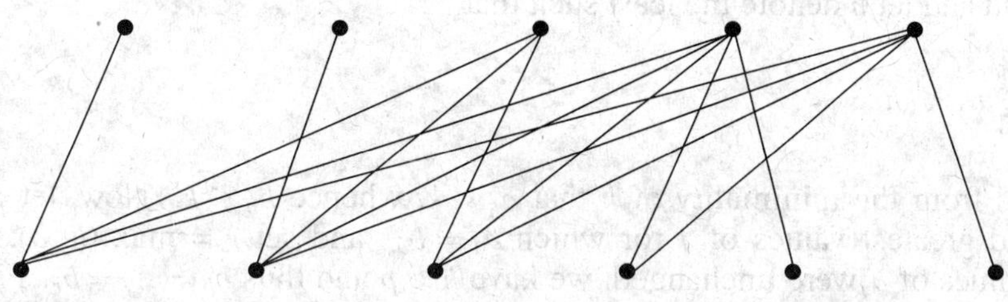

Fig. 12.7

A canonical tournament $T^*(A, B)$ has the following special property. In the subtournament $T^*_{r,n}$ induced by $\{x_1, \ldots, x_r\}$ and Y, if $x^*_r \to y^*_i$ and $y^*_j \to x^*_r$, then $s_{y^*_i} \leq s_{y^*_j}$, that is, $b_i \leq b_j$.

The next result is due to Beineke and Moon [20].

Theorem 12.14 If two bipartite tournaments have the same score sequences, then each can be transformed into the other by successively reversing the arcs of 4-cycles.

It can be noted that Theorem 12.14 does not imply that all bipartite tournaments with given score sequences have the same number of 4-cycles (they need not), although the corresponding statement does hold for 3-cycles in tournaments.

The next result first established by Moon [157] and then in the present form by Beineke and Moon [20] gives a simple criterion for determining whether a pair of sequences are realisable as scores.

Theorem 12.15 (Moon) A pair of sequences A and B of non-negative integers in non-decreasing order are the score sequences of some bipartite tournament if and only if

$$\sum_{i=1}^{k} a_i + \sum_{j=1}^{l} b_j \geq kl$$

for $1 \leq k \leq m$ and $1 \leq l \leq n$, with equality when $k = m$ and $l = n$.

Further more, the bipartite tournament is irreducible if and only if the inequality is strict except when $k = m$, and $l = n$.

Proof In any bipartite tournament T, the combined scores of any collection of k vertices from the first set and l from the second must be at least kl, so that the inequalities certainly hold. Further, if T irreducible, the inequality is strict unless $k = m$ and $l = n$.

Sufficiency If A and B satisfy the inequalities, we show that A' and B' satisfy the inequalities reordered as in construction of 12.13. It is easily seen that A' and B' are then in non-decreasing order, and further, their combined sum is

$$\sum_{1}^{m-1} a'_i + \sum_{1}^{h} b'_j = mn - a_m - (n - a_m) = (m-1)n.$$

For a fixed value of $k (1 \le k \le m-1)$, assume there is a value of l for which the inequality does not hold and let h denote the least such that

$$\sum_{1}^{k} a'_i + \sum_{1}^{h} b'_j < kh \,..$$

It follows from the minimality of h that $b'_h < k$, whence $b_h \le k$. Now, let p and q be the least and greatest values of j for which $b_j = b_{a_m}$ and set $r = \max\,(h, q)$. Since the first $p-1$ values of $b_j$were unchanged, we have $h \ge p$ and thus $b_h = \ldots = b_r$. Finally, let s denote the number of $j \le h$ such that $b'_j = b_{j-1}$. If $h \le q$, then $s \le q - a_m$, and if $h > q$, then $s = (h-q) + (q - a_m) = h - a_m$. In either case, $a_m + s \le r$. Therefore,

$$\begin{aligned}\sum_{1}^{k+1} a_i + \sum_{1}^{r} b_j &= \sum_{1}^{k} a'_i + \sum_{1}^{h} b'_j + \sum_{h+1}^{r} b_j + a_{k+1} + s < kh + (r-h)b_h + a_m + s \\ &\le kh + (r-h)k + r < (k+1)r,\end{aligned}$$

which is a contradiction. Therefore A' and B' satisfy the inequalities, as required.

It is easily seen that if the strict inequalities hold for A and B, no realisation can be reducible, completing the proof. ❑

The next criterion derived by Ryser [221] in the context of (0, 1)-matrices with prescribed row and column sums is equivalent to prescribed degrees in bipartite graphs.

Theorem 12.16 If A and B are sequences of non-negative integers with A in non-increasing order, then A and B are the score sequences of some bipartite tournament if and only if

$$\sum_{1}^{k} a_i \le \sum_{1}^{n} \min(k, m - b_j)$$

for $1 \le k \le m$, with equality when $k = m$. Further, the bipartite tournament is irreducible if and only if the inequality, is strict for all $k < m$ and $0 < b_j < m$ for all $j \le n$.

Remarks In general, one need not check the inequalities for all values of h and k, but only for those for which the next value in the sequence is different. Thus in order to show that [5, 5, 5, 3, 3, 2, 2] and [6, 5, 4, 1, 1, 0] belong to a bipartite tournament, we need to check the inequalities in Theorem 12.16 for $k = 3$, 5, and 7 only.

Theorem 12.17 If $A = [a_i]_1^m$ and $B = [b_j]_1^n$ are non-decreasing integer sequences with $0 \le a_i \le n$ and $0 \le b_j \le m$, and are such that

a. $A_m + B_n = mn$ and

b. $A_r + B_s \ge rs$, whenever $a_r < a_{r+1}$ and $b_s < b_{s+1}$.

Then (A, B) is realisable.

(Note that for a sequence $L = [x_i]_1^p, L_q = \sum_{i=1}^{q} x_i$ for $1 \le q \le p$ and $L_0 = 0$).

Proof We show that the inequality

$$A_k + B_x \ge kx \tag{4.17.1}$$

holds for all $1 \le k \le m$ and $1 \le x \le n$. If this is not the case for some k and x, let q and s be the smallest, and r and t be the largest indices such that $a_{q+1} = a_k = a_r$ and $b_{s+1} = b_x = b_t (q, s = 0)$. Now, $A_r + B_x < kx$. Claim that at least one of $A_k + B_s < ks$ and $A_k + B_t < kt$ holds. For otherwise, $(x - s)b_x < k(x - s)$ and $(t - x)b_x > k(t - x)$ which is impossible. Thus assume $(i)\ A_k + B_s < ks$.

Now, by hypothesis, (ii) $A_q + B_s \ge qs$ and (iii) $A_r + B_s \ge rs$ (observe that if $r = m$, then $A_m + B_n = mn$ and $0 \le b_j \le m$ together imply (iii). Then (i) and (ii) give $(k - q)a_k < (k - q)s$, while (i) and (iii) give $(r - k)a_k > (r - k)s$. These again lead to a contradiction. The case $A_k + B_t < kt$ can similarly be treated. ❑

The following result can be obtained from Theorem 12.16.

Corollary 12.4 If $C = [c_1, \ldots, c_m]$ and $D = [d_1, \ldots, d_n]$ be two non-increasing sequences having equal sum, then the following are equivalent.

i. $\sum_1^k c_i \le \sum_1^n \min(k, d_j)$, for $k = 1, \ldots, m$.

ii. $\sum_1^x d_j \le \sum_1^m \min(x, c_i)$, for $x = 1, \ldots, n$.

Now, different bipartite tournaments can have the same score sequences and they can differ only within irreducible components. That is, they must have the same numbers of components the same numbers of vertices within components, the same scores within components, and the same dominance between components. The general procedure here is to find a dominating component (a component is called dominating if it has no incoming arcs), delete its vertices and repeat. While an ordinary tournament has precisely one dominating component, the situation in the bipartite case is slightly different. It is described in the following result [19] and is a direct consequence of Theorem 12.15.

Theorem 12.18 Let $A = [a_1, \ldots, a_m]$ and $B = [b_1, \ldots, b_n]$ be score sequences (in non-decreasing order) of a reducible $m \times n$ bipartite tournament.

i. If $a_m = n$ or $b_n = m$, then there is a corresponding trivial dominating component, consisting of one vertex which dominates all the vertices in the other partite set.

ii. Otherwise, if k and x are the largest indices with $k < m$ and $x < n$ such that $\sum_{i=1}^{k} a_i + \sum_{j=1}^{x} b_j < kx$, then the non-trivial dominating component consists of all the vertices in the two partite sets with scores exceeding a_k and b_k respectively.

The following results can be found in [11].

Theorem 12.19 If $A = [a_i]_1^m$ and $B = [b_j]_1^n$ are realisable pair of score sequences with $0 < a_i < n$ and $0 < b_j < m$ and if $|a_i - a_k| \leq 1$ for any i, $k = 1, 2, \ldots, m$, then any bipartite tournament with score sequences A and B is irreducible.

Proof Assume T is a reducible bipartite tournament on partite sets X and Y with score sequences A and B respectively. Since $0 < a_i < n$ and $0 < b_j < m$, T has at least two non trivial components, say C and C', with C being the dominating one. If $x_i \in C \cap X$ and $x_k \in C' \cap X$, then x_i dominates all the vertices in Y dominated by x_k. Also, there exists $y_j \in C \cap Y$ and $y_l \in C' \cap Y$ such that $x_i \rightarrow y_j \rightarrow x_k$ and $x_i \rightarrow y_l \rightarrow x_k$. Thus, a_i = score $(x_i) \geq$ score $(x_k) + 2 = a_k + 2$. This contradicts the hypothesis, and the result follows. ❑

Theorem 12.20 Let $A = [a_i]_1^m$ (in non-decreasing order) and $B = [b^n]$ be sequences such that (A, B) is realisable. Let a_k, a_x be two entries in A with $a_k > 0$ and $a_x < n$. Define a new sequence $A' = [a_i']_1^m$ as follows.

$$a_k' = a_k - 1,\; a_x' = a_x + 1$$

and $a_i' = a_i$, for $i \neq k, x$. Then (A', B) is realisable.

Proof: It follows immediately from Theorem 12.17. ❑

Theorem 12.21 If (A, B) is irreducible, i. e., (A, B) is realisable and all its realisation are irreducible, and if A' is obtained from A by adding 1 to some entry and B' is obtained from B by subtracting 1 from some entry, then (A', B') is realisable.

12.8 Uniquely Realisable (Simple) Pairs of Score Sequences

If (A, B) is realisable, let T denote a realisation on partite sets X and Y. If a pair (A, B) is realisable and all its realisations are isomorphic, then (A, B) is called uniquely realisable.

The following observations can be found in [11].

Lemma 12.9 Let (A, B) be uniquely realisable. For any entry a_i in A and b_j in B, let X_i and Y_j be the subsets of X and Y consisting of vertices of scores a_i and b_j respectively. Then any cycle in T contains the same number of arcs from X_i to Y_j as from Y_j to X_i.

Proof If this were not the case for some cycle Z, then reversal of the arcs of Z would produce an (A, B) realisation non-isomorphic to T.

Lemma 12.10 If (A, B) is irreducible and uniquely realisable, then A or B is constant.

Proof If neither A nor B is constant, let X_1 be the set of vertices of minimum score in X and let $X_2 = X - X_1$, and similarly define Y_1 and Y_2. Since T is irreducible, every arc is contained in a cycle. Thus by Lemma 12.9, none of the four subtournaments $T(X_i, Y_i)$, $i, j = 1, 2$ is unanimous, i. e., has all its arcs directed from one partite set to the other.

Choose a vertex x_1 in X_1 of minimum score in $T(X_1, Y_1)$. Then x_1 dominates some $y_2 \in Y_2$. Consider two cases depending on whether or not y_2 dominates some vertex in X_2.

Case (i) Every vertex in X_2 dominates y_2. Let uv be an arc from Y_1 to X_2. Since score $(y_2) >$ score(u) in T, there exists an $x \in X_1$ such that $y_2 \to x \to u$ (Fig. 12.8).

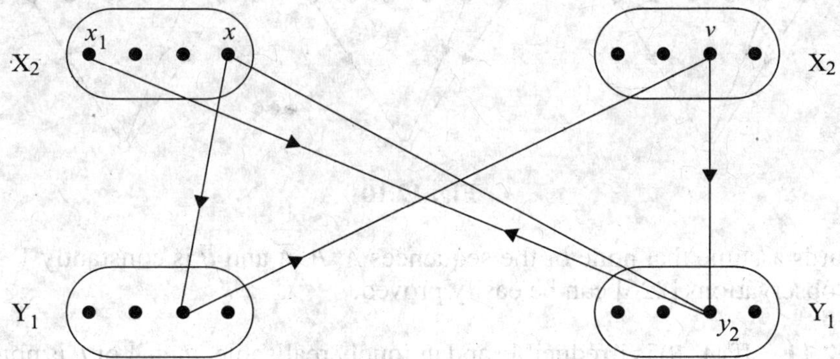

Fig. 12.8

But then $x \to u \to v \to y_2 \to x$ is a cycle which violates Lemma 12.9.

Case (ii) Some vertex $x_2 \in X_2$ is dominated by y_2. By the choice of x_1, there exists $y_1 \in Y_1$ such that $y_1 \to x_1$. If $x_2 \to y_1$, we again get a 4-cycle which has one arc from Y_1 to X_1, but no arcs in the other direction. So assume $y_1 \to x_2$ (Fig. 12.9). Since score $(y_2) >$ score (y_1) in T, there exists an $x \in X_1$ with $y_2 \to x \to y_1$. If $x \in X_2$, we again get a forbidden cycle $x_1 \to y_2 \to x \to y_1 \to x_1$. Thus $x \in X_1$. Likewise, there exists $y \in Y_1$ with $x_2 \to y \to x$. But then $x_1 \to y_2 \to x_2 \to y \to x \to y_1 \to x_1$ is a 6-cycle which violates Lemma 12.9.

Since all the possibilities have been exhausted, the result follows. ❑

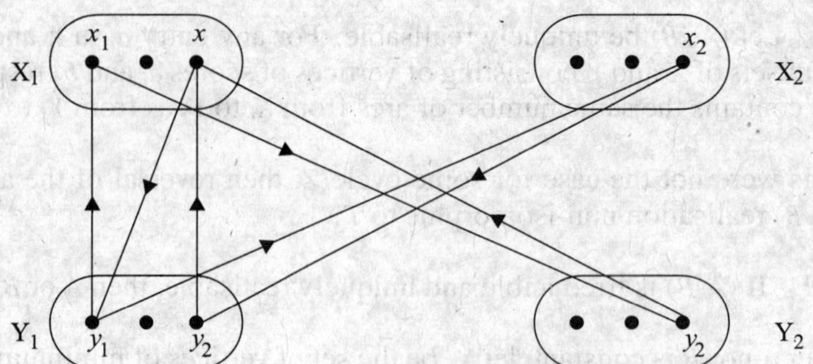

Fig. 12.9

Remarks We note that if in a realisable pair (A, B), one of the sequences has all entries as 1's (the sequence is constantly 1), then (A, B) is uniquely realisable. This is illustrated in Figure 12.10, where $A = [1, 1, \ldots, 1]$ and $B = [b_1, b_2, \ldots, b_n]$ and only X to Y arcs are shown.

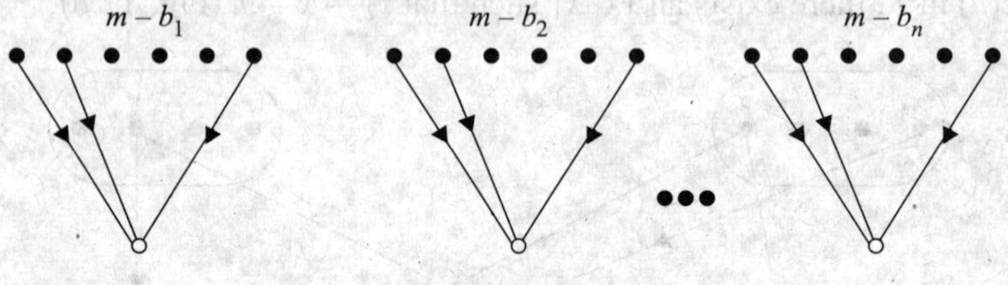

Fig. 12.10

Now onwards assume that none of the sequences A, B, $\overline{A}$ and $\overline{B}$ is constantly 1. Hence the following observations [226] can be easily proved.

Lemma 12.11 If (A, B) is irreducible and uniquely realisable, then A or B is non-constant.

Lemma 12.12 With A and B as above, the sequence B has precisely two distinct values.

Lemma 12.13 If (A, B) is irreducible, uniquely realisable and if $A = [a^m]$, $2 \le a \le n-2$, and $B = [b^r, c^s]$, $1 \le b < c \le m-1$, and $r, s > 0, r+s = n$, then $r = 1$ or $s = 1$.

Remarks It has been shown that if (A, B) is irreducible, uniquely realisable, then one of the sequences (or its dual) consists entirely of 1's, or one of the sequences is constant and the other has exactly two distinct values, one of which appears precisely once.

The following result due to Bagga and Beineke [11] gives necessary and sufficient conditions for unique realisability in the irreducible case.

Theorem 12.22 (Bagga and Beineke) An irreducible pair (A, B) of score sequences is uniquely realisable if and only if one of the following holds.

I. (without loss of generality) $A = [1^m]$ and B is arbitrary,

I′. the dual of (I), that is, $A = [(n-1)^m]$ and B is arbitrary,

II. (without loss of generality) $A = [1^{m-1}, a]$ and $B = [b^n]$,

II′. the dual of II,

III. (without loss of generality) $A = [1, a^{m-1}]$ and $B = [2^n]$,

III′. the dual of III.

Proof The sufficiency of (I) has already been noted in the remarks before Lemma 12.11 where Figure 12.10 shows the unique realisation. Now, let T be a realisation of $A = [1^{m-1}, a]$ and $B = [b^n]$ on partite sets $X = \{x_1, x_2, \ldots, x_m\}$ and $Y = \{y_1, y_2, \ldots, y_n\}$ respectively. If (say) x_m has score a and it dominates (say) $y_1, y_2, \ldots, y_n$, then $T - x_m$ has score sequences $A_1 = [1^{m-1}]$ and $B_1 = [(b-1)^{n-a}, b^a]$. Thus by (I), (A_1, B_1) is uniquely realisable. The unique realisability of (A, B) follows. This proves the sufficiency of (II). The proof of (III) is similar and the dual cases follow by the remarks before Lemma 12.11.

For proving necessity, induct on $m+n$. Since (A, B) is irreducible, so $m, n \geq 2$. If (say) m = 2, then $B = [1^n]$, and the result follows. Now, assume the result holds for all irreducible and uniquely realisable pairs of score sequences with combined length less than $m+n$, and consider such a pair (A, B) with $|A| = m$ and $|B| = n (m, n \geq 3)$.

Assume A and B are not of the type (I) or (I'). Then by the remarks after Lemma 12.13, we have, without loss of generality, $A = [a^m]$ and $B = [b^{n-1}, c]$, with $1 < a < n-1, 1 \leq b, c \leq m-1$ and $b \neq c$.

If y is the vertex of score c in a realisation T of (A, B), then $T - y$ has score sequences $A_1 = [(a-1)^{m-c}, a^c]$ and $B_1 = [b^{n-1}]$. Now, the unique realisability of (A, B) implies that of (A_1, B_1). Also, by Theorem 12.19, (A_1, B_1) is irreducible. Thus, by the induction hypothesis, A_1 and B_1 belong to one of the six given types. Consider these cases one by one.

i. If $B_1 = [1^{n-1}]$, then $B = [1^{n-1}, c]$, so that A and B are of type (II).

ii. If $B_1 = [(m-1)^{n-1}]$, then A and B belong to (II').

iii. If $B_1 = [b^{n-1}]$ and $A_1 = [1^{m-1}, a]$, then $c = 1$ and $a = 2$, so that $A = [2^m]$ and $B = [1, b^{n-1}]$. This is of type (III).

iv. If $B_1 = [b^{n-1}]$ and $A_1 = [d, (n-2)^{m-1}]$, we get A and B of type (III').

v. If $B_1 = [2^{n-1}]$ and $A_1 = [1, a^{m-1}]$, then $b = 2$, $a = 2$ and $c = m-1$. Thus, $A = [2^m]$ and $B = [2^{n-1}, m-1]$. Using Moon's theorem, we get $2m + 2(n-1) + (m-1) = mn$, so that $m = \frac{2n-3}{n-3}$. It follows that $n = 6$ and $m = 3$. But then A and B are both constant, a contradiction. Therefore this case is not possible.

vi. The possibility of $B_1 = [(m-2)^{n-1}]$ and $A_1 = [a^{m-1}, n-2]$ follows by duality.

This exhausts all the possibilities and hence by induction, the result is completely proved. □

Now, assume that (A, B) is a realisable pair and $Q_1, Q_2, \ldots, Q_p$ are the irreducible components of a realisation T of (A, B). Also, let Q_k has score sequences A_k and B_k, $1 \le k \le p$. Then (A, B) is uniquely realisable if and only if (A_k, B_k) is uniquely realisable for all k.

12.9 Score Sequences of Oriented Graphs

An oriented graph is a digraph with no symmetric pairs of directed arcs and with no loops. Avery [9] extended the concept of score structure to all oriented graphs.

Definition: Let D be an oriented graph with vertex set $V = \{1, 2, \ldots, n\}$, and let $d^+(v)$ and $d^-(v)$ be the outdegree and indegree respectively of vertex v. Then the *score* of vertex v denoted by a_v is defined as $a_v = n-1+d^+(v)-d^-(v)$ with $0 \le a_v \le 2n-2$. The sequence of scores is called the *score list*, and $A = [a_1, a_2, \ldots, a_n]$ arranged in non-decreasing order is called the *score sequence* of D.

Any oriented graph can be interpreted as the result of a round robin competition in which ties (draws) are allowed, that is, the participants play each other once, with an arc from u to v if and only if u defeats v. A player receives two points for each win and one point for each tie, as is frequently the case in sports such as soccer, ice hockey and cricket. With this scoring system , player v obtains a total of a_v points. An arc from u to v denoted by $u \to v$ is written as $u(1-0)v$, and $u(0-0)v$ means that neither $u \to v$ nor $v \to u$.

Definition: A *triple* in an oriented graph is an induced subdigraph with three vertices. A *cyclic triple* is an intransitive triple of the form $u \to v \to w \to u$. Any triple can be of the form $u(x_1-x_2)v(y_1-y_2)w(z_1-z_2)u$, where $0 \le x_i,\ y_i,\ z_i \le 1$ with $0 \le \sum x_i,\ \sum y_i,\ \sum z_i \le 1$.

The following result [9] extends a result of Ryser [228] which showed that if two tournaments have the same score structure, then each can be transformed to the other by successively reversing the arcs of appropriate cyclic triples.

Theorem 12.23 Let D and D' be two oriented graphs with the same score sequence. Then D can be transformed to D' by successively transforming appropriate triples in one of the following ways.

Either (a) by changing a cyclic triple $u(1-0)v(1-0)w(1-0)u$ to a transitive triple $u(0-0)v(0-0)w(0-0)u$, which has the same score sequence, or vice versa.

or (*b*) by changing an intransitive triple $u(1-0)v(1-0)w(0-0)u$ to a transitive triple $u(0-0)v(0-0)w(0-1)u$, which has the same score sequence, or vice versa.

The following result due to Avery [9] gives a constructive condition for a non-negative sequence in non-decreasing order to be a score sequence of some oriented graph. A short proof of this result is due to Pirzada et al. [194].

Theorem 12.24 (Avery) A sequence of non-negative integers in non-decreasing order is the score sequence of an oriented graph if and only if

$$\sum_{i=1}^{k} a_i \geq k(k-1)$$

for $1 \leq k \leq n$, with equality for $k = n$.

The following result can be found in [9].

Theorem 12.25 Among all oriented graphs with a given score sequence, those with the fewest arcs are transitive.

Proof Let A be a score sequence and let D be a realisation of A that is not transitive. Then D has an intransitive triple. There are two types of intransitive triples, a cyclic triple, which can be transformed by operation (a) of Theorem 12.23 to a triple with the same score sequence and three arcs fewer, and a triple $u(1-0)v(1-0)w(0-0)u$, which can be transformed by operation (b) of Theorem 12.23 to a triple with the same score sequence and one arc fewer. So in either case, we obtain a realisation of A with fewer arcs. ❑

The next result [9] provides a useful recursive test of whether a given sequence of non-negative integers is the score list of an oriented graph. We note that a transmitter is a vertex with indegree zero.

Theorem 12.26 Let A be a sequence of n integers between 0 and $2n-2$ inclusive and let A' be obtained from A by deleting the greatest entry $2n-2-r$ say, and reducing each of the greatest r remaining entries in A by one. Then A is a score list if and only if A' is a score list.

Proof Clearly, in a transitive oriented graph, any vertex of greatest score is a transmitter.

Let A' be a score list of some oriented graph D'. Then an oriented graph D with score list A can be obtained by adding a transmitter that is adjacent to just those vertices of whose scores are not reduced in going from A to A'.

For the converse, we show that there is an oriented graph with score list A in which a transmitter v with score $2n-2-r$ is adjacent to the (other) $n-1-r$ vertices with least scores. By Theorem 12.25, there is a transitive oriented graph D with score list A, in which a vertex v with greatest score $2n-2-r$ is a transmitter. Let U be the set of r vertices, apart from v, with the greatest scores in A, and let W be the set $V-\{v \cup U\}$.

Let v be adjacent in D to vertices $u_1, u_2, \ldots, u_k$ of U. Then there are exactly k vertices, say $w_1, w_2, \ldots, w_k$ of W not adjacent from v. Now, u_i cannot be adjacent to w_i, since D is transitive. Neither can w_i be adjacent to u_i, since taken together with the transitivity of D this implies that the score of w_i is greater than the score of u_i, which is contrary to the assumption. Thus $w_i(0-0)u_i$ for all i.

Now, transforming all triples $v(1-0)u_i(0-0)w_i(0-0)v$ to triples $v(0-0)u_i(0-1)w_i(0-1)v$, the vertex scores remain unchanged. This forms an (not necessarily transitive) oriented graph D_1 with score list A in which the transmitter v is adjacent to all vertices of W and none of U, as required. ❑

Theorem 12.26 provides an algorithm for determining whether a given non-decreasing sequence A of non-negative integers is a score sequence, and for constructing a corresponding oriented graph. At each stage, we form A' according to Theorem 12.26, such that scores of A' are also non-decreasing. If $a_n = 2n-2-r$, this means deleting a_n and reducing the r greatest remaining entries by one each to form $A' = |a'_1, a'_2, \ldots, a'_{n-1}|$ while ensuring that this is also non-decreasing. Arcs of an oriented graph are defined by $n \to v$ if and only if $a'_v = a_v$. If this procedure is applied recursively, then first it tests whether A is a score sequence and if A is a score sequence, an oriented graph $\Delta(A)$ with score sequence A is constructed.

Example Let $n = 5$, $A = [2, 4, 4, 4, 6]$.

Stage	A	B	Arcs of $\Delta(A)$
1	[2, 4, 4, 4, 6]	[2, 3, 3, 4]	$5 \to 4$, $5 \to 1$
2	[2, 3, 3, 4]	[2, 2, 2]	$4 \to 1$
3	[2, 2, 2]	[1, 1]	
4	[1, 1]	[0]	

Thus A is a score sequence.

We have the following observations [9] about $\Delta(A)$.

Theorem 12.27 The oriented graph $\Delta(A)$ is transitive for any score sequence A.

Theorem 12.28 There is no oriented graph with score sequence A which has fewer arcs than $\Delta(A)$.

One more method of constructing oriented graph with a given score sequence can be found in Pirzada [183].

The following is an equivalent statement of Theorem 12.24. A sequence of non-negative integers $A = [a_i]_1^n$ in non-decreasing order is a score sequence of an oriented graph if and only if for each subset $I \subseteq [n] = \{1, 2, \ldots, n\}$

$$\sum_{i \in I} a_i \geq 2\binom{|I|}{2}$$

with equality for $|I| = n$.

The following inequalities for scores in oriented graphs can be found in [229].

Theorem 12.29 A sequence $A = [a_i]_1^n$ of non-negative integers in non-decreasing order is a score sequence of an oriented graph if and only if for every subset $I = [n]$,

$$\sum_{i \in I} a_i \geq \sum_{i \in I} (i-1) + \binom{|I|}{2}$$

with equality when $I = [n]$.

Theorem 12.30 A sequence $A = [a_i]_1^n$ of non-negative integers in non-decreasing order is a score sequence if and only if for any subset $I \subseteq [n]$,

$$\sum_{i \in I} a_i \leq \sum_{i \in I} (i-1) + \frac{1}{2}|I|(2n - |I| - 1),$$

with equality for $I = [n]$.

Theorem 12.31 If $A = [a_i]_1^n$ is a score sequence of an oriented graph, then for each i, $i - 1 \leq a_i \leq n + i - 2$.

A necessary condition for a score sequence in oriented graphs to be self-converse, can be found in [187].

12.10 Score Sets in Oriented Graphs

Definition: The set A of distinct scores of vertices in an oriented graph D is called the *score set* of D.

Definition: A digraph D is *diregular* if $d_v^+ = d_v^- = k$ holds for each vertex v in D. In case of an oriented graph D with n vertices, $a_v = n - 1 + d_v^+ - d_v^-$, for each vertex v in D, and when $d_v^+ = d_v^- = k$ (say), then $a_v = n - 1 + k - k = n - 1$ for each v in oriented graph D. Thus an oriented graph D with n vertices is diregular if $a_v = n - 1$, for all v in D.

Now, we have the following result, the proof of which is obvious.

Lemma 12.14 The number of vertices in an oriented graph with at least two distinct scores does not exceed its largest score.

The following result is given by Pirzada and Naikoo [191].

Theorem 12.32 (a) (Pirzada and Naikoo) Let $A = \{a, ad, ad^2, \ldots, ad^n\}$, where a and d are positive integers with $a > 0$ and $d > 1$. Then there exists an oriented graph D with score set A, except for $a = 1, d = 2, n > 0$ and for $a = 1, d = 3, n > 0$.

Proof We induct on n. For $n = 0$, there is a positive integer $a > 0$, so that $a + 1 > 0$. Let D be a diregular oriented graph having $a + 1$ vertices. Then $a_v = a + 1 - 1 = a$, for all $v \in D$. Therefore score set of D is $A = \{a\}$. This proves the result for $n = 0$. If $n = 1$, then there are positive integers a and d with $a > 0$ and $d > 1$, and for $a = 1$, $d \neq 2, 3$.

Now, three cases arise: (I) $a > 1$, $d > 2$, (II) $a > 1$, $d = 2$ and (III) $a = 1$, $d > 3$.

(I) Let $a > 1$, $d > 2$. Therefore, $a+1 > 0$. Let D_1 be a diregular oriented graph having $a+1$ vertices. Then $a_v = a+1-1 = a$, for all $v \in D_1$.

Now, $ad - 2|V(D_1)| + 1 = ad{-}2(a+1) + 1 = ad - 2a - 1 \geq 3a - 2a - 1 = a - 1 > 0$, as $d \geq 3$ and $a > 1$. That is, $ad - 2|V(D_1)| + 1 > 0$. Let D_2 be a diregular oriented graph having $ad - 2|V(D_1)| + 1$ vertices. Then $a_u = ad - 2|V(D_1)| + 1 - 1 = ad - 2|V(D_1)|$, for all $u \in D_2$.

Let there be an arc from every vertex of D_2 to each vertex of D_1, so that we get an oriented graph D (which includes D_1 to D_2 together with all the new arcs from D_2 and D_1) having $|V(D_1)| + |V(D_2)| = a+1+ad-2|V(D_1)|+1 = a+1+ad-2(a+1)+1 = ad-a$ vertices with $a_v = a$, for all $v \in D_1$, and $a_u = ad - 2|V(D_1)| + 2|V(D_1)| = ad$, for all $u \in D_2$. Therefore score set of D is $A = \{a,\ ad\}$.

(II) Assume $a > 1$, $d = 2$. First take $a = 2$, $d = 2$. Then $ad = 4 > 0$. Let D be an oriented graph having ad = 4 vertices, say, v_1, v_2, v_3, and v_4 in which $v_1 \to v_3$ and $v_2 \to v_4$, so that $a_{v_1} = a_{v_2} = 2+4-2 = 4 = ad$, and $a_{v_3} = 4-2 = 2 = a$. Therefore D is an oriented graph having ad vertices with score set $A = \{a,\ ad\}$.

Now, take $a > 2$, $d = 2$. Let D_1 be a diregular oriented graph having 2 vertices, say v_1 and v_2. Then $a_{v_i} = 2-1 = 1$ for all $v_i \in D_1$, where $1 \leq i \leq 2$.

Again, $a > 2$ or $a-2 > 0$. Let D_2 be a diregular oriented graph having $a-2$ vertices, say $v_3,\ v_4,\ \ldots,\ v_a$. Then $a_{v_j} = a-2-1 = a-3$, for all $v_j \in D_2$, where $3 \leq j \leq a$.

Let there be an arc from every vertex of D_2 to each vertex of D_1, so that we get an oriented graph D_3 (which includes D_1 and D_2 together with all the new arcs from D_2 to D_1) having $2+a-2 = a$ vertices with $a_{v_i} = 1$, for all $v_i \in D_1$, where $1 \leq i \leq 2$, and $a_{v_j} = a-3+2(2) = a+1$, for all $v_j \in D_2$, where $3 \leq j \leq a$.

Again, $a > 2 > 0$. Let D_4 be a diregular oriented graph having a vertices, say $w_1, w_2, \ldots, w_a$. Then $a_{w_k} = a-1$, for all $w_k \in D_4$, where $1 \leq k \leq a$.

Let there be a arcs from a distinct vertices of D_4 to a distinct vertices of D_3 ($w_q \to v_q$, for all $q = 1, 2,\ \ldots,\ a$), so that we get an oriented graph D (which includes D_3 and D_4 together with all the new arcs from D_4 to D_3) having $a+a = 2a = ad$ vertices with $a_{v_i} = 1+a-1 = a$, for all $v_i \in D_3$, where $1 \leq i \leq 2$, $a_{v_j} = a+1+a+1 = 2a$, for all $v_j \in D_3$, where $3 \leq j \leq a$, and $a_{w_k} = a-1+2(1)+a-1 = 2a$, for all $w_k \in D_4$, where $1 \leq k \leq a$. Therefore score set of D is $A = \{a, 2a\} = \{a, ad\}$.

(III) Finally, let $a = 1$, $d > 3$. Therefore, $a+1 > 0$. Let D_1 be a diregular oriented graph having $a+1$ vertices. Then $a_v = a+1-1 = a$, for all $v \in D_1$.

Now, $ad - 2|V(D_1)| + 1 = ad - 2(a+1) + 1 = ad - 2a - 1 \geq 4a - 2a - 1 = 2a - 1 > 0$, as $d \geq 4$ and a = 1, i.e., $ad - 2|V(D_1)| + 1 > 0$. Then as in (I), we have an oriented graph D having $ad - a$ vertices with score set $A = \{a, ad\}$.

Hence in all these cases, we get an oriented graph D with score set $A = \{a, ad\}$. This shows that the result is also true for $n = 1$.

Assume the result to be true for all $p \geq 1$. We show that the result is true for $p + 1$.

Let a and d be positive integers with $a > 0$ and $d > 1$, and for $a = 1$, $d \neq 2, 3$. Therefore by induction hypothesis, there exists an oriented graph D_1 having $|V(D_1)|$ vertices with score set $\{a, ad, ad^2, \ldots, ad^p\}$.

Once again, we have either (I) $a > 1$, $d > 2$, or (II) $a > 1$, $d = 2$, or (III) $a = 1$, $d > 3$. Obviously, for $d > 1$, in all the above possibilities, $ad^{p+1} \geq 2ad^p$, and the score set of D_1, namely, $\{a, ad, ad^2, \ldots, ad^p\}$ has at least two distinct scores for $p \leq 1$. Therefore by Lemma 12.14, $|V(D_1)| \leq ad^p$. Hence, $ad^{p+1} \geq 2|V(D_1)|$, or $ad^{p+1} - 2|V(D_1)| + 1 > 0$.

Let D_2 be a diregular oriented graph having $ad^{p+1} - 2|V(D_1)| + 1$ vertices. Then $a_v = ad^{p+1} - 2|V(D_1)| + 1 - 1 = ad^{p+1} - 2|V(D_1)|$, for all $v \in D_2$.

Let there be an arc from every vertex of D_2 to each vertex of D_1, so that we get an oriented graph D (which includes D_1 and D_2 together with all the new arcs from D_2 to D_1) having $|V(D_1)| + |V(D_2)|$ vertices with $a, ad, ad^2, \ldots, ad^p$ as the scores of the vertices of D_1, and $a_v = ad^{p+1} - 2|V(D_1)| + 2|V(D_1)| = ad^{p+1}$, for all $v \in D_2$. Therefore score set of D is $A = \{a, ad, ad^2, \ldots, ad^p, ad^{p+1}\}$, proving the result for $p+1$. Hence the result follows. ❑

That no oriented graph exists when either $a = 1$, $d = 2$, $n > 0$ or $a = 1$, $d = 3$, $n > 0$, is proved in the following theorem.

Theorem 12.32 (b) There exists no oriented graph with score set $A = \{a, ad, ad^2, \ldots, ad^n\}$, $n > 0$, when either (i) $a = 1$, $d = 2$, or (ii) $a = 1$, $d = 3$.

We now have the following result [196].

Theorem 12.32 (c) If $a_1, a_2, \ldots, a_n$ are n non-negative integers with $a_1 < a_2 < \ldots < a_n$. Then there exists an oriented graph D with score set $A = \{a'_1, a'_2, \ldots, a'_n\}$, where

$$a'_i = \begin{cases} a_{i-1} + a_i + 1, & for\ i > 1, \\ a_i, & for\ i = 1. \end{cases}$$

Remarks

1. From Theorem 12.32 (c), it follows that every singleton set of non-negative integers is a score set of some oriented graph.
2. As we have shown in Theorem 12.32(b), i. e., the sets $\{1, 2, 2^2, \ldots, 2^n\}$ and $\{1, 3, 3^2, \ldots, 3^n\}$ cannot be the score sets of any oriented graph for $n > 0$. It follows, therefore, that the above results cannot be generalised to conclude that any set of non-negative integers forms the score set of some oriented graph. However, there can be other special classes of non-negative integers which can form the score set of an oriented graph, and the problem needs further investigations.

Pirzada and Naikoo [190] have obtained some results on degree frequencies in oriented graphs. More results on scores, score sets and kings in oriented graphs can be seen in [194, 196, 198, 209].

12.11 Uniquely Realisable (Simple) Score Sequences in Oriented Graphs

An oriented graph D is *reducible* if it is possible to partition its vertices into two nonempty sets V_1 and V_2 in such a way that there is an arc from every vertex of V_2 to each vertex of V_1. Let D_1 and D_2 be induced digraphs having vertex sets V_1 and V_2 respectively. Then D consists of D_1 and D_2 and arcs from every vertex of D_2 to each vertex of D_1. We write $D = [D_1, D_2]$. If this is not possible, then the oriented graph D is irreducible. Let $D_1, D_2, \ldots, D_k$ be irreducible oriented graphs with disjoint vertex sets. Then $D = [D_1, D_2, \ldots, D_k]$ denotes the oriented graph having all arcs of D_i, $1 \le i \le k$ and there are arcs from every vertex of D_j to each vertex of D_i, $1 \le i < j \le k$. Here $D_1, D_2, \ldots, D_k$ are called *irreducible components* of D. Such a decomposition is called as *irreducible component decomposition* of D, which is unique.

Definition: A score sequence A is said to be *irreducible* if all the oriented graphs D with score sequence A are irreducible.

In case of ordinary tournaments, the score sequence used to decide whether a tournament T having score sequence S, is strong or not. This is not true in case of oriented graphs. For example, the oriented graphs D_1 and D_2 in Figure 12.11, both have score sequence [2, 2, 2] but D_1 is strong and D_2 is not.

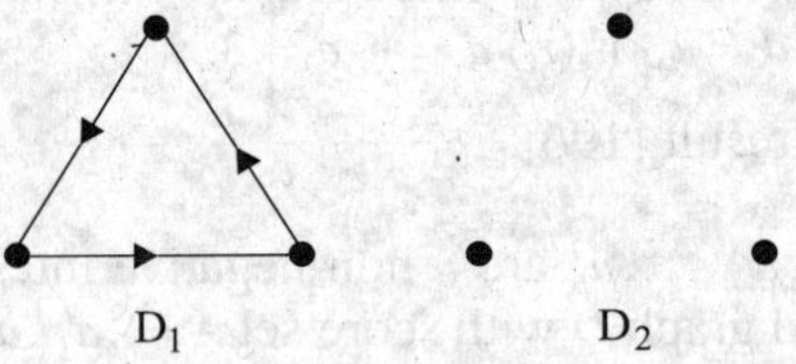

Fig. 12.11

The following result due to Pirzada [181] characterises irreducible oriented graphs.

Theorem 12.33 Let D be an oriented graph having score sequence. Then D is irreducible if and only if, for $k = 1, 2, \ldots, n-1$

$$\sum_{i=1}^{k} a_i > k(k-1) \tag{12.33.1}$$

and

$$\sum_{i=1}^{k} a_i = n(n-1) \tag{12.33.2}$$

Proof Suppose D is an irreducible oriented graph having score sequence $[a_i]_1^n$. Condition (12.33.2) holds since Theorem 12.24 has already established it for any oriented graph. To verify inequalities (12.33.1) we observe that for any integer $k < n$, the subdigraph induced by any set of k vertices has a sum of scores $k(k-1)$. Since D is irreducible, there must be an arc from at least one of these vertices to one of the other $n-k$ vertices, or there is no arc from these k vertices to other $n-k$ vertices. Thus, for $1 \le k \le n-1$

$$\sum_{i=1}^{k} a_i > k(k-1).$$

For the converse, suppose conditions (12.33.1) and (12.33.2) hold, we know by Theorem 12.24 that there exists an oriented graph D with these scores. Assume that such an oriented graph D is reducible. Let $D = [D_1, D_2, \ldots, D_k]$ be the reducible component decomposition of D. If m is the number of vertices in D_1, then $m < n$, and the following equation holds,

$$\sum_{i=1}^{k} a_i = m(m-1),$$

which is a contradiction. This proves the converse part. ❑

The following result due to Pirzada [181] can be proved easily.

Theorem 12.34 Let D be an oriented graph with score sequence $A = [a_i]_1^n$. Suppose that $\sum_{i=1}^{k} a_i = p(p-1)$, $\sum_{i=1}^{q} a_i = q(q-1)$ and for $p+1 \le k \le q-1$, where $0 \le p < q \le n$. Then the subdigraph induced by the vertices $v_{p+1}, v_{p+2}, \ldots, v_q$ is an irreducible component of D with score sequence $[a_{p+1} - 2_p, \ldots, a_q - 2_p]$.

Now, A is irreducible if D is irreducible and the irreducible components of A are the score sequences of the irreducible components of D. Theorem 12.34 shows that the irreducible components of A are determined by the successive values of k for which

$$\sum_{i=1}^{k} a_i = k(k-1),\ 1 \le k \le n. \tag{12.33.3}$$

We illustrate it with the following example.

Let $A = [1, 2, 3, 8, 8, 8, 13, 13]$. Equation (12.33.3) is satisfied for $k = 3, 6, 8$. Thus irreducible components of S are $[1, 2, 3]$, $[2, 2, 2]$ and $[1, 1]$ in ascending order.

Definition: A score sequence is *simple* if it belongs to exactly one oriented graph. We characterise simple score sequences of oriented graphs. First we have the following observation.

Lemma 12.15 The score sequence A of an oriented graph is simple if and only if every irreducible component of A is simple.

The following result due to Pirzada [181] determines which irreducible score sequences are simple.

Theorem 12.35 (S. Pirzada) Let A be an irreducible score sequence. Then A is simple if and only if it is one of [0], or [1, 1].

Proof Suppose A is an irreducible score sequence and let D be an oriented graph having score sequence A. We have three cases to consider. (1) D has $n \geq 3$ vertices, (2) D has two vertices, (3) D has one vertex.

Case (1) D has $n \geq 3$ vertices. Since A is irreducible, there exist vertices u, v and w such that D has a cyclic triple $u(1-0)v(1-0)w(1-0)u$; or an intransitive triple $u(1-0)v(1-0)w(0-0)u$; or a transitive triple $u(0-0)v(0-0)w(0-1)u$; or a transitive triple $u(0-0)v(0-0)w(0-0)$.

Now, if D contains the cyclic triple $u(1-0)v(1-0)w(1-0)u$, it can be changed to the transitive triple $u(0-0)v(0-0)w(0-0)u$ to form an oriented graph with the same score sequence, or vice versa. So the number of arcs in D and D' is different. If D contains the intransitive triple $u(1-0)v(1-0)w(0-0)u$, we can transform it to the transitive triple $u(0-0)v(0-0)w(0-0)u$, to form an oriented graph having the same score sequence, or vice versa. Here also the number of arcs in D and D' is different. Since in every case the number of arcs in D and is not same, so D is not isomorphic to D'. Thus A is not simple.

Case (2) D has two vertices. Then $A = [1, 1]$ is the only irreducible score sequence and it belongs to exactly one oriented graph, namely $u(0-0)v$.

Case (3) D has just one vertex. Then $A = [0]$ which is obviously simple.

Hence [0] and [1, 1] are the only irreducible score sequences that are simple. ❑

Corollary 12.5 The score sequence A is simple if and only if every irreducible component of A is one of [0], or [1, 1].

12.12 Score Sequences in Oriented Bipartite Graphs

An *oriented bipartite graph* is the result of assigning a direction to each edge of a simple bipartite graph. Let $X = \{x_1, x_2, \ldots, x_m\}$ and $Y = \{y_1, y_2, \ldots, y_n\}$ be the partite sets of an oriented bipartite graph D. For any vertex u in D, let $d^+(u)$ and $d^-(u)$ be the outdegree and indegree respectively. Define $a_x = n + d^+(x) - d^-(x)$ and $b_y = m + d^+(y) - d^-(y)$ as the scores of x in X and y in Y respectively. Clearly, $0 \leq a_x \leq 2n$ and $0 \leq b_y \leq 2m$. Then the sequences $A = [a_i]_1^m$ and $B = [b_j]_1^n$ in non-decreasing order are called a *pair of score sequences* of D. An arc from x to y, that is, $x \to y$ is denoted by $x(1-0)y$, and $x(0-0)y$ means neither $x \to y$ nor $y \to x$.

Definition: A *tetra* in an oriented bipartite graph is an induced subdigraph with two vertices from each partite set. Define tetras of the form $x(1-0)y(1-0)x'(1-0)y'(1-0)x$ and $x(1-0)y(1-0)x'(1-0)y'(0-0)x$ to be of α *-type*, and all other tetras to be of β *-type*. An oriented bipartite graph is said to be of α -type or β -type according as all of its tetras are of α -type or β -type respectively (Fig. 12.12).

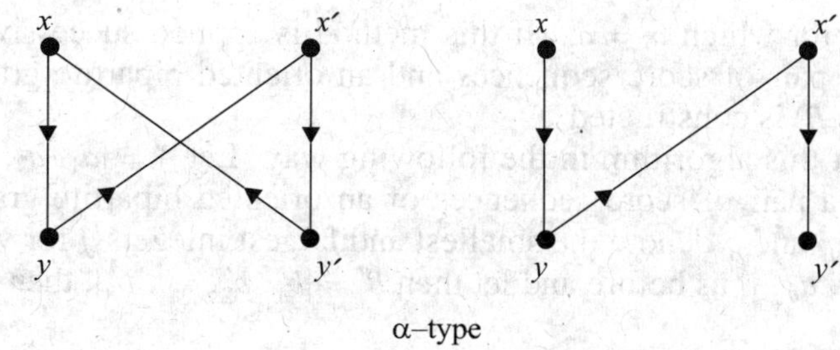

Fig. 12.12

We have the following simple observation.

Theorem 12.36 Among all oriented bipartite graphs with a given pair of score sequences, those with the fewest arcs are of β -type.

Proof Let (A, B) be a given pair of score lists and let D be a realisation of (A, B) that is not β -type. Then D has a tetra of α-type: $x(1-0)y(1-0)x'(1-0)y'(1-0)x$ or $x(1-0)y(1-0)x'(1-0)y'(0-0)x$. Since $x(1-0)y(1-0)x'(1-0)y'(1-0)x$ can be changed to $x(0-0)y(0-0)x'(0-0)y'(0-0)x$ with the same score sequences and four arcs fewer , and $x(1-0)y(1-0)x'(1-0)y'(0-0)x$ can be changed to $x(0-0)y(0-0)x'(0-0)y'(0-1)x$ with the same score sequences and two arcs fewer, so in either case we can obtain a realisation of (A, B) with fewer arcs. ❑

A *transmitter* is a vertex with indegree zero. In a β -type oriented bipartite graph with score sequences $A = [a_1, a_2, \ldots, a_m]$ and $B = [b_1, b_2, \ldots, b_n]$ either the vertex with score a_m, or the vertex with score b_n, or both may act as transmitter.

The next result due to Pirzada, Merajudin and Yin Jianhua [189] provides a useful recursive test to find whether a pair of lists is realisable.

Theorem 12.37 Suppose $A = [a_1, a_2, \ldots, a_m]$ and $B = [b_1, b_2, \ldots, b_n]$ be two sequences of non-negative integers in nondecreasing order. Let A' be obtained from A by deleting one entry a_m and B' be obtained from B by reducing $2n - a_m$ greatest entries of B by 1 each provided $a_m \geq n$ and $b_n \leq 2m - 1$. Then A and B are the score sequences of some oriented bipartite graph if and only if A' and B' are also score sequences of some oriented bipartite graph.

Theorem 12.37 provides an algorithm for determining whether a given pair of sequences (A, B) of non-negative integers in non-decreasing order is a pair of score sequences and for constructing a corresponding oriented bipartite graph. Suppose $A = [a_1, a_2, \ldots, a_m]$ and $B = [b_1, b_2, \ldots, b_n]$ be a pair of score sequences of an oriented bipartite graph with parts $X = \{x_1, x_2, \ldots, x_m\}$ and $Y = \{y_1, y_2, \ldots, y_n\}$, where $a_m \geq n$, $b_n \leq 2m - 1$. Deleting a_m and reducing $2n - a_m$ greatest entries of B by 1 each to form $B' = [b'_1, b'_2, \ldots, b'_n]$. Then arcs are defined by $x_m \to y_j$ for which $b_j = b'_j$. Now, if at least one of the conditions $a_m \geq n$ or $b_n \leq 2m - 1$ does not hold, then we delete b_n (obviously $b_n \geq m$, $a_m \leq 2n - 1$) and reduce $2m - b_n$ greatest entries of A by 1 each to form $A = [a'_1, a'_2, \ldots, a'_m]$. In this case arcs are defined by $y_n \to x_i$ for which $a_i = a'_i$. If this method is applied successively, then it tests whether (A, B) is a pair of score sequences and an oriented bipartite graph $\Delta(A,\ B)$ with score sequences (A, B) is constructed.

We can interpret this algorithm in the following way. Let $A = [a_1,\ a_2,\ \ldots,\ a_m]$ and $B = [b_1,\ b_2,\ \ldots,\ b_n]$ be a pair of score sequences of an oriented bipartite graph, where $a_m \geq n$, $b_n \leq 2m-1$. Let p and q denote the smallest and largest integers j for which $b_j = b_{a_m - n}$. Let $A' = [a_1,\ a_2,\ \ldots,\ a_{m-1}]$ as before and let then $B' = [b'_1,\ b'_2,\ \ldots,\ b'_n]$, then

$$b'_j = \begin{cases} b_j, & for\ 1 \leq j \leq p-1\ and\ p+q-(a_m-n) \leq j \leq q, \\ b_j - 1, & otherwise. \end{cases}$$

We illustrate this reduction and the resulting construction with the following example, beginning with lists A_1 and B_1. The oriented bipartite graph constructed is shown in Figure 12.13.

$A_1 = [4, 4, 5]$	$B_1 = [1, 1, 4, 5]$	$x_3 \to y_2$
$A_2 = [4, 4]$	$B_2 = [0, 1, 3, 4]$	$y_4 \to x_1, x_2$
$A_3 = [4, 4]$	$B_3 = [0, 1, 3]$	$x_2 \to y_1$
$A_4 = [4]$	$B_4 = [0, 0, 2]$	$y_3 \to x_1$
$A_5 = [4]$	$B_5 = [0, 0]$	$x_1 \to y_1, y_2$

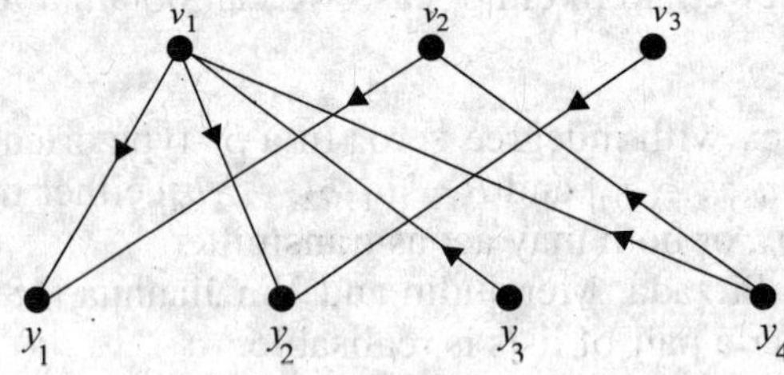

Fig. 12.13

Let D_i be the oriented bipartite graphs with disjoint parts X_i and Y_i for $1 \leq i \leq t$. Let $X = U_{i=1}^{t} X_i$ and $Y = U_{i=1}^{t} Y_i$. Clearly, $D = [D_1, D_2,\ \ldots,\ D_t]$ denotes the oriented bipartite graph with parts X and Y, obtained from D_i for $1 \leq i \leq t$ such that the arcs of D are the arcs of D_i and each vertex of Y_j is adjacent to every vertex of X_i for $j < i$ and each vertex of X_i is adjacent to every vertex of Y_j for $i < j$.

The next result [194] gives a criterion for determining whether a pair of sequences are realisable as scores.

Theorem 12.38 Let $A = [a_1,\ a_2,\ \ldots,\ a_m]$ and $B = [b_1,\ b_2,\ \ldots,\ b_n]$ be a pair of sequences of non-negative integers in non-decreasing order. Then A and B are scores sequences of some oriented bipartite graph if and only if

$$\sum_{i=1}^{k} a_i + \sum_{j=1}^{t} b_j \geq 2kl \qquad (12.3.1)$$

for $1 \leq k \leq m$ and $1 \leq l \leq n$, with equality when $k = m$ and $l = n$.

The characterisation of scores of oriented tripartite graphs can be found in [185] and scores (marks) in other types of digraphs can be found in [183, 196, 191].

12.13 Score Sequences of Semi Complete Digraphs

Definition: A *semi complete digraph* is a digraph with no directed loops and at least one arc between every pair of distinct vertices. Clearly, a tournament is a semi complete digraph in which there is exactly one arc between every pair of distinct vertices. Therefore every semi complete digraph contains at least one tournament on the same vertex set and is contained in the complete symmetric digraph on the same vertex set. The *score* of a vertex v in a semi complete digraph D is the outdegree of v.

The following result is due to Reid and Zhang [216].

Theorem 12.39 A sequence of non-negative integers $S = [s_i]_1^n$ in non-decreasing order is a score sequence of some semi complete digraph of order n if and only if

$$\sum_{i=1}^{k} s_i \geq \binom{k}{2} \text{ and } s_k \leq n-1, \tag{12.39.1}$$

for all $k, 1 \leq k \leq n$.

Proof

Necessity If S is a score sequence of some semi complete digraph D of order n, then any k vertices of D induce a semi complete digraph of order k which, in turn, contains a tournament W of order k. Therefore the sum of the scores in D of these k vertices is at least the sum of their scores in W which is the total number of arcs in W, $\binom{k}{2}$. Also, a vertex of D can dominate at most all of the other vertices, so no score in S can exceed $n-1$. Thus the conditions (12.39.1) are necessary.

We require the following result for proving sufficiency.

Lemma 12.16 If $S = [s_i]_1^n, n \geq 1$, is a sequence of integers in non-decreasing order satisfying (12.39.1), then there exists a tournament T with score sequence $s' = [s'_i]_1^n$, such that $s'_i \leq s_i$ for $1 \leq i \leq n$.

Proof Define an order $\preceq$ on all non-decreasing sequences of integers satisfying (12.39.1) (thus including all sequences satisfying conditions (12.1.2)) as follows. If $B = [b_1, b_2, \ldots, b_n]$ and m is the smallest index for which $b_m = b_n$ ($= \max\{b_i : 1 \leq i \leq n\}$), then B (strictly) covers the sequence $A = [a_1, a_2, \ldots, a_n]$, where A and B are identical such that $a_m = b_m - 1$. Note that if $m > 1$, then $b_{m-1} < b_m = b_{m+1} = \ldots = b_n$ and if $m = 1$, then $b_1 = b_2 = \ldots = b_n \geq (n-1)/2$.

Also, if B covers A, then $\sum_{i=1}^{n} a_i = \left(\sum_{i=1}^{n} b_i\right) - 1$.

This implies, by Landau's theorem, that if S satisfies (12.39.1), then S is the score sequence for some tournament if and only if S covers no sequence satisfying (12.39.1). And, if B is not the score sequence for any tournament, then B covers exactly one sequence satisfying (12.39.1). For two non-decreasing sequences of integers X and Y satisfying (12.39.1), define $X \preceq Y$ if either $X = Y$, or there is a sequence $X_0 = X, X_1, X_2, \ldots, X_{j-1}, X_j = Y$ of non-decreasing sequences of integers each satisfying conditions (12.39.1) such that X_i covers $X_{i-1}, 1 \le i \le j$.

Now, let $S = [s_i]_1^n$ be a sequence of integers in non-decreasing order satisfying conditions (12.39.1). Induct on the integer $e(S) \equiv \left(\sum_{i=1}^{n} s_i\right) - \binom{n}{2}$. If $e(S) = 0$, then by Landau's theorem, S itself is a score sequence for some tournament T. If $e(S) > 0$, then by the remarks above, S covers exactly one sequence $Z = [z_1, z_2, \ldots, z_n]$ satisfying (12.39.1), such that $z_i \le s_i$, for $1 \le i \le n$, and $e(Z) = \left(\sum_{i=1}^{n} Z_i\right) - \binom{n}{2} = \left(\sum_{i=1}^{n} s_i\right) - \binom{n}{2} - 1 = e(s) - 1$. By the induction hypothesis applied to Z, there is a score sequence $S' = [s_i']_1^n$ for some tournament T such that $s_i' \le z_i$, for $1 \le i \le n$. By the transitivity of $\le$, we have $s_i' \le s_i$, for $1 \le i \le n$, so and T suffice for S, as required. ❑

Sufficiency of Theorem 12.39 Let $S = [s_i]_1^n$, $n \ge 1$, be a sequence of integers in non-decreasing order, satisfying conditions (12.39.1). By Lemma 12.16, there is a tournament T of order n with score sequence S', where $S' \preceq S$ In T denote the vertex with score s_i' by v_i, $1 \le i \le n$. Since v_i has indegree $n - 1 - s_i' \ge n - 1 - s_i$, arcs can be added from v_i to any $n - 1 - s_i$ vertices in the inset of v_i in T so as to produce a semi complete digraph D with score sequence S.

12.14 Exercises

1. Prove that any n-tournament can be obtained from any other having the same scores by a sequence of arc reversals of 3-cycles.
2. If an n-tournament has every score s_i satisfying $\frac{1}{4}(n-1) \le s_i \le \frac{3}{4}(n-1)$ then show that it is irreducible.
3. Construct a proof for Theorem 12.2 and 12.6.
4. If $S = \{a,\ a+d,\ a+d+e\}$, where a, d, e are non-negative integers and $de > 0$, and if $(d,\ e) = g$, $d = a$ and $e \le a + d - d/2g + (1/2)$, then prove S is a score set of some tournament.
5. Prove that every set of three non-negative integers is a score set of some tournament.
6. If a, b, c, d are four non-negative integers with $bcd > 0$, prove that there exists a tournament T with score set $S = \{a, a+b, a+b+c, a+b+c+d\}$.
7. Construct a proof of Theorem 12.11.

8. Prove Lemma 12.7 and Lemma 12.8.

9. Construct a proof of Theorem 12.14.

10. Construct a proof of Theorem 12.16.

11. Construct proofs of Theorem 12.18 and 12.21.

12. If T is a bipartite tournament with score sequences $A = [a_i]_1^m$ and $B = [b_j]_1^n$ satisfying $n/4 < a_i < 3n/4$ for $1 \le i \le m$, and $m/4 < b_j < 3m/4$ for $1 \le j \le n$, then prove that T is irreducible.

13. Construct proofs of Theorem 12.37 and Theorem 12.38.

References

1. Akiyama, J. and Kano, M., Factors and factorization of graphs, *J. Graph Theory* 9, 1 (1985) 1–42.

2. Alavi, A. and Behzad, M., Complementary graphs and edge-chromatic numbers, *SIAM J. Apl. Math.* 20 (1971) 161–163.

3. Alspach, B. and Reid, K. B., Degree frequencies in digraphs and tournaments, *J. Graph Theory* 2, 3 (1978) 241–249.

4. Anderson, I., Perfect matching of a graph, *J. Combin. Theory Ser. B* 10 (1971) 183–186.

5. Appel, K. and Haken, W., Every planar map is four colorable, *Bull. Amer. Math. Soc.* 82 (1976) 711–712.

6. Appel, K. and Haken, W., Every planar map is four colorable, Part I, Discharging, *Illinois J. Math.* 21, 3 (1977) 429–490.

7. Appel, K. and Haken, W., Every planar map is four colorable, Part II, Reducibility, *Illinois J. Math.* 21, 3 (1977) 491–567.

8. Avery, P., Condition for a tournament score sequence to be simple, *J. Graph Theory* 4 (1980) 157–164.

9. Avery, P., Score sequences in oriented graphs, *J. Graph Theory* 15, 3 (1991) 251–257.

10. Baebler, F., Uber die Zerlegung regularer Streckenkomplexe ungerader Ordnung, *Comment. Math. Helve.* 10 (1938) 275–287.

11. Bagga, K. S. and Beineke, L.W., Uniquely realizable score lists in bipartite tournaments, *Czech. Math. Journal* 37, 2 (1987) 323–333.

12. Balakrishnan, R. and Paulraja, P., Chordal graphs and some of their derived graphs, *Congressus Numerantium* 53 (1986) 33–35.

13. Balakrishnan, R. and Ranganathan, K., *A Textbook of Graph Theory*, Springer-Verlag, New York (2000).

14. Barnette, D. W. and Grunbaum, B., On Steinitz's theorem concerning convex 3-polytopes and on some properties of planar graphs, *Lecture Notes in Math.* 110 (1969) 27–40.

15. Behzad, M. and Chartrand, G., *Introduction to the Theory of Graphs*, Allyn and Bacon, Inc., Boston, MA (1971).

16. Behzad, M. and Simpson, J. E., Eccentric sequences and eccentric sets in graphs, *Discrete Math.* 16 (1976) 187–193.

17. Behzad, M., Chartrand, M. G. and Lesniak-Foster, L., Graphs and Digraphs, Pindle, Weber and Schmidt Int. Series, Boston MA. (1979).

18. Beineke, L. W., Derived graphs and digraphs, in H. Sachs, H. Voss and H. Walther (eds), *Beitrage zur Graphentheorie,* Teubner, Leipzig (1968) 17–33.

19. Beineke, L. W., A tour through tournaments, or bipartite and ordinary tournaments, A comparative survey, *Combinatorics, London Math. Soc. Lecture Note Series* 52, Cambridge University Press (1981) 41–55.

20. Beineke, L. W. and Moon, J. W., On bipartite tournaments and scores, in G. Chartrand (ed.), *The Theory of Applications of Graphs, John Wiley and Sons, New York* (1981) 55–71.

21. Berge, C., Two theorems in graph theory, *Proc. Nat. Acad. Sci. U. S. A.* 43 (1957) 842–844.

22. Berge, C., *The Theory of Graphs and its Applications*, Methuen, London (1962).

23. Berge, C., *Graphs and Hypergraphs*, North-Holland, Amsterdam (1973).

24. Bermond, J. C. and Thomassen, C., Cycles in digraphs—a survey, *J. Graph Theory* 5, 1 (1981) 1–43.

25. Biggs, N. L., *Algebraic Graph Theory*, Cambridge University Press (1974).

26. Bjelica, M. and Lakic, S., Segments of scores sequences, *Novi Sad J. Math.* 30, 2 (2000) 11–14.

27. Bjelica, M. and Lakic, S., Segments of sets of scores with prescribed positions, *IMC Filomat* (2001) 26–30.

28. Boesch, F. T., Suffel, C. and Tindell, R., The spanning subgraphs of Eulerian graphs, *J. Graph Theory* 1, 1 (1977) 79–84.

29. Bollabas, B., *Extremal Graph Theory*, Acad. Press, New York (1978).

30. Bollobas, B., Uniquely colorable graphs, *J. Combin. Theory Ser.* B 24, 1 (1978).

31. Bollobas, B. and Catlin, P. A., Topological cliques of random graphs, *J. Combin. Theory Ser.* B 30 (1981) 224–227.

32. Bondy, J. A., Bounds on the chromatic number of a graph, *J. Combin. Theory* 7 (1969) 96–98.

33. Bondy, J. A., Properties of graphs with constraints on degrees, *Studia Sci. Math. Hungar*. 4 (1969) 473–475.

34. Bondy, J. A., Pancyclic graphs, *J. Combin. Theory Ser.* B11 (1971) 80–84.

35. Bondy, J. A., Short proofs of classical theorems, *J. Graph Theory*, 44, 3 (2003) 159–165.

36. Bondy, J. A. and Chvatal, V., A method in graph theory, *Discrete Math*. 15, 2 (1976) 111–135.

37. Bondy, J. A. and Halberstam, F. Y., Parity theorems for paths and cycles in graphs, *J. Graph Theory* 10 (1986) 107–115.

38. Bondy, J. A. and Thomassen, C., A short proof of Meyniel's theorem, *Discrete Math*. 19 (1977) 195–197.

39. Brooks, R. L., On coloring the nodes of a network, *Proc. Cambridge Phil. Soc*. 37 (1941) 194–197.

40. Brualdi, R. A. and Shen, J., Landau′s inequalities for tournament scores and a short proof of a theorem on transitive sub-tournaments, *J. Graph Theory* 38 (2001) 244–254.

41. Buckley, F. and Harary, F., *Distance in Graphs*, Addison-Wesley, Redwood City, CA (1990).

42. Buckley, F., Miller, Z. and Slater, P. J., On graphs containing a given graph as center, *J. Graph Theory* 5 (1981) 427–434.

43. Camion, P., Chemins et circuits Hamiltoniens des graphs complets, *C. R. Acad. Sci. Paris* 249 (1959) 2151–2152.

44. Cartwright, D. and Harary, F., On colorings of signed graphs, *Elem. Math*. 23 (1968) 85–89.

45. Cayley, A., A theorem on trees, *Quart. J. Math.* 23 (1989) 376–378; collected papers, Cambridge 13 (1877) 26–28.

46. Chang, L. C., The uniqueness and non uniqueness of the triangular association scheme, *Sci. Record* 3 (1959) 604–613.

47. Chartrand, G., On Hamiltonian line graphs, *Trans. Amer. Math. Soc*. 134 (1968) 559–566.

48. Chartrand, G. and Geller, D., Uniquely colorable graphs, *J. Combin. Theory* 6 (1969) 271–278.

49. Chartrand, G., Gavlas, H., Harary F. and Schultz, M., On signed degrees in signed graphs, *Czech. Math. Journal* 44 (1994) 111–117.

50. Chartrand, G. and Kronck, H. V., Randomly traceable graphs, *SIAM J. Appl. Math.* 16 (1968) 696–700.

51. Chartrand, G. and Stewart, M. J., Isometric graphs, in Capobianco et al., *Recent Trends in Graph Theory*, Springer-Verlag, Berlin, *Lecture Notes in Math.* 186 (1971) 63–67.

52. Chartrand, G. and Stewart, M. J., The connectivity of line graphs, *Math. Ann.* 182 (1969) 170–174.

53. Chartrand, G. and Schuster, S., Which graphs have unique distance trees, *Amer. Math. Monthly* 81 (1974) 53–56.

54. Chartrand, G. and Wall, C. E., On the Hamiltonian index of a graph, *Studia Sci. Math. Hungar.* 8 (1973) 43–48.

55. Chartrand, G. and White, A. T., Randomly traversable graphs, *Elem. Math.* 25 (1970) 101–107.

56. Chen, Y. L., A short proof of Kundus *f*-factor theorem, *Discrete Math.* 71 (1988) 177–179.

57. Choudum, S. A., A simple proof of the Erdos-Gallai theorem on graphic sequences, *Bull. Austral. Math. Soc.* 36 (1986) 67–70.

58. Chvatal, V., On Hamilton's ideals, *J. Combin. Theory Ser.* B 12 (1972) 163–168.

59. Clark, J. and Holton, D. A., *A First Look at Graph Theory*, World Scientific, Teaneck, NJ (1991).

60. Courant, R. and Robbins, H. E., *What is Mathematics?* Oxford Univ. Press, London (1941).

61. Cunningham, W. H., Matchings, matroids and extensions, *Math. Programming* B91 (2002) 515–542.

62. Deo, N., *Graph Theory with Applications to Engineering and Computer Science*, PHI, New Delhi (1974).

63. Dirac, G. A., A property of 4-chromatic graphs with some remarks on critical graphs, *J. London Math. Soc.* 27 (1952) 85–92.

64. Dirac, G. A., Short proof of Menger's graph theorem, *Mathematika* 13 (1966) 42–44.

65. Dirac, G.A., Some theorems on abstract graphs, *Proc. London Math. Soc.* 2 (1976) 111–135.

66. Dirac, G. A. and Schuster, S., A theorem of Kuratowski, *Nederl. Akad. Wetensch. Proc. Ser.* A 57 (1954) 343–348.

67. Edmonds, J. and Johnson, E. L., Matching, Euler tours and the Chinese postman, *Math. Programming* 5 (1973) 88–124.

68. Eplett, W. J. R., Self-converse tournaments, *Canad. Math. Bull.* 22 (1979) 23–27.

69. Erdos, P. and Fajtlowicz, S., On the conjecture of Hajos, *Combinatorica* 1 (1981) 141–143.

70. Erdos, P. and Gallai, T. G., Graphs with prescribed degrees of vertices(Hungarian), *Mat. Lapok* 11 (1960) 264–274.

71. Euler, L., Solutio problematis ad geometriam situs pertinent, *Comment. Academiae Sci. I Petropolitanae* 8 (1736) 128–140.

72. Euler, L., Demonstratio Nonnullarum Insignium Proprietatum QuibusSolida Hedris Planis Inclusa Sunt Praedita, *Novi Comm. Acad. Sci. Imp. Petropol* 4 (1758) 140–160.

73. Euler, L., The Konigsberg bridges, *Sci. Amer.* 189 (1853) 66–70.

74. Fary, I., On straight line representation of planar graphs, *Acta Sci. Math.* 11 (1948) 229–233.

75. Finck, H. J. and Sachs, H., Uber eine von H. S. Wilf angegebene Schranke fur die chromatische Zahl endlicher Graphen, *Math. Nachr.* 39 (1969) 373–386.

76. Fleischner, H., Elementary proofs of (relatively) recent characterizations of Eulerian graphs, *Discrete Applied Math.* 24 (1989) 115–119.

77. Fleischner, H., Eulerian graphs and related topics, *Annals of Discrete Math.* 45, North-Holland, New York (1990).

78. Ford, L. R. and Fulkerson, D. R., *Flows in Networks*, Princeton University Press, Princeton (1962).

79. Foulds, L. R., *Graph Theory Applications*, Springer-Verlag, New York (1992).

80. Fulkerson, D. R., Hofman, A. J. and Mc Andrew, M. H., Some properties of graphs with multiple edges, *Can. J. Math.* 17 (1965) 166–177.

81. Gale, D., A theorem on flows in networks, *Pacific J. Math.* 7 (1957) 1073–1082.

82. Gervacio, S. V., Score sequences: lexicographic enumeration and tournament construction, *Discrete Math.* 72 (1988) 151–155.

83. Grinberg, E. Ja., Plane homogenous graphs of degree three without Hamiltonian circuits (Russian), *Latvian Math. Yearbook* 4 (1968) 51–58.

84. Ghouila-Houri, A., Une condition suffisante d'existence d'un circuit Hamiltonien(French), *C. R. Acad. Sci. Paris* 25 (1960) 495–497.

85. Graver, J. E. and Jurkat, W. R., f-factors and related decompositions of graphs, *J. Combin. Theory Ser.* B 28 (1980) 66–84.

86. Griggs, J. R. and Reid, K.B., Landau's Theorem revisited, *Australasian J. Combinatorics* 20 (1999) 19–24.

87. Grotzsch, H., Zur Theorie der diskreten Gebilde VII. Ein Dreifar, bensatz fur dreikreisfreie Netze amf der Kugel (German) Ein Oreifarbensatz fur dreikreisfreie Netze auf der Kugel, txi Wiss. Z. Martin-Luther-Univ. Halle-Wittenberg Math.-Natur. *Reihe* 8 (1958) 109–120.

88. Grunbaum, B., Grotzschs Theorem on 3-colorings, *Michigan Math. J.* 10 (1963) 303–310.

89. Grunbaum, B., Graphs and Complex, Report of the University of Washington, Seattle, *Math.*, 572B, 1969.

90. Grunbaum, B., Problem 2 in combinatorial structures and their applications, Proc. Calgary International Conference, (1969), Gordon and Breach, New York.

91. Gupta, R. P., Bounds on the chromatic and achromatic numbers of complementary graphs, in W. T. Tutte (ed.), *Recent Progress in Combinatorics*, Acad. Press, New York 1969 (229–235).

92. Hadwiger, H., Uber eine Klassifikation der Streckenkomplexe (German), *Vierteljschr. Naturforsch Ges. Zurich* 88 (1943) 133–142.

93. Hager, M., On score sets for tournaments, *Discrete Math.* 58 (1986) 25–34.

94. Hajos, G., Uber eine Konstruktion nich n-farbarrer Graphen, *Wiss. Z. Martin-Luther-Univ. Halle-Wittenberg Math.-Nat. Reihe* 10 (1961) 116–117.

95. Hakimi, S. L., On realizability of a set of integers as degree of the vertices of a linear graph II. Uniqueness, *J. Soc. Indust. Appl. Math.*11 (1963) 135–147.

96. Hakimi, S., On the realizability of a set of integers as the degrees of the vertices of a linear graph, *J. Soc. Indust. Appl.Math*10 (1962) 496–506.

97. Hall, M. Jr, Distinct representatives of subsets, *Bull. Amer. Math. Soc.* 3 (1952) 584–587.

98. Hall, P., On representation of subsets, *J. London Math. Soc.* 10 (1935) 26–30.

99. Harary, F., A characterization of block graphs, *Canad. Math. Bull.* 6 (1963) 1–6.

100. Harary, F., *Graph theory*, Addison-Wesley, Reading, MA (1969).

101. Harary, F. and Frisch, I. T., *Communication, Transmission and Transportation Networks*, Addison-Wesley, Reading MA. (1971).

102. Harary, F. and Hedetniemi, S., The achromatic number of a graph, *J. Combin. Theory B* (1970) 154–161.

103. Harary, F., Hedetniemi, S. and Robinson, R. W., Uniquely colorable graphs, *J. Combin. Theory* 6 (1969) 264–270.

104. Harary, F. and Nash-Williams, C. St. J. A., On Eulerian and Hamiltonian graphs and line graphs, *Canad. Math. Bull.* 8 (1965) 701–710.

105. Harary, F. and Norman, R. Z., The dissimilarity characteristic of Husimi trees, *Ann. of Math.* 58 (1953) 131–141.

106. Harary, F., Norman, R. Z. and Cartwright, D., *Structural Models: An Introduction to the Theory of Directed Graphs*, Wiley, New York (1965).

107. Hasselbarth, W., Die verzweightheit von Graphen(Czech), *Match* 16 (1984) 3–17.

108. Havel, M., A remark on the existence of finite graphs, *Casopis Pest. Mat.* 80 (1955) 477–480.

109. Heawood, P. J., Map color theorem, *Qurat. J. Pure Appl. Math.* 24 (1890) 332–338.

110. Hedetniemi, S., On hereditary properties of graphs, *J. Combin. Theory, Ser. B 14(1973)94-99.*

111. Heirholzer, C., Ueber die Moglickkeit, Einen Linienzug ohne Wiederholung and ohne Unterrechung zu umfahren, *Math. Ann.* 6 (1893) 30–32.

112. Hoffman, A. J., On the exceptional case in a characterization of the arcs of complete graphs, *IBM J. Res. Develop.* 4 (1960) 487–496.

113. Hoffman, A. J., On the uniqueness of the triangular association scheme, *Ann. Math. Statist.* 31 (1960) 492–497.

114. Hoffman, A. J., On the line graph of the complete bipartite graph, *Ann. Math. Statist.* 35 (1964) 883–885.

115. Ivanyi, A., Reconstruction of complete interval tournaments, *Acta Univ. Sapientiae, Inform.*, 1, 1 (2009) 71–88.

116. Ivanyi, A., Reconstruction of complete interval tournaments II, *Acta Univ. Sapientiae, Math.*, 2, 1 (2010) 47–71.

117. Jaeger, F., A note on sub-Eulerian graphs, *J. Graph Theory* 3, 1 (1979) 91–93.

118. Jordan, C., Sur les assemblages de lignes, *J. Reine Angew. Math.* 70 (1969) 185–190.

119. Jung, H. A., Zu einem IsomorphiIsatz von Whitney fur Graphen, *Math. Ann.* 164 (1966) 270–271.

120. Kano, M., and Saito, A., [a, b]-factors of graphs, *Discrete Math.* 47, 1 (1983) 113–116.

121. Kano, M., and Saito, A., [a, b]-factorization of a graph, *J. Graph Theory 9* (1985) 129–146.

122. Kapoor, S. F., Polimeni, A. O. and Wall, C. E., Degree sets for graphs, *Fund. Math.* 95 (1977) 189–194.

123. Kasteleyn, P. W., Graph theory and crystal physics, in F. Harary (ed.) Chapter 2 in *Graph Theory and Theoretical Physics*, Acad. Press, London–New Yark (1967) 44–110.

124. Kempe, A. B., On the geographical problem of the four colors, *Amer. J. Math.* 2 (1879) 193–200.

125. Kleitman, D. J. and Wang, D. L., Algorithms for constructing graphs and digraphs with given valencies and factors, *Discrete Math.* 6 (1973) 78–88.

126. Koh, K. M. and Tan, B. P., The set and number of kings in a multipartite tournament, *Bull. Inst. Combin. Appl.* 13 (1995) 15–22.

127. Koh, K. M. and Tan, B. P., Kings in multipartite tournaments, *Discrete Math.* 147, 1-3 (1995) 171–183.

128. Koh, K. M. and Tan, B. P., Number of 4-kings in bipartite tournaments with no 3-kings, *Discrete Math.* 154 (1996) 281–287.

129. Koh, K. M. and Tan, B. P., The number of kings in multipartite tournaments, *Discrete Math.*, 167 (1997) 411–418.

130. Konig, D., Graphen and Matrizen, *Math. Fiz. Lapok* 38 (1931) 116–119.

131. Konig, D., Theorie der endlichen and unendlichen Graphen, B. G. Tenbner Verlags-gesllschaft, Leipzig.

132. Konig, D., Uber Graphen und ihre Anwendung auf determinantentheorie und Men-genlehre, *Math. Ann.* 77 (1916) 453–465.

133. Kotzig, A., Cycles in a complete graph oriented in equilibrium, *Mat. Fyz. Casopis SAV* 16 (1966) 175–182.]

134. Kotzig, A., The decomposition of a directed graph into quadratic factors consisting of cycles, *Acta F. R. N. Univ. Comen. Math.* 22 (1969) 27–29.

135. Kouider, M. and Lonc, Z, Stability number and [a, b]-factors in graphs, *J. Graph Theory* 46 (2004) 254–264.

136. Krausz, J., Demonstration nouvelle d'une theoreme de Whitney sur les reseaux, (Hungarian, French Summary) *Mat. Fiz. Lapok* 50 (1943) 75–85.

137. Kundu, S., Generalizations of the k-factor theorem, *Discrete Math.* 9 (1974) 173–179.

138. Kundu, S., The Chartrand-Schuster conjecture: Graphs with unique distance trees are regular, *J. Combin, Theory Ser.* B 22 (1977) 233–245.

139. Kundu, S., The k-factor conjecture is true, *Discrete Math.* 6 (1973) 367–376.

140. Kuratowski, C., Sur le probleme des courbes gauches en topologie, *Fund. Math.* 15 (1930) 271–283.

141. Landau, H. G., On dominance relations and the structure of animal socities: III. The condition for a score structure, *Bull. Math. Biophys.* 15 (1953) 143–148.

142. Lesniak-Foster, Linda M., Linda M. L., Eccentric sequences in graphs, *Period. Math. Hungar.* 64 (1975) 287–293.

143. Lesniak-Foster, Linda M. and Williamson, James E. and Williams, J. E., On spanning and dominating circuits in graphs, *Canad. Math. Bull.*20 (1977).

144. Lovasz, L., Subgraphs with prescribed valencies, *J. Combin. Theory* 8 (1970) 391–416.

145. Lovasz, L., Valencies of graphs with 1-factors, *Period. Math. Hungar.* 5 (1974) 149–151.

146. Lovasz, L., A remark on Menger′s theorem, *Acta Math. Acad. Sci. Hungar.* 21 (1970) 365–68.

147. Lovasz, L., Three short proofs in graph theroy, *J. Combin Theory Ser.* B 19, 3 (1975) 269–271.

148. Lovasz, L., *Combinatorial Problems and Exercises*, North-Holland, Amsterdam (1979).

149. Mathematisch Centrum, This Weeks Citation Classic, CC/Number 7, February 14, 1983, http://www.garfield.library.upenn.edu/.

150. Maurer, S. B., The king chicken theorems, *Math. Mag.* 53, 2 (1980) 67–80.

151. McCuaig, W., A simple proof of Menger′s theorem, *J. Graph Theory* 8, 3 (1984) 427–429.

152. Mckee, T. A., Recharacterizing Eulerian: Intimations of new duality, *Discrete Math.* 51, 3 (1984) 237–242.

153. Menger, K., Zur allgemeinen Kurventheoril, Fund. Math. 10 (1927) 96–115.

154. Menon, V., On repeated interchange graphs, *Amer. Math. Monthly* 13 (1966) 986–989.

155. Meyniel, M., Une condition sufficiante d'existance d'un circuit Hamiltonian dans un graphe oriente, *J. Combin. Theory Ser.* B 14 (1973) 137–147.

156. Mirsky, L., *Transversal Theroy, An Account of some aspects of combinational Mathematics*, Mathematics in Science and Engineering, vol. 75, Acad. Press, New York (1971).

157. Moon, J. W., On some combinatorial and probabilistic aspects of bipartite graphs, Ph.D Thesis, University of Alberta, Edmonton (1962).

158. Moon, J. W., On the line graph of the complete bigraph, *Ann. Math.* Statist. 34, 2 (1963) 664–667.

159. Moon, J. W., Various proofs of Cayley's formula for counting trees, in F. Harary and L. Beineke (eds), *A seminar on Graph Theory*, Holt, Rinehart and Winston (1967) 70–78.

160. Moon, J. W., *Topics on Tournaments*, Holt, Rinehart and Winsten, New York-Monmtrea;. Qie.-London (1968).

161. Naikoo, T. A., Pirzada, S., Samee, U., and Ivanyi, A., Imbalances in directed multigraphs, Acta Univ Sapientiae 2, 2 (2010) 133-145.

162. Nash-Williams, C. St. J. A., Edge-disjoint spanning trees of finite graphs, *J. London Math. Soc.* 36 (1961) 445–450.

163. Nash-Williams, C. St. J. A., Edge-disjoint Hamiltonian circuits in graphs with vertices of large valency, in *Studies in Pure Mathematics*, Acad. Press, London (1971).

164. Nash-Williams, C. St. J. A. and Tutte, W. T., More proofs of Menger's theorem, *J. Graph Theory* 1,1 (1977) 13–17.

165. Nebesky, L., On the line graph of the square and the square of the line graph of a connected graph, *Casopis. Pest. Mat.* 98 (1973) 285–287, 315.

166. Newman, D. J., A problem in graph theory, *Amer. Math. Monthly*, 65 (1958) 611.

167. Nordhaus, E. A. and Gaddam, J. W., On complementary graphs, *Amer. Math. Monthly* 63 (1956) 175–177.

168. O Neil, P. V., A new proof of Menger's theorem, *J. Graph Theory* 2 (1978) 257–259.

169. Ore, O., A problem regarding the tracing of graphs, *Elem. Math.* 6 (1951) 49–53.

170. Ore, O., Graphs and matching theorems, *Duke Math.* J. 22 (1955) 625–639.

171. Ore, O., Note on Hamilton circuits, *Amer. Math. Monthly* 67 (1960) 55.

172. Ore, O., *The Four Color Problem*, Acad. Press, New York (1967).

173. Ore, O., Theory of Graphs, *Amer. Math. Soc. Colloq. Publ.* Vol. XXXVIII American Mathematical Society, Providence, R1 (1962) Providence (1962).

174. Ore, O. and Stemple, G. J., Numerical methods in the four color problem, in W. T. Tutte (ed.) *Recent Progress in Combinatorics*, Acad. Press, New York (1969).

175. Parthasarathy, K. R., *Basic Graph Theory*, Tata McGraw-Hill, New Delhi (1994).

176. Petersen, J., Die Theorie der regulren Graphs, *Acta Math.* 15 (1891) 193–220.

177. Petrovic, V. and Thomassen, C., Kings in *k*-partite tournaments, *Discrete Math.* 98, 3 (1991) 237–238.

178. Petrovic, V., Decomposition of some planar graphs into trees, *Discrete Math.* 150, 1-3 (1996) 449–451.

179. Petrovic, V., Kings in bipartite tournaments, *Discrete Math.* 173, 1-3 (1997) 187–196.

180. Pirzada, S., Self converse score lists in oriented graphs, *J. China Univ. of Science and Tech.* 26, 3 (1996) 392–394.

181. Pirzada, S., Simple score sequences in oriented graphs, *Novi Sad J. Math.* 33, 1 (2003) 25–29.

182. Pirzada, S., Construction of oriented graphs, in R. Balakrishnan, R.J. Wilson and G. Sethuraman (eds) *Proc. National Conf. Graph Theory and Applications*, Narosa, (2004) 146–149.

183. Pirzada, S., Mark sequences in multidigraphs, *Discrete Math. Appl* 17, 1 (2007) 71–76.

184. Pirzada, S., On imbalances in digraphs, *Kragujevac J. Math.* 31 (2008) 143–14

185. Pirzada, S. and Merajuddin, Score lists in oriented tripartite graphs, *Novi Sad J. Math* 26, 2 (1996) 1–9.

186. Pirzada, S. and Samee, U., Mark Sequence in digraphs, Sem. Loth. Comb. 55(2006) Art. B55c, 13pp.

187. Pirzada, S., Merajuddin and Samee, U., On oriented graph scores, *Matematicki Vesnik* 60 (2008) 187–191.

188. Pirzada, S., Merajuddin and Samee, U., Inequalities in oriented graph scores, *Bull. Allahabad Mathematical Society* 23, 2 (2008) 389–395.

189. Pirzada, S., Merajuddin and Yin Jianhua, On the scores of oriented bipartite graphs, *J. Math. Study* 33, 4 (2000) 245–359.

190. Pirzada, S. and Naikoo, T. A., Degree frequencies in oriented graphs, *Thai J. Math.*. 2 (2004) 85–96.

191. Pirzada, S. and Naikoo, T. A., Inequalities on marks in digraphs, *J. Mathematical Inequalities and Applications* 9, 2 (2006) 189–198.

192. Pirzada, S. and Naikoo, T. A., Score sets in tournaments, *Vietnam J. Mathematics* 34, 2 (2006) 157–161.

193. Pirzada, S. and Naikoo, T. A., Score sets in k-partite tournaments, *J. Appl. Math. Comput* 22, 1-2 (2006) 237–245.

194. Pirzada, S. and Naikoo, T. A., Score sets in oriented k-partite graphs, *AKCE Int. J. Graphs Comb.* 3, 2 (2006) 135-145.

195. Pirzada, S. and Naikoo, T. A., Score sets for oriented graphs, *Appl. Anal. Discrete Math.* 2, 1 (2008) 107–113.

196. Pirzada, S., Naikoo, T. A. and Chishti, T. A., Score sets in oriented bipartite graphs, *Novi Sad J. Math.* 36, 1 (2006) 35–45.

197. Pirzada, S., Naikoo, T. A. and Dar, F. A., Signed degree sets in signed graphs, *Czech. Math. J.* 57, 3 (2007) 843–848.

198. Pirzada, S., Naikoo, T. A. and Shah, N. A., Score sequences in oriented graphs, *J. Appl. Math. Comput.* 22, 1–2 (2007) 257–268.

199. Pirzada, S., Naikoo, T. A. and Dar, F. A., Degree sets in bipartite and 3-partite graphs, *Oriental J. of Math. Sciences* 1, 1 (2007) 47–53.

200. Pirzada, S., Naikoo, T. A. and Dar, F. A., Signed degree sequences in signed bipartite graphs, *AKCE Int. J. Graphs and Comb.* 4, 3 (2007) 301–312.

201. Pirzada, S. Naikoo, T. A. and Dar, F. A., A note on signed degree sets in signed bipartite graphs, *Appl. Anal. and Discrete Math.* 2, 1 (2008) 114–117.

202. Pirzada, S. and Shah, N. A., Kings and serfs in oriented graphs, *Math. Slovaca* 58, 3 (2008) 277–288.

203. Pirzada, S. and Yin Jian Hua, Degree sequences in graphs, *J. Math. Study* 39, 1 (2006) 25–31.

204. Plesnik, J., Connectivity of regular graphs and the existence of 1-factors, *Mat. Casopis Sloven, Akad. Vied* 22 (1972) 310–318.

205. Posa, L., A theorem concerning Hamiltonian lines, *Magyar Tud. Akad. Mat. Kutato Int. Kozl.* 7 (1962) 225–226.

206. Prufer, H., Never Beweis eines Satzes ber Permutationen, *Arch. Math. Phys.* 27 (1918) 742–744.

207. Pym, J. S., A proof of Menger's theorem, *Monatsh. Math.* 73 (1969) 81–83.

208. Randic, M., Characterization of atoms, molecules and classes of molecules based on path enumerations, *Proceedings of Bremen Konferenz zur Chemie, (Univ. Bremen* 1978) Part II, Match No. 7 (1979) 5–64.

209. Rao, A. R. and Rao, S. B., On factorable degree sequences, *J. Combin. Theory Ser.* B 13 (1972) 185–191.

210. Redei, L., Ein Kombinatorischer Satz, *Acta Litterania Szeged*, 7 (1934) 39–43.

211. Reid, K. B., Score sets for tournaments, *Congressus Num.* 21 (1978) 607–618.

212. Reid, K. B. and Beineke, L.W., Tournaments, in L. W. Beineke and R. J. Wilson (eds), Chapter 7 in *Selected Topics in Graph Theory*, Acad. Press, London (1979) 169–204.

213. Reid, K. B., Tournaments with prescribed number of kings and serfs, *Congressus Numerantium* 29 (1980) 809–826.

214. Reid, K. B., Every vertex a king, *Discrete Math.* 38 (1982) 93–98.

215. Reid, K. B., Tournaments: Scores, kings, generalizations and special topics-a survey, *Congr. Numer.* 115 (1996) 171–211.

216. Reid, K. B. and Zhang, C. Q., Score sequences of semi complete digraphs, *Bull. Inst. Combin. Appl.* 24 (1998) 27–32.

217. Ringel, G. and Youngs, J. W. T., Solution of the Heawood map coloring problem, *Proc. Nat. Acad. Sci. USA* 60 (1968) 438–445.

218. Rizzi, R., A short proof of Konig's matching theorem, *J. Graph Theory* 33 (2000) 138–139.

219. Robertson, N., Sanders, D. P., Seymour, P. D. and Thomas, R., The four color theorem, *J. Combin. Theory Ser.* B. 70, 1 (1997) 2–44.

220. Rooij, Van and Wilf, H. A. C. M. S. The interchange graphs of a finite graph, *Acta. Math. Acad. Sci. Hungar.* 16 (1965) 263–269.

221. Ryser, H. J., Combinatorial properties of matrices of zeros and ones, *Canad. J. Math.* 9 (1957) 371–377.

222. Ryser, H. J., Matrices of zeros and ones in combinatorial mathematics, in *Recent Advances in Matrix Theory*, Univ. Wisconsin Press, Madison, WI (1964) 103–124.

223. Saaty, T. L., Thirteen colorful variations on Guthrie's four color conjecture, *Amer. Math. Monthly* 79 (1972) 2–43.

224. Saaty, T. L. and Kainen, P. C., *The Four Color Problem*, McGraw Hill, New York (1977).

225. Sabidussi, G., Graph derivatives, *Math.* Z. 76 (1961) 385–401.

226. Schnyder, W., Planar graphs and poset dimension, *Order* 5, 4 (1989) a. 323–343.

227. Seshu, S. and Reed, M., Linear Graphs and Electrical Networks, F. Harary(ed.), Addison-Wesley, Reading (1961) Acad. Press, London (1967) 44–110.

228. Slater, P. J., A counter-example to Randic's conjecture on distance degree sequences for trees, *J. Graph Theory* 6, 1 (1982) 89–92.

229. Sierksma, G. and Hoogeveen, H., Seven criteria for integer sequences being graphic, *J. Graph Theory* 15, 2 (1991) 223–231.

230. Sumner, D. P., 1-factors and antifactor sets, *J. London Math. Soc.* 13, 2 (1976) 351–359.

231. Szekeres, G. and Wilf, H. S., An inequality for the chromatic number of a graph, *J. Combin. Theory* 4 (1968) 1–3.

232. Tait, P. G., Remarks on the coloring of maps, *Proc. Roy. Soc. Edinburgh Sect.* A 10 (1880) 501–503, 729.

233. The Mathematics Center at Bell Labs, History of Mathematics at Bell Labs, http://cm.bell-labs.com/cm/ms/center/history.html

234. Thomassen, C., Kuratowski's theorem, *J. Graph Theory* 5, 3 (1981) 225–241.

235. Thomassen, C., Landau's characterization of tournament score sequences, in Chartrand, G., Alavi, Y., Goldsmith, D.L., Lesmak-Foster, L. and lick, D.R (eds) *The Theory and Applications of Graphs*, John Wiley and sons, New York (1981) 589–591.

236. Titov, V. K., A constructive description of some classes of graphs, Ph.D. Thesis, Moscow (1975).

237. Toida, S., Properties of an Euler graph, *J. Franklin Inst.* 295 (1973) 343–345.

238. Tripathi, A. and Vijay, S., A note on a theorem of Erdos and Galai, *Discrete Math.* 265 (1–3) (2003) 417–420.

239. Tripathi, A., Venugopalan, S. and West, D. B., A short proof of the Erdos-Gallai characterization of graphic lists, *Discrete Math.* 310 (2010) 843–844.

240. Turan, P., Eine Extremalaufgabe aus der Grapheneorie, *Mat. Fiz. Lapok* 48 (1941) 436–452 (1936), Reprinted Chelsea, New York (1950).

241. Tutte, W. T., A family of cubical graphs, *Proc. Cambridge Phil. Soc.* 21 (1946) 98–101.

242. Tutte, W. T. The factorization of linear graphs, *J. London Math. Soc.* 22 (1947) 107–111.

243. Tutte, W. T., The factors of graphs, *Canad. J. Math.* 4 (1952) 314–328.

244. Tutte, W. T., A short proof of the factor theorem for finite graphs, *Canad. J. Math.* 6 (1954) 347–352.

245. Tutte, W. T., On the problem of decomposing a graph into n connected factors, *J. London Math. Soc.* 36 (1961) 221–230.

246. Tutte, W. T., Graph factors, *Combinatorica* 1 (1981) 79–97.

247. Veblen, O., An application of modular equations in analysis situs, *Ann. of Math.* 14 (1912–13) 86–94.

248. Vergnas, M. L., An extension of Tuttes 1-factor theorem, *Discrete Math.* 23 (1978) 241–255.

249. Vergnas, M. L., M. Thesis, University of Paris, v1 (1972).

250. van Aardenne-Ehrenfest, T. and de Bruijn, N. G., Circuits and trees in oriented graphs, *Simon Stevin* 28 (1951) 203–217.

251. Vizing, V. G., On an estimate of the chromatic class of a p-graph (Russian) *Diskret. Analiz.* 3 (1964) 25–30.

252. Vizing, V. G., The chromatic class of a multigraph, *Cybernetics* 3 (1965) 32–41.

253. Wagner, K., Bemerkungen zum Vierfarbenproblem, *Jahresber Deutsch. Math. Verein* 46 (1936) 21–22.

254. Wang, D. L. and Kleitman, D. J., On the existence of n-connected graphs with prescribed degrees ($n > 2$), *Networks* 3 (1973) 225–239.

255. Welsh, D. J. A. and Powell, M. B., An upper bound for the chromatic number of a graph and its application to time-tabling problems, *Comput. J.* 10 (1967) 85–86.

256. West, D. B. *Introduction to Graph Theory*, Prentice Hall, Upper Saddle River, NJ. (1996).

257. Whitney, H., A theorem on graphs, *Annals Math.* 32 (1931) 378–390.

258. Whitney, H., Congruent graphs and the connectivity of graphs, *Amer. J. Math.* 54 (1932) 150–168.

259. Whitney, H., 2-isomorphic graphs, *Amer. J. Math.* 55, (1933) 245–254.

260. Whitney, H., Planar graphs, *Fund. Math.* 21 (1933) 73–84.

261. Wiener, N., A simplification of logic of relations, *Proc. Cambridge Phil. Soc.* 17 (1912–14) 387–390.

262. Wilson, R. J., *Introduction to Graph Theory*, Oliver and Boyd, Edinburgh (1972).

263. Woodall, D. R., Sufficient conditions for circuits in graphs, *Proc. London Math.Soc.* 24 (1972) 739–755.

264. Yan, J., Lih, K., Kuo, D. and Chang, G. J., Signed degree sequences in signed graphs, *J. Graph Theory* 26, 2 (1997) 111–117.

265. Yao, Tian Xing. On Reid conjecture of score sets for tournaments, *Chinese Sai. Bull*. 34, 10 (1989) 804-808.

266. Zhou, G., Yao, T. and Zhang, K, On score sequences of k-hypertournaments, *European J. Combin*. 21, 8 (2000) 993–1000.

Index